CLIMATE CHANGE LITIGATION IN EUROPE

CLIMATE CHANGE LITIGATION IN EUROPE

Regional, Comparative and Sectoral Perspectives

Edited by
Ivano Alogna
Carole Billiet
Matteo Fermeglia
Alina Holzhausen

INTERSENTIA
Cambridge – Antwerp – Chicago

Intersentia Ltd
8 Wellington Mews
Wellington Street | Cambridge
CB1 1HW | United Kingdom
Tel: +44 1223 736 170
Email: contact@larcier-intersentia.com
www.larcier-intersentia.com

Distribution for the UK and
Rest of the World (incl. Eastern Europe)
NBN International
1 Deltic Avenue, Rooksley
Milton Keynes MK13 8LD
United Kingdom
Tel: +44 1752 202 301 | Fax: +44 1752 202 331
Email: orders@nbninternational.com

Distribution for Europe
Lefebvre Sarrut Belgium NV
Hoogstraat 139/6
1000 Brussels
Belgium
Tel: +32 (0)2 548 07 13
Email: contact@larcier-intersentia.com

Distribution for the USA and Canada
Independent Publishers Group
Order Department
814 North Franklin Street
Chicago, IL 60610
USA
Tel: +1 800 888 4741 (toll free) | Fax: +1 312 337 5985
Email: orders@ipgbook.com

Climate Change Litigation in Europe. Regional, Comparative and Sectoral Perspectives

ISBN 978-1-83970-385-0
D/2023/7849/166
NUR 828

British Library Cataloguing in Publication Data. A catalogue record for this book is available from the British Library.

FOREWORD

A Beacon of Hope and Inspiration

Climate law scholars and practitioners master perhaps one of the most difficult law disciplines of our times. In essence, we have to cope with many developments, uncertainties and massive complexity regarding science, society and law. This is also true on the European continent. First, there is an enormous production and updating of regulatory tools, particularly by the EU legislator and subsequently the European Commission, but also by Member States and subnational entities. Meanwhile, the outcome of elections determining the political directions of those who occupy regulatory seats is uncertain yet tremendously important. Secondly, whether states, authorities and other actors addressed with obligations, including companies, will duly implement these climate laws is one of the most difficult questions of our time. As lawyers know, when a norm is adopted it is often not clear how it will play out in specific situations, including what (social and economic) efforts it will take to comply with it. Nonetheless, when non-compliance takes place, courts may be addressed to enforce the climate obligations. So indeed, thirdly, climate litigation is on the rise on the European continent, not only to enforce commitments, but also to step up the emission reduction actions of governments and companies. Climate change-related case law is present in many, if not all, national jurisdictions in Europe, as well as at the supranational level, such as before the Court of Justice of the European Union and the European Court of Human Rights. The fact that there is consideration about changing the competence for providing preliminary rulings specifically regarding the EU greenhouse gas emissions trading scheme, which is the flagship of the EU climate legislation, is a sign of a court busy with core climate change legislation.[1] More court action is, however, bound to follow: the further evolving legislative approaches to climate change will probably intensify the litigation before national and European courts on the interpretation, application and enforcement of the new provisions. That is not the only cause of court action: when insufficient regulatory action is taken, courts may be addressed about possibly filling these gaps, taking into consideration the protection of human rights. So either way, in cases of regulatory action or inaction, courts may be looked at as a beacon of hope.

1 Statute of the Court of Justice: amendment of Protocol No. 3, Legislative proposal published on 3 December 2022, procedure reference 2022/0906(COD).

In light of the above challenges, and particularly the challenge regarding the ever-increasing role of the courts, this book, *Climate Change Litigation in Europe*, developed by a dedicated team of editors and based on contributions by a mix of very senior as well as younger researchers, should be welcomed as a source of knowledge, inspiration and even encouragement. I invite the reader to take a step back from the hectic day-to-day legal and academic practice and indulge in the rich and varied insights provided in this book about whether and particularly how courts fulfil a meaningful role in addressing the climate change problem. Let us remain hopeful that the European legal community's approach, one underpinned by exhaustive research assessing the merits and drawbacks of various options, and a willingness to experiment with new and different strategies, will yield the most favourable and beneficial outcome.

Marjan Peeters
Professor of Environmental Policy and Law,
Maastricht University

CONTENTS

LIST OF CONTRIBUTORS

Ivano Alogna
Research Leader in Environmental and Climate Change Law, British Institute of International and Comparative Law (BIICL), United Kingdom; Lecturer in Environmental Law and Associated Member, Sorbonne Research Institute in International and European Law (IREDIES), University of Paris 1 Panthéon-Sorbonne, France

Carole Billiet
Head Environmental Law Unit, Hasselt University, Belgium; Member of the Brussels Bar

Farah Bouquelle
Assistant environmental law, Centre for Environmental and Energy Law, University of Ghent, Belgium; Board Member NGO Dryade

Dorien Coppens
Maastricht University, the Netherlands

Matteo Fermeglia
Assistant Professor of Climate Law and Governance, Amsterdam University, Faculty of Humanities, the Netherlands; previously (and throughout the book development) Post-Doctoral Assistant and Assistant Professor of International and European Environmental Law, Hasselt University, Faculty of Law, Belgium

Carlotta Garofalo
PhD Candidate, Institute of Public Law and Political Science, Clim:Law Graz, University of Graz, Austria

Giada Giacomini
Postdoctoral Researcher, Geneva Graduate Institute, Switzerland

Alexandru Gociu
PhD Candidate, School of Law, Trinity College Dublin, Ireland

Susann Handke
Independent Scholar

Alina Holzhausen
Researcher in Environmental and Climate Change Law, British Institute of International and Comparative Law (BIICL); PhD Candidate, University of Aberdeen, United Kingdom

Jannis Krüßmann
Student, University of Bonn, Germany

Konrad Lachmayer
Professor of Public Law, European Law and Foundations of Law, and Vice-Dean, Faculty of Law, Sigmund Freud University, Austria

Luc Lavrysen
President of the Constitutional Court of Belgium; Professor Emeritus, Centre for Environmental and Energy Law, University of Ghent, Belgium

Ander Maglica
PhD Candidate in Public Law, University of Milan, Italy and KU Leuven, the Netherlands

Marjan Peeters
Professor of Environmental Policy and Law, Maastricht University, the Netherlands

Suryapratim Roy
Assistant Professor, School of Law, Trinity College Dublin, Ireland

Rhonson Salim
Lecturer in Law, Aston University, United Kingdom

Joschka Schlake
PhD Researcher, Network of Competence on Future Challenges of Environmental Law (KomUR), Research Center for European Environmental Law, University of Bremen, Germany

Hendrik Schoukens
Professor of Environmental Law, Ghent University, Belgium; Solicitor at the Bar of Brussels; City Councillor in the municipality of Lennik

Jillian Sprenger
JD/BCL Candidate, Faculty of Law, McGill University, Canada; previously affiliated with the Department of Land Economy, University of Cambridge, United Kingdom

Patrick Thieffry
Independent Arbitrator; Member of the Paris and New York Bars

Maria Antonia Tigre
Global Climate Litigation Fellow, Sabin Center for Climate Change Law, Columbia Law School, United States

Marijn van der Sluis
Assistant Professor of Constitutional Law, Maastricht University, the Netherlands

Marta Zamorska
Graduate Assistant and PhD Candidate, University of Lausanne, Switzerland

Alan Żukowski
PhD Researcher, Centre for Legal Education and Social Theory, Department of Legal Theory and Philosophy of Law, University of Wrocław; Graduate Research Assistant, Institute of Philosophy and Sociology of the Polish Academy of Sciences, Poland

CLIMATE CHANGE LITIGATION IN EUROPE

An Introduction to Regional, Comparative and Sectoral Perspectives

Ivano Alogna, Carole Billiet, Matteo Fermeglia and Alina Holzhausen

1. ORIGIN, AIMS AND SPECIFICITY OF THIS VOLUME

Climate change litigation has come to the fore in recent decades as a global phenomenon, encompassing the societal striving for radical changes, the need to establish the responsibility of both private and public organisations in view of the compelling evidence of climate change, and the collective awareness of the significant efforts needed to achieve effective and ambitious greenhouse gas (GHG) emission reductions, in line with the best available climate science. In this regard, the initial wave of strategic climate change litigation is now leaving room for a more structural phenomenon, arguably enshrining climate change litigation as a transnational climate governance mechanism. Several underlying trends are being appraised, which underpin the always more considerable bulk of cases being brought before jurisdictions all over Europe at the regional and domestic levels.

This edited volume aims to contribute to the discussions on trends in climate change litigation in Europe, drawing from regional, comparative and sectoral perspectives. It builds on the conference entitled 'Climate Change Litigation in Europe: Comparative & Sectoral Perspectives and the Way Forward' held at

Hasselt University in Belgium on 18–19 February 2022, organised in cooperation with the British Institute of International and Comparative Law (BIICL) and Hasselt University.

The hybrid two-half-day event took stock of the current developments in climate change litigation in Europe while addressing systematically and comprehensively the latest relevant trends.[1] It focused on comparative perspectives by including the most significant domestic litigation experiences, as well as five sectoral perspectives: human rights, State responsibility, international trade and investment protection, corporate responsibility, and procedural hurdles. Bringing together practitioners, academics, judges and other experts in various panel discussions and five parallel sectoral-focused workshops, the suggestions and proposals provided by the conference participants not only set out the status quo but also provided the necessary framework to highlight the way forward.

The contributions in this volume stem, in Part I, from two keynote dialogues and one roundtable, focusing on regional and comparative perspectives before courts in climate change litigation. Part II covers the contributions of the above-mentioned sectoral perspectives, provided during the respective workshops on the event's second day. Together with the closing panel discussion, in which the workshop chairs presented remarks and the results of the parallel sectoral sessions, current trends and the way forward in climate change litigation in Europe are set out in Part III of this volume.

Therefore, this edited volume covers a variety of perspectives, combining chapters presenting academic analysis with contributions providing insights from legal practitioners involved with climate change cases. Moreover, it covers both domestic and regional developments in Europe, providing a solid legal basis for future comparative research with litigation trends in other world regions.

The next section offers a few preliminary comments on the definition of climate change litigation and its development worldwide (section 2), before introducing the content of the volume in more detail (section 3).

2. DEFINITION(S) AND DEVELOPMENT OF CLIMATE CHANGE LITIGATION

Climate change litigation can be understood in various ways, depending on its different definitions.[2] Applying a narrower definition, climate change litigation

---

1 Recordings of the conference are available at https://www.youtube.com/playlist?list=PLrRqwcJCpBFFo6K41rxiBB20mjV8OdFUr.

2 See for example J. Setzer and L. Vanhala, 'Climate Change Litigation: A Review of Research on Courts and Litigants in Climate Governance' (2019) *WIREs Climate Change* 6: 'There are as many understandings of what counts as "climate change litigation" as there are authors writing about the phenomenon'.

can be considered to be that kind of litigation 'directly and expressly' raising an issue related to climate change or climate change policy.[3] By contrast, its broader definition concerns those cases where there is an explicit reference to climate change not only in the proceedings or decisions, but also in the motivations of claimants, as well as those cases where climate change is not the central, but rather an 'additional' or 'secondary' concern, or where it is not even expressly mentioned.[4] According to Peel and Lin, 'there is a need for concepts of climate litigation that are able to capture lower-profile cases where climate change is more peripheral to arguments in, or the motivation for, the lawsuit'.[5] Such a broader definition is especially required when considering litigation in the Global South, 'where a significant number of the cases reflect a "peripheral" focus on climate change rather than having the issue at the "core" of the litigation'.[6] Golnaraghi and others classify climate change cases 'by motivation, by the type of litigants, and by the extent to which the case is about climate change'. They distinguish between private interest cases versus strategic cases, where the latter ones are filed to go beyond the result for the litigant and, for example, aim to advance climate policies.[7] The extent to which the case is about climate change depends on whether climate change is central (at the core of the legal strategy), peripheral (explicit reference to climate change but legal arguments based on other grounds) or just incidental (only practical yet implicit implications for climate change) in the case.[8]

Beyond the 'narrow' and 'broad' definitions of climate change litigation, Savaresi and Auz stress that among the various existing scenarios there can be reactive types of litigation, initiated to oppose particular changes in relation to climate change, or proactive ones, brought before courts to challenge States' failure to mitigate or address the impacts of climate change.[9] Other scholars define similar categories as pro-regulatory and anti-regulatory climate change

---

3 For example, the often-cited definition used by Markell and Ruhl refers to 'any piece of federal, state, tribal or local administrative or judicial litigation in which the party filing or tribunal decisions directly and expressly raise an issue of fact or law regarding the substance or policy of climate change causes and impacts'. D. Markell and J.B. Ruhl, 'An Empirical Assessment of Climate Change in the Courts: A New Jurisprudence or Business as Usual?' (2012) 64 *Florida Law Review* 15, 27.

4 For a more detailed discussion of these definitions, see J. Peel and J. Lin, 'Transnational Climate Litigation: The Contribution of The Global South' (2019) 113 *American Journal of International Law* 679.

5 Ibid., p. 691; see also K. Bouwer, 'The Unsexy Future of Climate Change Litigation' (2018) 30 *Journal of Environmental Law* 1.

6 J. Peel and J. Lin, above n. 4, p. 692.

7 M. Golnaraghi et al., 'Climate Change Litigation. Insights into the evolving global landscape' (2021) *The Geneva Association* 6.

8 Ibid.

9 A. Savaresi and J. Auz, 'Climate Change Litigation and Human Rights: Pushing the Boundaries' (2019) 9 *Climate Law* 244.

litigation.[10] While the reactive (and anti-regulatory) kind of climate change litigation has been common for a longer time, the proactive (and pro-regulatory) type has increased in the last decade, notably since the adoption of the Paris Agreement.[11]

In fact, whatever definition of climate change litigation has been used or considered, climate change cases have already been documented worldwide since the 1980s.[12] Until 2007, most climate change cases were filed before courts and tribunals in the United States. However, a surge in cases saw an expansion to European legal systems between 2007 and 2015, and eventually to other jurisdictions around the world.[13] As of August 2023, 2,509 climate change cases have been identified, of which 1,546 were filed before courts in the US and at least 285 before European national courts since 2015.[14] Notably, the most successful climate litigation pattern has taken place on the European continent. Following the landmark Dutch *Urgenda* case, other eminent decisions have been rendered by domestic courts, holding governments accountable for their (in)action against climate change, such as the *Neubauer* case in Germany, the French case *Notre Affaire à Tous*, the *Klimaatzaak* case in Belgium, and, last but not least, the UK High Court decision in the *Friends of the Earth* case.[15] These cases have been filed by a variety of claimants, such as individuals, non-governmental organisations (NGOs) and governments, mainly against governments, corporations, financial institutions and regulatory or supervisory authorities.[16] They

10 See for example J. Peel and H.M. Osofky, 'Litigation as a Climate Regulatory Tool' in C. Voigt (ed.), *International Judicial Practice on the Environment*, Cambridge University Press 2019.

11 A. Savaresi and J. Auz, above n. 9, p. 247.

12 M. Golnaraghi et al., above n. 7.

13 Ibid.

14 Please note that these numbers are retrieved from the two open-access, non-exhaustive climate change databases, the Grantham Research Institute Climate Change Laws of the World, available at https://climate-laws.org, and the Sabin Center Climate Change Litigation Database, available at http://climatecasechart.com/climate-change-litigation/. The data on European climate change litigation are drawn from J. Setzer, H. Narulla, C. Higham and E. Braaden, 'Climate Litigation in Europe: A summary report for the European Union Forum of Judges for the Environment', Grantham Research Institute on Climate Change and the Environment and Centre for Climate Change Economics and Policy, London School of Economics and Political Science and the European Union Forum of Judges for the Environment (2022).

15 *Urgenda Foundation v. The State of The Netherlands*, Supreme Court of the Netherlands, Case No. 19/00135 (20 December 2019); *Neubauer et al. v. Germany*, 1 BvR 2656/18, 1 BvR 78/20, 1 BvR 96/20, 1 BvR 288/20; *Notre Affaire à Tous*, Administrative Court of Paris, n° 1901967, 1904968, 1904972, 1904976/4-1 (14 October 2021); *VZW Klimaatzaak v. Kingdom of Belgium and Others* (2021), Brussels Court of First Instance, 2015/4585/A (24 March 2021); *Friends of the Earth et al. v. Secretary of State for Business, Energy and Industrial Strategy*, High Court [2022] EWHC 1841.

16 See for more information and detailed numbers and figures J. Setzer and C. Higham, 'Global trends in climate change litigation: 2023 snapshot', Grantham Research Institute on

are, thus, multifaceted due to the heterogeneity of the actors involved and objectives pursued: holding governments and private actors accountable to their legal obligations and engendering policy change, increasing the alignment of national laws and corporate commitments with the Paris Agreement, and obtaining compensation for damages caused by climate change.[17] To reach these various objectives, different areas of law have constituted important laboratories and offered interesting lessons to be learned, providing manifold causes of action, such as climate regulations and environmental legislation, tort law, consumer law and human rights law. The use of old and new legal tools and doctrines (public nuisance, public trust, greenwashing or climate-washing, information disclosures and fraud)[18] has also provided (and continues to offer) fruitful new avenues for this kind of litigation. The analysis of previous cases, coupled with the accelerating impacts of climate change and the related geopolitical context, suggests that various future directions for climate change litigation in the coming years are necessary and inevitable. The near future may hold, as seems likely from the current trends, consumer and investor fraud claims, product liability lawsuits, several implementation challenges, increased attention to climate attribution, pre- and post-disaster cases, and growing use of international adjudicatory bodies.[19] Looking more closely at climate change cases in Europe, the chapters in this edited volume aim to provide further insights into origins and developments, as well as current and future trends of climate change litigation.

3. STRUCTURE AND CONTENT

As already noted above, the volume is organised into three Parts. Part I, 'Climate Change Litigation in Europe: Regional and Comparative Perspectives', presents and examines climate change litigation and the role of courts, with a special focus on European regional courts as well as insights from legal practitioners in five European countries. Part II, 'Climate Change Litigation in Europe: Sectoral Perspectives', covers 18 contributions in the field of climate change litigation following the structure of the parallel workshops and dealing with human rights, State responsibility, international trade and investment protection, procedural

---

Climate Change and the Environment and the Centre for Climate Change Economics and Policy (2023).

17 For trends in climate change litigation, see the UN Environment Programme's latest report: UNEP, 'The Status of Climate Change Litigation – A Global Review' (2023), https://www.unep.org/resources/report/global-climate-litigation-report-2023-status-review.

18 See for further analysis of the relevant cases the contributions in I. Alogna, C. Bakker and J.-P. Gauci (eds), *Climate Change Litigation: Global Perspectives*, Brill 2021; F. Sindico and M.M. Mbengue (eds), *Comparative Climate Change Litigation*, Springer 2021.

19 UNEP, above n. 17, and Sabin Center, above n. 14.

rights, and corporate responsibility. Part III, 'Climate Change Litigation in Europe: The Way Forward', concludes the volume while highlighting the way forward.

3.1. PART I: CLIMATE CHANGE LITIGATION IN EUROPE: REGIONAL AND COMPARATIVE PERSPECTIVES

Part I focuses on the role of the courts in climate change litigation both from the point of view of European courts and domestic legal systems, thus providing regional and comparative perspectives. The target countries of this comparative overview are Belgium, France, Germany, the Netherlands and the United Kingdom, which offer additional insights from the claimants' side to the previous analysis on climate change litigation before the European courts.

Lavrysen and Bouquelle set the scene on the role of courts in climate change litigation, building and expanding on their research about the developments of this kind of litigation in the last few years. According to these authors, some general principles can be drawn from strategic climate change cases, as for the case of the human rights constituting a positive obligation to protect against environmental harm, including climate change. Looking ahead, they argue that in the decades to come both international and regional courts and national courts and tribunals will inevitably be increasingly confronted with climate cases. Shortly, the European Court of Human Rights (ECtHR) will clarify whether an approach based on Articles 2 and 8 European Convention on Human Rights (ECHR) is appropriate to address climate change.

Taking into consideration the developments before the ECtHR and the European regional level more broadly, Alogna and Billiet then focus on the ECtHR, as well as the Court of Justice of the European Union (CJEU). The authors take stock of the dialogue between the ECtHR Judge Tim Eicke and climate justice practitioner Marc Willers to stress the manifold features and challenges characterising the approach of the CJEU and the ECtHR when facing climate change litigation in terms of admissibility and merits of these claims.

In the last chapter of Part I, Fermeglia and Alogna lay out the comparative perspectives presented and discussed by a panel of legal practitioners during a comparative roundtable about some of the most interesting domestic experiences in Europe. This discussion addresses climate litigation in Europe from a diachronic perspective by looking at its past, present and future. Moreover, this chapter provides insights into the most relevant legal arguments successfully used in courts, the current legal challenges faced by claimants in different jurisdictions, and the future prospects for climate change cases in Europe, also looking beyond the realm of strategic litigation.

3.2. PART II: CLIMATE CHANGE LITIGATION IN EUROPE: SECTORAL PERSPECTIVES

Part II of this volume focuses on the sectoral perspectives of climate change litigation. The five sections on human rights, State responsibility, international trade and investment protection, procedural rights, and corporate responsibility cover contributions from various scholars and practitioners.

In the first section on 'Human Rights and Climate Change Litigation', Lachmayer examines the constitutional context of climate change litigation. Focusing on Germany and Austria, the chapter looks at the *Neubauer* case before the German Constitutional Court as well as at a case before the Austrian Constitutional Court, which led to the opposite outcome. By contrasting these examples, the author highlights that even though the constitutional texts in both countries could be compared as similar, the relevant human rights provisions and the constitutional reasoning differ significantly. According to Lachmayer, human rights-based climate change litigation requires a re-interpretation of constitutional law, as the whole range of constitutional provisions and reasoning must be taken into consideration to be successful. At the same time, these provisions and reasoning might (only) be relevant in the context of a certain constitutional culture.

In the following chapter, Roy and Gociu take an in-depth look at the *People v. Arctic Oil* case in Norway with a focus on the potential of strategic environmental assessments and the principle of non-regression in guiding energy policy.[20] Starting with a contextual background, the authors situate the case within the political scene of Norwegian oil policy, as well as within the legal scene of the Norwegian constitutional tradition, which bear on the interpretation of the right to a healthy environment. Continuing with a brief discussion of the respective court judgments, they demonstrate how the different levels of the judiciary expand, and narrow, the scope of this right. They then examine the unexplored potential of the role of law in strategic environmental assessment in terms of informing energy and climate policy, before finishing with the principle of non-regression and its role in this climate case.

Sprenger contributes to the section on rights-based climate change litigation with an examination of the human rights implications in global climate migration. Especially low- and middle-income countries will likely suffer climate change impacts to the worst extent, with their citizens being forced to leave their homes and relocate to Europe and other regions of the world, which are perceived as more resilient to climate change. By applying a socio-legal approach to climate migration and Europe's role toward climate migrants, Sprenger discusses climate

20 Norwegian Supreme Court (22 December 2020), *Greenpeace Nordic Association v. Ministry of Petroleum and Energy*, Case No. 20-051052SIV-HRET (*People v. Arctic Oil*).

migration and its causes as well as the legal challenges of applying refugee law to climate migrants. A case study focusing on climate migration in Sri Lanka underlines the argument that human rights law may be an alternative means to offer protection to climate migrants. Sprenger concludes the chapter with an assessment of relevant case law and its significance for future climate migration cases based on human rights law.

In the last chapter of this section, Giacomini puts the focus on human rights-based climate litigation and Indigenous peoples. The first part of her contribution analyses how Indigenous peoples' rights are not equally perceived and protected in supranational human rights system by the means of a comparison between European and Inter-American jurisprudence. Moreover, by examining how human rights standards are used by Indigenous peoples in climate change litigation and which hurdles would arise in cases before the ECtHR, Giacomini argues that a harmonisation between different human rights system is needed and proposes potential ways for future environmental and climate change litigation to be brought by Indigenous peoples in the European human rights system. Lastly, the second part of the chapter analyses just transition litigation cases brought by Indigenous people against European States and transnational energy companies.

In the second section on 'State Responsibility and Climate Change Litigation', Garofalo analyses the limits and prospects of aligning climate change litigation with justice in Europe. The author explores the limits of rights-based climate change litigation in the context of climate justice issues, while holding European countries accountable to their contribution to mitigating climate change. Garofalo argues that it is necessary to identify the cases' most ethically controversial aspects to find the appropriate legal tools to adjust climate policies to ethical standards. The chapter approaches this intuition in four sections, including seeing the national reduction pathway as a normative matter, showing to what extent identified moral issues cause legal uncertainty, laying out how courts deal with rights-based arguments and climate science used by claimants to overcome legal uncertainties, and exploring legal pathways that might support the judiciary in reviewing national mitigation policies while taking climate justice into consideration.

The following chapter focuses on State obligations to reduce carbon emissions. Guided by three landmark decisions in Europe, namely the *Urgenda* and *Milieudefensie* cases in the Netherlands,[21] and the *Neubauer* case in Germany, Krüßmann argues that a 'carbon reduction potential' should be used as a yardstick to assess State obligations for climate protection instead of mitigation targets for carbon emissions, or carbon budgets. In particular, while

---

21 *Milieudefensie et al. v. Royal Dutch Shell plc*, C/09/571932 / HA ZA 19-379 (26 May 2021).

most climate change policies and courts' assessments focus on territorial State emissions, the author highlights the role of indirect 'imported' emissions at the State level. As Krüßmann demonstrates, a 'carbon reduction potential' has already been laid out in case law, and further pending cases have the chance to address the points raised throughout the chapter.

Van der Sluis analyses States' obligations from a constitutional angle, focusing on environmental constitutionalism in the Netherlands and the EU. According to the author, climate change and mitigation measures have mainly been seen from a human rights perspective in constitutional law. However, as van der Sluis argues in this contribution, climate change-related issues have broader implications for constitutional law, as demonstrated by the ruling of the Dutch Supreme Court in the *Urgenda* case and by the European Green Deal (EGD). While focusing on identifying relevant questions, the chapter concludes with possibilities for future research on how constitutional law should, and can, engage with climate change.

Handke examines shifting principles related to climate cooperation in the context of the German Federal Constitutional Court's most famous ruling on intergenerational justice, and its implications as an inspiration for the UN climate regime. Focusing on the decision in the *Neubauer* case, the author compares the Court's arguments with the notion of development in the UN climate regime. Moreover, building on their normative differences, Handke illustrates how a set of three parameters outlining elements of climate and energy policy would help to balance different objectives when designing national policies and contemplating international cooperation.

Lastly in this section, Żukowski provides an examination of strategic climate change litigation in Poland, focusing on socio-legal communication before courts. After laying out the law applicable to strategic litigation in Poland, the author outlines the need for change in the Polish approach to strategic climate change litigation. Then, Żukowski examines the significance of the balance between social communication and legal argumentation for strategic climate change litigation, to conclude how this kind of litigation operates in Poland, and its consequences from a socio-legal system perspective.

The third section on 'International Trade and Investment Protection and Climate Change Litigation' starts with an examination by Thieffry of procedural improvements aiming at greater social acceptability of investment arbitration. Against the background of the development of several institutional projects pertaining to the procedural features of Investor-State Dispute Settlement (ISDS) in recent years, the author assesses the desirability of procedural measures aiming at ISDS's greater social acceptability. Moreover, Thieffry considers the trends and efforts towards the ISDS procedural reform. While it is difficult to anticipate the extent to which such reforms may succeed regarding the improvement of investment arbitration's social acceptability, the author argues that they could contribute to this goal and are worth observing.

In the fourth section on 'Procedural Rights and Climate Change Litigation', Schlake looks at climate change litigation before the CJEU in a 'complete system of remedies'. The author sheds light on the different paths for actions challenging the legality of EU climate change legislation before the CJEU. Schlake discusses the Court's interpretation of standing rules according to the *Plaumann* test and assesses whether this test constitutes a 'closed door' for climate change litigation, revealing a reasonable underlying logic. In addition, the author highlights to what extent the control of statutory climate protection measures based on fundamental rights can be achieved via the referral route.

Coppens reflects on the systematic public participation in the EU Taxonomy Regulation and Delegated Acts and focuses on how to avoid procedural hurdles that would hinder effective decision-making. In particular, the author assesses which procedural legal framework applies to the delegated decision-making regarding sustainable investments, especially in view of the second pillar of the Aarhus Convention: public participation. A case study based on the first Taxonomy Delegated Act is provided to demonstrate compelling climate-related arguments and to consider this European legislation as a chance to re-examine how the European integration system might fit the needs for a greener future by giving a voice to citizens throughout the process.

Project review, fossil infrastructure and climate change are put into context by Schoukens, who focuses on a Belgian planning dispute surrounding a petrol station as a lever to discuss the plethora of challenges that might arise when integrating climate consideration into specific planning and project decisions. The decision of the Flemish Council of Permit Disputes challenging the possibility to refuse a permit for fossil infrastructure with reference to climate-related considerations is discussed against the wider backdrop of other relevant Belgian climate change litigation, such as the *Klimaatzaak* case.

Salim answers the question concerning 'collective redress and climate change litigation in the EU – a promising future or more of the same?' The author considers that in light of the procedural reforms implemented by the Directive 2020/1828 for consumers,[22] Member States are presented with an opportunity to enact domestic procedural changes to effectively enable representative organisations to better act in claims relating to climate change. Salim contends that the Directive's approach to standing, information provision and redress remedies could enhance access to justice for climate change victims if transposed to the environmental sphere. In fact, effective climate change litigation for individuals can be facilitated by the empowerment of representative organisations to bring injunctive and monetary claims for the protection of

22 Directive (EU) 2020/1828 of 25 November 2020 on representative actions for the protection of collective interests of consumers and repealing Directive 2009/22/EC [2020] OJ L 409/1.

divisible interests. To advance these arguments, Salim takes stock of the findings from the *Urgenda* and *Milieudefensie* cases in the Netherlands, and from the main collective redress procedure in Poland.

In the last chapter of this section, Maglica offers an Italian perspective on climate change class actions in Europe. The author investigates the social, economic and institutional barriers preventing efficient climate change litigation in Europe, then presents class action mechanisms with a specific focus on Italy considering a recently introduced title in the Italian Civil Procedural Code. Finally, Maglica analyses the efficiency of class actions in overcoming the climate change litigation barriers set out in the chapter, and proposes his thoughts about social, statutory and institutional changes regarding the new Italian collective redress mechanisms.

In the fifth and last section of Part II on 'Corporate Responsibility and Climate Change Litigation', Tigre examines how *Urgenda*-type cases can inform the responsibility of private companies to mitigate climate change. The chapter expands on the questions whether emerging case law such as that stemming from *Neubauer* in Germany and *Notre Affaire à Tous* in France can inform private climate change litigation; whether, and to what extent, the strategies and arguments deployed in *Milieudefensie* are replicable outside the Netherlands; and whether human rights law and international climate law can be used to interpret a standard duty of care in other jurisdictions. In comparing these decisions, Tigre also considers how they can be replicated beyond the European context to jurisdictions in the Global South.

Finally, Zamorska examines the basis for climate change liability of financial institutions and discusses the role of various responsibility regimes which might be applicable in this context. While at the same time identifying gaps in existing liability schemes, the author sets out recommendations for policy reforms and explores new directions for tackling financial responsibility in fuelling carbon-intensive projects.

3.3. PART III: CLIMATE CHANGE LITIGATION IN EUROPE: THE WAY FORWARD

Lastly, Part III on 'Climate Change Litigation in Europe: The Way Forward' concludes this edited volume while highlighting the way forward. The conclusion chapter includes not only a summary of Parts I and II of the volume, but also important remarks made by the respective workshop chairs in the closing panel discussion on the second day of the hybrid conference. The concluding remarks from the editors of this volume, especially focused on the future of climate change litigation in Europe, round up the timely discussion on litigation trends in the context of climate change in Europe.

PART I

CLIMATE CHANGE LITIGATION IN EUROPE: REGIONAL AND COMPARATIVE PERSPECTIVES

CLIMATE CHANGE LITIGATION IN THE COURTS IN EUROPE

Luc Lavrysen and Farah Bouquelle*

1. INTRODUCTION

In the last decade we have seen a fast growth of climate litigation, understood as cases that relate to climate change mitigation, adaptation or climate science.[1] That rapid increase in climate litigation has occurred around the world. The 2017 UNEP Climate Litigation Report[2] identified 884 cases brought in 24 countries, comprising 654 cases in the United States of America and 230 cases in all other countries combined. As of 1 July 2020, the number of cases had nearly doubled, with at least 1,550 climate change cases filed in 38 countries (39 counting

* This chapter is an updated and expanded version of the following publications: L. Lavrysen and F. Bouquelle, 'Climate Change Litigation in Europe' in K. De Graaf et al. (eds), *Grensoverstijgende rechtsbeoefening. Liber Amicorum Jan Jans*, Uitgeverij Paris, Zutphen 2021, pp. 87–96, and L. Lavrysen and F. Bouquelle, 'Klimaatzaken van 2017 tot nu – zullen rechtbanken het tij keren?' in H. Schoukens and C.M. Billiet (eds), *Klimaatrechtspraak. Waarom Rechters het klimaat (niet) zullen redden. Huldeboek voor prof. Dr. Luc Lavrysen*, die Keure, Bruges 2021, pp. 19–30.

1 J. van Zeben, 'The Role of the EU Charter of Fundamental Rights in Climate Litigation' (2021) *German Law Journal* 1499.

2 UNEP, *The Status of Climate Change Litigation: A Global Review*, Nairobi 2017, pp. 10–11, https://wedocs.unep.org/handle/20.500.11822/20767.

the courts of the European Union). Those cases include approximately 1,200 filed in the US and over 350 filed in all other countries combined.[3] Outside of the US, Australia has seen the largest number of cases.[4] Although the number of cases in Europe, compared with the US and Australia, is lagging behind, probably the most iconic are nevertheless situated in Europe. In the last three years the numbers have gone up again.[5]

2. DEVELOPMENTS UNTIL 2017

The annual conference of the European Union Forum of Judges for the Environment (EUFJE) in Oxford in October 2017 focused on climate change.[6] It is striking that in several European countries – but certainly not all – and at EU level climate justice was developing gradually at that time, and it concerned almost exclusively very specific, often quite technical aspects of climate legislation, such as the European emissions trading system,[7] support mechanisms for renewable energies,[8] measures

---

3 UNEP, *Global Climate Litigation Report: 2020 Status Review*, Nairobi 2020, p. 4.

4 Ibid., p. 13.

5 J. Setzer and C. Higham, *Global trends in climate change litigation: 2023 snapshot. July 2023, Policy report*, Grantham Research Institute on Climate Change and the Environment and Centre for Climate Change Economics and Policy, London School of Economics and Political Science, London 2023.

6 In preparation of that annual conference, as usual, a detailed questionnaire was submitted to the members of EUFJE. Among other things, it aimed to assess the state of case law in this field in European countries. The national reports are available on the EUFJE website, and they give a reliable overview of the situation in 2017, so almost two years after the Paris Agreement, and almost a year after its entry into force. See https://www.eufje.org/images/docConf/ox2017/oxquestionnaireEN.pdf and https://www.eufje.org/index.php?option=com_content&view=article&id=48&Itemid=238&lang=en.

7 In 2017 we counted already more than 50 cases of the Court of Justice and the General Court of the EU in relation to Directive 2003/87/EC of the European Parliament and of the Council of 13 October 2003 establishing a system for greenhouse gas emission allowance trading within the Union and amending Council Directive 96/61/EC. Some of those cases dealt with the validity of certain aspects of the Directive, e.g. CJEU (Grand Chamber), 16 December 2008, C-127/07, *Arcelor Atlantique and Lorraine and Others* (equal treatment between industrial sectors); CJEU (Grand Chamber), 21 December 2011, C-366/10, *Air Transport Association of America and Others* (application of ETS to flights outside EU territory). In addition, on the national level there has been some case law in this field, e.g. Constitutional Court (Belgium), no. 92/2006, 7 June 2006, *Cockerill Sambre and Arcelor*; Constitutional Court (Belgium), no. 33/2011, 2 March 2011, *Brusselse Hoofdstedelijke Regering*. Meanwhile in the database of the CJEU 115 cases are reported.

8 In 2017 we counted already 20 cases of the Court of Justice and the General Court of the EU in relation to the relevant directives. Some of those cases have been of importance for the further development of EU renewable energy policies, e.g. CJEU, 31 January 2013, C-26/11, *Belgische Petroleum Unie and Others*; CJEU, 26 September 2013, C-195/12, *IBV & Cie*; CJEU (Grand Chamber), 1 July 2014, C-573/12, *Ålands Vindkraft*; CJEU, 11 September 2014, C-204/12, *Essent Belgium*.

to make mobility more sustainable,[9] permits for projects with a significant climate impact,[10] or, on the contrary, permits for climate-friendly projects.[11]

Some of these cases enjoyed international renown,[12] e.g. the *Vienna Airport extension* case. In its ruling of 2 February 2017 on the planned third runway for Vienna International Airport (Schwechat), Austria's Federal Administrative Court (Bundesverwaltungsgericht)[13] examined the expected changes in future air traffic, the emission impacts of those changes, and the extent to which it would be possible for the airport to control or otherwise limit various sources of emissions. It considered the economic benefits of the additional runway, the adverse impacts of climate change on Austria, and the state of Austria's and Europe's efforts to reduce greenhouse gas emissions generally and from air traffic. After reviewing several estimates, the Court concluded that a third runway would increase Austria's annual CO_2 emissions by 1.79%–2.02% by 2025. This is at odds, the Court noted, with Austria's 2020 transport sector emissions reduction target of 2.25%. The Court also observed that short-term gains in the form of commerce or jobs were easily outweighed by the economic consequences of a destabilised climate. Because authorising the runway would do more harm to the public interest than good, primarily because it would be contrary to Austria's national and international obligations to mitigate the causes of climate change, the application for the runway extension was dismissed in its entirety. The case has, however, been referred by Vienna International Airport and the State of Lower Austria to the Constitutional Court, which quashed the Federal Administrative Court's decision for violation of the constitutionally guaranteed right to equality before the law. The Constitutional Court held that the Federal Administrative Court had erred, because of its incorrect consideration of 'cruise emissions', by taking not directly applicable international and EU law regarding climate protection into consideration, through a misconception of 'public interests' in the framework of the Aviation Act, and by taking into account in the balancing of interests the non-competence-relevant State objectives and no normative documents.[14]

---

9 E.g. Constitutional Court (Belgium), no. 72/2013, 22 May 2013, *Alex De Wulf*; Constitutional Court (Belgium), no. 170/2014, 27 November 2014, *Federatie van de Belgische parkings* and *Beroepsvereniging van de Vastgoedsector*.

10 Justice Dove, 'Climate Change in the UK Courts: Perspectives of a Judge', Oxford 2017, pp. 4–7, https://www.eufje.org/images/docConf/ox2017/dovetxt.pdf.

11 CJEU, 21 July 2011, C-2/10, *Azienda Agro-Zootecnica Franchini* and *Eolica di Altamura*; CJEU, 27 October 2016, C-290/15, *D'Oultremont and Others*.

12 E. Colombo, 'Enforcing International Climate Change Law in Domestic Courts: A New Trend of Cases for Boosting Principle 10 of the Rio Declaration?' (2017) 35(1) *UCLA Journal of Environmental Law and Policy* 98, http://escholarship.org/uc/item/7g98s7f3.

13 http://climatecasechart.com/non-us-case/in-re-vienna-schwachat-airport-expansion/; UNEP, *Global Climate Litigation Report: 2020 Status Review*, Nairobi 2020, pp. 17–18.

14 https://www.ris.bka.gv.at/Dokumente/Vfgh/JFT_20170629_17E00875_00/JFT_20170629_17E00875_00.pdf; B. Hollaus, 'Austrian Constitutional Court: Considering Climate Change as a Public Interest is Arbitrary – Refusal of Third Runway Permit Annulled: Judgment of 29 June 2017, E 875/2017' (2017) 11(3) *ICL Journal* 467.

In Norway, an action was brought by Nature & Youth and Greenpeace Nordic against the Norwegian government, because it had just offered 13 companies oil and gas exploration licences, opening, for the first time in 20 years, a new area for the oil and gas industry in the Arctic Barents Sea. The case was pending before the Oslo District Court at the time of the EUFJE Conference in Oxford. The Oslo District Court ruled in favour of the Norwegian government on 4 January 2018. The Court recognised that Article 112 of the Norwegian Constitution is a rights provision but found that the government had not violated any relevant rights because it had fulfilled the necessary duties before making the licensing decision. The Court also declared that '[e]missions of CO_2 abroad from oil and gas exported from Norway are irrelevant when assessing whether the Decision entails a violation of Article 112.' In its assessment of whether the government had fulfilled its duties regarding traditional environmental harm or other climate effects, the Court noted that the Norwegian Parliament (Storting) had broadly agreed to open the southeast Barents Sea to licensing and had considered proposals to halt that licensing or review whether it was inappropriate in light of the goals of the Paris Agreement on climate change. The involvement of the Storting was found sufficient to indicate that the duty to take measures had been fulfilled. The Borgarting Court of Appeal confirmed the decision on 22 January 2020.[15] This case was finally decided much later, on 22 December 2020, by a judgment of the Norwegian Supreme Court, rejecting the request. The Court held that although the Norwegian Constitution protects citizens against environmental and climate damage, future emissions from exported oil are too uncertain to prevent the granting of these oil exploration licences.[16] Meanwhile, on 15 June 2021, six activists, Greenpeace and Young Friends of the Earth took Norway to the European Court of Human Rights (ECtHR). They argue that the Norwegian government, through the licences for oil and gas exploitation that will lead to emissions in 2035 and beyond, has violated their right to life (Art. 2 ECHR) and their right to the protection of private and family life (Art. 8 ECHR). In addition, they argue that the Norwegian courts have not assessed their claims and therefore they did not have access to an effective national remedy under Article 13 ECHR.[17] The case was communicated to the parties on 16 December 2021.[18]

---

15 H. Colby, A.S. Ebbersmeyer, L.M. Heim and M. Kielland Røssaak, 'Judging Climate Change: The Role of the Judiciary in the Fight Against Climate Change' (2020) *Oslo Law Review* 168, 178–79.

16 http://climatecasechart.com/non-us-case/greenpeace-nordic-assn-and-nature-youth-v-norway-ministry-of-petroleum-and-energy/; https://www.domstol.no/en/enkelt-domstol/supremecourt/news/2020/judgment-in-the-climate-lawsuit/.

17 http://climatecasechart.com/climate-change-litigation/non-us-case/greenpeace-nordic-assn-v-ministry-of-petroleum-and-energy-ecthr/.

18 ECtHR, application no. 34068/21, *Greenpeace Nordic and Others v. Norway*; J. Fraser and L. Henderson, 'The human rights turn in climate change litigation and responsibilities of legal professionals' (2022) *Netherlands Quarterly of Human Rights* 6.

A notable exception to the gradual development of climate litigation until 2017 was found in the Netherlands. In 2013, before the Paris Agreement, a small environmental association, the Urgenda Foundation, had started, together with nearly 900 natural persons, a civil procedure against the Dutch State, on the grounds of fault-based civil liability.[19] The claimants demanded that the State be required to make a 25–40% reduction in greenhouse gas emissions by the end of 2020, instead of the 16% EU reduction obligation for the Netherlands. The judgment of the Hague District Civil Court of 24 June 2015, partially accepted the request. The Court ordered the State to reduce the Netherlands' CO_2 emissions by 2020 by 25%. This judgment was because the State had argued in several policy statements that CO_2 emissions in the Netherlands should be reduced by at least 25% by 2020 but had failed to implement legislation or other measures to ensure this reduction. Given the State's duty of care to protect and improve the living environment, the Court decided the State needed to do more to avert the looming danger caused by climate change.[20]

3. CLIMATE CHANGE LITIGATION FROM 2018 ONWARDS

3.1. THE *URGENDA* CASE BEFORE THE COURT OF APPEAL AND THE SUPREME COURT

Since the EUFJE Conference in 2017, climate jurisprudence has really exploded. First, the Dutch State appealed against the decision in the *Urgenda* case by the District Court in The Hague.[21] The Hague Court of Appeal upheld the judgment on 9 October 2018, but, and this is particularly important, based it on other legal grounds, mainly on the European Convention on Human Rights (ECHR). The

---

19 The action was based on the thesis that the Dutch State had acted wrongly and negligently by not taking sufficient measures to reduce the CO_2 emissions of the Netherlands compared to 1990, thus engaging the tort liability of the State.

20 Rechtbank Den Haag 25 juni 2015, *Urgenda v. Nederlandse Staat* (2015) *Tijdschrift voor Milieurecht* 512; UNEP, *The Status of Climate Change Litigation: A Global Review*, Nairobi 2017, pp. 15, 29, 30, 38–39; A. Soete and H. Schoukens, 'Klimaatverandering in de rechtbank. De rechter als scherprechter bij een falend milieubeleid?' (2016) *Nieuw Juridisch Weekblad* 186; A. Soete and H. Schoukens, 'De klimaatzaak: een moeilijke evenwichtsoefening in rechterlijk activisme?' (2015) *Tijdschrift voor Omgevingsrecht en Omgevingsbeleid* 146; *Themanummer: Perspectieven op het Urgendavonnis* (2016) *Milieu & Recht* 199; H. Bortels, I. Goetelen, S. Smet and J. Theunis, '*Urgenda and beyond*: de rol van mensenrechten in klimaatrechtspraak' in H. Schoukens and C. Billiet (eds), *Klimaatrechtspraak. Waarom Rechters het klimaat (niet) zullen redden. Huldeboek voor prof. Dr. Luc Lavrysen*, die Keure, Bruges 2021, pp. 47–48; http://climatecasechart.com/non-us-case/urgenda-foundation-v-kingdom-of-the-netherlands/; http://blogs2.law.columbia.edu/climate-change-litigation/wp-content/uploads/sites/16/non-us-case-documents/2015/20150624_2015-HAZA-C0900456689_decision-1.pdf.

21 Many well-informed observers were sure: the Court of Appeal would undoubtedly reform this decision, which was considered by many to be incompatible with the separation of

Court of Appeal ruled that in accordance with Article 2 ECHR, the State has a positive obligation to protect the life of citizens under its jurisdiction, while Article 8 ECHR creates the obligation to protect the right to home and to privacy. This obligation applies to all activities, public and non-public, which could endanger the rights thus protected and certainly does apply if industrial activities, which are inherently dangerous, are at stake. When the government knows there is a real and imminent danger, the State must take preventive measures to avoid any damage as much as possible. Based on the reports of the Intergovernmental Panel on Climate Change (IPCC) and the work within the framework of the UN Framework Climate Change Convention and the Paris Agreement, the Court concluded that there is a real threat of dangerous climate change, posing a serious risk that the current generation of residents will face death and/or disruption of private and family life. After weighing all the elements of the State's defence, the Court of Appeal concluded that the State was acting illegally, contrary to the duty of diligence of Articles 2 and 8 ECHR, by failing to make further reductions by the end of 2020 and that the State should reduce emissions by at least 25%.[22]

Critics of this jurisprudence remained and focused on the separation of powers and the role of judges. It was up to the Dutch Supreme Court (Hoge Raad) to give the last word. Based on the very detailed conclusions of two advocates general (150 pages, almost 600 footnotes),[23] the Court dismissed the appeal in a judgment of 20 December 2019.[24] The Supreme Court based its judgment on the United Nations Framework Convention on Climate Change and on the State's legal obligations to protect the life and well-being of civilians in the Netherlands, enshrined in the ECHR. According to the Court, there is

---

powers, because the Court, by forcing the State to strengthen climate policy to achieve a more ambitious and quantified reduction in greenhouse gases, had taken the place of the executive, and even the legislature. However, the observers were wrong.

22 J. Verschuuren, 'The State of the Netherlands v Urgenda Foundation: The Hague Court of Appeal upholds judgment requiring the Netherlands to further reduce its greenhouse gas emissions' (2019) *RECIEL* 94; H. Bortels, I. Goetelen, S. Smet and J. Theunis, '*Urgenda and beyond*: de rol van mensenrechten in klimaatrechtspraak' in H. Schoukens and C.M. Billiet (eds), *Klimaatrechtspraak. Waarom Rechters het klimaat (niet) zullen redden. Huldeboek voor prof. Dr. Luc Lavrysen*, die Keure, Bruges 2021, pp. 49–51; B.W. Wegener, 'Urgenda – World Rescue by Court Order? The "Climate Justice" Movement Tests the Limits of Legal Protection' (2019) 16 *Journal for European Environmental & Planning Law* 125; H. Schoukens and A. Soete, 'Climate change litigation against states after *Urgenda*: the times they are a-changing?' (2018) *Aménagement-Environnement* 148; http://blogs2.law.columbia.edu/climate-change-litigation/wp-content/uploads/sites/16/non-us-case-documents/2018/20181009_2015-HAZA-C0900456689_decision-4.pdf.

23 http://blogs2.law.columbia.edu/climate-change-litigation/wp-content/uploads/sites/16/non-us-case-documents/2019/20190913_2015-HAZA-C0900456689_opinion-1.pdf.

24 https://uitspraken.rechtspraak.nl/inziendocument?id=ECLI:NL:HR:2019:2006; UNEP, *Global Climate Litigation Report: 2020 Status Review*, Nairobi 2020, pp. 17, 39–43; A. Nollkaemper and L. Burgers, 'A New Classic in Climate Change Litigation: The Dutch Supreme Court Decision in the Urgenda Case', *EJIL:Talk!*, 6 January 2020; https://www.ejiltalk.org/a-new-classic-in-climate-change-litigation-the-dutch-supreme-court-decision-in-the-urgenda-case/;

a broad consensus between science and the international community on the urgent need for developed countries to reduce greenhouse gas emissions by at least 25% towards the end of 2020. The State has not explained why a smaller reduction can be considered justified and may still achieve the ultimate objective accepted by the State. The State had defended the thesis that decision-making on the reduction of greenhouse gases belongs to policy-makers. However, the Court observes that the Constitution obliges the Dutch judge to apply the provisions of the ECHR. The judge's task of providing legal protection is an essential element of the democratic rule of law. This is what the Court of Appeal did in this case, according to the Dutch Supreme Court.

3.2. MORE AND MORE STRATEGIC CASES FILED

3.2.1. At the National Level

Since the first *Urgenda* judgment, in various countries in Europe more and more strategic cases on the main orientations of national climate policies have been brought based on human rights or fundamental conventional or constitutional rights. This is the case in Germany,[25] Belgium,[26] Spain,[27] France,[28] Ireland,[29] Italy[30] and Poland.[31]

C.W. Backes and G.A. van der Veen, 'Urgenda: the Final Judgment of the Dutch Supreme Court' (2020) 17(3) *Journal for European Environmental & Planning Law* 307; J. Spier, '"The 'Strongest' Climate Ruling Yet": The Dutch Supreme Court's Urgenda Judgment' (2020) *Netherlands International Law Review* 319; M. Wewerinke-Sing and A. McCoach, 'The State of the Netherlands v Urgenda Foundation: Distilling best practice and lessons learnt for future rights-based climate litigation' (2021) *RECIEL* 275; H. Colby, A.S. Ebbersmeyer, L.M. Heim and M. Kielland Røssaak, 'Judging Climate Change: The Role of the Judiciary in the Fight Against Climate Change' (2020) *Oslo Law Review* 168, 173–75; H. Bortels, I. Goetelen, S. Smet and J. Theunis, '*Urgenda and beyond*: de rol van mensenrechten in klimaatrechtspraak' in H. Schoukens and C.M. Billiet (eds), *Klimaatrechtspraak. Waarom Rechters het klimaat (niet) zullen redden. Huldeboek voor prof. Dr. Luc Lavrysen*, die Keure, Bruges 2021, pp. 51–53; N. de Sadeleer, 'Faculté ou obligation d'agir dans le chef de pouvoirs publics pour contrer le fléau climatique ? Quelques réflexions sur le droit comparé" in *L'environnement, le droit et le magistrat. Mélanges en l'honneur de Benoît Jadot*, Larcier, Brussels 2021, pp. 255–61; http://blogs2.law.columbia.edu/climate-change-litigation/wp-content/uploads/sites/16/non-us-case-documents/2020/20200113_2015-HAZA-C0900456689_judgment.pdf.

25 http://climatecasechart.com/non-us-case/family-farmers-and-greenpeace-germany-v-german-government/.

26 http://climatecasechart.com/non-us-case/vzw-klimaatzaak-v-kingdom-of-belgium-et-al/.

27 http://climatecasechart.com/non-us-case/greenpeace-v-spain/.

28 http://climatecasechart.com/non-us-case/notre-affaire-a-tous-and-others-v-total/; http://climatecasechart.com/non-us-case/commune-de-grande-synthe-v-france/.

29 http://climatecasechart.com/non-us-case/friends-of-the-earth-ireland-v-the-government-of-ireland-et-al/.

30 https://www.desmog.com/2021/11/04/italy-climate-lawsuit-giudizio-universale-human-rights/.

31 https://www.endseurope.com/article/1718850/warsaw-face-legal-challenge-climate-inaction.

In Ireland Friends of the Irish Environment (FIE) filed suit in the High Court, arguing that the Irish government's approval of the National Mitigation Plan in 2017 violated Ireland's Climate Action and Low Carbon Development Act 2015 ('the Act'), the Constitution of Ireland, and obligations under the ECHR, particularly the right to life and the right to private and family life.[32] On 31 July 2020, the Supreme Court reversed the lower court's decision rejecting FIE's argument and issued a ruling quashing the Plan. The Court determined that the Plan fell short of the sort of specificity the Act requires because a reasonable reader of the Plan would not understand how Ireland will achieve its 2050 goals. The Court explained that 'a compliant plan must be sufficiently specific as to cover climate policy over the whole period to 2050'.[33]

In France two cases should be mentioned. The first is a case which came before the Council of State (Supreme Administrative Court), *Commune de Grande-Synthe v. France*. On 23 January 2019, the municipality of Grande-Synthe sued the French government for insufficient action on climate change. The suit alleged that the French government's failure to further reduce greenhouse gas emissions violates domestic and international law, including the European Convention on Human Rights, the Paris Agreement, the French Environmental Code and the French Environmental Charter. Grande-Synthe asked the Council of State to direct the government to take legislative and regulatory measures to prioritise action on climate change and to prohibit actions that would increase greenhouse gas emissions. On 19 November 2020, the Council of State ruled that the case was admissible and instructed the government to justify, within three months, that it was taking adequate actions towards meeting its own 2030 climate goals. According to the Court, the coastal community's claims were admissible in part because the city is particularly exposed to the effects of climate change. The Court also accepted interventions by NGOs and other interested cities. The Court then noted that France had committed to a 40% reduction in greenhouse

32 FIE alleged that the National Mitigation Plan ('the Plan'), which seeks to transition to a low-carbon economy by 2050, was inconsistent with the Act and Ireland's human rights commitments because it is not designed to achieve substantial short-term emissions reductions. On 19 September 2019, the Court ruled for the government and rejected FIE's claim that the Plan was invalid for failing to achieve substantial short-term emissions reductions, concluding that the Act does not require specific intermediate targets.

33 The Court, however, determined that FIE lacks standing to bring its claims under the Constitution or ECHR. The Court also concluded that FIE had not made a compelling enough case for identifying an unenumerated right to a healthy environment, separate from the rights expressly conferred by the Irish Constitution, '[w]hile not ruling out the possibility that constitutional rights and obligations may well be engaged in the environmental field in an appropriate case'; UNEP, *Global Climate Litigation Report: 2020 Status Review*, Nairobi 2020, pp. 19, 40–41; H. Colby, A.S. Ebbersmeyer, L.M. Heim and M. Kielland Røssaak, 'Judging Climate Change: The Role of the Judiciary in the Fight Against Climate Change' (2020) *Oslo Law Review* 168, 176; http://climatecasechart.com/non-us-case/friends-of-the-irish-environment-v-ireland/.

gas emissions by 2030, compared to 1990 levels, and instructed the government to justify its ability to meet this goal without stricter measures. Although the Court signalled the decision would be driven by French and European law and not the Paris Agreement, the Court reasoned that the Paris Agreement must be considered in the interpretation of national law.[34] The Council of State issued a final decision on 1 July 2021 ordering the government to 'take all the measures necessary' by the end of March 2022 to bend the curve of greenhouse gas emissions to meet climate goals, including a 40% reduction by 2030. The Court annulled the government's implicit refusal to take the necessary measures, noting that the emissions decreases in 2019 and 2020 were not enough to ensure compliance with the required climate goals, and current climate regulations were insufficient to meet the target.[35]

The other case, *Notre Affaire à Tous and Others v. France*, was filed by non-profit organisations with the Administrative Court of Paris (Tribunal Administratif de Paris). On 3 February 2021, the Administrative Court of Paris issued a decision recognising that France's inaction had caused ecological damage from climate change and awarded the plaintiffs the requested one euro for moral prejudice caused by this inaction. The Court deferred the decision on whether to issue an injunction to order the French government to take stronger climate measures and ordered the government to disclose the steps it was taking to meet its climate targets within two months. As part of the decision, the Court held that France could be held responsible for failing to meet its own climate and carbon budget goals under EU and national law. But the Court rejected arguments that the government could be forced to meet more specific renewable energy and energy efficiency targets on the grounds that such sectoral measures cannot be independently directly linked to ecological damage. Furthermore, the Court declined the request to issue compensatory damages for ecological harm, as the Court found that the plaintiffs had not shown that the government would be unable to repair the harm caused. On 14 October 2021, the Administrative Court of Paris ordered the State to take immediate and concrete actions to comply with its commitments on cutting carbon emissions and repair the damages caused by its inaction by 31 December 2022. The Court determined that France

---

34 http://climatecasechart.com/non-us-case/commune-de-grande-synthe-v-france/; N. de Sadeleer, 'Le Conseil d'État de France condamne le report de la réduction des émissions de gaz à effet de serre par les autorités françaises', *Justice en ligne*, 8 January 2021, https://www.justice-en-ligne.be/le-Conseil-d-Etat-de-France; H. Bortels, I. Goetelen, S. Smet and J. Theunis, '*Urgenda and beyond*: de rol van mensenrechten in klimaatrechtspraak' in H. Schoukens and C.M. Billiet (eds), *Klimaatrechtspraak. Waarom Rechters het klimaat (niet) zullen redden. Huldeboek voor prof. Dr. Luc Lavrysen*, die Keure, Bruges 2021, pp. 53–55; N. de Sadeleer, 'Faculté ou obligation d'agir dans le chef de pouvoirs publics pour contrer le fléau climatique ? Quelques réflexions sur le droit comparé' in *L'environnement, le droit et le magistrat. Mélanges en l'honneur de Benoît Jadot*, Larcier, Brussels 2021, pp. 261–62.

35 http://climatecasechart.com/non-us-case/commune-de-grande-synthe-v-france/.

emitted 62 million extra tonnes of emissions in the period 2015–2018, though it lowered the amount to 15 million tonnes, taking into account the drop in emissions in 2020. The Court thus called on France to subtract the emissions caused in excess of its legislative commitments, adding these to the reduction of emissions planned between 2021 and 2022. France has committed to a reduction in greenhouse gas emissions of 40% by 2030, compared to 1990 levels, and to reaching carbon neutrality by 2050. Any future slippage of emissions beyond the legislative commitments must also be compensated. The Court rejected a request to have France pay €78 million per semester of delay in meeting the emissions goals, and said that it is up to the prime minister and the government to come up with the measures to fix the problem.[36]

In Germany, in February 2020, a group of young German people filed a legal challenge before the Federal Constitutional Court (Bundesverfassungsgericht) to Germany's Federal Climate Protection Act (Bundesklimaschutzgesetz or KSG), arguing that the KSG's target of reducing greenhouse gas emissions by 55% by 2030 compared to 1990 levels was insufficient. The complainants alleged that the KSG therefore violated their human rights as protected by the Basic Law, Germany's constitution. On 29 April 2021, the Federal Constitutional Court, in *Neubauer et al.*, struck down parts of the KSG as incompatible with fundamental rights for failing to set sufficient provisions for emissions cuts beyond 2030. The Court found that Article 20a of the Federal Constitution obliges the legislature to protect the climate and aim at achieving climate neutrality. Further, the Court stated that Article 20a 'is a justiciable legal norm that is intended to bind the political process in favour of ecological concerns, also with a view to the future generations that are particularly affected'. Accepting arguments that the legislature must follow a carbon budget approach to limit warming to well below 2°C and, if possible, to 1.5°C, the Court found that that the legislature had not proportionally distributed the budget between current and future generations, writing 'one generation must not be allowed to consume large parts of the CO_2 budget under a comparatively mild reduction burden if this would at

36 http://climatecasechart.com/non-us-case/notre-affaire-a-tous-and-others-v-france/; N. de Sadeleer, 'La Justice administrative française enjoint à l'État de réparer le préjudice écologique dû au réchauffement climatique', *Justice en ligne*, 26 April 2021, https://www.justice-en-ligne.be/La-Justice-administrative; H. Bortels, I. Goetelen, S. Smet and J. Theunis, '*Urgenda and beyond*: de rol van mensenrechten in klimaatrechtspraak' in H. Schoukens and C.M. Billiet (eds), *Klimaatrechtspraak. Waarom Rechters het klimaat (niet) zullen redden. Huldeboek voor prof. Dr. Luc Lavrysen*, die Keure, Bruges 2021, pp. 56–63; C. Cournil and M. Fleury, 'De "l'Affaire du siècle" au "casse du siècle" ? Quand le climat pénètre avec fracas le droit de la responsabilité administrative' (2021) *La Revue des droits de l'homme, Actualités Droits-Libertés*, http://journals.openedition.org/revdh/11141; N. de Sadeleer, 'Faculté ou obligation d'agir dans le chef de pouvoirs publics pour contrer le fléau climatique ? Quelques réflexions sur le droit comparé' in *L'environnement, le droit et le magistrat. Mélanges en l'honneur de Benoît Jadot*, Larcier, Brussels 2021, pp. 263–65; *Jurisprudence de Liège, Mons et Bruxelles* (2022), pp. 367–73, note D. Misonne.

the same time leave future generations with a radical reduction burden … and expose their lives to serious losses of freedom'. The Court ordered the legislature to set clear provisions for reduction targets from 2031 onward by the end of 2022.[37] Following that ruling and with a view to the new European climate target for 2030, the German federal government presented an amended Climate Change Act 2021 on 12 May 2021. The Bundestag approved the amendment to the Climate Change Act on 24 June 2021. On 25 June 2021 it was passed by the Bundesrat and the amended Act entered into force. The amended Climate Act[38] provides for raising the CO_2 emissions reduction targets. The target for 2030 is to be increased by 10 percentage points, to at least 65%. The climate goals are reviewed through continuous monitoring. Every two years, the Council of Experts for Climate Matters will present a report of the goals achieved, as well as measures and trends. For 2040 the reduction target is a minimum of 88%. Along the road to this goal, the Act lays down specific annual reduction targets during the 2030s. By 2045 Germany is to become greenhouse gas neutral. From 2050 onward, Germany aims to have a negative emissions balance, meaning that it would then remove more greenhouse gases using natural sinks than it emits.[39] On 24 January 2022, a group of German minors and young adults, supported by environmental organisation Deutsche Umwelthilfe filed a new constitutional challenge against the Amended Federal Climate Act. The claimants in this case – *Steinmetz et al.*[40] – argue that the amended greenhouse gas emissions reduction

37 L.J. Kotzé, 'Neubauer et al. versus Germany: Planetary Climate Litigation for the Anthropocene?' (2021) *German Law Journal* 1423; J. Peel and R. Markey-Towler, 'Recipe for Success?: Lessons for Strategic Climate Litigation from the *Sharma, Neubauer,* and *Shell* Cases' (2021) *German Law Journal* 1484; G. Winter, 'The Intergenerational Effect of Fundamental Rights: A Contribution of the German Federal Constitutional Court to Climate Protection' (2022) *Journal of Environmental Law* 209; H. Bortels, I. Goetelen, S. Smet and J. Theunis, '*Urgenda and beyond*: de rol van mensenrechten in klimaatrechtspraak' in H. Schoukens and C.M. Billiet (eds), *Klimaatrechtspraak. Waarom Rechters het klimaat (niet) zullen redden. Huldeboek voor prof. Dr. Luc Lavrysen*, die Keure, Bruges 2021, p. 56; J. Bäumler; 'Sustainable Development made justiciable: The German Constitutional Court's climate ruling on intra- and inter-generational equity', *EJIL:Talk!*, 8 June 2021, https://www.ejiltalk.org/sustainable-development-made-justiciable-the-german-constitutional-courts-climate-ruling-on-intra-and-inter-generational-equity/; N. de Sadeleer, 'Faculté ou obligation d'agir dans le chef de pouvoirs publics pour contrer le fléau climatique ? Quelques réflexions sur le droit comparé' in *L'environnement, le droit et le magistrat. Mélanges en l'honneur de Benoît Jadot*, Larcier, Brussels 2021, pp. 265–68; G. Roller, 'Les juges peuvent-ils sauver le climat ? Quelques réflexions concernant les actions juridiques en faveur du climat' in *L'environnement, le droit et le magistrat. Mélanges en l'honneur de Benoît Jadot*, Larcier, Brussels 2021, pp. 286–90; *Jurisprudence de Liège, Mons et Bruxelles* (2022), pp. 332–42, note C. Romainville; http://climatecasechart.com/non-us-case/neubauer-et-al-v-germany/; http://climatecasechart.com/non-us-case/family-farmers-and-greenpeace-germany-v-german-government/.

38 https://www.gesetze-im-internet.de/englisch_ksg/englisch_ksg.html.

39 C. Flachsland and S. Levi, 'Germany's Federal Climate Change Act' (2021) *30 Environmental Politics* 127.

40 http://climatecasechart.com/non-us-case/steinmetz-et-al-v-germany/.

paths are insufficient in light of Germany's constitutional and international legal obligations and that the new reduction path continues to infringe on their fundamental rights, as it will use up large parts of Germany's remaining CO_2 budget, as determined in accordance with Article 20a of the Basic Law.

On 17 June 2021, the Court of First Instance of Brussels gave its judgment in the Belgian *Klimaatzaak*.[41] The Brussels Court of First Instance condemned the various Belgian authorities for their negligent climate policy. However, the verdict did not directly lead to stricter climate targets. The Court ruled that Belgium's climate policy was inadequate and violated human rights, in particular Articles 2 and 8 ECHR. The Court found that Belgian climate policy was so substandard that it violated the legal duty of care and human rights. However, the verdict had no concrete consequences for the government. The State does not have to pay a fine and is not forced to tighten up the climate objectives and climate policy, as was the case in *Urgenda*.[42] On 17 November 2022, Klimaatzaak brought an appeal before the Court of Appeal in Brussels,[43] hoping to still be able to enforce specific emissions reduction targets. The citizens' collective is hoping to achieve stricter climate targets and is calling for a reduction of Belgian greenhouse gas emissions by at least 48% by 2025 and by 65% by 2030. The Brussels Court of Appeal has decided to give priority to the case. After a written conclusion round that will take 16 months, the case will be heard from 14 September to 6 October 2023. This is significantly faster than the average processing times of the Court.[44]

3.2.2. At the European Level

For the moment some important strategic cases have been brought before the ECtHR.[45] On 3 September 2020, six young Portuguese people filed an application

---

41 (2021) *Tijdschrift voor Milieurecht* 387–404; *Jurisprudence de Liège, Mons et Bruxelles* (2022), pp. 361–67, note M. Wuine.

42 P. Lefranc, 'Het klimaatzaakvonnis: wachten op "De man die bomen plantte"?' (2021) *Tijdschrift voor Milieurecht* 332; H. Bortels, I. Goetelen, S. Smet and J. Theunis, '*Urgenda and beyond*: de rol van mensenrechten in klimaatrechtspraak' in H. Schoukens and C. Billiet (eds), *Klimaatrechtspraak. Waarom Rechters het klimaat (niet) zullen redden. Huldeboek voor prof. Dr. Luc Lavrysen*, die Keure, Bruges 2021, pp. 64–67; E. de Kezel, 'De Belgische Klimaatzaak: het aansprakelijkheidsrecht als *gamechanger*' (2021) *Tijdschrift voor Omgevingsrecht en Omgevingsbeleid* 206; N. de Sadeleer, 'Faculté ou obligation d'agir dans le chef de pouvoirs publics pour contrer le fléau climatique ? Quelques réflexions sur le droit comparé' in *L'environnement, le droit et le magistrat. Mélanges en l'honneur de Benoît Jadot*, Larcier, Brussels 2021, pp. 269–72.

43 https://affaireclimat.cdn.prismic.io/affaireclimat/989e74fe-3d01-4cd0-9fff-d8642f974d8a_2021117_Reque%CC%82te+d%27appel_Def+DOCX_00832397+DOCX+-+PDF.pdf.

44 https://www.klimaatzaak.eu/en.

45 H. Bortels, I. Goetelen, S. Smet and J. Theunis, '*Urgenda and beyond*: de rol van mensenrechten in klimaatrechtspraak' in H. Schoukens and C. Billiet (eds), *Klimaatrechtspraak. Waarom Rechters het klimaat (niet) zullen redden. Huldeboek voor prof.*

before the ECtHR in the case *Duarte Agostinho and Others v. Portugal and 32 Other States.*[46] The objective was to recognise the responsibility of 33 European States in the climate crisis. The petitioners' complaint concerned the non-compliance by these States with their positive obligations under Articles 2 and 8 ECHR, read in the light of the commitments made under the Paris Agreement. On 30 November 2020, the Strasbourg Court notified the States concerned of the request, after the president of the section in charge of the case considered that this request should be examined as a matter of priority. The Court put three questions to the parties. The first is whether the facts of the complaint are of such a nature as to engage the responsibility of the States concerned 'taken individually or collectively because of their national or, as the case may be, European policies and regulations'. If so, the question arises as to whether the applicants suffer 'directly or indirectly and seriously' from the consequences of insufficient action by States to achieve the 1.5°C target of the Paris Agreement. Finally, if the answer to this is also positive, have the States fulfilled their obligations under the applicable provisions of the ECHR in the light of the principles of precaution and intergenerational equity? The requirement to exhaust domestic remedies compels individuals to first use available procedures under national law before bringing a complaint to the ECtHR. The applicants are lodging their case against 33 States directly before the ECtHR, because making use of domestic remedies in each of these States would take several years. As a result, the applicants, in this case, have not exhausted domestic remedies and are attempting to rely on an exception to this rule.[47]

In the meantime, a similar request was lodged on 26 November 2020 by a group of elderly Swiss women, after the Swiss Federal Administrative Court rejected their case in 2018, on the grounds that Swiss women over 75 are not the only population affected by the effects of climate change.[48] So in this case the requirement to exhaust

---

Dr. Luc Lavrysen, die Keure, Bruges 2021, pp. 44–47; S. Van Drooghenbroeck, 'We will see you in court: over klimaatzaken, mensenrechten en daadwerkelijke rechtsmiddelen' in H. Schoukens and C.M. Billiet (eds), *Klimaatrechtspraak. Waarom Rechters het klimaat (niet) zullen redden. Huldeboek voor prof. Dr. Luc Lavrysen*, die Keure, Bruges 2021, pp. 88–94; H. Keller and C. Heri, 'The Future is Now: Climate Cases Before the ECtHR' (2022) 40(1) *Nordic Journal of Human Rights* 153.

46 http://climatecasechart.com/non-us-case/youth-for-climate-justice-v-austria-et-al/. There are also two similar cases brought by Italian youngsters: *De Conto v. Italy and 32 other States* and *Uricchio v. Italy and 32 other States:* http://climatecasechart.com/non-us-case/de-conto-v-italy-and-32-other-states/; http://climatecasechart.com/climate-change-litigation/non-us-case/uricchio-v-italy-and-32-other-states/.

47 D. Stanculeso, 'The requirement to exhaust domestic remedies and the future of climate change litigation before the ECtHR', https://www.publicinternationallawandpolicygroup.org/lawyering-justice-blog/2021/4/26/the-requirement-to-exhaust-domestic-remedies-and-the-future-of-climate-change-litigation-before-the-ecthr; H. Keller and C. Heri, 'The Future is Now: Climate Cases Before the ECtHR' (2022) 40(1) *Nordic Journal of Human Rights* 153, 158–59; http://climatecasechart.com/non-us-case/youth-for-climate-justice-v-austria-et-al/.

48 On 20 May 2020, the Swiss Supreme Court dismissed the appeal. The Court concluded that the rights claimed by the plaintiffs had not been affected with sufficient intensity and that

national remedies has been fulfilled. The ECtHR communicated the case *Union of Swiss Senior Women for Climate Protection v. Swiss Federal Council and Others* (*Verein KlimaSeniorinnen Schweiz and Others v. Switzerland)* to the concerned State and raised some questions for the parties.[49] The main question is whether the applicant association and natural persons can be considered as actual or potential victims, within the meaning of Article 34 ECHR, of a violation of one of the ECHR rights invoked in this case because of the failure of the Swiss authorities to effectively protect them from the effects of global warming. In particular, did the applicants directly or indirectly and seriously suffer the consequences of insufficient action or inaction alleged by the respondent State? In the affirmative, has there been a violation of Articles 2 and 8 of the Convention in the present case and were these provisions applicable to the present case? Did the respondent State fail in its positive obligations to effectively protect the life (Article 2) and/or respect for private and family life, including the home (Article 8), of the applicants?[50] The Chamber to which the case had been allocated relinquished jurisdiction in favour of the Grand Chamber on 26 April 2022.[51]

Similar questions have been raised by the Court in the *Greenpeace Nordic and Others v. Norway* case.[52] Further cases are *Carême v. France*, a case brought by the former mayor of the city of Grande-Synthe in France, after the French Council of State in the *Grande-Synthe* case rejected that application insofar as it was brought by the applicant, on the grounds that he did not show his personal interest in the case since his claims were limited to the argument that, as an individual, his home was situated in an area likely to be subject to flooding by 2040.[53]

A similar action, the case of *Armando Carvalho and Others v. European Parliament and Council of the European Union*[54] was brought before the General Court of the European Union, on the one hand seeking the partial annulment of certain EU climate legislation deemed insufficient, and on the other hand seeking redress in the form of an injunction, obliging the co-legislators to adopt

---

the remedy they sought had to be obtained through political rather than legal means. http://climatecasechart.com/non-us-case/union-of-swiss-senior-women-for-climate-protection-v-swiss-federal-parliament/.

49 http://climatecasechart.com/non-us-case/union-of-swiss-senior-women-for-climate-protection-v-swiss-federal-council-and-others/.

50 http://climatecasechart.com/non-us-case/union-of-swiss-senior-women-for-climate-protection-v-swiss-federal-council-and-others/.

51 E. Schmid, 'Victim Status before the ECtHR in Cases of Alleged Omissions: The Swiss Climate Case', *EJIL:Talk!*, 30 April 2022, https://www.ejiltalk.org/victim-status-before-the-ecthr-in-cases-of-alleged-omissions-the-swiss-climate-case/. See also: https://strasbourgobservers.com/2021/10/22/third-party-intervention-in-pending-climate-case-the-human-rights-centre-of-ghent-university-submits-leave-to-intervene-in-klimaseniorinnen-v-switzerland/.

52 https://www.greenpeace.org/static/planet4-norway-stateless/2022/01/a45a392f-questions-to-the-parties-received-221221.pdf.

53 http://climatecasechart.com/climate-change-litigation/non-us-case/careme-v-france/.

54 http://climatecasechart.com/non-us-case/armando-ferrao-carvalho-and-others-v-the-european-parliament-and-the-council/.

measures 'imposing by 2030 a reduction in the level of greenhouse gas emissions included, at the very least, between 50% to 60% of their 1990 level'. The General Court declared the case inadmissible on 8 May 2019 for lack of standing based on the very strict '*Plaumann* test' applied by the EU courts.[55] The Court of Justice of the EU rejected the appeal against that decision on 25 March 2021.[56]

3.2.3. *Major Projects and Companies*

Apart from lawsuits challenging big projects, like the extension of Heathrow Airport,[57] more and more cases are being brought against major companies. The Climate Change Litigation database reported on 6 April 2022 78 non-US cases, of which 32 have been brought in Europe.[58]

On 26 May 2021, the Hague District Court rendered a ground-breaking judgment.[59] The Court ordered Royal Dutch Shell (RDS) to reduce the CO_2 emissions of the Shell group by net 45% in 2030, compared to 2019 levels, through the Shell group's corporate policy. This order was given in proceedings initiated by seven foundations and associations, i.e. the NGO Milieudefensie, as well as over 17,000 individual claimants.

The Court concluded that RDS was required to ensure through the Shell group's corporate policy that the CO_2 emissions of the Shell group, its suppliers and its customers would be reduced. This follows from the unwritten standard of care applicable to RDS, which the court interpreted based on the facts, widespread consensus and internationally accepted standards.[60]

---

55 CJEU, 8 May 2019, T-330/18, *Carvalho and Others v. Parliament and Council*; H. Schoukens, 'De People's Climate Case bij het Europees Hof van Justitie; over Kafka, Aarhus en de onfeilbaarheid van het Europese Klimaatbeleid' in H. Schoukens and C.M. Billiet (eds), *Klimaatrechtspraak. Waarom Rechters het klimaat (niet) zullen redden. Huldeboek voor prof. Dr. Luc Lavrysen*, die Keure, Bruges 2021, pp. 98–142; J. Fraser and L. Henderson, 'The human rights turn in climate change litigation and responsibilities of legal professionals' (2022) *Netherlands Quarterly of Human Rights* 9; J. van Zeben, 'The Role of the EU Charter of Fundamental Rights in Climate Litigation' (2021) *German Law Journal* 1506.

56 CJEU, 25 March 2021, C-565/19 P, *Carvalho and Others v. Parliament and Council*, http://climatecasechart.com/non-us-case/armando-ferrao-carvalho-and-others-v-the-european-parliament-and-the-council/.

57 N. de Sadeleer, 'Faculté ou obligation d'agir dans le chef de pouvoirs publics pour contrer le fléau climatique ? Quelques réflexions sur le droit comparé' in *L'environnement, le droit et le magistrat. Mélanges en l'honneur de Benoît Jadot*, Larcier, Brussels 2021, pp. 252–55; http://climatecasechart.com/non-us-case/plan-b-earth-others-v-secretary-state-business-energy-industrial-strategy/.

58 http://climatecasechart.com/non-us-case-category/corporations/page/5/.

59 O. Spijkers, 'Friends of the Earth Netherlands (Milieudefensie) v Royal Dutch Shell' (2021) *Chinese Journal of Environmental Law* 237; C.M. Billiet, 'Klimaatrechtspraak en bedrijven; het Shellvonnis in het tij' in H. Schoukens and C.M. Billiet (eds), *Klimaatrechtspraak. Waarom Rechters het klimaat (niet) zullen redden. Huldeboek voor prof. Dr. Luc Lavrysen*, die Keure, Bruges 2021, pp. 211–39.

60 According to the Hague District Court, the Shell group is one of the world's largest producers and suppliers of fossil fuels. The CO_2 emissions of the Shell group, its suppliers and customers

RDS has an obligation of result with respect to the Shell group's CO_2 emissions. As regards its suppliers and customers, RDS has a significant best-efforts obligation, which means that RDS must use its influence through the corporate policy for the Shell group, for instance by setting requirements on suppliers in its purchasing policy. RDS has complete freedom in how it meets its reduction obligation and shapes the Shell group's corporate policy. The required sacrifices outweigh the interest served by fighting dangerous climate change. The Court found that RDS is not presently in breach of its reduction obligation, as the claimants argued. RDS has improved the Shell group's policy and is working it out in more detail. However, seeing as the policy is not concrete, has many caveats and is based on monitoring social developments rather than the company's own responsibility for achieving CO_2 reduction, the Court found that there is an *imminent breach of the reduction obligation*. Therefore, the Court has ordered RDS to implement the above-mentioned emission reduction of the Shell group, its suppliers and its customers through its corporate policy.

This decision is ground-breaking. For the first time a court has decided that not only governments but also companies have a legal obligation to do their part against climate change. Shell has vowed to appeal the decision. The judgment is already binding, and the court can impose penalties. Legal scholars in the Netherlands expect that other such cases will arise.[61]

4. CONCLUSIONS

Looking at recent case law in strategic climate cases, it seems that some general principles can be deduced: (1) the protection of life and health includes protection against environmental pollution; (2) human rights constitute a positive obligation to protect against environmental harm, including the harm resulting from climate change; (3) emission cuts must not be postponed to later when only an extremely short time is left for radical transformations; and (4) reducing emissions is obligatory even if a State's share in global emissions is small.[62]

---

exceed those of many countries. This contributes to global warming, which causes dangerous climate change and creates serious risks to human rights, such as the right to life and the right to respect for private and family life. It is generally accepted that companies must respect human rights. This is an individual responsibility of companies, which is separate from States' actions. This responsibility also extends to suppliers and customers.

61 https://www.rechtspraak.nl/Organisatie-en-contact/Organisatie/Rechtbanken/Rechtbank-Den-Haag/Nieuws/Paginas/Royal-Dutch-Shell-must-reduce-CO2-emissions.aspx; https://uitspraken.rechtspraak.nl/inziendocument?id=ECLI:NL:RBDHA:2021:5337; http://climatecasechart.com/non-us-case/milieudefensie-et-al-v-royal-dutch-shell-plc/.

62 G. Roller, 'Les juges peuvent-ils sauver le climat ? Quelques réflexions concernant les actions juridiques en faveur du climat' in *L'environnement, le droit et le magistrat. Mélanges en l'honneur de Benoît Jadot*, Larcier, Brussels 2021, pp. 291–94.

In the near future, the ECtHR will be able to clarify whether the Dutch Supreme Court's approach, based on the positive duties derived from Articles 2 and 8 ECHR, is appropriate or not. These judgments of the ECtHR will have a decisive impact on the further development of climate litigation in Europe and elsewhere.

We can safely say that, in the decades to come, national courts and tribunals will also inevitably be increasingly confronted with climate cases.[63] As long as governments and companies[64] are not delivering as it is believed they should do – and recent climate change science tells us that we are indeed not on track to deliver on the Paris Agreement goals,[65] indeed far from it[66] – citizens and ENGOs will continue to bring strategic cases. Those cases will deal with a variety of issues. Public and private projects and policies will be scrutinised in terms of their impact on climate change, and the Environmental Impact Assessment and Strategic Environmental Assessment will play an ever more crucial role in it.[67] Because climate change is happening, adaptation measures must be taken,[68]

---

63 J. Setzer and C. Higham, *Global trends in climate change litigation: 2021 snapshot. July 2021, Policy report*, Grantham Research Institute on Climate Change and the Environment and Centre for Climate Change Economics and Policy, London School of Economics and Political Science, London 2021, p. 7.

64 See on the private law perspectives in relation to climate change cases: L. Burgers, *Justitia, the People's Power and Mother Earth. Democratic legitimacy of judicial law-making in European private law cases on climate change*, Universiteit van Amsterdam, Amsterdam 2020.

65 IPCC, *Climate Change 2022: Mitigation of Climate Change. Contribution of Working Group III to the Sixth Assessment Report of the Intergovernmental Panel on Climate Change* (P.R. Shukla, J. Skea, R. Slade, A. Al Khourdajie, R. van Diemen, D. McCollum, M. Pathak, S. Some, P. Vyas, R. Fradera, M. Belkacemi, A. Hasija, G. Lisboa, S. Luz and J. Malley, eds), Cambridge University Press, Cambridge/New York 2022, https://www.ipcc.ch/report/sixth-assessment-report-working-group-3/; IPCC, *Climate Change 2022: Impacts, Adaptation, and Vulnerability. Contribution of Working Group II to the Sixth Assessment Report of the Intergovernmental Panel on Climate Change* (H.-O. Pörtner, D.C. Roberts, M. Tignor, E.S. Poloczanska, K. Mintenbeck, A. Alegría, M. Craig, S. Langsdorf, S. Löschke, V. Möller, A. Okem and B. Rama, eds), Cambridge University Press, Cambridge/New York 2022, https://www.ipcc.ch/report/sixth-assessment-report-working-group-ii/; IPCC, *Climate Change 2021: The Physical Science Basis. Contribution of Working Group I to the Sixth Assessment Report of the Intergovernmental Panel on Climate Change* (V. Masson-Delmotte, P. Zhai, A. Pirani, S.L. Connors, C. Péan, S. Berger, N. Caud, Y. Chen, L. Goldfarb, M.I. Gomis, M. Huang, K. Leitzell, E. Lonnoy, J.B.R. Matthews, T.K. Maycock, T. Waterfield, O. Yelekçi, R. Yu and B. Zhou, eds), Cambridge University Press, Cambridge/New York 2021, https://www.ipcc.ch/report/sixth-assessment-report-working-group-i/.

66 UNEP, *The Heat Is On. A World of Climate Promises Not Yet Delivered. Emissions Gap Report 2021*, Nairobi 2021, https://www.unep.org/resources/emissions-gap-report-2021; European Environment Agency, *Report No 13/2021. Trends and projections in Europe 2021*, Copenhagen 2021.

67 H. Schoukens, 'Practice what you preach: de Langzame dans richting een bindende klimaattoets' in H. Schoukens and C.M. Billiet (eds), *Klimaatrechtspraak. Waarom Rechters het klimaat (niet) zullen redden. Huldeboek voor prof. Dr. Luc Lavrysen*, die Keure, Bruges 2021, pp. 177–209.

68 UNEP, *The Gathering Storm. Adapting to climate change in a post-pandemic world, Adaptation Gap Report 2021*, Nairobi 2021, https://www.unep.org/resources/adaptation-gap-report-2021.

and the impact of the related infrastructure works (construction of dykes, ponds, irrigation facilities, flood control measures, etc.) on the private life and property of citizens will lead to more litigation. In addition, public responses to emergencies will give rise to cases, including liability cases, when, for example, the response to a (predicted) flooding was believed not to be adequate.[69]

Even if strategic climate cases are won in the courts, the question arises as to how to enforce those judgments. What if the judicially imposed reduction targets are not met? What if a plan or a programme has been adopted by the government or corporation following the judgment, but is not or is insufficiently implemented? It was indeed no surprise that the Netherlands did not manage to respect the reduction targets imposed by the *Urgenda* judgments. The new preliminary figures for CO_2 emissions in 2021 show that emissions have again increased. Almost seven years after the *Urgenda* judgment of June 2015, the government is still not achieving the required 25% reduction in CO_2 emissions compared to 1990 levels. Will this give rise to follow-up cases and what types of remedies will be available?

69 https://www.brusselstimes.com/news/belgium-all-news/179395/criminal-investigation-into-flood-response-in-liege; https://www.swissinfo.ch/eng/german-officials-investigated-for-homicide-over-slow-flood-response/46848212.

CLIMATE CHANGE LITIGATION BEFORE EUROPEAN REGIONAL COURTS

An Expert Discussion

Ivano ALOGNA and Carole BILLIET

1. INTRODUCTION[1]

In recent years, climate-related litigation before European regional courts has increased and expanded swiftly.[2] To frame this context, four of the most significant cases in the field can be highlighted: two before the Strasbourg Court and two before the Luxembourg Court. Currently pending before the European Court of Human Rights (ECtHR) is the *Duarte Agostinho* case, in which six Portuguese youths filed a claim against 33 Council of Europe

---

1 This chapter builds on the discussion between Judge Tim Eicke KC and Marc Willers KC on climate change litigation before European regional courts, chaired by Professor Sanja Bogojevic, on the first day of the conference at the basis of this edited volume. Judge Tim Eicke KC is the United Kingdom's judge at the European Court of Human Rights (ECtHR) and Vice President of Section IV of the Court. Marc Willers KC is a UK barrister practising at Garden Court Chambers in London. Professor Sanja Bogojevic is a Fellow and Professor of Law at Lady Margaret Hall and the Faculty of Law at Oxford University. The authors wish to thank the speakers for contributing to the panel discussion, and particularly Mark Willers KC for his thoughtful and useful comments on the chapter.

2 See K. POUIKLI, 'Editorial: A Short History of the Climate Change Litigation Boom Across Europe' (2021) *Journal of the Academy of European Law* 569.

countries for neglecting to take adequate measures to combat climate change.[3] The Swiss *KlimaSeniorinnen* case is another climate case pending before the Strasbourg Court. It involves a group of senior women who have filed a lawsuit against the Swiss government, alleging that it has failed to uphold its obligations under the European Convention on Human Rights (ECHR) by failing to steer Switzerland onto a safe emissions reduction trajectory.[4] The petition by senior women observes that their demographic group is particularly vulnerable to heat waves due to climate change. The two cases before the Court of Justice of the European Union (CJEU) are the *People's Climate Case*, in which 10 families, including children from EU and non-EU countries, petitioned the EU courts for more stringent greenhouse gas regulations;[5] and the *EU Biomass Case*, in which plaintiffs from multiple EU countries challenged the Renewable Energy Directive on the grounds that it accelerated deforestation.[6] Both cases were deemed inadmissible on standing grounds.

The expert panel discussion at the conference focused on these cases, providing perspectives from a practitioner, a judge and an academic, and addressing various relevant points, including what makes a successful climate case, the main differences between the CJEU and the ECtHR, the enforcement of judgments and the role of courts, the interplay between regional and domestic courts and the role of science, and the risk of bringing climate cases to court, and concluding with some thoughts about cross-fertilisation among courts.

---

3 *Duarte Agostinho and Others v. Portugal and 32 Other States*, no. 39371/20 was lodged on 7 September 2020, given priority and communicated to the respondent States on 13 November 2020. The 33 respondent States include Portugal, the other 26 EU States, the UK, Switzerland, Norway, Russia, Turkey and Ukraine. The Grand Chamber will hear the parties' submissions on admissibility and merits on 27 September 2023. For more information, see https://youth4climatejustice.org/ and https://climatecasechart.com/non-us-case/youth-for-climate-justice-v-austria-et-al/.

4 *Verein Klimaseniorinnen v. Switzerland*, no. 53600/20 was lodged on 26 November 2020, given priority and communicated to the respondent States on 6 April 2021. The Grand Chamber heard the parties' oral arguments on admissibility and merits on 29 March 2023. For more information, see https://klimaseniorinnen.ch and http://climatecasechart.com/climate-change-litigation/non-us-case/union-of-swiss-senior-women-for-climate-protection-v-swiss-federal-parliament/.

5 Case T-330/18, *Armando Carvalho and Others v. European Parliament and Council of the European Union*, Order of the General Court (Second Chamber) of 8 May 2019; on appeal Case C-565/19 P, *Armando Carvalho and Others against the Order of the General Court*, Judgment of the Court (Sixth Chamber) of 25 March 2021.

6 Case T-141/19, *Peter Sabo and Others v. European Parliament and Council of the European Union*, Order of the General Court (Fourth Chamber) of 6 May 2020; on appeal Case C-297/20 P, *Peter Sabo and Others v. European Parliament and Council of the European Union*, Order of the Court (Eighth Chamber) of 14 January 2021.

2. WHAT MAKES A SUCCESSFUL CLIMATE CASE?

Marc Willers KC, as a climate justice practitioner, considered that the success of a case could be measured in various ways and that it was not all about winning before the judges and coming away with a resounding success. The two cases before the CJEU – the *People's Climate Case* and the *EU Biomass Case* – were both ruled inadmissible as they both fell afoul of the *Plaumann* doctrine on standing.[7] Nevertheless, both cases have made a significant positive impact outside of the courtroom: the former case played a part in persuading the EU to increase its greenhouse gas reduction target for 2030, compared with 1990 levels, from 40% to 55%;[8] the latter case helped push the EU to review its inclusion of biomass in the Renewable Energy Directive.[9] Despite the fact that the applicants were unsuccessful in having their cases heard on the merits, the reality is that they have achieved, before the court of public opinion, some of what they set out to achieve before the CJEU. However, Marc Willers KC considered that the CJEU's application of the *Plaumann* doctrine on standing will effectively preclude the possibility of individuals bringing future climate lawsuits before that court in the future; and he noted that Advocate General Jacobs and others, including the Aarhus Convention Committee, have expressed a strong need for the CJEU to revise the *Plaumann* doctrine.[10]

As for the pending applications before the ECtHR, it is important to appreciate that admissibility has not yet been determined in any of those cases, though they have been communicated to the respondent States. There is hope that at least one of them will be ruled admissible and be determined on its merits and that the ECtHR will go at least as far as the Dutch Supreme Court in the *Urgenda* case did, and, indeed, adopt much of what the Supreme Court said in that case.[11]

---

7 For an application brought by an individual to be considered admissible before the CJEU the contested act must affect a natural or legal person 'by reason of certain attributes that are peculiar to them or by reason of circumstances in which they are differentiated from all other persons, and by virtue of these factors distinguishes them individually just as in the case of the addressee.' Case 25/62, *Plaumann & Co. v. Commission* [1963] ECR 95.

8 Art. 4(1) Regulation (EU) 2021/1119 of the European Parliament and of the Council of 30 June 2021 establishing the framework for achieving climate neutrality and amending Regulations (EC) No 401/2009 and (EU) 2018/1999 ('European Climate Law').

9 Directive (EU) 2018/2001 of the European Parliament and of the Council of 11 December 2018 on the promotion of the use of energy from renewable sources.

10 See ACCC/C/2008/32 European Union, Part II – Findings adopted on 17 March 2017, https://unece.org/env/pp/cc/accc.c.2008.32_european-union.

11 *Urgenda Foundation v. The State of the Netherlands*, Hague District Court, Case No. C/09/456689 / HA ZA 13-1396, 24 June 2015; *The State of the Netherlands v. Urgenda Foundation*, Hague Court of Appeal, Case No. C/09/456689 / HA ZA 13-1396, 9 October 2018; *The State of the Netherlands v. Urgenda Foundation*, Supreme Court, Case No. 19/00135,

Speaking more generally, Marc Willers KC said that for a climate case to succeed, there was a need for resilient and committed clients because the journey is generally long. Another important requirement is a great communications strategy and team in order to maximise awareness amongst the public of the issues at stake. Thirdly, it is vital that brilliant scientific experts are engaged who can explain why the applicants will be affected by climate change, and why it is the respondent State's fault that they will be affected by climate change in a significant way. The scientific experts must be able to provide that explanation in a way which is coherent and clear for lawyers and judges to understand. Finally, it is critical that expert lawyers are instructed so that the legal arguments are properly presented for the best chance of a successful climate change case, one that may succeed in front of the judges or at least nudge States into taking climate change seriously.

Judge Tim Eicke KC, the UK's judge at the ECtHR, agreed that there is more to litigation than winning in the courts. As widely acknowledged and extensively discussed in the literature, the ECtHR poses considerable challenges in terms of admissibility and merits that a case must surmount to achieve victory. However, it is evident that the discussion around the *Duarte Agostinho* case, particularly in the media and in the public sphere, has undeniably exerted an influence. The generation of that public discussion could already be considered a successful consequence of the plaintiffs' application, albeit that it may not necessarily align with the level of success they aspire to attain. However, it is obvious that these cases will take some time to be determined. Consequently, successes can arise during the process, whether or not the case is ultimately successful in Strasbourg.

3. DIFFERENCES BETWEEN THE CJEU AND THE ECtHR

The CJEU and the ECtHR exhibit certain similarities. However, they also manifest notable differences. Apart from the already mentioned prohibitive CJEU standing rules, it is worth noting that the potential remedies for climate cases can vary significantly depending on the jurisdiction, and that the ECtHR lacks the extensive range of legal tools available to the Luxembourg Court.

---

20 December 2019; see http://climatecasechart.com/non-us-case/urgenda-foundation-v-kingdom-of-the-netherlands/. See also C. Bakker, 'Climate Change Litigation in the Netherlands' in I. Alogna, C. Bakker and J.-P. Gauci (eds.), *Climate Change Litigation: Global Perspectives*, Brill 2021, pp. 199–224.

Judge Eicke KC agreed that the two courts are very different but drew attention to the fact that, within the broader context of climate change litigation, there is a dialogue between the international, regional and domestic courts, the challenges they encounter, and the strategies employed to overcome them. By way of example, Judge Eicke KC noted that although there were divergent outcomes of the *Urgenda* case and the case presented before the UN Committee on the Rights of the Child,[12] in both cases the tribunals made significant pronouncements that could influence other courts in future proceedings.

The main difference between the CJEU and the ECtHR is that the former functions as the supreme court of a legal order, overseeing the establishment and implementation of an intricate and comprehensive legal system encompassing various matters, including climate change, whereas the ECtHR primarily focuses on monitoring the adherence of its Member States to the commitments they have undertaken under the ECHR. So the focus of the two regional courts is somewhat different, and as a result the decisions reached by each court may appear to diverge.

In its current form, the Convention does not include provisions for a right to a healthy environment or any other mechanism specifically addressing climate change. Consequently, the cases before the ECtHR invoke: Articles 2 and 8 of the ECHR, which protect the right to life and the right to respect for private and family life, respectively, as well as arguments based upon Article 6 of the ECHR, which guarantees the right of access to court and Article 1 of Protocol 1, which safeguards the right to the peaceful enjoyment of one's property.

Marc Willers KC, commenting on the remedies available to the regional courts, highlighted that, unlike the CJEU, the ECtHR does not have the power to strike down legislation and has significant limitations regarding the remedy it can provide to a successful applicant. He also noted that the applicants in the *Agostinho* case seek a declaration that their rights, as guaranteed by Articles 2, 3, 8 and 14 of the Convention, have been infringed. They have not asked the ECtHR to issue an order specifying the actions the 33 respondent Member States should undertake to address climate change and enhance their targets for reducing greenhouse gas emissions. The responsibility for deciding what steps should be taken lies with the Member States, which, in the event of a successful outcome, will be required to revise and reformulate their policies.

Judge Eicke KC also noted that an examination of the ECtHR's jurisprudence on remedies and Article 41 of the ECHR (the right to just satisfaction) demonstrates that the main remedies issued by the Court are declaratory judgments and/or monetary awards.

---

12 *Sacchi et al. v. Argentina, Brazil, France, Germany and Turkey* (2021); see http://climatecasechart.com/non-us-case/sacchi-et-al-v-argentina-et-al/.

4. ENFORCEMENT OF JUDGMENTS

The execution of the ECtHR's judgments is supervised by the Committee of Ministers and is a process which is non-judicial and more politically oriented. That process serves again to highlight the inherent differences between the two regional courts, where the CJEU enforces a legal instance within a hierarchical legal system, equipped with a comprehensive array of tools, while the ECtHR enforces minimum standards under a public international law treaty, with no substructure and a very limited legislative basis on which it can operate.

Marc Willers KC stated that the political nature of the enforcement of ECtHR judgments can lead to difficulties when it comes to the implementation of its decisions. Cases involving the Roma community were mentioned by Marc Willers KC as a compelling illustration of situations in which the ECtHR has consistently and persistently rendered judgments, yet the implementation of these judgments has not been realised. Similar problems may arise if the applicants in the climate change cases pending before the ECtHR achieve victory.

Professor Bogojevic noted that there are also inherent limitations in the enforcement capabilities of the Luxembourg Court, notwithstanding its relatively more robust powers.

Judge Eicke KC stated that these issues raised a fundamental question regarding the role of the regional courts in the context of climate change. The regional courts do not have the democratic legitimacy comparable to that held by domestic governments and their legislature when enacting climate change-related policy and law, and the question is to what extent it is feasible, suitable, legitimate and desirable for the regional courts to engage in these matters.

5. INTERPLAY BETWEEN REGIONAL AND DOMESTIC COURTS AND THE ROLE OF SCIENCE

Professor Bogojevic stressed that one advantage of having a regional court is that its judgments have a broader judicial scope, resulting in the CJEU's judgments effectively becoming binding law in all Member States. However, it is important to consider the extent to which the presence of national courts may still constrain a regional court. The CJEU frequently relies on references to the decisions of national courts in its judgments as a means of asserting that the European Union ensures effective judicial protection. As for the ECtHR, it is necessary to exhaust all national remedies before resorting to Strasbourg.[13] There exist inherent limits

13 Art. 35(1) ECHR (Admissibility criteria): 'The Court may only deal with the matter after all domestic remedies have been exhausted, according to the generally recognised rules of international law, and within a period of four months from the date on which the final

that undoubtedly influence the capacity of regional courts to deliver outcomes and shape our expectations of their performance.

Judge Eicke KC agreed that, in both regional courts, there is a significant reliance on the decisions of domestic courts. This is evident in the ECtHR through the obligation to exhaust domestic remedies and the principle of subsidiarity, which has been incorporated into the preamble of the Convention since the entry into force of Protocol 15 (although it was already an integral part of the Court's jurisprudence).[14] The principle of subsidiarity is considered to be particularly important. First of all, it relates to the previously made point about the legitimacy of climate judgments, and, more particularly, their foundation in democratic legitimacy. Another practical point is that the regional courts rely upon domestic courts to fulfil a fact-finding role. For regional courts to reach conclusions on climate-related matters without the benefit of domestic courts having done what they do best – namely, hearing evidence and determining the factual situation – would place them in a challenging and practical position when attempting independently to ascertain these matters. That is one of the reasons why the exhaustion of domestic remedies is so important. A third aspect to consider is the principle of public international law, which provides that governments should be given the opportunity to address any shortcomings or failures of compliance before being subjected to international court proceedings.

Addressing this factual point, Marc Willers KC highlighted that the scientific consensus is well established. It is supported by the Intergovernmental Panel on Climate Change (IPCC) reports.[15] Additionally, the Member States, having

decision was taken.' Note that '[t]he exhaustion rule may be described as one that is golden rather than cast in stone. The Commission and the Court have frequently underlined the need to apply the rule with some degree of flexibility and without excessive formalism, given the context of protecting human right' – ECtHR, *Practical Guide on Admissibility Criteria*, updated 31 August 2022, p. 27, https://www.echr.coe.int/documents/d/echr/admissibility_guide_eng.

14 Preamble to the ECHR, as amended by the provisions of Protocol 15: 'Affirming that the High Contracting Parties, in accordance with the principle of subsidiarity, have the primary responsibility to secure the rights and freedoms defined in this Convention and the Protocols thereto, and that in doing so they enjoy a margin of appreciation, subject to the supervisory jurisdiction of the European Court of Human Rights established by this Convention.'

15 As is widely known, the IPCC publishes General Assessment Reports (ARs) and thematic reports, called Special Reports (SRs). These reports come with a Summary for Policy Makers (SPMs) and Technical Summaries (TCs), the ARs additionally with a Synthesis Report (SYR) (with specific SPM). The most recent AR is AR6, published in August 2021 (report of Working Group I, 'The Physical Science Basis'), February 2022 (report of Working Group II, 'Impacts, Adaptation and Vulnerability') and April 2022 (report of Working Group III, 'Mitigation of Climate Change'). Its Synthesis Report was adopted in March 2023. The most well-known thematic report is the Special Report '1.5°C' of 2018, which studies the differences between global heating of 1.5°C and global heating of 2°C. The reports are submitted to a double peer review. They are approved in plenary meetings of the Member States of the IPCC: 'Conclusions drawn by IPCC Working Groups and any Task Forces are not official IPCC views until they have been accepted by the Panel in a plenary meeting': Principles Governing

ratified the Paris Agreement, have essentially acknowledged the validity of this scientific consensus. Consequently, they have committed themselves to employing their utmost efforts to address climate change, aiming to limit global warming to well below 2°C and ideally to 1.5°C. Marc Willers KC observed that the applicants in the two cases pending before the ECtHR had avoided the risk of any respondent State disputing the scientific evidence (and the Court being placed in the uncomfortable position of having to determine such a dispute) by relying upon the fact that the respondent Member States had committed to the temperature limit outlined in the Paris Agreement. Nevertheless, he noted that the scientific evidence actually demonstrates that a 1°C increase in global temperature has led to hazardous climate change and that in the United States the lawyers of Our Children's Trust have consistently argued in the youth cases they have brought before the US courts that a 1°C increase in temperature is excessive and contributes to the occurrence of dangerous climate change.[16]

According to Judge Eicke, despite ongoing debates on the scientific consensus, it is important to acknowledge that there are still dissenting opinions on the technical intricacies, particularly where the subject matter under consideration does not pertain to the broader field of scientific inquiry, nor does it adhere to the established guidelines set forth by the IPCC or the standards outlined in the Paris Agreement. For example, in the context of a case brought by a resident of an urban area, it is necessary to demonstrate personal impact to claim victim status in order to engage the protection of Article 8. That issue needs to be established on the available evidence, and national courts are better placed than the ECtHR to conduct that exercise. Therefore, the debate regarding scientific evidence does not relate to the global picture but rather to the matters that need to be proved for a case to be admitted by the Court.

Nonetheless, from Marc Willers KC's perspective, there is potential for young individuals and their advocates to argue that a government's climate change mitigation policy that heavily relies on untested, speculative and high-risk measures, such as negative emission technology and carbon capture and storage, may impose a significant burden on youth and future generations. Such a policy could potentially place young people in a situation where they bear the

---

IPCC Work, last updated 2013, https://www.ipcc.ch/site/assets/uploads/2018/09/ipcc-principles.pdf. The approval of the reports in plenary meeting actively involves the IPCC Member States. Professor W. Thiery (Université Libre of Brussels), a member of the Belgian delegation at the plenary meeting of March 2023 where the SYR of the AR6 and its SMP were approved, described the validation process as moving forward 'sentence by sentence': T. Ysebaert, 'Er is geen tijd meer, de uitstoot moet dalen', *De Standaard*, 21 March 2023, p. 3, '*zin per zin*'.

16 Today, the average global surface warming has reached 1.1°C above pre-industrial levels. IPCC, AR6 SYR, SPM, *sub* A.1, https://www.ipcc.ch/report/ar6/syr/downloads/report/IPCC_AR6_SYR_SPM.pdf.

consequences of these risks and face considerable challenges in achieving the target of net-zero emissions by 2050. In that scenario, wherein one is assessing the future prospects of young people who have presented a case before the ECtHR, it is arguable that an exhaustive fact-finding endeavour may not be imperative in order for the Court to conclude that these individuals are being disproportionately affected due to their age. The decision rendered by the German Constitutional Court in the *Neubauer* case[17] was effectively based on the same line of reasoning.

Judge Eicke made the point that the approach the ECtHR might adopt in the cases pending before it is uncertain. He noted that the Swiss *KlimaSeniorinnen* case is currently under consideration due to the denial of standing to the victims by the Supreme Court of Switzerland, which applied the Strasbourg test as established in two earlier Swiss decisions. Additionally, the UN Committee on the Rights of the Child has dismissed complaints brought before it on the grounds of failing to exhaust available domestic remedies.[18] He said that the significance of such judgments cannot be lightly disregarded. The ECtHR relies on national courts and the exhaustion of domestic remedies is such an important principle that the Court's approach to it may require alteration, adjustment or modification in order to facilitate the consideration of certain cases.

6. RISK OF BRINGING CLIMATE CASES TO COURT

Prof. Bogojevic highlighted a potential risk associated with the phenomenon known as 'climate populism', as discussed by Chris Hilson and other scholars.[19] This concept includes the utilisation of courts in policy-related matters such as climate change and poses the inherent danger of instrumentalising the judicial system in the political game and raises the question of the possible hazards of employing the courtroom for such specific purposes.

On one side, Judge Eicke, referring to the already mentioned concept of democratic legitimacy, stressed the potential risk of bringing climate cases to court. Even a successful climate lawsuit may entail a risk that it will not be accepted or adhered to by relevant societal stakeholders. That is particularly so if it is not considered proper for a court to intervene or engage to such a significant extent. This subject must be acknowledged and carefully considered, particularly in light of the current resistance to judicial overreach.

---

17 *Neubauer et al. v. Germany* (2021), http://climatecasechart.com/non-us-case/neubauer-et-al-v-germany/.

18 *Sacchi et al. v. Argentina, Brazil, France, Germany & Turkey*, above n. 12.

19 See for instance C. Hilson, 'Climate Populism, Courts and Science' (2019) 31 *Journal of Environmental Law* 395.

On the other side, Marc Willers KC examined the matter again through the lens of youth, as exemplified by the global activism of Greta Thunberg and the Fridays for Future movement. Despite their consistent and unwavering efforts in advocating for change every Friday, it is evident that their voices are not being adequately acknowledged or heeded. Consequently, it is to be expected that individuals will resort to legal professionals, both lawyers and judges, to compel States to fulfil their responsibilities. Therefore, it is unlikely that courts can evade the responsibility of addressing a climate-related issue when they are presented with it. Otherwise, the potential outcome is that the younger generation's perception of the rule of law will decline. Of course, as mentioned, there are significant procedural obstacles on the way. However, to effectively contribute to resolving this intergenerational dilemma, Marc Willers KC considers it necessary for the ECtHR to grapple with the issues and demonstrate creativity in its approach to the claims brought before it. At the very least, Marc Willers KC hoped that the Court would rule on the issue of climate change and provide domestic courts with explicit guidance on how they should determine climate-related human rights claims brought before them. If the Strasbourg Court provides consistent guidance on how to approach these cases, it would greatly benefit individuals at the domestic level who are otherwise engaging in street protests on Fridays in an attempt to persuade politicians to take appropriate action.

7. CONCLUSION: CROSS-FERTILISATION AMONG COURTS

To conclude, this expert discussion on climate change litigation before European regional courts focused on the cross-fertilisation among courts in the EU and abroad. Indeed, according to Marc Willers KC, the jurisprudence pertaining to climate change from both the Strasbourg and the Luxembourg Courts would be likely to exert a mutual influence, wherein the judgments rendered by one court in this domain will inevitably impact the other court. There is also another possible avenue for interaction, which may arise as a result of the EU's accession to the ECHR, unrealised thus far but close to a successful conclusion.[20] In fact, it is conceivable that a scenario may arise wherein a legal dispute is brought before the ECtHR by individuals challenging the actions or policies of the EU, notably in the context of a climate change case.

However, the *Plaumann* doctrine and the already mentioned admissibility hurdles imposed by the CJEU remain a significant obstacle to individual climate change cases being brought before the Luxembourg Court.

---

20 See https://www.coe.int/en/web/human-rights-intergovernmental-cooperation/accession-of-the-european-union-to-the-european-convention-on-human-rights.

Concerning the exchange of legal precedents, it is important to note that there exists a significant level of consciousness regarding global developments in the realm of judicial decision-making, according to Judge Eicke KC. The ECtHR maintains a connection with the Inter-American Court of Human Rights, enabling both courts to stay informed about their respective judgments, to share knowledge and be cognisant of the respective legal principles. Naturally, applicants will present and rely upon judgments from other jurisdictions in an attempt to convince the ECtHR to adopt a comparable approach. The Court has a track record of considering pertinent international law in its rulings, with the aim of comprehensively examining the relevant legal landscape in relation to the specific issue at hand. There exists a heightened consciousness regarding climate change litigation that extends beyond the confines of Europe, and the Court has a well-established practice of engaging with this body of legal precedents. However, it is crucial to carefully analyse and consider these judgments, being fully aware of the different legal systems in which they have been formulated, as well as the similarities that could be utilised to construct a compelling argument in favour of reaching a resolution in accordance with the ECHR.

Furthermore, Marc Willers KC highlighted that the need for lawyers specialising in this domain to utilise jurisprudence from many global jurisdictions also has major importance for the evolution of this field. By way of example he referred to a recent case in the United Kingdom concerning the question whether an environmental impact assessment of an oil production project required the developer to assess the impact of downstream emissions arising from the combustion of the oil.[21] In that case the claimants' representatives drew upon American and Australian legal precedents, including a ruling by Justice Preston, Chief Judge of the Land and Environment Court of New South Wales,[22] and presented this body of jurisprudence before the Appeal Court for consideration. Although such judgments are not binding on UK courts, the fact is that they are persuasive and serve a useful purpose by demonstrating how the approach to novel issues has been developed in other jurisdictions, and may also serve to improve judicial understanding of the scientific evidence and consequences of dangerous climate change. Moreover, where the approach adopted in various jurisdictions is uniform, its persuasive force will be more powerful and may embolden judges to make decisions favouring the claimant. It is also important to acknowledge the significance of cross-fertilisation between claimants, whether they are from diverse age groups, such as youth or grandparents, or different parts of the globe, thanks to the help of the numerous NGOs that are actively

---

21 *Finch on behalf of the Weald Action Group and Others v. Surrey County Council and Others*, http://climatecasechart.com/non-us-case/r-finch-v-surrey-county-council/. The case is pending before the UK Supreme Court, which in August 2022 granted leave to appeal against the Court of Appeal verdict of 17 February 2022. A hearing was held on 21 June 2023.

22 See https://www.lec.nsw.gov.au/about-us/judicial-officers-and-decision-makers.html.

disseminating information and raising awareness on this matter. In addition to Greta Thunberg and the Fridays for Future movement, many NGOs such as ClientEarth, Greenpeace, Friends of the Earth and Our Children's Trust are effectively equipping individuals of all ages with the knowledge and necessary resources to hold their respective governments accountable.

Finally, Marc Willers KC noted that it is unsurprising that young individuals are at the forefront of this movement since they recognise that they do not bear any responsibility for the future consequences they will face, and they are acutely aware that immediate action is vital to prevent dreadful conditions from befalling them.

CLIMATE CHANGE LITIGATION IN EUROPE

Comparative Perspectives

Matteo FERMEGLIA and Ivano ALOGNA

1. INTRODUCTION

Climate change litigation is booming across Europe under its different tenets and manifestations. At least 119 climate change lawsuits have been filed in 20 European countries since 2015 to seek more ambitious climate action by governments and companies in line with the best available climate science.[1]

This chapter builds on a high-level roundtable held at the conference 'Climate Change Litigation in Europe: Comparative & Sectoral Perspectives and the Way Forward' at Hasselt University on 18 February 2022.[2] It aims to analyse key topics surrounding climate litigation in five European jurisdictions. The roundtable, moderated by the authors, comprised the following speakers,

---

1 J. SETZER, H. NARULLA, C. HIGHAM and E. BRAADEN, 'Climate Litigation in Europe: A summary report for the European Union Forum of Judges for the Environment', Grantham Research Institute on Climate Change and the Environment and Centre for Climate Change Economics and Policy, London School of Economics and Political Science and the European Union Forum of Judges for the Environment, 2022.

2 The authors wish to thank all the participants at the UHasselt-BIICL Conference roundtable for their vibrant and insightful discussion, which has undoubtedly contributed to fostering knowledge on climate change litigation. We hope that this chapter will provide a fair representation of that discussion.

all high-level lawyers involved directly in climate change litigation cases in their respective jurisdictions:

- Carole Billiet, Equal Partners, Belgium;
- Sébastien Mabile and François de Cambiaire, Seattle Avocats, France;
- Roda Verheyen, Rechtsanwalte Günter, Germany;
- Sarah Mead, Urgenda Foundation, the Netherlands; and
- Nigel Pleming KC, 39 Essex Chambers, the United Kingdom.

In addition to the synchronic comparative perspective, the approach followed at the roundtable discussion, as reflected in this chapter, looks at climate change litigation in Europe from a diachronic perspective. Thus, it aims to address past, present and future trends in climate litigation. Section 2 deals with selecting legal instruments for climate litigation in different legal systems and their successful deployment in courtrooms. Section 3 focuses on existing procedural and substantive hurdles, both legal and 'meta-legal' (or extra-legal), currently undermining climate change litigation in the above legal systems. Section 4 outlines potential legal and meta-legal elements, increasing the chances for successful climate change litigation in different European jurisdictions. Section 5 concludes by laying down a set of common threads of climate litigation in Europe.

2. PAST TRENDS IN CLIMATE CHANGE LITIGATION IN EUROPE

The outbreak and successful uptake of litigation as a national as well as transnational phenomenon entail a series of elements that often transcend the law in the books and its use in courtrooms.[3] Social unrest and mobilisation in light of the unfolding climate emergency have proven as a significant element to foster litigation in most European countries, with the notable example, among others, of the Netherlands and Belgium. Yet the collective claim of climate change as a threat to humanity altogether and climate litigation as an attempt to enforce such claim has implications for the choice of legal instruments in court. In Belgium, for example, the fact that a vast multitude of Belgian citizens signed up for the *Klimaatzaak* case[4] – more than 60,000, the most significant number of plaintiffs in a strategic climate litigation case globally – proved conducive to the selection

3 See, *inter alia*, J. Peel and H. Osofsky, 'A Rights Turn in Climate Change Litigation?' (2018) 7(1) *Transnational Environmental Law* 37.

4 *VZW Klimaatzaak v. Kingdom of Belgium & Others* (2021), Brussels Court of First Instance, 17 November (Belgium), http://climatecasechart.com/non-us-case/vzw-klimaatzaak-v-kingdom-of-belgium-et-al/.

of a specific legal ground for action, which allow for injunctive relief in case of manifest violation of environmental law or the threat thereof. Similarly, in the *Urgenda* case,[5] a key enabler of the case was a dedicated provision in the Dutch Civil Code (Article 3:305a) specifically allowing for public interest litigation.

Yet substantive law requirements are relevant for climate litigation, too. In this respect, the pioneering 2017 Duty of Vigilance Law[6] enacted in France was successfully invoked in one of the first ambition cases brought against Total by the French NGO Notre Affaire à Tous and others.[7] This law, which amended the French Commercial Code (adding Articles L. 225-102-4 and L. 225-102-5), sets the specific obligation for large companies (in terms of manpower and turnover) to adopt specific measures to monitor, address and communicate any risks for human rights and the environment across their supply chain, both domestically and abroad. All the relevant information should then be collected in an *ad hoc* document, the Vigilance Plan, which must then be made publicly available. These legal obligations certainly herald accountability and transparency of the private sector – especially private finance – also in light of the non-binding commitments adopted under the UNFCCC Glasgow Climate Pact.[8] Furthermore, they provide additional arguments to establish companies' duty of care under the different tort law regimes across legal systems about their awareness of conduct against the risks posed by climate change. This French regime has heavily informed the key EU legislative proposal on corporate sustainability due diligence, which will ideally provide a harmonised framework to this end, given that similar legislation is present only in a few other European States (e.g. Germany).[9]

Such strategies have also been successfully paired with approaches based on carbon budgeting as a universal concept, which has clear legal implications and has begun to be appreciated across jurisdictions. The carbon budget approach was applied in the landmark *Neubauer* case against the German

5 *Urgenda Foundation v. State of the Netherlands* (2019), Supreme Court of the Netherlands, Case No. 19/00135, 20 December (Netherlands), http://climatecasechart.com/non-us-case/urgenda-foundation-v-kingdom-of-the-netherlands/.

6 Law no. 2017-399 of 27 March 2017 (Loi n° 2017-399 du 27 mars 2017 relative au devoir de vigilance des sociétés mères et des entreprises donneuses d'ordre), available in the French original version at: https://www.legifrance.gouv.fr/jorf/id/JORFTEXT000034290626/.

7 *Notre Affaire à Tous and Others v. France* (2021), Administrative Court of Paris, Nos 1904967, 1904972, 1904976/4-1, 21 October (France), http://climatecasechart.com/non-us-case/notre-affaire-a-tous-and-others-v-france/.

8 United Nations Framework Convention on Climate Change, *Report of the Conference of the Parties on its Twenty-Sixth Session, Held in Glasgow from 31 October to 13 November 2021*, 8 March 2022, FCCC/CP/2021/12/Add.1, https://unfccc.int/sites/default/files/resource/cp2021_12_add1_adv.pdf.

9 See European Commission, *Proposal for a Directive on Corporate Sustainability Due Diligence amending Directive 2019/1937/EU*, COM(2022) 71 final.

federal government,[10] and in the legal action against Volkswagen[11] in Germany, as well as in the already famous lawsuit against Royal Dutch Shell in the Netherlands.[12] Addressing the issue of public and private entities' responsibility for climate change by looking at a neutral yet well-established metric such as the remaining gap of greenhouse gas (GHG) emissions compared to the expected emission trends can provide a meaningful common ground for action. However, while this might be the case in Germany after the decision of the Bundesverfassungsgericht (German Federal Constitutional Court) in *Neubauer*, it might not be the case in other jurisdictions that do not have a proper constitutional framework for such a legal obligation. And even so, more than that might be needed under certain circumstances. In the UK, despite the introduction of a statutory duty for the Secretary of State to achieve climate neutrality by 2050 under the Climate Change Act 2008, attempts to dispute the Secretary of State's lack of fulfilment of such obligations have fallen short when seeking judicial review of government policy as construed narrowly by English courts, for example in the case concerning the Heathrow Airport expansion.[13]

Nonetheless, the critical legal element that might distinguish a successful climate litigation case against public and private entities in court is the elastic concept of duty of care under tort law in different jurisdictions. It has been widely recognised that the very open notion of duty of care arising from Article 6:162(2) of the Dutch Civil Code and interpreted by Dutch courts has proven conducive to successful cases such as *Urgenda v. the Kingdom of the Netherlands* and *Milieudefensie v. Royal Dutch Shell*. In both cases, the Dutch courts developed an unwritten standard of care encompassing positive obligations under the human rights framework, particularly Articles 2 and 8 of the European Convention on Human Rights (ECHR). Such a standard has then been appraised against the scientific findings of the IPCC as to the GHG emission reduction targets needed to avoid the risks and damages associated with climate change. Whether the Dutch legal system will manage to export such a line of reasoning outside its borders to countries with different legal cultures, narrower conceptions of the tort liability clauses and systems less open to collective redress remains to be seen.

---

10 *Neubauer et al. v. Germany* (2021), Federal Constitutional Court of Germany, 29 April (Germany), http://climatecasechart.com/non-us-case/neubauer-et-al-v-germany/.

11 *Kaiser et al. v. Volkswagen AG* (2021), Regional Court of Braunschweig, 11 November (Germany), http://climatecasechart.com/non-us-case/kaiser-et-al-v-volkswagen-ag/.

12 *Milieudefensie et al. v. Royal Dutch Shell plc* (2022), The Hague District Court, C/09/571932 / HA ZA 19-379, 25 April (Netherlands), http://climatecasechart.com/non-us-case/milieudefensie-et-al-v-royal-dutch-shell-plc/.

13 *Friends of the Earth and Others v. Secretary of State for Transport* (2020), Supreme Court, [2020] UKSC 52, 16 December (United Kingdom), http://climatecasechart.com/non-us-case/plan-b-earth-v-secretary-of-state-for-transport/.

3. CURRENT TRENDS IN CLIMATE CHANGE LITIGATION IN EUROPE

As a super-wicked problem and a ground-breaking phenomenon,[14] climate change poses and faces several challenges in courtrooms. Obstacles to climate change litigation may arise from structural deficiencies in the social and economic context surrounding the pursuit of litigation and the legal system in which the same litigation is expected to be launched. In fact, the financial ability and resilience of plaintiffs, who are typically individual citizens and NGOs with limited manpower and financial means, is a crucial element that should be factored in cross-cuttingly. In addition, the legal cost allocation system in many jurisdictions is still based on the 'loser pays' rule. This must also be underscored in light of the potential long timeframe that characterises such cases, which exposes potential plaintiffs to a significant financial risk related to litigation.

The broader issue of time thus comes into play. Time causes yet another potential roadblock – or limitation – to climate change litigation due to the apparent mismatch between the timeline of justice in several European jurisdictions and the timeframe of global climate action. According to the IPCC, immediate action should be taken on climate change mitigation and adaptation, with the first milestones in both respects to be achieved by 2030.[15] However, an entire legal proceeding before domestic courts in Europe lasts at least three years on average. The Belgian climate case reached a first-instance decision only after five years, while the *Urgenda* case was officially closed with the judgment by the Dutch Supreme Court six years after it was launched. The timeframe might be significantly longer when issues of extraterritoriality and jurisdiction arise, for example in cases brought against multinationals operating in several countries.[16] When putting the timeline of justice on the scale of the window of opportunity afforded by climate science, it is clear that procedures providing a meaningful result in a relatively short period are increasingly necessary. An

---

14 See R. Lazarus, 'Super Wicked Problems and Climate Change: Restraining the Present to Liberate the Future' (2009) 94 *Cornell Law Review* 1153.

15 IPCC, *Climate Change 2021: The Physical Science Basis. Contribution of Working Group I to the Sixth Assessment Report of the Intergovernmental Panel on Climate Change*, Cambridge University Press, 2021; IPCC, *Global Warming of 1.5°C. An IPCC Special Report on the impacts of global warming of 1.5°C above pre-industrial levels and related global greenhouse gas emission pathways, in the context of strengthening the global response to the threat of climate change, sustainable development, and efforts to eradicate poverty*, Cambridge University Press, 2018.

16 See J. Setzer, 'The Impacts of High-Profile Litigation against Major Fossil Fuel Companies' in C. Rodríguez-Garavito (ed.), *Litigating the Climate Emergency: How Human Rights, Courts, and Legal Mobilization Can Bolster Climate Action*, Cambridge University Press, 2022, pp. 206–20; R. Verheyen and J. Franke, 'Climate Change Litigation: A Reference Area for Liability' in P. Gailhofer, D. Krebs, A. Proelss, K. Schmalenbach and R. Verheyen (eds), *Corporate Liability for Transboundary Environmental Harm*, Springer, 2023, pp. 353–418.

alignment of the rules of procedure across jurisdictions to recognise the global climate emergency is something that could be appraised against legal systems' country-specific discrepancies.[17]

Most of the substantial legal obstacles to litigation relate to the peculiarities of domestic tort law systems across different States. The longstanding difficulty in establishing causality for climate change impacts is well known and has been widely explored, including comparatively.[18] Another relevant legal issue relates to the distinction between different GHG emissions from upstream to downstream operations. The main issue in this regard relates to expanding the extent of liability to Scope 3 GHG emissions. Scope 3 emissions include those arising from assets not directly owned or controlled by a reporting organisation, which are indirectly affected by that organisation's value chain. The broad interpretation adopted by the Hague court in the *Shell* case allowed for an affirmative response to this question. However, this might not be the case in other jurisdictions with a narrower liability test and in the absence of a written standard of care in this regard.[19]

Alongside the notorious issue of causation, another major hurdle identified at different latitudes is the separation of powers. This doctrine is foundational to the rule of law as we understand it and apply it today in the West. However, climate change litigation inevitably blurs the boundaries between different powers insofar as enforcement of governmental action is at stake. Setting climate mitigation targets and policies to achieve them is clearly a task that falls within the competence of the legislative and executive branches. The problem then arises as to the justiciability of such conduct by the judiciary. This is a challenge in England as judicial practice shows a conservative approach to the pivotal rationality test. Accordingly, courts would review the exercise of discretion or judgement by the government only when such activity is considered irrational. Differently, the *Urgenda* case has heralded domestic courts' power to assess whether the same executive and legislature have exceeded and/or failed to exercise their powers. Human rights have also provided a meaningful compass for such an assessment beyond Dutch borders (e.g. in Belgium), although leading to slightly diverging outcomes and remedies. In the *Neubauer* case in Germany, the discussion has been framed in light of the rights of future generations. Yet these are all standards that can be made more objective to guide judges to ensure

---

17 See I. Alogna, C. Bakker and J.-P. Gauci (eds), *Climate Change Litigation: Global Perspectives*, Brill, 2021.

18 See, among others, R. Lord, S. Goldberg, L. Rajamani and J. Brunée (eds), *Climate Change Liability: Transnational Law and Practice*, Cambridge University Press, 2012; F. Sindico and M.M. Mbengue (eds), *Comparative Climate Change Litigation: Beyond the Usual Suspects*, Springer, 2021.

19 See M.-P. Weller and M.-L. Tran, 'Climate Litigation against companies' (2022) 1(14) *Climate Action* 15.

the justiciability of climate change policies when faced with the separation of powers question.[20]

Another issue that arises comparatively is the double-edged sword role played by the evolving climate governance set up in the European Union. Since 2015, the European Union has established increasingly stringent obligations and requirements imposed upon its Member States. The three legal pillars of such obligations are the EU Governance Regulation (No. 2018/1999/EU), the European Climate Law (Regulation No. 2021/1119/EU) and the Effort Sharing Regulation (No. 2018/842/EU). All these EU legal tools interact heavily with domestic law and further crystallise GHG emission reduction targets as binding obligations upon domestic authorities. Where such developments might streamline access to courts in strategic litigation cases, however, they also shift the focus to more technical disputes, thus fending off principle- and human-rights-based litigation. This leads to the compelling issue of enforcement. Enforcement assumes a prospective approach to litigation and judicial action as it points to whether or not judges might be willing to go beyond general ideas of what law can (or shall) do or what it cannot (or shall not) do. And at this stage, different judiciaries operating under different power allocation systems and in different legal cultures might tend to be frontrunners or laggards in replying to this underlying question.

4. FUTURE TRENDS IN CLIMATE CHANGE LITIGATION IN EUROPE

As an unfolding and multifaceted phenomenon, several future trends can be pinpointed in European climate change litigation. Overall, a growing cultural shift is apparent in judicial bodies as regards the legal challenges presented by climate change. Dealing with climate change pushes judges to question charted territories of law-making and decision-making by embracing new principled perspectives on both the merits and the procedural side. An interesting legal construction for climate litigation is the triangular intersection between human rights, separation of powers and the right to an effective remedy. Nobody can deny that substantive climate policies of public authorities and companies can be framed as human rights issues. As pointed out above, some consensus appears to be emerging in European courts on how to deal with the separation of powers to strike a balance between focusing on goal setting, on the one hand, and a more pervasive stance

20 I. Alogna, N.K. Arnould and A. Holzhausen, 'The Role of Judges in Implementing Climate Policies: A Comparative Perspective on the Separation of Powers' in O. Quirico and F. Baber (eds), *Implementing Climate Policies: Designing and Deploying the European Green Deal in the Post-Paris Environment*, Cambridge University Press, forthcoming.

encroaching upon instrument of choice, on the other hand. Yet all European legal systems and judiciaries also operate under the obligation to provide an effective remedy, which is relevant in Europe both under the European Convention on Human Rights (ECHR, Article 13) and the EU Charter of Fundamental Rights (EU CFR, Article 47). Hence a construction whereby climate mitigation would be understood as the only effective way to provide remedies against the existential threat of climate change as a human rights violation under the ECHR and the EU CFR could lead to promising developments domestically in countries where judicial action is not as far-reaching as others – for instance, in Belgium.

Moreover, a human rights trend in climate change litigation is also beginning to emerge in European common law jurisdictions such as the UK. However, in the UK significant obstacles remain, as posed by the existing climate policy framework under the Climate Change Act 2008. In addition, the stance of British courts against enforcing action by public authorities would hamper further far-reaching decisions by courts.

Furthermore, a new era is ahead for climate science in courtrooms. The IPCC's findings have already been used by courts, particularly in Europe, to determine the minimum standard to assess governments' and companies' (in)actions on climate change. However, IPCC reports might be regarded as arbitrary, although a political consensus has been reached after the Paris Agreement on the 1.5°C global temperature goal. The additional complexity of this approach consists in applying IPCC findings appropriately to European countries individually while factoring in the issues of common but differentiated responsibilities and equity with regard to historical contributions to global warming. Hence additional evidence can be provided, for example, by the Climate Analytics reports.[21] These reports, which draw on the IPCC's methodology, provide an aggregated and analytical account of different countries' vulnerability to current and future impacts of climate change based on scientific standards. The reports have been used in climate litigation in Italy and Poland. These studies would provide courts with more meaningful evidence to further craft their intervention to mandate more ambitious action and come up with effective enforcement of the countries' (and companies') long-term climate targets.

Finally, looking at the more material prospective legal avenues for litigation, at least two promising trends can be identified.

The first trend of cases – albeit not yet widespread in Europe – relates to environmental permitting for GHG-intensive projects. Judges' burgeoning awareness of and education on complex technical issues related to climate change and global warming and the steep learning curve of public authorities are conducive to these cases. A hypothetic legal ground for such litigation is the appraisal of Scope 2 and Scope 3 GHG emissions within the Environmental

---

21 All the reports are available at the following link: https://climateanalytics.org/publications/.

Impact Assessment (EIA) framework. Article 3 of the EIA Directive (No. 2011/92/EU) arguably allows projects' lifecycle GHG emissions to be assessed under the umbrella of indirect environmental impacts. A preliminary ruling by the Court of Justice of the European Union providing interpretation in this direction could be a breakthrough. Moreover, permitting litigation bypasses any enforcement obstacle since it deals only with the issuing or non-issuing of the permit. Therefore, climate change permitting cases will join strategic, *Urgenda*-like cases to deliver the whole ambition on the ground. The landmark judgment of the Dutch Court in the *Shell* case has undoubtedly led to a legacy of addressing the private sector in other countries (e.g. in the UK). Hence, project-based litigation will target industries beyond the power sector to encompass all projects that ultimately undermine the long-term GHG emission targets.

The second trend of cases includes claims aiming to enhance the accountability and transparency of corporations in both GHG-emitting and financial sectors. More specifically, one major development relates to the adoption of climate neutrality commitments by both States and corporations by mid-century. Such commitments might acquire utmost relevance in the context of legislation posing specific obligations to control, monitor and prevent environmental and climate change impacts throughout supply chains, such as the French due diligence law. Likewise, an option that deserves further investigation relates to the EU Directive on unfair commercial practices,[22] which might be the legal basis to prevent greenwashing claims, such as companies' untruthful or misleading commercial statements on carbon neutrality. Another significant development relates to the emergence of challenges brought by shareholders against corporations (e.g. in the UK)[23] regarding their failure to disclose the climate change effects of

---

22 Directive 2005/29/EC of the European Parliament and of the Council of 11 May 2005 concerning unfair business-to-consumer commercial practices in the internal market and amending Council Directive 84/450/EEC, Directives 97/7/EC, 98/27/EC and 2002/65/EC of the European Parliament and of the Council and Regulation (EC) No 2006/2004 of the European Parliament and of the Council (Unfair Commercial Practices Directive). The Directive has been amended by Directive (EU) 2019/2161 of 27 November 2019 on better enforcement and modernisation of Union consumer protection rules, part of the 'Review of EU consumer law – New Deal for Consumers'.

23 Where ClientEarth filed a derivative action against Shell's board of directors for violation of their duties to promote the best interest of the company by not properly managing climate risk. *ClientEarth v. Shell Board of Directors* (2023), UK High Court [2023] EWHC 1137 (Ch), 12 May (United Kingdom), https://assets.caselaw.nationalarchives.gov.uk/ewhc/ch/2023/1137/ewhc_ch_2023_1137.pdf. The case was rejected by the UK High Court, which found that ClientEarth had failed to satisfy the Court that it had a *prima facie* case, as it did not demonstrate that the '[d]irectors' current approach falls outside the range of reasonable responses to climate change risk and will cause harm to Shell's members'. Following this decision, the oral hearing of the application was heard by the Court, which on 24 July 2023 maintained its previous decision. ClientEarth are currently requesting permission to appeal. See Simmons & Simmons, 'ClientEarth v Directors of Shell: Oral hearing takeaways', 1 August 2023, https://www.simmons-simmons.com/en/publications/clksecr2v00liu2s88db4ovnk/clientearth-v-directors-of-shell-oral-hearing-takeaways.

their investments. This is an interesting development as it shifts the position of climate litigation from an external, civil society-driven component questioning companies' conduct to the inherent dynamics of economic undertakings.

5. CONCLUSIONS

This chapter has contributed to the burgeoning body of literature aiming to appraise the different legal, social and institutional dynamics underpinning climate change litigation across jurisdictions. As a super-wicked problem, climate change is challenging to address from a comparative legal and historical standpoint. Climate change challenges traditional legal concepts developed in a world with CO_2 levels well below 400 ppm. Nonetheless, the collective quest for justice pursued for more than 30 years in courts provides us with a clear set of legal arguments and strategies, which share inherent common features regardless of the domestic specific legal setting and cultures in which they are filed, debated and eventually upheld.

Three main elements can be underscored to summarise the findings of this chapter, which can provide guidance for future research agendas on the topic. In line with the chapter's approach, such elements look at the past, present and future prospects for climate change litigation.

First, and looking at the past, climate change litigation is aimed at a clear set of goals, namely public and private entities' accountability, enforcement of climate change goals, and – to a lesser extent – tort liability for the losses derived from climate change and the adaptation costs to prevent climate change impacts. The first two objectives are chiefly pursued by the strategic (or ambition) cases, which snowballed across most European jurisdictions starting from the 2015 decision in the *Urgenda* case in the Netherlands. This approach has also been adopted to target private entities since the 2021 *Milieudefensie v. Royal Dutch Shell* decision. Not surprisingly, both cases were held in the same country and before the same court (The Hague District Court). Thus, a snowball effect is also being generated by the *Shell* case in other countries (e.g. France and the UK), which, however, will undoubtedly witness a somewhat different legal construction not only in terms of the underlying black-letter rule but also as to the interpretation thereof by domestic judges and regarding procedural aspects. Liability claims are also rising in Europe, starting from the landmark *Lliuya v. RWE* case in Germany.[24] As climate change impacts continue to reveal themselves, liability claims will most likely confront judges and legal systems with the unfolding consequences of climate change, as they will address concrete economic and non-economic

[24] *Luciano Lliuya v. RWE AG* (2022), Higher Regional Court of Essen, Case No. 2 O 285/15, on appeal, May (Germany), http://climatecasechart.com/non-us-case/lliuya-v-rwe-ag/.

losses. Hence, regardless of the different legal rules, doctrines and concepts to be deployed in all these lawsuits, a case for a common functional legal ground is clearly taking shape.

Second, and looking at the present, climate change litigation in Europe faces resistance from substantive and procedural rules that are conceived to establish and regulate social constructions in a society striving for arguably opposite goals. Most legal provisions and procedures being relied upon for European climate litigation draw on Western socio-economic thinking, which pursues a neoliberal legal order, free market, economic optimality, individual well-being and collective growth, and corrective justice within given territorial boundaries. This is simply the socio-economic system that Europeans have conceived and crafted, at least since the Industrial Revolution. Yet the inequalities posed by climate change and the urgency of the fight against global warming shake the foundations of all these assumptions while requiring a prompt and effective response in a timeframe that aligns well with the timeline of justice.

Third, and looking at the future, climate change litigation is an ever-changing phenomenon. As such, it is prone to spark legal innovations and ground-breaking legal thinking against evolving political momentum, scientific evidence and social awareness. This might sound a rather obvious statement for everyone involved in the area, though it is all but a given within the context of other traditional strands of litigation. In other words, filing a climate change litigation case in 2023 is an entirely different exercise than it was a decade ago (when the *Urgenda* case was filed) or in 1992 (when the UNFCCC was signed). Likewise, future climate change lawsuits filed five or 10 years from now will see significant shifts in the legal strategies deployed, the scientific and economic underpinnings of such strategies, and even the actors prompting those claims. After a first wave of litigation filed mostly by individuals, local communities and environmental NGOs, we now witness claims filed by companies, cities and even investors and shareholders pursuing different interests, against the emerging risks posed by climate change. Nonetheless, these cases depart from the compelling evidence of climate change based on established climate science and endorsed through clear-cut commitments by governments and private entities.

In conclusion, all the above elements call for legal scholarship to address the current and future trajectories of climate litigation with an open mind, thus looking at the different legal traditions and various legal formants involved, not only from a 'horizontal' comparative perspective but also from an 'evolutionary' perspective, taking into account the potential economic, social, scientific and governance developments in Europe.

PART II

CLIMATE CHANGE LITIGATION IN EUROPE: SECTORAL PERSPECTIVES

Human Rights and Climate Change Litigation

THE CONSTITUTIONAL CONTEXT OF CLIMATE CHANGE LITIGATION

A Comparative Analysis of Germany and Austria

Konrad LACHMAYER

1. THE ROLE OF DOMESTIC CONSTITUTIONAL LAW

In a recent tort law case regarding the approval of the extension of a coal mine, the Federal Court of Australia[1] decided unanimously[2] – by overturning a judgment of a single judge[3] – that the imposition of a 'duty of care' regarding 'human safety' has to be rejected in the context of climate change. The Court backed up the claim made by the Minister for the Environment that it 'is one of core, indeed high, policy-making for the Executive and Parliament involving questions of policy (scientific, economic, social, industrial and political) which are unsuitable for the Judicial branch to resolve in private litigation by reference to the law of torts and potential personal responsibility for indeterminate damages, if harm eventuates in decades to come.'[4] One might question the relevance of this climate change case in private law when the focus of the following analysis lies in constitutional law. The Australian case, however, perfectly illustrates the effect of the lack of constitutional law concerning climate rights of individuals. Australian constitutional law does not provide a fundamental rights catalogue of its own[5] and was unable to provide a constitutional basis for climate change litigation.[6]

Constitutional law and tort law are just two examples of the possible ways to address climate change in courts.[7] The international human rights perspective seems to be dominant in addressing climate change. Domestic constitutional law and constitutional rights, however, might differ significantly from an international human rights perspective. The success or failure of domestic climate change litigation is closely linked to the constitutional context of the country

---

1 The Federal Court of Australia is a lower federal court in Australia with a wide jurisdiction including cases on constitutional matters (unlike the case in question), since constitutional adjudication is not centralised at the High Court of Australia; see on the Australian judicial system N. Owens, 'The Judicature' in C. Sanders and A. Stone (eds), *The Oxford Handbook of the Australian Constitution*, Oxford University Press, Oxford 2018, p. 654.

2 Federal Court of Australia, 15.03.2022, *Minister for the Environment v. Sharma* [2022] FCAFC 35.

3 Federal Court of Australia, 27.05.2021, *Sharma by her litigation representative Sister Marie Brigid Arthur v. Minister for the Environment* [2021] FCA 560; see also J. Peel and R. Markey-Towler, 'A Duty to Care: The Case of Sharma v Minister for the Environment [2021] FCA 560' (2021) 33 *Journal of Environmental Law* 727.

4 Ibid., para. 15.

5 See C. Saunders, *The Constitution of Australia. A Contextual Analysis*, Hart, Oxford 2011, pp. 257, 274; S. Stephenson, 'Rights Protection in Australia' in C. Sanders and A. Stone (eds), *The Oxford Handbook of the Australian Constitution*, Oxford University Press, Oxford 2018, p. 905.

6 But see successful judgments based on statutory law, e.g. New South Wales Land and Environment Court, 08.02.2019, *Gloucester Resources Limited v. Minister for Planning*.

7 See e.g. W. Kahl and M.-P. Weller (eds), *Climate Change Litigation. A Handbook*, Beck/Hart/Nomos, Munich 2021; F. Sindico and M.M. Mbengue (eds), *Comparative Climate Change Litigation: Beyond the Usual Suspects*, Springer, Cham 2022.

in question. Human rights arguments in domestic climate change litigation are related to the systematic and interpretative context of the particular constitution. There are important differences in both the selection of constitutional rights relevant to climate change and other constitutional provisions[8] which might be key when addressing climate change on a constitutional level. Climate change litigation must consider these constitutional particularities to be able to develop successful strategies.

The role of constitutional law and its interpretation by the courts are crucial in domestic constitutional adjudication.[9] As the following analysis will show, climate protection on a constitutional level relates to various human rights or other constitutional law provisions. The specific challenge of climate change litigation is the need to change existing constitutional reasoning in more than one aspect. These elements of constitutional reasoning concern, for example, the scope of rights protection, the involvement of the international dimension of climate change (e.g. in terms of the group of applicants or the legal sources considered), the duties of the State to fight climate change, and the normative relevance of certain rights or State objectives.

From the perspective of constitutional reasoning, there are numerous possibilities to go beyond the existing case law. At the end of the day, judges not only need to understand the dramatic situation faced by the planet and its inhabitants, but also need to show their willingness to further develop constitutional law by judicial intervention.

Constitutional reasoning is not only an 'exercise in persuasion'; it also depends on the 'judges' skills and creativity in crafting [legal] arguments'.[10] On the one hand, plaintiffs fighting climate change have to put new legal arguments forward. In doing so, they have to consider the existing legal culture.[11] On the other hand, judges of supreme and constitutional courts have to transform existing case law into new constitutional reasoning to integrate the climate change perspective.

This chapter compares the German and Austrian examples in climate change litigation to illustrate these constitutional challenges. While the existing constitutional texts could be viewed as being similar (section 2), the constitutional reasoning that has been developed differs significantly. The Federal Constitutional Court of Germany (FCC) recently opened up the possibilities for

8 E.g. constitutional principles, such as the rule of law or the separation of powers principle.

9 See e.g. the in-depth analysis of 18 countries in A. Jakab, A. Dyevre and G. Itzcovich (eds), *Comparative Constitutional Reasoning*, Cambridge University Press, Cambridge 2017.

10 See A. Jakab, A. Dyevre and G. Itzcovich (eds), *Comparative Constitutional Reasoning*, Cambridge University Press, Cambridge 2017, pp. 1, 18–19.

11 See regarding the concept of legal culture J.Ø. Sunde, 'Managing the Unmanageable – An Essay Concerning Legal Culture as an Analytical Tool' in S. Koch and J.Ø. Sunde (eds), *Comparing Legal Cultures*, 2nd ed., Fagbokforlaget, Oslo 2021, pp. 23–40.

climate change litigation[12] (section 3); in contrast to this milestone, the Austrian Constitutional Court (ACC) closed all (existing) possibilities of climate change adjudication some years ago[13] (section 4). In a comparative analysis of relevant particularities, the different approaches will be investigated (section 5), leading to conclusions on climate change litigation (section 6).

2. COMPARING THE CONSTITUTIONAL STARTING POINT

2.1. A CONSTITUTIONAL ANCHOR?

Climate change litigation has many different possible ways to address climate change on a legal basis. Constitutional adjudication is only an option when a constitutional anchor exists, as the Australian example at the beginning illustrated. If constitutional law does not provide any foundation to address climate change, other legal options – like tort law – have to be prioritised.[14]

While an international and European human rights perspective indicates that a rights-based approach is most promising, the particularities of domestic constitutional law have to be taken into consideration. Different human rights or civil liberties enshrined in domestic constitutional law offer a legal basis for climate change litigation. Moreover, other constitutional dimensions, for example State objectives such as sustainability clauses, or constitutional principles, such as the rule of law or the separation of powers principle, might prove decisive.

The concrete case law analysed in this chapter shows that the textual starting points in Austria and Germany are quite similar. Both constitutions provide a significant number of human rights, including the right to life, and include environmental protection and sustainability as State objectives.

2.2. THE RIGHT TO LIFE

The right to life, prominently mentioned by the German Constitutional Court in the climate change judgment, is enshrined in Article 2 paragraph 2 of the German Basic Law: 'Every person shall have the right to life and physical integrity. Freedom of the person shall be inviolable. These rights may be interfered with only pursuant to a law.' According to Austrian constitutional

12 See Federal Constitutional Court of Germany, 24.03.2021, 1 BvR 2656/18.

13 See Austrian Constitutional Court, 29.06.2017, E 875/2017.

14 Climate change litigation, however, will use all possible options.

law,[15] the right to life as an Austrian fundamental right is guaranteed by Article 2 of the European Convention on Human Rights (ECHR): 'Everyone's right to life shall be protected by law.'[16]

Although the German Basic Law and the Austrian Constitution are based on different concepts (own rights catalogue in Germany; an implemented international treaty on a constitutional level in Austria), the texts for the right to life are quite similar. Concrete statements concerning climate change are lacking and the textual starting points can be described as neutral.

2.3. PROTECTION OF FUTURE GENERATIONS AS A STATE OBJECTIVE

In contrast to this text-neutral approach to human rights, both constitutions contain explicit, value-based references to the challenges of environmental protection, sustainability and future generations. Article 20a of the German Basic Law states that, '[m]indful also of its responsibility towards future generations, the state shall protect the natural foundations of life and animals by legislation and, in accordance with law and justice, by executive and judicial action, all within the framework of the constitutional order.' The Austrian Constitution contains a (separate) Federal Constitutional Act on sustainability (FCA Sustainability), animal protection, comprehensive environmental protection, water and food security, and research.[17] Section 1 of this FCA Sustainability states that '[t]he Republic of Austria ... is committed to the principle of sustainability in using natural resources to ensure that future generations will also benefit from optimal quality of life.'[18]

Textual similarities are easy to spot. Both provisions refer to future generations and natural resources and thus claim to provide for a sustainable approach by the State to be established through legislation and government. In both countries, the provisions have been understood as mere State objectives which are not justiciable.

---

15 The ECHR is formally part of the Austrian Constitutional Law (in a German version of the text). See M. Stelzer, *The Constitution of the Republic of Austria. A Contextual Analysis*, Hart, Oxford 2011, p. 211.

16 Regarding the interference with physical integrity, the Austrian Constitution refers to the right to private life in terms of Art. 8 ECHR.

17 Austrian Federal Law Gazette I No. 111/2013.

18 See also sec. 3 paras 1 and 2 FCA Sustainability: '(1) The Republic of Austria (federal government, federal provinces and municipalities) is committed to comprehensive environmental protection. (2) Comprehensive environmental protection means the prevention of harmful effects on the natural environment as the basic resource of the human being. Comprehensive environmental protection consists particularly in measures to ensure the cleanliness of air, water and soil as well as to prevent noise disturbance.'

2.4. DIFFERENT CONSTITUTIONAL REASONING

Although more or less the same constitutional anchors exist, the interpretation of the provisions by the two constitutional courts regarding climate change could not have been more different. While the interpretation of the FCC can be understood as a step forward in climate change protection, the ACC decided to go the other way. Constitutional reasoning with regard to climate change calls courts to go beyond the existing understanding of constitutional law and constitutional interpretation, which requires an extra effort in constitutional reasoning (see the FCC) or even risks rejection by the constitutional court if it does not accept the new reasoning of the lower court (see the ACC).

3. THE GERMAN CLIMATE CHANGE JUDGMENT – A STEP FORWARD

3.1. OPENING UP CLIMATE CHANGE LITIGATION

In its recent climate decision in 2021,[19] the FCC declared certain provisions of the Federal Climate Change Act to be void. The plaintiffs of the German Constitutional Court judgment directly challenged the (German) Federal Climate Change Act and were not opposing a concrete infrastructure project.[20] As the Court explained, they argued that 'the state has not introduced a legal framework sufficient for swiftly reducing greenhouse gasses, especially carbon dioxide (CO2) – a legal framework they claim is necessary to limit the increase in global temperature to well below 2°C and preferably to 1.5°C'.[21] The Court therefore had to deal with the overall strategy of the German government for dealing with climate change.

The Court judgment can be understood as part of (domestic) constitutional case law, which opens up climate change as a topic of constitutional adjudication. Courts are not only empowering themselves to play a role in an environmental transition, but are also reacting to the groups and individuals who are actively pushing the climate change agenda forward. In that regard, the FCC followed the crucial judgment of the Supreme Court of the Netherlands in the case *State of the Netherlands v. Urgenda Foundation*.[22]

---

19 Federal Constitutional Court of Germany, 24.03.2021, 1 BvR 2656/18.

20 But see the Austrian case below.

21 Federal Constitutional Court of Germany, 24.03.2021, 1 BvR 2656/18, para. 1.

22 Supreme Court of the Netherlands, 20.12.2019, *State of the Netherlands v. Urgenda Foundation*, ECLI:NL:HR:2019:2007. In this leading case the Dutch Supreme Court also had to deal with percentages of greenhouse gas emissions and confirmed the decision of the Court of Appeal

Crucially, the FCC's decision was built upon the particularities of the German Basic Law. While the Court – to a certain extent – followed the reasoning of the Dutch Supreme Court (with regard to the right to life), the decisive argumentative element of constitutional interpretation in Germany concerned the environmental State objective provided in Article 20a of the German Basic Law.[23]

In that regard, the FCC argued that the right to life (Article 2 paragraph 2 of the German Basic Law) includes 'an objective duty to protect future generations', but, moreover, asserted that the State objective of the protection of future generations (Article 20a of the German Basic Law) 'obliges the state to take climate action'. The FCC linked this State objective with 'any state interference with fundamental rights'.[24]

3.2. CONSTITUTIONAL REASONING

In a first step, the FCC clarified the State's duty to grant protection against the risks of climate change as part of the right to the protection of life and health.[25] This was a major step towards activating the fundamental right to life as a constitutional guarantee of climate protection.[26]

The FCC, however, did not detect a general violation of this obligation by the German legislator. It found the Federal Climate Change Act 'not manifestly unsuitable for safeguarding the interests protected under Art. 2'[27] of the Basic Law. Nevertheless, certain details have been identified as unconstitutional because the legislator failed 'to take sufficient precautionary measures to manage the obligations to reduce emissions in ways that respect fundamental rights obligations that could be substantial in later periods due to the emissions allowed by law until 2030.'[28]

---

that 'the State is in any case obliged to achieve the aforementioned reduction of at least 25% by 2020'. In its reasoning the Court argued that this obligation can be based on Arts 2 and 8 ECHR.

23 See below section 3.2.

24 Federal Constitutional Court of Germany, 24.03.2021, 1 BvR 2656/18 (headnote 3).

25 Interestingly enough the Court addressed neither Art. 1 German Basic Law (concerning human dignity) nor Art. 2 para. 1 German Basic Law (concerning the general freedom of action), although the plaintiffs claimed a 'fundamental right to a future consistent with human dignity (*menschenwürdige Zukunft*)' or a 'fundamental right to an ecological minimum standard of living'. See Federal Constitutional Court of Germany, 24.03.2021, 1 BvR 2656/18, paras 38, 60, 113–14.

26 'The fundamental right to the protection of life and health enshrined in Art. 2(2) first sentence GG obliges the state to afford protection against the risks of climate change. The state must combat the considerable potential risks emanating from climate change by taking steps which – with the help of international involvement – contribute to stopping human-induced global warming and limiting the ensuing climate change. These steps must be supplemented by positive measures aimed at alleviating the consequences of climate change ("adaptation measures").' Ibid., para. 144.

27 Ibid., para. 154.

28 Ibid., para. 182.

In order to argue the violation of this right, the Court included the State objective of the protection of future generations regarding Article 20a of the German Basic Law in its consideration.[29]

The Court determined the normative relevance of Article 20a of the German Basic Law and explained its substantive significance in relation to climate protection. The FCC derived an obligation of the State to take climate action from Article 20a of the German Basic Law.[30]

Although the Court did not derive any international responsibility with regard to the effects of climate change in other countries, it understood the global dimension and included this international perspective in its argumentation.[31] The Court identified the global average temperature as 'one key indicator' and noted the necessity to introduce temperature limits as part of taking climate action.[32]

In conclusion, the German Federal Constitutional Court set up a fully fledged constitutional framework for climate change litigation. The Court activated the State objective regarding Article 20a of the German Basic Law, intended to protect future generations, as a 'justiciable legal provision designed to commit the political process to a favouring of ecological interests'.[33] Moreover, the Court developed and enriched the normative contents of Article 20a of the German Basic Law as obliging the State to take climate action.

3.3. REACTION IN SCHOLARSHIP

Constitutional law scholars reacted mainly positively to the judgment of the FCC.[34] Some critics, however, were concerned that the Court had not done

29 'However, any such exercise of freedom is subject to limits that the legislator must impose in order to take climate action in accordance with Art. 20a GG and to fulfil duties of protection arising from fundamental rights. … In this respect, the relevant aspect in terms of constitutional law is the obligation to take climate action enshrined in Art. 20a GG.' Ibid., para. 185.

30 Ibid., para. 193.

31 'Art. 20a GG obliges the state to take climate action. The fact that no state can resolve the problems of climate change on its own due to the worldwide nature of the climate and global warming does not invalidate the obligation to take climate action, but it does have an effect on the obligation's content. Since the German legislator would not on its own be capable of protecting the climate as required under Art. 20a GG due to the global nature of climate change, Art. 20a GG also requires that solutions be sought at the international level.' Ibid., para. 197.

32 Ibid., para. 198.

33 Ibid., para. 197.

34 See regarding a critical analysis e.g. C. Möllers und N. Weinberg, 'Die Klimaschutzentscheidung des Bundesverfassungsgerichts' (2021) 76 *Juristenzeitung* 1069; L.J. Kotzé, 'Neubauer et al. versus Germany: Planetary Climate Litigation for the Anthropocene?' (2021)

enough given the international dimension of the situation.[35] It might seem obvious that, in terms of climate change, societal reactions qualify the judgment as too little, too late; from a constitutional law perspective, the FCC not only took a major step forward but also created a convincing line of constitutional reasoning which could serve as a blueprint[36] for other courts in other countries.

The Court activated a provision that had been a 'mere goal' of the constitution (*Staatszielbestimmung*)[37] and 'built a robust connection between this merely aspirational provision and the fundamental rights of the Basic Law. Even though the FCC still does not allow individuals to bring cases based directly on Article 20a, the provision is of utmost relevance now as part of the objective law against which restrictions of fundamental rights need to be measured.'[38] The newly involved concept of intertemporality was qualified as 'a doctrinal innovation'.[39] However, only 'the rights of younger generations living now' are involved and not those of future unborn generations.[40] Moreover, the international dimension of the topic was not only accepted but integrated into the overall constitutional reasoning. The Court 'stresses … that if no international solutions are attainable, this would not absolve the German state from its obligation to adopt climate protection measures … [M]ost importantly, inaction by other states does not affect this obligation.'[41]

Criticism was also aimed at the fact that 'the court's inability to narrow down the available national budget impeded meaningful judicial control of

---

22 *German Law Journal* 1423; R. Krämer-Hoppe, 'The Climate Protection Order of the Federal Constitutional Court of Germany and the North-South Divide' (2021) 22 *German Law Journal* 1393; J. Peel and R. Markey-Towler, 'Recipe for Success?: Lessons for Strategic Climate Litigation from the Sharma, Neubauer, and Shell Cases' (2021) 22 *German Law Journal* 1484; J. van Zeben, 'The Role of the EU Charter of Fundamental Rights in Climate Litigation' (2021) 22 *German Law Journal* 1499; R. Sinder, 'Anthropozänes Verfassungsrecht als Antwort auf den anthropogenen Klimawandel. Besprechung von BVerfG, Beschluss v. 24. 3. 2021 – 1 BvR 2656/18 u. a.' (2021) 76 *Juristenzeitung* 1078; C. Calliess, 'Das "Klimaurteil" des Bundesverfassungsgerichts: "Versubjektivierung" des Art. 20a GG?' (2021) 32 *Zeitschrift für Umweltrecht* 355; J. Krüszmann, 'Das Bundesverfassungsgericht betrachtet die falschen CO2-Emissionen', *Juwissblog* (2021), https://www.juwiss.de/100-2021/.

35 See e.g. R. Krämer-Hoppe, 'The Climate Protection Order of the Federal Constitutional Court of Germany and the North-South Divide' (2021) 22 *German Law Journal* 1393.

36 See regarding legal transplants and the migration of constitutional ideas A. Watson, *Legal transplants: An approach to comparative law*, 2nd ed., University of Georgia Press, Athens 1993, pp. 95–101; S. Choudhry, 'Migration as a new metaphor in comparative constitutional law' in S. Choudhry (ed.), *The migration of constitutional ideas*, Cambridge University Press, Cambridge 2006, pp. 1–35.

37 See C. Calliess, 'Das "Klimaurteil" des Bundesverfassungsgerichts: "Versubjektivierung" des Art. 20a GG?' (2021) 32 *Zeitschrift für Umweltrecht* 355.

38 H. Aust, 'Climate Protection Act Case' (2022) 116 *American Journal of International Law* 150.

39 Ibid., p. 4.

40 Ibid.

41 Ibid.

Germany's climate policy. The only relief for plaintiffs found by the Court was the legislator's obligation to set the reduction path earlier and by different means to allow plaintiffs and society to adapt accordingly.'[42] This claim of the judgment was, however, very limited.

> The 2021 German climate change case demonstrates that judges at the German Constitutional Court were unwilling to resolve disputes about the targets in the Paris Agreement. The Court gave the government a deadline of the end of 2022 to address post-2030 emissions and left the government a significant degree of leeway. The decision seems to have prompted a political response that may go beyond the parameters of the court case. Judicial remedies set the floor and not the ceiling on governmental efforts to counter climate change.[43]

In conclusion, the decision of the German Constitutional Court can be understood as a starting point, opening the door for further climate change litigation.[44] Inspired by the Dutch ruling, the German Court created new constitutional reasoning regarding the German case law on climate change and integrated this reasoning into the context of German constitutional law.

4. THE AUSTRIAN ANTI-CLIMATE CHANGE JUDGMENT – A STEP BACKWARDS

4.1. CLOSING DOORS

In contrast to this decision by the German Federal Constitutional Court, a case before the Austrian Constitutional Court led to the opposite outcome.[45] The decision by the ACC concerned a concrete infrastructure project. The relevant environmental impact assessment procedure led to a ground-breaking decision by the Federal Administrative Court,[46] which had rejected the construction of an

---

42 A. Buser, 'Of Carbon Budgets, Factual Uncertainties, and Intergenerational Equity – The German Constitutional Court's Climate Decision' (2021) 22 *German Law Journal* 1409, 1422; in its decision the FCC required the legislator to set the path to reducing emissions after 2030 earlier and by different means but did not find a breach of any positive obligations requiring the legislator to narrow down the available carbon budget.

43 K. Roach, 'Judicial Remedies for Climate Change' (2021) 17 *Journal of Law and Equity* 105, 129.

44 L.J. Kotzé, 'Neubauer et al. versus Germany: Planetary Climate Litigation for the Anthropocene?' (2021) 22 *German Law Journal* 1423, 1425.

45 Austrian Constitutional Court, 29.06.2017, E 875/2017; see also B. Hollaus, 'Austrian Constitutional Court: Considering Climate Change as a Public Interest is Arbitrary – Refusal of Third Runway Permit Annulled' (2017) 11 *ICL Journal* 467.

46 The Federal Administrative Court is an administrative court of first instance. The judgment of the court can be appealed at the Austrian Constitutional Court (VfGH) and the Supreme Administrative Court (VwGH). See U. Giera and K. Lachmayer, 'The Principle of Effective

additional airstrip at the Vienna International Airport, the only internationally relevant airport in Austria, for climate change-related reasons.[47] The Federal Administrative Court took international environmental treaties, like the Paris Agreement, into consideration and argued that the airport expansion would have significant negative effects on climate change.[48] In its balancing of the different interests concerning Austrian aviation law, the Federal Administrative Court concluded that the application to build a third runway had to be rejected.[49]

The applicants appealed and were successful. The ACC rejected the reasoning of the Federal Administrative Court and identified a violation of the right to equal treatment before the law. The ACC argued that the specific constitutional provisions regarding sustainability and future generations (FCA Sustainability) do not enjoy priority and have no relevance at all in the relevant Court decision. The Court did not link the case with fundamental rights, rejected the relevance of international and European law concerning the balancing of interests, and concluded that the decision of the administrative court was arbitrary.[50]

In comparison to the Austrian case, there have been similar cases in Norway and Australia concerning concrete infrastructure projects as well. In both cases, the courts of last instance rejected the relevance of climate change argumentation.[51] In the Norwegian case, the permission for offshore oil exploration in the Arctic Ocean was granted.[52] In Australia – as mentioned above – a tort case regarding the extension of a coal mine was rejected due to legal concerns.[53]

4.2. THE REASONING OF THE COURT

If one looks further into the details of the case, the ACC interpreted the relevant provisions in quite the opposite way to the FCC. The ACC rejected any particular relevance of the sustainability principle enshrined in the FCA Sustainability.

Legal Protection in Austrian Administrative Law' in K. Lachmayer and Z. Szente (eds), *The Principle of Effective Legal Protection in Administrative Law*, Routledge, Oxford 2016, pp. 3, 87–88. See below section 6.2.

47 Austrian Federal Administrative Court, 02.02.2017, W109 2000179-1/291E.

48 Ibid.

49 Ibid.; see also B. Hollaus, 'Austrian Constitutional Court: Considering Climate Change as a Public Interest is Arbitrary – Refusal of Third Runway Permit Annulled' (2017) 11 *ICL Journal* 467, 468.

50 See for the reasoning for the Court in detail below section 4.2.

51 Partly brought up by lower courts.

52 Norwegian Supreme Court, *Greenpeace Nordic Association v. Ministry of Petroleum and Energy* (2020), Case No. 20-051052SIV-HRET (*People v. Arctic Oil*). See e.g. C. Voigt, 'The First Climate Judgment before the Norwegian Supreme Court: Aligning Law with Politics' (2021) 33(3) *Journal of Environmental Law* 697.

53 Federal Court of Australia, 15.03.2022, *Minister for the Environment v. Sharma* [2022] FCAFC 35.

While the Court recognised its general constitutional relevance, the Court did not activate it as a justiciable norm. The ACC even thwarted the State objective, with the effect that it became legally irrelevant in that case.[54] All in all, the ACC followed a scaling-down approach to sustainability.[55]

While the reasoning of the Court at first suggests that the (Austrian) Aviation Act should be read in conformity with the State objective of sustainability, the Court relativised the concrete superiority and concluded that it is not relevant in the context of the Aviation Act.[56] As a consequence of the irrelevance of the constitutional State objective of sustainability, the Court concluded that only public interests relevant to this particular Act have to be considered. Furthermore, the Court rejected the relevance of Article 37 of the Charter of Fundamental Rights of the European Union (CFR) as it makes no additions to the Austrian constitutional State objective of sustainability.[57]

The argumentation of the Federal Administrative Court that international law on environmental law and climate change should be taken into consideration was also rejected by the ACC following the same narrow understanding of 'public interests' that could be considered in regard to the Aviation Act. The ACC concluded that the judgment of the Federal Administrative Court was arbitrary for considering these aspects and therefore unlawful.[58]

---

54 '[A]n absolute priority of environmental protection interests over other decision-making determinants incumbent on the administration can be derived neither from the [old] Federal Constitutional Act on Comprehensive Environmental Protection nor from Sec 3 Federal Constitutional Act on Sustainability'. Austrian Constitutional Court, 29.06.2017, E 875/2017, para. 206.

55 'It is therefore constitutionally necessary to include comprehensive environmental protection both in the interpretation of the considered interests that are relevant for balancing, which are to be perceived according to the Aviation Act, and in the subsequent weighting of these interests if the interests determined to be decisive have a link to environmental protection. The stated state objective does not extend the interests to be taken into account beyond the group of interests to be safeguarded under the Aviation Act, nor does the framework for emissions or other effects expand the interests that are to be examined under the Aviation Act.' Ibid., para. 208.

56 The crucial restriction is that the relevance of sustainability only exists 'if the interests determined to be decisive have a link to environmental protection'. The ACC comes (without any convincing argument) to the result that sustainability is not of further relevance.

57 Austrian Constitutional Court, 29.06.2017, E 875/2017, para. 232: 'In the present case, Art. 37 GRC – apart from the fact that its legal relevance as a principle in proceedings before a member state court is limited (cf. Art. 52 para. 5 CFR) – does not add up any content that goes beyond the Federal Constitutional Act on Sustainability. Regarding this it is not necessary to examine whether Art. 37 CFR is applicable at all in the present case.'

58 'The approach of the Federal Administrative Court, in a procedure according to Sec. 71 Aviation Act to consider standards, which on the one hand originate from not directly applicable international conventions and on the other hand which are not applicable to emissions from aircraft, for the assessment of the effects of assumed emissions, lacks a legal basis; Thus, these considerations have to be understood as arbitrariness (in the meaning of the established case law of the Constitutional Court).' Ibid., para. 221.

In conclusion, the ACC refused to consider environmental protection and climate change as they could not be manifested in a concrete provision of the Aviation Act.

4.3. REACTION AMONG AUSTRIAN SCHOLARS

From an international perspective, the Austrian case might appear to be of no further interest as it was unsuccessful; however, the decision could be of crucial importance when seeking to avoid following a dead end. As it cannot serve as a best-practice example, the overall international discussion of the case has remained limited.[59] In contrast, there has been a lively scholarly debate about the matter in Austria.[60]

Criticism concerned the restrictive interpretation of public interests in the Austrian Aviation Act, which did not consider the existing case law of the Supreme Administrative Court.[61] Moreover, the ACC did not consider the existing concept of balancing different public interests, the relevance of European law (especially concerning environmental impact assessment) and existing State objectives concerning sustainability.[62] Another criticism concerned the fact that the ACC agreed to issue a decision at all, as the questions mainly related to interpretation not of constitutional law but of statutory law, which should primarily be reviewed by the Supreme Administrative Court.[63] The missed opportunity to initiate a preliminary procedure at the Court of Justice of the European Union (CJEU) was also the subject of criticism.[64]

---

59 But see e.g. P. de Vilchez Moragues, *Climate in Court. Defining State Obligations on Global Warming Through Domestic Climate Litigation*, Edward Elgar, Cheltenham 2022, p. 26; B. Hollaus, 'Austrian Constitutional Court: Considering Climate Change as a Public Interest is Arbitrary – Refusal of Third Runway Permit Annulled' (2017) 11 *ICL Journal* 467.

60 See e.g. F. Merli, 'Ein seltsamer Fall von Willkür: Die VfGH-Entscheidung zur dritten Piste des Flughafens Wien' (2017) 31 *Wirtschaftsrechtliche Blätter* 682; V. Madner and E. Schulev-Steindl, 'Dritte Piste – Klimaschutz als Willkür? Anmerkungen zu VfGH 29.06.2017, E 875/2017, E 886/2017' (2017) 72 *Zeitschrift für Öffentliches Recht* 589; E. Wagner, 'Die Judikatur zur „3. Piste" – vom Senkrechtstart zur Bruchlandung in Sachen Klimaschutz' (2017) 4 *Zeitschrift der Verwaltungsgerichtsbarkeit* 282; E. Wagner, 'Was bislang geschah: Staatszieldebatte / VfGH hebt Urteil Dritte Piste auf' (2017) 4 *Recht der Umwelt* 149.

61 V. Madner and E. Schulev-Steindl, 'Dritte Piste – Klimaschutz als Willkür? Anmerkungen zu VfGH 29.06.2017, E 875/2017, E 886/2017' (2017) 72 *Zeitschrift für Öffentliches Recht* 589, 596.

62 See e.g. F. Merli, 'Ein seltsamer Fall von Willkür: Die VfGH-Entscheidung zur dritten Piste des Flughafens Wien' (2017) 31 *Wirtschaftsrechtliche Blätter* 682.

63 See e.g. F. Merli, 'Ein seltsamer Fall von Willkür: Die VfGH-Entscheidung zur dritten Piste des Flughafens Wien' (2017) 31 *Wirtschaftsrechtliche Blätter* 682; see also V. Madner and E. Schulev-Steindl, 'Dritte Piste – Klimaschutz als Willkür? Anmerkungen zu VfGH 29.06.2017, E 875/2017, E 886/2017' (2017) 72 *Zeitschrift für Öffentliches Recht* 589, 600; A. Balthasar, 'Zu kurz gegriffen. Besprechung VfGH 29.06.2017, E 875/2017, E 886/2017' (2017) 72 *Zeitschrift für Öffentliches Recht* 577, 586.

64 A. Balthasar, 'Zu kurz gegriffen. Besprechung VfGH 29.06.2017, E 875/2017, E 886/2017' (2017) 72 *Zeitschrift für Öffentliches Recht* 577, 582–83.

The flaws of the judgment became evident in the academic analysis. The Constitutional Court reached its decision too hastily and did not really deal with the constitutional issues of the case, focusing instead on statutory questions (which the Supreme Administrative Court would have to decide upon).[65] Moreover, the ACC based its decision on outdated literature and judgments from the 1970s. It failed to deal with existing European provisions (regarding the Environmental Impact Assessment Directive)[66] and ignored existing case law (of the Supreme Administrative Court) regarding the involvement of international law. The Court did not start preliminary proceedings at the CJEU or initiate interim proceedings to review the statutory act in terms of its constitutionality.

In conclusion, the ACC not only denied the relevance of climate change as a constitutional argument but also excluded the possibility of considering it in general. The argumentative way out is that its considerations only concerned the Austrian Aviation Act. In another case, the ACC would be able to distinguish it from the existing case and could introduce an argumentation that takes climate change into account.

5. COMPARING CONSTITUTIONAL PARTICULARITIES

5.1. DIFFERENT STARTING POINTS

Although there was no major difference between the constitutional starting positions in the two countries, the results of the two constitutional court judgments could not have been more distinct. The FCC developed the existing constitutional provisions in the direction of active climate change adjudication, whereas the ACC not only ignored the relevance of climate change concerning the existing provision, but also shut down various possibilities for constitutional reasoning.

A comparison of the facts of the two cases shows how different they were. While in Germany the FCC had to decide directly on the recently enacted Climate Change Act,[67] the ACC's decision concerned an infrastructure project, which had been the source of much dispute for more than 15 years.[68]

65 See e.g. F. Merli, 'Ein seltsamer Fall von Willkür: Die VfGH-Entscheidung zur dritten Piste des Flughafens Wien' (2017) 31 *Wirtschaftsrechtliche Blätter* 682, 686; see the final decision of the Austrian Supreme Administrative Court, 06.03.2019, Ro 2018/03/0031-0038, Ro 2019/03/0007-0009.

66 See Directive 2011/92/EU on the assessment of the effects of certain public and private projects on the environment [2012] OJ L 26/1.

67 See the Federal Climate Change Act (Bundes-Klimaschutzgesetz, KSG) of 12.12.2019 (Federal Law Gazette, Bundesgesetzblatt – BGBl I, p. 2513).

68 S. Stadlmeier, 'Zur dritten Piste des Flughafens Wien' (2019) 74(1) *Zeitschrift für Öffentliches Recht* 21, 24–25.

The Austrian judgment occurred four years earlier, when – at least from the perspective of Austrian politics and public discussion – the relevance of climate change was not yet as significant.[69] Yet the ACC's decision did come after the Paris Agreement.[70] Moreover, the ACC had to review a pro-climate protection judgment by the Federal Administrative Court, which was ground-breaking by Austrian standards. Instead of supporting the Federal Administrative Court, the ACC fell back on old-fashioned arguments, not only maintaining judicial restraint but actively opposing any new possibilities.[71]

5.2. RIGHTS SELECTION

Climate change litigation requires, *inter alia*, a re-interpretation not only of constitutional law, but of many strands of law, challenging existing constitutional interpretation as well as the constitutional culture of the particular country. A rights-based approach must take the whole range of constitutional provisions and constitutional reasoning into consideration to be successful. This includes all possible human rights as well as other constitutional provisions, which might be (only) relevant in the context of a certain constitutional culture.

The human rights selection has to be understood as crucial. While the FCC derived State duties from the right to life (Article 2 paragraph 2 of the German Basic Law), environmental protection can also be based on the right to private life (Article 8 ECHR). The ACC did not even involve the case law of the ECtHR. From an Austrian perspective, the right to equal treatment (Article 7 of the Austrian Constitution) would be the most likely provision to develop rights in a new direction. In the last 40 years, the Court focused predominantly on Article 7 of the Austrian Constitution for the purposes of judicial activism and to go beyond the current state of constitutional rights.[72] Most recently, the ACC derived the right to an autonomous decision for a humane death from the right to equality.[73]

---

69 After the Paris Agreement, the Fridays for Future movement drew public attention to climate change. See e.g. M. Wahlström, P. Kocyba, M. De Vydt and J. de Moor (eds), *Protest for a future: Composition, mobilization and motives of the participants in Fridays For Future climate protests on 15 March, 2019 in 13 European cities. Project Report*, Keele Research Repository, 2019, https://eprints.keele.ac.uk/6571/.

70 See the Paris Agreement, https://unfccc.int/sites/default/files/english_paris_agreement.pdf.

71 The FCC in contrast struck out in a new direction and develop new dimensions of rights interpretation.

72 K. Lachmayer, 'The Austrian Constitutional Court' in A. Jakab, A. Dyevre and G. Itzcovich (eds), *Comparative Constitutional Reasoning*, Cambridge University Press, Cambridge 2017, pp. 75, 106–07.

73 See Austrian Constitutional Court, 11.12.2020, G 139/2019; the ACC followed the case law of the German Constitutional Court but developed its own constitutional interpretation on a different conceptual foundation (Art. 7 Austrian Constitution). See also the judgment of the Federal Constitutional Court of Germany, 26.02.2020, 2 BvR 2347/15.

The constitutional rights relevant to climate change, therefore, might be completely different in different States and the range of possible rights is broad;[74] the interpretative result could, however, be very similar.

5.3. THE CULTURE OF CONSTITUTIONAL REASONING

The German Constitutional Court has been following an activist approach for decades.[75] The Court is well aware of its global 'beacon function' in constitutional law; it presents arguments in detail and is willing to develop new concepts and forms of constitutional reasoning based on case law established over the decades.[76] Moreover, the German Constitutional Court rests on a highly developed doctrine of public law, which regularly gives varied input and criticism.[77]

In contrast to this, the ACC plays a minor role among the European supreme and constitutional courts. If the Court develops its case law, it often follows the European courts (CJEU as well as ECtHR) and is inspired by judgments by the FCC.[78] The heyday of judicial activism of the ACC (1980s to early 2000s) has passed and the Court returned to an approach of judicial restraint almost 10 years ago.[79] Remarkably, the Court does still uphold its activist approach in a few cases of societal importance.[80]

Based on the overall approach to law, and thus the particular legal culture of a country,[81] the specific culture of constitutional reasoning diverges significantly in different legal systems.[82] Even countries like Austria and Germany, which

---

74 'Indigenous rights litigation also has potential to address the harms of climate change.' K. Roach, 'Judicial Remedies for Climate Change' (2021) 17 *Journal of Law and Equity* 105, 129.

75 See e.g. O. Lembcke, 'The German Federal Constitutional Court: Authority transformed into power?' in K. Pócza (ed.), *Constitutional politics and the judiciary: Decision-making in Central and Eastern Europe*, Routledge, Abingdon/Oxford 2019, pp. 61–88; M. Hailbronner and S. Martini, 'The German Federal Constitutional Court' in A. Jakab, A. Dyevre and G. Itzcovich (eds), *Comparative Constitutional Reasoning*, Cambridge University Press, Cambridge 2017, pp. 356–93.

76 M. Jestaedt, O. Lepsius et al., *The German Federal Constitutional Court: The court without limits*, Oxford University Press, Oxford 2020.

77 Ibid.

78 See A. Gamper, 'Foreign Precedents in Austrian Constitutional Litigation' (2015) 9 *ICL Journal* 27, 29–30, 33–39.

79 H. Eberhard, 'Judicial activism und judicial self restraint in der Judikatur des VfGH' in E. Bernat et al. (eds), *Festschrift Christian Kopetzki*, Manz Publishing, Vienna 2019.

80 S. Gstöttner and K. Lachmayer, 'A Human Rights Stronghold Despite Becoming Judicial Restraint. The Austrian Constitutional Court 1990–2020' in K. Pócza (ed.), *Judicial Constraints on Legislatures in Europe 1990–2020*, Routledge, Abingdon 2024 (forthcoming).

81 See in general S. Koch and J.Ø. Sunde (eds), *Comparing Legal Cultures*, 2nd ed., Fagbokforlaget, Oslo 2021.

82 See A. Jakab, A. Dyevre and G. Itzcovich (eds), *Comparative Constitutional Reasoning*, Cambridge University Press, Cambridge 2017.

share many similarities and a common past, approach constitutional law in different ways.[83]

An example of how differently both courts approach constitutional reasoning can be seen in their approach to simple State objectives. While the FCC has started to enrich the substance of Article 20a of the German Basic Law, the ACC has not only ignored the FCA Sustainability, but has even gone so far as to thwart the FCA's role. An escape from the constitutional deadlock in Austria will not be achieved by overcoming the approach to State objectives, but requires a completely different form of constitutional reasoning.[84]

6. CONCLUSIONS

6.1. THE CONSTITUTIONAL CLIMATE TURNAROUND?

Four years have passed between the two judgments, but it seems that the overall approach has changed significantly. As Aust argues, 'since the Urgenda decisions of the Dutch courts, the tide seems to be turning'.[85] Nevertheless, the urgent need for further improvement of climate change litigation will pose a challenge for both countries. While Austria will have to find a way out of its climate change deadlock, Germany can – at least – build upon its first steps towards a constitutionally grounded climate change path.

Climate change litigation as constitutional adjudication needs a constitutional anchor and new forms of constitutional reasoning which open up existing constitutional argumentation to address climate change. Nevertheless, the developments of climate change litigation and related constitutional reasoning are still in their infancy and will have to improve quickly to support the measures necessary to turn the situation around.

6.2. AN OUTLOOK FOR AUSTRIA?

As the ACC shut down the possibilities of climate change litigation, it is up to the coalition government (which includes the Austrian Green Party) to take

83 See A. Jakab, 'Die österreichische öffentlich rechtliche Dogmatik aus deutschem Blickwinkel. Ex contrario fiat lux' (2007) 46(2) *Der Staat* 268; E. Wiederin, 'Denken vom Recht her. Über den *modus austriacus* in der Staatsrechtslehre' in H. Schulze-Fielitz (ed.), *Staatsrechtslehre als Wissenschaft, Die Verwaltung Beiheft 7*, Duncker & Humblot, Berlin 2007, pp. 293–317; K. Lachmayer, 'The Austrian Constitutional Court' in A. Jakab, A. Dyevre and G. Itzcovich (eds), *Comparative Constitutional Reasoning*, Cambridge University Press, Cambridge 2017, pp. 75–114.

84 See below section 6.2.

85 H. Aust, 'Climate Protection Act Case' (2022) 116 *American Journal of International Law* 150.

climate action by stopping new infrastructure projects.[86] The Austrian Minister of Climate Change has started taking such steps but faces opposition from many figures in the Austrian administration.

The ACC will therefore remain a key player in terms of climate change in Austria. When it comes to potential steps forward in its constitutional adjudication, four different possibilities for constitutional reasoning can be suggested to break the existing deadlock:

- *The change of time argument:* The Constitutional Court could argue that the foundation of constitutional reasoning has changed as climate change has become an imminent threat to humanity that must be taken into consideration.
- *The comparative argument:* While in 2017 the ACC was not aware of climate change litigation, the situation has changed significantly. From an Austrian perspective, the German decision is of particular relevance as the ACC regularly orients itself towards the FCC.
- *The equality argument:* The Austrian Constitutional Court has to follow its own case law and its own way of constitutional reasoning. The right to equal treatment plays an important role in the case law of the ACC. There are many possibilities for arguing within Austrian constitutional law that the equality principle is violated by ongoing climate change: for example, that the principle of reasonability has to be interpreted in the light of ongoing climate change or that the right to equal treatment has to take younger generations (or even future generations) into account. Recent case law regarding the COVID-19 crisis shows that the ACC is willing to include scientific predictions in its understanding of reasonability of law.
- *The European argument:* The easiest way to overcome the constitutional deadlock would be to refer to EU law. In recent years, many new EU regulations and directives concerning climate change have been enacted.[87] It would be easy for the ACC to draw upon new European legislation and to argue with regard to the direct effect and new obligations under EU law that the Austrian Constitution has to be re-interpreted. It is unlikely that the ACC will come up with a re-interpretation of Article 37 of the CFR,

---

86 See K. Lachmayer and C. Müller, 'Austria's Struggle to Respond to Climate Change', *Verfassungsblog on Matters Constitutional* (2022), https://verfassungsblog.de/austrias-struggle-to-respond-to-climate-change/.

87 See the judgment of the ACC regarding the CFR, VfSlg 19.632/2012: while the ACC declared that the rights of the Charter of Fundamental Rights, which correspond to the rights of the ECHR, have to be understood as fundamental rights regarding the Austrian Constitution, the ACC excluded other rights and principles like Art. 37 CFR. Developments of the case law of the ECtHR regarding climate protection are, however, crucial for the further acceptance of Art. 37 CFR in Austria.

but if the CJEU in particular starts to revitalise this provision,[88] it would be reasonable to expect that the ACC would embrace the new dimensions of this provision.[89]

6.3. THE POTENTIAL AND RISK OF A CONSTITUTIONAL RIGHTS APPROACH

Climate change litigation focuses – at least to a certain extent – on rights, especially human rights. Human rights litigation and case law of many different domestic and international courts over the last decades have seemed to be a promising way to approach climate change. The first positive decisions of courts, such as those in the Netherlands and Germany, support this impression and illustrate the potential of a constitutional approach to climate change. In addition, several pending cases before the ECtHR[90] related to climate change could potentially facilitate the use of Convention rights as a tool for climate change litigation before national courts.

Memories of global social rights adjudication in the 1990s and 2000s should, however, serve as a warning against being too optimistic about constitutional adjudication.[91] While to begin with there were high hopes for the potential of social rights adjudication, for example in South Africa,[92] these expectations have

88 J. van Zeben, 'The Role of the EU Charter of Fundamental Rights in Climate Litigation' (2021) 22 *German Law Journal* 1499, 1505: 'However, close analysis of Article 37, its relationship to the other Charter provisions, Article 11 TFEU and EU law more generally, and its appearance – or lack thereof – in CJEU jurisprudence, indicates that Article 37 currently does not provide any limits or obligations on actors with respect to environmental protection or integration. Nevertheless, the potential of Article 37 for "greening" actions of EU actors via the Charter is considerable, given the EU's environmental, and climate, ambitions; the fact that there is virtually no area of environmental policy that is not dominated by EU law; and that the scope of Article 37 arguably extends far beyond environmental legislation.'

89 See A. Gamper, 'Foreign Precedents in Austrian Constitutional Litigation' (2015) 9 *ICL Journal* 27, 29–30.

90 See e.g. the case *Duarte Agostinho and Others v. Portugal*, no. 39371/20, pending before the Grand Chamber of the ECtHR.

91 See e.g. V. Gauri and D.M. Brinks, *Courting Social Justice: Judicial Enforcement of Social and Economic Rights in the Developing World*, Cambridge University Press, Cambridge 2008; A. Nolan (ed.), *Economic and social rights after the global financial crisis*, Cambridge University Press, Cambridge 2014; J. King, *Judging social rights*, Cambridge Studies in Constitutional Law series, Cambridge University Press, Cambridge 2012.

92 See e.g. D.M. Davis, 'Socio-Economic Rights' in M. Rosenfeld and A. Sajó (eds), *The Oxford Handbook of Comparative Constitutional Law*, Oxford University Press, Oxford 2012, pp. 1020, 1027–30, 1033–34; E. Cameron, 'A South African Perspective on the Judicial Development of Socio-Economic Rights' in L. Lazarus, C. McCrudden and N. Bowles (eds), *Reasoning rights: Comparative judicial engagement*, Hart, Oxford 2014, pp. 319–38.

not been fully realised in ongoing developments.[93] While constitutional courts conceded the constitutional relevance of social rights initially, they accepted the limited application of social rights in favour of parliamentary and governmental restrictions. In all the cases discussed in this chapter, the relevance of the parliament and the government in deciding on the application of measures concerning climate change played a significant role. The risk of climate change litigation is therefore that it quickly reaches the limits of the courts' ability and willingness to intervene in governmental strategies concerning climate change.

There is still a great need for judges to develop existing case law and to re-interpret the constitution, taking into consideration of a new ecological understanding. The consistent worsening of the global situation might serve as an increasing motivation for constitutional and supreme courts to develop constitutional reasoning to fight climate change. The role of the courts, however, will be decisive in developing new concepts that take into account intergenerational justice as an immanent part of existing human and fundamental rights catalogues.

---

93 J. Berger, 'Litigating for social justice in post-Apartheid South Africa: a focus on health and education' in V. Gauri and D.M. Brinks, *Courting Social Justice: Judicial Enforcement of Social and Economic Rights in the Developing World*, Cambridge University Press, Cambridge 2008, pp. 38, 95: 'Although litigation remains an indispensable tool, without which the inertia of a flawed political process may never be broken, it becomes most effective when its use is limited and targeted. Simply put, broad social change will not be won in the courts alone.'

TAKING *PEOPLE v. ARCTIC OIL* SERIOUSLY

The Potential of Strategic Environmental Assessments and the Principle of Non-Regression in Guiding Energy Policy

Suryapratim Roy and Alexandru Gociu

1. INTRODUCTION

People v. Arctic Oil is a full-bench judgment and decision delivered by the Norwegian Supreme Court in December 2020.[1] It was a case where Greenpeace and Nature & Youth (joined by Grandparents' Climate Movement and Friends of the Earth Norway as interveners) filed an application to quash licences issued by the Norwegian government for petroleum exploration in the Barents Sea during the 23rd Licensing Round (Licensing Decision). The case began its trajectory before the Oslo District Court with a fair bit of publicity – there was an ice sculpture with a '112' inscription found outside the courthouse,[2] signifying Article 112 of the Norwegian Constitution on the right to a healthy environment. Thus, the case was framed by the petitioners as a climate rights case where both rights under the European Convention of Human Rights (ECHR) as well as

---

1 Norwegian Supreme Court, 22 December 2020, *Greenpeace Nordic Association v. Ministry of Petroleum and Energy*, Case No. 20-051052SIV-HRET (*People v. Arctic Oil*). Unofficial translation at www.klimasoksmal.no/wp-content/uploads/2021/01/judgement_translated.pdf.

2 https://media.greenpeace.org/archive/People-vs-Arctic-Oil-Court-Case-Ice-Sculpture-in-Oslo-27MZIFJX62PAG.html.

constitutional rights were in play. The case then went up to the Borgarting[3] Court of Appeal, and finally to the Supreme Court. The case was decided in favour of the government at all three stages. Aggrieved by the decision, young Norwegians have filed an application before the European Court of Human Rights (ECtHR) on a similar cause of action, focusing on Article 2 (right to life) and Article 8 (right to private family life) of the ECHR.[4]

The Supreme Court judgment prompted a fair bit of criticism. This is primarily for three reasons: (1) given the aim of achieving a net-zero level of emissions by 2050, further exploration of oil is counterproductive, and hence there is an emerging international trend against oil exploration;[5] (2) the deferential stance taken by the Court in favour of the government is not representative of climate change judgments in other jurisdictions where rights have informed policy;[6] and (3) the Licensing Decision pertains to blocks in the Arctic, which is a vulnerable ecosystem.[7] It is not surprising that the judgment has been found to be 'backward-looking'.[8] However, there has also been some support for the judgment. At a domestic level, it has been argued that, given Norway's oil revenues fuel both its welfare system and its transition to renewables, energy and climate policy need to be balanced.[9] At the international level, it has been argued that human rights are unsuitable in dealing with questions of transnational climate and energy diplomacy.[10]

On the issue of international climate and energy policy, the 2022 Russian invasion of Ukraine[11] has happened since the judgment was delivered. This

---

3 Norway has six courts of appeal, each with jurisdiction on specific Norwegian counties. The Borgarting Court of Appeal has jurisdiction over Oslo and western Viken.

4 A copy of the application is available at: https://climatecasechart.com/wp-content/uploads/non-us-case-documents/2021/20210615_Application-no.-3406821_petition-1.pdf.

5 R. Frost, 'The End of Fossil Fuels: Which countries have banned exploration and extraction?', *Euronews*, 12 August 2021, https://www.euronews.com/green/2021/08/12/the-end-of-fossil-fuels-which-countries-have-banned-exploration-and-extraction.

6 P. Minnerop and I. Røstgaard, 'In Search of a Fair Share: Article 112 Norwegian Constitution, International Law, and an Emerging Inter-Jurisdictional Judicial Discourse in Climate Litigation' (2021) 44 *Fordham International Law Journal* 847.

7 D. Shapovalova, 'Arctic Petroleum and the 2°C Goal: A Case for Accountability for Fossil-Fuel Supply' (2020) 10 *Climate Law* 282.

8 C. Voigt, 'The First Climate judgment before the Norwegian Supreme Court: Aligning law with politics' (2021) 33 *Journal of Environmental Law* 697, 698.

9 A. Gociu, 'The Norwegian Petroleum Regulatory Framework and the Transition to Green Energy' (2021) 1 *Queen Mary Law Journal* 33.

10 A. Zahar, 'A Leakage Case Litigated as a Human Rights Case', Paper presented at the 'Climate Litigation as Governance Tool' Conference, held at Duke Kunshan University, Suzhou, China, 24–25 October 2020, https://papers.ssrn.com/sol3/papers.cfm?abstract_id=3714290.

11 For a collection of legal issues on the invasion, see Symposium papers on Ukraine and the International Order hosted by American Journal of International Law Unbound, https://www.cambridge.org/core/journals/american-journal-of-international-law/ajil-unbound-by-symposium/ukraine-and-the-international-order.

invasion has resulted in an interest in Europe in energy security.[12] Such interest in energy security would entail enhancement of energy efficiency measures, and ramping up renewable energy investments.[13] Such measures, however, cannot phase out the need 'to ensure the security of oil'.[14] With respect to Norway, rethinking the dependence on Russian oil and gas by countries in the EU has led to the question of whether there should be greater reliance on Norwegian oil and gas. This period has been characterised as a 'boom time'[15] for Norway, with Equinor (the State-owned Norwegian energy company) reporting profits 10 times that of the previous year.[16] Even though the process of oil exploration and exploitation takes more than a decade, Norway might have found itself in an unusual position if it had increased sales of oil and gas, and at the same time was prohibited from further exploration by the Supreme Court.

It appears from the above that the *People v. Arctic Oil* judgment has gone against developments in climate law, but is in keeping with concerns on European energy security and domestic welfare policy. This chapter unsettles this binary. Specifically, it argues that energy policy and climate policy do not necessarily have to be at loggerheads. Rather, environmental law can inform both. Further, it is possible to pursue energy policy without being detrimental to climate goals. Specifically, to support this argument the chapter focuses on two aspects of the judgment that have not received scholarly scrutiny – the role of the European Union Strategic Environmental Assessment Directive (SEA Directive),[17] and the principle of non-regression. The SEA Directive is explicitly discussed in the judgment, and is central to the reasoning adopted by Judge Webster in a dissenting opinion. The principle of non-regression is not discussed in the judgment, but given the facts and circumstances of the case, the chapter argues that this principle would be of explanatory value. Further, the principle is related to the principle of progressive development of climate action found in the Paris Agreement, which the Court discusses.

---

12 M. Mišík, 'The EU Needs to Improve its External Energy Security' (2022) 165 *Energy Policy* 112930.

13 European Commission, 'Communication from the Commission to the European Parliament, the European Council, the Council, the European Economic and Social Committee and the Committee of the Regions: RepowerEU Plan', COM(2022) 230.

14 Ibid.

15 'In Europe, Norway would be at the front of the queue to step in if the continent were to start refusing hydrocarbons from Russia.' N. Ferris, 'Boom time in Norway as the West cracks down on Russian oil', *The New Statesman*, 10 March 2022.

16 N. Adomaitis and N. Buli, 'Equinor shareholders to get $10 bln payout as energy prices soar', *Reuters*, 9 February 2022, https://www.reuters.com/business/equinor-posts-record-q4-hikes-dividend-share-buybacks-2022-02-09/.

17 Directive 2001/42/EC of the European Parliament and of the Council of 27 June 2001 on the assessment of the effects of certain plans and programmes on the environment.

The chapter proceeds as follows. Section 2 provides a contextual background to the case, and section 3 presents a brief discussion of the judgment as it made its way from the District Court to the Supreme Court, highlighting the contribution of each court, and especially the radical contribution of a dissenting opinion penned by Judge Webster at the Supreme Court. Section 4 looks to the unexplored potential of the role of the law on strategic environmental assessments in informing energy and climate policy, and section 5 suggests that the issues central to the case may be effectively understood using the principle of non-regression. The chapter points to how the framing of energy policy versus decarbonisation is misplaced once it is realised that both climate and energy policy need to happen in a certain way. Specifically, it is argued that the guiding framework of 'realist sustainability' central to Norwegian energy policy is compatible with the principle of non-regression.

2. BACKGROUND TO THE CASE: THE NORWEGIAN 'PARADOX'

Norway's relationship with carbon emissions is considered paradoxical – within the boundaries of the State, 98% of its energy comes from renewable sources. *National Geographic* has dubbed it the world's greenest nation.[18] Norway has ratified the Paris Agreement, and recently updated its climate targets.[19] Norway participates in the European Union Emissions Trading Scheme (EU ETS) and has domestic climate and renewable policies which are at the forefront of national climate action. The infrastructure for oil exploitation uses energy from renewable sources, and a sizable percentage of the proceeds is used for investments in renewables.[20] The proceeds in general from the sale of fossil fuels are fed into Norwegian Government Pension Fund Global (GPFG) – a sovereign wealth fund that is a central pillar of the Norwegian welfare system.[21] The Norwegian Parliament has devised ethical criteria for investments made by the GPFG, and the management body of the GPFG seeks to divest its assets from companies that are not doing enough to combat climate change.[22] In contrast

---

18 M. Carroll, 'Norway's leading the charge on a sustainable electric future', *National Geographic*, 27 June 2019.

19 In February 2020, Norway updated its nationally determined contribution under the Paris Agreement to reduce emissions by at least 50% and up to 55% by 2030, compared to 1990 levels.

20 'Norway's wealth fund to double green energy investment cap', *The Local*, 6 April 2019.

21 For an overview, see M. Takle, 'The Norwegian Petroleum Fund: Savings for future generations' (2020) 30 *Environmental Values* 147.

22 S. Chesterman, 'The Turn to Ethics: Disinvestment from Multinational Corporations for Human Rights Violations – The Case of Norway's Sovereign Wealth Fund' (2007) 23 *American University International Law Review* 577; 'Norway's $1 trillion fund to cut oil and gas investments', *BBC News*, 8 April 2019.

with all of this is a simple fact: Norway is the third-largest oil exporter in the world, and is the seventh-largest exporter of greenhouse gas emissions[23] due to the combustion of the embodied emissions of its oil exports.

The paradox described above is not a legal paradox if looked at from the perspective of international climate treaties, where there is only an obligation to be 'clean at home', and the international emissions accounting framework is one that is based on a producer-based territorial model.[24] Following this model, States are accountable for direct emissions at source within their territorial boundaries, and where such emissions do not have to include extraterritorial combustion emissions. Thus, it is perfectly legal for a rich State to be clean at home and be dirty outside from the perspective of international climate treaties. This may explain why Norway has historically been a 'frontrunner' in international climate negotiations,[25] and was proactive in the adoption of the framework of nationally determined contributions during the negotiations of the Paris Agreement.[26] The producer-based territorial model of emissions accounting used in the UN system is in Norway's favour. Energy policy premised on simultaneously continuing oil production and adopting higher climate targets has enjoyed the support of larger political parties,[27] Equinor[28] and trade unions.[29] It is not hard to see why scholars have critiqued this model, and have offered alternatives such as an income-based model where a State would bear responsibility in line with the income it earns from emissions-causing activities.[30] At a more general level, it is not hard to see why scholars are turning away from the United Nations Framework Convention on Climate Change (UNFCCC) as the only way to appreciate international climate

23 H. McKinnon, G. Muttitt and K. Trout, 'The Sky's Limit Norway: Why Norway should lead the way in a managed decline of oil and gas extraction', *Oil Change International Report*, 9 August 2017, http://priceofoil.org/2017/08/09/the-skys-limit-norway-why-norway-should-lead-the-way-in-a-managed-decline-of-oil-and-gas-extraction/.

24 For a discussion of the principle and alternatives, see S. Bastianoni, F.M. Pulselli and E. Tiezzi, 'The Problem of Assigning Responsibility for Greenhouse Gas Emissions' (2004) 49 *Ecological Economics* 253.

25 B. Lahn and E. Wilson Rowe, 'How to be a "front-runner": Norway and international climate politics' in B. de Carvalho and I.B. Neumann (eds), *Small States and Status Seeking: Norway's quest for international standing* (Routledge 2014).

26 A. Brun, 'Conference Diplomacy: The making of the Paris Agreement' (2016) 4 *Politics and Governance* 115.

27 With the exception of the Progress Party, no Norwegian political party has opposed climate obligations. They have also simultaneously supported oil exploitation. R. Eckersley, 'Poles Apart?: The Social Construction of Responsibility for Climate Change in Australia and Norway' (2013) 59 *Australian Journal of Politics and History* 382, 386.

28 A. Nissen, 'A Greener Shade of Black? Statoil, the Norwegian government and climate change, 1990–2005' (2021) 46 *Scandinavian Journal of History* 408.

29 For an account of varying degrees of petroleum dependence among different unions, see C. Roueland, D. Jordhus-Lier and F. Hambro Angell, 'Solidarity tested: The case of the Norwegian Confederation of Trade Unions (LO-Norway) and its contradictory climate change policies' (2021) 53 *Area* 413.

30 A. Marques, J. Rodrigues, M. Lenzen and T. Domingos, 'Income-based Environmental Responsibility' (2012) 84 *Ecological Economics* 57.

law – environmental principles in other international treaties could be mobilised for finding climate obligations,[31] and national court judges have been playing an active role in devising climate law.[32]

Given the division into domestic energy policy and international climate law which Norway embraces while being compliant with international law and the EU ETS, it may be asked what changed in the recent past that prompted the lawsuit. There is a combination of transnational and domestic factors. Taking a cue from the above discussion, the recent spate of climate lawsuits in which transnational non-governmental organisations (NGOs) have played a part is certainly a factor.[33] Norway was the site for such a case; the lawsuit was initiated by the Norwegian branches of transnational NGOs, and the petition filed before the District Court of Oslo references climate cases filed in other jurisdictions.[34] What distinguishes this case from climate cases in other jurisdictions is the focus on emissions from a particular sector, namely petroleum. In this regard, this case is a first; it was only in 2019 that the lawsuit against Shell was filed in the Hague District Court, and the decision given in 2021.[35] Domestic developments within Norway appear to have played a role. With respect to party politics, the Green Party gained a seat in the Storting (the Norwegian Parliament), with oil drilling opposition as its primary campaign.[36] Though operating under the Ministry of Climate and Environment, the Norwegian Environment Agency (NEA)[37]

---

31 A. Boyle and N. Singh Ghaleigh, 'Climate Change and International Law beyond the UNFCCC' in K. Gray, R. Tarasofsky and C. Carlarne (eds), *The Oxford Handbook of International Climate Change Law* (OUP 2016).

32 S. Mead and L. Maxwell, 'Climate Change Litigation: National Courts as Agents of International Law Development' in E. Sobenes, S. Mead and B. Samson (eds), *The Environment Through the Lens of International Courts and Tribunals* (T.M.C. Asser Press 2022), pp. 617–48.

33 Following the Netherlands, there has been an explosion of climate cases globally filed by citizens and NGOs, with lawsuits filed in Belgium, France, Germany, Ireland, Pakistan, Spain and the UK, before the European Court of Justice (CJEU) and the ECtHR, among others. For an overview, see UNEP, *Global Climate Litigation Report 2020 Status Review*, https://www.unep.org/resources/report/global-climate-litigation-report-2020-status-review; 'Climate change litigation cases spreading around the world', Grantham Research Institute on Climate Change and the Environment, Press Release, July 2021, https://www.lse.ac.uk/granthaminstitute/news/climate-change-litigation-cases-spreading-around-the-world/.

34 Writ of Summons before the Oslo District Court, https://action4justice.org/wp-content/uploads/2018/01/Claim-form-People-v-Arctic-Oil-Norway-legal_writ_english_final_20161018-low-res.pdf.

35 District Court of The Hague, 26 May 2021, *Milieudefensie et al. v. Royal Dutch Shell plc*, C/09/571932/HA ZA 19-379; English version (*Milieudefensie v. RDS*), available at https://climatecasechart.com/wp-content/uploads/non-us-case-documents/2021/20210526_8918_judgment-1.pdf.

36 T. Solsvik, 'Norway's anti-oil Green Party could hold key to election outcome', *Arctic Today*, 23 August 2017.

37 The Norwegian Environment Agency is an independent government agency under the Ministry of Climate and Environment with a mainly advisory and implementation role in the field of climate and environmental policy.

expressed concern that oil reserves may become 'stranded assets' and warned against further licensing.[38] Based on these observations, Bang and Lahn conclude that there is a new policy coalition between the Greens, the NEA and NGOs.[39] The concern over 'stranded assets' is notable – although the intention of the NEA might have been to warn against more exploration, it may well have had a counter-effect as the government could have issued more licences in the short term. In fact, the number of licences issued in the 23rd licensing round pertaining to the Licensing Decision[40] was substantially higher than those issued earlier.[41] This is perhaps not only a reaction to the fear of oil in the Arctic becoming a stranded asset, but also due to Norwegian relations with Russia. A 44-year-old border dispute with Russia was settled in 2011 that led to a substantial area of the Barents Sea becoming available for exploration.[42] It may well be that the government felt it was time to open this area up for exploration. The spike in the number of licences issued in the recent past is a departure from Norwegian practice, based on a 'go slow' policy of oil exploitation,[43] which has allowed Norway to escape the short-termism that leads to a resource curse.[44] The chapter will return to the issue of a spike in licences when discussing the principle of non-regression.

3. JURISPRUDENTIAL TAKEAWAYS

There was no legal hurdle in the plaintiffs securing standing to litigate this case. The decision even at the District Court level was on the merits.[45] Central to standing and the reasoning of the District Court was Article 112 of the

---

38 G. Bang and B. Lahn, 'From oil as welfare to oil as risk? Norwegian petroleum resource governance and climate policy' (2020) 20 *Climate Policy* 997.

39 Ibid.

40 Ministry of Petroleum and Energy, 'Announcement 23rd Licensing Round Awards', Government.no, 18 May 2016, www.regjeringen.no/en/aktuelt/announcement-23rd-licensing-round-awards/id2500936/.

41 B. Lahn, 'Norwegian Petroleum Policy in a Changing Climate', Center for International Climate Research Report, 2019, p. 27, https://cicero.oslo.no/no/publications/internal/2890.

42 Arctic Forum Foundation, 'Delimitation agreement: A new era in the Barents Sea and the Arctic?', http://eu-arctic-forum.org/allgemein/delimitation-agreement-a-new-era-in-the-barents-sea-and-the-arctic/.

43 In June 1974, the Finance Ministry's White Paper No. 25, 'The Role of Petroleum Activity in Norwegian Society' outlined a detailed petroleum strategy introducing the concept of a 'go slow' policy, essentially moderate and controlled petroleum development in order to facilitate strongest possible Norwegian participation in petroleum production. For a discussion, see A. Gociu, above n. 9.

44 T.L. Karl, *The Paradox of Plenty: Oil Booms and Petro-States* (University of California Press 1997).

45 Oslo District Court, 4 January 2018, *Greenpeace Nordic Association v. Ministry of Petroleum and Energy Case*, Case No. 16-166674TVIOTIR/06.

Norwegian Constitution. Given that this provision animates the case, it might be useful to take a look at the text of the Article:

> Every person has the right to an environment that is conducive to health and to a natural environment whereby productivity and diversity are maintained. Natural resources shall be managed on the basis of comprehensive long-term considerations, which will safeguard this right for future generations as well.
>
> In order to safeguard their right in accordance with the foregoing paragraph, citizens are entitled to information on the state of the natural environment and on the effects of any encroachment on nature that is planned or carried out.
>
> The authorities of the state shall take measures for the implementation of these principles.

Article 112 was recognised as a substantive rights-bearing provision, where both citizens and organisations secure standing to query the State's policies if they do not satisfy their corresponding duty of care to secure rights,[46] given the Article enjoins the State to take measures to implement the principles contained in it. Thus, unlike some other jurisdictions where a distinction has been made between citizens and organisations in litigating personal rights,[47] the District Court judgment allows claims for both. This is already of jurisprudential interest as *People v. Arctic Oil* is the first case that discussed and ruled on the scope of Article 112. Notwithstanding the recognition of Article 112 as a rights-bearing provision that entails a corresponding duty of care on the part of the State, the District Court ruled in favour of the State. This was firstly due to deference to the government in deciding how to satisfy its duty of care,[48] and second to the irrelevance of extraterritorial emissions in meeting its environmental obligations.[49]

The decision was appealed by the plaintiffs, and the Borgarting Court of Appeals also decided in favour of the State, but not without a substantial difference in its reasoning. The Court of Appeals first maintained the District Court's view that Article 112 is a rights-bearing provision, and in an unprecedented interpretive step recognised that the State's duty of care under Article 112 may apply to environmental harms caused due to extraterritorial emissions from fossil fuels exported and consumed outside Norwegian territory.[50] Voigt suggests

---

46 Ibid., para. 9.

47 This is found in the Irish climate case. *Friends of the Irish Environment v. Ireland* [2020] IESC 49. For a discussion, see S. Roy, 'The Domestic Life of Climate Law: *Friends of the Irish Environment v. Ireland*' (2022) 3 *Irish Supreme Court Review* 141.

48 Oslo District Court, above n. 45, para. 28.

49 Borgarting Court of Appeal, 22 January 2020, *Greenpeace Nordic Association v. Ministry of Petroleum and Energy*, Case No. 18-060499ASD-BORG/03.

50 Ibid., para. 11.

that this observation was in an *obiter dictum*,[51] as it did not aid in the decision reached by the Court in favour of the government. However, the authors of this chapter partially disagree. It is true that this observation did not have any bearing on the final decision, but that is primarily because the decision was premised on the separation of powers. The Norwegian Petroleum Regulations[52] under the Petroleum Act require the Norwegian Ministry of Petroleum and Energy to conduct an impact assessment during the process of opening up the blocks.[53] Given there is existing legislation on the issue, and that there is legislation on Norway's international climate commitments, the Court observed that Article 112 was not violated. Thus, there is a considerable burden of proof on the plaintiff to demonstrate a violation of the right to a healthy environment[54] – there is a high threshold that needs to be overcome to challenge existing policy against Article 112.

A full-judge bench of the Supreme Court heard arguments in a plenary session, with a majority decision given in favour of the government by 11 judges, with a dissenting opinion penned by Judge Webster supported by three other judges. The focus of the majority decision was the interpretation and applicability of Article 112, with observations on the role of the ECHR, and whether there were any procedural errors with respect to impact assessments. The dissenting opinion focused primarily on impact assessments understood in the light of Article 112. A substantial portion of the judgment focused on the interpretation of Article 112 using parliamentary history. This is a feature inimical to Norwegian constitutional tradition; there is heavy reliance on preparatory works[55] and legislative history on the adoption and amendment of constitutional provisions.[56] Following an examination of materials that led to the adoption of Article 110B (the predecessor to Article 112), and its amendment to the current form, the Court concluded that Article 112 is a 'safety valve' when there is gross disregard by the government of environmental harm.[57] However, this threshold of gross disregard is difficult to establish. The Licensing Decision was characterised as a form of delegated legislation, where a majority vote in the parliament arrived at a Royal Decree to permit the grant of licences.[58] Further, the process of oil exploration has a legislative framework to assess environmental

51 C. Voigt, above n. 8, p. 5.

52 Chapter 2a.

53 Section 6c, first paragraph, (b) and (e) of the Regulations.

54 Ibid.

55 For a definitive treatment on the use of preparatory works, see K. Bergo, *Høyesteretts forarbeidsbruk* (Cappelen Akademisk Forlag 2000).

56 Voigt critiques this approach for being a backward interpretative method that does not take into account developments since the adoption of the provision. C. Voigt, above n. 8, p. 7.

57 Norwegian Supreme Court, above n. 1, para. 142.

58 Ibid., para. 236.

impacts. Given that such legislation is in place, a gross disregard of Article 112 is difficult to maintain. On the issue of extraterritorial emissions, the Court was of the opinion that Article 112 applies only to harm within Norway; environmental harm as a result of extraterritorial emissions could fall within the scope of the Constitution if such harm was because of government activities that caused direct environmental damage. The 'direct' damage element was used to interpret the ECHR: the Court did not find any infringement of the right to life under Article 2 as infringement requires evidence of 'real and immediate' harm to citizens, where 'real and immediate' was interpreted to mean 'proximate harm', which was not made out in this case.[59]

The inclination of the Court to limit its engagement to issues within Norway informed its appreciation of the role of impact assessment. The Court found that there are obligations to conduct impact assessments under the Petroleum Act read with the SEA Directive. However, the effects of emissions outside Norway was beyond the scope of judicial review: 'the net impact of Norwegian exports of oil and gas on global emissions is complex and debated';[60] it would be 'up to the Ministry and the Government to decide whether it was appropriate to refer to and deal with the question of climate effects at an overarching level.'[61] As to what considerations might be at play, the Court identified competition between States on supply of fossil fuels.[62] Thus, the issue of whether impact assessments should account for combustion emissions of its oil exports is a matter of government policy, and specifically foreign policy, over which the Court has no remit. This reasoning was complemented by a narrow temporal interpretation of whether there is procedural infirmity given that the Licensing Decision did not account for environmental harm due to climate effects. The Court observed that the Licensing Decision 'does not grant an unconditional right to production even if commercially exploitable discoveries are made';[63] actual production would require approvals on specific Plans for Development and Operations (PDOs) presented by developers. Given that the existence and commercial viability of oil reserves would be assessed on a case-by-case basis at that stage, the majority found this lawsuit premature.[64]

What can be seen from the above is that the temporal and spatial reach of impact assessments was read narrowly, and the guiding principle for appreciating combustion emissions from oil exports is deference to legislative discretion in

59 Ibid., para. 170.
60 Ibid., para. 234.
61 Ibid.
62 Ibid.
63 Ibid., para. 218.
64 For a discussion, see A. Gociu and S. Roy, 'Extraterritoriality of Oil Constitutionalism in People v Arctic Oil', *EJIL:Talk!*, 16 February 2021, https://www.ejiltalk.org/extraterritoriality-of-oil-constitutionalism-in-people-v-arctic-oil/.

determining energy policy where a host of 'overarching concerns' are at play, not least of which are foreign policy concerns. It is in this respect that the dissenting opinion presents a radical departure, in that impact assessments are informed by *law* rather than *policy*. Specifically, the primary points of reference were Article 112 and CJEU jurisprudence on the SEA Directive. There is no doubt that any discussion on legislative decisions happens in the shadow of constitutional law: '[t]he procedural rules in the petroleum legislation *must* be assessed in the light of Article 112 of the Constitution' (emphasis added).[65] As to how the right to a healthy environment has a bearing, Judge Webster identified an unexpected component of the text of Article 112 as key: 'citizens are *entitled to information* on the state of the natural environment and *on the effects of any encroachment on nature that is planned* or carried out' (emphasis added). Given there is a constitutional entitlement to be informed on 'any encroachment on nature that is planned', it is imperative that citizens must be informed of the effects of licensing decisions from the earliest stages. In this way, the two-stage temporal distinction made by the majority as to the stage at which exploratory licences are granted and a subsequent stage when specifics of development are approved is collapsed. The removal of the two-stage distinction is further supported by CJEU jurisprudence on the SEA Directive. Judge Webster referred to an opinion by the CJEU on a preliminary reference by Belgium on whether broad plans require an SEA.[66] This opinion explains the difference between the scope of the SEA Directive and the Environmental Impact Assessment Directive (EIA Directive): the SEA Directive applies to policy-level plans where details may not be ferreted out, while the EIA Directive applies to specific projects. Following this line of reasoning, the Licensing Decision falls within the scope of the SEA Directive, while approvals for specific PDOs would fall within the scope of the EIA Directive. On the issue of extraterritoriality and the spatial scope of impact assessments, the minority opinion pointed to the need to take into account 'climatic factors' when assessing the effects of plans and programmes on the environment. Here, combustion emissions from exported oil are interpreted to fall within the scope of climatic factors by virtue of a footnote in Annex II of the SEA Directive, which advises accounting for 'secondary, cumulative and long-term effects' in understanding what environmental effects are to be included while conducting an impact assessment.[67] This interpretive step of bringing combustion emissions into the scope of the SEA Directive via a potent footnote is truly a radical moment in the history of climate law.

---

65 Norwegian Supreme Court, above n. 1, para. 255.

66 Case C-671/6, *ASBL Inter-Environnement Bruxelles*, ECLI:EU:C:2018:403.

67 Norwegian Supreme Court, above n. 1, para. 263.

4. ROLE OF SEAs AND RIGHTS

As discussed above, jurisprudence on strategic environmental assessment had a limited role to play in the majority judgment of the Supreme Court, but it was central to the minority opinion. In the majority judgment, impact assessments were understood as a component of domestic policy and discretion. The Petroleum Act requires impact assessments. Further, whether combustion emissions from oil exports should be included was characterised as an overarching concern of foreign policy, and hence outside the remit of the Court. The minority opinion understood impact assessments as a creature of constitutional law and European law, the requirements of which exist prior to and outside the specifics of policy considerations.

Was it necessary to apply the SEA Directive via Article 112? Or, to put it another way, given the constraints on judicial review, why was it necessary to invoke constitutional doctrine? There are two responses to this. The first is that the SEA Directive (and interpretation of the Directive) would not have direct effect as Norway is not a member of the EU. By virtue of the European Economic Agreement, EU law is substantively followed, but for Judge Webster to find the SEA Directive to have direct effect would have been a step too far. The second reason is that there is no direct jurisprudence on the issues discussed in relation to the SEA Directive by the CJEU – there is no jurisprudence on 'climatic factors', or long-term and cumulative effects. Given this constraint, relying on the SEA Directive on its own would not be sufficient to develop the line of reasoning that there needs to be early and continuous assessment for long-term and cumulative effects.

It appears that this novel combination of rights and SEA jurisprudence may be specific to Norway, as other jurisdictions may not have the same obligations about informing the citizenry of the effects of State initiatives in terms of encroachment on the environment as Article 112 does. It is submitted that the SEA Directive read in the light of the procedural rights protected under the Aarhus Convention[68] would allow citizens this entitlement independent of specific constitutional provisions on the right to environmental information. Further, any constitutional right to a healthy environment without specific wording on a right to information about effects on the environment would also entail a similar obligation read in the light of the Aarhus Convention. The interpretation on including extraterritorial combustion emissions within the scope of the SEA Directive by combining provisions on 'climatic factors' and 'secondary, cumulative, and long-term effects' is not contingent on specific provisions in

[68] The United Nations Economic Commission for Europe (UNECE) Convention on Access to Information, Public Participation in Decision-making and Access to Justice in Environmental Matters, 1998. This has been implemented in the EU through two Directives and changes to existing legislation. See https://ec.europa.eu/environment/aarhus/legislation.htm.

Norwegian law. This is indeed a novel and contentious interpretation as the spatial scope of the SEA Directive appears to be restricted to the territory of the State which formulates the plan or programme that triggers the need for an impact assessment.[69] The exception seems to be Article 7, where States can engage in transboundary consultations on impact assessments where there are extraterritorial effects.[70] Having said that, this interpretation is not incompatible with the principle of curtailing harm to citizens – extraterritorial emissions are a concern because they exacerbate climate change, which can in turn damage the Norwegian environment and the health of its citizens. This possibility was acknowledged by the Borgarting Court of Appeals.[71] The difference between the majority decision by the Supreme Court and the minority opinion is that while the majority focused on the *direct* harm that fossil fuel decisions pose to citizens, the minority focused on *indirect* harm due to the secondary, cumulative and long-term effects of decisions on fossil fuels. This interpretation has radical potential in a sectoral approach to account for transnational emissions, given that any sectoral policy would be preceded by a plan that would fall within the scope of the SEA Directive. In *People v. Arctic Oil*, the relief sought was the quashing of licences already issued, and the minority opinion saw this as a possibility because an improper impact assessment pointed to an infringement of Article 112. In other jurisdictions and future cases not tied to this particular relief, the relationship between SEAs and climate effects articulated in this case may play a greater role at an earlier stage when policy options are being considered.

5. PRINCIPLE OF NON-REGRESSION AND PROGRESSIVE DECARBONISATION

It was noted earlier that the Licensing Decision entailed a spike in the number of licences issued for oil exploration in the Barents Sea. It was suggested that this could have been due to fears of oil in the Arctic becoming a 'stranded asset', or it could have been due to these blocks being open to exploration after a bilateral resolution with Russia. There has also been speculation that Norway issued more licences than usual given fears about Russia's stance towards the

---

69 Such restrictions are evident in empirical work on SEAs, such as difficulties in including multi-sectoral cumulative effects, see C. Fidler and B. Noble, 'Advancing strategic environmental assessment in the offshore oil and gas sector: Lessons from Norway, Canada, and the United Kingdom' (2012) 34 *Environmental Impact Assessment Review* 12, 19.

70 Kramer finds this provision anachronistic as affected countries should have 'the direct right to give an opinion or voice objections to a draft plan.' He argues that '[i]t is wrong to pass via the neighboring government for such a consultation. After all, the environment has no frontiers.' L. Kramer, 'An Important Planning Instrument: Strategic Environmental Assessment (EU Directive 2001/42)' (2019) *Hungarian Yearbook of International and European Law* 13, 27.

71 See discussion in section 3 on the decision by the Court of Appeals.

Arctic after the annexation of Crimea.[72] Irrespective of the reason, the spike in licences issued is uncharacteristic of Norway's energy policy, and it stands to reason that the issuance of more licences can only mean more carbon dioxide emissions attributed to the Licensing Decision. At the very least, there can be no doubt that an increase in licences is not going to result in a decrease in emissions. The decision appears to be at odds with Norway's own 'oil constitutionalism' or a historical commitment to the slow, gradual exploitation of oil with a transition to renewables and maintenance of high environmental standards. Even with respect to the current political climate in the wake of Russia's invasion of Ukraine, there is opposition by political parties and among the public to a production increase in natural gas to replace dependence on Russian gas.[73] This resistance is in keeping with Norway's approach to energy over the 20th century. The 'go slow' policy was so imbedded in the Norwegian policy culture related to oil that when the government announced the increase of oil activities to deal with the oil crisis in 1977,[74] criticism emerged on environmental and safety grounds.[75] However, the increase was necessary to mitigate the effects of the international recession on the Norwegian economy, and to maintain the real increase of wages and the general living standards.[76] 1981 witnessed a situation similar to the current scenario; the US sought to encourage a reduction of European dependence on Soviet oil, and turned to Norway.[77] Norway was urged by the US to start production as soon as possible but the 'go slow' policy and the principle of sustainability imposed a much slower development pace than the US expected, including imposition of a depletion cap – Norway followed its national interests regardless of the international pressure it was subjected to. It appears, therefore, that there is resistance against short-termism in Norway's policy culture. But how can it be

---

72 A. Østhagen, 'Norway's Arctic Policy: Still high North, low tension?' (2021) 11 *The Polar Journal* 75, 82; J. Wilhelmsen and K. Gjerde, 'Norway and Russia in the Arctic: New Cold War Contamination?' (2018) 9 *Arctic Review on Law and Politics* 382. This concern may be more than speculation given Russia's statements to this effect: 'In a competition for resources, it cannot be ruled out that military force could be used to resolve emerging problems that would destroy the balance of forces near the borders of Russia and her allies.' Communication from the Kremlin, cited and discussed in Y. Morozov, 'Arctic 2030: What are the consequences of climate change?: The Russian response' (2012) 68 *Bulletin of the Atomic Scientists* 22.

73 C. Duxbury, 'Norway's political tussle over new gas supplies', *Politico*, 12 June 2022, https://www.politico.eu/article/norway-political-tussle-new-gas-supplies/.

74 O. Noreng, *The Oil Industry and Government Strategy in the North Sea* (International Research Center for Energy and Development, 1980), p. 56.

75 Ibid., p. 57.

76 Ibid.

77 CIA, *The Soviet Gas Pipeline in Perspective*, RF-22-7 (1982), https://www.cia.gov/readingroom/docs/DOC_0000273322.pdf; and CIA, *Analysis of Ability of U.S./CoCom Oil/Gas Controls to Impede Soviet Oil/Gas Production*, 22 October 1981, https://www.cia.gov/readingroom/docs/CIA-RDP83M00914R002000090018-6.pdf.

ensured that domestic or international political interests do not detract from decarbonisation? It is submitted that if a policy decision triggers a chain of events that leads to an unjustified increase in emissions, then that decision could be said to violate the requirement of progressive decarbonisation found in the Paris Agreement, and the principle of non-regression.

The Supreme Court found that Norway was compliant with the Paris Agreement.[78] One of the principles of the Paris Agreement is progressive achievement of decarbonisation.[79] Such progressive achievement appears to be collective,[80] as well as individual.[81] The individual aim is tethered to nationally determined contributions,[82] and Norway could be said to satisfy such progressive decarbonisation as it has increased its targets. The Climate Change Act 2017 requires the government to present updated climate targets to the parliament every five years based on the best available scientific knowledge,[83] and requires that these represent a progression from the preceding targets in the lead-up to 2050.[84] The collective element would be in question if Norwegian policies were to lead to an increase in emissions, irrespective of where such increase takes place. Here, it would be prudent to bring in the geopolitical context that the Court alluded to (but refrained from pronouncing on) when it observed that 'overarching concerns' such as competition between States affect fossil fuel supplies. As observed earlier, given Russia's current invasion of Ukraine, there is intent at the EU and Member State level to move away from dependence on Russian energy. If this shift entails a greater dependence on Norwegian oil and gas, then it could be argued that at a collective level there would still be a reduction of emissions internationally, given that policy decisions on the production of Russian oil and gas do not have strong legal procedures to account for climate impacts,[85] nor is there transparency on what happens to the

---

78 Norwegian Supreme Court, above n. 1, para. 59.

79 One of the recitals of the Agreement reads: 'Recognizing the need for an effective and progressive response to the urgent threat of climate change on the basis of the best available scientific knowledge.'

80 Article 3 provides: 'The efforts of all Parties will represent a progression over time, while recognizing the need to support developing country Parties for the effective implementation of this Agreement.'

81 Article 4(3) provides: 'Each Party's successive nationally determined contribution will represent a progression beyond the Party's then current nationally determined contribution and reflect its highest possible ambition, reflecting its common but differentiated responsibilities and respective capabilities, in the light of different national circumstances.'

82 Ibid.

83 Climate Change Act § 5.

84 Ibid.

85 There are some areas of Russian environmental regulation that are stricter than Norway. However, there are general issues of weak authorities and compliance. A. Moe, 'Russian and Norwegian Petroleum Strategies in the Barents Sea' (2010) 1 *Arctic Review* 225, 238. On the specific issue of accounting for climate impacts due to oil exploration and exploitation, there is no strategic environmental impact assessment system in Russia. B. Noble and K. Hanna,

proceeds. As discussed earlier in the chapter, some of the proceeds from the sale of Norwegian oil are invested in renewable energy, and there are ethical criteria for divesting from companies not engaged in climate action.

Having said the above, the international climate regime is premised on nationally determined contributions and the production-based territoriality principle discussed earlier in the chapter. This framework does not provide doctrinal guidance on how to inform energy policy. For this, the potential of the principle of non-regression is explored. The principle of non-regression was initially developed in international human rights law and constitutional jurisprudence,[86] and has gradually drifted into environmental law,[87] not least because of the increasingly deeper connection between human rights and environmental law. The International Union for the Conservation of Nature (IUCN), notably, had set up a working group under its Environmental Law Commission to investigate the principle,[88] and adopted a resolution on non-regression.[89] The crux of the principle is that there should not be backsliding on the level of protection afforded by law, unless there is a proper and proportionate justification for doing so.[90] Regression can take several forms, such as withdrawing from treaties, or relaxing procedures in place, or diluting standards.[91] As to whether an increase in fossil fuel use without explicit change in environmental law would violate such a principle is a moot point, primarily because regression is assessed in relation to law rather than actual environmental degradation.[92] Bryner notes that the Costa Rican Supreme Court rooted the principle of non-regression in 'preventing harm to the environment, as opposed to simply preventing changes in the law'[93] in a case challenging an amendment to the Forest Act that reduced its protected area.[94] Within the European legal space, if a State signatory to the Aarhus Convention makes changes to its

'Environmental Assessment in the Arctic: A Gap Analysis and Research Agenda' (2015) 68 *Arctic* 341, 343.

86 For a critical treatment of the nuances of the principle within constitutional discourse, see J. Jeffries and D. Levinson, 'The Non-Retrogression Principle in Constitutional Law' (1998) 86 *California Law Review* 1211.

87 M. Vordermayer-Riemer, *Non-Regression in International Environmental Law* (Intersentia 2020); L. Collins, 'Principle of Non-regression' in J. Morin and A. Orsini (eds), *Essential Concepts of Global Environmental Governance* (2nd ed., Routledge 2020).

88 For an overview, see M. Prieur, 'Non-regression in Environmental Law' (2012) 5 *Surveys and Perspectives Integrating Environment and Society*, https://journals.openedition.org/sapiens/1405.

89 IUCN World Conservation Congress Resolution on the 'Need for non-regression in environmental law and policy', WCC-2012-Res-128-EN.

90 N.S. Bryner, 'Never Look Back: Non-regression in environmental law' (2022) 43 *University of Pennsylvania Journal of International Law* 555.

91 M. Prieur, above n. 88.

92 For the distinction between regression and degradation, see N.S. Bryner, above n. 90, n. 12 and corresponding text.

93 Ibid., pp. 18–19.

94 Sala Constitucional, Voto No. 7294-98 de las 16:15 horas del 13 de octubre de 1998, cited in N.S. Bryner, above n. 90, p. 18.

energy policy that would likely result in greater environmental degradation, such a policy would invariably constitute environmental information,[95] and would in turn trigger environmental principles. To clarify, the principle of non-regression would not automatically result in a cessation of activities due to energy policy. Rather, it would instil a 'culture of justification'[96] with respect to energy policy. This principle would require a justification when there is either a legislative or administrative decision to dilute environmental standards, or a decision that would result in a lowering of environmental standards. For administrative decisions, the principle is easier to apply, as a decision that lowers environmental standards is akin to creating a new policy.[97] For legislative decisions, the principle has less force, as it is within the remit of legislative power to change the course of policy.[98] There would, however, be need for legislative authorities to justify environmental backsliding if the requirement to do so flows from international law or a constitutional mandate. In both explicit endorsement in international legal instruments and implicit development in the understanding of the precautionary principle and sustainable development, the doctrinal form the principle takes is that there is a strong presumption against retrogression.[99] Within the ambit of Article 112, taking a cue from the minority opinion, a weak version of non-regression would be that the citizenry would need to be apprised of what 'overarching concerns' would lead to a departure from a 'go slow' approach to the issuance of licences. A stronger version would be that such a departure would not be permitted unless the court is satisfied with the evidence that a departure would not interfere with a right to a healthy environment. At the cost of being speculative, an evidentiary requirement on non-degradation can be met if Norway can demonstrate that a possible increase in emissions would be offset domestically through other means,[100] or internationally if there is less dependence on sources that have higher emissions. If such evidence cannot be furnished, then the government would need to demonstrate that there would be grave consequences (such as energy poverty) were it not for a policy decision to step up oil exploration.[101] In both

---

95 For a recent treatment, see S. Whittaker, *The Right of Access to Environmental Information* (Cambridge University Press 2021).

96 On the role of proportionality in fostering a shift from a culture of authority to a culture of justification, see M. Cohen-Eliya and I. Porat, 'Proportionality and the Culture of Justification' (2011) 59 *American Journal of Comparative Law* 463.

97 N.S. Bryner, above n. 90, pp. 25–30.

98 For the argument that the American Supreme Court uses non-regression as a way to create policy, see J. Jeffries and D. Levinson, above n. 86; N.S. Bryner, above n. 90, pp. 30–32.

99 See L. Collins and D. Boyd, 'Non-regression and the Charter Right to a Healthy Environment' (2016) 29 *Journal of Environmental Law and Practice* 285, 294–98.

100 For the potential of new mitigation practices, see E. Hermansen and G. Sundqvist, 'Top-down or bottom-up? Norwegian climate mitigation policy as a contested hybrid of policy approaches' (2022) 171 *Climatic Change* 1.

101 With respect to policy considerations outside rights, there is evidence to suggest that a transition away from oil exploration will have a positive effect on Norway's sovereign wealth

cases, the principle of non-regression would play an information-forcing role. As the reader will suspect, the authors' intuition is that the principle of non-regression can be a check on short-termism through the need for justification – something to look out for in other jurisdictions where there are instances of decarbonisation backsliding.

6. CONCLUSION

Climate change jurisprudence is susceptible to transnational borrowing – it develops incrementally,[102] and diagonally,[103] and the decisions of lower courts, and even overturned judgments, influence court rulings in other jurisdictions.[104] From *People v. Arctic Oil*, one message that one can take away is that courts have a limited role to play in subjecting energy policy to climate considerations, and especially so with respect to specific policy decisions. However, this message is contingent on context – the path-dependence of the Norwegian welfare state on oil, and even the jurisprudential context of interpreting constitutional provisions in the light of parliamentary history. Given this context, it appears that what might be of equivalent value is the gradual development of jurisprudence – the recognition of the right to a healthy environment as entailing corresponding duties of the State to prevent climate harm, the possibility of extraterritorial emissions causing harm and thereby infringing the right to environment as articulated by the Borgarting Court of Appeals, and the radical potential of rights-based strategic environmental assessments in requiring information on extraterritorial emissions brought about by energy policy to be provided to the citizenry. Environmental law in the time of climate change also plays a crucial role in informing energy policy. In this chapter, the information-forcing role of the principle of non-regression when decisions on energy could result in decarbonisation backsliding has been highlighted.

---

fund in the medium to long term. P. Stoknes, I. Aslaksen, U. Goluke, J. Randers and P.A. Garnåsjordet, 'Plausible Futures for the Norwegian Offshore Energy Sector: Business as Usual, Harvest or Rebuild?', Discussion Paper 958, Statistics Department Norway (2021), https://ssb.brage.unit.no/ssb-xmlui/bitstream/handle/11250/2787745/DP958_web.pdf?sequence=1.

102 P. Minnerop and I. Røstgaard, above n. 6, p. 890.

103 H. Osofsky, 'Is Climate Change International – Litigation's Diagonal Regulatory Role' (2008) 49 *Virginia Journal of International Law* 585.

104 Though overturned by the Supreme Court, the Court of Appeals for the Second Circuit judgment in *Connecticut v. American Electric Power* informed the arguments in the *Urgenda* case. S. Roy and E. Woerdman, 'Situating *Urgenda v. the* Netherlands in Comparative Climate Litigation' (2016) 34 *Journal of Energy and Natural Resources Law* 165, 178.

CLIMATE CHANGE AND MIGRATION

A Socio-Legal Approach to Understanding Europe's Responsibilities Toward Climate Migrants

Jillian SPRENGER

1. INTRODUCTION

The issue of climate migration (forced displacement due to climatic events) has long been discussed in academic circles. It became a salient policy issue as early as the 1990s with the publication of the first United Nations Intergovernmental Panel on Climate Change (IPCC) Assessment Report.[1] The report stated that 'the gravest effects of climate change may be those on human migration as millions will be displaced'.[2] Now, as the climate becomes increasingly volatile and climate

1 E. PIGUET, A. PÉCOUD and P. DE GUCHTENEIRE, 'Migration and Climate Change: An Overview' (2011) *Refugee Survey Quarterly* 30(3): 1–23.

2 IPCC, *Climate Change: The IPCC Impacts Assessment*, 1990, p. 20, http://www.ipcc.ch/ipccreports/far/wg_II/ipcc_far_wg_II_full_report.pdf.

change is an even more pressing issue on global policy agendas, the issue of climate migration is rapidly drawing international attention.

There are three categories of climatic events that drive climate migration. The first includes rapid-onset events such as tropical cyclones, severe storms and floods. These events tend to lead to shorter-term displacements, typically within national or regional borders.[3] They overwhelmingly affect vulnerable individuals in lower-income countries, many of whom lack the financial resources to permanently relocate.[4] Many of these individuals return to the site of the event shortly after it occurs, even rebuilding their homes in the disaster zone.[5] The second category of displacement-inducing climatic event is drought and desertification, which can cause shortages of both drinking water and water for irrigation. These phenomena occur over a longer period of time.[6] Their progressive nature tends to also lead to progressive mobility patterns: over time, more and more people from affected regions relocate permanently as their environment becomes increasingly inhospitable.[7] Finally, the third major category of climatic event driving migration is sea level rise. It has been shown that due to the irreversible and progressive nature of this phenomenon, coastal communities globally are finding themselves with no choice but to move to regions less at risk.[8] The threat of disappearance of island nations is a particularly well-documented instance of this.

The climatic events described above are known to be significant drivers of migration. Importantly, there are also many other drivers which are often deeply intertwined with climatic events. For example, food insecurity, political instability, violent conflict and health challenges can each be compounded by climate change and may also contribute to an individual's decision to migrate.[9] Thus, in many cases, identifying the primary driver of migration can be difficult, if not impossible: migration is the result of a complex interplay of factors which together render life in a given place extremely challenging.

Most climate migrants are internally displaced within their countries of origin.[10] However, as the climate crisis continues to wreak havoc on global ecosystems, a subset of individuals will also be forced to relocate internationally,

---

3 E. Piguet, A. Pécoud and P. de Guchteneire, above n. 1.
4 Ibid.
5 Ibid.
6 L. Nishimura, '"Climate Change Migrants": Impediments to a Protection Framework and the Need to Incorporate Migration into Climate Change Adaptation Strategies' (2015) *International Journal of Refugee Law* 27(1): 107–34.
7 E. Piguet, A. Pécoud and P. de Guchteneire, above n. 1; L. Nishimura, above n. 6.
8 E. Piguet, A. Pécoud and P. de Guchteneire, above n. 1.
9 B. Mayer, 'The International Legal Challenges of Climate-Induced Migration: Proposal for an International Legal Framework' (2011) *Colorado Journal of International Environmental Law and Policy* 22(3): 360–415.
10 E. Piguet, A. Pécoud and P. de Guchteneire, above n. 1; B. Mayer, above n. 9.

particularly to regions perceived as less climatically volatile, including Europe. Currently, the legal protection afforded to international or cross-border migrants only applies to those who qualify under the definition of a 'refugee'.[11] This raises the urgent question of whether those who are forced to move due to climate change can be protected under the mandates of international refugee agreements, or alternatively whether they should be afforded any other forms of legal protection. This is a controversial issue: there is significant debate over the nuances of the definition of 'refugee', whether the definition includes those displaced by climate change, and whether States have a legal or moral duty to protect these individuals. This is also a politically contentious issue, as each State's position on this, and their interpretation of international legal agreements, is driven by political considerations.

2. THE CONCEPT OF 'CLIMATE REFUGEE'

The 1951 Refugee Convention and the 1967 Protocol Relating to the Status of Refugees define a 'refugee' as an individual who is unable or unwilling to return to their country of origin due to a well-founded fear of persecution, for reasons including race, religion, nationality, membership in a social group or political opinion.[12] Claims to refugee status must be considered on an individual basis to determine whether sending a person back to their country of origin would cause them to experience persecution. Particular attention is paid to whether the person would likely be subject to deprivation of life, torture, or cruel, inhuman or degrading treatment upon their return. States Parties to the Convention and Protocol are obliged to allow refugees who have arrived in their territory to stay. This is the principle of non-refoulement: refugees must not be forced to return to their country of origin. No reservations or exceptions may be permitted.[13]

There are several problems when considering refugee law in the context of climate migration. The formal definition of a refugee, in addition to a large body of case law, clearly identifies a requirement for the threat or harm to be persecutory. As described above, the individual must experience the threat

[11] B. Felipe Pérez, 'Beyond The Shortcomings of International Law: A Proposal for the Legal Protection of Climate Migrants' in S. Behrman and A. Kent (eds), *Climate Refugees: Beyond the Legal Impasse?*, Routledge 2018, pp. 214–29; I.I. Berchin, I.B. Valduga, J. Garcia and J.B.S.O. de Andrade Guerra, 'Climate Change and Forced Migrations: An Effort towards Recognizing Climate Refugees' (2017) *Geoforum* 84: 147–50.

[12] United Nations High Commissioner for Refugees, 'Convention and Protocol Relating to the Status of Refugees' (2010), https://www.unhcr.org/uk/3b66c2aa10; E. Piguet, A. Pécoud and P. de Guchteneire, above n. 1; B. Felipe Pérez, above n. 11.

[13] United Nations High Commissioner for Refugees, above n. 12.

(or persecution) because of their race, religion, nationality, membership in a social group or political opinion.[14] Climate migrants do not meet any of these criteria and, as such, do not qualify for protection under this legal framework. In certain court cases, lawyers have attempted to argue that climate migrants are persecuted by developed countries, in that these countries have historically contributed to climate change (and continue to do so) in ways that severely and disproportionately affect individuals in low-income countries.[15] However, these arguments have not been successful as they have been unable to demonstrate a direct intent to discriminate or persecute.[16] Furthermore, the level of severity of an event must be such that it could be considered 'persecution'.[17] This has been addressed in a number of cases where it was found that the climatic impacts in the countries of origin were not severe enough that the claimant could be said to be persecuted if they were to be returned.[18] These decisions have focused on the potentially delayed onset of climatic events, as well as uncertainty over the likelihood that climatic events will actually occur. Finally, the difficulty in establishing a direct causal link between greenhouse gas emissions, extreme weather and harm befalling individuals in poor countries has been another major challenge in efforts to protect climate migrants under refugee law.[19]

From the above, it is evident that climate migrants do not readily fall under the scope of the 1951 Refugee Convention and the 1967 Protocol. As a result, alternatives must be considered in order to provide legal protection to these individuals. One option would be to update the law so as to create an entirely new legal category of 'climate refugees'. Unfortunately, this idea is unlikely to gain traction. There is a general lack of willingness on the part of developed countries to engage with it because of its ensuing legal obligations to assist a new group of migrants.[20] In many cases, there is a political element to this position:

---

14 B. Felipe Pérez, above n. 11; J.B. Cooper, 'Environmental Refugees: Meeting the Requirements of the Refugee Definition' (1998) *New York University Environmental Law Journal* 6: 480–529; L. Nishimura, above n. 6.

15 B. Felipe Pérez, above n. 11; M. Scott, 'Refuge from Climate Change-Related Harm: Evaluating the Scope of International Protection within the Common European Asylum System' in C. Bauloz, M. Ineli-Ciger, S. Singer and V. Stoyanova (eds), *Seeking Asylum in the European Union: Selected Protection Issues Raised by the Second Phase of the Common European Asylum System*, Brill 2015, pp. 195–221.

16 J. McAdam, 'Climate Change Displacement and International Law: Complementary Protection Standards', United Nations High Commissioner for Refugees 2011, p. 16, https://www.unhcr.org/4dff16e99.pdf; M. Scott, above n. 15.

17 J. McAdam, above n. 16, p. 12.

18 UN Human Rights Committee, 'Views Adopted by the Committee under Article 5 (4) of the Optional Protocol, Concerning Communication No. 2728/2016', 2020, https://climatecasechart.com/non-us-case/un-human-rights-committee-views-adopted-on-teitiota-communication/; M. Scott, above n. 15.

19 B. Mayer, above n. 9; L. Nishimura, above n. 6.

20 L. Nishimura, above n. 6.

many States' populations and political bodies have strong anti-immigration sentiment.[21] The political climate in these States is such that they have a vested interest in maintaining the status quo and refusing responsibility for these individuals. This makes the advancement of new refugee protections extremely difficult. Furthermore, as the international refugee regime is voluntary in the sense that States must agree to sign on to the Refugee Convention before they can be legally bound to its obligations,[22] there is no possibility of requiring unwilling States to take part. Any similar system for 'climate refugees' would likely have the same voluntary nature. Even if these political challenges were to be overcome, creating a climate refugee category would involve many technical challenges. For example, it would be difficult to operationally define 'climate refugee', and in practice to identify climate change as the driver of one's migration (except in very few specific cases, such as where sea level rise has destroyed one's home). Clearly defining the level of causation required between climatic events and displacement, as well as the type of evidence needed to support such claims, would also be very challenging.[23]

Despite the political challenges described above, the expected increase in climate migration in the coming years means that more cases addressing these issues will likely come through international and domestic courts.[24] This may provide a different means of developing new protections for climate migrants. Lawyers will need to advance new and creative arguments to help establish a clear link between climate change and forced migration. Committed efforts in this regard may help to establish a new body of case law, which could then establish the need to offer legal protections to climate migrants. It is worth considering, however, the ethical implications of courts being at the forefront of the development of this area of law, particularly as only certain individuals have access to the resources needed to bring a case to court. The law may also develop differently in various jurisdictions, thus presenting an additional challenge of a piecemeal approach to dealing with climate migrants.

The problems inherent in the previous approaches necessitate the consideration of an additional avenue to offer protection to climate migrants. Considering climate migration in the context of human rights law may be an effective way of doing so. All countries signatory to international human rights agreements

---

21 H. Locke, 'Use of Force in Crisis: A Comparative Look at the Domestic and International Laws Governing the Use of U.S. Military Force to Respond to Mass Climate Refugee Migration' (2019) *Hastings Environmental Law Journal* 26: 27–46.

22 L. Nishimura, above n. 6.

23 H. Locke, above n. 21.

24 J. Setzer and R. Byrnes, 'Global Trends in Climate Change Litigation: 2020 Snapshot', Grantham Research Institute on Climate Change and the Environment 2020, https://www.lse.ac.uk/granthaminstitute/wp-content/uploads/2020/07/Global-trends-in-climate-change-litigation_2020-snapshot.pdf.

are obligated to protect those at risk,[25] and since many climate migrants do experience severe violations of their human rights, countries may have a duty to protect these individuals. Importantly, the international human rights principle of non-refoulement states that individuals cannot be sent back to countries where they would face these human rights violations, regardless of their status as refugees or otherwise.[26]

In the European context, there are several articles of the European Convention on Human Rights (ECHR) that should be considered. In particular, Article 2 (right to life) and Article 8 (right to respect for private and family life), are highly relevant in connection with climate migration. These articles are typically invoked in human rights-based environmental cases heard in European courts, including the European Court of Human Rights (ECtHR):[27] the links between these articles and environmental issues have thus been previously examined. Also important is Article 3 ECHR, which states that 'no one shall be subjected to torture or to inhuman or degrading treatment or punishment'.[28] European courts have significant flexibility to determine what constitutes inhuman or degrading treatment under this article: the nature and context of the treatment, as well as its effects (both physical and mental) can be taken into account.[29] In the climate migration context, severe climate-related events and disasters certainly lead to inhuman treatment involving 'actual bodily harm or intense physical and mental suffering'.[30] Evidence that climate migration leads to violations of Article 3 ECHR could provide an additional way for lawyers to advocate for the protection of climate migrants, particularly as the ECtHR has already demonstrated an openness to considering Article 3 ECHR in climate-related contexts.[31]

With sufficient evidence showing that climate migrants indeed experience human rights violations, there is reason to believe that international and regional human rights law frameworks could be an avenue through which to offer protection to these individuals. States are obligated to protect those experiencing these violations, regardless of their refugee status (or lack thereof).

---

25 Office of the High Commissioner of Human Rights, 'The Principle of Non-Refoulement under International Human Rights Law' (n.d.), https://www.ohchr.org/Documents/Issues/Migration/GlobalCompactMigration/ThePrincipleNon-RefoulementUnderInternationalHumanRightsLaw.pdf.

26 Ibid.

27 P. Siwior, 'The Potential of Application of the ECHR in Climate Change Related Cases' (2021) *International Community Law Review* 23(2): 197–208.

28 European Court of Human Rights, 'European Convention on Human Rights', 1953, https://www.echr.coe.int/documents/convention_eng.pdf.

29 *A. v. United Kingdom*, no. 25599/94, European Court of Human Rights 1998.

30 Council of Europe, 'Prohibition of Torture and Inhuman and Degrading Treatment (Article 3)', 2014, http://echr-toolkit.coe.int.

31 C. Heri, 'The ECtHR's Pending Climate Change Case: What's Ill-Treatment Got to Do with It?', *EJIL:Talk!*, 2020, https://www.ejiltalk.org/the-ecthrs-pending-climate-change-case-whats-ill-treatment-got-to-do-with-it/.

Relying on this domain of law may also be more politically palatable: framing climate migration as a human rights issue rather than a refugee issue may help to change societal norms,[32] and may garner more public support. Human rights law frameworks may thus be an effective way of protecting those vulnerable to climate-induced displacement.

3. CASE STUDY OF CLIMATE MIGRATION IN SRI LANKA: EVIDENCE OF HUMAN RIGHTS VIOLATIONS

The following anthropological case study of climate migration in Sri Lanka, conducted by the author in 2018, allows for a more nuanced perspective on the challenges facing climate migrants. It also provides clear evidence that climate migration can lead to violations of human rights, including those set out in the ECHR. While the ECHR is a regional framework and thus does not directly apply to Sri Lankan citizens, the human rights violations they experience may still be relevant in the context of the principle of non-refoulement. Furthermore, the human rights issues observed in this case study indicate that similar harms may affect climate migrants in other contexts. This implies that Europe may have a duty to protect these individuals, and it supports the contention that human rights law may provide a new avenue through which to offer protection to climate migrants.

3.1. A SUMMARY OF CLIMATE MIGRATION IN SRI LANKA

Sri Lanka, a small South Asian country, faces particularly adverse climatic events. It is prone to all three types of climatic disruption previously described: it experiences severe drought in its Dry Zone and frequent flooding in hilly regions (both of which have been worsening in recent years), and as an island nation it is exposed to rising sea levels which threaten coastal towns and industries.[33] As a result of these climatic threats, human mobility patterns are changing, and the number of climate migrants is rapidly increasing. Many migrate due to sudden events such as floods or landslides, and others migrate due to longer-term loss of livelihoods linked to climate change (mainly failed agricultural harvests due to drought).[34] The majority migrate domestically (typically to cities such as Colombo).[35] Most Sri Lankan climate migrants

---

32 H. Locke, above n. 21.

33 SLYCAN Trust, 'Climate Change and Human Mobility in Sri Lanka: Policies, Laws, and Processes', August 2020.

34 Ibid.

35 Ibid.

face intractable challenges in their day-to-day lives. Their living situation is precarious, with most relying on day-labour jobs or other forms of informal employment and living in extremely poor conditions.

3.2. DEMOGRAPHIC AND TEMPORAL PATTERNS OF CLIMATE MIGRATION

Most Sri Lankan climate migrants are men. Many have families to support and send remittances home to help make ends meet. Their migration tends to be temporary: individuals displaced by one-time climate disasters usually attempt to rebuild and move back to their homes if possible, whereas those who migrate due to loss of agricultural livelihood tend to do so seasonally, returning to their farms during the harvest season. The work taken up by climate migrants is usually day labour, construction or driving. Nearly all face significant challenges in urban areas. This point is particularly salient in the context of human rights: in interviews, several individuals described a lack of safe housing, appropriate toilet facilities and affordable food. Many are homeless upon arrival at their destination and have to resort to begging for leftover food from restaurants in order to survive. Additionally, their precarious living situation means that many climate migrants are at high risk of illness and disease. The physical and mental suffering described by the climate migrants amounts to 'actual bodily harm or intense physical and mental suffering'[36] as described under Article 3 ECHR.

3.3. CLIMATE MIGRATION AND MENTAL HEALTH

Mental health issues are a significant (and often neglected) effect of climate migration. These issues affect both climate migrants themselves and their families. Too often, the focus is simply on the physical challenges that migration brings, but depression and other mental health concerns can be just as problematic. According to several interviewees, the stress of poverty and vulnerability is just one factor contributing to these mental health struggles. Another major cause is the family separation that tends to occur with climate migration. Several women spoke of the depression they experienced as a result of being separated from their husbands, and one child described a feeling of loss and of extreme difficulty concentrating in school during his father's absences. The issue of forced family separation may be in contravention of Article 8 ECHR, and the mental health issues resulting from this and from extreme vulnerability may be deemed 'intense mental suffering'[37] as described under Article 3 ECHR.

---

[36] Council of Europe, above n. 30.

[37] Ibid.

3.4. CLIMATE MIGRATION AND GENDER

The issue of climate migration can also be explored through a gendered lens. Several interviewees described the challenges specific to women, particularly in the context of the women who are left behind when men migrate. Forced to take on additional labour as well as the responsibilities of heading the household, women are often left in a state of vulnerability to harassment or violence from other men in the community. Again, this arguably demonstrates a violation of human rights: the threats to women's lives, as well as the physical and mental suffering they experience, are in contravention of Articles 2 and 3 ECHR. Furthermore, it could also be argued that these challenges experienced by women (specifically because they are women) amount to discrimination on the basis of gender.

3.5. THE POOREST ARE THE MOST VULNERABLE

The poorest individuals contribute the least to the carbon emissions that drive climate change, and yet are the most vulnerable to its effects. This is true globally; however, many interviewees emphasised the relevance of this point in Sri Lanka. The country has a rapidly growing economy, and at the time of interviews national data showed that it was on track to become upper-middle income within the next few years.[38] However, the national aggregate data obscured the reality of a widening wealth gap, as well as the fact that the majority of the population of 22 million lives just above the national poverty line.[39] Over 80% of the population lives in rural areas.[40] These individuals in particular remain in a state of extreme vulnerability, and they lack resilience to climatic shocks. Recognising this is very important: the scale of the problem is vast and is likely underestimated. As the poorest and most vulnerable individuals are forced to move due to climate change, the human rights issues described above will become reality for a growing proportion of the population in Sri Lanka and elsewhere.

4. CLIMATE MIGRATION, HUMAN RIGHTS AND LITIGATION

The Sri Lanka case study provides strong evidence that climate migration indeed leads to human rights violations. This in turn implies a responsibility on the

---

38 Asian Development Bank, 'Sri Lanka: Country Partnership Strategy (2018–2022)', 2018, https://think-asia.org/bitstream/handle/11540/8848/cps-sri-2018-2022.pdf?sequence=1.

39 Ibid.

40 World Bank, 'World Development Indicators Sri Lanka', 2021, https://databank.worldbank.org/reports.aspx?source=world-development-indicators.

part of receiving States to protect climate migrants under human rights law. The assertion that human rights law represents an avenue through which to offer protection to these individuals is further supported by a recent case heard by the UN Human Rights Committee, *Teitiota v. New Zealand*. The views adopted by the Committee emphasise the importance of upholding and protecting human rights in climate migration cases. This case may have ramifications for the treatment of climate migrants in the coming years and, as such, is worthy of discussion.

In 2013, Ioane Teitiota, a citizen of the island nation of Kiribati, applied for refugee status in New Zealand on the grounds that sea level rise driven by climate change was rendering Kiribati uninhabitable and had forced him to flee.[41] Each level of the court in New Zealand denied the claimant's request due to his inability to demonstrate the fact that he was being persecuted.[42] Following the loss of his appeal at the New Zealand Supreme Court in 2015, Mr Teitiota filed a Communication before the UN Human Rights Committee.[43]

The Committee declined to reverse the New Zealand Court's decision, as it did not find a violation of international human rights law: Mr Teitiota had failed to provide sufficient evidence that he would immediately face life-threatening conditions upon return to Kiribati.[44] In spite of the Committee's final decision, its views are extremely important because of their implications for future litigation related to climate migration. The decision, rather than focusing on the definition of a 'refugee' and whether Mr Teitiota should be entitled to this status, emphasised that States must not expel an individual when there are substantial grounds for believing that the person is at risk of harm.[45] The Committee referred to Article 6 (right to life) and Article 7 (prohibition of torture and cruel, inhuman or degrading treatment or punishment) of the International Covenant on Civil and Political Rights (ICCPR)[46] in its decision.[47] Most importantly, the Committee stated that the obligation not to expel individuals pursuant to Article 6 ICCPR 'may be broader than the scope of the principle of non-refoulement under international refugee law'.[48] This is to say that this protection should be given to individuals whose human rights (and particularly the right to life) are being violated, even if they are not entitled to formal refugee status. This is extremely important: the Committee emphasised the importance of identifying the human rights violations

---

41 UN Human Rights Committee 2020, above n. 18; J. Setzer and R. Byrnes, above n. 24, p. 17.

42 M. Scott, above n. 15.

43 J. Setzer and R. Byrnes, above n. 24, p. 17.

44 UN Human Rights Committee 2020, above n. 18.

45 Ibid.

46 Office of the United Nations High Commissioner for Human Rights, 'International Covenant on Civil and Political Rights', 1966, https://www.ohchr.org/en/professionalinterest/pages/ccpr.aspx.

47 UN Human Rights Committee 2020, above n. 18.

48 Ibid.

facing climate migrants and the potential to offer protection under international human rights law rather than under refugee law. Though Mr Teitiota did not succeed in demonstrating that his human rights were being violated in this way, the Committee affirmed that climate migrants should indeed be protected against removal to their country of origin if their human rights are at real risk.

The Committee's findings are an important step forward in determining the protection that can be offered to those displaced due to climate change. While the Committee's judgments are not binding on States Parties,[49] they do represent a strong normative force in that their decisions are acknowledged to be the authoritative interpretation of the ICCPR (and thus international human rights law). As such, this decision may set a precedent and may be relied upon in future cases seeking to establish States' responsibilities toward those forced to move due to climate change.

Though this is a largely positive development, some academics and legal practitioners have expressed reservations about opening the 'floodgates'[50] if cases start to be decided in favour of climate migrants. There are two important points in response to this concern. The first is that the scope of this influx will be much smaller than such alarmist comments suggest. The majority of climate migrants are displaced internally within their country of origin.[51] Many migrate seasonally, and most express a lack of desire to leave their homes (a point which is especially evident through the Sri Lanka case study). Furthermore, climatic events have different impacts based on the characteristics of the individuals they affect. Climate change does not always trigger displacement, and it would be incorrect to equate populations at risk with those that will actually migrate.[52] The second important point is that there should be a shift in the normative approach to this issue: there must be a stronger focus on protecting human rights and on the obligations of States to do so. All countries signatory to international human rights agreements are obligated to protect those at risk, and the principle of non-refoulement clearly states that individuals cannot be sent back to countries where they would face these human rights violations.[53] Whether this protection exists in practice is a separate question, but regardless, international norms indicate that countries should uphold these rights. Each person requesting asylum on the grounds of climate migration should be given a fair opportunity to provide evidence of their situation.

---

49 Office of the United Nations High Commissioner for Human Rights, 'Individual Communications: Human Rights Treaty Bodies' (n.d.), https://www.ohchr.org/EN/HRBodies/TBPetitions/Pages/IndividualCommunications.aspx#whathappens.

50 M. Scott, 'LUMIN Final Report: Climate Change Related Displacement and Strategic Litigation', Migration Law Network 2015, p. 6, http://migrationlawnetwork.org/wp-content/uploads/2015/07/scott-short-summary.pdf.

51 L. Nishimura, above n. 6.

52 E. Piguet, A. Pécoud and P. de Guchteneire, above n. 1.

53 Office of the United Nations High Commissioner for Human Rights, above n. 24.

5. THE EUROPEAN COURT OF HUMAN RIGHTS AND THE PRINCIPLE OF NON-REFOULEMENT

In the European context, it is instructive to consider existing jurisprudence on the principle of non-refoulement. This can help to clarify the opportunities and limitations that may exist for a future climate migration case involving this principle. The ECtHR has addressed non-refoulement in many contexts other than that of climate migration: the Strasbourg Court has in fact produced a very large body of case law on the principle over the past several decades.[54] As demonstrated through this corpus of work, the ECtHR has primarily considered non-refoulement in the context of Article 3 ECHR (the prohibition of torture and inhuman or degrading treatment or punishment).[55] The Court is thus very familiar with, and has a noted history of considering the importance of, protecting individuals from being subjected to this sort of treatment, regardless of their status as refugees or otherwise.

The ECHR does not include a formal definition either of torture, or of inhuman or degrading treatment.[56] However, the large and ever-evolving body of non-refoulement-related case law of the ECtHR has enabled the Court to establish several factors that can qualify as this type of treatment. These will be discussed in more detail below, but it is important to first note that the harm or mistreatment must meet a certain level of severity for it to fall within the scope of Article 3 ECHR and trigger the principle of non-refoulement. This level of severity, however, is relative and somewhat subjective, in that the circumstances of the case are of critical importance. Relevant circumstances may include the nature and duration of the harm, its physical and mental traumatic effects, and the applicant's physical characteristics (e.g. age, sex and health status).[57]

The Court employs different tests to establish torture, inhuman treatment and degrading treatment, since each of these is defined differently and thus has unique implications. Torture is considered to be the most severe case covered by Article 3 ECHR, and it must involve sufficient intensity, intent and purpose to be considered as such. There will be no further discussion of torture in this chapter as it is not particularly applicable to the discussion of non-refoulement as may be related to a future climate migration case. Furthermore, most cases in which the Court has found a violation of Article 3 ECHR have not concerned torture, but instead have involved inhuman or degrading treatment.[58] The

54 F. de Weck, 'Introduction' in *Non-Refoulement under the European Convention on Human Rights and the UN Convention Against Torture*, Brill 2016, p. 3.

55 Ibid.

56 F. de Weck, 'The Nature of the Harm Triggering the Application of the Non-Refoulement Principle under the ECHR and the CAT' in *Non-Refoulement under the European Convention on Human Rights and the UN Convention Against Torture*, Brill 2016, p. 138.

57 Ibid., p. 140.

58 Ibid., p. 143.

ECtHR has determined that, for treatment to be considered inhuman (the level of severity below torture), it must involve serious physical and mental suffering.[59] In terms of degrading treatment, the minimum boundary for such harm to fall under the scope of Article 3 ECHR has been difficult to establish and has led to some inconsistencies in the Court's case law, including in the context of non-refoulement.[60]

The Court has issued several decisions that may have implications for future climate migration cases. These decisions may be relevant because of how they identify and address violations of Article 3 ECHR, and because of how this relates to non-refoulement. Firstly, the destruction of homes or property (such as that which may be experienced by climate migrants) may be deemed inhuman treatment within the scope of Article 3 ECHR if it has caused a severe level of suffering. In the judgment in *Bilgin v. Turkey*, the Court considered the fact that the plaintiff's home had been destroyed by State security forces, depriving him of his livelihood and forcing him to leave the region in which he lived. The Court found that this destruction caused the plaintiff suffering of sufficient severity that it was deemed inhuman treatment. As such, this was considered to be a violation of Article 3 ECHR.[61] Since climate migrants may also experience destruction of homes or property, this case may set an important precedent in the future. The Court has also made important and relevant decisions on the implications of deportation on an applicant's health.[62] In *D. v. United Kingdom*, the Court found that deporting an individual to their home country would amount to inhuman treatment and would cause a violation of Article 3 ECHR, since the individual would not be able to access appropriate medical care for their health condition.[63] This may also be applicable to climate migrants, who may also experience limited access to crucial healthcare in their home countries, particularly in the context of climate disasters which have damaged infrastructure. Furthermore, the Court has also indicated that, in some cases, if asylum seekers are to experience dire living conditions upon their return, then the principle of non-refoulement may be triggered under Article 3 ECHR.[64] This was the case in *M.S.S. v. Belgium and Greece*, in which it was found that removing an Afghan asylum seeker from Belgium to Greece amounted to degrading treatment under Article 3 ECHR, due to the living and detention conditions in the latter country.[65] This was also the case in *Tarakhel v. Switzerland*, in which the ECtHR determined that deporting an Afghan family from Switzerland to Italy would potentially

59 Ibid., p. 143.

60 Ibid., p. 152.

61 *Bilgin v. Turkey*, no. 23819/94, European Court of Human Rights 2000.

62 F. de Weck, above n. 56, p. 168.

63 *D. v. United Kingdom*, no. 30240/96, European Court of Human Rights 1997.

64 F. de Weck, above n. 56, p. 168.

65 *M.S.S. v. Belgium and Greece*, no. 30696/09, European Court of Human Rights 2011.

violate Article 3 ECHR.[66] It is important to note that the Court has stated that poor socio-economic and humanitarian conditions do not necessarily mean that an individual is at risk of ill-treatment within the scope of Article 3 ECHR. However, the phrasing of 'not necessarily' leaves open the possibility that, under some circumstances, socio-economic and humanitarian conditions may indeed fall within the scope of Article 3 ECHR.[67]

While environmental and climate matters have never explicitly been considered by the ECtHR, one particular case has addressed related issues. In *Sufi and Elmi v. United Kingdom*, the Court addressed the question of whether two Somali complainants would be at risk of human rights violations should they be returned from the UK to an internally displaced persons camp in Somalia. The Court found that the deplorable humanitarian conditions there would lead to a real risk of Article 3 ECHR violations for the complainants, noting in particular the limited access of camp residents to food, water and shelter.[68] These findings may be relevant for future climate migration cases since climate migrants may face similar humanitarian conditions. Furthermore, while not the central focus of the case, it is significant that the Court also noted the potential relevance of the causes of Somalia's poor humanitarian conditions. Although they are primarily attributable to intentional acts and conflict, if they had instead been the result of the State's lack of ability to deal with natural phenomena (including drought), this may have been a factor to consider.[69] This differentiation is important because it may open the door for a future argument in support of climate migrants' right to remain in host countries: natural phenomena and environmental issues, as well as States' capacity to address them, have been acknowledged as potentially relevant factors in non-refoulement cases.

As shown above, the ECtHR's body of case law on non-refoulement mostly pertains to Article 3 ECHR. However, it should be noted that the Office of the United Nations High Commissioner for Human Rights (OHCHR) has made it clear that there are several fundamental rights likely to be violated by climate change in the coming years. These include the rights to life, to adequate food, to water, to health, to adequate housing and to self-determination.[70] In order to trigger the principle of non-refoulement for one of these other rights, one must clearly establish a causal link between environmental degradation and the enjoyment of one of these rights. Furthermore, the Committee has also advised

---

66 *Tarakhel v. Switzerland*, no. 29217/12, European Court of Human Rights 2014.

67 F. de Weck, above n. 56, p. 168.

68 *Sufi and Elmi v. United Kingdom*, nos. 8319/07 and 11449/07, European Court of Human Rights 2011; F. de Weck, above n. 56, p. 177.

69 *Sufi and Elmi v. United Kingdom*, above n. 68; F. de Weck, above n. 56, p. 183.

70 C. Caskey, 'Non-Refoulement and Environmental Degradation: Examining the Entry Points and Improving Access to Protection', The Graduate Institute Geneva 2020, p. 2, https://www.graduateinstitute.ch/sites/internet/files/2020-11/C%20Caskey%20Research%20Paper%20-%20No.%2026%20-%20Final%20v2.pdf.

that one should be able to demonstrate that the risk is personal in nature rather than simply due to general conditions in the State of origin.[71] Given the commonly accepted knowledge that the impacts of climate change disproportionately affect the most vulnerable members of society,[72] these individuals may be able to make a claim to this personal risk. A cumulative approach (i.e. a compilation of all the risks faced by the applicant, both in terms of environmental conditions and personal circumstances) may be a successful way of demonstrating the risk of harm.[73] Those migrating to another country and asking for protection from climate change should be presumed to be vulnerable[74] and given a fair opportunity to demonstrate this.

While the ECtHR has yet to hear a case specifically addressing climate migration, it is of note that some domestic European courts have heard such cases, and thus have begun to grapple with new questions pertaining to non-refoulement. A particularly interesting case comes from Italy's Supreme Court of Cassation, which ruled on a case pertaining to 'environmental migration' in early 2021. This case allowed for the development and advancement of the Court's jurisprudence, as it specifically recognised a category of 'environmental refugees' for the first time.[75] In this case, an individual of Nigerian origin applied for asylum in Italy. The applicant complained of environmental destruction in their home country: militant attacks on oil production sites in the region had led to environmentally disastrous oil spills. The Court relied on precedent set in a 2018 case, in which it was determined that Italy should protect an applicant from being returned to their country of origin if the applicant risked violation of their essential rights to life and human dignity due to the social, political or environmental context.[76] A violation of human dignity should thus trigger the provision of a residence permit for humanitarian protection.[77] In the 2021 case, the Court extended this by developing a test to determine whether a given environmental condition would threaten human dignity and life. One of three criteria must be met for this to be the case: an ecosystem's balance must be irreversibly altered, the alteration of the ecosystem must be very costly to fix or only achievable with exceptional measures, or there must be a risk to public safety as a result of the destruction of the ecosystem.[78] This decision and the

71 Ibid., p. 11.
72 Ibid., p. 24.
73 Ibid., p. 22.
74 Ibid., p. 24.
75 A. Ciervo, 'Verso Il Riconoscimento Dei "Rifugiati Ambientali"? Note a Prima Lettura Ad Una Recente Ordinanza Della Corte Di Cassazione', Accademia Diritto e Migrazioni 2021, http://www.adimblog.com/2021/05/31/verso-il-riconoscimento-dei-rifugiati-ambientali-note-a-prima-lettura-ad-una-recente-ordinanza-della-corte-di-cassazione/.
76 Ibid.
77 Ibid.
78 Ibid.

development of this test represent important steps forward in Italy's domestic law. Offering protection to those migrating due to environmental issues has come to be recognised as a logical and evolutionary development of the principle of non-refoulement.[79] It is likely that similar cases will be brought forward to other domestic European courts, as well as to the ECtHR, in the near future.

6. CONCLUSION

Adverse environmental conditions caused by climate change will inevitably force an increasing number of people to migrate in search of safety. However, current international frameworks for the protection of refugees do not readily apply to people moving in this context. This poses a major challenge for the protection of these individuals. It is thus necessary to explore the various legal avenues that may be used to increase the protection that may be offered to them. Formally updating refugee law such that it encompasses those forced to migrate due to climate change is one possibility, but there are significant limitations to this approach. Initiating renegotiations on the international refugee framework would be politically contentious, particularly in developed nations (many of which have general anti-immigration sentiment).[80] This also runs the risk that certain countries may attempt to use such an opportunity to weaken existing refugee protections.[81]

Rather than modifying existing refugee law frameworks, creating an entirely new legal category of climate refugees may be possible. This, however, could trigger the same political issues as above. This approach also has its own set of challenges: the concept of the 'climate refugee' is somewhat problematic in and of itself, as it implies a degree of mono-causality between climate change and migration. As previously discussed, climate change is a complex matter that intersects with other problems including food insecurity, violence and political strife, among others.[82] Given this reality, asking the international community to operationalise a definition for 'climate refugee' could lead to fraught and inconclusive debate.

The options above are clearly problematic as they would be very difficult to implement. It may instead be more effective to use existing human rights frameworks to protect climate migrants. In particular, the principle of non-refoulement has the scope to cover these individuals: those experiencing significant violations of their human rights should be protected by this principle and should not be removed from receiving States. The UN Human Rights

---

79 Ibid.

80 H. Locke, above n. 21.

81 Ibid.

82 B. Mayer, above n. 9.

Committee's findings in *Teitiota v. New Zealand* support this contention. In the coming years, this case (and eventually other human rights-based climate migration cases) will likely serve an important role in the development of this field. The large body of established ECtHR case law on the principle of non-refoulement will also be critical as more cases are brought forward in Europe.

There are certainly problems with relying solely on litigation to advance the law, in that the legal cultures and systems of States play a large role in case outcomes. The ethical implications of relying on certain individuals to bring their cases to court (and conversely the fact that many individuals do not have the resources to do so) should be considered as well. This is not to deny the fact that litigation will certainly be an important tool in protecting those forced to move due to climate change, but rather to add nuance and further considerations to the discussion about the avenues available for ensuring these protections.

The world is increasingly experiencing climatic volatility: addressing the protection of those most vulnerable to its effects is a highly pressing matter. Human rights law is certainly a promising means of offering legal protection to climate migrants. However, a global agreement or framework should also be developed by international bodies to explicitly acknowledge that they are entitled to legal protection under human rights law. Such a framework could help clarify States' responsibilities toward these vulnerable individuals and reduce States' abilities to deny them protection. Developed countries have a moral duty to take on such a task: they are largely responsible for driving climate change through their historical and contemporary emissions and should thus be equally responsible for helping those experiencing the worst of its effects.

HUMAN RIGHTS-BASED CLIMATE LITIGATION AND INDIGENOUS PEOPLES

Comparative Perspectives and New Trends for Climate Justice in Europe

Giada GIACOMINI

1. INTRODUCTION

Climate change is one of the many aspects of biotic impoverishment, which directly weakens human communities through reduced quality of life, environmental injustice and political instability.[1] Because of such important consequences for basic human rights, in recent years there has been a growing number of cases brought before national, regional and international courts that aim to hold States and private entities responsible for their actions and omissions regarding climate change policies. Human rights-based climate

1 J.R. KARR, 'Ecological integrity: an essential ingredient for humans' long-term success' in L. WESTRA, K. BOSSELMANN and C. SOSKOLNE (eds), *Globalisation and Ecological Integrity in Science and International Law*, Newcastle upon Tyne: Cambridge Scholars Pub., 2011.

litigation aligned with climate objectives uses international and national human rights law to request governments and corporations to reduce their greenhouse gas emissions on the basis that climate change causes significant breaches of international human rights law. However, human rights-based climate litigation also includes those lawsuits not aligned with climate objectives, aimed at opposing green development projects that have a negative impact on human rights. In such lawsuits, even though the plaintiffs are not objecting to climate action being undertaken, they are criticising how such climate-related projects are being implemented.[2]

At present, several such complaints have been filed before the European Court of Human Rights (ECtHR), seeking redress for climate injustices that have caused serious human rights violations.[3] As of May 2021, there were as many as 112 cases (out of 1,841 cases) relying in whole or in part on human rights revindications.[4] This 'rights turn' in climate change litigation aims at regulating climate policies, whereas the international legal regime does not provide for enforcement or accountability tools when States do not meet their emissions reduction obligations.[5] Because of the important obligations of settler States deriving from international human rights law, Indigenous peoples' claims in climate litigation have – so far – been framed in such terms. As a matter of fact, international human rights law sees States as duty bearers concerning environmental protection.[6]

This chapter aims to present an overview of current climate litigation discourses and cases brought forward by Indigenous peoples, intending to criticise the limits of the ECtHR when it comes to protecting Indigenous peoples' environmental human rights. It also aims to show how Indigenous peoples have been the protagonists of transnational just transition litigation cases characterised by an infringement of human rights due to the installation of wind farms. The case law analysed is limited to international and supranational cases (for litigation aligned with climate objectives) and to two national cases (for litigation not aligned with climate objectives).

---

2 A. Savaresi and J. Setzer, 'Rights-based litigation in the climate emergency: mapping the landscape and new knowledge frontiers' (2021) *Journal of Human Rights and the Environment* 1.

3 Several cases have been filed before the ECtHR but not yet decided: *Mex M. v. Austria* (2021); *Duarte Agostinho and Others v. Portugal and 32 Other States* (2020); *Greenpeace Nordic Association v. Ministry of Petroleum and Energy* (2016); *Union of Swiss Senior Women for Climate Protection v. Swiss Federal Council and Others* (2016).

4 See Karr, n. 1.

5 J. Peel and H. Osofski, 'A Rights Turn in Climate Change Litigation?' (2018) *Transnational Environmental Law* 37.

6 K.A. Gwiazdon, 'The state versus the environment: the ethical and legal implications for state non-action in protecting the foundations of life' in L. Westra, K. Bosselmann, J. Gray and K. Gwiazdon (eds), *Ecological Integrity, Law and Governance*, Oxon/New York: Routledge, 2018, pp. 7–18.

The difficulties Indigenous peoples face in being recognised as subjects of rights in the international law realm resonate with the issues raised in this chapter. Their struggle for recognition as human beings first, and, more recently, as people with their own systems of laws, language and culture based on a specific ontological and epistemic dimension demonstrate that Western law still has to overcome its limits and limitations. These problems translate into access to justice issues,[7] production of Indigenous stereotypes and forced translation of Indigenous cosmovision to fit into Western legal standards, which fosters further epistemic violence against Indigenous peoples.[8] Such aspects are particularly true for the ECtHR when it comes to effectively protecting Indigenous peoples' rights by granting access to and use of their ancestral territories. Moreover, Indigenous peoples have traditionally been excluded from international climate negotiations and decision-making in climate strategies, and their holistic views and environmental demands are disregarded.[9]

The chapter is thus divided into two parts. In the first part, it will be argued that Indigenous peoples' rights are not equally perceived and protected in supranational human rights systems. To demonstrate this point, a comparison between European and Inter-American jurisprudence will be carried out to argue that harmonisation between these different human rights systems is highly desirable when it comes to protecting Indigenous peoples' rights. The chapter will also assess how human rights standards are being brought to the fore by Indigenous peoples in climate change litigation, in order to analyse the limits such narratives would have in a potential case before the ECtHR. It will therefore propose potential ways for the European human rights justice system to diverge from its exclusively Western-based legal culture in view of future environmental and climate litigation.

The second part will analyse just transition litigation cases brought forward by Indigenous peoples against European States and transnational energy companies.

---

7 J. Gilbert, *Indigenous peoples' land rights under international law: from victims to actors*, Leiden: Brill, 2006; J. Gilbert, 'Litigating indigenous peoples' rights in Africa: Potentials, challenges and limitations' (2017) 66 *International and Comparative Law Quarterly* 657; J. Gilbert and B. Begbie-Clench, 'Mapping for Rights: Indigenous Peoples, Litigation, and Legal Empowerment' (2018) 11 *Erasmus Law Review* 6; J. Gilbert, 'Land rights and nomadic peoples: Using international law at the local level' (2012) 16(2) *Nomadic People* 78; J. Gilbert, *Natural Resources and Human Rights: An Appraisal*, Oxford: Oxford University Press, 2018.

8 M.C. Petersmann, 'Contested Indigeneity and Traditionality in Environmental Litigation: The Politics of Expertise in Regional Human Rights Courts' (2021) 21(1) *Human Rights Law Review* 132.

9 F. Mihlar, *Voices that must be heard: minorities and indigenous people combating climate change*, Minority Rights Group International, 2008; C. Betzold and A. Flesken, 'Indigenous peoples in international environmental negotiations. Evidence from biodiversity and climate change' in T. Kaime (ed.), *International Climate Change Law and Policy*, Oxon/New York: Routledge, 2014; C.M. Doyle, *Indigenous Peoples, Title to Territory, Rights and Resources*, Oxon/New York: Routledge, 2015; M. Brugnach, M. Craps and A. Dewulf, 'Including indigenous peoples in climate change mitigation: addressing issues of scale, knowledge and power' (2017) 140 *Climatic Change* 19.

Such cases are relevant insofar as they demonstrate, for example, how the Supreme Court of Norway has successfully defended the Saami's rights as well as the importance of grievance redress mechanisms (GRMs) to secure accountability of human rights, participatory parity, and environmental and social standards in the realisation of climate change projects in Indigenous territories.

2. COMPARATIVE PERSPECTIVES BETWEEN THE EUROPEAN AND THE INTER-AMERICAN SYSTEM ON HUMAN RIGHTS

2.1. EUROPEAN COURT AND COMMISSION OF HUMAN RIGHTS

This section focuses on the jurisprudence specifically aimed at protecting Indigenous peoples from displacement and securing their right to their ancestral lands. To this end, it pursues a comparative perspective between the European and the Inter-American system. This type of consideration will pave the way for reflections on the interlinkage between Indigenous human rights and climate change which are at the core of contemporary climate litigation cases. As an example, the ECtHR and the European Commission of Human Rights (ECmHR) have wide and extremely varied jurisprudence regarding the protection of environmental human rights.[10] Such rights should include Indigenous peoples' rights because of their complex relationship with nature: Indigenous peoples' legal, social, economic and cultural systems are inextricably linked and dependent on the environment and the preservation of biodiversity. But Indigenous peoples and their rights are suffering a sort of 'invisibilisation' in Europe, given that the States in which they reside (except Norway) have not yet ratified the International Labour Organization Convention 169 on Indigenous and Tribal Peoples (ILO Convention 169),[11] and Indigenous peoples have not received legal redress from supranational European institutions when seised, mainly because of procedural hurdles.[12]

In fact, the ECtHR and the ECmHR have addressed complaints brought forward by Indigenous peoples like the Inuit, the Saami and other Russian groups.[13] However, when it comes to protecting Indigenous peoples' rights,

10 O.W. Pedersen, 'The European Court of Human Rights and International Environmental Law' in J.H. Knox, and R. Pejan, *The human right to a healthy environment*, Cambridge: Cambridge University Press, 2018, pp. 86–96.

11 See ratification status at https://www.ilo.org/dyn/normlex/en/f?p=NORMLEXPUB:11300:0::NO::P11300_INSTRUMENT_ID:312314.

12 R. Grote, 'On the Fringes of Europe: Europe's Largely Forgotten Indigenous Peoples' (2007) 31(2) *American Indian Law Review* 425.

13 In the late 1980s, several complaints concerning European Indigenous peoples were heard before the European Commission on Human Rights, namely: *G. & E. v. Norway*, also known

the decisions of the Court seem ill-suited to deal with the complex problems that characterise Indigenous human rights, especially with respect to their cosmovision and the holistic relationship they have with their territory. Notwithstanding these relevant aspects, only a very few cases have reached the merits stage. In the *Alta* case (1983),[14] the first Saami application submitted to the ECmHR, the human rights violations were not interpreted as threatening the Saami's cultural rights and freedoms, but rather as a very slight interference with their economic life – reindeer herding was, according to the Commission, an economic activity carried out in a 'comparatively small area which will be lost by the Applicants'[15] due to the construction of the Alta dam. In the *Johtti* case (2005)[16] and in the *Handölsdalen* case (2010),[17] the ECmHR expected the Saami peoples to have already established their ancestral territorial rights through their domestic jurisdiction.[18] In the latter case, the Court affirmed that the issue of the burden of proof of the territorial rights of Indigenous peoples lay with the Saami. Such an affirmation relied on the fact that 'the rules on the burden of proof, as laid down in Sweden in the old Land Code of 1734, that is, long before any recognition of indigenous peoples emerged, were perfectly able to govern the situation'.[19]

Other ECtHR cases have concerned issues related to forced relocation. In *Hingitaq 53 and Others v. Denmark* (2006), the claim was submitted by the Inughuit of Greenland as a result of their forced relocation that occurred in the 1950s.[20] The applicants argued that Denmark had dispossessed them of their aboriginal lands, violating the right to a peaceful enjoyment of possessions under Protocol 1 of the International Covenant on Civil and Political Rights (ICCPR), as well as their rights to privacy and family life, a fair trial, and an effective remedy under the ECHR. This case was deemed admissible, and the merits analysed. However, the ECtHR found that Denmark had not committed any breach of the Inughuits' right to peaceful enjoyment of their property, and the dispossession of their ancestral lands was not an arbitrary measure. This decision appears in stark contrast with the international law normative contents

as the *Alta* case (1983), *O.B. and Others v. Norway* (1993), *Konkima and 38 Other Saami Villages v. Sweden* (1996); and *Halvar FROM v. Sweden* (1998). None of these cases ruled in favour of Indigenous peoples.

14 ECmHR, *G. and E. v. Norway*, nos 9278/81 and 9415/81 (joined), 3 October 1983.

15 Ibid.

16 ECtHR, *Johtti Sapmelaccat Ry and Others v. Finland*, no. 42969/98, 2005.

17 ECtHR, *Handölsdalen Sami Village and Others v. Sweden*, no. 39013/04, 30 March 2010.

18 T. Koivurova, 'Jurisprudence of the European Court of Human Rights Regarding Indigenous Peoples: Retrospect and Prospects' (2011) 18(1) *International Journal on Minority and Group Rights* 1.

19 *Handölsdalen Sami Village and Others v. Sweden*, n. 17.

20 The Inughuit of Greenland are one of the smallest Indigenous groups in the world, cf. also T. Ngiviu, 'The Inughuit of Northwest Greenland: An Unacknowledged Indigenous People' (2014) 6(1) *The Yearbook of Polar Law Online* 142.

of ILO Convention 169 and United Nations Declaration on the Rights of Indigenous Peoples (UNDRIP) regarding the rights of Indigenous peoples to their ancestral lands.

The case *Chagos Islanders v. United Kingdom* (2012) originated with the construction of the Diego Garcia US naval base in the 1960s, which obliged the inhabitants of the Chagos Islands to leave their ancestral native land starting in 1967. This case is quite unique because the Chagos Islands, although located in the Indian Ocean, have been under the administration of the United Kingdom since the early 19th century. Such former colonies are now considered by the United Kingdom as 'dependencies'.[21] After pursuing domestic means of justice without positive results in order to be able to return to their homeland, the Chagossians appealed to the ECtHR, basing their lawsuit on violations of Articles 3, 6, 8 and 13 of the ECHR and on Article 1 of Protocol 1 ECHR. The ECtHR dismissed the case on procedural grounds, since the UK had not extended to that dependency – i.e. the Chagos Islands – the legal jurisdiction of the ECtHR. Once again, a lawsuit brought by Indigenous peoples did not reach the merits stage even though human rights violations had occurred.

Moreover, a similar approach was also used in *Könkämä and 38 Other Saami Villages v. Sweden* (1996).[22] The Saami villagers complained against the revision of the Swedish legal regime for hunting, fishing and herding, which would necessitate licences when such activities occurred within the territorial boundaries of the State. The ECtHR again dismissed the case on procedural grounds before reaching the merits stage since the complainants had not exhausted local remedies. Finally, the ECtHR declared the complaint in *Muonio Saami Village v. Sweden* (2000) admissible, although it did not reach the merits stage since an agreement was reached between the government and Saami people.[23]

This brief case law review demonstrates that the substantive merits of Indigenous rights have not been properly dealt with by the ECtHR because of procedural hurdles that have blocked access to justice, meaning that the Court has avoided dealing with Indigenous peoples' rights.[24] Even in the cases that reached the merits stage, the approach of the ECtHR is not adequate to effectively protect Indigenous peoples' rights for several reasons. The most striking aspect

---

21 P. Kovács, 'Indigenous Issues under the European Convention of Human Rights Reflected in an Inter-American Mirror' (2015) 48 *George Washington International Law Review* 781.

22 ECmHR, *Könkämä and 38 Other Saami Villages v. Sweden*, no. 27033/95.

23 ECtHR, *Muonio Saami Village v. Sweden*, no. 28222/95.

24 Again, in the Inter-American system the procedural requirements are less stringent. The IACtHR has stated that in the case of Indigenous peoples, they must exhaust only those remedies that respond to their particular characteristics, either economic or social, including their customary laws and values. Cf. F. Hampson et al., 'Inaccessible apexes: Comparing access to regional human rights courts and commissions in Europe, the Americas, and Africa' (2018) 16(1) *International Journal of Constitutional Law* 161.

is the lack of recognition of the important interlinkage between ancestral lands and Indigenous peoples' views, values and cultural identity. In addition, it must be noted that the land disputes and geographical recognition of ancestral lands cannot rely exclusively on the Indigenous people who have brought the claim. Indeed, the Committee on the Elimination of Racial Discrimination noted its concerns about the Saami case when addressing Sweden.[25] For these reasons, Indigenous peoples have traditionally preferred to bring their claims before the UN Human Rights Committee.[26] The contrast between Indigenous peoples' international human rights standards protected under international law and the ECtHR decisions is surprising and should raise important questions about the extent to which Indigenous peoples are protected in Europe.

2.2. INTER-AMERICAN COURT AND COMMISSION OF HUMAN RIGHTS

Unlike the European system, the Inter-American human rights system has a long history of protection of Indigenous peoples' rights and is regarded as a progressive institution in terms of recognition and protection of Indigenous peoples. An important feature distinguishing this judicial system from other international adjudicatory bodies is the peculiar *locus standi* it affords to plaintiffs. In fact, Article 44 of the American Convention on Human Rights allows '[a]ny person or group of persons, or any nongovernmental entity legally recognized in one or more member states of the Organization [of American States]' to file claims with the Inter-American Commission on Human Rights (IACmHR). Consequently, the petitioner and victim need not necessarily be the same person. This broad *locus standi* substantially differs from that of the ECtHR, insofar as it allows NGOs to act as petitioners on behalf of, for example, Indigenous people. This feature is important because it promotes the passing of the preliminary stage of those cases based on a general and communitarian environmental interest.[27] This signals that the IACmHR and the IACtHR have much less stringent procedural hurdles to overcome for complainants compared to the European system.

---

25 CERD, *Concluding observations of the Committee on the Elimination of Racial Discrimination, Seventy-third session consideration of Reports Submitted by States Parties under Article 9 of the Convention* (28 July–15 August 2008) (Sweden), para. 20.

26 HRC cases: *Kitok v. Sweden*, UN Doc. CCPR/C/33/D/197/1985 (1988); *Chief Bernard Ominayak and Lubicon Lake Band v. Canada*, UN Doc. CCPR/C/38/D/167/1984 (1990); *Ilmari Länsman et al. v. Finland*, UN Doc. CCPR/C/52/D/511/1992 (1994); *Apirana Mahuika et al. v. New Zealand*, UN Doc. CCPR/C/70/D/547/1993 (2000); *Poma Poma v. Peru*, UN Doc. CCPR/C/95/D/1457/2006 (2009).

27 The ECtHR has recently remarked that an NGO cannot rely in its own name on the right to respect for private life and home (Art. 8 ECHR). Unlike the right to a fair trial, Art. 8 can only be relied on by natural persons. See *Yusufeli İlçesini Güzelleştirme Yaşatma Kültür Varlıklarını Koruma*

The IACtHR and IACmHR have decided quite a large number of cases in favour of Indigenous peoples by interpreting the ILO Convention 169 and other human rights treaties in a progressive and evolutive way. Such interpretation includes broadening the scope of international human rights law to embed collective rights to culture and land. Such decisions have been incorporated in domestic legislation and adopted by courts in Latin America, contributing to the standardisation of minimum requirements established by the American Convention on Human Rights.[28]

Important and well-known decisions related to the violation of Indigenous peoples' rights are *Awas Tingni*,[29] *Maya Communities of Belize*,[30] *Sarayaku*[31] and *Saramaka*.[32] In addition to these cases, other relevant Indigenous applications have been made to the IACtHR. *Yakye Axa*,[33] *Sawhoymaxa*[34] and *Xakmok Kasek*[35] are all related to the relocation of the Indigenous groups in the Chaco paraguayano area. The Court affirmed the applicability of the international right law dispositions enshrined in the ILO Convention 169 related to the right to land, affirming that when a relocation is taking place, Indigenous peoples have the right to receive other land of the same quality and value. The IACtHR also stressed the importance of land as a vehicle for the replication of Indigenous culture, cosmovision, religion and cultural identity. Moreover, the IACtHR stressed the importance of respecting the participatory and procedural rights of Indigenous peoples, including free prior and informed consent (FPIC), which is prescribed by UNDRIP. Generally, we can affirm that the Indigenous applications and the IACtHR decisions have revolved around violations of the right to property (individual and collective) due to the dispossession of ancestral lands in favour of private firms, with the consequence of the forced relocation of Indigenous peoples. Lastly, in *Lhaka Honhat Association* (2020) the

---

Derneği v. Turkey, no. 37857/14, 7 December 2021. See also R. Pavoni, 'Environmental jurisprudence of the European and Inter-American Courts of Human Rights: Comparative insights' in B. Boer, *The Environmental Dimension of Human Rights*, Oxford: Oxford University Press, 2015, pp. 70–106.

28 S. Herencia Carrasco, 'Public Interest Litigation in the Inter-American Court of Human Rights: The Protection of Indigenous Peoples and the Gap between Legal Victories and Social Change' (2015) *Revue Quebecoise de Droit International* 199.

29 IACtHR, *Mayagna (Sumo) Awas Tingi Community v. Nicaragua*, judgment of 1 January 2000, Ser. C No. 66; judgment of 31 August 2001, Ser. C No. 79.

30 IACtHR, *Maya Indigenous Communities v. Belize*, Case 12.053, Report No. 78/00, OEA/Ser.L/V/II.111, doc. 20, rev. (2000).

31 IACtHR, *The Kichwa Peoples of Sarayaku v. Ecuador*, Petition 167/03, Report No. 62/04, OEA/Ser.L/V/II.122, doc. 5, rev. 1 (2004).

32 IACtHR, *Saramaka People v. Suriname*, judgment of 28 November 2007, Ser. C No. 172.

33 IACtHR, *Comunidad Indígena Yakye Axa v. Paraguay*, judgment of 17 June 2005, Ser. C No. 125, para. 188; and *Case Masacre de Plan de Sánchez v. Guatemala*, judgment of 19 November 2004.

34 IACtHR, *Sawhoyamaxa Indigenous Community of the Enxet-Lengua people v. Paraguay*, judgment of 29 March 2006, Ser. C No. 146, IHRL 1530 (IACHR 2006).

35 IACtHR, *Xákmok Kásek Indigenous Community v. Paraguay*, 24 August 2010, Ser. C No. 214, 2010.

IACtHR enforced Indigenous groups' rights to communal property, a healthy environment, cultural identity, food and water.[36]

2.3. INDIGENOUS PEOPLES' NARRATIVES IN LITIGATION ALIGNED WITH CLIMATE OBJECTIVES: EXAMPLES FROM THE INTER-AMERICAN SYSTEM

Human rights-based approaches to climate change are a tool that is increasingly being used before international human rights courts in order to obtain justice and redress deriving from climate harm. Thus, human rights-based approaches can represent a viable mean to achieve climate justice, if international courts are progressive enough to recognise at the legal level the important interlinkage between the negative impacts of climate change, violation of human rights and States' failure to respect climate change objectives.[37] It is now widely demonstrated that climate change has the potential to endanger the enjoyment of fundamental human rights, such as the right to life, the right to property and adequate housing, and the right to a livelihood. Indigenous peoples are already confronting the loss of their traditional ways of life, their culture and identity, and their ancestral lands due to the negative repercussions of climate change impacts.[38]

Indigenous peoples living in Europe in a future not even so distant might be the plaintiffs of new climate change litigation cases, as they are already suffering the impacts of climate change, which are irreversibly damaging their ancestral lands.[39] Elsewhere, Indigenous peoples are employing climate litigation as a tool to bring States before international human rights courts, arguing for the redress of significant violations of their rights as a consequence of climate change impacts when the State did not provide for effective remedies.

In the Inter-American system, Indigenous peoples have brought, as of the time of writing, two human rights-based climate litigation cases, the *Inuit* case

---

36 IACtHR, *Lhaka Honhat Association v. Argentina*, 6 February 2020, Ser. C No. 420, 2020.

37 E.A. Posner, 'Climate change and international human rights litigation: a critical appraisal' (2006) 155 *University of Pennsylvania Law Review* 1925; B.J. Preston, 'The evolving role of environmental rights in climate change litigation' (2018) 2(2) *Chinese Journal of Environmental Law* 131; A. Savaresi and J. Auz, 'Climate change litigation and human rights: pushing the boundaries' (2019) 9(3) *Climate Law* 244; C. Rodríguez-Garavito, 'Human rights: The global south's route to climate litigation' (2020) 114 *American Journal of International Law* 40; K. Yoshida and J. Setzer, 'The trends and challenges of climate change litigation and human rights' (2020) 2 *European Human Rights Law Review* 140.

38 J. Williams, 'The impact of climate change on Indigenous people – The implications for the cultural, spiritual, economic and legal rights of Indigenous people' (2012) 16(4) *The International Journal of Human Rights* 648.

39 I. Markkula, M. Turunen and S. Rasmus, 'A review of climate change impacts on the ecosystem services in the Saami Homeland in Finland' (2019) *Science of the Total Environment*

and the *Athabaskan* case. Such lawsuits are framed in human rights terms as defending the groups' social, economic and cultural rights by linking the impacts of global warming, severe weather events and environmental degradation to an immediate threat to their survival. While these cases have been rejected or not yet decided, they are relevant insofar as they show how human rights have contributed to shaping the justice discourse related to Indigenous peoples and climate change.

The *Inuit* and the *Athabaskan* cases were both presented before the IACmHR. They are united by similar geographical and climatic settings, as well as by the fact that climate change is already impacting both Indigenous groups' territory, thus causing severe human rights violations. As a matter of fact, the UN Human Rights Council has ascertained that the negative impacts of climate change tend to be more severe depending on the vulnerability of the population of a determined territory.[40] The Arctic ecosystems are particularly endangered as they are currently experiencing the highest rates of global warming, with a dramatic increase in temperature between 2°C and 4°C occurring in the last 60 years.[41] In the Arctic, temperatures are rising twice as fast as compared to the rest of the world's continents.[42] The IPCC's special report from 2018 reads: 'Populations at disproportionately higher risk of adverse consequences with global warming of 1.5°C and beyond include disadvantaged and vulnerable populations, some Indigenous peoples, and local communities dependent on agricultural or coastal livelihoods (high confidence). Regions at disproportionately higher risk include Arctic ecosystems'.[43]

By using human rights-based litigation as a tool to achieve climate justice, the *Inuit* and *Athabaskan* petitions rely on the rights prescribed in the American Declaration of the Rights and Duties of Man. This is because the Declaration, a non-binding instrument, is the only legal document enforceable against the United States and Canada, since they are not parties to the Inter-American Convention on Human Rights.[44]

1070; J.J. Jaakkola, S. Juntunen and K. Näkkäläjärvi, 'The holistic effects of climate change on the culture, well-being, and health of the Saami, the only indigenous people in the European Union' (2018) 5(4) *Current Environmental Health Report* 401.

40 UN Human Rights Council (UNHRC) Res. 26/27, *Human Rights and Climate Change*, UN Doc. A/HRC/26/L.33, 23 June 2014, p. 3.

41 See generally IPCC, *Climate Change 2021: The Physical Science Basis. Contribution of Working Group I to the Sixth Assessment Report of the Intergovernmental Panel on Climate Change*, Cambridge: Cambridge University Press, 2021.

42 Ibid.

43 IPCC, 'Summary for Policymakers' in *Global Warming of 1.5°C: An IPCC Special Report on the impacts of global warming of 1.5°C above pre-industrial levels and related global greenhouse gas emission pathways, in the context of strengthening the global response to the threat of climate change, sustainable development, and efforts to eradicate poverty*, Cambridge: Cambridge University Press, 2018.

44 The 1979 statute of the IACmHR provides the Commission with the faculty to uphold the rights protected in the ADRIP, following the principles contained in Article 1. See also Statute

The Inuit Petition to the IACmHR was filed in December 2005 on behalf of Inuit peoples in the US and Canada.[45] The petition aimed to compel the US to take climate control action since global warming directly affects the natural environment upon which Inuits' lives are dependent, impacting their fundamental human rights. Even if the Inuit are present in multiple nation-states and they are all represented in the Inuit Circumpolar Conference, the petition was filed only by those living in the US and Canada, as Greenland and Russia are not subject to the authority of the IACmHR.

Inuit people argued that permanent environmental changes in the Arctic are directly causing severe violations of their fundamental human rights, mainly their right to a home, their freedom of residence and movement, the right to property and the right to their own means of subsistence. What makes this case particular and the first of its kind is that in order to apply the Declaration in the multifaceted climate change context, the Inuit Petition relied on the complex relationships between environmental protection and human rights at multiple geographical and political scales. Here, the Indigenous people's nation-states (scattered across different countries) confront national and supranational authorities (the US and the Inter-American Court).[46] This petition hence went beyond the traditional judicial boundaries of the nation-state by appealing to a supranational court, which has traditionally shown great responsiveness to linking environmental harm and Indigenous peoples' rights. Additionally, the petition represents an important means of tracking down climate change effects in the Arctic from the perspective of the Inuit, by linking the deteriorating conditions of the environment to the loss of their ancestral land and culture.

The Inuit Petition was rejected in 2006 in a two-paragraph decision[47] because the plaintiffs could not establish specific causation between the US's failure to lower emissions and violations of Inuit human rights. However, the petition has been praised as a tool to raise awareness of climate change impacts on the Inuit and to link these impacts to human rights violations, especially after the two hearings on the topic requested by the Inuit.[48]

---

of the Inter-American Commission on Human Rights, OAS Res. 447 (IX-0/79), OAS Off. Rec. OEA/Ser.P/IX.0.2/80 (1979), Vol. 1, p. 88.

45 For a full account on the Petition documents, see Climate Case Chart website, http://climatecasechart.com/non-us-case/petition-to-the-inter-american-commission-on-human-rights-seeking-relief-from-violations-resulting-from-global-warming-caused-by-acts-and-omissions-of-the-united-states/.

46 H.M. Osofsky, 'The Inuit Petition as a Bridge? Beyond dialectics of Climate Change and Indigenous Peoples' Rights' in B. William and H.M. Osofsky (eds), *Adjudicating Climate Change: State, National, and International Approaches*, Cambridge: Cambridge University Press, 2009.

47 IACmHR, Decision, 16 November 2006, http://blogs2.law.columbia.edu/climate-change-litigation/wp-content/uploads/sites/16/non-us-case-documents/2006/20061116_na_decision.pdf.

48 J. Gordon, 'Inter-American Commission on Human Rights to Hold Hearing after Rejecting Inuit Climate Change Petition' (2007) 7(2) *Sustainable Development Law & Policy* 55.

The Athabaskan Petition, which has not yet been decided, similarly alleges that Canada has failed to effectively regulate black carbon emissions, which is causing significant changes in the Arctic environment and in turn violates the Athabaskans' human rights. The petition could succeed if, on the one hand, the Athabaskans unequivocally establish a specific interlinkage between Canada's actions and the violation of human rights and, on the other hand, the IACmHR expands its interpretation of international human rights law.[49] Regarding the latter aspect, it must be noted that in an Advisory Opinion the IACtHR recognised the important interlinkage between human rights and the environment, including the right to a healthy environment, and States' obligations regarding environmental protection.[50] The contents of this Advisory Opinion are relevant for the Athabaskan case and potentially for other human rights-based litigation, since the IACtHR established clear obligations related to environmental degradation, the right to life and the right to personal integrity. Moreover, the IACmHR has recently adopted Resolution 3/21, entitled 'Climate emergency: scope of inter-American human rights obligations'. The resolution is the first document of the Inter-American human rights system specifically dedicated to the issue of climate change, and it recognises that climate change is a human rights emergency, constituting one of the greatest threats to the full enjoyment of human rights by present and future generations, for the health of ecosystems and all species that inhabit the planet.

2.4. COMPARATIVE REMARKS

The analysis proposed here has firstly shown the differences in the approach of two international human rights courts to the protection of Indigenous peoples' rights, especially when it comes to relocation without ensuring adequate consultations and FPIC. Such differences are crucial to investigate the potential of human rights-based climate litigation as another facet of the interaction between human rights, the environment and access to traditional lands. In the context of the Inter-American human rights system, such a case has not yet been decided; however, one might assume from the analysis below that Indigenous peoples' rights in the climate change context will still have a higher protection level at the Inter-American level than at the European level. Because of the different treatment Indigenous people receive in Europe, they might be discouraged from bringing claims before the ECtHR. However, vulnerable communities should not be discouraged from filing cases before national and European courts because

---

49 D. McCrimmon, 'The Athabaskan Petition to the Inter-American Human Rights Commission: using human rights to respond to climate change' (2016) 6(2) *The Polar Journal* 398.

50 IACtHR, Advisory Opinion OC-23/17, 15 November 2017, Requested by the Republic of Colombia.

this might constitute a way to foster an operative human rights dimension for climate change. Hopefully, in time courts will be more receptive to such cases and be willing to accept them.[51] In any case, such premises may merit some comparative remarks and potential ways to expand the human rights scope of the ECtHR when it comes to the protection of Indigenous peoples' rights.

First, the collective nature of Indigenous peoples' rights and their attachment to their territory is something that can hardly be protected in the excessively individualistic, State-centred European justice system. European courts might be ill-suited to address such cultural and spiritual complexities. And, of course, such aspects would also necessarily need to face the inherent problems of a type of litigation, i.e. climate change litigation, that is relatively novel in relation to human rights claims. Perhaps the differences in the Inter-American and European systems are not only to be found in their substantial and procedural grounds, but also in the very different social, economic and cultural contexts that characterise the two geographical areas.

Second, an important difference between the Inter-American and the European systems lies in the fact that the ECHR does not guarantee a substantive right to a healthy environment, nor are any of its provisions expressly constructed to ensure a general environmental protection. However, notably, the ECtHR has repeatedly recognised that a healthy environment is a fundamental precondition for the enjoyment of a great number of human rights, foremost the right to private and family life according to Article 8 ECHR.[52] At the domestic level, European States have recognised the right to a healthy environment by broadening of the scope of the ECHR.[53] In this respect, the European human rights-based justice system could be an important venue for climate litigation. The doctrine of positive obligations requires States to actively protect human rights within their jurisdictions 'through an interpretive design of using the human health and integrity consideration as the prism through which the effects of environmental degradation are measured onto the realisation of the full scope of the protected rights'.[54] Nation-states' positive obligations as prescribed by ECtHR case law include procedural and substantive

51 Cf. H. Keller and A.D. Pershing, 'Climate Change in Court: Overcoming Procedural Hurdles in Transboundary Environmental Cases' (2021) 3(1) *European Convention on Human Rights Law Review* 23.

52 K. Morrow, 'After the Honeymoon: The Uneasy Marriage of Human Rights and the Environment Under the European Convention on Human Rights and in UK Law Under the Human Rights Act 1998' (2013) *Revue générale de droit* 317.

53 D. Shelton, 'Human Rights, Health and Environmental Protection Linkages in Law and Practice' (2007) 1(9) *Human Rights and International Legal Discourse* 9.

54 See also *Hatton and Others v. United Kingdom*, no. 360022/97, 8 July 2003; *Fadeyeva v. Russia*, no. 55723/00, 9 June 2005; *Borysiewicz v. Poland*, no. 71146/01, 1 July 2008; and *Leon and Agnieszka Kania v. Poland*, no. 12605/03, 21 July 2009. Cf. K. Braig and S. Panov, 'The Doctrine of Positive Obligations as Starting Point for Climate Litigation in Strasbourg: The European Court of Human Rights as a Hilfssheriff in Combating Climate Change?' (2020) 35 *Journal of Environmental Law and Litigation* 261.

duties related to information,[55] participation,[56] access to justice,[57] conducting environmental impact assessments[58] and the obligation to prosecute environmental polluters.[59] While this list is not exhaustive, it indicates that human rights-based climate litigation could rightfully – and perhaps successfully – be brought before the ECtHR.

Third, while the doctrine of positive obligations might have beneficial effects on human rights-based climate litigation, several challenges persist regarding the protection of Indigenous peoples' rights at the ECtHR level. For instance, Indigenous peoples have traditionally been excluded from international environmental and climate change decision-making processes, and have had their holistic views concerning the environment disregarded. Furthermore, they face insurmountable difficulties in trying to access the human rights justice system because of issues related to the burden of proof, demonstration of territorial rights and *locus standi*. This appears to conflict with Kobylarz's affirmation that, through the procedural rights and obligations that are considered crucial for the practical fulfilment of substantive rights, European human rights law would strengthen the fundamental principles and concepts of international and community environmental law, such as citizens' participation in a decision-making process, access to information and justice, and environmental impact assessment.[60]

The ECtHR and European States' practice, through the development of relevant jurisprudence that would help Indigenous peoples address environmental – and climate – injustice, might be a useful way to address such complex contemporary issues. In particular, it is desirable that the ECtHR and the IACtHR cite each other's case law: in fact, the ECtHR has a long tradition in the assessment and protection of human rights and the environment (although within the limits of a strong anthropocentric matrix), while the IACtHR has demonstrated that it will ensure adequate protection standards and reparations for Indigenous peoples.[61] The ECtHR is already referring to the IACtHR in matters

55 *Guerra v. Italy*, no. 14967/89, 19 February 1998. See also the framework established by the Aarhus Convention in this regard.

56 *Hatton v. United Kingdom*, no. 36022/97, 8 July 2003.

57 *Moor v. Switzerland*, no. 52067/10, 11 March 2014.

58 *Tatar v. Romania*, no. 67021/01, 27 January 2009.

59 *Oneryildiz v. Turkey*, no. 48939/99, 30 November 2004.

60 See generally N. Kobylarz, 'The European Court of Human Rights: An Underrated Forum for Environmental Litigation' in H. Tegner Anker and B. Egelund Olsen, *Sustainable Management of Natural Resources: Legal Instruments and Approaches*, Cambridge: Intersentia, 2018.

61 As Pavoni has pointed out, this cross-fertilisation between the European and the Inter-American system has already taken place, for example in the *Kawas-Fernandez* judgment of the IACtHR, where the Court asserted: 'in accordance with the case law of this Court and the European Court of Human Rights, there is an undeniable link between the protection of the environment and the enjoyment of other human rights.' See R. Pavoni, 'Environmental jurisprudence of the European and inter-American courts of human rights: Comparative insights' in B. Boer, *The Environmental Dimension of Human Rights*, Oxford: Oxford University Press, 2015.

such as forced disappearances, and nothing would prevent it from also taking such inspiration in potential cases brought by Indigenous peoples.[62] This aspect would be crucial in relation to the collective attachment of Indigenous peoples to their lands and its environmental and spiritual significance, as prescribed by ILO Convention 169 and by UNDRIP. In fact, harmonisation with international human rights standards contained in these two instruments is highly desirable.[63] According to Gismondi, there are two tactics commonly followed by the ECtHR in the interpretation of the human rights provisions.[64] The first approach is to treat the ECHR as a living document, taking into consideration how international law is applied. The second one, more Eurocentric, relies on the enforcement of European values. She argues that in the cases involving Indigenous peoples before the ECtHR (especially *Hingitaq 53*, *Chagos Islanders* and *Handdlsdalen Sami Village*) the second approach prevailed, resulting in a narrow interpretation of Protocol 1 ECHR, which undermined the cultural preservation and land rights of Indigenous peoples. This is also because it is impossible to reach a European consensus on Indigenous peoples' rights, since Indigenous peoples in Europe are located only in certain areas, thus leaving nation-states a wide margin of appreciation.

The current situation of Indigenous peoples' rights outlined above clearly indicates that a critical re-examination of the ECtHR application of the European human rights system is needed to devise potentially satisfactory human rights-based litigation for Indigenous peoples in Europe. Yet how can the European justice system be rethought in such a way as to not spread further lack of consideration for Indigenous peoples' needs in the current epoch of climatic change? How can we halt the epistemic violence, which traditionally overlooks the crucial relationship between Indigenous peoples and their ancestral lands? How can we realise a non-exclusionary but all-embracing model of climate governance that also includes Indigenous views of the environment?

This process should be inspired by the laws and principles aimed at protecting Indigenous peoples' rights in international law, and by relevant established jurisprudence. Such inspiration would potentially foster the enforcement of Indigenous land rights, and the recognition of the interlinkage between their knowledge, cosmovision and laws and their ancestral lands. Such a process aimed at securing justice and remedies should be preceded by the actual enforcement of Indigenous peoples' participatory rights in environmental and climate change

---

62 P. Kovács, 'Indigenous Issues under the European Convention of Human Rights Reflected in an Inter-American Mirror' (2016) 48 *George Washington International Law Review* 781.

63 The ILO Convention 169 has been ratified, in Europe, by Norway in 1990 and very recently by Germany, with entry into force on 23 June 2022.

64 G. Gismondi, 'Denial of justice: The latest Indigenous land disputes before the European Court of Human Rights and the need for an expansive interpretation of Protocol 1' (2016) 18 *Yale Human Rights and Development Law Journal* 1.

decision-making. Crucially, this would in turn give room for a non-Westernised, non-anthropocentric conceptualisation of the environment.[65] While the latter is a long-term objective, it must be recognised that at present human rights-based climate litigation is one of the most powerful tools to achieve climate justice. As this contribution has shown, the human rights system remains rooted in a series of application flaws, which make human rights standards subject to change depending on national and regional circumstances. This translates into completely different approaches to Indigenous peoples' human rights in Europe and in the Americas. Therefore, re-interpreting and applying human rights-based approaches to justice in the light of the jurisprudence of different international justice systems, such as the Inter-American one, is sorely needed in order for Indigenous peoples in Europe to obtain justice and redress, including in light of environmental and climate impacts.

3. INDIGENOUS PEOPLES, PARTICIPATORY PARITY AND 'JUST TRANSITION LITIGATION' IN EUROPE

This section analyses two cases brought by Indigenous peoples in the realm of human rights-based climate litigation not aligned with climate objectives. The use of human rights and social standards to prevent, oppose and redress the negative impacts on Indigenous and local communities due to the implementation of green transition and climate adaptation and mitigation projects is already at the centre, for example, of the work of relevant international quasi-judicial mechanisms and GRMs such as the Independent Redress Mechanism (IRM)[66] of the Green Climate Fund (GCF).[67] In recent years, this trend concerning

65 At present, there is an ongoing debate in Europe about non-anthropocentric conceptualisation of the environment and Rights of Nature. For example, the European Parliament's Policy Department for Citizens' Rights and Constitutional Affairs, at the request of the JURI Committee, required the drafting of a report to explore the concept of 'Rights of Nature' (RoN). See also 'Can Nature get it Right? A Study on Rights of Nature in the European Context', https://www.europarl.europa.eu/thinktank/en/document/IPOL_STU(2021)689328.

66 The IRM is the independent, quasi-judicial mechanism that ensures accountability for GCF actions. Among its key functions, it addresses complaints and grievances from persons and communities adversely impacted by GCF projects or programmes. When a complaint arises, the IRM mediates with a view to reaching a mutually satisfactory outcome. If parties are unwilling or unable to resolve the issues, the IRM might carry out an investigation to identify any non-compliance with GCF policies or procedures in relation to the complaint and recommends appropriate redress. To access the case database consult https://irm.greenclimate.fund/case-register.

67 The GCF has adopted relevant social and environmental standards that specifically protect Indigenous peoples in the context of green development projects. See also G. Giacomini, 'Free prior and informed consent in the Green Climate Fund: the implementation of a project in the Datém del Marañón, Peru' (2020) *CUHSO (Temuco)* 102. The Indigenous Peoples Policy can be consulted at https://www.greenclimate.fund/document/indigenous-peoples-policy.

just transition litigation has also been the central argument put forward by individuals at the national level and at the transnational level.[68]

For example, in 2018 Mexican Indigenous peoples challenged the French State, asking for the transnational energy company EDF to be ordered to fulfil its obligations under French due diligence legislation, the 'Duty of Vigilance Act'.[69] In this case, representatives of the Indigenous communities of Unión Hidalgo filed a specific complaint against the EDF Group and its subsidiary EDF Renewables concerning a project for the construction of a wind farm located in the territory of two municipalities of the district of Juchitán de Zaragoza in the State of Oaxaca. They appealed to the French OECD (Organisation for Economic Co-operation and Development) National Contact Point (NCP), which is the body for the non-judicial grievance mechanism for the implementation of the OECD Guidelines for Multinational Enterprises.[70]

The issues at stake concerned the fact that the scope of the project would cover plots of land that are part of the customary community land tenure (*tierra comunal*). According to the complainants, the company should have informed and consulted the assembly of the *comuneros* since the early stages of the project. The complainants argued that the right to information and to the FPIC of the Unión Hidalgo's Indigenous community had not been respected in the implementation of the EDF project. According to the referral, EDF and EDF Renewables had not correctly carried out their due diligence regarding the risk of adverse effects on human rights. This situation led to tensions within the Indigenous communities and the other stakeholders involved in the project, insofar as some landowners have been granted a rent and some people are therefore benefiting from the project (owners, local economic sectors), whereas the rest of the population is not. The plaintiffs invoked their human rights recognised in the Mexican Constitution, contained in ILO Convention 169 and in UNDRIP.

In its recommendation, the NCP adopted a strong participatory approach, in conformity with what is prescribed by the OECD Guidelines. It recommended that EDF 'make arrangements for engaging with all stakeholders potentially concerned by these projects, particularly with those bearing social and cultural interests'.[71] Moreover, it noted that the issue at stake should be addressed in

---

68 *Fägerskiöld v. Sweden*, no. 37664/04; *Vecbaštika and Others v. Latvia*, no. 52499/11; *Quechan Tribe v. US Dept. of Interior*, 755 F. Supp. 2d 1104 (S.D. Cal. 2010); and see generally the Corporate Legal Accountability database curated by the Business and Human Rights Resource Centre: https://old.business-humanrights.org/en/case-studies-renewable-energy.

69 The case documentation can be accessed at http://mneguidelines.oecd.org/database/instances/fr0026.htm.

70 The guidelines can be accessed at https://www.oecd.org/corporate/mne/.

71 'EDF and EDF RENEWABLES IN MEXICO', Final Statement of the French National Contact Point, 10 March 2020, non-official translation, https://www.tresor.economie.gouv.fr/Institutionnel/Niveau3/Pages/8fd9ecb1-2cb5-4e35-95b7-587b6793f341/files/bd60d487-1d03-44b1-9bf2-13ea02ed7f01.

an appropriate framework in the context of the Indigenous consultation to prevent future litigation. This case stressed the importance of GRMs to make transnational companies (and development funds) accountable for their human rights and due diligence obligations when implementing green development projects. However, the power of GRMs can present crucial limitations. In fact, in this specific case the NCP highlighted that 'NCPs are not competent to review decisions of administrative authorities. Some of the issues raised by this specific instance do not fall strictly within its jurisdiction'.

In another case, again concerning a wind farm, the Saami people filed a suit before the Supreme Court of Norway.[72] In this case, the Saami questioned whether the construction of the Storheia and Roan wind farms on the Fosen peninsula amounted to a violation of the reindeer herders' right to enjoy their own culture under Article 27 ICCPR. The Court found that the wind power development would have a significant adverse impact on the reindeer herders' opportunity to practise their culture on Fosen. Against that background, the Supreme Court found that the herders' rights would be violated if satisfactory remedy measures were not implemented.[73] Additionally, the construction of the wind farm was supported by international investments, including from BKW, a Swiss energy company. BKW holds shares in Nordic Wind Power DA – the European consortium of investors founded by Credit Suisse Energy Infrastructure Partners – which in turn holds a 40% stake in the joint venture Fosen Wind DA. In 2020, the Society for Threatened Peoples (STP) filed a complaint with the Swiss NCP against BKW. This case represents another attempt at redress through a GRM. In August 2021, the STP website reported that it had concluded the arbitration process with BKW. As a result, BKW is committed to protecting the rights of Indigenous communities and improving due diligence. In fact, FPIC will soon be included in BKW's internal guidelines.[74]

This brief overview of just transition litigation cases highlights how Indigenous peoples' rights are facing threats not only because of climate change impacts, but also because of the implementation of climate change mitigation measures. The respect of international human rights standards such as FPIC represent the *minimum* threshold that transnational companies and States should

---

72 Supreme Court judgment, 11 October 2021, HR-2021-1975-S (Case No. 20-143891SIV-HRET, Case No. 20-143892-SIV-HRET and Case No. 20-143893SIV-HRET). The Court of Norway had already protected Indigenous peoples' rights to their collective lands in at least another two decisions: *Erik Anderson v. The Norwegian State*, No. 5B/2001 (5 October 2001) and *Jon Inge Sirum v. Esslan Reindeer Pasturing District*, No. 4B/2001 (21 June 2001).

73 Supreme Court of Norway, HR-2021-1975-S (Case No. 20-143891SIV-HRET, Case No. 20-143892SIV-HRET and Case No. 20-143893SIV-HRET), text of the decision available at https://www.domstol.no/globalassets/upload/hret/decisions-in-english-translation/hr-2021-1975-s.pdf.

74 The STP's website is available at https://www.gfbv.ch/en/media/news/bkw-corporate-responsibility/ and BKW's press statement at https://www.bkw.ch/en/about-us/news/media/press-releases/bkw-boosts-its-commitment-to-sustainable-conduct.

apply when implementing projects in Indigenous peoples' ancestral lands. FPIC represents a way to achieve just and equitable participatory parity insofar as it should be applied from the early stages of project design with the participation and meaningful involvement of Indigenous peoples. It does not entail just the mere 'consent' of Indigenous peoples, but a broad 'spectrum of participation' that takes into account the right of self-determination pertaining to Indigenous peoples.[75] In the case of transnational corporations and investors, it is of the utmost importance that GRMs are accessible and reliable in investigating the violation of human rights and social and environmental standards in the context of green development projects. The cases presented in this section – especially those concerning the Court of Norway – might also be of inspiration for the ECtHR when addressing Indigenous peoples' environmental rights, cultural identity and interconnection with ancestral lands.

4. CONCLUSIONS

In its first part, this chapter showed how Indigenous rights are protected in a different manner by the ECtHR compared to the standards applied by the IACtHR and the IACmHR, the latter being much more receptive to Indigenous peoples' contemporary issues related to access to their ancestral lands, relocation, and the deep intertwinement between territory, cosmovision and identity. This perspective has demonstrated how Indigenous rights are often overlooked in Europe. Thus, the comparative perspective offered may be useful in examining the potential regulatory impacts of human rights-based climate litigation aligned with climate objectives and its limits. Therefore, the argument can be made that a critical rethinking of the role of the European justice system is due when it comes to protecting Indigenous peoples' rights, especially in the context of achieving environmental and climate justice. Such critical rethinking might be achieved by means of a 'decolonisation' of the ECtHR, where the European human rights justice system may take inspiration from international law on Indigenous rights or the Inter-American system, with a view to harmonising its decision with international human rights standards concerning Indigenous peoples.

In its second part, this chapter focused on cases brought by Indigenous peoples in so-called 'just transition litigation' cases, underscoring how GRMs and quasi-judicial mechanisms play a key role in holding private companies and development funds accountable and redressing injustices related to the

---

75 See generally F. Cittadino, *Incorporating Indigenous Rights in the International Regime on Biodiversity Protection: Access, Benefit-sharing and Conservation in Indigenous Lands*, Leiden: Brill, 2019.

implementation of projects in Indigenous territories. In fact, human rights standards should be permeated by a just and fair participatory parity when it comes to the implementation of green development projects in Indigenous ancestral lands. Respect of FPIC and participatory rights is a potential tool to avoid injustices related to climate change law and policies, and such participation should include environmental decision-making and participation in project design from an early stage.

PART II

CLIMATE CHANGE LITIGATION IN EUROPE: SECTORAL PERSPECTIVES

State Responsibility and Climate Change Litigation

FROM RIGHTS-BASED CLAIMS TO CLIMATE JUSTICE: AN UNEASY PATH

Limits and Prospects to Align Climate Litigation to Justice in Europe

Carlotta GAROFALO*

* The author is particularly grateful to Sarah Mead, Carole Billiet and Laura García Portela, and to the editors, for their insightful comments and feedback on this chapter, and wishes

1. INTRODUCTION

Despite a widespread sense of urgency in the climate discourse, the latest national climate pledges set the world on track for a global temperature increase of 2.7°C.[1] Thus, the realistic chances of delivering the 1.5°C target are fast decreasing, with alarming implications for the most vulnerable populations and ecosystems in the world.[2] Against this background, the number of climate cases challenging national mitigation policies have recently grown into a new wave of climate litigation.[3] Following the lead of the *Urgenda* case, in Europe alone 15 cases have been filed with the aim of compelling more ambitious and thorough policies.[4] These cases, defined by Maxwell, Mead and Van Berkel as 'systemic mitigation cases',[5] go as far as requesting that governments comply with specific reduction pathways, in line with the most ambitious 1.5°C target.[6]

---

to acknowledge the Austrian Science Fund (FWF), who funded this research under the Research Grant W1256 (Doctoral Programme Climate Change: Uncertainties, Thresholds and Coping Strategies).

1 UNEP, *Emissions Gap Report 2021: The Heat Is On – a World of Climate Promises Not Yet Delivered* (United Nations Environment Programme 2021).

2 L. Warszawski et al., 'All Options, Not Silver Bullets, Needed to Limit Global Warming to 1.5 °C: A Scenario Appraisal' (2021) 16 *Environmental Research Letters* 064037.

3 According to a recent 'scenario-based' categorisation, such cases can be described as public climate lawsuits where the plaintiff considers that their State is breaching the law by having an overall climate policy that is not ambitious enough to mitigate and/or adapt to climate change. https://www.c2li.org/c2li-scenarios/. When focusing on mitigation policies, such cases have also been defined as 'systemic mitigation cases.' L. Maxwell, S. Mead and D. Van Berkel, 'Standards for Adjudicating the Next Generation of Urgenda-Style Climate Cases' (2022) 13 *Journal of Human Rights and the Environment* 35.

4 *VZW Klimaatzaak v. Kingdom of Belgium and Others* (Tribunal de première instance francophone de Bruxelles); *Verein Klimaseniorinnen v. Federal Department of the Environment, Transport, Energy and Communications* (Federal Supreme Court); *Carvalho and Others v. European Parliament and Council of the European Union* [2019] European Court of Justice (Second Chamber) T-330/18; *Family Farmers and Greenpeace Germany v. Germany* [2019] Administrative Court of Berlin 10 K 412.18; *Notre Affaire à Tous v. France* [2021] Tribunal Administratif de Paris n° 1904967, 1904968, 1904972, 1904976/4-1; *Friends of the Irish Environment v. Ireland* [2020] Supreme Court of Ireland 205/19; *Neubauer et al. v. Germany (unofficial English translation of the complaint)* (Federal Constitutional Court); *Commune de Grande Synthe v. France* [2021] Council of State 427301/2021; *Duarte Agostinho and Others v. Portugal and 32 Other States* (pending) European Court of Human Rights no. 39371/20; *Klimatická žaloba ČR v. Czech Republic* (Prague Municipal Court); *A Sud et al. v. Italy* (Civil Court of Rome); *Górska et al. v. Poland* (District Court of Warsaw); *Steinmetz et al. v. Germany* (Federal Constitutional Court).

5 L. Maxwell, S. Mead and D. Van Berkel (n. 3).

6 *VZW Klimaatzaak v. Kingdom of Belgium and Others* (Tribunal de première instance francophone de Bruxelles); *Verein KlimaSeniorinnen Schweiz et al. v. Federal Department of the Environment, Transport, Energy and Communication* [2018] Federal Administrative Court of Switzerland A 2992/2017; *Carvalho et al. v. European Parliament and Council* [2019] European Court of Justice T-330/18; *Family Farmers and Greenpeace Germany v. Germany* [2019] Administrative Court of Berlin 10 K 412.18; *Neubauer et al. v. Germany (unofficial English translation of the complaint)* (Federal Constitutional Court); *A Sud et al. v. Italy* (Civil Court of Rome); *Górska et al. v. Poland* (District Court of Warsaw).

Overall, systemic mitigation lawsuits pursue a climate justice purpose: to make industrialised countries take responsibility for climate change: a global problem for which they were major contributors, but whose consequences will hit more severely those who are the least responsible for it. Their goals are both material and symbolic, as they aim to change policies while also influencing the political discourse. As emphasised by Tessa Khan, former co-director of the Climate Litigation Network, by exposing the governments and fossil fuel industry's contribution to the climate crisis, these cases support the climate justice movement in drawing 'a clear narrative of responsibility'.[7] Furthermore, systemic mitigation cases in Europe have often been based on human rights arguments. Plaintiffs claim that the insufficient action taken by their governments threatens the citizens' capability to enjoy their fundamental rights, both in the present and the future. Secondly, they argue that, with their current climate policies, European States violate their fair share of obligations vis-à-vis climate change, i.e. that their efforts fall below the level of ambition and responsibility that is expected of them as industrialised countries, given their historical responsibilities and economic resources.

Against this background, the chapter explores the limits of rights-based litigation in tackling climate justice issues and, eventually, holding European countries accountable for their (insufficient) contribution to mitigating climate change. The chapter follows the intuition that, to be achieved, the climate justice aims underlying systemic mitigation cases need to be understood as moral questions before legal ones. To put it simply, to understand how to adapt climate policies to ethical standards, it is first necessary to identify their most ethically controversial aspects.

This intuition is set out over four sections. Section 2 argues that the definition of a national reduction pathway is a normative matter. It does so by describing the moral assumptions behind different temperature goals and burden-sharing approaches. Section 3 shows how and why the moral issues identified still cause legal uncertainty. Furthermore, it shows how claimants have tried to resolve such uncertainties, by resorting to rights-based arguments and climate science. Section 4 shows how courts have reacted to the latter arguments, particularly to rights claims. In that way, the section assesses the adequacy of rights-based arguments in tackling issues related to climate justice in court. Finally, section 5 explores two alternative legal pathways that might support judges in reviewing national mitigation policies, while taking climate justice issues into account. In particular, the section looks into the potential use of scientific studies considering different burden-sharing approaches, as well as into the proportionality principle as a way to balance anthropocentric and eco-centric interests.

---

7 T. Khan, 'Litigation Is a Powerful Tool for Holding Those Responsible for the Climate Crisis to Account', *Time* 25 September 2019, https://time.com/5686087/courtroom-climate-change-litigation/.

2. DEFINING A NATIONAL REDUCTION PATHWAY: WHAT ETHICAL CONSIDERATIONS?

Given the current knowledge about the climate system's sensitivity to CO_2, global mitigation pathways show how the maximum amount of CO_2 emissions available without exceeding a certain temperature increase, i.e. the global carbon budget, can be distributed over time. Namely, national pathways allocate greenhouse gas (GHG) emissions in a specific national territory. Furthermore, the trajectory of national pathways depends on at least four variables: (1) the global temperature goal; (2) the scientific method used for the calculation of the global carbon budget; (3) the approach used for its distribution among nations; and (4) the reduction pace.

All these variables, in turn, are to some extent dependent on moral intuitions or assumptions. The following section focuses on the ethical dimensions concerning the setting of a temperature target and the choice on how to distribute the global carbon budget among countries ('fair share issue'). These two aspects are particularly salient to show the problems that arise when courts are asked to assess value-laden choices through a human rights lens.

2.1. TEMPERATURE GOAL: DANGEROUS CLIMATE CHANGE TO WHOM?

The authors of the Third IPCC Assessment Report noted that, while 'sciences can provide essential information for decisions on what constitutes dangerous anthropogenic interference with the climate system', these are ultimately 'value judgements … taking into account considerations such as development, equity, and sustainability'.[8] After two decades of negotiations, the Paris Agreement turned the ambiguous notion of 'dangerous climate change' into a quantitative target.[9] Under Article 2.2 of the Paris Agreement, the Parties committed to hold the temperature increase well below 2°C above pre-industrial levels and to pursue efforts to limit it within 1.5°C. Thus, despite welcoming the vulnerable countries' requests to include the 1.5°C target, the Agreement left some leeway to States on where exactly to set their national targets.

Furthermore, multiple scholars argue that the provision does not impose a specific mitigation obligation upon States, instead establishing a strong normative expectation that the Parties will gradually increase their ambition to comply

---

8 IPCC, *Climate Change 2001: Synthesis Report. A Contribution of Working Groups I, II and III to the Third Assessment Report of the Intergovernmental Panel on Climate Change* (IPCC 2001).

9 L. Rajamani and E. Guèrin, 'Central Concepts in the Paris Agreement and How They Evolved' in D. Klein et al. (eds), *The Paris Agreement on Climate Change: Analysis and Commentary* (Oxford University Press 2017).

with the collective goals.[10] Adopting a positivist approach to the interpretation of international law, Benoit Mayer has argued that the temperature goals can help to assess whether governments have complied with their due diligence obligations, only insofar as they are reflected in States' practice.[11]

Nonetheless, leaving national governments a broad margin of leeway in defining the temperature target has significant normative implications. As shown by the Special IPCC Report on 1.5°C, the choice to set the temperature goal at well below 2°C rather than 1.5°C is likely to lead to particularly adverse consequences for poor communities, exposed regions and threatened ecosystems. Except for heat-related morbidity, the risks associated with extreme weather events are projected to be higher in Global South regions, with heatwaves, droughts and sea level rise hitting Sub-Saharan Africa, the Mediterranean and Southern African regions, and small island States and Southeast Asia, respectively, more severely.[12] Moreover, climate risks including floods and food shortages, as well as water scarcity, are expected to hit the lower latitudes and poorer communities in countries at all levels of development.[13] Finally, warmer scenarios are associated with potentially irreversible impacts on coral reefs and arctic ecosystems, and a higher risk of reaching several tipping points.[14]

2.2. THE ALLOCATION OF THE CARBON BUDGET: ACCORDING TO WHICH PRINCIPLES OF EQUITY?

Determining how to distribute the global carbon budget among countries is probably the most complex value judgement regarding national reduction

---

10 H. Thorgeirsson, 'Objective (Art. 2.1)' in D. Klein et al. (eds), *The Paris Agreement on Climate Change: Analysis and Commentary* (Oxford University Press 2017). The author refers to Art. 2(2) as establishing a general obligation, and a guiding principle for the implementation of all the other provisions in the Agreement; N. Singh Ghaleigh, 'Article 2: Aims, Objectives and Principles' in G. Van Calster and L. Reins (eds), *The Paris Agreement on Climate Change: A Commentary* (Edward Elgar Publishing 2021) p. 81: 'Article 2, and in particular the temperature goal, is not asserted in unequivocal language which might impose an obligation upon a given party.' B. Mayer, 'Temperature Targets and State Obligations on Mitigation of Climate Change' (2021) 33 *Journal of Environmental Law* 585. Mayer argues that the vagueness of the provision 'makes it challenging to translate temperature targets into an emission budget with any degree of precision.'

11 B. Mayer (n. 10). The author underlines that the positivist approach, according to which customary law must be grounded on consistent State practice, is in line with the prevalent doctrine and judiciary practice (p. 6).

12 O. Hoegh-Guldberg, T. Jacob and M. Taylor, 'Impacts of 1.5°C of Global Warming on Natural and Human Systems' in *Global Warming of 1.5°C. An IPCC Special Report on the impacts of global warming of 1.5°C above pre-industrial levels and related global greenhouse gas emission pathways, in the context of strengthening the global response to the threat of climate change, sustainable development, and efforts to eradicate poverty* (IPCC 2018), pp. 237–39.

13 Ibid., p. 255.

14 O. Hoegh-Guldberg, T. Jacob and M. Taylor (n. 12), pp. 229–33, 262–64.

pathways. Political philosophers have been debating the notion of international equity for decades, leading to a co-existence of interpretations and scenarios in the literature.[15] The complexity of such decisions is demonstrated by the fact that, after 30 years of political negotiations, the Parties to the United Nations Framework Convention on Climate Change (UNFCCC) and to the Conference of the Parties (COP) have not yet agreed on the exact meaning and operationalisation of the principle of common but differentiated responsibilities (CBDR). Historically, it can be said that, while developing countries have emphasised the industrialised States' 'historical, moral, and legal responsibility to pay', developed countries have rather seen the principle as 'a pragmatic problem-solving formula based on relative ability to pay'.[16]

Following the normative literature,[17] the Fifth IPCC Assessment Report: Mitigation of Climate Change (AR5 Climate Change: Working Group III 2014) identified five effort-based approaches, i.e. 'responsibility', 'capability', 'equality', 'responsibility-capability-need', and an 'equal cumulative per capita'.[18]

Respectively based on the 'polluter pays' principle and ability to pay principle, the responsibility approach distributes mitigation costs taking into consideration the historical responsibility of industrialised countries,[19] whereas the capability approach considers the different and evolving economic capacities, based on indexes such as a country's gross domestic product (GDP).[20] An egalitarian part of the literature, on the other hand, embraces 'equal-per-capita' emission rights, i.e. implying that every person should have an equal right to emit.[21] Moreover, to avoid imposing unsustainable burdens on populous developing countries,

---

15 H. Shue, 'Global Environment and International Inequality' (1999) 75 *International Affairs* 531; S.M. Gardiner, *Debating Climate Ethics* (Oxford University Press 2016).

16 J. Brunnée and C. Streck, 'The UNFCCC as a Negotiation Forum: Towards Common but More Differentiated Responsibilities' (2013) 13 *Climate Policy* 589, 592; L. Rajamani, 'The Nature, Promise, and Limits of Differential Treatment in the Climate Regime' (2005) 16 *Yearbook of International Environmental Law* 81.

17 N. Höhne, M. den Elzen and D. Escalante, 'Regional GHG Reduction Targets Based on Effort Sharing: A Comparison of Studies' (2014) 14 *Climate Policy* 122.

18 L. Clarke et al., *Climate Change 2014: Mitigation of Climate Change. Contribution of Working Group III to the Fifth Assessment Report of the Intergovernmental Panel on Climate Change* (IPCC 2014). The five approaches are illustrated in depth at pp. 317–19. For an illustration of the application of the five approaches to reduction pathways, see pp. 456–62.

19 Among others, T. Wei et al., 'Developed and Developing World Responsibilities for Historical Climate Change and CO_2 Mitigation' (2012) 109 *Proceedings of the National Academy of Sciences* 12911; L. Meyer, 'Why Historical Emissions Should Count' (2013) 13 *Chicago Journal of International Law* 598.

20 P. Hayes and K.R. Smith (eds), *The Global Greenhouse Regime: Who Pays?: Science, Economics and North-South Politics in the Climate Change Convention* (Earthscan Publications/United Nations University Press 1993); P. Baer, 'Greenhouse Development Rights: A Framework for Climate Protection That Is "More Fair" than Equal per Capita Emissions Rights' in S.M. Gardiner et al. (eds), *Climate Ethics: Essential Readings* (Oxford University Press 2010).

21 M. Grubb, *The Greenhouse Effect: Negotiating Targets* (2nd ed., Royal Institute of International Affairs 1992); A. Agarwal and S. Narain, *Global Warming in an Unequal World: A Case of Environmental Colonialism* (Centre for Society and Environment 1991, reprint in 1996).

some studies propose that the latter reduce their emissions only after their per-capita emissions exceed a certain level (contraction and convergence).[22] A further variation is the 'equal-cumulative-per-capita' approach, which includes historical emissions in the equation, thus narrowing the carbon budget available to developed nations.[23] Finally, the 'equality-capability-need' approach prioritises the interests of poor communities and countries in meeting their basic needs.[24] According to the latter, rich countries should reduce their emissions the most, while other countries' emissions could temporarily increase.

Quite interestingly, in the lack of international consensus on one of those burden-sharing approaches, some have argued that scientists should bear the responsibility to create methods to assess fairness.[25] As a matter of fact, some scholars have crafted different methods to fairly distribute the global carbon budget, mainly referring to the five main approaches identified by the Fifth IPCC Report. Some of their studies have been used by think tanks to show the level of compliance of individual countries with their fair share.[26] However, even if scientists can provide a valuable contribution by translating ethical and legal principles into concrete scenarios, the distribution of the global carbon budget is ultimately a matter of distributive justice that needs to be treated as such.[27]

2.3. CONCLUDING REMARKS

Among other scholars, Stephen Gardiner has expressed the view that climate injustice manifests itself in at least three levels: the international, intergenerational, and ecological dimensions.[28] The essence of climate injustice consists in the

22 A. Meyer, 'Briefing: Contraction and Convergence' (2004) 157 *Proceedings of the Institution of Civil Engineers – Engineering Sustainability* 189.

23 S. Bode, 'Equal Emissions per Capita over Time – A Proposal to Combine Responsibility and Equity of Rights for Post-2012 GHG Emission Entitlement Allocation' (2004) 14 *European Environment* 300.

24 H. Winkler, T. Letete and A. Marquard, 'A South African Approach – Responsibility, Capability and Sustainable Development' in H. Winkler et al. (eds), *Equitable access to sustainable development: contribution to the body of scientific knowledge* (BASIC expert group 2011).

25 P. Lawrence and M. Reder, 'Equity and the Paris Agreement: Legal and Philosophical Perspectives' (2019) 31 *Journal of Environmental Law* 511.

26 H.O. Pörtner and D.C. Roberts, *Climate Change 2022: Impacts, Adaptation, and Vulnerability. Contribution of Working Group II to the Sixth Assessment Report of the Intergovernmental Panel on Climate Change (Summary for Policymakers)* (IPCC 2022), p. 2387.

27 Ibid. Besides noting the existence of different fairness criteria in the literature, the Sixth Assessment Report focuses extensively on the distributional implications of mitigation policies, within and between countries. P.R. Shukla et al., *Climate Change 2022: Mitigation of Climate Change. Contribution of the Working Group III to the Sixth Assessment Report of the Intergovernmental Panel on Climate Change* (IPCC 2022), p. 43.

28 S.M. Gardiner, *A Perfect Moral Storm: The Ethical Tragedy of Climate Change* (Oxford University Press 2011).

fact that those who contributed the least or not at all to climate change will suffer the most severe consequences. While having been caused for the most part by rich countries from the Industrial Revolution onwards, climate change threatens to have its worst effects on the poorest communities, developing economies, future generations and threatened ecosystems, who did not contribute or contributed the least to the problem. Therefore, to craft climate policies according to moral standards requires in the first place to fully consider their larger implications. The analysis conducted in the paragraphs above shows that the design of a national reduction pathway affects all the dimensions of climate justice. Climate policies aiming at the least ambitious targets and ignoring the different responsibility, capacity and needs of global and social actors, while benefiting the least exposed and high-emitting countries in the short term, will produce the most negative and potentially irreversible impacts on the most vulnerable subjects, i.e. the people living in the Global South, future generations and ecosystems at risk of exceeding their tipping points.

3. CLIMATE POLICIES' AMBITION AND FAIRNESS IN CLIMATE LITIGATION BETWEEN LEGAL CREATIVITY AND UNCERTAINTY

The choice of the global temperature goal and the distribution of the global carbon budget has been the subject of legal argumentation in systemic mitigation cases. The present section explains, firstly, how the mentioned issues create legal uncertainty. Secondly, it discusses the creative solutions that plaintiffs have used to overcome them.

3.1. THE TEMPERATURE TARGET: USING RIGHTS TO JUSTIFY AMBITION?

The publication of the IPCC Special Report on 1.5°C in 2018 (SR 1.5°) marked a turning point for climate litigation in Europe. Taking its warnings seriously, many climate lawsuits filed after the SR 1.5° have requested that national policies comply with the 1.5°C target.

Nonetheless, the idea that pursuing the 1.5°C target is necessary to protect the rights of European citizens is to some extent arguable. While the effects of a 2°C scenario will be undoubtedly severe in the Global South and in the Mediterranean area, climate impacts on North and Central European countries appear to be generally milder. Against this argument, one could object that climate change, even at the present temperature increase, is already causing human rights violations in both Global North and Global South countries.[29] If that is true, exceeding the 2°C temperature threshold would violate human rights to a greater extent than exceeding 1.5°C. However, a further counter-argument (see section 4.2) could be that the rights of the citizens living in less exposed and richer countries might not be violated if appropriate adaptation measures are taken. As noted already in the 2001 Third IPCC Assessment Report, a country's resilience to climate change impacts depends primarily upon its social, institutional and economic resources to cope with them.[30]

In the *Klimaatzaak v. Belgium* case, the plaintiffs referred to the indirect impacts of a 2°C-warmer scenario on the political and economic security of Europe and in particular Belgium. Nonetheless, the fact that the alleged risks, such as potential interruptions to the national food supply, will affect Belgian citizens' human rights does not appear self-evident. This is not only true because proving the connection between human rights violations and specific climate change impacts in court might be challenging from the evidentiary perspective.[31] It is also true because, in the case at stake, public policies aiming, for example, to subsidise national agricultural production and promote adaptation might mitigate the impacts of climate change on national food security. Incidentally, Belgium appears to have a strong adaptive capacity concerning other climate change impacts. Recent studies have shown that the country has one of the most advanced planning policies against sea level rise, and that several additional feasible measures might be taken to prevent flooding disasters like the one that occurred in the summer of 2021.[32] Similar remarks have been made with regard to the claim, in the *Urgenda* case, that low-lying regions of the Netherlands might become uninhabitable due to sea level

---

29 Extreme weather events attributed to climate change have also caused multiple casualties in Northern and Central Europe, as for example in the floods that hit Northern Germany in July 2021, or in the 2003 heatwave, which hit urbanised areas in Central Europe more severely. See P.A. Stott, D.A. Stone and M.R. Allen, 'Human Contribution to the European Heatwave of 2003' (2004) 432 *Nature* 610; H. Else, 'Climate Change Implicated in Germany's Deadly Floods' [2021] *Nature* d41586.

30 H.O. Pörtner and D.C. Roberts (n. 26), p. 280. Countries with limited economic resources, low levels of technology, poor information and skills, poor infrastructure, unstable or weak institutions, and inequitable empowerment and access to resources have little capacity to adapt and are highly vulnerable.

31 *Report of the Office of the United Nations High Commissioner for Human Rights on the Relationship between Climate Change and Human Rights*, UN Doc. A/HRC/10/61(2009), para. 70, p. 23. The study notes that 'it is virtually impossible to disentangle the complex causal relationships linking historical greenhouse gas emissions of a particular country with a specific climate change-related effect, let alone with the range of direct and indirect implications for human rights'.

32 S. McEvoy, M. Haasnoot and R. Biesbroek, 'How Are European Countries Planning for Sea Level Rise?' (2021) 203 *Ocean & Coastal Management* 105512; M. Kuebler, 'How Can We Prepare for Extreme Flooding?', *DW* (19 July 2021), https://www.dw.com/en/germany-belgium-floods-climate-crisis-adaptation/a-58318340.

rise if global warming is not stopped to well below 2°C. Namely, an author noted that only in exceptional circumstances would the predicted sea level rise be as threatening as predicted, while in normal circumstances dykes would be sufficient to protect citizens.[33]

Given the indirect, uncertain and comparatively milder effects of climate change in North and Central Europe, and the high capacity to adapt of European countries, it is at least arguable that a 1.5°C scenario would harm the human rights of the current population, if appropriate adaptation measures would be taken. Hence, when concerning least exposed countries, the protection of citizens' human rights might constitute a flawed argument, when used alone, to request more ambitious and possibly very costly climate action.

3.2. THE NATIONAL DISTRIBUTION OF THE CARBON BUDGET: ON THE IMPOSSIBILITY OF ESCAPING ETHICAL CHOICES

When allocating a carbon budget to their respective countries, climate litigators are forced to choose an approach for the distribution of the global carbon budget. As noted in the Sixth IPCC Assessment Report: Mitigation of Climate Change (AR6 Climate Change 2022: Working Group III),[34] national emissions pathways can only be linked to a global long-term temperature goal, according to a distributive, or 'effort-sharing', approach. Furthermore, as argued above, to select any distributive criterion means to make a value judgement.

By contrast, in *Neubauer*, the complainants made the case that to calculate a country's minimum contribution was possible in a morally neutral way, by directly relying on the global pathways to achieve 1.5°C included in the IPCC's SR 1.5°. As noted in the literature,[35] this method represents one of the two approaches to which climate litigants have so far resorted in Europe: the 'global average approach', and 'effort-sharing methodologies'. While claims based on the former explicitly avoid referring to equity-based criteria, those based on the latter generally calculate national carbon budgets according to the effort-sharing approaches identified by the AR5 Climate Change: Working Group III 2014 (cf. section 2.2).

Following the global average approach, in the *Neubauer* case, the claimants defined Germany's fair share as its part of what is globally necessary to keep the temperature increase within 1.5°C.[36] They calculated the country's share

---

33 J. Spier, '"The 'Strongest' Climate Ruling Yet": The Dutch Supreme Court's Urgenda Judgment' (2020) 67 *Netherlands International Law Review* 319.

34 P.R. Shukla (n. 27).

35 L. Maxwell, S. Mead and D. Van Berkel (n. 3), pp. 19–22.

36 *Neubauer et al. v. Germany (unofficial English translation of the complaint)* (n. 6), p. 115.

considering the average between three out of the four global reduction pathways included in SR 1.5°C (P1–P3). As admitted by the complainants, by disregarding both historical emissions and other countries' development rights, such an approach left Germany with a significantly more generous carbon budget compared to the scenarios based on notions of equity.[37] Similarly, other claimants have explicitly avoided referring to equity-based criteria, in order to overcome the separation of powers objection. In *Greenpeace et al. v. Spain*,[38] and in the appeal of the judicial decision in *Klimaatzaak*,[39] the claimants differentiated the concepts of 'minimum' and 'fair' shares, and on that basis requested the courts to only impose on the respective governments their minimum obligations, according to the global average or similar approaches.

On the other hand, in *A Sud et al. v. Italy*, the claimants relied on an *ad hoc* report based on an effort-sharing methodology.[40] The report calculated Italy's fair share based on the application of the five criteria recognised in the AR4 Climate Change 2014.[41] Referring to a previous study by Höhne et al., the report identified five categories of effort-sharing approaches, based on three equity principles: responsibility, capability and equality. The authors thus calculated a fair share range by aggregating the different criteria, and then narrowed it down based on the objective of achieving the 1.5°C target with a probability of at least 50%.[42] The study adjusted the fair share range to the consideration that, if all States were to choose the minimum end of the range, the 1.5°C target would be missed.[43] A similar approach was also used in the *Duarte v. Austria et al.* case (also known as the *Young Portuguese Children* case), where the claimants referred to the fair share studies provided by Climate Action Tracker.[44]

---

37 Ibid., p. 118.

38 *Greenpeace v. Spain I (complaint)* [2020] Supreme Court (Third Section) Rec. 2/265/2020, p. 104.

39 *Klimaatzaak v. Belgium (appeal)*, pp. 35–36.

40 G. Guanti et al., *Italy's Climate Targets and Policies in Relation to the Paris Agreement and Global Equity Considerations* (Climate Analytics 2021).

41 K. Akimoto et al., 'Assessing Transformation Pathways' in *Climate Change 2014: Mitigation of Climate Change. Contribution of Working Group III to the Fifth Assessment Report of the Intergovernmental Panel on Climate Change* (Cambridge University Press 2014), p. 457. The report refers to six categories: 'responsibility', 'capability', 'equality', 'responsibility, capability and need', 'equal cumulative per capita emissions', 'staged approaches', and 'equal marginal abatement costs'. However, the report does not quantify emission scenarios based on 'responsibility', i.e. only considering the country's historical responsibilities. For this reason, many following studies refer to the 'five effort-sharing categories' presented in the IPCC.

42 Ibid., p. 3. Grandfathering (also known as constant emissions ratio) is a 'status-quo approach that allocates equal emission mitigation rates to all countries'.

43 Y. Robiou du Pont and M. Meinshausen, 'Warming Assessment of the Bottom-up Paris Agreement Emissions Pledges' (2018) 9 *Nature Communications* 4810, p. 3. The authors show that if all countries were to follow the least-stringent equity approach, global warming would reach a temperature increase between 2 and 2.3°C, and thus would exceed the Paris Agreement objective.

44 *Duarte Agostinho and Others v. Portugal and 32 Other States* (pending) European Court of Human Rights no. 39371/20.

Generally, European climate litigators have opted to use the global average approach, or else request that their governments comply with commitments and benchmarks set down in national laws.[45] This is because, following *Urgenda*, multiple litigators have pushed forward the idea that courts are allowed to review climate policies to the extent that they violate a 'minimum reasonableness standard'.[46] However, while clear and easily enforceable by courts, such standards are also inadequate from a climate justice perspective. The global average approach, applying the same reduction rate to all countries, resembles the grandfathering approach, i.e. 'a status quo approach that allocates equal emission rates to all countries',[47] based on the idea that 'prior emissions increase the entitlement to future emissions'.[48] Furthermore, while widely considered unjust, and 'not openly supported by any country, [the grandfathering approach] implicitly matches many developed countries' targets.'[49] In this context, the judicial endorsement of the global average approach risks providing a legal justification to the maintenance of insufficient and unjust climate pledges.

4. LIMITS OF RIGHTS-BASED LITIGATION IN DEFINING FAIR AND AMBITIOUS CLIMATE POLICIES

So far, European national courts have asserted their competence to review national reduction pathways, when they are based on national legislation and threaten to interfere with constitutional and human rights. In three climate cases, national courts have found the respective national climate policies to be illegitimate based on human rights standards. In the *Urgenda* and *Klimaatzaak* cases, the respective courts found that the Dutch and Belgian States had violated their positive duties under the European Convention of Human Rights, by adopting inadequate climate policies. In the *Neubauer* case, the Constitutional Court of Germany found that the State had interfered with the constitutional freedoms of the generations living after 2030, by imposing on them a disproportionate burden to mitigate climate change. While the novelty and importance of such arguments have been emphasised elsewhere in the literature,[50] the present section aims to show, through the example of the three decisions, that rights-based arguments may be partially ill-suited to achieve climate justice in its international, intergenerational and ecological dimensions.

45 *Friends of the Irish Environment v. Ireland* [2019] High Court of Ireland 793/2017; *Notre Affaire à Tous v. France* [2021] Tribunal Administratif de Paris n° 1904967, 1904968, 1904972, 1904976/4-1.

46 L. Maxwell, S. Mead and D. Van Berkel (n. 3).

47 Y. Robiou du Pont and M. Meinshausen (n. 42).

48 C. Knight, 'What Is Grandfathering?' (2013) 22 *Environmental Politics* 410.

49 Y. Robiou du Pont and M. Meinshausen (n. 42).

50 See, among others, J. Peel, H. Osofsky and M. Hari, 'A rights turn in climate change litigation?' (2018) 7(1) *Transnational Environmental Law* 37.

4.1. HUMAN RIGHTS REVIEW AND THE IDEA OF THE 'MINIMUM'

In *Urgenda*, the Dutch Court of Appeals turned the legal basis from tort law to a rights-based one, by doing so influencing the scope of its judicial review. Following the European Court of Human Rights' practice, the Court of Appeals considered that, due to the broad margin of appreciation to be left to the government on environmental matters, its role was limited to make sure that the minimum measures to protect fundamental rights had been taken (i.e. 'minimum reasonableness standard').[51] As noted by Burgers, '"the minimum principle" aims to make sure that a minimum level of human rights protection is guaranteed, while preserving the separation of powers'.[52] Despite being based on constitutional law rather than on human rights law, the standard of judicial review applied by the German Federal Constitutional Court was similar. In assessing whether the government had fulfilled its duty to protect the right to life (Article 2), the Court applied the *Untermaßverbot* principle. Following the latter, the Court's role is limited to making sure that the government has not adopted 'wholly inappropriate or unsuitable measures' to protect the right at stake. A similar judicial review structure was adopted in *Greenpeace Nordic Association v. Norway*, where the Court considered that, to set aside a law, the legislative body must have grossly disregarded its duties under Article 112 of the Norwegian Constitution.[53]

Nonetheless, while providing a standard against which national policies can be assessed, the mere compliance with the minimum standard will be insufficient to ensure sufficient climate protection. Recent studies have shown that if all countries were to only deliver their minimum fair share, total emissions would be higher than required to deliver the temperature target between 1.5°C and well below 2°C.[54] More precisely, a 2018 study noted that 'systematic court decisions that governments must follow the least-ambitious end of an equity range would be insufficient to achieve the Paris Agreement'.[55]

---

51 L. Maxwell, S. Mead and D. Van Berkel (n. 3).

52 L. Burgers, 'The Minimum Principle', *Völkerrechtsblog* (2022), https://intr2dok.vifa-recht.de/receive/mir_mods_00011745.

53 P. Minnerop, 'In Search of a Fair Share: Article 112 Norwegian Constitution, International Law and an Emerging Inter-Jurisdictional Discourse in Climate Litigation' [2020] *SSRN Electronic Journal* 879.

54 Y. Robiou du Pont and M. Meinshausen (n. 42); L. Rajamani et al., 'National "Fair Shares" in Reducing Greenhouse Gas Emissions within the Principled Framework of International Environmental Law' (2021) 21 *Climate Policy* 983.

55 Y. Robiou du Pont et al., 'Equitable Mitigation to Achieve the Paris Agreement Goals' (2017) 7 *Nature Climate Change* 38, p. 2.

4.2. THE ADAPTABILITY ARGUMENT AND THE ANTHROPOCENTRISM OF HUMAN RIGHTS

In *Neubauer*, the claimants argued that sticking to the 1.5°C target was necessary to protect their rights to life, property and a dignified future. On the other hand, the Court considered that only aiming for the Paris Agreement targets, i.e. between well below 2°C and preferably 1.5°C, might have been sufficient to protect human life and health. It added that the State might be able to protect its citizens from climate-related risks concerning their human health.[56] Interestingly, while recognising the importance of sticking to 1.5° in order not to exceed the global tipping points, and thus to avoid climate instability, the Court concluded that the constitutional rights to life and health might not be the appropriate tool to protect 'a climate that is favourable to the environment, animals and humans'.[57]

Regarding the claim that crossing tipping points violated their fundamental right to a dignified future, the Court denied that the government's action was bound to create an apocalyptic future in which free agency would be made impossible by adverse environmental conditions.[58] Following its jurisprudence on the right to dignity, it argued that a violation of the right to a dignified future could have only taken place in a scenario where adaptation measures had become insufficient to protect life, physical integrity, property and the other prerequisites of the German citizens' social, cultural and political life.[59] Thus, the German Federal Constitutional Court concluded that aiming for 1.5°C is not an absolute necessity under constitutional law. Conversely, aiming for the Paris Agreement targets would be sufficient, if the legislative and executive branches would take consistent action to achieve them, and climate impacts in Germany could be alleviated through adaptation.

In short, in the absence of a constitutional right to a healthy or balanced environment, other human rights might be a flawed instrument for the purpose of enhancing environmental protection. This is firstly because the interest to respect planetary boundaries involves a different and wider range of interests

---

56 *Neubauer et al. v. Germany* (n. 6), para. 167. 'It is not evident that the health consequences arising from 2°C global warming and from the associated climate change in Germany could not be alleviated by supplementary adaptation measures in a manner that would be sufficient under constitutional law.'

57 Ibid., para. 163.

58 *Neubauer et al. v. Germany (unofficial English translation of the complaint)* (n. 6). Conversely, the normative interest to avoid tipping points was arguably subsumed under the State's objective to duty to climate protection (Art. 20a). Following the latter, the Court argued that the State's discretion in defining the carbon budget finds a limit when there are even mere indications pointing to the possibility of serious or severe impairments to the environment, as long as they are sufficiently reliable (para. 229).

59 *Neubauer et al. v. Germany* (n. 6), para. 114.

than human ones, for example the protection of human health. Secondly, given that in the German and in other European constitutions,[60] the protection of the natural foundations of life, and thus of climate stability, constitutes a political objective rather than a right, the State enjoys a broader discretion, so long as it guarantees a minimum level of protection of the affected rights.

4.3. THE AMBIGUOUS IMPLICATIONS OF EXTRATERRITORIALITY IN EUROPEAN HUMAN RIGHTS AND CONSTITUTIONAL LAW

A further limit to a fair determination of the national reduction pathways consists in the territoriality of human rights obligations. Although the transboundary validity of human rights obligations is increasingly recognised by international institutions in the context of climate change,[61] extraterritoriality still represents a controversial legal subject in international human rights law. In contrast with the international case law, expressed for example in the recent Advisory Opinion OC-23/17 of the Inter-American Court of Human Rights,[62] at the European level, the picture is more ambiguous.[63] Most recently, the European Court of Human Rights has adopted a conservative interpretation of the notion of jurisdiction in *Georgia v. Russia*,[64] raising concerns of a judicial retrogression compared to the international trends.[65]

In *Urgenda*, the extraterritoriality issue emerged in connection with the foundation's standing, as well as with the scope of the government's obligations. The District Court of The Hague noted that the association's statutory goal to strive for a sustainable society had an inherent international dimension.[66] Thus,

---

60 M. Liselot and L. Reins, 'Local Liability for Global Consequences? Climate Change Litigation in Belgium' in *Comparative Climate Change Litigation: Beyond the Usual Suspects* (Springer 2021).

61 N. Jauer, 'Two Milestones in Favour of the Environment in Just a Few Days?', *Völkerrechtsblog* (2021), https://intr2dok.vifa-recht.de/receive/mir_mods_00011348.

62 Advisory Opinion OC-23/17 (Inter-American Court of Human Rights).

63 L. Raible, 'Extraterritoriality between a Rock and Hard Place' (2021) 82 *Questions of International Law* 7.

64 *Georgia v. Russia* [2021] European Court of Human Rights no. 38263/08. Different scholars have considered the decision as being arbitrary or flawed from a legal perspective, while clearly motivated by political considerations. In the case, the Court concluded that Russia was not bound to its obligations under the European Convention with regard to the military acts that occurred during the active hostilities in Georgia, since they took place in a 'context of chaos'.

65 M. Milanovic, 'Georgia v. Russia No. 2: The European Court's Resurrection of Bankovic in Contexts of Chaos', *EJIL:Talk!* (25 January 2021), https://www.ejiltalk.org/georgia-v-russia-no-2-the-european-courts-resurrection-of-bankovic-in-the-contexts-of-chaos/. L. Raible (n. 63), pp. 21–24.

66 *Urgenda v. Netherlands* [2015] The Hague District Court C/09/456689, para. 4.7. 'The interests Urgenda wants to defend appear to be – from its objective formulated in its by-laws – primarily but not solely Dutch interests. Moreover, the term "sustainable society" has an inherent

the court recognised the Urgenda foundation's standing to represent people living outside of the Netherlands, besides Dutch nationals and future generations. However, the courts of second and last instance only confirmed the association's standing with regard to the present generations living in the Netherlands.[67] Furthermore, in *Milieudefensie v. Shell*, the same District Court of The Hague denied extraterritorial standing to the association, revealing an unresolved legal ambiguity around the issue.[68]

In *Neubauer*, the German Federal Constitutional Court admitted that the German State has responsibility for the effects of its GHG emissions abroad. Despite its limitations, the Court's position on extraterritoriality has been welcomed in the literature as a positive, and hopefully incremental, legal change.[69] Nonetheless, when compared against international trends, the Court's reasoning presents some level of conservatism, even more so considering that it concerned German citizens living abroad, rather than third-country nationals.[70] The Court distinguished between the State's negative and protective duties, noting that the exact content of the latter depends on the specific circumstances of the case.[71] Thus, it considered that, due to its limited capacity to take adaptation measures in foreign countries, and the broad margin of discretion generally assigned to the State concerning protective and preventive duties, Germany had not violated its obligations vis-à-vis its citizens living in Bangladesh and Nepal.[72]

In *Greenpeace Arctic v. Norway*,[73] the Norwegian Supreme Court, while recognising the extraterritorial consequences of Norway's exploration policies, considered that the State had not violated its constitutional duties to protect the right to a healthy environment (Article 112).[74] Considering the calculation

---

international (and global) dimension. As based on its by-laws Urgenda is defending the interest of a "sustainable society", it actually protects an interest that by its nature crosses national borders.'

67 *Urgenda v. Netherlands* [2018] The Hague Court of Appeal 200.178.245/01; *Urgenda v. Netherlands* [2019] Hoge Raad 19/00135, para. 2.3.2.

68 L. Burgers (n. 52).

69 P. Minnerop (n. 53); J. Bäumler, 'Sustainable Development Made Justiciable: The German Constitutional Court's Climate Ruling on Intra- and Inter-Generational Equity', *EJIL:Talk!* (8 June 2021), https://www.ejiltalk.org/sustainable-development-made-justiciable-the-german-constitutional-courts-climate-ruling-on-intra-and-inter-generational-equity/; J. Mührel, 'All That Glitters Is Not Gold', *Völkerrechtsblog* (2021), https://intr2dok.vifa-recht.de/receive/mir_mods_00010533.

70 L. Raible (n. 63). Namely, when considering that nationality has been used as a criterion to establish the extraterritorial validity of human rights obligation in two recent communications by the Committee on the Human Rights of the Child. See pp. 13–16.

71 *Neubauer et al. v. Germany* (n. 6), paras 176–77.

72 Ibid., paras 178–81.

73 *Greenpeace Nordic Ass'n v. Ministry of Petroleum and Energy (People v. Arctic Oil)* (Supreme Court of Norway).

74 P. Minnerop (n. 53), p. 871.

of future emissions outside of the national territory to be too uncertain, the Court ultimately upheld the decision authorising the excavation activities in the Barents Sea.[75]

The three cases show that, while courts are slowly starting to recognise the extraterritorial validity of the right to be protected from climate change, the exact implications for States' obligations remain unclear or dissatisfactory. Thus, even evolutive interpretations of human rights and constitutional law do not yet offer the tools to modify or annul climate policies when they are inadequate to protect the rights of vulnerable people in foreign countries. Conversely, as shown by the *Neubauer* case, the minimum approach, supported by constitutional and human rights law, can even provide a sound legal justification for climate policies that disregard completely the rights to development and basic needs of the people living in Global South countries.

5. LEGAL PATHWAYS TO OVERCOME THE LIMITS OF RIGHTS-BASED LITIGATION

The previous section illustrated the existence of a mission dissonance in rights-based climate change litigation. Namely, it pointed out that, while aiming to protect human rights from the effects of climate change and safeguard climate stability as far as possible, human rights litigation might contribute to setting benchmarks that will be insufficient to protect the rights of those most affected by climate change. Secondly, human rights litigation in Europe, having its basis in existing individual rights, might not be adequate yet to safeguard against the exceedance of global tipping points, and thus against severe climate instability. The present section proposes two legal pathways that might help the judiciary to directly tackle climate justice issues, and possibly align climate policies with climate justice standards.

5.1. TAKING EQUITY SERIOUSLY: JUSTIFYING THE FAIRNESS OF NATIONAL MITIGATION PATHWAYS ACCORDING TO THE BEST AVAILABLE SCIENCE AND INTERNATIONAL LAW PRINCIPLES

As already noted, there is not a strong normative consensus nor a legally valid agreement on the exact meaning of the principle of common but differentiated responsibilities. Nonetheless, recently scholars have come to agree on certain benchmarks and methodologies to assess the 'fairness' of mitigation policies and, more specifically, of nationally determined contributions (NDCs).

---

75 *Greenpeace Nordic* (n. 73), para. 168.

On the one hand, despite the lack of agreement on one distributive approach, there is some agreement, among normative scholars, that developed countries should take the lead on climate change.[76] On a similar note, scholars have noted that in *Urgenda*, the Dutch Supreme Court identified the 'leadership role' of developed countries as the normative core of the principle of common but differentiated responsibilities.[77]

On the other hand, several studies have started assessing the compatibility of NDCs with the Paris Agreement targets and proposing their own calculations of national fair shares, based on the most widely recognised interpretations of equity in the literature. If some studies have assessed the countries' NDCs against the average of all the effort-sharing principles published, including cost-effectiveness,[78] others consider the different criteria individually.[79] The two methodologies have been used, respectively, by Climate Action Tracker and the Paris Equity Check project.[80] More recently, a study published by Rajamani and other scholars went a step further, as it calculated and then narrowed down States' fair share ranges according to international environmental law principles.[81] The authors took into account that if all States only complied with the minimum end of the fair share, that would not be sufficient to achieve the global temperature objectives, and thus avoid transboundary harm. Thus, based on the principle of harm prevention and precaution, they narrowed down the fair share to a range that would still make it possible to collectively achieve the global temperature objectives. In *A Sud et al. v. Italy*, a systemic mitigation case arguing the insufficiency of Italy's mitigation policies, the plaintiffs applied a similar methodology to calculate the national fair share. As in the study by Rajamani et al., the fair share was calculated by aggregating the different equity approaches found in the literature, and then narrowed down taking into consideration the final temperature goals. In particular, the study appended to the case simulated a situation in which all countries adopted the same level of ambition.[82]

---

76 S.M. Gardiner (n. 14), p. 100.

77 P. Galvão Ferreira, '"Common But Differentiated Responsibilities" in the National Courts: Lessons from *Urgenda* v. *The Netherlands*' (2016) 5 *Transnational Environmental Law* 329, 347–49. *Urgenda v. Netherlands* [2019] Hoge Raad 19/00135. See para. 4.57: 'The principle of fairness also expresses that industrialized countries have to take the lead in combating climate change and its negative impact. The justification for this, lies first and foremost in the fact that from an historical perspective the current industrialized countries are main causes of the current high greenhouse gas concentration in the atmosphere and that these countries also benefited from the use of fossil fuels, in the form of economic growth and prosperity'.

78 N. Höhne et al., 'Assessing the Ambition of Post-2020 Climate Targets: A Comprehensive Framework' (2018) 18 *Climate Policy* 425.

79 Y. Robiou du Pont et al. (n. 55).

80 *Urgenda v. Netherlands* [2019] Hoge Raad 19/00135; http://paris-equity-check.org/multi-equity-map.html#.

81 L. Rajamani et al. (n. 54).

82 G. Guanti et al. (n. 40), pp. 25–26.

The three illustrated methodologies have recently been included in the Sixth IPCC Assessment Report.[83] It needs to be pointed out that, given the demandingness and scope of the measures recommended therein, domestic courts lack the democratic mandate to order national governments to directly implement them. Nonetheless, their recognition in the latest IPCC Report, and thus their status as the best available science, makes it at least plausible that courts will refer to such standards as an interpretative aid in judicial reviews.

In *Urgenda*, the Supreme Court considered that the positive duties under Articles 2 and 8 ECHR also imply that the government has an obligation to show that the policy pursued meets the State's own duties.[84] Such requirements, in *Urgenda*, were identified in the compliance with (at least) the lower end of the State's fair share. Similar justifications have been required in other climate decisions, where courts asked the respective governments to justify their planned policies, by setting a specific pathway consistent with the selected carbon budgets. In *Neubauer*, even denying that the State has an autonomous obligation to justify its legislative action, the Constitutional Court required it to define a carbon budget that would respect the rights of the people living after 2030.[85] Furthermore, in *Friends of the Earth v. Ireland*, as well as in *Notre Affaire à Tous v. France*,[86] the Irish and French courts ordered the government to specify and disclose the measures they planned to adopt, in order to comply with their own legislative targets.

In a similar way, national courts could ask governments to disclose how they intend to meet the fairness criteria in their mitigation policies, in light of the internationally recognised normative and scientific standards. Thus, if in *Urgenda* the government was only obliged to prove that its contribution was above the lower limit of its fair share, following the most recent climate science, national governments will have been bound to much more ambitious standards, to realistically aim towards the Paris Agreement objectives. The Italian case, in which, following effort-sharing methodologies, the complainants asked for a 91% reduction of the national GHG targets by 2030, provides a good example.

Ultimately, if courts were to take equity seriously, and apply the effort-sharing methodologies according to international environmental law principles, they would find themselves in the uncomfortable and arguably undemocratic position of imposing radical and immediate reduction measures on the population.

---

83 P.R. Shukla et al. (n. 27), p. 616.

84 *Urgenda v. Netherlands* [2019] Hoge Raad 19/00135, para. 6.5.

85 As noted in the literature, 'the Court did not require the legislature to offer any reasons beyond meeting the substantive requirements of fundamental freedoms under the German Constitution.' C. Eckes, 'Separation of Powers in Climate Cases', *Verfassungsblog: On Matters Constitutional* (2021), https://intr2dok.vifa-recht.de/receive/mir_mods_00010591.

86 *Friends of the Irish Environment v. Ireland* [2020] Supreme Court of Ireland 205/19, paras 6.20, 6.41; *Notre Affaire à Tous v. France* [2021] Tribunal Administratif de Paris n° 1904967, 1904968, 1904972, 1904976/4-1, para. 39.

Considering that exceeding the fair share will be politically unavoidable, one could imagine that, in a dialogic spirit, courts could request governments to provide explanations for how they plan to compensate for their excessive territorial emissions, for example by cutting emissions abroad, or providing funds for mitigation measures in other countries.[87]

5.2. VALUE FORMALISM AND ECO-PROPORTIONALITY: DIRECTLY BALANCING HUMAN AND ECOLOGICAL INTERESTS AGAINST ONE ANOTHER

National courts, particularly in rights-based cases, have limited powers and tools to navigate the complex normative dimensions of national mitigation policies. Such limits are partly due to the separation of powers doctrine, namely to the idea that ethical questions should be left to the political and legislative domain only. Partly, they have to do with the very structure and function of rights and with their judicial review. Human rights, being anthropocentric, territorial and, at least in their European interpretations,[88] bound to the individual sphere, might be an inadequate tool for reviewing policies responsible for transnational, ecological and diffuse harms. Furthermore, when assessing climate policies' compatibility with rights, courts have restricted themselves to verifying their compliance with the minimum reasonableness standard.

This section proposes a scenario in which courts resort to the proportionality analysis to balance against one another the wide spectrum of interests involved in climate change policies. Namely, the interest to emit GHG emissions might be balanced directly against the human and more-than-human interest to preserve climate stability. The proportionality principle, providing a solid logical framework to assess and 'measure' values,[89] offers a valid argument against the separation of powers doctrine, particularly with the argument that courts should not deal with ethical questions to avoid arbitrariness. Furthermore, it provides a tool to review climate policies beyond their minimum reasonableness.

---

87 See L. Rajamani et al. (n. 54), p. 1000: 'If their fair share is not reachable with domestic emissions, these states would need to support others to reduce their emissions to make their fair share contribution.'

88 F. Francioni, 'International Human Rights in an Environmental Horizon' (2010) 21 *European Journal of International Law* 41. The author distinguishes between an individualistic and anthropocentric, and a more communitarian and eco-centric approach to the protection of human rights in relation to the environment.

89 M. Hailbronner, 'Rethinking the Rise of the German Constitutional Court: From Anti-Nazism to Value Formalism' (2014) 12 *International Journal of Constitutional Law* 626. The author refers to value formalism as a particular style of jurisprudence reconciling transformative constitutionalism with a hierarchical idea of authority. According to the author, value formalism would offer the tools for a flexible interpretation of the law while 'conveying an illusion of legal certainty and judicial determinacy.' See p. 647.

Following an ecological approach to the law, one could imagine a scenario in which the proportionality analysis is oriented towards eco-centric interests, such as the interest in climate stability. Following the framework proposed by Gerd Winter,[90] the 'eco-proportionality' analysis would aim to control the extent to which society at large intrudes on nature. In that framework, citizens would not be conceived of only as rights holders, but also as duty bearers towards nature. Furthermore, environmental protection would be considered a separate interest to be balanced against broader societal goals, including those of the State, individual citizens and businesses.

Reframed in this way, the proportionality test may allow an assessment of whether the interference with the interest in climate stability is justified in light of competing societal interests.[91] Furthermore, national reduction pathways could be considered as policies aiming to distribute a socially useful but stranded resource, i.e. CO_2 emissions, among different people in time and space. Thus, when carrying out their review, courts would have to ensure that the social goal of guaranteeing the fundamental freedoms associated with emitting CO_2 does not override to a disproportionate extent the interest in climate stability.

Generally, proportionality analysis involves the assessment of the legitimacy, necessity and proportionality *stricto sensu* of a public measure.[92] In an ecological approach, to be legitimate, a societal goal has to be 'understandable in view of the ever-growing scarcity of natural resources'.[93] In that sense, one could imagine that reduction policies that do not sustainably allocate CO_2 emissions over time and space could be assessed as illegitimate. Given the scarcity of the global GHG budget, such an approach might require the State to prove that the allocation of CO_2 to a country or to a 'generation' does not infringe other countries and generations' fundamental freedoms.

Secondly, following the necessity test, courts may have to assess whether the reduction policy at stake could be replaced by an alternative one that is less intrusive on climate stability. Given the political leeway to choose a reduction target between 1.5°C and 2°C, the necessity test might imply a preference for the most ambitious reduction pathways, to the extent that they are equally economically feasible. As the exceedance of tipping points will be more likely at a global warming level above 1.5°C,[94] most ambitious reduction pathways would be less intrusive on climate stability. Thirdly, the proportionality test *stricto sensu*

90 G. Winter, 'Ecological Proportionality: An Emerging Principle of Law for Nature?' in C. Voigt (ed.), *Rule of Law for Nature* (Cambridge University Press 2013).

91 J. Rockström et al., 'Planetary Boundaries: Exploring the Safe Operating Space for Humanity' (2009) 14 *Ecology and Society* article 32. Planetary boundaries have been described as the Earth system's limits in guaranteeing a 'safe operating space for humanity to live on Earth.'

92 R. Alexy, 'Constitutional Rights and Proportionality' [2014] *Revus* 5165.

93 G. Winter (n. 90), p. 115.

94 Ibid.

might guide courts in assessing whether a reduction pathway does not infringe to a disproportionate extent on climate stability, given the social importance of certain carbon-intensive activities. This last test might help in evaluating how specific climate policies affect different groups for whom reduction policies may be either too slow or too fast, such as future generations or workers in carbon-dependent sectors and economies. Regarding the latter, scholars have pointed out that, to aim towards the 1.5°C target, a rapid phase-out of fossil fuels will be unavoidable in both developed and developing countries.[95] In this scenario, balancing climate stability with the threatened fundamental freedoms might mean aiming to make sure that the mitigation costs are not transferred to poor developing countries, without the provision of financial assistance, or to affected workers, without adequate welfare and labour policies helping the transition.

6. CONCLUSION

The first section of this chapter showed that, even when based on the best available science, the definition of a national reduction pathway is never a purely scientific matter. Indeed, the definition of a long-term temperature goal and the choice of an approach to distribute CO_2 emissions imply making choices with moral implications for both human and more-than-human interests. Accordingly, the form taken by national reduction pathways will change depending on the importance attributed to the interests not to exceed tipping points, or not to disproportionately harm poor people in the most climate-vulnerable countries, as well as on the weight given to the interests of future vis-à-vis present generations. Against this background, rights-based climate litigation in Europe has increasingly been used to push governments to replace existing climate policies with more responsible, ambitious and equitable ones. However, as shown in the second and third sections, human rights strategies might not always be an appropriate or effective tool to enhance climate justice. In fact, when used as a main legal basis for the claim, they might lead to sometimes flawed or even counterproductive legal strategies. On the one hand, the human rights implications of climate change in Europe might be an insufficient argument to compel governments to enhance their mitigation plans. On the other hand, human rights obligations might prove ineffective because, by only requiring a minimum standard of protection, they might provide a legal justification to insufficient climate pledges. Finally, the anthropocentric and often territorial interpretation of human rights seems to hinder courts from fully considering the normative interests of those who are most vulnerable to climate change. Given

---

95 G. Muttitt and S. Kartha, 'Equity, Climate Justice and Fossil Fuel Extraction: Principles for a Managed Phase Out' (2020) 20 *Climate Policy* 1024, 1033.

such limits, the last section of this chapter has illustrated two legal pathways that might support judges in navigating climate justice issues in mitigation cases. Respectively, fair share calculations based on equity standards and international environmental law, and an ecological approach to the proportionality principle might serve as an appropriate reference or as a methodology for judges willing to enter into the normative merits of national mitigation policies.

STATE OBLIGATIONS TO REDUCE CARBON EMISSIONS

Using their 'Carbon Reduction Potential' Instead of Territorial Emissions as a Yardstick

Jannis KRÜßMANN*

1. INTRODUCTION

In times of rapidly increasing climate change, not only do parliaments and governments have to play their part in combating the emerging crisis, but also

* The author wants to express his thanks to Martje Köppen and Frida Mühlhoff for their helpful comments and insights. This chapter is in parts based on ideas first expressed in a

courts: the number of climate change-related cases is growing worldwide.[1] Since climate change is a global problem that requires a global solution, it is of the utmost importance to assess internationally effective carbon reduction ambitions of nation-States as well as companies. Many national courts in recent years seem to have been well aware of the problem that their respective States cannot stop climate change on their own, but still acknowledge that this does not release them from any reduction obligations. This is an important first step towards internationally minded climate protection by States. Nevertheless, most courts struggle in finding an appropriate yardstick for State obligations beyond national borders. Apparently, this is not necessarily the case when assessing *corporate* reduction obligations, where indirect Scope 3 emissions – occurring anywhere in the supply chain of a product – can already be included, such as in the *Milieudefensie* case.

While most national climate protection policies as well as courts focus in their assessments only on territorial State emissions, this chapter attempts to highlight the role of indirect 'imported' emissions at State level. By including them in national policies, the national impact area increases substantially and reflects the true potential of national climate protection measures in enforcing international climate action.

Therefore, instead of mitigation targets for carbon emissions or even carbon budgets, the perspective of a 'carbon reduction potential' as a yardstick is preferable when assessing State obligations for climate protection. In the following, the author shows – guided by three landmark recent decisions in Europe – why the foundation for this 'carbon reduction potential' has in fact already been laid out and what advantages and implications this may have.

2. STATE'S NATIONAL RESPONSIBILITIES ACCORDING TO THE HOGE RAAD AND BVERFG

On 20 December 2019, the Dutch Supreme Court (Hoge Raad) ruled in a landmark decision in *Urgenda et al. v. The Netherlands* that the State had to reduce its carbon emissions more rapidly. The Hoge Raad laid out in detail the dangerous consequences of climate change, its global dimension, international agreements, and what State obligations regarding carbon emission reduction derive from that.

The German Federal Constitutional Court (BVerfG) ruled on 24 March 2021 in *Neubauer et al. v. Germany* that the German Federal Climate Protection Act

---

blog post by the same author: J. KRÜSSMANN, 'Das Bundesverfassungsgericht betrachtet die falschen CO2-Emissionen', JuWissBlog No. 100/2021 of 11 November 2021, https://www.juwiss.de/100-2021/.

[1] http://climatecasechart.com/climate-change-litigation/non-us-climate-change-litigation/.

was in breach of the German Basic Law (Grundgesetz, GG). This was due to the fact that its carbon emission reduction pathway violated the freedom of future generations by shifting most of the reduction obligations disproportionally into the future. The Court also emphasised the international dimension of climate change and demanded that the legislator act internationally upon climate change.

Finally, on 26 May 2021, The Hague District Court (Rechtbank Den Haag) rendered its judgment in *Milieudefensie et al. v. Royal Dutch Shell plc*, ordering Royal Dutch Shell (RDS) to reduce its direct and indirect carbon emissions (Scope 1, 2 and 3) by 45% by 2030 relative to 2010. According to the Court, this was due to a violation of the unwritten standard of care deriving from Article 6:162 of the Dutch Civil Code. In the meantime, RDS has lodged an appeal.

Both the Hoge Raad in *Urgenda v. The Netherlands* and the BVerfG in *Neubauer v. Germany* highlighted that climate change is a problem that needs to be solved internationally. Even though neither State can do so on its own, this does not release them from their individual national responsibility.

2.1. TERRITORIAL EMISSIONS AS A YARDSTICK FOR STATES

First of all, it has to be made clear that whenever either of the Courts addressed the national carbon reduction obligation, this only encompassed the respective national *territorial* emissions: territorial emissions are those that occur on the territory of the State directly.[2] They do not include those emissions that are caused during the production of goods in foreign countries, even if these goods are then imported and used in the respective State. The implications of this approach become clear when considering an example. Following this territorial approach, technically, a (small) country could reduce its territorial emissions radically by replacing its production with carbon-intensive imports (goods, energy, etc.) from abroad. This way, there would be next to no carbon emissions occurring from its national territory. In return, the emissions of other (surrounding) States would increase by the same amount.

In light of these explanations, it seems questionable to what extent these territorial emissions – which can be deceptive and easily manipulated – can even be an appropriate measure for a State's reduction obligations. Nevertheless, the Hoge Raad stated several times explicitly that its decision, as well as the whole dispute, is only about territorial emissions.[3]

On the other hand, the BVerfG referred in its argumentation mostly to a global carbon budget calculated by the Intergovernmental Panel on Climate Change

2 For a thorough overview: https://ourworldindata.org/consumption-based-co2.

3 *Urgenda*, paras 2.3.2, 5.6.3, 5.7.7, 6.1, 6.3.

(IPCC) to limit global warming to 1.5°C or 2°C.[4] From this global carbon budget, the German Advisory Council on the Environment (Sachverständigenrat für Umweltfragen der Bundesregierung, SRU) derived a national carbon budget for Germany.[5] The SRU did so by using a per-capita approach and simultaneously stated that it only focused on territorial emissions for Germany.[6]

Furthermore, the German Federal Climate Protection Act (Klimaschutzgesetz, KSG) covers only territorial emissions, as §1 KSG mentions as the goal of 'ensuring achievement of the national climate targets'.[7] These national climate targets are specified in Annex 2 KSG, 'Permissible annual emission budgets for the years 2020 to 2030', but according to numbers from the German Environment Agency (Umweltbundesamt, UBA), these targets only cover territorial emissions from Germany.[8]

As a result, the territorial approach from both the advisory council and the climate protection act was adopted by the BVerfG. But unlike its Dutch equivalent, the German Federal Constitutional Court at least proved to be aware of the fact that there would be other ways to assess States' reduction possibilities.[9] However, that does not change the fact that the BVerfG's use of a national carbon budget in the end only included territorial emissions.

2.2. STATE'S TERRITORIAL CARBON REDUCTION OBLIGATIONS

According to the Hoge Raad, 'the Netherlands are obliged to do "its part" in order to prevent dangerous climate change, even if it is a global problem'.[10] The Court also referred to the United Nations Framework Convention on Climate Change as well as Article 3 of the Paris Agreement to support its argument that every country will have to do what is necessary pursuant to the principle of partial responsibility.[11] At the same time, the Hoge Raad rejected the government's defence that since other countries also do not comply with their share of their partial responsibility, the Netherlands may do the same.[12] No matter how small the impact of one country reducing emissions may be on a global scale, this circumstance may not be used as an excuse to reduce national carbon emissions

4 *Neubauer*, para. 219.
5 Ibid.
6 SRU, *Für eine entschlossene Umweltpolitik in Deutschland und Europa*, Umweltgutachten 2020, p. 51; *Neubauer*, para. 225.
7 https://www.gesetze-im-internet.de/englisch_ksg/englisch_ksg.html.
8 https://www.umweltbundesamt.de/daten/klima/treibhausgas-emissionen-in-deutschland.
9 *Neubauer*, para. 225.
10 *Urgenda*, para. 5.7.1.
11 Ibid., paras 5.7.2 et seq.
12 Ibid., para. 5.7.7.

to a lesser degree, the Court stated.[13] In fact, it went on to say that 'no reduction is negligible', since it means that the remaining global carbon budget stays bigger, thus enabling more flexibility globally.[14]

Differently, the BVerfG found that climate change calls for global action.[15] Moreover, this would be constitutionally demanded by Article 20a GG, a principle of the German Constitution, on which this decision is grounded. Namely, Article 20a GG contains 'a duty that necessarily looks beyond the domestic legal system under the sole responsibility of the individual state … pointing towards the level of international activity'.[16] This means that the German government is explicitly obliged to promote international climate action by using any possible means.[17] The BVerfG even provided examples for this, namely 'through negotiations, via treaties or in organisations'.[18] In line with the Hoge Raad, the BVerfG stated that Germany's 2% share of global carbon emissions does not mean that the German contribution could be neglected on a global scale – quite the opposite: the BVerfG explicitly underscored the role that the German contribution may play in achieving an 'overall drive' to fight climate change globally.[19] It then continued – referring not only to the Hoge Raad itself, but also to other (non-)German courts – that 'the state may not evade its responsibility here by pointing to greenhouse gas emissions in other states'.[20]

2.3. CALL FOR AN INTERNATIONALLY ACTIVE ROLE OF STATES

Altogether, both Courts found that the respective national emission reduction obligations have to be seen in a broader, international scheme. Neither the fact that their emissions are relatively small, nor the assumption that not all States will live up to their responsibilities can reduce each individual States' duties (see above). The BVerfG even more than the Hoge Raad demanded that the respective State actively foster international action.[21] For example, the German Federal Constitutional Court called explicitly for international agreements like the Paris Agreement and for Germany to hold up its end of these agreements to build mutual trust between the countries involved.[22] Consequently, Germany must 'avoid

13 Ibid.
14 Ibid., para. 5.7.8.
15 *Neubauer*, para. 199.
16 Ibid., para. 200.
17 Ibid.
18 Ibid.
19 Ibid., para. 201.
20 Ibid., para. 202.
21 Ibid.
22 Ibid.

creating incentives for other states to undermine this [international] cooperation'.[23] In a new construction, the BVerfG explained that by passing the German Federal Climate Protection Act (including the Paris Agreement's temperature target), the German legislator specified a minimum standard of Article 20a GG regarding climate action.[24] By pointing this out, the Court reminded us of the role that international agreements must play.

The Hoge Raad, on the other hand, also underlined the importance of international agreements (even if they are not binding and it seems, therefore, fit for the Court to be more restraining),[25] but reminded the Dutch government that the Netherlands does not depend on such international agreements to reduce its national carbon emissions and that it has its own obligation to do so anyway.[26] Possibly, the Hoge Raad envisaged a scenario where it seemed impossible for (all) States to come to an agreement and, therefore, already wanted to make sure that this would not be used as an excuse by governments to halt their climate action altogether.

Interestingly, while the German State is called on to foster more climate action internationally, the Dutch State was mandated to perform more effective climate action nationally due to international climate ambitions: the Hoge Raad laid out that several international agreements on climate change (mostly the Conferences of Parties to the United Nations Framework Convention on Climate Change, but also agreements within the EU) require developed States to aim for a 25–40% reduction by 2020 relative to 1990.[27] Therefore, following this 'high degree of international consensus [regarding the climate ambitions]'[28] the Netherlands must reduce its emissions by at least 25%.[29]

Even though the interaction between national climate action and international agreements seems to have a slightly different focus in each Court's view, the Hoge Raad and the BVerfG expect both of their respective States to treat climate action as an international endeavour and to take an active role.

3. ROYAL DUTCH SHELL'S CARBON EMISSIONS AND REDUCTION OBLIGATIONS

3.1. DIFFERENT TYPES OF CARBON EMISSIONS: SCOPE 1, 2 AND 3

When assessing the scope of a company's reduction obligations concerning carbon emissions, it is of the utmost importance to differentiate between the

23 Ibid.
24 Ibid., paras 120, 197, 208 et seq.
25 *Urgenda*, para. 6.6.
26 Ibid., para. 6.3.
27 Ibid., paras 7.2 et seq.
28 Ibid., para. 7.2.7.
29 Ibid., para. 7.5.1.

company's Scope 1, 2 and 3 emissions. This can be done using the standards and definitions of the Greenhouse Gas (GHG) Protocol.[30]

While Scope 1 emissions include 'direct emissions' from operations that are owned or controlled by the company (e.g. vehicles, furnaces, etc.), Scope 2 emissions include those from the generation of energy by third companies (e.g. heating and purchased electricity).[31]

Scope 3 emissions include so-called 'indirect emissions' that occur anywhere throughout the value chain of the company (excluding Scope 2 emissions), for example during the production and transportation of purchased or sold goods or materials as well as the consumption of products.[32] They can be differentiated into 'upstream' (occurring *before* the respective company) or 'downstream' emissions (*after* the respective company).[33]

According to Royal Dutch Shell's own reports, the share of indirect Scope 3 emissions was roughly 85% in 2018, as was also acknowledged by the Rechtbank Den Haag.[34] This is due to RDS's encompassing business model, since RDS is active in the field of exploration, production and, most importantly, trading and marketing of oil and gas. Therefore, most of its emissions fall under Scope 3 (which are at the same time the Scope 1 emissions of the respective end-users). From 1988 to 2015, RDS's carbon emissions (including Scope 3) were the ninth-biggest of all companies globally, with roughly 1.67% of global carbon emissions in this timespan.[35]

3.2. THE YARDSTICK OF SHELL'S REDUCTION OBLIGATIONS ACCORDING TO THE RECHTBANK DEN HAAG

The Rechtbank Den Haag proved to be well aware of the fact that one of the main disputes in the *Shell* case concerned the scope of RDS's reduction obligations, or in the words of the Court itself: 'the case revolves around the question whether or not RDS has the obligation to reduce … all emission Scopes (1 through to 3)'.[36]

First of all, RDS itself had already stated in 1998 in an internal report that '[Shell companies] must play their part in the necessary precautionary measures to limit greenhouse gas emissions', meaning that they should 'reduce emissions

30 https://ghgprotocol.org/standards/scope-3-standard.

31 GHG Protocol, *Corporate Value Chain (Scope 3) Accounting and Reporting Standard*, 2011, p. 28.

32 Ibid.

33 Ibid., p. 29.

34 *Milieudefensie*, para. 2.5.5.

35 https://www.theguardian.com/sustainable-business/2017/jul/10/100-fossil-fuel-companies-investors-responsible-71-global-emissions-cdp-study-climate-change.

36 *Milieudefensie*, para. 4.1.1.

of greenhouse gases in their own operations as well as helping their customers to do the same'.[37] Thus, RDS had already admitted back then that it had an impact on its Scope 3 emissions. This is also in line with the Court's finding that 'companies subsequently should take "appropriate action" on the basis of their findings and assessments'[38] and that the latter also needed to include the company's Scope 3 emissions.[39]

Moreover, the Rechtbank Den Haag also stated that RDS's reduction obligations for its Scope 3 emissions are not mitigated by the end-users' individual responsibility for their own emissions (which are their Scope 1) emissions.[40] Since RDS can directly affect its indirect emissions by changing the composition of its energy package, it does have an impact on its indirect Scope 3 emissions.[41]

RDS's argument that its reduction obligation will have no effect because its competitors might just take its place in the global markets was also rejected by the Rechtbank Den Haag: the Court leaves it open whether this seems reasonable but insists that 'this will not benefit RDS' and certainly this hypothetical scenario will 'not absolve RDS of its individual partial responsibility'.[42]

In sum, the Court left no doubt regarding the yardstick of RDS's greenhouse gas reduction obligations: the company also must reduce its indirect Scope 3 emissions. RDS is, therefore, not only responsible for its direct emissions, but rather has to exploit its complete 'carbon reduction potential', including indirect emissions. That is despite the fact that the latter could perhaps be more easily reduced by those actors that account for these emissions as their direct Scope 1 (or even 2) emissions. The assumption is that it is easier for an organisation to reduce Scope 1, Scope 2 and Scope 3 emissions in light of its proximity to the occurrence of these emission types.

4. APPLYING THE YARDSTICK FOR COMPANIES TO STATES: CREATING A 'CARBON REDUCTION POTENTIAL'

When comparing all of the above-mentioned decisions regarding the greenhouse gas emissions reduction obligations of States and companies, it is obvious that the yardstick for companies is stricter: it also has to account for its indirect emissions, even though others (e.g. end-users) could affect them more easily. At the same time, States are only responsible for their direct emissions.

37 Ibid., para. 2.5.9.
38 Ibid., para. 4.4.21.
39 Ibid., para. 4.4.20.
40 Ibid., para. 4.4.24.
41 Ibid., para. 4.4.25.
42 Ibid., para. 4.4.49.

Thus, the following subsection attempts to apply the yardstick for companies (including responsibility for indirect emissions) to the State level. By doing so, a 'carbon reduction potential' is created, also including a State's possible impact on its indirect emissions.

4.1. INDIRECT EMISSIONS ON STATE LEVEL?

First and foremost, it needs to be clarified what the State equivalent to indirect emissions on the corporate level could be. As laid out above, both the Hoge Raad in the Netherlands and the BVerfG in Germany only focused on territorial emissions from the respective State. Nevertheless, besides these territorial emissions, there are also those emissions that are 'imported' into these two countries in the form of goods, for example. As pointed out above, they do not count into the 'official' (territorial) State emissions since the emissions themselves occurred during the production abroad. Still, these emissions benefit the national welfare of the importing State, since this is where the goods are being consumed.

This effect can be shown using an example. The emissions that occur during the production of a car in Germany count as part of the German territorial emissions. If the car is then sold and transported to the Netherlands, where it is used on Dutch territory, the emissions occurring during its use count as Dutch territorial emissions. The emissions of the production remain German territorial emissions, even though the car is being completely used in the Netherlands and contributes to its welfare.

As a result, these 'imported' emissions can be described as a State's indirect emissions: the State does not emit them itself, but profits from them and could also affect them (see below). This is just what the Rechtbank Den Haag demanded that RDS do: include its Scope 3 emissions within its reduction obligation. However, those are not being emitted by RDS directly but benefit it (in a financial way) and can be addressed by RDS (see section 4.2 above). Since these indirect emissions can also be affected by the State, they can be counted under its 'carbon reduction potential', meaning those emissions that can be reduced by the State: both its direct and indirect emissions.

The question remains whether these 'imported' emissions are actually worth addressing. Dutch carbon emissions were roughly 210 Mt in 2015, while the 'imported' carbon dioxide (CO_2) accounted for an additional 185 Mt in the same year.[43] Therefore, if those 'imported' emissions were to be included in the State's 'carbon reduction potential', it would be 87% higher than the Dutch territorial emissions.

---

43 B. Fortuński, 'The impact of foreign trade on the Netherlands' real CO_2 emissions' (2019) *Central European Review of Economics and Management* 141, 143.

In Germany, according to the advisory council SRU, imported carbon emissions were as high as 904 Mt and 'imported' emissions another 506 Mt in 2015,[44] increasing the German 'carbon reduction potential' by 56% relative to the German territorial emissions in the same year.

Even though the increase of each 'carbon reduction potential' relative to its respective territorial emissions is not as high as RDS's share of indirect Scope 3 emissions relative to Scopes 1 and 2, the inclusion of these 'imported' emissions on a State level is substantial and crucial for the assessment of State obligations for emission reductions.

4.2. EQUALISATION OF IMPORTS AND EXPORTS?

At the same time, it must not be forgotten that this method of 'carbon reduction potential' only adds 'imported' emissions to territorial emissions: would hence it not be appropriate to subtract 'exported' emissions, which are part of the territorial emissions? While German 'exported' emissions are slightly bigger that its 'imported' emissions, the opposite is the case in the Netherlands.

In this respect, when discussing the need for a German CO_2 budget, the SRU makes the values of emission imports and exports equal to simplify its considerations. This logic makes sense for a national CO_2 budget but does not apply to the 'carbon reduction potential': as a matter of fact, Germany can impact *both* its 'imported' and 'exported' emissions (the latter in fact more easily). Therefore, both have to be included in the German 'carbon reduction potential'.

When applying this method of a 'carbon reduction potential', a certain amount of emissions are subject to double-counting – in other words, they are included in two or more different States' 'carbon reduction potential'. Yet this is not the case when using a carbon budget approach to assess States' reduction obligations: while all carbon budgets added should make up for the global carbon budget, all 'carbon reduction potentials' added together are bigger than the carbon budget. This is due to the fact that many – maybe even most – emissions can be influenced directly and indirectly by more than one State.

In the example of a car being imported from Germany to the Netherlands, Germany could affect the emissions caused during production by increasing the share of renewable energies in the power generation, but the Netherlands could also, for example, put in place an import ban on carbon-intensive goods.

---

44 SRU, *Für eine entschlossene Umweltpolitik in Deutschland und Europa*, Umweltgutachten 2020, p. 51.

Adding to that, in the words of the Rechtbank Den Haag, '[RDS's] obligation is not removed or reduced by the individual responsibility of the business relations, including the end-users, for their own CO_2 emissions'.[45]

4.3. COMPARING STATE AND CORPORATE RESPONSIBILITIES

Generally speaking, it seems appropriate to let States bear greater obligations than companies. Moreover, States that are led by a democratically elected parliament not only have greater legitimation than shareholder-led companies, but can also be expected to meet higher duties of care regarding the protection of their citizens and their human, constitutional and simple-law rights. Furthermore, when looking at the balance of power between those two players, States can more easily affect carbon emissions by individuals – at least within their national boundaries – using their legislative power (and State monopoly of coercing means) over both citizens and companies. This is also acknowledged by the Rechtbank Den Haag, which states '[this] emphasizes that states determine the playing field and the rules for private parties'.[46]

Thus, it seems reasonable to apply a stricter yardstick to States than to companies. Interestingly, the opposite is the case in the case law: while the Hoge Raad and the BVerfG ordered the Netherlands and Germany to only reduce their direct territorial emissions, the Rechtbank Den Haag ruled that RDS must also reduce its indirect Scope 3 emissions. In consequence, this must mean that the standard for States would have to be all the stricter.

Finally, addressing 'imported' emissions seems not only appropriate with regard to the comparison of State–corporate obligations, but also concerning the progress of climate change and the need for international climate action that was emphasised so heavily by both the Hoge Raad and the BVerfG in their judgments (see section 3.3 above).

4.4. POSSIBLE IMPLEMENTATIONS AND IMPLICATIONS

The decision on the design of any possible system to reduce these 'imported' indirect emissions by States should, of course, be left up to the legislator. But before any laws can be passed, it seems necessary to find a way to assess the numbers of 'imported' and 'exported' emissions in the first place. A uniform global standard seems most suited for this purpose. In a second step, these emissions can then be addressed.

45 *Milieudefensie*, para. 4.4.24.

46 Ibid., para. 4.4.51.

Ideas for the implementation of EU-wide measures to address these 'imported' emissions already exist in the form of the Carbon Border Adjustment Mechanism (CBAM).[47] This makes particular sense in the light of the Single European Market. Although the CBAM was not (only) initially designed to address 'imported' emissions but to avoid carbon leakage and to protect EU-domestic industries, it can now also serve as an example of a climate instrument.

Therefore, it would seem inappropriate – and would certainly lead to conflicts within the EU – if national courts like the Hoge Raad or the BVerfG were to demand that their respective States address their 'imported' emissions nationally. Given the European integration, it would instead make sense to require the Netherlands and Germany to promote EU-wide action on 'imported' emissions. Just because these emissions cannot be addressed properly by nation-States that are part of the EU, this does not mean that national courts should not mention the issue at all and demand that their respective State act on this topic. As long as EU Member States act according to their duties arising from the Paris Agreement, there is no need to apply these standards to the domestic market for intra-European imports-exports.

The CBAM intended by the EU is supposed to put a tax on carbon-intensive imports to reduce the 'imported' (or consumption-based) emissions of the EU. In addition to that, it also follows the economic interests of the EU by decreasing the so-called 'carbon leakage': the fear of industries moving from the EU abroad to avoid climate-related (and price-raising) restrictions on their production.

Therefore, the implementation of the CBAM or any similar systems would also meet the demands of the BVerfG, which stated that Germany 'must avoid creating incentives for other states to undermine this [international] cooperation', in this example to allow carbon-leaking (see above).[48] This fits in with the fact that the Hoge Raad correctly rejected the Dutch government's argument that other States were not living up to their responsibilities to set low targets themselves.[49]

5. CONCLUSION: 'CARBON REDUCTION POTENTIAL' INSTEAD OF TERRITORIAL EMISSIONS AS A YARDSTICK

Another aspect that should not be underestimated is the role that the highest national courts like the Hoge Raad and the BVerfG play on the international

---

47 https://ec.europa.eu/taxation_customs/green-taxation-0/carbon-border-adjustment-mechanism_en.

48 *Neubauer*, para. 202.

49 *Urgenda*, para. 5.7.7.

stage: these courts are capable of being beacons and inspiration not only to lower courts of all branches in their respective States, but also to foreign or international courts. That way, the yardstick of a decision regarding (State) obligations can serve as legal precedent in other cases which are not necessarily State-related. Lastly, in a global issue like climate change, courts also refer to each other internationally: the *Urgenda* decision triggered similar cases all over the world. By publishing its press release and the full text of the *Neubauer* decision also in English and French, the BVerfG proved to be well aware of its international impact. This is also in line with the aim of creating an 'overall drive' or international climate action, as suggested by the BVerfG itself.

In the absence of coercive means to enforce climate protection internationally, economically relatively strong States such as Germany and the Netherlands (and even more so the EU) also have an obligation to act beyond their borders: it seems very likely that some States will refuse to take the necessary climate protection measures in good time. That is why acting States must exhaust all available means (see section 4.4 above) to still influence their emissions indirectly. This seems especially urgent in the light of the IPCC's recent insights regarding the progression of climate change.

Finally, it must be said that the current system of allocating national responsibilities for carbon emissions mostly concerns territorial emissions, as is also stated by, for example, Article 4(2) of the Paris Agreement. Nonetheless, as shown above, this system and its standard of State responsibilities only for territorial emissions has proven to be inadequate in recent years and in the light of an ever-worsening climate crisis. Therefore, if the system does not meet the needs anymore, there is a need to change the system.

In summary, both the Hoge Raad and the BVerfG correctly emphasised the international dimension of successful climate protection, but did not draw the right conclusion from this: while looking only at territorial emissions of their respective State, they substantially underestimated the State's impact at the global level. The decisive factor and yardstick for national influence on global climate action is less the respective State's carbon budget, but more its 'carbon reduction potential', including indirect 'imported' emissions.

The Rechtbank Den Haag provided a template for how to deal with indirect emissions (globally): by assessing the company's scope of influence on these indirect emissions, it concluded that RDS's reduction obligation also encompassed Scope 3 emissions. It cannot be that companies have to bear greater reduction obligations than democratically elected States; therefore, the latter also need to include their indirect emissions into their (inter)national climate policies. In this respect, States must abandon the budget approach in favour of their 'carbon reduction potential'.

With currently pending cases such as *Deutsche Umwelthilfe v. BMW*,[50] as well as the recent constitutional complaint challenging the German National Climate Protection Act,[51] courts will have the chance to revise and internationally adjust their decisions in this regard. The same applies to whatever suits may arise from the recent threats of legal action against Dutch companies by Milieudefensie.[52]

50 http://climatecasechart.com/non-us-case/deutsche-umwelthilfe-duh-v-bmw.

51 https://www.duh.de/vbklima.

52 https://en.milieudefensie.nl/news/logo-the-solution-is-less-pollution-milieudefensie-friends-of-the-earth-netherlands-demands-climate-plan-from-30-major-climate-polluters.

CLIMATE CHANGE AS A CONSTITUTIONAL TOPIC

Environmental Constitutionalism in the Netherlands and the EU

Marijn van der Sluis

1. INTRODUCTION

Climate change is becoming a hot topic in constitutional law. In a ground-breaking ruling, the Dutch Supreme Court[1] ordered the Dutch State in December 2019 to quickly reduce carbon dioxide (CO_2) emissions in the Netherlands. This decision was followed in Europe by similar rulings from the French Council of State[2] and the German Constitutional Court.[3] In France, a citizen assembly had moreover already been used to come up with climate change mitigation measures that would have

1 Hoge Raad (Netherlands), 20 December 2019, *Urgenda*, 19/00135, ECLI:NL:HR:2019:2006.

2 Conseil d'État (France), 19 November 2020, 427301, ECLI:FR:CECHR:2020:427301.20201119.

3 Bundesverfassungsgericht (Germany), 24 March 2021, *Neubauer*, 1 BvR 2656/18, ECLI:DE:BVerfG:2021:rs20210324.1bvr265618.

wide popular support. Similar assemblies had been used in Ireland, albeit as part of a series of assemblies, and in the UK.[4] These developments come on top of a steady trend of integrating *environmental* objectives and rights into constitutions over the last decades.[5] Climate change mitigation is also rising as a priority for many governments and organisations, for example in the EU through the European Green Deal (EGD). This may lead to conflicts concerning the priority of climate change mitigation vis-à-vis (other) constitutional objectives and rights.

A comprehensive account of the relevance of climate change for constitutional law is lacking. Currently, climate change and mitigation measures are mainly seen in constitutional law from the perspective of human rights. The point of this chapter is to show that climate change has broader ramifications for constitutional law and that a human rights approach is therefore too narrow. This is shown by analysing several of the developments mentioned above: the ruling by the Dutch Supreme Court (section 2), and the European Green Deal (section 3). The last section (section 4) sets out a direction for constitutional scholarship to engage with the new questions and discusses the role of citizen councils.

2. THE *URGENDA* JUDGMENT

The Dutch Supreme Court ruled in December 2019 that on the basis of Articles 2 and 8 of the European Convention on Human Rights (ECHR), the Dutch State is required to reduce CO_2 emissions in the Netherlands by 25% by 2020 compared to 1990 levels.[6] The ruling was the result of a private lawsuit filed by the environmental organisation Urgenda, and 886 Dutch citizens. The District Court first found that, as a private organisation, Urgenda could not rely on the ECHR but nonetheless ruled in its favour on the basis of non-contractual liability. The Court of Appeal and later the Supreme Court determined, however, that Urgenda could rely on the ECHR. The case has been at the centre of attention in the Netherlands since the first ruling by the District Court in 2015. Whilst most of the political parties in parliament found that more action was indeed necessary to reduce CO_2 emissions, a distinct aspect of the debate concerned the role of the courts and the separation of powers. Opponents of the ruling pointed to the long tradition in the Netherlands of judicial deference to politics.

4 R. Willis, *Too Hot to Handle? The Democratic Challenge of Climate Change*, Bristol University Press 2020.

5 J.R. May and E. Daly, *Global Environmental Constitutionalism*, Cambridge University Press 2014.

6 For an extensive English-language discussion of the case, see J. Spier, '"The 'Strongest' Climate Ruling Yet": The Dutch Supreme Court's Urgenda Judgment' (2020) 67 *Netherlands International Law Review* 319.

It is paradoxical that such a ground-breaking ruling arose in the Netherlands. The argument put forward in this chapter is that, from the perspective of Dutch constitutional law, the judgment is not simply a human rights case, but primarily a climate case. The following parts of this section set out the traditional views on the role of the judiciary in the Netherlands and the separation of powers critique on the *Urgenda* judgment, before describing how a broader view of the constitutional effects of climate change negates the separation of powers critique of the *Urgenda* judgment.

2.1. JUDICIAL DEFERENCE IN THE NETHERLANDS

The traditionally unassertive position of the judiciary in the Netherlands is largely the result of Article 120 of the Dutch Constitution, which prohibits the judiciary from reviewing legislation and treaties against the Constitution.[7] The Dutch Constitution is an outlier in this regard, compared to the large majority of constitutions around the world. The Constitution in effect requires parliament and government as co-legislators to check the conformity of the laws they jointly adopt with the Constitution, aided by advice of the Council of State. The text of Article 120 leaves open the possibility for constitutional review through the back door, for example by reviewing legislation against the Charter for the Kingdom of the Netherlands, which sets out the relations between the Netherlands and the three other countries in the Kingdom, and which hierarchically stands above the Constitution. Another option for review would be general principles of law. The Supreme Court, however, has ruled that legislation cannot be reviewed against these sources of law, due to the general 'tradition of non-reviewing' in the Netherlands.[8] Rules adopted by bodies other than the formal legislator, such as municipal councils, can be reviewed against the Constitution.

The absence of constitutional review of legislation must, however, be seen in light of the constitutional openness towards international law. Article 94 of the Constitution states that legislation is not applicable if it conflicts 'with provisions of treaties or of resolutions by international institutions that are binding on all persons'. Provisions of international treaties that seek to give rights to individuals function directly in the Dutch legal order and may be used as a standard to review legislation. Hence, judicial human rights protection in the Netherlands is largely the result of international law. The tradition of 'non-reviewing' is thus tempered by the monistic approach to international law, and of course by the prominent position of European Union (EU) law in the national

7 Art. 120 Dutch Constitution: 'The constitutionality of Acts of Parliament and treaties shall not be reviewed by the courts' (translation provided by the Dutch Government).

8 Hoge Raad (Netherlands), 14 April 1989, *Harmonisatiewet-arrest*, ECLI:NL:HR:1989:AD5725.

legal order. However, the judicial deference to politics is also seen in relation to international law. Many international human rights treaties offer a minimum level of protection and do not seek to prevent national constitutions from offering a higher level of protection. The Dutch courts have adopted the technique of mirroring the rulings of the European Court of Human Rights (ECtHR) in the interpretation of the ECHR.[9] As a result, the situation provided for by Article 94 of the Constitution, where legislation is deemed inapplicable because it violates an international obligation, is rare.[10] Moreover, finding legislation inapplicable does not always lead to an outcome desired by the applicant. For example, in cases where legislation authorises subsidies for one group, but not for another, the inapplicability of the legislation rarely solves the problem at hand. On this issue, the Supreme Court developed a view on the manner in which the judiciary can signal legal problems and 'ask' for a legislative solution before coming up with a judicial solution. However, the Supreme Court still noted that under the Dutch separation of powers doctrine, it is not possible for the judiciary to order the legislator to act.[11]

2.2. UNDERSTANDING *URGENDA*

It is against this background that the importance of the *Urgenda* judgment in the Dutch constitutional order becomes visible. The Supreme Court appears to cast aside previous reservations about intervening in political decision-making in several ways. First, in interpreting Articles 2 and 8 ECHR, the Supreme Court took little guidance from the ECtHR. As the ECtHR has not (yet) ruled on climate change as a threat to human rights, the Supreme Court took the initiative to provide an expansive reading of Articles 2 and 8 ECHR. Second, the Supreme Court ordered the State to act to (quickly) reduce CO_2 emissions. Technically, the Supreme Court has not ordered the legislature to act, but only the State as such. Non-legislative measures can of course also be useful in taking climate action; for example, under current legislation there might already be discretion to reject permits for high-emitting activities. Given the scale of the challenge and the limited timeframe in which the judgment should be executed, it was, however, unrealistic to expect that the ruling could be implemented without

9 Hoge Raad (Netherlands), 10 August 2001, ECLI:NL:HR:2001:ZC3598, para 3.9. See also J. Gerards, 'Spiegel of Lachspiegel? Over Het EVRM En Het Urgenda-Arrest', *Montaigne Centrum Blog*, 5 February 2020, https://blog.montaignecentre.com/nl/spiegel-of-lachspiegel-over-het-evrm-en-het-urgenda-arrest.

10 M. Claes, A.W. Heringa, M. van der Sluis and M. Stremler, 'Rechtsvergelijkend Onderzoek Constitutionele Toetsing', Ministerie van Binnenlandse Zaken en Koninkrijksrelaties, 2021, https://www.rijksoverheid.nl/documenten/rapporten/2021/03/01/rechtsvergelijkend-onderzoek-constitutionele-toetsing.

11 Hoge Raad (Netherlands), 21 March 2003, *Waterpakt*, ECLI:NL:HR:2003:AE8462, para. 3.5.

legislation. Lastly, the Supreme Court set aside considerations of proportionality. Were the Netherlands to indeed reduce CO_2 emissions, this would hardly affect the position of those in the Netherlands threatened by climate change. Reductions in CO_2 emissions in the Netherlands might actually even lead to increased emissions elsewhere. Especially since the Netherlands is part of the EU Emissions Trading System (EU ETS), unused emission rights may be sold to other emitters in the EU, leading to intra-EU carbon leakage.[12]

If the *Urgenda* judgment is analysed without taking into account the context of Dutch constitutional law, the judgment is (merely) one of the first of what might be a long line of climate rulings by supreme courts to protect (new) human rights.[13] However, in the Dutch constitutional order it does more: it overturns a long tradition of judicial deference. A proper understanding of the *Urgenda* case thus has to go beyond viewing climate change as a threat to human rights, because if climate change was simply that, it would not have had such a constitutional impact in the Netherlands. The difficulty here is that the Supreme Court itself does not explain why in this case a new approach to human rights was warranted. Hence, the ruling has attracted criticism from many constitutional scholars in the Netherlands on the basis of a separation of powers doctrine (even from progressive voices). Some prominent constitutional scholars have defended the judgment, but not primarily because of its substantive contribution to climate change mitigation, but because the judgment represents a new form of constitutionalism. Neither the critique nor the responses sufficiently engage with the dilemmas of the judgment.

2.2.1. Urgenda *and Separation of Powers*

The critique based on the tradition of the separation of powers in the Netherlands is misguided as it equates climate change to other human rights. The reasoning in *Urgenda* indeed departs from many established precedents, but whether or not that is justified depends on how the constitutional significance of climate change is viewed. Besselink, for example, compares the judgment to human rights cases dealing with smoking in bars (right to health), and the refusal of a conservative Christian political party to include women on their election list (right to equality and non-discrimination).[14] The problem, according to Besselink, is that the Court

---

12 The issue of carbon leakage is discussed in the recent IPCC report on mitigation: IPCC, *Climate Change 2022: Mitigation of Climate Change. Contribution of Working Group III to the Sixth Assessment Report of the Intergovernmental Panel on Climate Change*, 2022. Specifically for carbon leakage to other Member States of the EU, see C.W. Backes and G.A. Van der Veen, 'Urgenda: the Final Judgment of the Dutch Supreme Court' (2020) 17 *Journal for European Environmental & Planning Law* 307, 316–17.

13 See e.g. J. Spier, above n. 6.

14 L.F.M. Besselink, 'Machtenscheiding in de Urgenda-Zaak' (2020) 11 *Tijdschrift voor Constitutioneel Recht* 128.

overruled political decision-making and prioritised one common interest over others.[15] This critique does not consider the fact that the reasoning of the Court continuously emphasised the challenges of climate change. In a final paragraph, the Supreme Court stressed that climate change creates an *exceptional* situation.[16] In other words, the Supreme Court (apparently) diverged from its previous case law because the situation is different, since climate change is unlike other human rights challenges. In any case, the assertion that climate change represents 'just' a common interest is implausible and requires justification. Certain climate change scenarios imply such a high level of devastation throughout the world that it is difficult to maintain that climate change is merely one amongst several constitutional objectives.

2.2.2. Urgenda *as 'New Constitutionalism'*

The response that the judgment represents an embrace of a new type of constitutionalism or 'law-finding' (being seen as a good thing) also largely overlooks the fact that climate change was the driving force behind the judgment.[17] While it is correct to note that the judgment took place in a changing legal environment in which societal problems or constitutional values invite the judiciary to be less deferential to political decision-making, that reasoning also disregards the central role played by climate change in the ruling of the Supreme Court.

2.2.3. Urgenda *and Human Rights*

Discussing the *Urgenda* judgment mainly in light of human rights protection also has great appeal, but in the end only offers part of the justification of the *Urgenda* judgment. As noted in the introduction, environmental human rights have made remarkable progress in constitutions and constitutional law over the last decades. Whereas post-World War II human rights instruments such as the ECHR and the Universal Declaration of Human Rights (UDHR) did not explicitly incorporate environmental rights, constitutions and international treaties have over in recent decades increasingly begun to emphasise environmental rights, both individually and in relation to the fulfilment of other rights. In the literature, the growing prominence of environmental rights has been central to the development of concepts such as

---

15 Ibid.

16 Hoge Raad, *Urgenda*, above n. 1, para. 8.3.4.

17 M. Stremler, 'Urgenda-Arrest Is Voorbeeld van Nieuw Constitutionalisme', *Nederland Rechtsstaat*, 8 January 2020, https://www.nederlandrechtsstaat.nl/urgenda-arrest-is-voorbeeld-van-nieuw-constitutionalisme. See also the commentary by Van Gestel and Loth after the ruling in 2015: M. Loth and R. Van Gestel, 'Urgenda: Roekeloze Rechtspraak of Rechtsvinding 3.0?' (2015) *Nederlands Juristenblad* 2598.

environmental constitutionalism,[18] the *Umweltstaat* or the *milieurechtsstaat*.[19] The predominant line of thinking in this literature is that the environment must receive legal protection in the form of rights. The emphasis is thus on the negative aspects of constitutionalism, whereby legal rules are employed to protect against an overbearing government or against problems in political or democratic decision-making. Less attention is then devoted to the positive aspects of constitutionalism, which seek to organise and activate democratic decision-making. The concept of 'green democracy' is then largely left to political scientists and political economists.[20] Environmental constitutionalism thus needs to be completed so as to integrate the positive aspects of constitutionalism, which is further elaborated in section 4.

Focusing on the *Urgenda* judgment, an explanation that relies on the importance of climate change in light of human rights is insufficient. If the *Urgenda* judgment were primarily a judgment about human rights, it ought to have had a transformative effect on the Dutch constitutional order. The ruling would then be the rising tide that lifts all human rights in the Netherlands. There is, however, no indication that the Supreme Court sought to bring about such a broad change in Dutch constitutional law, apart from on the issue of climate change. Although it is certainly possible that the Supreme Court might use the *Urgenda* judgment to justify other innovations at a later point, such a change is for now not evident, for example in relation to lower courts. If the judgments by the Appeals Court and the Supreme Court were clarion calls for strengthened human rights protection in the Netherlands, the lower courts have certainly not listened. The main exception where the lower courts again creatively intervened to protect human rights is the recent case against Shell,[21] again concerning climate change.

The *Urgenda* judgment thus relies on human rights to require the Dutch State to act on climate change mitigation, but the perspective of human rights protection cannot explain crucial aspects of the judgment. This might also explain the irritation the judgment has caused within Dutch constitutional law. The Supreme Court relies in its reasoning on human rights, but without

---

18 L.J. Kotzé, *Global Environmental Constitutionalism in the Anthropocene*, Hart Publishing 2016; J.R. May and E. Daly, above n. 5.

19 J. Verschuuren, *Het Grondrecht Op Bescherming van Het Leefmilieu*, WEJ Tjeenk Willink 1993.

20 F. Fisscher, *Climate Crisis and the Democratic Prospect: Participatory Governance in Sustainable Communities*, Oxford University Press 2017; J. Wainwright and G. Mann, *Climate Leviathan: A Political Theory of Our Planetary Future*, Verso 2018; R. Eckersley, *The Green State: Rethinking Democracy and Sovereignty*, MIT Press 2004.

21 District Court The Hague (Netherlands), *Milieudefensie v. Shell*, 26 May 2021, ECLI:NL:RBDHA:2021:5337. See for an overview of cases J. Krommendijk, 'Beyond Urgenda: The Role of the ECHR and Judgments of the ECtHR in Dutch Environmental and Climate Litigation' (2021) 31 *Review of European, Comparative and International Environmental Law* 60, 70–72. He argues that in the Netherlands there has been an uptick in the use of the ECHR in environmental law cases since 2017, but that the substantive impact of the 'turn to rights' is limited (p. 11).

explaining why the application of human rights protection *in this case* diverges so strongly from how human rights protection in the Netherlands ordinarily functions. In other words, the judgment is revolutionary, without the Supreme Court offering a proper explanation for the innovative character of the judgment. The key issue of the judgment is then that climate change is not only a threat to human rights, but a broader challenge for constitutional law. The judgment thus offers few clues about the place of climate change within constitutional law.

3. THE EUROPEAN GREEN DEAL

In December 2019, nine days before the Supreme Court's *Urgenda* judgment, EU Commission President Von der Leyen presented the EGD.[22] The name of the plans refers to the New Deal in the US from President Roosevelt, which sought to tackle the deep economic recession in the 1930s in the US. The EGD starts from the premise that dealing with climate change and related environmental challenges is 'this generation's defining task',[23] and strives for net-zero emissions of greenhouse gases and a decoupling of economic growth from resource use. The EGD is the hallmark plan of this Commission, with numerous proposals, plans and initiatives having been produced under its banner since it was launched. Although the EGD is primarily a regulatory project that utilises well-known instruments of EU law, it raises several constitutional questions. This section aims to show that the constitutional aspects of the EGD are crucial to its success, after first outlining three of its components.

3.1. OBJECTIVES, RULES AND FUNDING

The EGD is not an open-ended action plan, but revolves around goal-setting, with the ultimate goal of net-zero greenhouse gas emissions in the EU in 2050. This is stipulated in the European Climate Law (Regulation 2021/1119), adopted in June 2021. The Commission is made responsible for proposing, setting and monitoring further targets to be achieved by the Member States over the coming decades. The Commission is also obliged to check the conformity of *all* its draft measures and legislative proposals with the climate-neutrality objective. By July 2021, the Commission was furthermore obliged to review all relevant EU legislation. This resulted in the second aspect

22 European Commission, Communication from the European Commission, 'European Green Deal', COM(2019) 640 final, 11 December 2019.

23 Ibid.

described here: the 'Fit for 55'[24] package of legislative proposals that aims at reducing CO_2 emissions by 55% by 2030 compared to 1990 levels. The set of legislative proposals seeks to amend or recast numerous legal instruments on different topics, including the EU ETS, energy taxes, forests, transport, land use, renewable energy, a social climate fund, and a carbon border adjustment mechanism to avoid carbon leakage to non-EU countries. Other policies are also being actively reviewed, for example in banking supervision with regard to climate risks on the balance sheets of banks,[25] and in competition law with regard to the guidelines for State aid for energy.[26]

The third relevant aspect of the EGD is the allocation of private and public funding. The EGD aims to steer private funds, Member State funds and European funds towards sustainable investments. In the example of banking regulation, the imposition of new rules to protect financial stability against climate change-related risks should also have the effect of steering private funds towards activities that are less likely to be affected by climate change. The recently adopted Taxonomy Regulation furthermore aims to clarify under which conditions an economic activity or investment therein can be deemed environmentally sustainable, thereby promoting private investments. The Taxonomy Regulation might be of help to, for example, pension funds or other (public) investors that seek to make green investments. To be qualified as sustainable, an investment must substantially contribute to one of several environmental goals, and not significantly hurt the other goals. The Taxonomy Regulation sets several goals, without creating a hierarchy amongst them, namely: climate change mitigation, climate change adaptation, pollution control, protection of biodiversity, and the transition to a circular economy. The EGD also includes a fund to compensate regions that suffer as a result of the economic transition.[27] Current EU funding instruments, including those created to tackle the economic effects of the COVID-19 pandemic, are also employed to promote green investments. Hence, the Corona Recovery Fund (Resilience and Recovery Fund) stipulates that Member States should use 37% of the funding they receive for their green transition.[28]

---

24 European Commission, Communication from the Commission, '"Fit for 55": delivering the EU's 2030 Climate Target on the way to climate neutrality', COM(2021) 550 final, 14 July 2021.

25 See e.g. European Banking Authority, EBA report on management and supervision of ESG risks for credit institutions and investment firms, EBA/REP/2021/18, 23 June 2021.

26 European Commission, Commission Press Release, 'State aid: Commission invites interested parties to provide comments on proposed draft Climate, Energy and Environmental State aid Guidelines', IP/21/2784, 7 June 2021.

27 Regulation (EU) 2021/1056 of the European Parliament and of the Council of 24 June 2021 establishing the Just Transition Fund [2021] OJ L 231/1.

28 Art. 18(4)(e) Regulation (EU) 2021/241 of the European Parliament and of the Council of 12 February 2021 establishing the Recovery and Resilience Facility [2021] OJ L 57/17.

3.2. THE CONSTITUTIONAL ASPECTS OF THE EGD

The EGD is promoted and discussed primarily as a matter of policy. Constitutional and institutional aspects are barely touched upon in the proposals so far, except for perfunctory references to the need for public participation. For those following the developments in the European Union over the last decade, this absence of constitutionality-talk comes as a breath of fresh air.[29] The eurozone crisis, the migration crisis, Brexit and lastly the rule of law crisis: all revolved in one way or another around fundamental constitutional questions, including dis-integration. Such issues do not afflict the EGD, yet for the EGD, too, constitutional issues are unavoidable.[30] These issues can be split into three groups.

A first set of issues concerns rather common questions of legality and legal consequences in the EU. Is the EU actually allowed to implement the EGD as it is proposed, and can it be enforced?[31] Standard constitutional topics concern the allocation of competences (including objectives), proportionality and procedure. In the EU, competences attributed to the institutions are often accompanied by specific objectives: powers may only be employed in the service of specific goals.[32] An example is Article 127 of the Treaty on the Functioning of the European Union (TFEU), which states that the primary objective of monetary policy is to maintain price stability. Hence, the promise in the announcement of the EGD in December 2019 that *all* EU policies will be revisited in light of the EGD finds the EU Treaties in its path.[33] On monetary policy, for example, the Commission has no policy-making powers, and the European Central Bank (ECB) may be limited in its ability to incorporate climate change-related objectives. Although monetary policy *adaptation* to climate change is helpful for the achievement of its primary objective, maintaining price stability, it is doubtful that the ECB may aim for climate change *mitigation* through its policies.[34] A monetary policy aimed at adaptation is more likely to conform to the principle of proportionality.

---

29 G. Davies, 'Editorial Note: Can Climate Policy Give Europe Its Mojo Back?' (2021) 17 *Croatian Yearbook of European Law and Policy* VII.

30 A. Sikora, 'European Green Deal – Legal and Financial Challenges of the Climate Change' (2021) 21 *ERA Forum* 681.

31 M. Chamon and M. Peeters, 'The European Climate Law: Too Much Power for the Commission?', *Maastricht University Law Faculty Blog*, 30 March 2020, https://www.maastrichtuniversity.nl/blog/2020/03/european-climate-law-too-much-power-commission.

32 For a critique on the democratic nature of linking the exercise of competences to specific objectives, see G. Davies, 'Democracy and Legitimacy in the Shadow of Purposive Competence' (2015) 21 *European Law Journal* 2.

33 European Commission, European Green Deal, above n. 22.

34 M. van der Sluis, 'The ECB Should Combat Climate Change, Because It Can' (2021) 73 *EU Law Live – Weekend Edition*. See for a broader discussion on the possibilities of greening monetary policy: D. Schoenmaker, 'Greening Monetary Policy' (2021) 21 *Climate Policy* 581.

Many other EU competences must be employed in light of not one but a wide array of objectives, and there is significant leeway in reorienting the policies towards the goal of sustainability. However, treaty provisions may set limits on new policies or shape the manner in which they are implemented. For example, in competition law the treaties require that the benefits of an agreement between undertakings which restricts competition flow back to the consumer in the relevant market (rather than the population as a whole).[35] This does not block the greening of competition law as such, but does restrict in what way that can be done. With regard to the goal-setting aspects of the EGD, an open question is what exactly the consequences of a failure of a Member State to reach a certain goal could be. What could enforcement look like in such a case, given the peculiarities of the specific goal?[36]

A second set of concerns centres around the functioning of the EU institutions, especially in relation to their democratic legitimacy. Although complaints about the lack of democratic legitimacy are often not matched by the actual practice of EU institutions, there is a long history of valid concerns about the democratic quality of the EU.[37] The EGD will complicate several aspects of the democratic nature of the EU institutions. Firstly, by shifting from market integration as the predominant theme in EU integration to climate mitigation and environmental concerns, the (economic) output legitimacy of European integration may be weakened. Although in recent years various attempts have been made to strengthen the non-market aspects of EU integration and the input and throughput legitimacy of the institutions, the economic growth and improvement of living standards associated with membership of the internal market remains a key pillar of the legitimacy of the Union. Where climate policies distract from economic growth in Member States, they may hamper the output legitimacy of the EU.[38] The announcement in 2019 stresses that the EGD

---

[35] S. Holmes, 'Climate Change, Sustainability, and Competition Law' (2020) 8 *Journal of Antitrust Enforcement* 354.

[36] The emphasis on the targets as legally binding is only helpful in order to distinguish them from soft law or political targets. It remains to be seen how such legally binding targets could be enforced. For a discussion on the legal status of the targets, see M. Peeters and N. Athanasiadou, 'The Continued Effort Sharing Approach in EU Climate Law: Binding Targets, Challenging Enforcement?' (2020) *Review of European, Comparative and International Environmental Law* 201.

[37] F.W. Scharpf, 'After the Crash: A Perspective on Multilevel European Democracy' (2015) 21 *European Law Journal* 384.

[38] 'Editorial Comments: The European Climate Law – Making the Social Market Economy Fit for 55?' (2021) 58 *Common Market Law Review* 1321. See the reference therein to G. Majone, *Dilemmas of European Integration: The Ambiguities and Pitfalls of Integration by Stealth*, Oxford University Press 2005. Majone states (p. 117): 'What is most striking about the development of the EU environmental policy is the amount of legislation that has been enacted in the absence, not only of a firm legal basis until the late 1980s but also of a clear rationale for action at the European level.'

is a new growth model, squaring climate policies with economic growth through the concept of 'decoupling'. It is doubtful whether an effective climate policy can live up to that promise, given the required speed with which emissions should be reduced. Although emission reduction in the past has coincided with economic growth, this is no guarantee that economic growth can continue in the next phases of emission reduction. An argument can be made that future emission reduction requires a deeper economic transformation, as the previous reductions were the metaphorical 'low-hanging fruit'. In any case, the debate about the viability of the strategy of decoupling resource use from economic growth is not settled.[39] The EGD also includes a component focused on 'justice', which encompasses for example a Just Transition Fund.[40] In addition, the EU's Recovery and Resilience Facility, part of NextGenEU, requires Member States to use a significant part of the funds they receive from the EU for the green transition. Member States can, therefore, use EU funding for their own climate plans. Despite the fact that these sums are not insignificant, it is doubtful that they can fully compensate for the asymmetric socio-economic effects of the economic transition envisioned by the EGD.[41] The impact of the EGD will be asymmetric, as certain regions in the EU will be economically more heavily affected by the necessary economic transformations than others.

Besides changing demands concerning EU spending, the goals of the EGD are also the driving force behind new initiatives to complement the EU's own income with new sources. Starting with the new multiannual EU budget in 2028, the EU will have to find a solution to repay the debts it has taken on to finance the Corona Recovery Fund. As part of the political agreement on the Corona Recovery Fund, the Member States agreed to seek new sources of income for the EU. In July 2021, the Commission proposed to use the income from the ETS as a new source of income for the EU, as well as income from the proposed Carbon Border Adjustment Mechanism (CBAM). The greening of the EU is becoming enmeshed with other constitutional developments, here regarding the functioning of the Economic and Monetary Union.[42]

Another institutional concern is to what extent climate policies can rely on the model of 'integration through law'. Law has played a vital role in the construction of European integration in depoliticising conflicts, empowering economic actors and citizens vis-à-vis governments, and employing national

39 For introductory texts on the issue see J. Hickel, *Less Is More – How Degrowth Will Save the World*, Cornerstone 2020; W. Nordhaus, *The Spirit of Green: The Economics of Collisions and Contagions in a Crowded World*, Princeton University Press 2021.

40 Regulation (EU) 2021/1056 of 24 June 2021 of the European Parliament and the Council establishing a Just Transition Fund [2021] OJ 231/1.

41 See R.C. Fleming and R. Mauger, 'Green and Just? An Update on the "European Green Deal"' (2021) 18 *Journal for European Environmental & Planning Law* 164.

42 B. De Witte, 'The European Union's Covid-19 Recovery Plan: The Legal Engineering of an Economic Policy Shift' (2021) 58 *Common Market Law Review* 635.

institutions in the service of European integration.[43] The central role of law in European integration has also meant that the Member States remained the primary addressees of Union policies, with national courts acting as EU courts for the purpose of giving effect to EU rules and rights. The policies promoted through the EGD appear *prima facie* to require a different kind of governance, where the EU itself is tasked with executing governmental and administrative tasks. To give one example, a deep change in transportation in Europe probably requires a well-functioning high-speed rail network across the EU. This would require a deeper integration of the rail networks of the Member States, which may be unlikely in the absence of a stronger EU institutional presence.[44] Sustainable economic development is a more elusive concept than market integration and appears to require a more constant involvement of the EU and the Member States in the economy. It should be noted here that other EU policies have already led to a shift in how EU policies are executed. The banking union, for example, is relatively centralised around the ECB, but with many operating responsibilities for national authorities. The legal difficulties arising from this type of cooperation have brought about constitutional innovation, for example in relation to the issue of judicial protection.[45]

Lastly, the aforementioned issues point to a more fundamental question about the nature and purpose of European integration. Where do environmental sustainability and climate change mitigation fit into the values and objectives of the European Union?[46] Are they part of the (constitutional) values that the EU has already enshrined in the treaties, namely 'human dignity, freedom, democracy, equality, the rule of law and respect for human rights', or should sustainability be seen as a distinct constitutional value that requires a re-balancing of EU constitutional dogmas? Currently, sustainability is framed as an objective of EU policy, in Article 3 of the Treaty on European Union (TEU) and Article 11 TFEU, and as a human right in Article 37 of the Charter of Fundamental Rights of the EU. Article 11 TFEU is part of the 'provisions having general application', alongside promoting a high level of employment, prohibiting religious discrimination, and consumer protection. Where Article 11 TFEU certainly empowers institutions to take some action to promote sustainability, it is unclear whether Article 11 TFEU as such can lead to a re-balancing of priorities under the Treaties. In other words,

---

43 M. Cappelletti, M. Seccombe and J. Weiler, 'Integration Through Law: Europe and the American Federal Experience' in M. Cappelletti, M. Seccombe and J. Weiler (eds), *Integration Through Law*, Vol. 1, Book 1, De Gruyter 1986.

44 It must be noted that improving rail connections is not at the forefront of the EGD at the moment. See also the report 'Fostering the Railway Sector through the European Green Deal' by the European Union Agency for Railways.

45 F. Brito Bastos, 'Derivative Illegality in European Composite Administrative Procedures' (2018) 55 *Common Market Law Review* 101.

46 E. Chiti, 'Managing the Ecological Transition of the EU: The European Green Deal as a Regulatory Process' (2022) 59 *Common Market Law Review* 19.

what legal form is required for sustainability to not only enable new actions, but to also restrict or displace existing parts of EU law? Does the EGD simply come on top of the existing structures of EU law, or can it more fundamentally restructure EU law, where necessary?

The conclusion is not that the EGD is undemocratic or illegitimate, but that it overturns long-held notions of what makes the EU legitimate and democratic (or democratically acceptable). For the EGD to be successful, a new view on the purpose, functioning and legitimacy of the EU is needed. In other words, the EGD needs a constitutional foundation.

4. NEGATIVE AND POSITIVE ENVIRONMENTAL CONSTITUTIONALISM

The *Urgenda* judgment and the EGD both raise questions about the connection between climate change and constitutional law, albeit from different perspectives. In the *Urgenda* judgment, the constitutional relevance is the reason for its prominence. For the EGD, its constitutional significance is hidden behind technical proposals and ambitious press releases. What is missing in both developments is an understanding of how constitutional law can enable decision-making on climate change mitigation. Where there is an emphasis on constitutional law in mitigating climate change, the focus is on constitutional law as limiting the role of politics or the scope of political decision-making.[47] This was the case both for the *Urgenda* judgment in the Netherlands and the *Neubauer* judgment by the German Constitutional Court. In both cases the courts restricted the possibilities for political decision-making by requiring that a certain result should be reached. The emphasis in negative constitutionalism is on imposing constraints on decision-making through democratically elected or controlled institutions. This *negative* perspective should be complemented by a *positive* view of constitutionalism that is concerned with organising and empowering these institutions. The argument presented in this section is that environmental constitutionalism should likewise also focus on both sides. Enveloped in this argument is the critique that the focus of environmental constitutionalism as developed until today is too narrow.

It would be incorrect to say that the positive, enabling aspect of constitutionalism is wholly absent from the debate on how constitutional law and decision-making processes affect the environment. There are several developments that point towards a broader understanding of constitutionalism in relation to sustainability and the environment. The Aarhus Convention

[47] See e.g. R. Cox, *Revolution Justified*, Stichting Planet Prosperity Foundation 2012.

on Access to Information, Public Participation in Decision-Making and Access to Justice in Environmental Matters of 1998 has been key to shaping environmental decision-making in Europe.[48] However, the Aarhus Convention is also limited in this regard, as it approaches the issue only through the prism of good governance. A similar problem occurs in the book by Kotzé on global environmental constitutionalism. The focus of this book is not entirely on the negative aspect of constitutionalism. The book recognises the importance of democratic institutions in creating an effective climate policy: democracy improves the distribution of environmental costs and benefits throughout society.[49] This part of the book is then best seen in opposition to the view, defended by other authors, that democracy is unable to take effective environmental/climate action and that some form of authoritarianism is thus necessary and justified.[50]

The blind spot of this approach nevertheless remains that it envisions democracy as a black box that transforms public opinion into legislation and decisions. Within this view, there is little that constitutional law, or constitutional scholarship, can do to shape the functioning of democracy itself. Democratic institutions are seen as a given, with the task of constitutional law being to respond to whatever comes out of the black box. This neglects the fact that democratic institutions are themselves shaped by rules that favour some interests over others or set priorities. Environmental constitutionalism should be about shaping the rules of democracy, not to circumvent it, but to strengthen it.

The key is to recognise democracy as being created through rules and procedures. A constructivist approach to democracy denies that there is an *a priori* will of the people that can then be translated through voting and representation into policy.[51] Rather, the will of the people, or even the people as such, can come into existence only through democratic procedures. And once created in that manner, democratic procedures also help shape the rules themselves, for example by changing voting rules, creating advisory agencies for

---

48 On the relevance of the Aarhus Convention for EU climate law, see S. Nóbrega, *EU Climate Law through the Lens of the Aarhus Convention: Access to Environmental Information and Public Participation in EU Climate Change Decision Making*, Maastricht University 2020.

49 L.J. Kotzé, above n. 18, p. 170.

50 For the evolution of this position, see the description in J.M. Meyer, 'Political Theory and the Environment' in J.S. Dryzek, B. Honig and A. Phillips (eds), *The Oxford Handbook of Political Theory*, Oxford University Press 2008. See also R. Mittiga, 'Political Legitimacy, Authoritarianism, and Climate Change' (2021) 16 *American Political Science Review* 998. For a concise argument against 'coercive environmentalism', see Y. Li and J. Shapiro, *China Goes Green: Coercive Environmentalism for a Troubled Planet*, Polity Press 2020.

51 F. Wolkenstein, 'Revisiting the Constructivist Turn in Political Representation' (2021) *European Journal of Political Theory* 1. Kotzé does recognise this aspect of constitutionalism, for example in relation to the making of global environmental democracy. L.J. Kotzé, above n. 18, p. 237.

legislation and by limiting or expanding the mandate of courts. These procedural adjustments or innovations are rarely *neutral*.[52] They are adopted to engage with a specific problem, in light of a specific analysis that highlights or disregards certain (economic) positions over others.

In the Netherlands, a prime example of how democracy reformed itself in light of certain economic ideals is the Socio-Economic Council (Sociaal-Economische Raad, SER). The SER was created in 1950 through legislation, with the goal of providing advice on matters concerning, amongst other things, labour relations.[53] Representation in the Council consists of employers' organisations, employee organisations and experts (government appointees). The political influence of the SER can be seen, for example, in the current reforms of the Dutch pension system. The key characteristics of the reform were negotiated in the SER and are now in the process of being adopted in legislation. The SER thus has a central place in Dutch politics, based on a form of economic representation, without negating the legislative powers of parliament. The influence of the SER has also fluctuated over time, in part as a result of legislative changes concerning the role of the SER.

Democracy is, therefore, a process that not only involves citizens in decision-making, but which can also adapt in light of specific challenges. The key constitutional question is what a green democracy looks like.

One proposal that is gaining momentum in this regard, especially within several green or sustainability movements, is the use of citizen councils. As noted in the introduction, in France and Ireland these citizen councils have been employed to come up with proposals for, amongst other things, climate change mitigation. In the EU, deliberative citizen panels were used in the Conference on the Future of Europe. In the Netherlands, the use of a citizen council for climate policy is being researched and discussed.[54]

For a citizen council, a group of citizens are selected by lottery in order to deliberate upon a specific topic and propose a set of solutions.[55] As these

52 This is also a key point within the historical institutionalist approach to constitutional law, as the development of constitutional law is a product of political decision-making. See e.g. R.M. Smith, 'Historical Institutionalism and the Study of Law' in G.A. Caldeira, D.R. Kelemen and K.E. Whittington (eds), *The Oxford Handbook of Law and Politics*, Oxford University Press 2008.

53 Wet op de Sociaal-Economische Raad (Act on the Socio-Economic Council) of 27 January 1950. The SER was also authorised for some time to make binding rules on certain topics.

54 E. Rovers, *Nu Is Het Aan Ons: Oproep Tot Echte Democratie*, De Correspondent 2022; Adviescommissie Burgerbetrokkenheid bij klimaatbeleid, 'Betrokken Bij Klimaat: Burgerfora Aanbevolen' (2021), https://www.rijksoverheid.nl/documenten/publicaties/2021/03/21/adviesrapport-betrokken-bij-klimaat; C. Van Es, K. Hagen and I. Bakker, 'Een Stem Voor Burgers in de Strijd Tegen Klimaatverandering' (2021) 27 *Nederlands Juristenblad* 1978.

55 O. Doyle and R. Walsh, 'Constitutional Amendment and Public Will Formation: Deliberative Mini-Publics as a Tool for Consensus Democracy' (2022) 20 *International Journal of Constitutional Law* 398.

citizens are selected by chance (taking into account at least certain distinctions, such as gender and age) they are supposed to represent the citizenry as a whole, albeit in a different way than elected representatives in parliament. During their meetings, the Council may invite experts to support their deliberations, both on the analysis of the problem and on the solutions. The proposals resulting from these citizen councils are then expected to find broader popular support, as this process is thought to be less likely to be captured by vested interests. Moreover, as these selected citizens do not have an interest in re-election, they will be less incentivised to play into political or societal divisions, but instead to overcome them. The experience so far appears to indicate that the proposals from citizen councils are more ambitious with regard to climate policy.[56]

Proposals for the creation of citizen councils often start with an analysis of the current democratic system and identify certain structural problems that stand in the way of these democratic systems adopting proper climate policies. As citizen councils are not afflicted by these problems, they should lead to better climate policies. Hence, the emphasis lies on citizen councils being *outside* the ordinary democratic process. However, what has so far remained unclear is how citizen councils can be integrated into the constitutional and democratic systems. To be successful over the long term, citizen councils must find a place within the constitutional system, rather than stand outside them. These councils are currently positioned as advisory bodies, rather than as legislative bodies. Hence, they will rely on existing political institutions for their mandate, funding and of course for the implementation of their proposals. In France, the citizen council on climate policy was an initiative of the President, who also supported most of their proposals. However, the French Senate did not, and few proposals were ultimately transformed into policy.[57]

As discussed above, the Socio-Economic Council in the Netherlands has played a crucial role in Dutch socio-economic relations, despite its mostly advisory role. Hence, the fact that citizen councils are conceived of as advisory does not necessarily stand in the way of their effectiveness. However, it does require that attention be paid to their embedding within the larger democratic system.

5. CONCLUSION

This contribution has sought to bring together several seemingly disparate developments. Although all these developments deserve to be analysed in depth, the point I have sought to make here is that they all relate to the question of how

56 R. Willis, above n. 4.

57 H. Landemore, *Open Democracy: Reinventing Popular Rule for the Twenty-First Century*, Princeton University Press 2020, p. 118.

constitutional law should engage with the topics of climate change and climate change mitigation.

This chapter does not offer any specific solutions or answers to the question of how constitutional law should engage with climate change. Rather, the attempt is to show the relevance of climate change for various constitutional debates. Climate change is, or will become, enmeshed with several constitutional developments. What is needed is an overall perspective on the relationship between climate change and constitutionalism, in order for these debates to progress in a coherent manner.

As this chapter has focused on identifying relevant questions rather than providing answers, a key issue that has been left open is the extent to which constitutional law, and the ideas on which it is based, requires a fundamental overhaul, or whether less intrusive reforms are sufficient. Nor did we discuss what those options actually entail in relation to combating climate change and promoting sustainability. It would go beyond the purview of this conclusion to make any suggestions on this matter here, except to say that it would seem imprudent to *prima facie* deny the possibility that climate change as such cannot prompt deep changes in constitutional law and constitutionalism. There is a tendency within constitutional scholarship to see constitutional law as a more or less finished affair: we know what democracy and rule of law look like, even if they function differently in different countries. Especially since democracy and the rule of law are under severe threat, there is a need to stand firmly behind the key principles of democracy and the rule of law. However, such a response should not preclude genuine discussion on how constitutional law can aid the mitigation of climate change.

SHIFTING PRINCIPLES OF CLIMATE COOPERATION

A Court Ruling on Intergenerational Justice as Inspiration for the UN Climate Regime

Susann HANDKE

1. INTRODUCTION

In late 2021, the 26th Conference of the Parties to the UN climate regime (COP26) took place in Glasgow. This conference's number, together with the fact that these events take place annually,[1] reminds us that the international community has been debating the problem of climate change for more than a quarter of a century. The UN climate regime forms the institutional context of these deliberations. Many issues that shaped the evolution of the three treaties[2]

1 COP26 was delayed by one year because of the disruptions that resulted from the outbreak of the COVID-19 pandemic in early 2020.

2 The three treaties are the 1992 United Nations Framework Convention on Climate Change (UNFCCC), the 1997 Kyoto Protocol, and the 2015 Paris Agreement. See United Nations Framework Convention on Climate Change, 9 May 1992, 1771 UNTS 107, 31 ILM 849 (1992); Kyoto Protocol to the UN Framework Convention on Climate Change, 11 December 1997,

and decisions[3] of the UN climate regime reoccurred during the annual climate conferences and preparatory meetings, generally putting developed and developing countries in opposing camps. One example is the vaguely defined right to development, as will be shown below. In the context of mitigating climate change, this right is about preserving a carbon-intensive path to economic growth, in order to realise social progress for future generations.

During the climate negotiations in the late 1990s, government representatives of developing countries insisted that their countries first needed to achieve economic growth before they would be able to address climate change, as was the case with other forms of environmental degradation. At the time, climate negotiators understood the phenomenon of human-induced climate change as an environmental problem. The institutionalisation of international climate cooperation thus followed the model of other multilateral environmental agreements. The need to balance development and environmental protection has influenced the evolution of the UN climate regime from the outset.

During the final session of COP26, representatives from China and India once again pointed to the pursuit of economic development as their core concern when they watered down a provision on the phase-out of unabated coal use in the electricity sector. As a result, the final declaration of COP26 calls on the parties to transition towards a 'phasedown' of unabated coal use to produce power.[4] Although this looks like a minor semantic adjustment, legal scholars will be aware of the underlying development debate and its legacy in the context of international climate cooperation.

After about three decades of international efforts to address climate change, other principles and concepts that guide the Parties' cooperation under the UN climate regime might help to consider a refined approach to the notion of development. Undoubtedly, the reality of both the global energy business and the increasingly imminent threat of climate change indicate a need to give greater emphasis to the principle of intergenerational justice, which, as one of the core principles of the UN climate regime, is stipulated in Article 3(1) of the United Nations Framework Convention on Climate Change (UNFCCC).

In an effort to highlight the importance of intergenerational justice for international climate cooperation, this chapter collects legal arguments that justify an increased emphasis on intergenerational justice. The contribution

---

2303 UNTS 148, 37 ILM 22 (1998); and Decision 1/CP.21 – Adoption of the Paris Agreement (FCCC/CP/2015/10/Add.1), 29 January 2016.

3 The annual COP – as the plenary body of the UN climate regime – takes decisions that implement the treaties and shape the regime based on the treaties, especially by referring to the principles of the UNFCCC, by adding specific issues that the treaties address insufficiently.

4 United Nations Climate Change, 'Glasgow Climate Pact – Advance Unedited Version', para. 36, https://unfccc.int/sites/default/files/resource/cma3_auv_2_cover%20decision.pdf.

draws inspiration from a decision[5] at which Germany's federal constitutional court (Bundesverfassungsgericht, hereafter the Court) arrived a few months before COP26. This decision considers the rights of future generations in the context of Germany's path to climate neutrality. The chapter follows the Court's train of thought, which is particularly interesting for the international debate. The chapter argues that instead of adhering to an outdated definition of development, leaders and people from the developing world gain most by embracing intergenerational justice as a guiding principle when engaging in international climate cooperation. This is particularly true when they have to take decisions about the structure of the energy system, as was attempted during the debate about coal use at COP26. To illustrate this interlinkage, this chapter relates the application of the principle of intergenerational justice to vital parameters of energy and climate policy design.

The chapter develops its analysis as follows. The next section briefly describes the methods and theoretical framework that the chapter deploys to arrive at and present its reasoning. The third section summarises the Court's decision on the German climate law. Then, the fourth section shifts the attention to the premise of development in the evolution of the UN climate regime. The fifth section contrasts the Court's arguments with the notion of development in the UN climate regime, imagined as a conversation between the judges' reasoning and the interpretation of the principle of intergenerational justice under the UN climate regime. Building on the findings of the previous sections, the sixth section illustrates how a set of three parameters that outline elements of climate and energy policy helps to balance different objectives, when both designing national policies and contemplating international cooperation. The seventh section concludes.

2. CONSIDERING NATIONAL JURISPRUDENCE AS A REALITY CHECK FOR THE UN CLIMATE REGIME

Climate laws that national legislators and governments draft do not evolve in isolation from international legal developments. In fact, the adoption of both the Kyoto Protocol and Paris Agreement were preceded and followed by a flurry of national legislative and regulatory activities to either anticipate or implement the policy changes that the international climate treaties required. The scope of socio-economic change and the depth of the measures that meaningful cooperation under the Paris Agreement entails have been reasons for the

5 Bundesverfassungsgericht (BVerfG), Order of the First Senate of 24 March 2021, 1 BvR 2656/18, paras 1–270, https://www.bundesverfassungsgericht.de/e/rs20210324_1bvr265618en.html.

adoption of extensive climate laws in many States since 2015. The European Parliament and the national governments of the Union's Member States adopted the 'Clean Energy for All Europeans' legislative package[6] in 2019. This package implements the Energy Union, including the objectives of the Paris Agreement.[7] Thus, rule-making efforts at the international and EU levels inspired EU Member States to pass national climate laws.

These laws are comprehensive and generally seek to guide the decarbonisation of the entire economy. As a result, society as a whole is affected. This, in turn, requires the balancing of rights, interests and various objectives of socio-economic policies. In Europe, courts will most likely continue to decide whether policy-makers and legislators made the right choices in aligning the protection of fundamental rights and the implementation of climate measures. This was the case when the German Constitutional Court considered complaints against the country's federal climate law. Several individuals, supported by three non-governmental organisations, had submitted complaints. One legal basis for the complaints was the duty of the State to protect freedom rights of young people.[8]

By assessing the Court's reasoning, various arguments can be found that help enrich the debate on international climate cooperation. To show how the Court's findings relate to the UN climate regime and its principles, this chapter contrasts the reasoning with the concept of development. This concept has had a great influence on the evolution of the UN climate regime, while the principle of intergenerational justice as one of the core principles of the regime has played a less prominent role thus far.

By linking the results of this juxtaposition with the reality of the global energy transition, the chapter chooses a novel approach. It considers an example of a court case against a national climate law – decided by a country's highest court – and evaluates some of the court's findings in the light of rule-making to promote climate cooperation at the international level. Scholarly assessments of both topics are generally divided by the legal realms that they analyse. Research on intergenerational justice in the context of climate change mitigation usually takes a moral or philosophical approach, while national debates that inspire court rulings often delve into practical, technical facets of the energy transition,

---

6 See for an overview, European Commission, 'Clean Energy for All Europeans Package', https://energy.ec.europa.eu/topics/energy-strategy/clean-energy-all-europeans-package_en.

7 Pursuant to Articles 2(1)(a) and 4(1) of the Paris Agreement, the main objectives that the Parties to the Agreement agreed to achieve are the limitation of global warming to 1.5–2°C, compared to pre-industrial levels, and accomplishing climate neutrality in the second half of the 21st century.

8 The Court specifically considered the question of whether the German climate law 'offloads significant portions of the greenhouse gas reduction burdens required under Art. 20a GG [Basic Law] onto the post-2030 period' and, by doing so, would place the complainants 'under enormous (additional) strain' and 'comprehensively' jeopardise complainants' 'freedom protected by fundamental rights'. See BVerfG, above n. 5, para. 117.

and carbon budgets, which is also exemplified by the factual part on which the German Constitutional Court bases its reasoning.[9]

To contextualise an imagined conversation between the national and international legal levels, this chapter draws on the application of John Rawls's theorising[10] to intergenerational justice under the threat of global environmental crises. This approach is meaningful, mainly because it helps to combine the Court's practical considerations with theoretical thinking. By doing so, the presentation of the findings can cross the divide between national and international climate rule-making. Moreover, the inclusion of Rawls's theory of justice provides new avenues for thinking about development, the needs of future generations, and finite natural resources to sustain human life.

Accordingly, this chapter creates a space for debate. It fills this space with the arguments that national judges from one European country present in their ruling on the prospects for future generations in a climate-constrained world and subsequently contrasts the judges' approach with considerations that proponents of development rights frequently raise during the deliberations under the UN climate regime. The application of Rawlsian theorising about the rights of future generations helps to both contextualise this imagined conversation and arrive at some general conclusions for the organisation of international climate cooperation. To facilitate the presentation of the chapter's main findings with respect to the structuring of international climate cooperation, the sixth section includes an illustration of essential parameters that condition international climate action.

For the purpose of engaging with the concept of intergenerational justice, the German Constitutional Court's decision is useful, mainly because it takes a broad perspective on freedom rights of the next generation that will be affected if the government postpones decisive climate measures. The chapter considers the judges' reasoning in the context of international climate cooperation by correlating their conclusions with references to the 'right to development' in decisions by annual COPs of the UN climate regime.

No doubt it would also be possible to discuss statements by negotiators on behalf of individual States or negotiation coalitions during the annual COPs. However, COP decisions are more relevant to the evolution of the UN climate regime – and the progress of the debate – than sole government statements during the negotiation rounds, even if they are supported by a number of States. COP decisions generally energise future negotiation trajectories.

---

9 The German Constitutional Court deploys the notion of a national carbon budget as basis for its reasoning. See BVerfG, above n. 5, para. 216.

10 J. Rawls, *A Theory of Justice*, Belknap, Cambridge, MA 1971.

To put intergenerational justice into perspective, this chapter relies on theorising that is inspired by John Rawls's thinking. In conceptualising what he calls a 'well-ordered society' that provides justice to its constituents, Rawls is neutral towards the choices that individuals make.[11] In other words, the pursuit of a good life for each individual is merely constrained by institutions that guarantee and thus maintain the Rawlsian well-ordered society. Maintaining and promoting just institutions is part of social development. Thus, the need to uphold just institutions can form a path to extend Rawls's theory to consider the challenges of a climate-constrained world.[12]

Rawlsian-inspired theorising on intergenerational justice is helpful, mainly because authors that apply his notion of justice to future generations are able to link this concept with global environmental crises and future generations' ability to design choices to lead their lives, individually and – as a consequence – translated into policies that constitute collective results of individual choices. Two concepts that form the basis for this chapter's analysis in its sections 5 and 6 derive from Rawlsian thinking – i.e. interrelated factors of *societal stability* and *resource depletion* as a threat to future generations' life designs and the need to preserve policy space for them. The interpretation of Rawlsian thought by Hyunseop Kim[13] and Britta Clark[14] inform the Rawlsian interpretation of these two concepts in this chapter's analysis.

To apply Rawls's theory to a climate-constrained world, its scope needs to be extended. Kim shows that, in order to discuss climate change, environmental considerations need to be added to Rawlsian theorising.[15] In addition, Clark relates the Rawlsian notion of neutrality to the availability of natural resources in the future: actions today must not make particular ways of life impossible for future generations to pursue. This needs to be the standard of just treatment between subsequent generations.[16]

In his theory of justice, Rawls did not include environmental concerns. The well-ordered society persists without institutions that regulate the impact that people's individual choices have on the environment. However, Kim shows that

---

11 According to Rawls, a society is well ordered 'when it is not only designed to advance the good of its members but when it is also effectively regulated by public conception of justice.' In this society, 'everyone accepts and knows that the others accept the same principles of justice. Moreover, 'the basic social institutions generally satisfy and are generally known to satisfy these principles.' See J. Rawls, above n. 10, pp. 4–5.

12 S.M. Gardiner, 'Rawls and Climate Change: Does Rawlsian Political Philosophy Pass the Global Test' (2011) 14 *Critical Review of International Social and Political Philosophy* 125, 142.

13 H. Kim, 'An Extension of Rawls's Theory of Justice for Climate Change' (2019) 11 *International Theory* 160.

14 B. Clark, 'Neutrality, Nature, and Intergenerational Justice' (2021) 30 *Environmental Politics* 307.

15 H. Kim, above n. 13, pp. 163–68.

16 B. Clark, above n. 14, pp. 319–20.

in the case of climate change this omission would render the maintenance of a well-ordered society improbable.[17] The main argument for including concerns for the climate in the institutional fabric that maintains the well-ordered society is the existential threat that climate change poses to human existence. Thus, the damage that the consequences of climate change can cause is sufficiently severe that potential disruptions imperil the stability of the well-ordered society.[18]

This extension of Rawlsian thought is permissible. In fact, Rawls was aware of the necessity to extend his theory of justice. In a late article, he reconsidered his theory in the context of 'reasonable pluralism' in liberal societies that his account of justice failed to acknowledge.[19] This openness of Rawls's theory allows us to include further, environmental aspects that emerge as relevant to societal stability. In this sense, extending Rawlsian thought in the face of disastrous climate change is justified and even logical. Hence, societal developments in a climate-constrained world require this extension of Rawlsian theorising to account for the maintenance of stability under these new and challenging circumstances.

Another valid argument for taking environmental concerns into account when considering the ability of young people to make their own life choices is the threat that climate change poses to the room for manoeuvre that will be available to future generations, mainly because global warming will (potentially) completely deplete the natural resources that facilitate these choices.[20] The application and interpretation of Rawls's theory on which Kim and Clark build their arguments are consistent and coherent. It is thus possible to draw on Rawls's thinking to assess justice issues in the context of climate change that pertain to future generations, despite the fact that Rawls did not extend his theory of justice to institutions that manage natural resources.

Finally, Rawls's theory of justice is helpful for developing this chapter's argument, as he considers justice both in well-ordered national societies and in the 'Society of Peoples'[21] – i.e. the international realm. The simultaneousness of justice implications at the national and international levels characterises the task of mitigating climate change and dealing with the consequences of global warming. Questions about just treatment arise intragenerationally and intergenerationally. Thus far, the UN climate regime has primarily been shaped by intergenerational matters. The above-mentioned decades-long debate about the premise of national development and the wish to pursue inexpensive

17 H. Kim, above n. 13, p. 166.

18 Ibid., p. 165.

19 J. Rawls, 'The Idea of Public Reason Revisited' (1997) 64 *The University of Chicago Law Review* 765.

20 B. Clark, above n. 14, pp. 319–20.

21 H. Kim, above n. 13, pp. 160, 168.

development trajectories based on the consumption of fossil fuels exemplify this observation. Hence, the extension of Rawlsian theorising to institutions that deal with climate change offers a theoretical framework to consider national aspects of intergenerational justice, while also acknowledging injustices in international affairs that relate to the fossil economy.

By doing so, this chapter presents a comprehensive account of the utility of climate litigation to reconsider justice and related policy implications in a world that is increasingly adversely affected by global warming. The chapter embeds legal arguments in philosophical thoughts in order to bridge the legal and policy realms. Indeed, the policy-focused account at the end of this chapter's analytical part applies justice considerations to the design of broader climate measures. Thus, section 6 reconnects the justice-inspired philosophical discussion with the description of parameters, which, if well-balanced, define meaningful climate action. In essence, the question of how policy-makers and legislators achieve this balance forms the core of many recent climate litigation cases. This chapter offers one interpretation of this tricky balancing act.

3. THE GERMAN CONSTITUTIONAL COURT'S DECISION

National climate laws in EU Member States help to implement the Union's energy and climate policy, which aims to achieve climate neutrality by 2050. Legislators in the Member States are required to transpose the EU climate and energy legislation into national law and policy measures. The 2019 climate law[22] that the German federal government drafted was part of this Union-wide effort. It entailed measures until 2030 to reduce emissions. It goes without saying that this law of the then coalition government was a compromise catering to divergent interests in society, especially coal-producing regions and the security of affordable energy supplies for Germany's (heavy) industry. It thus covered the main constituencies of the ruling Christian-democratic and social-democratic grand coalition.

Climate activists did not hesitate to challenge the federal government's climate law before the German constitutional court soon after its adoption. On 24 March 2021, the Court issued its order in response to complaints by several young individuals against the climate law.[23] Non-governmental organisations, such as Germanwatch, Greenpeace and Protect the Planet, supported the legal action that the young people had initiated.

22 Bundes-Klimaschutzgesetz (Federal Climate Protection Law), Federal Law Gazette – BGBl. I S. 2513.

23 BVerfG, above n. 5.

The Court considered to what extent the German climate law would fulfil the country's contribution to the global efforts in the context of the Paris Agreement and the law's effects on freedom rights. The Court based its reasoning on Article 20a of the Basic Law (Germany's constitution), which stipulates that the State's responsibility includes the protection of the 'natural foundations of life ... by legislation'.[24]

According to the Court, the State failed to fulfil this responsibility with respect to the 2019 climate law, mainly because the measures do not sufficiently take into account the temperature limit that the Paris Agreement sets.[25] In determining the State's failure to fulfil its responsibility, the Court translates the temperature limit into an 'emission measurement'[26] to 'measure whether the emission amounts allowed' in the climate law 'are compatible with the temperature limit' of the Paris Agreement.[27] The path that the climate law set for the implementation of climate measures was only detailed until 2030.

After 2030, the planned reductions would have been issued by ordinance, a legal instrument that requires less public participation and debate than the legislative procedure in the federal parliament. The Court considers the unpredictability of the further emissions reduction trajectory based on this legal instrument to be in violation of Article 20a of the Basic Law, as 'the specific updating process has not been sufficiently laid out' in the climate law.[28] Therefore, the envisioned procedure 'does not meet the constitutional requirements for a structuring mechanism aimed at providing sufficient orientation for further development going forward.'[29] The legal framework failed to 'satisfy the requirements of fundamental rights ... on the updating of the reduction targets from 2031 until the point when climate neutrality is reached as required' by the constitution.[30]

The Court holds that by only vaguely outlining how the annual reduction targets will be set for the period from 2030 onwards, the climate law did not

24 Article 20a Basic Law: 'Der Staat schützt auch in Verantwortung für die künftigen Generationen die natürlichen Lebensgrundlagen und die Tiere im Rahmen verfassungsmäßigen Ordnungen durch die Gesetzgebung und nach Maßgabe von Gesetz und Recht durch die vollziehende Gewalt und die Rechtsprechung.' Official English translation: 'Article 20a of the Basic Law [Protection of the natural foundations of life and animals] – Mindful also of its responsibility towards future generations, the state shall protect the natural foundations of life and animals by legislation and, in accordance with law and justice, by executive and judicial action, all within the framework of the constitutional order.' See Federal Ministry of Justice, https://www.gesetze-im-internet.de/englisch_gg/englisch_gg.html#p0116.

25 BVerfG, above n. 5, para. 213.

26 Ibid., para. 215.

27 Ibid., para. 216.

28 Ibid., para. 256.

29 Ibid.

30 Ibid., para. 266.

sufficiently protect future generations' fundamental rights. The reduction requirements after 2031 would have been too extensive. Furthermore, given the short period until climate neutrality has to be achieved, they would entail a potential far-reaching violation of freedom rights of young people who already live today. The comparatively small volume of carbon dioxide (CO_2) emissions reductions that were required by 2030 would leave a great deal of work to do in the short period between that year and 2050, when climate neutrality should be achieved. The burden was to a large extent shifted onto the next generation.

Accordingly, the Court concludes that the task of quickly reducing large volumes of carbon dioxide emissions would place the next generation 'under enormous (additional) strain' and comprehensively jeopardise their freedom that is protected by fundamental rights.[31] Since greenhouse gas emissions result from 'virtually all aspects of human life', 'all forms of freedom are potentially affected'.[32] In any case, the 'general freedom of action' of Article 2(1) of the Basic Law was threatened.[33]

The fact that the climate law allowed the present generation to consume a considerable part of the carbon budget would have narrowed the next generation's freedom, the exercise of which involves carbon dioxide emissions, and would have shortened 'the time left for initiating and completing a socio-technological transformation'.[34] Thus, larger volumes of greenhouse gases emitted until 2030 would have resulted in a diminishing room for manoeuvre, at which point the next generation would be required to consider substantive policy choices, while being left with a narrowing window to accomplish the transition to climate neutrality. This line of thought that the Court presents is the finding on which this chapter primarily builds its argument relating to the pursuit of intergenerational justice, as section 5 will show. Before this consideration, the next section gives an overview of the international context.

4. THE PREMISE OF DEVELOPMENT IN THE UN CLIMATE REGIME

The UN climate regime explicitly acknowledges the right of developing countries to development. In its third preambular paragraph, the UNFCCC points to the 'still relatively low' level of per-capita emissions in developing countries at the time when the UNFCCC was adopted in the 1990s and continues to stipulate

31 Ibid., para. 117.
32 Ibid.
33 Ibid.
34 Ibid., para. 122.

that 'the share of global emissions originating in developing countries will grow to meet their social and development needs.'[35] Thus, developing countries were provided with a space to develop their economies without limiting the emission of greenhouse gases. This reasoning is based on the conviction that 'economic development is essential for adopting measures to address climate change', which Article 3(4) UNFCCC reiterates.[36]

Article 4 UNFCCC lists the commitments of the Parties under the UNFCCC and stipulates in its paragraph 7 that 'the extent to which developing country Parties will effectively implement their commitments under the Convention will take fully into account that economic and social development and poverty eradication are the first and overriding priorities of the developing country Parties.'[37] Thus, from the outset, climate cooperation under the UN climate regime was based on the notion that developing countries could pursue their – implicitly carbon-intensive – economic development. Only at a later moment in time would they join developed countries in their efforts to limit and reduce annual greenhouse gas emissions.

This notion was reiterated on several occasions in the evolution of the UN climate regime. Most notably, the 'development space' that developing countries could enjoy was included in the Berlin Mandate, which formed the basis for negotiating the Kyoto Protocol.[38] This treaty for the first time established concrete binding emissions reduction obligations of the Parties under the UN climate regime. However, the Kyoto Protocol excluded developing countries from obligations to achieve a reduction of their greenhouse gas emissions compared to the 1990 level. As a result, the notion of providing developing countries time and space to pursue economic development based on emission-intensive processes shaped the cooperation during the first and second commitment periods of the Kyoto Protocol – from 2008 to 2012 and 2013 to 2020 respectively. In fact, this arrangement would eventually spell the Protocol's failure. Increasing greenhouse gas emissions from large developing economies outpaced the reductions that developed countries were able to make. Dissatisfaction with the arrangements of the Kyoto Protocol led to the adoption of the Paris Agreement in 2015.

In the Paris Agreement, the right to development is reiterated in the 11th preambular paragraph. However, this paragraph goes beyond economic development as a State goal. It points to the task to 'respect, promote and consider their respective obligations on human rights, the right to health, the rights

35 UNFCCC, above n. 2, third preambular paragraph.

36 Ibid., Article 3(4).

37 Ibid., Article 4(7).

38 The Berlin Mandate: Review of the Adequacy of Article 4, paragraph 2 (a) and (b), of the Convention, Including Proposals Related to a Protocol and Decisions on Follow-up, Decision 1/CP.1 (FCCC/CP/1995/7/Add.1), para. 1(1)(a).

of indigenous peoples, local communities, migrants, children, persons with disabilities and people in vulnerable situations and the right to development, as well as equality, empowerment of women and intergenerational equity', when the Parties take action to address climate change.[39]

The debate during the final hour of the Glasgow COP26 and this conference's overall outcome show that the meaning of the right to development and its position in the UN climate regime remain contested. Thus far, the spirit of the Paris Agreement has failed to alter the perception of the interlinkage between development and the need to mitigate climate change, especially among some developing countries with large economies. Hence, more arguments are needed to further strengthen the debate in the context of the UN climate regime.

The refinement of the definition of key concepts and principles that shape the UN climate regime is an arduous and lengthy process, as the refinement of the principle of common but differentiated responsibilities shows. In fact, during the first two decades of climate action under the UN climate regime, developing countries' obligations to engage in limiting and reducing greenhouse gas emissions were closely related to the interpretation of the principle of common but differentiated responsibilities. Only the adoption of the Paris Agreement changed this situation.

The principle of common but differentiated responsibilities is included in Article 3 UNFCCC and belongs to the core principles of the UN climate regime. By refining its interpretation in the Paris Agreement,[40] the Parties to the UN climate regime created rule-making space to include developing countries in efforts to limit and reduce annual greenhouse gas emissions. Now, the application of the principle allows the Parties to 'self-differentiate' the extent to which they engage in emissions reduction action.[41] Thus, based on their own assessment of their capabilities to contribute to global climate action, developing countries can re-interpret the relationship between climate action and economic development. This adjustment of developing countries' positioning with respect to their responsibilities unlocks a new perspective on development and intergenerational justice, as the following section will show.

---

39 Paris Agreement, above n. 2, para. 11.

40 This was achieved by adding the clause 'in the light of different national circumstances' to the original formulation of the principle. See, for instance, Article 4(3) of the Paris Agreement, which stipulates the commitments of the Parties. The Paris Agreement is based on the notion that *all* Parties have the commitment to submit nationally determined contributions to global efforts to mitigate climate change.

41 See for an in-depth account, L. Rajamani, 'Ambition and Differentiation in the 2015 Paris Agreement: Interpretative Possibilities and Underlying Politics' (2016) 65 *International and Comparative Law Quarterly* 493.

5. CONVERSING ABOUT INTERGENERATIONAL JUSTICE

Altering the definition of key concepts of the UN climate regime is a process that unfolds during the sessions of the plenary and subsidiary bodies that serve the regime as well as in numerous dialogues that have been created to address specific aspects of climate cooperation. Rather than expressing a clearly defined legal meaning, more often than not the concepts and formulations of principles in treaties and decisions convey an ideational meaning. In this sense, there is a semantic openness for input from beyond the UN climate regime. For the sake of the meaningful, future-minded evolution of the regime, it seems necessary to foster such input.

5.1. DIALOGUE BETWEEN LEGAL REALMS

The fate of future generations and their right to development – at least implicitly – informed the establishment of the UN climate regime. When international climate cooperation was first institutionalised in the early 1990s, many considered the onset of threatening and materialising consequences of climate change a distant affair. Three decades into climate cooperation, the impact of a global temperature rise is increasingly tangible. The effects of climate change are generally associated with the destruction caused by changing weather patterns and phenomena, such as frequently occurring prolonged periods of drought and heat that feed wildfires in California and the Russian Arctic regions, stronger typhoons in South-East and East Asia, unusual monsoon seasons in South Asia, and floods after extreme rainfall in western Europe.

The destructive force of these weather phenomena recontextualises the linkage between the right to development and the concept of intergenerational justice. Indeed, a broad global public turned its attention to this interrelationship following massive climate strikes and protests that teenagers organised on all inhabited continents in 2018 and 2019. The young protesters rightly questioned the rationale for expanding fossil infrastructure in the name of economic development. Many of these massive protests took place in large cities across South and South-East Asia. Still, State and business elites from these parts of the world have most recently advocated for the expansion of carbon-intensive modes of development. It comes as no surprise that, at the international level and especially at annual climate summits, these countries' representatives hardly speak up for their young people's interests.

As seen during COP26 in Glasgow, representatives from large developing countries prefer to highlight the right to development. They generally argue that only sufficient economic development would provide their countries with the means to also engage in environmental protection. This notion of a gradual evolution of developing countries' contribution to climate action is based on two propositions. First, the proponents of this thinking adhere to the understanding that climate change is an environmental problem. Second, building on the experiences of developed countries during the second half of the 20th century, they suggest that environmental pollution is part of an initial phase of development. After acquiring adequate means, governments would enact policies to protect the environment.

Both propositions are erroneous. First, although the UN climate regime considers climate change as an environmental problem, solving this problem requires a restructuring of the entire economy, transitioning from carbon-intensive modes of growth to climate-neutral processes. Thus, combating global warming is above all about transforming national fossil fuel-based economies. Second, the scope of climate change as a cumulative global crisis exceeds the environmental problems that emerged during phases of industrialisation in developed countries. Hence, the mitigation of climate change goes far beyond small-scale efforts to, for instance, restore polluted rivers or improve the ecology of environmentally degraded areas next to chemical plants.

In its reasoning, the German Constitutional Court presents an argument that relates to the linkage between economic development and climate change, including the implications for future generations. The Court repeatedly emphasises the irreversibility of climate change. The judges acknowledge that carbon dioxide emissions 'make an essentially irreversible contribution towards global warming.'[42] The legislator, under constitutional law, 'may not allow climate change to progress *ad infinitum* without taking action.'[43] The Court thus recognises that there is no way of denying the adverse effects of carbon-intensive economic development. It is the task of the legislator to take measures. Furthermore, the Court highlights the fact that 'provisions that allow CO2 emissions in the present pose an irreversible legal risk to future freedom.'[44]

Interestingly, the Court links the irreversibility of climate change with an 'irreversible' threat to others' freedom rights. It expects that 'at some point' any exercise of freedom that causes the emission of carbon dioxide will 'have to be prohibited', as climate change can only be mitigated if carbon dioxide concentrations in the atmosphere 'do not rise any further'.[45] Only the protection of fundamental rights would justify 'any overshoot of the critical temperature for preventing climate change', as it is commonly known 'that climate change is almost entirely irreversible'.[46]

---

42 BVerfG, above n. 5, para. 185.
43 Ibid.
44 Ibid., para. 186.
45 Ibid.
46 Ibid., para. 198.

In this case, a balancing process seems to be necessary. When considering such proceedings, the Court notices that 'the obligation to take climate action is accorded increasing weight as climate change intensifies.'[47] Hence, carbon-intensive activities, under conditions of ongoing global warming, are permissible if they serve the protection of fundamental rights. Citing the need to develop a country's economy might not be sufficient to fulfil this threshold, in particular for developing countries with large economies.

Given the irreversibility of climate change, the Court points to the duty of the State to protect the 'right to life and physical integrity' and the inviolability of people's freedom rights, pursuant to Article 2(2) of Germany's Basic Law. This duty 'is also oriented towards the future', as it 'can also establish a duty to protect future generations', which is 'all the more applicable where irreversible processes are at stake'.[48]

To drive this point home, the Court creates a useful vehicle – the notion of an 'advance interference-like effect'.[49] The Court uses this vehicle to link the State's responsibility for the protection of future generations' freedom rights with the severe, irreversible impact of climate change on freedom rights.[50] Thus, allowing the large-scale emission of greenhouse gases today and in the near future has an advanced interference-like effect on the freedom of younger people and future generations. This degree of interference is only permissible by law. When drafting such legislation, the legislator would be required to balance the severity of climate measures, which affect the current generation, with the freedom rights of future generations. Moreover, the emission of greenhouse gases 'can ultimately only be reconciled with the potentially affected fundamental freedoms if precautionary measures are taken in order to manage the reduction of burdens … in ways that respect fundamental rights.'[51]

In other words, in a climate-constrained world the pursuit of carbon-intensive economic development is conditional on a set of steps that governments need to take. Even in developing countries, policy-makers and legislators need to be cognisant of the adverse effects of their carbon-intensive policy measures, in terms of the consequences for their own constituents and potential global impacts. Therefore, governments should be prepared to present a justification of these fossil fuel-based development policies in relation to the potential impact on

47 Ibid.

48 Ibid., para. 146.

49 Ibid., para. 183; see also K. Kotulla and M. Kotulla, 'Bundesverfassungsgericht und Klimaschutz: Wenn die Zukunft über die Gegenwart mitentscheiden darf' (Federal constitutional court and climate protection: The present is allowed to co-decide on the future) (2022) 44 *Natur und Recht* 1, 8, 10.

50 P. Minnerop, 'The "Advance Interference-Like Effect" of Climate Targets: Fundamental Rights, Intergenerational Equity and the German Federal Constitutional Court' (2022) 34 *Journal of Environmental Law* 135, 148–50.

51 BVerfG, above n. 5, para. 245.

the freedom rights of future generations. This would involve showing evidence of balancing proceedings that policy-makers and legislators have conducted ahead of adopting the policies in question. Furthermore, when enacting carbon-intensive development policies, governments need to combine these policies with precautionary measures, in order to manage the burden on future generations.

To sum up, in the 2020s it is increasingly questionable whether carbon-intensive modes of economic development are still viable. In a climate-constrained world, the pursuit of carbon-intensive economic policies is only justifiable when these policies help to protect fundamental rights. The adoption and implementation of such policies requires a balancing process, weighing current constituents' fundamental rights and those of future generations. If carbon-intensive policies are implemented, precautionary measures are essential to sufficiently contain the damage – i.e. the emission of additional greenhouse gases into the atmosphere. To be sure, claiming a right to unabated carbon-intensive development is behind the times. The German Constitutional Court's findings and the description of 'development' in the Paris Agreement put forward arguments for a more refined debate at the international level.

5.2. A RAWLSIAN PERSPECTIVE ON INTERGENERATIONAL JUSTICE

The German Constitutional Court emphasised the irreversibility of climate change. Indeed, this characteristic of global warming proves to be a valid starting point for justice considerations when assessing the consequences of climate change for governing the well-ordered societies that Rawls describes.

The interpretation and extension of Rawls's theory that Clark and Kim propose offer two viewpoints concerning the just treatment of future generations in a climate-constrained world – one concerns individual freedom and another pertains to society as a whole. Both analyses build on the extension of Rawlsian thinking on justice to the very environmental features that sustain the well-ordered society.

On an individual basis, just treatment in a liberal, well-ordered society needs to entail the availability of natural resources that enable individual life choices. Clark discerns from the liberal premise of neutrality regarding individual preferences the obligation of the present generation to preserve natural resources that make the pursuit of individual life designs possible.[52] Natural resources provide 'ecological spaces' for these choices.[53]

Yet individual life designs become impossible after the irreversible destruction of resources that are essential for particular choices. Thus, following Clark's thought, the Rawlsian liberal postulate to remain neutral regarding individual choices demands that the well-ordered society establish institutions

52 B. Clark, above n. 14, p. 308.

53 Ibid., p. 314.

that sustain those choice-enabling ecological spaces, in order to continue to guarantee the availability of particular choices and designs. In other words, the present generation has an obligation to guarantee that future generations can pursue 'any reasonable conception of the good'.[54] The institutional setup of society that the present generation maintains and passes to the next one must include institutions that preserve natural resources. Hence, in this interpretation of Rawlsian thought, rules that require the mitigation of climate change to avoid a dangerous global temperature rise are essential for a just treatment of future generations.

When considering society as a whole, preserving the physical environment in which society functions is vital to maintain societal stability. Kim holds that guaranteeing essential environmental background conditions is necessary for retaining the basic institutional structure of the well-ordered society.[55] Only a resilient society that can sustain its institutions and rules is able to provide justice 'in perpetuity'.[56]

The effects of climate change can potentially destabilise society. Avoiding a dangerous rise in temperatures thus constitutes a precondition for societal stability and the provision of justice. Only a stable society treats people fairly. Thus, the institutional structure of society in a climate-constrained world must include measures that preserve those environmental conditions that are essential for maintaining stability. Societal stability is the threshold for determining the extent of institutions and rules to mitigate climate change.[57]

To sum up, from a Rawlsian perspective, just treatment of future generations requires the present generation to take measures to avoid dangerous climate change. Efforts in this regard are essential to enable future generations to enjoy freedom rights and choose life designs that characterise a liberal society. Therefore, the protection of favourable environmental conditions needs to be part of the basic institutional fabric of a well-ordered society. To elaborate climate policies that balance different concerns and aims, the next section discusses the parameters of an institutional framework that helps to take into account the rights of future generations.

6. A FUTURE-MINDED FRAMEWORK FOR INTERNATIONAL CLIMATE COOPERATION

The responsibility of the State clearly includes care for future generations when considering environmental impacts of policy measures and, in particular, when

---

54 Ibid., p. 316.

55 H. Kim, above n. 13, p. 161.

56 Ibid., p. 164.

57 Ibid., p. 178.

initiating a timely response to climate change. However, governments have to deal with a whole range of policy objectives and public services that the State is expected to provide to its citizens. The provisions of the Paris Agreement include some guidance regarding the balancing of components that shape climate action. This section ponders how insights regarding the relationship between the right to development and intergenerational justice in the context of climate change mitigation can help inform meaningful energy and climate policies. Together with the provisions of the Paris Agreement, the findings of the previous sections can indeed form a basis for imagining parameters that help guide future climate action.

The transition to climate neutrality entails the transformation of the entire fossil fuel-based economy. This long-term process has far-reaching socio-economic and environmental consequences. The German Constitutional Court's reasoning gives present-day policy-makers and legislators a clear task: policies and laws that are adopted today need to take into account room for manoeuvre[58] for future policy choices. This will allow the next generation to fulfil its obligation of accomplishing the reduction of greenhouse gas emissions towards climate neutrality. Leaving little policy space for the next generation will most likely force today's youth to endure far-reaching measures, which sooner or later will considerably impair their fundamental rights.

The consideration of societal stability, environmental impacts and the energy system's structure alludes to three parameters that future policies should take into account – i.e. climate and transition resilience, the precautionary concept, and the adequacy of energy provision. Figure 1 depicts these three parameters in a triangular relationship that needs to be balanced, with respect to both policy design and implementation activities.

The parameters of this figure need to find themselves in balance when contemplating national measures, and their balancing needs to inform international climate cooperation as well. The components of this framework are reflected in the Paris Agreement.

The temperature target stipulated in Article 2(1)(a) of the Paris Agreement resembles a precautionary approach. The article describes the objective of the Paris Agreement as '[h]olding the increase in the global average temperature to well below 2°C above pre-industrial levels and pursuing efforts to limit the temperature increase to 1.5°C above pre-industrial levels, recognizing that this would significantly reduce the risks and impacts of climate change.'[59]

The framework's component 'precautionary concept' relates to climate change in two ways. First, it concerns measures to mitigate climate change. In this

---

58 The German Constitutional Court calls this 'leeway'. See BVerfG, above n. 5, paras 152, 162, 211.

59 Paris Agreement, above n. 2, Article 2(1)(a).

Figure 1. Components of (international) climate action

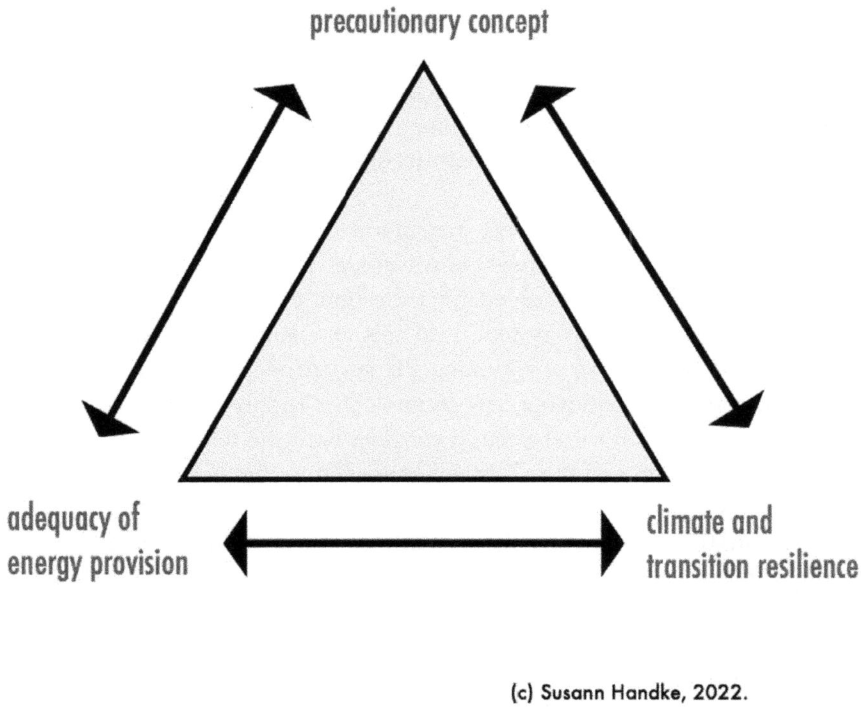

Source: Produced by the author.

context, the 1.5–2°C threshold is relevant, as is the need to reduce greenhouse gas emissions to avoid dangerous climate change. Thus, the precautionary concept is reflected in the notion of national carbon budgets and the task of the Parties to the Paris Agreement to make nationally determined contributions to mitigate climate change. Second, the concept also concerns measures that are taken in response to the increasing threat of global warming. Climate action in this regard relates to negative-emissions technologies (far-reaching interventions in the environment to reduce carbon dioxide in the atmosphere) as well as geo-engineering to interfere with weather patterns. Climate measures are not necessarily benign in terms of their environmental impacts. Therefore, all stakeholders must take sensible precautions.

Article 4(19) of the Paris Agreement links the objective of the Agreement with the Parties' task to 'formulate and communicate long-term low greenhouse gas emission development strategies.'[60] Thus, government measures to reduce emissions can be considered as a precautionary policy. These measures are part

60 Ibid., Article 4(19).

of a country's economic policy. Yet they also have a societal facet, as the final part of this section shows.

Policies to target carbon dioxide emissions first and foremost influence the structure of the energy sector, mainly because this sector is responsible for the largest share of greenhouse gas emissions related to human activity. Thus, implementing policies and adopting laws to alter the structure of the energy system, especially a phase-out of coal use, are an essential contribution to the mitigation of climate change.

The decarbonisation of energy generation can be achieved by deploying measures to capture carbon dioxide or transition to low-carbon fuels. However, in the course of the low-carbon energy transition, other policy goals must not be disregarded. The energy system must remain stable. Energy supplies must be reliable, affordable and environmentally sustainable. Thus, throughout the transition and when deploying new technologies, supply disruptions must be avoided. Transition measures need to consider both the reliability of (climate-neutral) fuel supplies and the affordability of energy. The former might include foreign policy adjustments, while the latter concerns the competitiveness of the domestic economy and the prevention or reduction of energy poverty among vulnerable groups. These are the main considerations that the triangular framework comprises in its component 'adequacy of energy provision'.

Finally, the third component, 'climate and transition resilience', concerns societal stability in the context of experiencing and mitigating climate change. Thus, it touches upon efforts to deal with the consequences of climate change (adaptation) and the challenges of the transition towards climate neutrality. This component points to a range of considerations, such as equitable burden-sharing regarding the implementation of climate measures and the costs of global warming. In addition, ongoing global warming requires some degree of preparedness for security threats that arise from climate change. Given that the protection of fundamental rights pertains to the stability of society, regard for intergenerational justice in the design of climate measures is thus part of the framework's 'climate and transition resilience' component.

To sum up, caring about future generations' freedom rights includes the preservation of the environmental conditions that enable future generations to enjoy these rights. Following the German Constitutional Court's reasoning concerning the duty of the State to protect fundamental rights of future generations, today's policies need to envision a fast and far-reaching reduction of greenhouse gases that leaves policy space for the final years before 2050 when climate neutrality needs to be achieved. The policy-making process needs to take into account the environmental impact of climate measures and the importance of a stable energy system for running a climate-neutral economy. Climate litigation plays a vital role in guiding this transformation process, as the decision of the German Constitutional Court illustrates. Only judges are in a position to authoritatively balance freedom rights against economic objectives and environmental concerns with an eye to future generations.

7. CONCLUDING REMARKS

By clarifying and refining elements that shape policy trajectories, climate litigation can help guide the transition to climate neutrality. This chapter considered the arguments of the German Constitutional Court regarding the responsibility of the State for the protection of future generations' fundamental rights when designing climate policies. The main thrust of the Court's reasoning concerns the legislators' task to leave sufficient policy space to the next generation when designing today's climate policies. Fulfilling this task will help prevent a situation in which the next generation would have to make 'drastic' efforts to achieve climate neutrality, which would possibly amount to a violation of future generations' fundamental rights.[61]

Accordingly, a timely transition to climate neutrality preserves the physical environmental conditions in which future generations will be able to enjoy their freedom rights. Early and determined climate action can help to protect the fundamental rights of future generations. Thus, when the negotiators of the Glasgow Climate Pact opted for a 'phasedown' of unabated coal use in the power sector instead of arriving at a phase-out, their behaviour was not informed by the principle of intergenerational justice. In a climate-constrained world, carbon-intensive policies require a balancing of policy objectives, a proper justification and precautionary measures to limit environmental impacts.

This chapter has demonstrated that the legal realms of national jurisprudence and international rule-making can interact fruitfully. This interaction can inspire the refinement of legal principles and the process of rule-making. In the future, national efforts to implement climate measures will be regularly assessed as part of the global stocktake under the Paris Agreement. International cooperation will need to take into account both technical aspects of the transition to climate neutrality and the interpretation of core principles of the UN climate regime. Climate negotiators from Europe should be bold: balanced policies to mitigate climate change foster societal stability today and in the future. Accelerating the pace of achieving climate neutrality is the right thing to do, for both developed *and* developing countries. The protection of the freedom rights of future generations is impossible unless it is a global effort.

---

61 See BVerfG, above n. 5, para. 245.

STRATEGIC CLIMATE LITIGATION IN POLAND

In Search of a Proper Socio-Legal Communication before Courts

Alan Żukowski

1. INTRODUCTION

The primary purpose of this chapter is to analyse how strategic climate litigation operates in Poland and its consequences for the socio-legal system. Strategic litigation is a process initiated to change the direction of politics; it is a legal dispute before a court that is motivated by social forces and the main goal is not to win the case, but to achieve broad public support. Strategic litigation changes the way social problems are understood, as individual claims become a social paradigm of normative change.[1] This is possible by focusing activities on three aspects: naming (the social issue in legal terms), claiming (before the court) and blaming (political institutions).[2] The first aspect indicates a dichotomy, in that litigation can either be defined as a strategy of fighting for the recognition of fundamental rights or as a strategy of obtaining the correct application of existing law.[3] Legal claiming defines the boundaries of the dispute, which indicate the need to resolve a specific issue or the need for a fundamental systemic change. The last aspect is related to the attribution of responsibility (to public authorities and/or private entities).

This chapter is divided into three parts. The first deals with the law applicable to strategic litigation in Poland (section 2). Next, the (potential) need for change in the Polish approach to strategic climate litigation will be outlined (section 3). Finally, the significance of the balance between social communication and legal argumentation for strategic climate litigation-based storytelling will be examined (section 4).

2. STRATEGIC CLIMATE LITIGATION IN POLAND

This section presents a typology of the law applicable to suing the Republic of Poland for failure to comply with international climate-friendly obligations before Polish courts or equivalent institutions. This typology results from an empirical study of cases – pending before Polish courts between 2018 and 2021 – and indicates three established legal grounds for claiming. Next, the chapter explains how the liability of public authorities for negative impacts on the climate is assessed.

2.1. THE TYPOLOGY OF CASES: FROM NAMING TO CLAIMING

The first type of cases are those based on the Polish Civil Code.[4] In the cases studied, smog was the source of deteriorating health, physical well-being and reduced comfort. This type of claim is based on two equivalent legal grounds. The first is a causal link between the unlawful act and the violation

---

1 L. Mather and B. Yngvesson, 'Disputes, Social Construction and Transformation of the Social Behavioral Sciences' in *International Encyclopedia of Social and Behavioral Sciences*, Elsevier 2005.

2 W. Felstiner, R. Abel and A. Sarat, 'The Emergence and Transformation of Disputes: Naming, Blaming, Claiming' (1981) 15(2/3) *Law & Society Review* 631.

3 Cf. A. Hatano, *Can strategic human rights litigation complement social movements? A case study of the movement against racism and hate speech in Japan*, Routledge 2020.

4 Act of 23 April 1964 – Polish Civil Code (Ustawa z dnia 23 kwietnia 1964 r. – Kodeks Cywilny), Journal of Law 2019, item 1145 et al.

of personal interests of human beings (*dobra osobiste*) – the right to live in a clean environment.[5] The second combines the public authorities' wrongdoings and the need for remedy or compensation for the damage.[6] An example of this type of litigation is the case of actress Grażyna Wolszczak against the Polish Exchequer.[7] In this case, the court found that the legal grounds the plaintiff had sought to rely on were inappropriate due to the substantive vagueness of the allegations. Nonetheless, the judgment was ultimately in favour of the plaintiff. The court emphasised that it was more appropriate to base the claims on a specific act incorporating an EU directive into the Polish legal system. This directive, in turn, specifies international obligations – including those of Poland – to implement an anti-smog policy. Irrespective of the substantive assessment of the judgment, attention should be paid to the legal trend of separating the right to live in a climate-safe State from the open catalogue of personal interests contained in the Polish Civil Code.[8] The resolution of the Polish Supreme Court[9] unambiguously indicated that the right to live in a clean environment is not among the personal interests. Therefore, the failure to implement climate protection standards (e.g. regarding air quality) cannot be the basis of a litigant's claim to protect personal interests. The court's reasoning relies on the assertion that while health is a protectable personal interest, the fact of breaching air quality obligations imposed on the Republic of Poland does not imply that specific persons will suffer bodily injury or health disorders. Therefore, demonstrating the causal relationship between breaching air quality obligations and consequent injury is crucial to the tort law-based regime.[10] Briefly, the Supreme Court points to the subordinate and abstract nature of the State's international commitments to protect the climate. The judgment focuses on the notion of a tort and whether the State's international commitments give rise to a duty of care. However, the weight of the proper legal argumentation in this case should have rested on the relationship between two facts: the unlawful act and the violation of an open catalogue of personal interests. It could invigorate the (self-contained) legal significance of fundamental rights. The Supreme Court argues that it aims to define precisely the relationship between the form of protection and the limits of what constitutes a violation of personal interests. In practice, it is a method that makes the consideration of observance of climatic obligations abstract. It is worth emphasising that waiting for the physical impact of climate change

5 Articles 23 and 24 in relation to Article 448 Polish Civil Code.

6 Article 417 Polish Civil Code.

7 Warszawa-Śródmieście Regional Court Judgment, 24 January 2019, Case No. VI C 1043/18.

8 Article 24 Polish Civil Code.

9 Resolution of the Supreme Court – Civil Chamber, 28 May 2021 (Uchwała Sądu Najwyższego – Izba Cywilna z dnia 28 maja 2021 r.), Case No. III CZP 27/20.

10 Recognised interpretation of Article 448 Polish Civil Code.

to be felt on the security of personal interests is risky in a climate catastrophe scenario.

The second type of cases focus on environmental law[11] as a self-contained litigation premise. The legal ground consists of causing a direct threat to the environment and failing to provide ecological infrastructure (installation of special equipment or facilities).[12] This procedure of adjudication rests on the strict liability principle. This means that the adjudication is to determine whether the entity taking the particular action has considered its impact on the environment. The simple construction of the provision and the intuitive conviction of the need to ensure that investment projects adhere to environmental safeguards do not affect the practical significance of this legal ground. Litigation cases based on this ground take a very long time. Two cases of strategic climate litigation based on this legal ground will be examined in the following.

The first litigation on such grounds was initiated on 23 September 2019 by the Polish environmental foundation ClientEarth before the District Court in Łódź. The organisation demanded the reduction of greenhouse gas emissions by the Bełchatów power plant – Europe's largest, owned by PGE Polish Energy Group (Polska Grupa Energetyczna). According to ClientEarth's calculations, Bełchatów burns 45 million tonnes of lignite annually. Over the power plant's entire lifespan, this translates into approximately 1 billion tonnes of carbon dioxide. These are emissions of an unprecedented global scale. ClientEarth accuses PGE Polish Energy Group of failing to present an official plan to reduce its negative impact on the climate. This litigation aims to counteract the consequences of lignite burning and to reduce emissions. The goal is to meet international climate commitments by 2035 and the general obligation of public authorities to protect the common good, namely a safe environment. The court committed the parties to negotiations, which ended on 22 September 2020 with no compromise.[13] It should be noted that the court abandoned a conclusive decision and shifted the burden of responsibility of the public authority to the outcome of non-binding talks between two private parties.

The second lawsuit was filed on 11 March 2020 in the District Court in Łódź by Greenpeace Poland against PGE Górnictwo i Energetyka Konwencjonalna. This is a joint stock company subsidiary of the PGE Polish Energy Group. The primary demand is to stop all fossil fuel investments and achieve net-zero greenhouse gas emissions from existing coal-fired power plants by 2030. The

---

11 Act of 27 April 2001 – Law on Environmental Protection (Ustawa z dnia 27 kwietnia 2001 r. – Prawo ochrony środowiska), Journal of Laws 2020, item 1219 et al.

12 Article 323 Law on Environmental Protection.

13 Note on the failure of negotiations between ClientEarth and Polish Energy Group GiEK, https://www.clientearth.pl/najnowsze-dzialania/artykuly/zakonczyly-sie-negocjacje-pomiedzy-fundacja-clientearth-prawnicy-dla-ziemi-a-pge-giek/ (in Polish).

case is pending.[14] This litigation is part of a global trend of seeking court rulings on the need for energy companies to reorganise their business profiles.[15] The changes companies make should take into account the global need for a just transition. This means that the main goal currently is pushing energy companies to achieve net-zero emissions and to make this a fundamental part of their business operations.

The third type of cases combine Polish commercial law[16] and corporate regulation. This allows strategic climate litigation to be decided in the courts and outside of them – during negotiations between private entities within the framework provided by the competent institutions.

This legal combination provided the foundation for the case of *ClientEarth v. Enea S.A.*[17] The claimant argued that the general meeting of shareholders' decision to build a power plant in Ostrołęka harmed the company's economic interests. Financial risks related to the increase in prices of carbon dioxide emissions and the global competitiveness of renewable energy sources in ensuring energy security were indicated as the reasons. ClientEarth unequivocally stressed that the potential economic damage was deliberately concealed from the shareholders by the company's main shareholder and the initiator of the power plant construction, i.e. the Exchequer. The court – pronouncing a verdict invalidating the decision to build the power plant – pointed to the Exchequer's special obligation to provide information in line with current scientific knowledge on climate change.

The second procedure that could be substantially (despite the judiciary's disengagement) defined as strategic climate litigation is the so-called 'good offices' procedure.[18] This procedure is provided within the framework of the National Contact Point of the Organisation for Economic Co-operation and Development (OECD) and is based on the OECD Guidelines for Multinational Enterprises (a core example of corporate regulations).[19] The most significant Polish strategic climate litigation has been the case brought by the Development

---

14 Information on the website of Greenpeace Poland, https://www.greenpeace.org/poland/aktualnosci/27697/greenpeace-pozywa-pge-za-zmiany-klimatu-koncern-musi-odejsc-od-wegla-do-2030-r/.

15 *Milieudefensie/Friends of the Earth Netherlands et al. v. Royal Dutch Shell plc*, ECLI:NL:RBDHA:2021:5337.

16 Significantly Article 422 para. 1 Act of 15 September 2000 – Commercial Companies Code (Ustawa z dnia 15 września 2000 r. – Kodeks spółek handlowych), Journal of Laws 2019, item 505 et al.

17 Judgment of the District Court in Poznań – IX Commercial Division, 31 July 2019, Case No. IX GC 1118/18.

18 The OECD NCP monitoring memorandum in the case of the Development YES – Open-Pits NO foundation against PZU S.A., Warsaw, 18 February 2021, https://www.gov.pl/attachment/67d3e088-6ec9-4918-967f-5dcfd8c56a26.

19 2011 Update of the OECD Guidelines for Multinational Enterprises, https://www.oecd.org/daf/inv/mne/oecdguidelinesformultinationalenterprises.htm.

YES – Open-Pits NO foundation (Rozwój TAK – Odkrywki NIE) against the Common Insurance Company Capital Group (Powszechny Zakład Ubezpieczeń S.A.), whose strategic shareholder is the Polish Exchequer. The main complaint, which the National Contact Point upheld, pointed to the lack of insurance coverage for high-climate-risk enterprises in the report on the non-financial undertakings of the company.

2.2. BLAMING: THE UNITY OF RESPONDENTS

The Polish authorities' politics is based on the discursive myth of representation.[20] The government's official messages emphasise the close relationship between social expectations and political decisions. Strategic climate litigation is prone to contradict this message as it reveals the gap between the actions taken by the government and the actions that are socially needed to counteract the climate catastrophe.

The concept of legal mobilisation seems adequate to address this issue.[21] However, promoting the socio-legal agenda does not depend solely on the number of cases. The number of cases is pivotal so long as there is a plan for the convergence of targets. Each case should call for a specific response from public authorities and build the social proximity of legal problems. Strategic climate litigation cannot make its effectiveness dependent on winning a case in court. The task is to convince the authorities of the social significance of the judgment. Strategic climate litigation must be firmly rooted in the social fabric. In short, strategic litigation cannot be a legal transplant of a social idea.[22]

Moreover, the strategic litigants' allegations against Poland do not point only to climate regulatory passivity. The role of the Polish Exchequer (the respondent) is to carry out public tasks (it has a policy-making-oriented responsibility) and it is also a dominant shareholder in strategic commercial companies (with responsibility for where investment is directed). Unfortunately, the Exchequer equates the public interest with momentary profit from (ill-conceived) commercial investments. Therefore, the role of climate social movements is to represent the true public interest. The public should have access to reliable information about the climate catastrophe and opportunities for participation in the decision-making process. Strategic climate litigation should clarify the limits of State action, as well as the State's law-based duty to society to counteract the

---

20 C. Mudde, 'The Populist Zeitgeist' (2004) 39(4) *Government and Opposition* 541.

21 Cf. M. McCann, 'Litigation and Legal Mobilisation' in G.A. Caldeira et al., *The Oxford Handbook of Law and Politics*, Oxford University Press 2008.

22 This practice is not appropriate for promoting a socio-legal agenda. Cf. I. Krastev and S. Holmes, *The Light That Failed: Why the West Is Losing the Fight for Democracy*, Pegasus Books 2020.

climate catastrophe. It aims to empower the social foundation (social justice), stop the ecological overshoot (climate justice) and regenerate the democratic space for current and future generations.[23]

3. SIGNIFICANT PROBLEMS WITH STRATEGIC CLIMATE LITIGATION IN POLAND

This section examines the significant problems with strategic litigation in Poland to date. Firstly, it reflects on the position of legal mobilisation in the face of opposition from Poland's populists in power. Second, Polish litigants' need for the latest climate litigation strategies and the role of the ClientEarth-led #ClimateOurCase (#KlimatNaszaSprawa) initiative in challenging the current approach to strategic climate litigation will be recognised. Finally, actions taken by Poland's populists against strategic climate litigation will be analysed.

3.1. CHALLENGING POLAND'S POPULISTS IN POWER

This subsection focuses on charting the role of legal mobilisation in light of Poland's populists in power. Legal mobilisation is a well-constituted civil society strategy that translates into concrete legal action.[24] Such action is strategic climate litigation. However, strategic legal mobilisation requires institutional conditions. First, the legal system does not correspond to the socially shared ideas behind taking specific actions. In addition, the law does not enable the integration of these ideas into the political discourse. Therefore, legal mobilisation within strategic litigation is politics by other means.[25] Second, the legal system validates the political system. The political system – in turn – lies in paradigms defined within the boundaries of the legal system. In this framework, there must be formal conditions for the presentation of legally momentous arguments (rules of the game)[26] and institutional space for the independent adjudication of their validity (rule of law).[27] The third condition links legal mobilisation with social

---

[23] K. Raworth, *Doughnut Economics: Seven Ways to Think Like a 21st-Century Economist*, Chelsea Green Publishing 2017, pp. 34–36, 80–82.

[24] Cf. J. Handmaker, 'Researching legal mobilisation and lawfare', ISS Working Paper Series No. 641, 2019.

[25] R. Abel, *Politics by Other Means: Law in the Struggle Against Apartheid, 1980–1994*, Routledge 1995, pp. 70–71.

[26] Cf. J. Setzer and L.C. Vanhala, 'Climate change litigation: A review of research on courts and litigants in climate governance' (2019) 10(3) *WIREs Climate Change* e580.

[27] Cf. P. Sands, 'Climate change and the rule of law: Adjudicating the future in international law' (2016) 28(1) *Journal of Environmental Law* 19.

agency, which results from institutional (judicial) recognition of politically excluded claims.

Implementing the above conditions in Poland is hampered in the context of the above-mentioned phenomenon of populists in power.[28] The purpose of this discussion is neither to describe this phenomenon in depth nor to identify its links with climate-friendly politics. In this chapter, populists in power are treated as a particular form of the politico-legal regime that undermines the essence of legal mobilisation against the dominant politics. Poland's populists in power fit into the traditional canon of this phenomenon. For this reason, the populists' three techniques of governing[29] are the basis for the Polish government's politics.

The first technique involves the occupation of the State.[30] This concept undermines the ethos of independence and legalistic apoliticism of State institutions. This results in the instrumentalisation of political practices (democratic decision-making, official narrative) and the legal order (opposition to the legal system and hierarchy of norms).

The second is discriminatory legalism, which aims at the repression of civil society.[31] The State institutions are reorganised in a way that allows populists to dominate political discourse. Populists use the instruments of the political-legal system (electoral participation, law-making, staffing of institutions), on a critique of which they build the populist social agenda. Practically, this means that the populists aim to give a new meaning to the established politico-legal order.

The last technique is called clientelism.[32] It is a reversed form of corruption. Populists indicate whom they represent and the possibility of political representation depends on the exclusion of other (precisely defined) groups and preferences.

The three populist techniques of governing generate normative consequences for strategic climate litigation in Poland. In this context, the legal perspective and the social perspective will be distinguished.

The legal approach analyses the relationship between legal argumentation and its translation into social reality. The basic thesis is that the law is not taken seriously by populists in power.[33] The law is understood – in parallel with the

---

28 Meaning that a political group has come to power through populist slogans and has excluded the demo-liberal paradigms to maintain power. It comes from the book D. Albertazzi and D. McDonnell, *Populists in Power*, Routledge 2015.

29 J.-W. Müller, *What Is Populism?*, Penguin Books 2016, pp. 43–44.

30 Ibid., pp. 44–46.

31 Ibid., pp. 47–49.

32 Ibid., pp. 46–47.

33 J. Zajadło, '"Nie biorąc prawa poważnie" – uwagi w związku z wyrokiem TSUE w sprawach połączonych C-585/18; C-624/18; C-625/18' ('Not taking the law seriously' – remarks in relation to the CJEU's judgment in joint cases C-585/18; C-624/18; C-625/18), Portal Konstytucyjny.pl, 2020, https://konstytucyjny.pl/jerzy-zajadlo-nie-biorac-prawa-powaznie-uwagi-w-zwiazku-z-z-wyrokiem-tsue-w-sprawach-polaczonych-c-585-18-c-624-18-c-625-18/.

political system – both as a social system and as the outcome of the application of the law by official institutions. The above thesis explains the strategy of Poland's populists in power towards their supranational environment. This strategy appears to be a peculiar paradox. The Polish government questions the legitimacy of decisions (made by the EU institutions or independent internal bodies) that undermine the legality of its actions. The significant argument is the allegation of the political nature of such decisions. On the other hand, Poland's populists in power define the political neutrality of institutions as an acceptance of the dominance of government-centric politics over legal reflection.[34] Such a position seems cynical in itself. But it is related to the social perspective of normative consequences for strategic climate litigation in Poland.

The social approach stems from populists emphasising that legal actions can undermine the will of the people. Poland's populists emphasise their democratic legitimacy and oppose legal decision-making on social problems. According to the populists, the recognition of problems as socially momentous should be exclusively their political decision. Accepting such an approach makes strategic climate litigation an art for art's sake. In this way, the concept of legal representation resembles the use of idioms that do not affect communication and, moreover, are ignored by populists in power. Moreover, the acceptance of a populist idiom requires the acceptance of preconditions that make social discourse dependent on the political will of governing populists. Therefore, strategic climate litigants should explicitly identify their legal action before the courts as politics to counteract the democratic exclusion from populist official discourses.

3.2. POLISH LITIGANTS' NEED FOR CLIMATE LITIGATION STRATEGIES: FINDING THE RIGHT DIRECTION TOWARDS THE RIGHTS TURN

Challenging the position of populists in power is about looking at strategic climate litigation as an opportunity for questioning the populists' techniques of governing concerning the above socio-legal aspects. The aim of strategic climate litigation in contemporary Poland is not to find a legal settlement to uncertainties in countering the climate crisis. Rather, it aims at articulating socio-legal arguments against official politics. Therefore, reflecting on the right direction for the Polish litigants' climate strategy is to rethink the space for social actors and the legal ground for making a claim before the courts.

---

34 Cf. P. Blokker, 'Populism as a constitutional project' (2019) 17(2) *International Journal of Constitutional Law* 536.

The space for social actors includes helping to create a form of organisation around litigation and introducing legal professionalisation[35] to better articulate demands. Current trends in strategic climate litigation confirm that lawsuits are initiated by emerging new social movements.[36] The new social movements bring together people with different views and they are (instrumentally) objective-oriented.[37] The Dutch Urgenda Foundation is an example of a new social movement that started from the (rather political) project of the green European transition[38] and initiated actions (including strategic climate litigation) for legal climate protection that have inspired strategic litigants globally.[39] The idea of the new social movement is to act simultaneously in different spheres of public life (e.g. lobbying, education, expertise, litigation) and to redefine the public interest from the bottom up.[40] However, this idea does not fit into contemporary Poland. The new social movement is firmly rooted in the participatory nature of society. Social participation was not popular in Poland before 2015. On the other hand, the idea of strategic climate litigation in Poland is equally new. What is worth emphasising is that Polish climate initiatives emerge around a dialogue between distinct social groups – i.e. climate activists, social facilitators and legal professionals. Looking at the legal claiming process from the perspective of these three groups of actors could help to reject a strictly formal assessment of applicable laws (legal approach) and create a social context around conflicts over politico-legal agency in populism (social approach).

The Polish specificity of strategic climate litigation presents climate issues as peripheral vis-à-vis more momentous social matters.[41] The formal nature of the laws applicable to the (above) three types of cases indicates this phenomenon. The litigation process and the final judgment provide a clear account of the strength of the parties' arguments, showing that the strategic litigants have a well-reasoned, legally sound argument. However, this argumentation is

---

35 Cf. L. Guinier and G. Torres, 'Changing the Wind: Notes Toward a Demosprudence of Law and Social Movements' (2014) 123 *Yale Law Review* 2740.

36 J. Setzer and C. Higham, *Global trends in climate change litigation: 2021 snapshot,* Grantham Research Institute on Climate Change and the Environment and Centre for Climate Change Economics and Policy 2021, pp. 18–21.

37 M. Wieviorka, 'The resurgence of social movements' (2012) 3(2) *Journal of Conflictology* 13.

38 S. Rothman, J. Rotmans and B.A. van Asselt, *Scenario Innovation: Experiences from an Experimental Garden*, CRC Press 2005.

39 Cf. J. Spier, 'The "Strongest" Climate Ruling Yet: The Dutch Supreme Court's Urgenda Judgement' (2020) 67 *Netherlands International Law Review* 319.

40 C. Offe, 'New Social Movements: Challenging the Boundaries of Institutional Politics' (1985) 52(4) *Social Research* 817.

41 Cf. J. Peel and J. Lin, 'Transnational Climate Litigation: The Contribution of the Global South' (2019) 113(4) *American Journal of International Law* 690. The authors name a theoretical approach to strategic climate litigation rooted in the 'peripheral' nature of climate issues to wider disputes over politico-legal challenges.

constrained by the legal system (which strategic litigants hope to change) and the government's position is exposed as ignorant. Making the climate crisis the main axis of contention in strategic climate litigation rests on reflecting the main trends of current public debate. In the context of a country with a populist government, considering the legal system as a space for raising political arguments (outside politics) seems particularly interesting. This implies the need to ground claims on the discourse of fundamental rights. The ongoing climate catastrophe opens up a new space for thinking about fundamental rights and the limits of their protection. Grounding climate claims on fundamental rights is a global phenomenon – named the revolution of rights.[42] Another term – which highlights the determination of strategic litigants to persuade the courts to expand the normative scope of climate rights – is the rights turn.[43] This term expresses a new quality in thinking about the role of strategic climate litigation within the politico-legal discourse and the appropriateness of courts hearing social demands. Briefly, even if the law is not taken seriously in populist Poland, perhaps there will be space for taking (climate) rights seriously.[44]

The changes in Polish litigants' strategies presented here are not solely abstract ideas. ClientEarth has realised that the existing lawsuits translate neither into strengthening the politico-legal discourse nor into raising the standard of fundamental rights protection in Poland. For this reason, in mid-2021, ClientEarth launched the #ClimateOurCase initiative.[45] The initiative is the fruit of a dialogue between ClientEarth, five activists (of different ages and affected by climate change in different ways) and the Warsaw-based law firm GESSEL, and it combined social demands with climate rights-based legal argumentation. This initiative may change the approach to and consequences of strategic climate litigation in Poland. The pending nature of this case does not allow for an in-depth analysis of it. However, the aim is to boost awareness that the Polish legal mobilisation against the climate catastrophe is a vibrant and scientifically attractive matter. The Polish perspective is particularly relevant because of the ongoing creativity of social actors in the face of the diminution of law and rights by populists in power.

---

42 D.R. Boyd, *The Environmental Rights Revolution: A Global Study of Constitutions, Human Rights, and the Environment*, UBC Press 2012.

43 J. Peel and H.M. Osofsky, 'A Rights Turn in Climate Change Litigation?' (2018) 7(1) *Transnational Environmental Law* 37.

44 This conclusion follows the findings of the seminal book by R. Dworkin, *Taking Rights Seriously*, Harvard University Press 1977.

45 Information on the #KlimatNaszaSprawa initiative on the website Noizz.pl, https://noizz.pl/klimatnaszasprawa.

3.3. BETWEEN FORMAL STRUCTURE AND SUBSTANTIVE OBSTACLES

Legal mobilisation to oppose political institutions takes place in two steps.[46] The first one uncovers pivotal narratives that reinforce the institutional regime. The second step involves a democratic dialogue to contest these narratives. In the case of Poland, the populist vision of social disputes equates challenging the populist narrative with challenging the public interest.[47]

Current guidelines from the Polish General Prosecutor's Office instruct lower-level units to join ongoing strategic climate lawsuits on the side of the Polish Exchequer.[48] The argument conflates the public interest with the stability of public finances. This stability, according to the Polish Prosecutor's Office, is compromised by the increase in the number of climate cases lost by the Polish Exchequer and the need to pay damages (or make restitution) for this.[49] Paradoxically, it is in the public interest to have a just transition that would make public finances more resilient during climate catastrophes.

Populist legal argumentation consists of vague concepts. The prosecution declares a desire to protect the public interest, a component of the rule of law. The rule of law is a vague concept that defines the legal limit of political action. A well-established line of case law[50] guarantees that the General Prosecutor's Office is unlimited in the assessment of situations in which the rule of law and, consequently, the public interest are threatened. Moreover, political decisions do not require justification (contrary to adjudication) and are verified only during elections.[51] The General Prosecutor's decision to join strategic climate litigation on the side of the Polish Exchequer does not require the Office to justify why it perceives there to be a risk of breaching the rule of law. In this way, legal concepts – as part of the political game – can be subject to definitional manipulation (*Etikettenschwindel*).[52] This manipulation aims to make the public

---

46 E. Lehoucq and W.K. Taylor, 'Conceptualising Legal Mobilisation: How Should We Understand the Deployment of Legal Strategies?' (2020) 45(1) *Law and Inquiry* 166.

47 M. Krygier, 'What's the Point of the Rule of Law?' (2019) 67 *Buffalo Law Review* 743, 759–68.

48 M. Adamski, 'Znana aktorka wygrała sprawę o smog. Ziobro składa skargę nadzwyczajną' (Famous actress wins smog case. Ziobro files an extraordinary complaint), Rzeczpospolita, https://www.rp.pl/w-sadzie-i-w-urzedzie/art35889761-znana-aktorka-wygrala-sprawe-o-smog-ziobro-sklada-skarge-nadzwyczajna.

49 It is justified on the ground of Article 7 para. 1 Act of 17 November 1964 – Code of Civil Procedure (Ustawa z dnia 17 listopada 1964 r. – Kodeks Postępowania Cywilnego), Journal of Laws 2021, item 1805.

50 Judgments of the Polish Supreme Court of 2 August 2007, Case No. V CSK 109/07; 9 March 1993, Case No. I CR 3/93; and 3 December 2014, Case No. IV CSK 365/14.

51 Cf. P.J. Steinberger, *The Concept of Political Judgement*, University of Chicago Press 1993.

52 Cf. K. Skrzydłowska-Kalukin, interview with Ewa Łętowska: 'Naruszanie niezależności sądów nazywają reformą' (They call the violation of judicial independence a reform),

interest and the axiology of the law dependent on the will of the populists in power and the non-environmental enterprises they manage. The uncertainty of adversarial litigation within the framework of strategic climate litigation hinders the achievement of the ultimate goal, i.e. the implementation – underpinned by court decisions in favour of strategic climate litigants – of State-led actions to combat climate change.

4. A NARRATIVE APPROACH: BETWEEN SOCIAL COMMUNICATION AND LEGAL ARGUMENTATION

A narrative approach uses the formal structure as a tool to overcome substantive obstacles.[53] The storytelling-oriented method presents a strongly axiological basis for strategic climate litigation. Setting out the differences between allies and bad actors reveals the spaces and boundaries of the dialogue on climate catastrophe prevention. Proper communication within the framework of strategic litigation influences the follow-up processes to adjudication.

4.1. STORYTELLING: ALLIES AND BAD ACTORS

The recognition of strategic climate litigation as one form of storytelling could be an interesting solution.[54] Firstly, the moral of the story appeals to society more than hermetic legal arguments. Second, strategic litigation shows two extreme perspectives of a social problem that are subject to stark judgments. Third, strategic litigation finds its validity in the injustice of its opponents' actions. Ultimately, strategic litigation is a prism that helps laypersons understand what the point of countering climate catastrophe is.

Strategic climate litigation as storytelling starts with distinguishing between allies and bad actors. Even a superficial analysis of the narratives of the new social movements indicates that this is not a problem.[55] The moral legitimacy of strategic litigation facilitates this process in climate catastrophes. The new

---

Kultura Liberalna, https://kulturaliberalna.pl/2021/11/30/naruszanie-niezaleznosci-sadow-nazywaja-reforma/.

53 Cf. P. Paiement, 'Urgent agenda: how climate litigation builds transnational narratives' (2020) 11(1–2) *Transnational Legal Theory* 121.

54 J.B. Baron, 'Storytelling and Legal Legitimacy' (1998) 25(1) *Law, Literature, and Interdisciplinarity* 63; P.B. Meyer, 'How to shape your legal storytelling', *ABA Journal*, 2014, https://www.abajournal.com/magazine/article/shaping_your_legal_storytelling.

55 Cf. B. Doherty, J. de Moor and G. Hayes, 'The "new" climate politics of Extinction Rebellion?', *Open Democracy*, 2014, https://www.opendemocracy.net/en/new-climate-politics-of-extinction-rebellion/.

social movements place themselves on the side of the good and identify the bad actors. The competition between good and evil is the basis of storytelling and the construction of legal arguments. However, this chapter aims to discuss the importance of storytelling for inclusive and democratic debates about the law. Theoretical inspiration goes back to legal functionalism, which considered law from the bad man's perspective.[56] Legal functionalism presented the law as a tool to avoid or minimise responsibility. New social movements want to emphasise this perspective and classify their initiatives as a process of counteracting the instrumentalisation of law by bad actors. Therefore, strategic litigation uses the law as a tool to fight against evil. The indicated practice requires constant references to bad actors. The strategic climate litigants' allies do not speculate but articulate the losses that result from the actions of bad actors. Law can be helpful and fatal at the same time. The legitimacy of allies' claims stems from social mobilisation, an act of opposition to the power of bad actors. The real opponents in strategic litigation are the institutional limitation of the social will versus its substantive expression. The first one manipulates the law. The latter discovers the meaning of the law based on the fundamental rights discourse and restores – in the communicative and argumentative layer – the law for society.

4.2. THE TWO FACES OF PROPER COMMUNICATION

Socio-legal communication makes it possible to determine how to use the law to mobilise society around strategic climate litigation and to identify the actors obliged to implement solutions in line with society's demands. Briefly, this process precedes the legal argumentation for climate protection and allows for its deliberative preparation.

The essence of communication is mutual understanding among the debating actors that appears in two spaces. The first is the space of communication between lawyers. The second provides the legal framework for strategic climate litigation within the social context.

Communication between professionals is intersubjective. This concept implies the ability to use specialised language within a commonly recognised discourse. The intuitive basis for this kind of communication is a semantic agreement, which concerns the applicable law (naming), the way claims are justified (claiming) and the indication of the limits of blame and expected actions from the respondent (blaming). At this stage, a debate about narrative space is possible. The legal world lies within two alternative spaces: system

---

56 Cf. S.R. Perry, 'Holmes versus Hart: The Bad Man in Legal Theory' in S.J. Burton, *The Path of the Law and its Influence The Legacy of Oliver Wendell Holmes, Jr*, Cambridge University Press 2009, pp. 158–96.

and lifeworld.[57] The system focuses on instrumental validity and the technical correctness of arguments. This means that the system's effectiveness derives from the correct application of the law and the ability to counter violations of the law. The lifeworld makes legal effectiveness dependent on properly articulating a coherent discourse of fundamental rights. Reconciliation of the system and the lifeworld means that legal rationale ceases to be an abstract dialogue between specialists and becomes part of the social debate. In this way, strategic climate litigation gains a constituent force to empower rights and laws.

The second space of understanding relies on the relationship between the consequences of strategic litigation and the perception of the people (participants in new social movements) supporting it. The goal of strategic climate litigation is the instrumental use of legal acts for argumentative law-finding. Three types of law-finding (legal interpretation)[58] can be distinguished.

Law-finding 1.0 understood the law as the effects of court adjudication based on a formal and substantive evaluation of the litigants' and respondents' arguments.[59] Space for discussion was limited within the judicial discourse. The narrative had to meet the formal conditions and convince only the court.

Law-finding 2.0 stems from the neoliberal belief in the existence of one right answer, which reveals the interpretive links between rules and standards.[60] The correct interpretation of the law is the key to solving all social problems. The law is to be objectively communicated and respected by society.

Law-finding 3.0 relies on social participation to reveal the value of law.[61] Socio-legal networks are visible. Strategic litigation is not just a courtroom performance. It is a complex articulation of fundamental rights discourse within the narratives adopted by new social movements. The role of the court is to decide the case. The adjudication relies on the political conflicts depicted by the litigants and assesses the validity of the fundamental rights claimed. Proper communication is to use socio-legal resources and the multidimensional spaces of narrative legal argument design.

4.3. SOCIO-POLITICAL FEEDBACK TO LEGAL ARGUMENTS

Strategic climate litigation has narrative, argumentative and epistemic boundaries. Narrative-based boundaries boil down to identifying opposing

---

57 Cf. J. Habermas, 'The Uncoupling of System and Lifeworld' in J. Habermas, *Lifeworld and System: A Critique of Functionalist Reason*, Beacon Press 1985, pp. 153–98; H. Baxter, 'System and lifeworld in Habermas's theory of law' (2002) 23(473) *Cardozo Law Review* 563.

58 M. Loth and R. van Gestel, '*Urgenda*: Roekeloze Rechtspraak of Rechtsvinding 3.0?' (2015) 1849(37) *Nederlands Juristenblad* 2598, 2604.

59 Cf. O.W. Holmes Jr, 'The Path of the Law' (1897) 10 *Harvard Law Review* 457.

60 R. Dworkin, 'Is There Really No Right Answer in Hard Cases?' (1978) 53 *NYU Law Review* 1.

61 M. Loth and R. van Gestel, '*Urgenda*: Roekeloze Rechtspraak of Rechtsvinding 3.0?' (2015) 1849(37) *Nederlands Juristenblad* 2598.

actors and explicitly valuing their actions. Argumentatively, strategic litigation reduces social debate to protecting the discursively accepted boundaries of public authority actions. The epistemic element reveals knowledge that reinforces the articulation of claims and warns against the consequences of fostering climate catastrophe. However, the most important boundary of strategic litigation relates to the conclusive end of the process before the court. This means that adjudication is the final frontier of strategic litigation. Acceptance of the above thesis dispels doubts about whether new social movements want to operate outside democratic political institutions.[62] Strategic litigation stimulates democratic decision-making processes and strengthens them with socially expected legal arguments. This action facilitates post-litigation change in the law in the climate catastrophe context.

This section aims to reflect on the expected end of strategic litigation. Winning a case in court is an unqualified success. The narrative victory of good against evil mobilises a new social movement and convinces it of the validity of the socio-legal agenda. Each climate-friendly adjudication weakens hegemonic (populist) discourses. However, only direct and democratic actions can subvert hegemonic discourses.[63] Citizens' assemblies are the space for such actions. The above-mentioned social institutions are an alternative to the political institutions that maintain the system (which is in strategic litigation). Citizens' assemblies implement the postulate 'go beyond politics', as they allow a debate on mitigation-oriented policies based on an exchange of views between randomly selected individuals over scientific recommendations to respond to climate catastrophe.[64] It is a deeply democratic engagement process with climate activists, the outcomes and course of which consolidate participatory inclusion with evidence-based social expertise. The subversion of hegemonic discourses relies on the inclusive rethinking of how democracy, reason and politics are understood by activists.[65] In the context of Poland's populists in power, the adjudication does not imply the normative change of a specific situation. The specificity of Polish strategic climate litigation distinguishes the tension between the strategic litigants' motivation behind legal mobilisation and the populists in power's political ignorance of climate rights-based legal arguments. Therefore, a participatory debate in citizens' assemblies on how to implement a legal ruling resulting from strategic climate litigation seems an enticing innovation.

---

62 Such doubts were raised in L. Burgers, 'Should Judges Make Climate Change Law?' (2020) 9(1) *Transnational Environmental Law* 55.

63 Cf. C. Mouffe, 'Deliberative Democracy or Agonistic Pluralism?' (1999) 66(3) *Social Research* 745.

64 R. Wells, C. Howarth and I. Brand-Correa, 'Are Citizen Juries and Assemblies on Climate Change Driving Democratic Climate Policymaking? An Exploration of Two Case Studies in the United Kingdom' (2021) 168(3–4) *Climatic Change* 1.

65 W. Ufel, 'Are Citizens' Assemblies a Good Strategy for Climate Activists?' (2021) 2 *Interfere* 78.

In this way, strategic climate litigation appears as a process that has reclaimed the possibility of social decision-making to protect fundamental rights. Belief in the problem-solving approach to strategic climate litigation excludes the discursive character of fundamental rights.[66] Consequently, strategic climate litigation determines the legal momentousness of climate issues and opens the political space to address them. However, the political tensions are not to interfere with undebatable fundamental rights but result from proper socio-legal communication around climate rights.

5. CONCLUSION

To sum up, strategic climate litigation in Poland has not produced the successful results seen in other countries. There is an elaborate social trend and interest in the institutional fight against climate catastrophe. However, the impact of legal mobilisation on wider social groups is not significant. This is possibly because judicial discourse is equated with political practice in society. Therefore, promoting and co-creating a socio-legal agenda beyond pure (in terms of executive or legislative powers-led) politics is complex. Moreover, there is no coherent social movement in Poland that could smoothly move from intersubjective communication to legal argumentation. The potential to change this state of affairs and to effect (climate rights-based) change through strategic climate litigation in Poland could rest on the shoulders of the ClientEarth foundation and its #ClimateOurCase initiative. In this situation, it is necessary to focus on resources that combine the force of scientific knowledge with climate activists' momentum. Strategic climate litigation is of vital importance to (re)gain climate rights for people and revive a (subsequent) democratic debate about counteracting climate catastrophe. This is the only way to transcend the narrow focus of (legal) adjudication on the individual rights and remedies of individual claimants, in favour of future-oriented socio-legal (systemic) change in Poland.

---

66 W. Simon, 'Solving Problems vs. Claiming Rights: The Pragmatist Challenge to Legal Liberalism' (2004) 46 *William & Mary Law Review* 127.

PART II

CLIMATE CHANGE LITIGATION IN EUROPE: SECTORAL PERSPECTIVES

International Trade and Investment Protection and Climate Change Litigation

PROCEDURAL IMPROVEMENTS AIMING AT INVESTMENT ARBITRATION'S GREATER SOCIAL ACCEPTABILITY

Patrick THIEFFRY

1. INTRODUCTION

Amid the controversies surrounding investment arbitration, the single most salient criticism is probably that of a perceived impairment of sovereign States' power to legislate in highly sensitive public interest areas such as human rights, human health, the environment or the energy transition, including so-called 'procedural chill'. Testament to the extent of what can be described as investment arbitration's crisis are the many attempts at inserting and/or strengthening responsive substantive provisions in investment protection agreements, including the recognition of environmental protection as a treaty objective, the right of States to regulate environmental matters, or the continuing duty of States to enforce and promote environmental protection measures. These attempts have been thoroughly described,[1] but they do not appear to have remedied the situation, at least not to a sufficient extent.

Climate change considerations, although they may not have been as present in actual disputes so far, are more or less directly relevant to all these highly sensitive public interest areas: climate change may have adverse impacts on human rights, health, the environment or the energy transition. Conversely, a 'climate litigation'

1 See e.g. C.L. BEHARRY and M.E. KURITZKY, 'Going Green: Managing the Environment Through International Investment Arbitration' (2015) 30(3) *American University International Law Review* 383.

trend[2] relies on a wide array of legal bases, including increasingly human rights and fundamental rights, in an attempt to trigger stronger responses from public authorities[3] and from the private sector.[4] Indeed, substantive provisions relating to climate change have also been considered in the context of investment protection treaties, such as the 2018 Netherlands Model Bilateral Treaty according to which 'Contracting Parties reaffirm their obligations under the multilateral agreements in the field of environmental protection ..., such as the Paris Agreement'. Yet the prospects for international arbitration of climate-related disputes are hardly doubtful and have already been established.[5]

The Permanent Court of Arbitration's (PCA) 2001 Optional Rules for Arbitration of Disputes Relating to Natural Resources and/or the Environment (PCA Environmental Rules)[6] may obviously apply to climate change-related disputes as a particular kind of environmental dispute. The PCA has indeed administered a number of cases thereunder, concerning both State and non-State actors and dealing with environmental disputes. In 2019, the International Chamber of Commerce (ICC) issued a report entitled 'Resolving Climate Change Related Disputes through Arbitration and ADR' (ICC Task Force Report).[7] In short, that report not only verified the capability of arbitration to offer adequate solutions in climate change-related disputes, but also explored 'potential procedural innovations and guidance for arbitration and ADR' in such disputes.[8] It is worth mentioning at this stage that, in the closely related area of human rights, the Hague Rules on Business and Human Rights Arbitration, which were also completed in 2019, provide for the administration of arbitrations concerning disputes related to the impact of business activities

2 See e.g. the report issued in 2020 by UN Environment and the Columbia University's Sabin Center for Climate Change Law, which mentions 1,550 cases in 38 countries: *Global Climate Report – 2020 Status Review*, https://www.unep.org/resources/report/global-climate-litigation-report-2020-status-review.

3 Most noted were a few court decisions, such as the *Urgenda* case, Hoge Raad, 20 December 2019, ECLI:NL:HR:2019:2006; see also Bundesverfassungsgericht, 29 April 2021, *Neubauer et al.*, http://climatecasechart.com/non-us-case/neubauer-et-al-v-germany/.

4 The Hague, 26 May 2021, *Milieudefensie et al. v. Royal Dutch Shell plc*, ECLI:NL:RBDHA:2021:5337 (English translation: ECLI:NL:RBDHA:2021:5339).

5 See e.g. P. Thieffry, 'International Arbitration of Climate-related Disputes: Prospects for Alternative Dispute Resolution' in I. Alogna, C. Bakker and J.-P. Gauci (eds), *Climate Change Litigation: Global Perspectives*, Brill 2021, p. 462.

6 https://docs.pca-cpa.org/2016/01/Optional-Rules-for-Arbitration-of-Disputes-Relating-to-the-Environment-and_or-Natural-Resources.pdf.

7 ICC, *Resolving Climate Change Related Disputes through Arbitration and ADR*, Report of the ICC Task Force on Arbitration of Climate Change Related Disputes, https://iccwbo.org/wp-content/uploads/sites/3/2019/11/icc-arbitration-adr-commission-report-on-resolving-climate-change-related-disputes-english-version.pdf. The author was a co-chair of that task force.

8 ICC Task Force Report, above n. 7, para. 5.5.

on human rights.[9] This should be viewed as further evidence of the capability of arbitration to provide dispute resolution where the public interest is salient. These comments relate to commercial arbitration as well as to investment arbitration or investor-State dispute settlement (ISDS).[10]

In the meanwhile, several institutional projects pertaining to ISDS's procedural features have developed. On 21 March 2022, the International Centre for Settlement of Investment Disputes (ICSID),[11] having conducted 'extensive dialogue' with its membership and the public, adopted resolutions to amend its Convention Arbitration and Conciliation Rules (ICSID Arbitration Rules). As amended, the ICSID Arbitration Rules would allow, *inter alia*, greater transparency in the conduct and outcome of proceedings, new disclosure requirements for third-party funding, and expedited arbitration rules for parties wishing to further shorten the procedural timescale.[12] Already in 2014, the United Nations Commission on International Trade Law (UNCITRAL), a major legislative body for arbitration,[13] had adopted the Rules on Transparency in Treaty-based Investor-State Arbitration (UNCITRAL Rules on Transparency), the application of which is promoted by United Nations Convention on Transparency in Treaty-based Investor-State Arbitration, also known as the Mauritius Convention on Transparency.[14] Currently, what has become known as UNCITRAL's Working Group III is actively involved in preparing an 'Investor-State Dispute Settlement Reform' with a view to introducing major changes to ISDS arbitral procedure.[15]

Against such a background, it is relevant to try and assess the desirability of procedural measures aiming at ISDS's greater social acceptability (section 2), before considering the trends and efforts towards the procedural reform of ISDS (section 3).

---

9 The Hague Rules on Business and Human Rights Arbitration, https://docs.pca-cpa.org/2019/12/The-Hague-Rules-on-Business-and-Human-Rights-Arbitration.pdf.

10 ICC Task Force Report, above n. 7, para. 2.7.

11 The ICSID was established in 1966 by the Convention on the Settlement of Investment Disputes between States and Nationals of Other States (ICSID Convention), and it is the only global institution dedicated to international investment dispute settlement.

12 https://icsid.worldbank.org/news-and-events/news-releases/icsid-submits-amended-rules-administrative-council-vote.

13 Major UNCITRAL contributions to the arbitration legal framework include the Convention on the Recognition and Enforcement of Foreign Arbitral Awards (New York, 1958), its 1985 Model Law on International Commercial Arbitration, which inspired to a great extent the legislation on arbitration in approximately 85 countries, and the UNCITRAL Arbitration Rules, which are widely used in *ad hoc* arbitrations as well as administered arbitration. See https://uncitral.un.org/en/texts/arbitration/contractualtexts/arbitration.

14 https://uncitral.un.org/en/texts/arbitration/conventions/transparency.

15 https://uncitral.un.org/working_groups/3/investor-state.

2. ISDS'S NEED FOR GREATER SOCIAL ACCEPTABILITY

Academics have now been struggling for years with the difficult task of researching what an author has characterised as 'a shy, yet sufficiently discernible, change of mindset regarding the place granted to environmental considerations in investment litigation' and consolidating such change in 'an "upgraded" traditional approach to the relations between international investment law and environmental protection'.[16] Accordingly, 'environmental protection has to evolve within the space granted to it by international economic law but, unlike a merely "traditional" approach, within a constantly growing space'.[17] The same author concludes an extensive review of arbitral awards by noting 'a number of recurrent themes and issues, such as the diligence that can be expected from the investor, the deference that must be accorded to state authorities, the normality and legality of environmental regulatory change over time or environmental justifications for differential treatment'.[18]

Indeed, the 'traditional approach' of ISDS as a means of protecting investors' interests against undue interferences of the host State could easily be noted in early cases until approximately the middle of the 2000s, when investors generally prevailed in their claims for compensation on such grounds as indirect expropriation or breach of fair and equitable treatment.[19] States' attempts to rely on environmental protection or similar grounds as justification for their actions were not accepted. As one award stated, '[t]hat the actions of the Respondent are legitimate or lawful or in compliance with the law from the standpoint of the Respondent's domestic laws does not mean that they conform to the Agreement or to international law'.[20]

Then came a series of cases in which claims from investors no longer systematically prevailed, and a more 'balanced approach' may have seemed to develop, albeit for various reasons. In a nutshell, leaving aside the many but untypical 'solar cases', three broad categories of responses arose in matters where the respondent States availed themselves of environmental justifications. Some awards relied upon the failure of the investor to conduct appropriate prior due

---

16 J.E. Viñuales, 'Foreign investment and the environment in international law: The current state of play', C-EENRG Working Papers 2016-1, Cambridge Centre for Environment, Energy and Natural Resource Governance, University of Cambridge, 2016, p. 8.

17 Ibid.

18 Ibid., p. 36.

19 See *Southern Pacific Properties (Middle East) Limited v. Egypt*, ICSID Case No. ARB/84/3, Award, 20 May 1992; *Compañia del Desarrollo de Santa Elena S.A. v. Republic of Costa Rica*, ICSID Case No. ARB/96/1, Award, 17 February 2000; *Metalclad Corporation v. United Mexican States*, ICSID Case No. ARB(AF)/97/1, Award, 30 August 2000; *Técnicas Medioambientales Tecmed, S.A. v. Mexico*, ICSID Case No. ARB(AF)/00/2, Award, 29 May 2003.

20 *Técnicas Medioambientales Tecmed, S.A. v. Mexico*, ICSID Case No. ARB(AF)/00/2, Award, 29 May 2003, para. 120.

diligence, or to more broadly take account of the general policy and legislative context, and to act accordingly.[21] Other awards dismissed investors' claims based on a failure of the investor to conduct a proper environmental impact assessment, or to act accordingly.[22] Yet other awards just found the claims meritless in view of the plain legitimacy of the State's actions and of the failure of the investor to meet the requirements of the applicable investment protection agreement.[23] Altogether, those awards could have been understood as revealing an arbitral practice far from being biased against States, since they prevailed.

In addition, recent investment arbitrations have been addressing novel situations, to some extent akin to a reinvention of ISDS as it originally presented itself.[24]

First, environmental claims, as opposed to investment protection ones, have been asserted in ISDS, a remarkable development since investor protection is generally perceived as antagonistic with environmental protection. The case of *Peter A. Allard v. Barbados* was emblematic of this new development: the investor, having purchased and developed land for an eco-tourism project, claimed that the State failed to take reasonable and necessary environmental protection measures and thus contributed to the site's contamination, annihilating the value of the investment. While that claim was dismissed on the ground that the claimant felt short of establishing material deterioration,[25] that matter shows that, in the proper circumstances, an investment protection claim can have its roots in environmental protection or environmental law. Even the prospect of 'mass arbitrations' brought by multitudes of foreign investors cannot be ruled out as a possibility in climate change-related disputes, since there do not seem to be insurmountable obstacles for such proceedings. Thus, an investment protection claim could arguably be based on climate change considerations, such as a failure of the host State to adopt and implement appropriate adaptation measures.

---

21 *Methanex v. United States*, UNCITRAL/NAFTA, Final Award, 3 June 2005; *Parkerings-Compagniet AS v. Lithuania*, ICSID Case No. ARB/05/8, Award, 11 September 2007; *Plama Consortium Limited v. Bulgaria*, ICSID Case No. ARB/03/24, Award, 27 August 2008; *David R. Aven et al. v. Costa Rica*, Case No. UNCT/15/3, Award, 18 September 2018.

22 *Emilio Agustín Maffezini v. The Kingdom of Spain*, ICSID Case No. ARB/97/7, Award, 13 November 2000; *Cortec Mining Kenya Limited, Cortec (PTY) Limited and Stirling Capital v. Kenya*, ICSID Case ARB/15/29, Award, 22 October 2018; *Bilcon of Delaware et al. v. Canada*, PCA Case No. 2009-04, Award on jurisdiction and liability, 17 March 2015, and Award on damages, 10 January 2019.

23 *Glamis Gold, Ltd. v. US*, UNCITRAL/NAFTA, Award, 8 June 2009; *Chemtura v. Canada*, UNCITRAL/NAFTA, Award, 2 August 2010; *Mamidoil Jetoil Greek Petroleum Products Société S.A. v. Albania*, ICSID ARB/11/24, Award, 30 March 2015; *Urbaser S.A. and Consorcio de Aguas Bilbao Bizkaia, Bilbao Biskaia Ur Partzuergoa v. The Argentine Republic*, ICSID Case No. ARB/07/26, Award, 8 December 2016.

24 In some respects, investment arbitration could be seen as acting as a 'sword' for environmental protection in such situations, as opposed to a shield against such protection: see P. Thieffry, above n. 5.

25 *Peter A. Allard (Canada) v. The Government of Barbados*, PCA Case No. 2012-06, Award, 27 June 2016.

Second, counterclaims have also been pursued by States against investors on the grounds of environmental damages caused by the latter. In the *Urbaser* case, the respondent State asserted that the investor, which had secured the Buenos Aires water distribution and sanitation concession, failed to make adequate investments, which affected not only contractual provisions but also basic human rights, the health and the environment of thousands of persons, most in extreme poverty. However, the award found that, while companies are no longer immune from putting their policies in line with legal rules on human rights, it remains the State's obligation that is based on the fundamental right to water, but the obligations of investors remain strictly based on contract and are not derived from human rights.[26] By contrast, Ecuador successfully filed environmental counterclaims in the sister cases separately brought by Burlington Resources and Perenco Ecuador, two members of a consortium for the same project. In short, the host State claimed that the consortium members abandoned the site, leaving behind a massive environmental catastrophe, and it was awarded compensation for damages to the soils, underground waters and infrastructures. That amount was thus offset by what the State was ordered to pay under the main investors' claims. Beyond the very fact of the compensation granted to the respondent State for environmental damages, these awards are remarkable in that they have broached difficult issues that did not have ready-made responses under the applicable law or the case law of the local courts, for example the risk of double compensation or the use of the proceeds for cleaning up the site.[27] Again, somewhat similar issues might arise in climate-related arbitrations.

It thus appears that there is a perception of ISDS in matters with environmental considerations which may not be well informed. While ISDS may deserve all or part of the criticism it is facing, this ought not to be taken for granted without further consideration in view of the above background. And, as to climate change-related disputes, there does not seem to be any reason why similar situations and issues could not arise. Yet there is clearly a case to be made for improvements of a procedural nature that could contribute to removing such rejection, or at least mitigating it.

3. ISDS PROCEDURAL REFORM TRENDS

In addition to the above-mentioned attempts at inserting and/or strengthening responsive substantive provisions in investment protection agreements, the urge

---

26 *Urbaser S.A. and Consorcio de Aguas Bilbao Bizkaia, Bilbao Biskaia Ur Partzuergoa v. The Argentine Republic*, ICSID Case No. ARB/07/26, Award, 8 December 2016.

27 *Burlington Resources Inc. v. Republic of Ecuador*, ICSID Case No. ARB/08/5, Decision on Counterclaims, 7 February 2017; *Perenco Ecuador Limited v. Republic of Ecuador*, ICSID Case No. ARB/08/6, Interim Decision on the Environmental Counterclaim, 11 August 2015, and Final Award, 27 September 2019.

for some change in ISDS has been so strong as to prompt upheaval proposals. The most radical proposal was put forward by the EU with 'the establishment of a multilateral investment tribunal and appellate mechanism for the resolution of investment disputes',[28] most likely to be composed of former judges with strong international public and trade law backgrounds.[29] Falling short of such radical proposals, a number of procedural improvements that may contribute to enhancing investment arbitration's social acceptability are under consideration in several forums. Indeed, this other avenue for reforming ISDS appears in the shape of a massive revisitation of many of its procedural aspects.

As already mentioned, the ICC Task Force Report explored 'potential procedural innovations and guidance for arbitration and ADR in climate change related disputes',[30] some of which were readily implemented by the ICC. The amendments to the ICSID Arbitration Rules[31] and UNCITRAL's ongoing Investor-State Dispute Settlement Reform[32] follow somewhat similar paths. However, where the ICC Task Force Report contemplates improvements relevant to both commercial and investment arbitration, the ICSID and UNCITRAL projects by their nature focus on investment arbitration. Yet there appears to be a common direction to all of these projects, which converge towards a more socially acceptable arbitration procedural framework.

In short, when considering arbitration of climate change-related disputes, a few major trends can be noted. The first relevant trend, and a widely shared one, consists in alleviating the burden on parties faced with manifestly ill-founded, if not frivolous, claims by allowing their early disposition or by ensuring the possible compensation of procedural costs by the claimant ('security for costs'). The second relevant trend seeks the opening up of arbitration to third parties in a passive way, at different levels, since the various arbitration institutions involved started in this respect from different baselines, from the mere publication of basic information, sometimes of redacted awards, to that of party submissions, expert reports, hearing transcripts and even attendance at hearings. The third trend advances this opening up through the active participation of third parties, by incorporating into the rules the existing practice of *amicus curiae* and taking

---

28 Article 8.29 of the Comprehensive Economic and Trade Agreement (CETA) between Canada, of the one part, and the European Union and its Member States, of the other part [2017] OJ L 11/23. See also Article 3.9 of the EU-Singapore Investment Protection Agreement.

29 Including equally nationals of a Member State, nationals of Canada, and nationals of third countries, all qualified in their respective countries for appointment to judicial office or who are jurists 'of recognized competence' having demonstrated expertise in public international law, and preferably in international investment law, in international trade law and the resolution of disputes arising under international investment or international trade agreements (Article 8.27 CETA; Article 3.9 EU-Singapore Investment Protection Agreement).

30 ICC Task Force Report, above n. 7, para. 5.5.

31 See above n. 12.

32 https://uncitral.un.org/working_groups/3/investor-state.

the first steps towards their formal involvement as regular parties to the dispute, such as through easier consolidation of separate arbitrations.

From a chronological viewpoint, the first major step taken was UNCITRAL's effort to allow greater transparency in investment arbitration in recognition of the underlying public interest in investment protection. Thus, the UNCITRAL Rules on Transparency formalise procedural steps such as the publication not only of benchmark information, but also of parties' and non-disputing parties' submissions, witness statements, expert reports, transcripts and all decisions rendered by the tribunal. Public attendance at hearings is even considered. These procedural devices apply in two procedural situations. The first situation is that of cases conducted under the UNCITRAL Arbitration Rules pursuant to investment treaties concluded since 1 April 2014, unless the parties to the treaty opt out. The second is that in which the Mauritius Convention on Transparency provides that the UNCITRAL Rules on Transparency apply to ISDS pursuant to a treaty concluded before 1 April 2014.

The next most significant step has been the adoption of the amendments to the ICSID Arbitration Rules. The ICSID adopted the amended rules on 21 March 2022. They now allow, *inter alia*, greater transparency in the conduct and outcome of proceedings, new disclosure requirements for third-party funding, and expedited arbitration rules for parties wishing to further shorten the procedural timescale. Some of the amendments to the ICSID Arbitration Rules aim at alleviating the burden sustained by respondent host States in defending investors' claims, where this is deemed appropriate. Under the revised rules, a party is able to object that a claim is manifestly without legal merit, whether as to the substance of the claim, the jurisdiction of the centre or the competence of the tribunal, within 45 days after the constitution of the tribunal, and the tribunal shall decide on that objection within 60 days after the latter of its constitution or the last submission on the objection.[33] This should allow respondent host States to avoid wasting the resources (time and costs) needed to deploy extensive defences against frivolous cases. Indeed, the prevailing party – and thus the said respondent host State, as the case may be – shall furthermore be awarded its reasonable costs 'unless the Tribunal determines that there are special circumstances justifying a different allocation of costs'.[34] And, along the same lines, but with a longer-term perspective in mind, upon request, the tribunal may order a party to provide security for costs in relevant circumstances, including in view of that party's ability or willingness to comply with an adverse decision on costs, the effect that providing security for costs may have on that party's ability to pursue its claim or counterclaim, and the conduct of the parties.[35]

33 ICSID Arbitration Rules as revised, Rule 41.
34 Ibid., Rule 52(2).
35 Ibid., Rule 53.

Other amendments to the ICSID Arbitration Rules aim more directly at the public perception of the proceedings, working under the assumption that their lack of transparency would contribute to undesirable practices. Thus, the 'observation of hearings' by third parties as well as the publication of recordings or transcripts become the general rule. Attendance by individuals 'in addition to the parties, their representatives, witnesses and experts during their testimony, and persons assisting the Tribunal' are allowed 'unless either party objects', and subject to 'procedures to prevent the disclosure of confidential or protected information'.[36] By contrast, recordings or transcripts of hearings will only be made publicly available upon request of a party, and with the consent of the other party.[37] Finally, and in a less novel fashion, *amicus curiae*, which tribunals have been allowing as a matter of practice and subject to conditions determined on a case-by-case basis, will henceforth be provided for as 'submissions of non-disputing parties'. Such submissions will be subject to prior authorisation of the tribunal, which 'shall consider all relevant circumstances', including most notably their relevance to the subject matter of the dispute.[38]

Among the many items of the Investor-State Dispute Settlement Reform currently considered by UNCITRAL's Working Group III,[39] the most advanced one seems to be that of a code of conduct for arbitrators. While still under consideration, one of the options being considered for that code of conduct as regards one of the most highly criticised arbitral practices would be the full prohibition of 'double-hatting', i.e. the fact that arbitrators act as counsel in other, unrelated, investment arbitrations. Other advanced projects include a multilateral advisory centre, which would provide assistance to State respondent parties in an effort to offset their perceived inadequate defence resources as compared to those at the disposal of investors. Likewise, stand-alone review or appellate mechanisms are under discussion as a response to the lack of uniformity between arbitral tribunals' substantive positions in respect of similar or comparable legal issues, i.e. the absence of arbitral case law and of appellate processes that could provide more of a level playing field. Yet other topics of discussion in Working Group III include such possible features as the requirement of prior exhaustion of local remedies, a procedure to address frivolous claims, including summary dismissal (as in the amended ICSID Arbitration Rules), restrictions against multiple, parallel proceedings, reflective losses, and counterclaims by respondent States.

These ICSID and UNCITRAL procedural improvements, actual or potential, should clearly contribute to allaying the perception that ISDS is genetically

36 Ibid., Rule 65(1) and (2).
37 Ibid., Rule 65(3).
38 Ibid., Rule 67.
39 https://uncitral.un.org/en/working_groups/3/investor-state.

biased in favour of investors – and, conversely but more critically, against the interests of respondent host States deemed consistent with public interest – not only substantively, as a result of one-sided guarantees provided for in investment protection agreements, but also in terms of procedural features, some of which are now more or less condemned as unfair or illegitimate.

As a matter of fact, these procedural improvements coincide to some extent with those considered in the ICC Task Force Report. Looking at the broader category of climate change-related disputes, i.e. including commercial arbitration as opposed to investment arbitration only, arbitration at first sight appears perhaps even less as a primary forum for public interest disputes. However, it offers advantages, such as the ability to provide early or urgent resolution of disputes, to allow appropriate scientific and other expertise, and to improve the understanding of relevant climate policy and law. Increased transparency may be provided where appropriate, as well as third-party involvement.[40]

4. CONCLUSION

The 'right to legislate' of host States has drawn much attention in the last few years, though repeatedly reaffirmed. Yet this right to legislate may have to be adjudicated in investment arbitration at some expense and with an undeniable risk of procedural chill. Investment law has proven its ability to address novel situations and to create new types of substantive safeguards and treaty interpretation. Nevertheless, an ISDS reform is underway on the procedural side, and this seems to be welcome. Such procedural changes as a code of conduct for arbitrators with an optional prohibition of 'double-hatting', early dismissal of frivolous claims, security for costs, increased transparency, observation of hearings, third-party involvement through *amicus curiae* or even joinder of concerned citizens, etc. clearly aim at improving investment arbitration's social acceptability. While it is difficult to anticipate the extent to which such reforms may succeed in this respect, they could contribute to this goal and, as such, they are worth observing.

40 ICC Task Force Report, above n. 7.

PART II

CLIMATE CHANGE LITIGATION IN EUROPE: SECTORAL PERSPECTIVES

Procedural Rights and Climate Change Litigation

CLOSED DOORS IN LUXEMBOURG?

Climate Change Litigation before the CJEU in a 'Complete System of Remedies'

Joschka SCHLAKE

1. INTRODUCTION

Following the 'rights turn'[1] in climate change litigation in Europe, several national courts have made it clear that legislation on climate protection can also be reviewed in the light of fundamental rights.[2] In contrast, recent decisions by the Court of Justice of the European Union (CJEU)[3] have rejected

1 J. PEEL and H.M. OSOFSKY, 'A Rights Turn in Climate Change Litigation?' (2018) 7 *Transnational Environmental Law* 37.

2 See for instance the cases of *Neubauer*, BVerfG, 1 BvR 2656/18, para. 5, and *Urgenda*, Rechtbank Den Haag, *Stichting Urgenda v. Government of the Netherlands*, ECLI:NL:RBDHA:2015:7145, C/09/456689 / HA ZA 13-1396.

3 In the following referred to as CJEU, intending to include both the Court of Justice of the European Union and the Court of First Instance (CFI).

similar actions.[4] Prominently, in its decision of 25 March 2021, the CJEU refused to declare the action in the *People's Climate Case* admissible, and in doing so, also made it clear that direct actions against EU climate change law in principle have no prospect of being successfully contested by individual plaintiffs.[5] '*Plaumann* means *Plaumann* means *Plaumann*' seems to be the unshakable position of the Court regarding the interpretation of individual action possibilities, pointing to the indirect route to the CJEU with an action before a national court and the possibility of referral as a preliminary ruling. Since the Court has essentially not changed its position on standing within the past 60 years, this approach has often been described with a reference to Franz Kafka,[6] creating an image of standing rules before the CJEU as being as insurmountable as the gatekeeper in the parable *Der Prozeß*.[7] But is this image truly accurate or is there a comprehensive explanation for this restrictive approach?

This chapter takes the opportunity to shed light on the different paths to the CJEU in the EU judicial system for actions that aim to challenge the legality of EU legislation to improve efforts to combat climate change. This includes the Court's interpretation of standing rules in direct actions according to the *Plaumann* test, whether it in fact creates a 'closed door' for climate change litigation, and whether it reveals a reasonable underlying logic. Further, this chapter discusses to what extent the control of statutory climate protection measures on the basis of fundamental rights can be achieved via the referral route.

2. DIRECT ACTIONS

2.1. INDIVIDUAL CONCERN AND FUNDAMENTAL RIGHTS: NO MATCH MADE IN HEAVEN

Article 263(4) of the Treaty on the Functioning of the European Union (TFEU) opens up the possibility for individuals to bring an action directly before the CJEU. In general, all acts by EU organs are reviewable, including legislative acts. Unlike privileged and semi-privileged applicants, as set out in Article 263(2) and (3), individuals are non-privileged applicants and must, therefore, claim to be individually and directly affected. This formulation of the provision has

---

4 Case C-297/20 P, *Sabo and Others v. Parliament and Council*, ECLI:EU:C:2021:24; Case C-565/19 P, *Carvalho and Others v. Parliament and Council*, ECLI:EU:C:2021:252.

5 Ibid.

6 H. Schoukens, 'Access to Justice in Environmental Cases After the Rulings of the Court of Justice of 13 January 2015: Kafka Revisited?' (2015) 31 *Utrecht Journal of International and European Law* 46; N. Grundhewer, *Torhüter zur Verwaltungsgerichtsbarkeit*, Duncker & Humblot, Berlin 2020, p. 23.

7 F. Kafka, *Der Prozeß*, Die Schmiede, Berlin 1925.

long been interpreted by the European courts according to the well-known formula in the *Plaumann* case: an individual is only impacted if the act affects them 'by reason of certain attributes that are peculiar to them or by reason of circumstances in which they are differentiated from all other persons, and by virtue of these factors distinguishes them individually just as in the case of the addressee'.[8] Accordingly, individual concern is not to be understood in terms of 'different' concern but rather in terms of 'similar to the addressee', so that a plaintiff is only sufficiently individualised if their position is really 'unique among many'.

This has resulted in private actions being consistently found inadmissible by the Court, especially when private applicants suffering environmental harm have attempted to challenge EU acts that were not addressed to them.[9] In legal scholarship, it has often been pointed out that in such cases the hurdles set by the *Plaumann* test are difficult to overcome. This is certainly the case, yet it should be noted that the requirement for individual concern is not to be mistaken for a mere higher substantiation of a violation of rights. Rather, the criterion of individual concern is an entirely different category that is not tied to intensity. In the Court's case law, three types of cases can be identified.[10] First, individual concern can be caused by formal participation in the administrative procedure leading to a legal act.[11] Secondly, the fact that at the time of the adoption of a legal act a protected group of individuals has already been conclusively determined can bring about a position that is 'similar to the addressee' in the sense of the *Plaumann* test.[12] Thirdly, the Court has granted *locus standi* in cases in which the applicants were noticeably affected in their market position or in specific positions, such as trademark rights.[13]

The key criterion is, therefore, that applicants must be members of a closed category of people.[14] It is due to this fact that applicants have not been able to be accepted as individually concerned with the argument that an EU act violates their fundamental rights. In the *Carvalho* case, the applicants challenged the targets of the EU climate protection laws as not being sufficiently ambitious

---

8 Case 25/62, *Plaumann v. Commission*, ECLI:EU:C:1963:17.

9 A. Arnull, 'Private applicants and the action for annulment since Codorniu' (2001) 38 *Common Market Law Review* 7; K. Lenaerts and J. Gutiérrez-Fons, 'The general system of EU Environmental Law enforcement' (2011) 30 *Yearbook of European Law* 3, 11.

10 A. Thiele, '§9 Die Nichtigkeitsklage' in S. Leible and J.P. Terhechte (eds), *Enzyklopädie Europarecht. Band 3: Europäisches Rechtsschutz- und Verfahrensrecht*, 2nd ed., Nomos, Baden-Baden 2021, pp. 297–300.

11 Case C-26/76, *Metro SB-Großmärkte v. Commission*, ECLI:EU:C:1977:167.

12 Case C-11/82, *Piraiki-Patraiki v. Commission*, ECLI:EU:C:1985:18.

13 Case C-358/89, *Extramet Industrie v. Council*, ECLI:EU:C:1991:214; Case C-309/89, *Codorníu v. Council*, ECLI:EU:C:1994:197.

14 A. Albors-Llorens, 'Judicial protection before the Court of Justice of the European Union' in C. Barnard and S. Peers (eds), *European Union Law*, 3rd ed., Oxford University Press, Oxford 2020, p. 299.

because they enable greenhouse gas emissions and are, therefore, partly responsible for climate change-related harmful conditions for certain groups of people, resulting in violation of their fundamental rights to life, physical and mental integrity, occupation, property, and equal treatment.[15] The Court did in fact acknowledge that the appellants are affected differently by climate change, yet this in itself was not sufficient to establish standing.[16] Instead, the Court argued that because climate change is likely to affect everyone, no individual could claim to be distinguished as the addressee in the sense of individual concern, and a different approach would render the requirements of Article 263 TFEU meaningless.[17] This led to the Court dismissing the case as inadmissible without further review of the substantive issues.

Despite this result seeming frustrating, as *locus standi* is impossible the more individuals are affected, it shows that 'individual' concern asks for more than 'different' concern, and that even a violation of fundamental rights can never result in a sufficient individualisation. Fundamental rights are composed in an abstract-objective way, and, therefore, everyone in the group of addressees has in common that they are all holders of fundamental rights. Thus, no one within this group can be identified as unique.

Another example showing that a fundamental rights approach is not suitable to overcome the standing requirements in actions for annulment is the *Sabo* case.[18] In this case, it was argued that Directive 2018/2001,[19] which includes forest biomass among the sources of renewable energy, had resulted in the destruction of forests. Some applicants claimed they were affected not just in those fundamental rights as relied upon in the *Carvalho* case. Rather, the threat to the forests would also lead to an infringement of their private family life and their right to ensure the education of their children, in breach of Articles 7 and 14(3) of the EU Charter of Fundamental Rights (CFR) due to the family's deep personal connection to the forests of the region, which is passed on to their children as a philosophical conviction. The Court eventually rejected this reasoning in the same way as in previous cases. Despite such threats being serious, this claim illustrates an approach in strategic climate change litigation which aims to select plaintiffs with the 'most unique' exposure to climate change to overcome the *Plaumann* test. Since fundamental rights have not yet been able to constitute *individual concern*, strategies based on fundamental rights likely do not have a chance of success before the CJEU.

---

15 Case C-565/19 P, *Carvalho and Others v. Parliament and Council*, ECLI:EU:C:2021:252.

16 Ibid., para. 40.

17 Ibid., para. 48.

18 Case C-297/20 P, *Sabo and Others v. Parliament and Council*, ECLI:EU:C:2021:24.

19 Directive (EU) 2018/2001 of the European Parliament and of the Council of 11 December 2018 on the promotion of the use of energy from renewable sources.

2.2. THE *PLAUMANN* TEST AS A TARGET OF CRITICISM

With this finding, it is not surprising that the issue of *locus standi* before European courts and the high hurdles set by the *Plaumann* doctrine have been a controversial issue for decades. A very prominent attempt to overcome *Plaumann* occurred during the 'hot summer of 2002',[20] when Advocate General Francis Jacobs pledged a broader interpretation of Article 263(4) TFEU in the *UPA* case.[21] AG Jacobs's criticism focused on general disadvantages of the option of indirect access to the Court via preliminary references in terms of cost issues, the duration of proceedings and the involvement of third parties. Shortly after, the idea to redefine the criterion of individual concern found approval by the Court of First Instance (CFI) in the *Jégo-Quéré* case.[22] In its judgment, the Court reversed previous case law and held that the lack of individual concern should simply be irrelevant to the question of admissibility if otherwise no effective legal protection can be achieved. However, in its final judgment on appeal, the CJEU declared both actions inadmissible, referring to the possibility of indirect action.[23] This might have been a way to pass the ball to the Convention on the Future of Europe, which was working on a draft treaty establishing a Constitution for Europe between February 2002 and July 2003.[24] The working group on fundamental rights discussed the specific issue of access by individuals to the CJEU, but ultimately voted against the implementation of a fundamental rights complaint against legislative acts.[25] Still, the slight revision of the provision as manifested in the Lisbon Treaty grants access to the CJEU to individuals without the requirement of individual concern when they are directly concerned by regulatory acts that do not entail implementing measures. Even though this raised hopes for the end of the *Plaumann* test,[26] the position of individuals has

---

20 N. Van den Broek, 'A Long Hot Summer for Individual Concern? The European Court's Recent Case law on Direct Actions by Private Parties ... and a Plea for a Foreign Affairs Exception' (2003) 30 *Legal Issues of Economic Integration* 61, 68.

21 Opinion of Advocate General Jacobs, Case C-50/00 P, *Unión de Pequeños Agricultores (UPA) v. Council*, ECLI:EU:C:2002:197, para. 59.

22 Case C-263/02 P, *Commission v. Jégo-Quéré*, ECLI:EU:C:2004:210.

23 Case C-50/00 P, *Unión de Pequeños Agricultores v. Council*, ECLI:EU:C:2002:197; Case C-263/02 P, *Commission v. Jégo-Quéré*, ECLI:EU:C:2004:210.

24 F.C. Mayer, 'Individualrechtsschutz im Europäischen Verfassungsrecht' (2004) *Das Deutsche Verwaltungsblatt* 606, 609.

25 See the Final Report of Working Group II, CONV 350/02; H.H. Fredriksen, 'Individualklagemöglichkeiten vor den Gerichten der EU nach dem Vertrag über eine Verfassung für Europa' (2005) 19 *Berliner Online-Beiträge zum Europarecht* 30, https://www.jura.fu-berlin.de/forschung/europarecht/bob/berliner_online_beitraege/Paper19-Fredriksen/Paper19---Individualklagemoeglichkeiten-vor-den-Gerichten-der-EU-nach-dem-Vertrag-ueber-eine-Verfassung-fuer-Europa.pdf.

26 M. Kottmann, 'Plaumanns Ende: Ein Vorschlag zu Art. 263 Abs. 4 AEUV' (2010) 70 *Zeitschrift für ausländisches öffentliches Recht und Völkerrecht* 547.

not significantly altered, as the CJEU made clear that regulatory acts do not include acts that have been adopted through a legislative procedure.[27]

To date, the Court's interpretation has been criticised for being overly restrictive and not handled consistently in its application. Observers claim that, in the past, the CJEU sometimes assumed that non-privileged plaintiffs were individually affected if economic interests were involved.[28] In contrast, in the case of general interests, the Court has always held that there is no standing if the legal interests of many individuals are affected.[29] As shown above, the requirement for 'individual concern' in fact privileges economic interests over public or ecologic interests. In addition, the requirement as interpreted by the Court has not always proven to be consistent even within its own logic.[30] Despite some results being frustrating regarding the need for judicial enforcement in the area of general interests, there is no evidence of an unequal treatment of certain policy areas by the Court for political or ideological reasons.[31] The requirement of individual concern asks for individualisation alone and remains applicable regardless of the nature of the interests affected.[32] The primary function of the action for annulment is to guarantee access to justice in relation to acts of the EU administration that are usually single-case decisions. Legislative acts are included for cases with a similar effect but a coincidentally different legal nature, which is why the individualisation criterion serves as a safeguard for comparability. Regardless of the importance of the legal interests involved, fundamental rights that every individual holds differ from certain economically relevant positions such as trademark rights in terms of individualisation, as the latter are more suitable for clearly distinguishing an

27 Case C-583/11 P, *Inuit v. Parliament and Council*, ECLI:EU:C:2013:625; see also J. Wildemeersch, 'Standing Requirements of Private Parties in Actions for Annulment Concerning Regulatory Acts: The State of Affairs 10 Years After the Entry into Force of the Lisbon Treaty' in D. Sarmiento, H.R. Fabri and B. Hess (eds), *Yearbook on Procedural Law of the Court of Justice of the European Union – 2019*, MPILux Research Paper Series 2020(2), p. 49.

28 Case C-309/89, *Codorníu v. Council*, ECLI:EU:C:1994:197; P. Craig and G. De Búrca, *EU Law*, 7th ed., Oxford University Press, Oxford 2020, p. 550.

29 Cf. regarding the almost cynical result in the case of an action against a nuclear test, Case T-219/95, *Danielsson and Others v. Commission*, ECLI:EU:T:1995:219, para. 70. Further L. Krämer, 'The Environment before the European Court of Justice' in C. Voigt (ed.), *International Judicial Practice on the Environment*, Cambridge University Press, Cambridge 2019, pp. 25, 31.

30 This is illustrated by the *Extramet* case, Case C-358/89, *Extramet Industrie v. Council*, ECLI:EU:C:1991:214, where it is not clear why the plaintiff, as the largest importer of calcium metal, challenged anti-dumping duties on its imports that were supposed to be part of a closed category. As a comparison to the original *Plaumann* case, it could be argued that anyone could theoretically become an importer of calcium as well. It should be noted that the Court did not apply this approach to other cases, referring to the exceptional circumstances of the case, see A. Albors-Llorens, above n. 14, pp. 301–02.

31 In this vein L. Krämer, above n. 29, p. 25; I. Hadjiyianni, 'Judicial Protection and the Environment in the EU Legal Order: Missing Pieces for a Complete Puzzle of Legal Remedies' (2021) 58 *Common Market Law Review* 777, 786.

32 Case T-585/93, *Greenpeace and Others v. Commission*, ECLI:EU:T:1995:147, para. 50.

individual from others in a similar way to an addressee of a single-case decision. It is, therefore, not a more generous interpretation by the CJEU of individual concern but the requirement of individual concern itself that privileges economic interests over public interests such as environmental concerns.

While the CJEU's view on standing in direct actions has not changed since the *Plaumann* case, the recent case law, especially in environmental cases, provides many examples where the Court has tended to strengthen the access to justice of individuals and environmental non-governmental organisations (ENGOs) before national courts within the scope of the Aarhus Convention.[33] This was pointed out as a double standard compared to what is required of national courts and of the CJEU itself when it comes to ensuring effective judicial protection.[34] Such decisions involve sensitive questions of national procedural rules. However, there is a clear connection between the narrow access to the Court with direct actions and broader standing criteria before national courts as a prerequisite for indirect access to the Court. As discussed in the following subsection, the different handling of standing requirements serves the functioning of the decentralised judicial system as set out in the Treaties.

2.3. THE FUNCTION OF THE *PLAUMANN* TEST AS A FILTER IN THE EU SYSTEM OF LEGAL PROTECTION

In the past, the Court has rejected all attempts to establish an interpretation of the requirement of individual concern that deviates from the *Plaumann* test. The Court itself uses a recurring argumentation, according to which 'the FEU Treaty has established a complete system of legal remedies and procedures designed to ensure judicial review of the legality of acts of the institutions, and has entrusted such review to the Courts of the European Union', which

> may not, without going beyond their jurisdiction, interpret the conditions under which an individual may institute proceedings against an act of the Union in a way which has the effect of setting aside those conditions, which are expressly laid down in the FEU Treaty, even in the light of the principle of effective judicial protection.[35]

---

33 Starting with Case C-237/07, *Janecek v. Freistaat Bayern* and recently with a preliminary climax in Case C-535/18, *IL and Others v. Land Nordrhein-Westfalen*; see further F. Lecomte, 'The contours of ecological justice before EU courts in the light of recent case-law' (2021) 21 *ERA Forum* 737, 746; J. Berkemann, 'EuGH stärkt erneut Klagebefugnisse im Umweltrecht' (2021) *Das Deutsche Verwaltungsblatt* 1.

34 M. Ruffert, 'Umweltrechtsschutz ohne methodische Grundlage? Zur neueren Rechtsprechung des EuGH und ihren Folgen für Deutschland' (2019) *Das Deutsche Verwaltungsblatt* 1033.

35 Case C-565/19 P, *Carvalho and Others v. Parliament and Council*, ECLI:EU:C:2021:252, paras 68–70; Case C-50/00 P, *UPA v. Council*, ECLI:EU:C:2002:462, para. 44.

The argument that the wording of the provision of Article 263(4) TFEU in itself prohibits a different interpretation has been invalidated, as the Court has already created standing rights contrary to the wording of the provision for the European Parliament.[36] Furthermore, focusing on the context with the Convention on the Future of Europe does not offer a conclusive explanation. Indeed, in the latest amendment of standing provisions with the Lisbon Treaty, the Member States did not decide in favour of a reformulation of the standing provisions, as the Court has indicated in its *UPA* decision.[37] However, this cannot be used to give the last word on the interpretation due to the *ad hoc* character of the considerations in the working groups.[38] Rather, it is then necessary to ask what the core content of the *Plaumann* test is, which, according to the Court, leads to its 'constitutional status'.[39]

The key to answering this question is to assess the role that the *Plaumann* test plays within the judicial system of the EU. Bogojević has highlighted the concept of judicial subsidiarity to explain why the Court refuses to improve access to justice with direct actions.[40] While the existence of judicial division of powers is a well-known feature of EU law,[41] judicial subsidiarity goes further and can be seen as an interpretative principle to structure the judicial system in a way that prioritises the decentralised approach over direct actions. Accordingly, this compromises broad access to national courts and narrow access directly to the CJEU itself. From this point of view, the *Plaumann* test is the downside of the judicial law enforcement by national courts as a substantive feature of the success story that is the law of the EU.

Thus, what are the benefits of the decentralised system of judicial review? It has shown that the *Plaumann* test works as a pinhole to ensure that the CJEU receives most cases via preliminary references from national courts. Thereby, national courts are included within the judiciary of the EU. This circumstance is crucial for the success of the enforcement of EU law in the Member States because, unlike the Member States, the EU has no ability to enforce its law

36 Case C-70/88, *Parliament v. Council*, ECLI:EU:C:1990:217; see also U. Haltern, *Europarecht. Dogmatik im Kontext. Band II*, 3rd ed., Mohr Siebeck, Tübingen 2017, para. 508.

37 Case C-50/00 P, *Unión de Pequeños Agricultores v. Council*, ECLI:EU:C:2002:197, para. 45.

38 G. Winter, 'Not fit for purpose. Die Klagebefugnis vor dem Europäischen Gericht angesichts kollektiver Gefahren' (2022) *Europarecht* 367, 394.

39 Cf. K. Lenaerts and J. Gutiérrez-Fons, above n. 9, pp. 22–23.

40 S. Bogojević, 'Judicial Protection of Individual Applicants Revisited: Access to Justice through the Prism of Judicial Subsidiarity' (2015) 34 *Yearbook of European Law* 5; see also the text of the oral intervention of the then President of the CJEU, R. Iglesias, before the Discussion Circle, CONV 572/03, 4; similar B. Wegener, 'Art. 19 EUV' in C. Calliess and M. Ruffert (eds), *EUV/AEUV. Das Verfassungsrecht der Europäischen Union mit Europäischer Grundrechtecharta. Kommentar*, 6th ed., C.H. Beck, Munich 2022, para. 68.

41 Cf. K. Lenaerts, 'The Rule of Law and the Coherence of the Judicial System of the European Union' (2007) 44 *Common Market Law Review* Band 1, C.H. Beck, Munich 1625.

by compulsion.[42] Including national courts not only links EU law with national law enforcement tools, but also involves individuals.[43] This way, the end of a proceeding is marked by the judgment of a national court even though the relevant questions have mainly been determined in Luxembourg.[44] Still, this enables judicial problems to be resolved closer to the citizen, and ultimately to promote trust in EU law.[45]

Beyond that, this mechanism affects the way EU law is shaped by interpretation and judicial law-making. As a generalist court, the CJEU can make use of the particular qualifications of specialised courts in domestic jurisdictions, and operate together as a community of interpretation, in which the CJEU and the courts in Member States play complementary roles.[46] By giving an opinion on the question they pose, national courts can indicate to the CJEU the specifics of the perspective of their own legal system and serve as a stimulus for the development of European law.[47] This corresponds to the pluralistic reality of the EU legal order with its various conceptions of legal rules and culture.[48]

However, it must be borne in mind that the idea of a right of individuals to challenge legislative acts with a direct complaint is not shared in all of the Member States.[49] Beyond that, the EU is not a State and references to the principle of effective legal protection cannot lead to evaluating the EU by the same standards as its Member States. The legislative process in the EU is in particular characterised by complex political compromises and is therefore susceptible to

---

42 U. Everling, 'Referat' in Ständige Deputation des Deutschen Juristentages (eds), *Verhandlungen zum 60. Deutschen Juristentag*, Band 1, C.H. Beck, Munich 1994, n. 9.

43 J.H.H. Weiler, 'Journey to an Unknown Destination: A Retrospective and Prospective of the European Court of Justice in the Arena of Political Integration' (1993) 31 *Journal of Common Market Studies* 417, 421.

44 C. Franzius, *Europäisches Verfassungsrechtsdenken*, Mohr Siebeck, Tübingen 2010, p. 107; see further U. Haltern, above n. 36, para. 513.

45 S. Bogojević, above n. 40, pp. 5, 21. See for the dimension of trust in this sense A. Wallermann Ghavanini, 'Power Talk: Effects of Inter-Court Disagreement on Legal Reasoning in the Preliminary Reference Procedure' (2020) 5 *European Papers* 887.

46 D. Kraus, 'Die kooperative Sicherung der Rechtsstaatlichkeit der Europäischen Union durch die mitgliedstaatlichen Gerichte und die Gemeinschaftsgerichte' (2008) 3 *Europarecht-Beiheft* 109, 128; critically U. Haltern, 'Verschiebungen im europäischen Rechtsschutzsystem' (2005) 96 *Verwaltungsarchiv* 311, 344; see further D. Classen, 'Effektive und kohärente Justizgewährleistung im europäischen Rechtsschutzverbund' (2006) *Juristenzeitung* 157, 165.

47 J. Schwarze, 'Zwischen Tradition und Zukunft: Die Rolle allgemeiner Rechtsgrundsätze im Recht der Europäischen Union' (2011) *Das Deutsche Verwaltungsblatt* 721, 723; U. Haltern, above n. 36, para. 514.

48 S. Bogojević, above n. 40, p. 24.

49 U. Wölker, 'Rechtsschutz Privater gegenüber dem europäischen Gesetzgeber' (2003) *Die Öffentliche Verwaltung* 570, 574.

being disturbed by numerous lawsuits brought by individuals.[50] By declaring a legislative act invalid, the CJEU overrules not only the European Parliament, but also the Member States, whose representatives have given their approval in the Council. In this regard, the self-limitation of the CJEU by excluding its judicial decision-making power from such cases can be seen as conscious self-restraint in deference to the political process.[51]

Access to the CJEU has to be balanced with the issues of legal certainty, the acceptance of standard-setting, and the control of the workload of the European Courts.[52] Still, such reasons cannot alone justify the restriction of individual actions as set by the *Plaumann* test. Standing criteria have an impact that goes beyond solely filtering the cases that reach the CJEU. The essence of the restriction of direct actions lies in the fundamental decision in favour of the decentralised system of judicial review. Opening up the opportunities for direct actions could put the objective of involving national courts and strengthening the preliminary reference procedure at risk.

Despite the fact that actions against legislative acts are theoretically included in the Treaty provisions, an amendment that would result in a general fundamental rights complaint would, therefore, fundamentally change the structure of judicial competences in the EU as it affects the question of who is allowed at which level to intervene in the regulatory processes. Such a case would actually have the result of rendering the requirements of Article 263 TFEU meaningless, contradicting the principle of judicial subsidiarity. The CJEU does not only exercise judicial subsidiarity when the position of applicants before national courts is improved. Likewise, the narrow access to the Court via direct actions has the function of a pinhole to ensure the allocation of judicial competences.

As shown, the decision in favour of decentralised judicial review instead of a broad possibility to address direct actions to the European Courts plays a key role in the EU legal order. But still, the CJEU also refers to its effectiveness

---

50 Cf. E. Pache, '§11 Prozessuale Durchsetzung der Unionsgrundrechte' in S.M. Heselhaus and C. Nowak (eds), *Handbuch der Europäischen Grundrechte*, 2nd ed., C.H. Beck, Munich 2020, para. 53; M. Nettesheim, 'Effektive Rechtsschutzgewährleistung im arbeitsteiligen System europäischen Rechtsschutzes' (2002) *Juristenzeitung* 929; M. Browoski, 'Die Nichtigkeitsklage gem. Art. 230 Abs. 4 EGV' (2004) *Europarecht* 879, 893; S. Lenz and S. Staeglich, 'Kein Rechtsschutz gegen EG-Verordnungen? Europäische Rechtsschutzdefizite und ihr Ausgleich durch die Feststellungsklage nach §43 I VwGO' (2004) *Neue Zeitschrift für Verwaltungsrecht* 1421, 1422.

51 U. Haltern, above n. 36, paras 518, 522.

52 M. Rhimes, 'The EU courts stand their ground: why are the standing rules for direct actions still so restrictive?' (2016) 9 *European Journal of Legal Studies* 103, 157; J. Schwarze, 'Der Rechtsschutz Privater vor dem Europäischen Gerichtshof: Grundlagen, Entwicklungen und Perspektiven des Individualrechtsschutzes im Gemeinschaftsrecht' (2002) *Das Deutsche Verwaltungsblatt* 1297, 1308.

and points out that the 'FEU Treaty has established a complete system of legal remedies and procedures designed to ensure judicial review of the legality of acts of the institutions, and has entrusted such review to the Courts of the European Union'.[53] As this also includes judicial review of legislative acts, the next section examines whether such acts can effectively be addressed in preliminary references in the first place or specifically in climate change cases.

3. INDIRECT ACTIONS

3.1. A 'COMPLETE SYSTEM OF REMEDIES'?

Can the lack of legal action be compensated for by referring to national legal proceedings and the possibility of a referral according to Article 267 TFEU? A closer look leads to the conclusion that decentralised judicial review is not suitable for achieving the goals of climate change litigation. Most of the traditional arguments against the effectiveness of the preliminary reference procedure, such as the subordinate position of the complainants or the long duration of the proceedings, turn out to make actions impractical rather than actually impossible, and do not lead to a gap of judicial protection. It is instead the structural conception of this way of legal protection that excludes climate change litigation cases from accessing the CJEU.

According to Article 267 TFEU, a reference requires an admissible action before a national court and a corresponding question that is relevant for those particular proceedings, which is then sent to the CJEU by the national court involved. The decision whether to refer to the CJEU is generally left to the discretion of the national court. An obligation to refer applies only to courts of last instance, and in cases where the national court considers an EU act to be invalid and the court is inclined to not apply the EU act as the basis for its ruling.[54] The appellants, therefore, have no possibility of forcing a referral. Even if a referral can be suggested during the proceedings, they are dependent on the court at least having doubts about the validity of the Union act in question and making use of its right of referral.[55] Due to the *erga omnes* effect of CJEU judgments, a decision on the conformity of a Union legal act with higher-ranking

---

53 Case C-565/19 P, *Carvalho and Others v. Parliament and Council*, ECLI:EU:C:2021:252, para. 68.

54 Case 314/85, *Foto Frost*, ECLI:EU:C:1987:452, para. 14.

55 K. Rennert, 'Effektivität des Rechtsschutzes und Vorabentscheidungsverfahren vor dem EuGH – Die Perspektive der nationalen Gerichtsbarkeit' (2008) *Europäische Grundrechtezeitschrift* 385, 388; regarding sanctions to safeguard the duty to refer see further A. Betz, *Die verfassungsrechtliche Absicherung der Vorlagepflicht*, Mohr Siebeck, Tübingen 2013.

law applies in all Member States, so that in any case it would not be necessary to take legal action in each individual Member State.[56]

Provided that an EU act has been transposed into national law, it is possible to bring an action before a national court against the transposing act or against a measure adopted on the basis of that act. Without a national implementation, this possibility basically does not exist. In accordance with the dual legal protection structure of the Union, a Union legal act cannot be the subject of an action directly before a national court.[57] However, Article 19(1) of the Treaty on European Union (TEU), which was newly inserted by the Treaty of Lisbon, codifies the CJEU's jurisdiction in the *UPA* case and requires Member States to create legal remedies to ensure effective legal protection against acts of the Union with direct effect.[58] This goes as far as to mean that, where appropriate, national procedural rules under which a national measure would not otherwise be open to judicial challenge must be interpreted in such a way as to allow for incidental review.[59] For this reason, differences of national standing rules cannot be used as a valid argument against the decentralised approach to judicial protection, as it is not dependent on national law.[60] However, interpreting national procedural rules in this way could at any rate lead to admissible actions before national courts in constellations such as those in which an action was inadmissible in the past. This certainly only applies to actions that were aimed at avoiding a burden imposed by certain provisions.[61]

The climate lawsuit constellation examined in this chapter is different. It concerns the question of what happens when a violation of fundamental rights is alleged by an EU provision itself, without this provision restricting or prohibiting certain conduct. Irrespective of all the difficulties of bringing an action aiming at the incidental control of EU law before a national court, the decisive point lies in the relevance of the reference question. The preliminary ruling procedure is

---

56 G. Winter, 'Armando Carvalho et alii versus Europäische Union: Rechtsdogmatische und staatstheoretische Probleme einer Klimaklage vor dem Europäischen Gericht' (2019) *Zeitschrift für Umweltrecht* 259.

57 Cf. A. Vosskuhle and J. Schemmel, '§6 Die Rolle der nationalen Gerichte im Europarecht' in S. Leible and J.P. Terhechte (eds), *Enzyklopädie Europarecht. Band 3 Europäisches Rechtsschutz- und Verfahrensrecht*, 2nd ed., Nomos, Baden-Baden 2021, para. 22.

58 Case C-50/00 P, *Unión de Pequeños Agricultores v. Council*, ECLI:EU:C:2002:197; B. Wegener, above n. 40, para. 67; C. Koch, 'Locus standi of private applicants under the EU Constitution' (2005) 30 *European Law Review* 511, 518.

59 Case C-50/00 P, *UPA v. Council*, ECLI:EU:C:2002:462. This means that actions have to be declared admissible to enable an incidental decision via the preliminary reference procedure, despite being inadmissible due to national procedural rules. Cf. A. Vosskuhle and J. Schemmel, above n. 57, para. 22.

60 For this argument see the Opinion of Advocate General Jacobs, Case C-50/00 P, *UPA v. Council*, ECLI:EU:C:2002:197, para. 53.

61 See for instance Case C-263/02 P, *Commission v. Jégo-Quéré*, ECLI:EU:C:2004:210, regarding a ban on the use of certain fishing nets, or Case C-583/11 P, *Inuit v. Parliament and Council*, ECLI:EU:C:2013:625, where the import of seal products was challenged.

designed to clarify the interpretation or validity of Union acts that are relevant to the original legal dispute. In principle, the decision on this is at the subjective discretion of the court or tribunal.[62] Only in exceptional cases can the CJEU refuse such a request.[63] However, a referral is inadmissible if the interpretation or assessment of a Community provision has no connection with the subject matter of the main proceedings.[64]

This is the case for climate lawsuits against public authorities that typically aim to achieve more ambitious climate protection, whether it be through higher climate protection targets or through more efficient measures to reach those targets. A referral from a national court would, therefore, have to ask whether EU legal acts on the issue of climate protection are compatible with higher-ranking EU law such as the CFR. This would affect the national dispute only if the EU law were to stand in the way of a more ambitious national framework for climate protection. Instead, as prescribed by Article 193 TFEU, the Member States are allowed to introduce more stringent protective measures regarding environmental problems and combating climate change. Consequently, the EU legal framework for climate protection is based on the principle of minimum harmonisation. This again leads to the fact that if a question challenges the violation of higher-ranking law by an EU legislative act due to insufficient climate protection measures, the answer cannot at the same time be relevant to a national legal dispute.[65] When a national implementation law can go beyond the EU legal framework, an answer that confirms either the validity or invalidity of this framework can technically not affect the validity of the implementing act. The national court has to decide on this question solely on the basis of higher-ranking national law.[66] This explains the decision by the German Federal Constitutional Court (BVerfG) in the *Neubauer* case, in which it declared the German Federal Climate Change Act incompatible with national fundamental rights without sending a preliminary reference to the CJEU, although it admitted that the challenged law in fact implemented EU legislation.[67] From this point of view, the lack of referral was due to the absence of an admissible question rather than avoidance of judicial dialogue.[68] Admittedly, this outcome could be seen to be based on a quite technical understanding of the procedural rules.

---

62 A. Middeke, '§10 Das Vorabentscheidungsverfahren' in H.W. Rengeling, A. Middeke and M. Gellermann, *Handbuch des Rechtsschutzes in der Europäischen Union*, 3rd ed., C.H. Beck, Munich 2014, para. 53.

63 Cf. P. Thomy, *Individualrechtsschutz durch das Vorabentscheidungsverfahren*, Nomos, Baden-Baden 2009, p. 68.

64 Ibid., p. 70.

65 G. Winter, above n. 38, p. 378.

66 Ibid., p. 378.

67 BVerfG, 1 BvR 2656/18, para. 5.

68 In this vein J. van Zeben, 'The Role of the EU Charter of Fundamental Rights in Climate Litigation' (2022) 22 *German Law Journal* 1499, 1510.

A more practical perspective could raise the question: would the CJEU really have rejected a preliminary question by the BVerfG or the Hoge Raad as inadmissible? However, the answer remains hypothetical.

In the *T & L Sugars and Sidul Açúcares* case, the CJEU held that standing requirements cannot be made conditional on the existence of a legal remedy within the legal systems of the Member States by which the legality of an EU act may be contested, as this would require the CJEU to interpret national procedural law.[69] Judgments on national law certainly go beyond the Court's jurisdiction. Apart from that, the situation is different when the possibility of calling the validity of an EU act into question is blocked due to the absence of an admissible question. In this case, the root of the problem lay in Article 267 TFEU itself, and, therefore, within the scope of the CJEU's jurisdiction. It is for this reason that, contrary to the CJEU's judgment in the *Carvalho* case, where the Court upheld the argument of the 'complete system of remedies', there is in fact a gap in judicial protection based on the TFEU provisions themselves which the CJEU has avoided addressing.[70]

3.2. VALIDITY QUESTIONS IN PRELIMINARY RULINGS

However, despite the hurdles in this particular case, defending the concept of decentralised judicial protection should not be understood as an attempt to overlook the general problems with the preliminary reference procedure. Instead, the consequences of judicial subsidiarity result in a situation where access to the CJEU is in many ways more complicated than direct actions. To ask litigants to bring a case before a national court, which then sends a referral to the CJEU, naturally adds to the duration of the procedure and its costs.[71] However, with average durations of 19.2 months for direct actions and 15.8 months for preliminary rulings, the issue of time-consuming proceedings cannot be expected to be solved through a direct action.[72]

A striking issue is the applicant's dependency on the actual willingness of a national court to submit a reference to the CJEU. Not only do applicants have no possibility of obtaining a referral, they also have no influence on how the question

69 Case T-279/11, *T & L Sugars and Sidul Açúcares v. Commission*, ECLI:EU:T:2013:299, paras 68–70.

70 G. Winter, above n. 38, p. 377.

71 See for the effect of costs on access to justice, J. Darpö, 'Effective Justice? Synthesis Report of the Study on the Implementation of Articles 9.3 and 9.4 of the Aarhus Convention in the Member States of the European Union', European Commission/DG Environment, 2013-10-11/Final, 2013; C. Backes, 'Possible Initiatives on Access to Justice in Environmental Matters and Their Socio-Economic Implications', European Commission, DG ENV.A.2/ETU/2012/009rl, 2013.

72 CJEU, 'Annual Report 2020', p. 14, https://curia.europa.eu/jcms/upload/docs/application/pdf/2021-04/ra_jud_2020_en.pdf.

is formulated and what arguments are part of the national court's opinion.[73] While the question of how and why the preliminary reference procedure is in fact used by national courts has been considered a 'black box'[74] in the past, recent research has shed light on these decisions, yet indicating that extra-legal motives nevertheless play a role in one way or another.[75] It is crucial for the functioning of the decentralised judicial system that national courts live up to their responsibility and play their part within the judicial partnership with the CJEU.[76] This means identifying appropriate questions and using the preliminary reference mechanism whenever the case requires it. As shown above, validity questions in the field of environmental protection are not necessarily hampered by the unwillingness of national judges to refer due to reasons of legal culture but rather by an unfortunate interplay between the principle of minimum harmonisation and the question being required to be decisive for the national proceedings.[77] In any case, empirical findings indicate that the possibility of validity checks in the field of environmental law is only used in very few cases.[78]

Still, one could ask whether it is convincing to involve national courts in questions on the validity of EU acts. There have been arguments in favour of broader direct access to the CJEU that suggest that a legal problem is better solved on the level at which it is located, including the collection of evidence.[79] National courts themselves have no jurisdiction to decide on the validity of EU acts and, as opposed to interpretation questions, the problem of a validity question primarily certainly affects the EU level and not the implementation of EU requirements into the national legal order.[80] However, this should not obscure the fact that it is primarily the national courts that are intended to

---

73 Opinion of Advocate General Jacobs, Case C-50/00 P, *UPA v. Council*, ECLI:EU:C:2002:197, paras 59 et seq.; E. Dikaios, *Überindividueller Umweltrechtsschutz am Beispiel der altruistischen Verbandsklage in der deutschen, griechischen und europäischen Rechtsordnung*, Duncker & Humblot, Berlin 2018, p. 913.

74 M. Bobek, 'EU Law in National Courts: Viking, Laval and Beyond' in M. Freedland and J. Prassl (eds), *Viking, Laval and Beyond*, Hart Publishing, Oxford 2013, pp. 323, 324.

75 See for the motives of national courts to refer J. Krommendijk, *National Courts and Preliminary References to the Court of Justice*, Elgar Online, https://www.elgaronline.com/view/9781800374164.xml, and on why courts decide against a referral K. Leijon and M. Glavina, 'Why passive? Exploring national judges' motives for not requesting preliminary rulings' (2022) 29(2) *Maastricht Journal of European and Comparative Law* 263. On the question of how national courts behave when they render a follow-up judgment, see L. Squintani and J. Rakipi, 'Judicial cooperation in environmental matters: Mapping national courts behaviour in follow-up cases – the United Kingdom' (2018) 20 *Environmental Law Review*, 89.

76 S. Bogojević, above n. 40, p. 24.

77 Cf. I. Hadjiyianni, above n. 31, p. 811.

78 Ibid., p. 806.

79 See in this vein the Opinion of Advocate General Bobek, Case C-352/19 P, *Région de Bruxelles*, ECLI:EU:C:2020:588, para. 143.

80 Case 314/85, *Foto Frost*, ECLI:EU:C:1987:452, para. 20.

play the role of the ordinary EU courts, in other words as the true courts *de droit commun européen*.[81] They are to be involved in questions of validity as well. This is demonstrated by the fact that the courts' obligation to engage in a dialogue extends in particular to questions of fundamental rights.[82] It follows from Article 6(3) TEU and Article 52 CFR that the interpretation of European fundamental rights is based on the constitutional traditions common to the Member States. Referrals from national courts are a way to introduce such traditions into the European debate,[83] which is why generally discarding the decentralised system of legal protection in favour of a direct action, even if only for questions of validity, would leave the interpretation of the CFR solely in the hands of the CJEU.

With this finding, it may be concluded that the decentralised judicial system of the EU not only exists for procedural-economic reasons, but is inherent to fundamental features of the EU legal order. This affects the relationship between national and European courts, the interlocking of legal orders, and the way EU law is enforced. This also applies to questions of interpretation and validity, and a reform leading to a centralised judicial system is beyond the CJEU's law-making competences. Still, the system reveals gaps in judicial protection, as shown for actions in climate change litigation, that are not within the area of responsibility of the Member States, but rather of the EU itself, leaving this issue to be targeted by the CJEU.

3.3. ROOM FOR AMENDMENTS?

Since a treaty amendment to create broader access to the CJEU seems unlikely at the moment, it remains to ask whether there is another way to improve judicial protection in environmental and climate change matters within the interpretative space of the Court.[84] As this chapter argues, the actual gap where judicial protection through the CJEU cannot be achieved at all solely encompasses the constellation as seen in the *Carvalho* case, where an EU legislative act that only requires minimum harmonisation is to be reviewed for its (in)validity, which results from whether there is a violation of higher-ranking law due to the legal framework being not ambitious enough to meet the

---

81 C. Lycourgos, 'Building intra-judicial dialogue: the relationship between the ECJ and Cypriot national courts' (2016) 41 *European Law Review* 623.

82 P.M. Huber, 'Die gemeinsamen Verfassungsüberlieferungen der Mitgliedstaaten – Identifizierung und Konkretisierung' (2022) *Europarecht* 145, 163.

83 Cf. K. Lenaerts, 'Grundrechte-Charta im System eines pluralistischen Grundrechtsschutzes' (2014) 10 *Anwaltsblatt* 772, 783.

84 See on the limits of the Court's interpretative space on standing issues M.J. Van Wolferen, *To Justify the Wayes of God to Men: Limits to the court's powers of interpretation*, PhD thesis, University of Groningen 2018, https://research.rug.nl/files/66168969/Complete_thesis.pdf.

requirements of the protection of fundamental rights. From this perspective, two possibilities remain to be considered. First, the CJEU could accept a validity reference from a national court that has been addressed to review the legality of an implementing act, such as the German Federal Constitutional Court in the *Neubauer* case. Again, the national court decides within its discretion when referring to the CJEU, including its opinion being the relevant criterion for assessing the necessity of the question.[85] Nevertheless, referring a question that is not necessary for the national proceedings would be explicitly *contra legem* to Article 267 TFEU.

Instead, the interpretation of standing requirements should be guided by a more far-sighted perspective. The CJEU should take the structural limitations of the preliminary reference into account, rather than using boilerplates that refer to the completeness of the judicial system and the Court's inability to make any variations to its traditional interpretation.[86] Bearing in mind the restrictions on interpretative space, a divergent interpretation could not render the standing requirements for actions for annulment meaningless, even if the wording of Article 263 TFEU itself does not prohibit any deviation. 'Individually concerned' could be interpreted in a way that includes an exception to the traditional *Plaumann* test, whenever legal protection cannot be granted due to EU law itself. This would only apply to the rather limited gap as identified in this chapter, and, therefore, not result in a direct action that has the effect of an individual fundamental rights complaint as it exists within the Member States. Further, such an interpretation would not go beyond the Court's jurisdiction, as it would not include the interpretation of national procedural law, but only EU law. In this regard, the *Carvalho* case has to be seen as a missed opportunity, as the Court refused to consider the possibility of a reference in this case even though the applicants explicitly pointed this out.

As the CJEU has correctly held, Article 47 CFR does not necessarily require that individuals are entitled to bring an action for annulment directly before the CJEU.[87] Still, the right to an effective remedy requires that the combination of remedies as offered by the treaties guarantees complete judicial protection for natural and legal persons against illegal acts of the institutions.[88] In other words, this means that if direct access is blocked, indirect access has to be granted. Vice versa, if indirect access is blocked for reasons that reach beyond the sphere of the Member States or beyond practicability issues, direct access has to be granted. This is not only required by the Union's commitment to fundamental rights and

---

85 A. Middeke, above n. 62, para. 53.

86 Case C-50/00 P, *UPA v. Council*, ECLI:EU:C:2002:462, para. 40; Case C-583/11 P, *Inuit v. Parliament and Council*, ECLI:EU:C:2013:625, para. 92; Case C-565/19 P, *Carvalho and Others v. Parliament and Council*, ECLI:EU:C:2021:252, para. 53.

87 Case C-583/11 P, *Inuit v. Parliament and Council*, ECLI:EU:C:2013:625, para. 105.

88 A. Albors-Llorens, above n. 14, p. 286.

the rule of law, but also by the case law of the Court itself, which repeatedly refers to the completeness of the system of remedies. While the restriction of direct judicial protection is justified by judicial subsidiarity, it has to be kept in mind that the principle of subsidiarity does not only have restricting effects. Bearing in mind that according to Article 5(3) TEU the Union shall only act if the objectives of proposed actions can 'be better achieved at Union level', the fact that decentralised judicial protection cannot always be granted conversely supports the idea of turning to the action for annulment as a substitute in exceptional cases.[89]

Furthermore, excluding EU legislative acts from judicial protection would deny that the European legal framework does in fact have a significant impact on the lived realities of European citizens on its own. This is illustrated by feedback loops in harmonisation and implementation of EU law. Despite the fact that Member States implement EU law through their own legislation, it is not a common practice within the Member States to lay down more stringent standards than required, especially in environmental protection law.[90]

It is true that courts cannot replace political measures and should not have the power to overrule decisions of the democratic will of the majority.[91] However, with regard to climate change litigation, the aim is not to replace politics, but to leave political decisions about fundamental issues within the scope of a monitoring institution. Sensitivity regarding issues of democracy can be expressed through judicial restraint in the actual decision-making. Leaving gaps in the access to justice is, therefore, neither suitable nor necessary for balance in the division of powers.

4. CONCLUSION

After the recent CJEU decisions on actions challenging EU climate protection laws, the issue of access to justice remains a topic that is both emotional and difficult to reconstruct. The aim of this chapter was to review common arguments against the CJEU's restrictive approach to standing in direct actions, in search of a more consistent approach to improve judicial protection. It has shown that in the current situation the goals of strategic climate change litigation have

---

89 G. Winter, above n. 38, p. 380.

90 J.H. Jans et al., '"Gold Plating" of European Environmental Measures?' (2009) 6 *Journal for European Environmental & Planning Law* 417; see for a critical analysis regarding 'no-gold-plating policies' in Germany, M. Payrhuber and U. Stelkens, '„1:1-Umsetzung" von EU-Richtlinien: Rechtspflicht, rationales Politikkonzept oder (wirtschafts)politischer Populismus? – zugleich zu Unterschieden zwischen Rechtsangleichungs- und Deregulierungs-richtlinien' (2019) *Europarecht* 190.

91 Cf. J. Waldron, 'The Core of the Case Against Judicial Review' (2006) 115 *Yale Law Journal* 1346.

no prospects of being achieved through direct actions for annulment, since the concept of individual concern in line with the *Plaumann* interpretation is incompatible with a fundamental rights-based argumentation on standing. It remains the case that subjective (fundamental) rights that potentially entitle all individuals cannot constitute *locus standi*. Such an interpretation would lead to a fundamental change in the EU judicial system in a way that is not inherent to the EU legal order. It has thus been revealed that the *Plaumann* test has a function in the EU judicial system that goes beyond the strategic protection of acts that have been adopted through a legislative procedure. Instead, it can be seen as a structural condition for the systemic approach to judicial protection in the EU that focuses on broad access to decentralised, national courts while confining direct access to the CJEU. The result is the division of labour between EU and national courts as an essential structure of the application of law in Europe, which is why the solution for the improvement of access to justice cannot be found in a German-modelled fundamental rights complaint. From this point, two aspects are crucial for the functioning of the EU judicial system: first, national courts should be effectively included in the common jurisdiction and development of EU law via preliminary references; and second, the CJEU should take an overall view when interpreting rules on standing.

HARNESSING PUBLIC PARTICIPATION IN THE EU TAXONOMY REGULATION DELEGATED ACTS

Mobilising Sustainable Investments and Mobilising People

Dorien COPPENS*

1. INTRODUCTION

The European Green Deal aims to reshape the functioning of the EU towards sustainable development so as to face urgent climate-related and environmental challenges.[1] Chiti points out that this ambitious regulatory project not only

* This chapter is based on the author's Master's thesis written to obtain an LLM in European Law at Maastricht University in 2021 under supervision of Prof. Dr Marjan Peeters and Dr Marijn van der Sluis, to whom the author is very grateful for their guidance. The chapter does not reflect the views of the author's current employer, the Court of Justice of the European Union.

1 European Commission, 'Communication from the Commission to the European Parliament, the European Council, the Council, the European Economic and Social Committee and the Committee of the Regions: The European Green Deal', COM(2019) 640 final (12.11.2019); J. JENDROŚKA, M. REESE and L. SQUINTANI, 'Towards a New Legal Framework for Sustainability under the European Green Deal' (2021) *The Opole Studies in Administration and Law* 87, 87.

deals with environmental protection, but in a sense brings about a transition from the current phase of European integration to another, with the intention of establishing a new societal order.[2] The European Commission states that to make the Green Deal policies work and be accepted, active public participation is 'paramount'.[3] The importance placed upon participation raises questions as to how citizens will be effectively involved in the process of complex environmental decision-making in the creation of this new societal order under the European Green Deal.

Such complex environmental decision-making arises, for example, in mobilising climate-dedicated funding and facilitating sustainable investments to make the ambitions of the European Green Deal a reality. One of the key tools in this context concerns the Taxonomy Regulation.[4] The Taxonomy Regulation aims at founding a unified EU green classification framework for investments, which entrusts the Commission with adopting delegated acts to determine whether or not an economic activity is sustainable in light of the regulation.

While the Taxonomy Regulation aims to classify environmentally sustainable investments and therefore has a potential influence on the internal market and individuals, the path for citizens to get involved in implementing this instrument is not so straightforward. Whereas Articles 10(3) and 11(1)–(3) of the Treaty on European Union state that citizens should be included in the democratic life of the Union,[5] specifically in the field of environmental law the ratification of the Aarhus Convention by the EU in 2005 provides civil society with the opportunity to take part and to control the quality of decision-making.[6] Legal literature on the interplay with the Aarhus Convention's procedural rights is, however, limited in areas where regulations on the financial and environmental dimensions collide.

Whilst many legal questions arise under the Taxonomy Regulation, a solid and reliable procedural framework is deemed indispensable to improving substantive

---

2 E. Chiti, 'Managing the ecological transition of the EU: the European Green Deal as a regulatory process' (2022) *Common Market Law Review* 19, 20–21.

3 European Commission, 'Communication from the Commission to the European Parliament, the European Council, the Council, the European Economic and Social Committee and the Committee of the Regions: The European Green Deal', COM(2019) 640 final (12.11.2019), p. 2.

4 Regulation (EU) 2020/852 of the European Parliament and of the Council of 18 June 2020 on the establishment of a framework to facilitate sustainable investment, and amending Regulation (EU) 2019/2088 [2020] OJ L 198/13.

5 For a further exploration of the idea of public participation imbedded in the Treaties, see *inter alia*: J. Mendes, 'The Making of Delegated and Implementing Acts: Legitimacy beyond Institutional Balance' in C.F. Bergström and D. Ritleng (eds), *Rulemaking by the European Commission*, Oxford University Press, Oxford 2016, p. 246; J. Makowiak, 'Participation in Environmental Decision Making in European Law' in L. Paddock (ed.), *Decision Making in Environmental Law*, Edward Elgar, Northampton 2016, pp. 334–35.

6 The UNECE Convention on Access to Information, Public Participation in Decision-making and Access to Justice in Environmental Matters (Aarhus Convention), 25.06.1998.

law in achieving the Green Deal's aims. This chapter will delve into the core of the Taxonomy Regulation by assessing what procedural legal framework applies to the delegated decision-making regarding sustainable investments, particularly in view of the spirit of the second pillar of the Aarhus Convention, i.e. public participation.

2. AARHUS CONVENTION AND TAXONOMY DELEGATED ACTS: KINDRED SPIRITS?

2.1. IMPLEMENTING THE TAXONOMY REGULATION

The Taxonomy Regulation's criteria for determining environmentally sustainable economic activities should be granular and tailored to the different economic activities covered. Given the inherently fast-changing nature of both science and technology, these criteria should be regularly updated.[7] This flexibility is accompanied by the requirement for further rule-making through implementation. The Commission is formally entrusted with the task of adopting delegated acts to set out criteria for investments labelled as 'environmentally sustainable'.[8] As this chapter aims to focus on the opportunities for the public to participate in the decision-making process, the focus will be on notions of public participation already included in the Taxonomy Regulation's provisions on implementation.

Throughout the text of the Taxonomy Regulation, two obligations for the Commission stand out regarding public participation: the Commission (1) *shall* carry out consultations and gather all necessary expertise and (2) *shall* respect certain time limits.

First, the Taxonomy Regulation sets out obligations focusing on public consultation throughout the process of adopting a delegated act. The text of the Taxonomy Regulation references the principles laid down in the Interinstitutional Agreement on Better Law-Making[9] and mentions the importance of carrying out appropriate consultations during the Commission's preparatory work and gathering all the necessary expertise.[10] It can be noted that no clear indications on what is deemed 'appropriate' consultation are given, nor a complete definition or view on what expertise is considered 'necessary'. However, this first set of 'shall' obligations makes public involvement in the decision-making process

7 See also Recital 38 Taxonomy Regulation.

8 Articles 8(4), 10(3), 11(3), 12(2), 13(2), 14(2), 15(2) and 23 Taxonomy Regulation.

9 Interinstitutional agreement between the European Parliament, the Council of the European Union and the European Union and the European Commission of 13 April 2016 on Better Law-Making [2016] OJ L 123/1.

10 Articles 23(4) and 24 Taxonomy Regulation.

mandatory to a certain extent and recognises its value as part of the procedure to create a qualitative delegated act.

Second, time limits are imposed on the otherwise broad delegation with regard to filling out the Taxonomy Regulation's framework. For example, the Commission *shall* adopt the first delegated acts by 31 December 2020, to ensure their application from 1 January 2022.[11] In this case, the first set of delegated acts concern climate change mitigation and adaptation. These deadlines show the need and urgency to implement climate laws, in order to provide the financial market with more certainty about what can be labelled as sound sustainable investments.

These two kinds of obligations for the Commission in the adoption procedure of Taxonomy delegated acts bring about an intrinsic dilemma, namely how an urgently required implementation measure with a high degree of technicality should be produced in a timely manner, whilst also, in an ambitious way, enabling the public to take part in this decision-making process.

2.2. ARTICLE 8 AARHUS CONVENTION

To scope out the full extent of the latter part of the dilemma found in the previous section, this section will delve into the concept of public participation, using the second pillar of the Aarhus Convention as the main legal consolidation of measures to enhance public participation regarding administrative decision-making in environmental matters.[12] In this respect, this section aims to capture the lessons learned from the Aarhus Convention for the implementation of the Taxonomy Regulation.

The regime on public participation set out in Article 8 Aarhus Convention on 'the preparation of executive regulations and/or generally applicable legally binding normative instruments' is addressed to the executive branch of government in law-making and sparks possible relevance for the Taxonomy delegated acts.

The provision states (emphasis added):

> Each Party shall *strive to promote* effective public participation at an appropriate stage, and while options are still open, during the preparation by public authorities of executive regulations and other generally applicable legally binding rules that may have a significant effect on the environment.

---

11 Articles 10(6) and 11(6) Taxonomy Regulation.

12 B.J. Richardson and J. Razzaque, 'Public Participation in Environmental Decision-Making' in B.J. Richardson and S. Wood (eds), *Environmental Law for Sustainability*, Hart Publishing, Oxford 2005, p. 174.

To this end, the following steps should be taken:

(a) *Time frames sufficient* for effective participation should be fixed;
(b) *draft rules* should be *published* or otherwise made publicly available; and
(c) the public should be given the opportunity to comment, *directly or through representative consultative bodies.*

The result of the public participation *shall* be *taken into account as far as possible.*

Key elements of this provision will be addressed, linked to EU endeavours to promote public participation, and with an analysis of the extent to which these elements are relevant for Taxonomy delegated acts.

Regarding the EU's endeavours in this field, the European Commission's approach to public consultations[13] has been amended as part of the updated version of the Better Regulation Agenda, which was implemented through the November 2021 Better Regulation Guidelines and Toolbox.[14] With the first Taxonomy Climate Act being adopted before the implementation of the November 2021 Better Regulation Agenda and its Complementary Delegated Act being adopted on 9 March 2022, i.e. after said implementation, this chapter offers a timely opportunity to examine the systematics of public participation in one of the Green Deal's main instruments interacting with the principles of the Aarhus Convention.

2.2.1. Obligation of Effort

Article 8 Aarhus Convention is an obligation of effort for the Parties to *strive to promote* effective participation. Parties are not bound by a certain standard of public participation. The nature of this specific provision has also influenced the EU's implementation of the Aarhus Convention, which was done through the Aarhus Regulation.[15] In the proposal of this Regulation, the Commission mentioned that Article 8 Aarhus Convention did not provide any legally binding

13 The notion of 'public participation' in general is hard to define, as participation by the public in decision-making procedures exists in different forms and varieties. For the purpose of this chapter, a broad understanding will be used, seeing *inter alia* 'public consultation' as a synonym for public participation. For further reading on the spectrum of participation opportunities, see for example, S.R. Arnstein, 'A Ladder of Citizen Participation' (1969) 35 *Journal of the American Institute of Planners* 216.

14 European Commission, 'Better Regulation Guidelines', SWD(2021) 305 final (03.11.2021); European Commission, 'Better Regulation "Toolbox" Which Complements the Better Regulation Guidelines Presented in SWD(2021) 305 Final' (11.2021).

15 Regulation (EC) No 1367/2006 of the European Parliament and of the Council of 6 September 2006 on the application of the provisions of the Aarhus Convention on Access to Information, Public Participation in Decision-making and Access to Justice in Environmental Matters to Community institutions and bodies [2006] OJ L 264/13.

requirement.[16] Therefore, no EU provisions contain an explicit implementation of this article.

The 2021 amendments to the Aarhus Regulation[17] are focused on compliance with Article 9(3) Aarhus Convention regarding the review (process) of administrative acts and aim to broaden the possibilities for NGOs to seek administrative review.[18] Although no explicit mention of Article 8 Aarhus Convention is found, this does offer NGOs the opportunity to challenge the public participation in the act in question, if, in their view, it falls short of offering the public the opportunity to adequately participate, or even lacks this possibility altogether. Regarding the delegated acts under the Taxonomy Regulation, ClientEarth has already launched two requests for internal review regarding Taxonomy delegated acts so far,[19] although neither of those two directly mention public participation concerns. Since this chapter focuses on public participation during the process of getting to the Taxonomy delegated acts and the opportunity for internal review only presents itself after the acts have been adopted, the extended opportunity for internal review by NGOs will not be discussed in further detail. It should however be noted that this enlarged possibility for administrative review could provide an interesting reparative route for (E)NGOs.

---

16 European Commission, 'Proposal for a Regulation of the European Parliament and of the Council on the Application of the Provisions of the Aarhus Convention on Access to Information, Public Participation in Decision-Making and Access to Justice in Environmental Matters to EC Institutions and Bodies', COM(2003) 622 final, C 96/22 (2004), p. 13.

17 Regulation (EU) 2021/1767 of the European Parliament and of the Council of 6 October 2021 amending Regulation (EC) No 1367/2006 on the application of the provisions of the Aarhus Convention on Access to Information, Public Participation in Decision-making and Access to Justice in Environmental Matters to Community institutions and bodies [2021] OJ L 356/1. The amendments brought about by this Regulation 2021/1767 did not concern public participation, so Article 8 of the Aarhus Convention remains not explicitly implemented in EU law.

18 European Commission, 'Proposal for a Regulation of the European Parliament and of the Council on amending Regulation (EC) No 1367/2006 of the European Parliament and of the Council of 6 September 2006 on the application of the provisions of the Aarhus Convention on Access to Information, Public Participation in Decision-making and Access to Justice in Environmental Matters to Community institutions and bodies', COM(2020) 642 final (14.10.2020), p. 1.

19 The first request for internal review concerned the labelling of bio-energy and bio-plastics as done in the first Taxonomy Climate Delegated Act and was submitted to the CJEU in February 2022 after rejection by the Commission. The second request for internal review was filed regarding the classification of gas as sustainable in the Taxonomy Complementary Delegated Act on 19 September 2022. The NGOs involved deemed the subsequent reply of the Commission in February 2023 insufficient and launched a procedure before the CJEU in April 2023. See also ClientEarth, 'EU Commission taken to court over unlawful decisions on bio-energy and bio-plastics', Press Release (16.09.2022), https://www.clientearth.org/latest/press-office/press/eu-commission-taken-to-court-over-unlawful-decisions-on-bio-energy-and-bio-plastics/; and ClientEarth, 'EU Taxonomy: Environmental groups take EU to court over "green" gas label', Press Release (18.04.2023), https://www.clientearth.org/latest/press-office/press/eu-taxonomy-environmental-groups-take-eu-to-court-over-green-gas-label/.

Without there being an explicit implementation, some scholars view Article 8 Aarhus Convention more as a guideline for public participation mechanisms, which makes them reluctant to further discuss the provision in light of implementation and compliance with EU law.[20] As Nóbrega points out, this perception does not, however, exempt the EU from the general obligation to strive to promote public participation.[21]

Public participation in acts adopted by the Commission is regulated through soft law instruments such as communications and guidelines. The Taxonomy Regulation mentions the Commission's Better Regulation Agenda concerning public participation and the Interinstitutional Agreement on Better Law-Making.[22] In general, 'better regulation principles' originated from the desire for better European governance but also – and closely linked to the Taxonomy Regulation's ambitions – anchoring sustainable development in the Union's policy-making.[23] In general, appropriate public participation can be a crucial step towards sustainable development, given that the proposed development will be structured based on the demands and needs of the stakeholders, which include the considerations for future generations.[24]

Regarding this obligation of effort, it should be pointed out that the Commission retains considerable discretion in deciding whether, when and how to hold a public consultation following its own Better Regulation Agenda. As Tabb notes, it is not abnormal for government actors, in general, to retain considerable discretion in fashioning procedures to implement participation mandates.[25] However, Article 8 Aarhus Convention does not leave room for such discretion when the executive measure may significantly affect the

20 B. Toth, 'Public Participation and Democracy in Practice – Aarhus Convention Principles as Democratic Institution Building in the Developing World' (2010) 30 *Journal of Land Resources & Environmental Law* 295, 303; J. Jendrośka, 'Public Participation in Environmental Decision-Making: Interactions between the Convention and EU Law and Other Key Legal Issues in Its Implementation in the Light of the Opinions of the Aarhus Convention Compliance Committee' in M. Pallemaerts (ed.), *The Aarhus Convention at ten: interactions and tensions between conventional international law and EU environmental law*, Europa Law Publishing, Groningen 2011, p. 97.

21 S. Nóbrega, 'EU Climate Law through the Lens of the Aarhus Convention: Access to Environmental Information and Public Participation in EU Climate Change Decision Making', Maastricht University 2020, p. 126. The author is grateful to this work for pointing out a large amount of relevant literature and insights on the workings of public participation under the Aarhus Convention.

22 Article 23 Taxonomy Regulation.

23 European Commission, 'Communication on Impact Assessment', COM(2002) 276 (05.06.2002), p. 2.

24 A. Marzuki, 'Challenges in the Public Participation and the Decision Making Process' (2015) 53 *Sociologija i Prostor* 21, 22.

25 W.M. Tabb, 'Public Participation in Environmental Decision Making' in L. Paddock, R.L. Glicksman and N.S. Bryner, *Elgar Encyclopedia of Environmental Law: Volume II*, Edward Elgar, Northampton 2016, p. 325.

environment. Regardless, in an early analysis of the Commission's participatory regime under the 2021 Better Regulation Agenda, Christopolou points out that the Commission's discretion is augmented since it intends to hold consultations only once during the policy cycle.[26]

As Article 8 Aarhus Convention constitutes an obligation of effort, the determination of compliance depends on the concrete steps taken to achieve this goal.[27]

2.2.2. *Basic Procedural Framework*

Article 8(2) Aarhus Convention gives additional guidance for effective public participation by providing a basic procedural framework consisting of three minimum requirements.

First, *sufficient timeframes* are needed to ensure effective participation, with the establishment of such time limits left to the executive.[28]

In this regard, the 2017 and 2021 Better Regulation Agendas mention the Commission launching public consultations for draft delegated acts on its website for a four-week period, parallel to consultations of experts in Member States.[29] This timeframe applies to all implementing acts regardless of their complexity, while Article 8 prescribes a timeframe 'sufficient' for effective participation. The 2021 Better Regulation Agenda echoes this by making 'sufficient time for participation' one of the five minimum standards of consultation, but does not make any substantial changes to the four-week timeframe.[30]

Admittedly, flexibility in timeframes would make the Commission's system more complex. However, the rigidity in relation to the timeframe may amount to insufficient time for effective participation to make sound decisions, especially relating to complex technical elements in environmental matters.

The second requirement entails making draft rules *publicly available*. This element is less controversial, as the 2017 and 2021 Better Regulation 'Toolboxes' foresee publication of the drafts of implementing acts.[31]

---

26 A.-E. Christopoulou, 'Public Consultations Unpacked: The Commission's Participatory Regime under the 2021 Better Regulation Agenda', *European Law Blog* (20.01.2022), https://europeanlawblog.eu/2022/01/20/public-consultations-unpacked-the-commissions-participatory-regime-under-the-2021-better-regulation-agenda/.

27 J. Ebbesson, H. Gaugitsch, J. Jendrośka, F. Marshall and S. Stec, *The Aarhus Convention: an implementation guide*, 2nd ed., United Nations, Geneva 2014, p. 181.

28 Ibid., p. 183.

29 European Commission, 'Better Regulation "Toolbox" Which Complements the Better Regulation Guidelines Presented in SWD(2017) 350', pp. 441–42; European Commission, 'Better Regulation "Toolbox" Which Complements the Better Regulation Guidelines Presented in SWD(2021) 305 Final', p. 447.

30 European Commission, 'Better Regulation Guidelines', SWD(2021) 305 final (03.11.2021), p. 14.

31 European Commission, 'Better Regulation "Toolbox" Which Complements the Better Regulation Guidelines Presented in SWD(2017) 350', p. 444; European Commission, 'Better

Third, the public should be allowed to comment, *directly or through representation*. At the EU level, the Commission decided to give 'the public at large' the possibility to react to the draft act.[32] The 2021 Better Regulation Agenda underlines that this feedback requirement also applies to very technical acts, where the public at large is given the possibility to react to the draft act, even though, in reality, only comments from a specialised group of stakeholders are expected.[33]

The Commission's aim of including all citizens can be seen as ambitious, but it might also be a factor constraining effective participation. Efficiency and effectiveness could be compromised by the public struggling to understand technical reports, which, in the context of Taxonomy delegated acts, are likely to contain granular and technical screening criteria for environmentally sustainable activities.[34]

2.2.3. *Taking Results into Account 'as Far as Possible'*

Lastly, Article 8(3) Aarhus Convention states that the result of public participation shall be taken into account as far as possible. The Implementation Guide specifies that this is a relatively high burden of proof.[35] In practice, the final document adopting the rules should explain the public participation process and how its results were accounted for.[36] Interestingly, the Implementation Guide deduces from the phrase 'as far as possible' an acknowledgement of politics in law-making.[37] This part of the provision, therefore, does not force the decision-maker – i.e. the Commission in the case of the Taxonomy delegated acts – to pledge the impossible.

On the materialisation of the 'as far as possible' requirement, the Aarhus Convention Compliance Committee has oversight, albeit non-binding.[38] Members of the public are therefore able to raise this issue before the Compliance

Regulation "Toolbox" Which Complements the Better Regulation Guidelines Presented in SWD(2021) 305 Final', pp. 449, 451.

32 European Commission, 'Better Regulation "Toolbox" Which Complements the Better Regulation Guidelines Presented in SWD(2017) 350', p. 144.

33 European Commission, 'Better Regulation "Toolbox" Which Complements the Better Regulation Guidelines Presented in SWD(2021) 305 Final', p. 451.

34 A. Marzuki, 'Challenges in the Public Participation and the Decision Making Process' (2015) 53 *Sociologija i Prostor* 21, 22.

35 J. Ebbesson, H. Gaugitsch, J. Jendrośka, F. Marshall and S. Stec, *The Aarhus Convention: an implementation guide*, 2nd ed., United Nations, Geneva 2014, p. 185.

36 Aarhus Convention Compliance Committee, 'Compilation of Findings of the Aarhus Convention Compliance Committee Adopted 18 February to Date' (05.02.2021), p. 14.

37 J. Ebbesson, H. Gaugitsch, J. Jendrośka, F. Marshall and S. Stec, *The Aarhus Convention: an implementation guide*, 2nd ed., United Nations, Geneva 2014, p. 185.

38 J. Makowiak, 'Participation in Environmental Decision Making in European Law' in L. Paddock (ed.), *Decision Making in Environmental Law*, Edward Elgar, Northampton 2016, p. 333.

Committee. However, it is not clear whether they also have access to the Court of Justice of the European Union based on the fact that they have a right to submit comments through the public consultation.[39] Moreover, following case law, including the *Eurofer*[40] and the *WWF-UK* case,[41] although on different subjects, it is likely that even if the public accesses the Court of Justice, the Court's supervision would be limited to a test of the procedure at hand. However, it can be argued that the wording 'shall be taken into account as far as possible' in and of itself poses an obligation that lends itself to judicial review. This issue of enforcement requires further case law.

According to the 2017 Better Regulation Agenda, the Commission also needs to explain how it has taken the feedback into account.[42] The 2021 Better Regulation Agenda qualifies this accountability, together with openness, as a general principle of consultation to make the consultation process and how it has affected policy-making transparent to those involved and the general public.[43] Delegated acts should therefore include an explanatory memorandum.[44]

Such accountability is likely to comply with Article 8(3) and its obligation of effort in taking the result of public participation into account as far as possible. The actual determination of compliance will be based on a case-by-case assessment. Regarding public participation under the implementation of the Taxonomy Regulation, the following section will therefore serve as a case study of the experiences under the first Taxonomy Delegated Act and its Complementary Delegated Act.

3. PUBLIC PARTICIPATION: EXPERIENCES UNDER THE FIRST TAXONOMY DELEGATED ACT

On 4 June 2021, the first Taxonomy Delegated Act (partially) spanning the technical criteria related to the first two environmental objectives of the Taxonomy Regulation[45] was formally adopted, missing its deadline of 31 December 2020.[46]

---

39 G. Bándi, 'The Three Pillars of Environmental Democracy in a European Perspective' in G. Bándi (ed.), *Environmental democracy and law: public participation in Europe*, Europa Law Publishing, Groningen 2014, p. 58.

40 Case T-381/11, *Eurofer v. Commission*, ECLI:EU:T:2012:273.

41 Case T-105/95, *WWF v. UK*, ECLI:EU:T:1997:26.

42 European Commission, 'Better Regulation "Toolbox" Which Complements the Better Regulation Guidelines Presented in SWD(2017) 350', pp. 441–43.

43 European Commission, 'Better Regulation Guidelines', SWD(2021) 305 final (03.11.2021), p. 14.

44 European Commission, 'Better Regulation "Toolbox" Which Complements the Better Regulation Guidelines Presented in SWD(2021) 305 Final', p. 353.

45 Articles 10 and 11 Taxonomy Regulation.

46 European Commission, 'Commission Delegated Regulation (EU) 2021/2139 of 4 June 2021 Supplementing Regulation (EU) 2020/852 of the European Parliament and of the Council by

Additionally, a Complementary Climate Delegated Act covering nuclear and gas activities – sectors missing from the initial Taxonomy Delegated Act – was formally adopted by the European Commission on 9 March 2022.[47] Taking the lead-up to these acts as a guiding example, this section will evaluate whether and how the public was able to participate in the drafting and implementation of these delegated acts by the Commission.

Public participation took place at several stages throughout the process of getting to the first Delegated Act. From the Technical Expert Group on Sustainable Finance asking for public feedback on its initial reports in 2018,[48] to impact assessments,[49] all the way through to public consultation on the draft Delegated Act,[50] public participation seems to have been promoted, and drafts were published to be commented on by the public. It is encouraging to see that the obligation of effort established by the Aarhus Convention and the EU's response through soft law did not lead to public participation initiatives slowly fading away under the first Taxonomy Delegated Act.

It should, however, be noted that for the Complementary Climate Delegated Act, the Commission built on the findings of the public consultation as part of the preparation of the initial Taxonomy Climate Delegated Act and no separate public consultation was held. In its explanatory memorandum, the Commission noted that the technical screening criteria for natural gas were initially included in the draft Taxonomy Climate Delegated Act and were subject to the four-week feedback period. Regarding the technical criteria for nuclear energy, no such public consultation was held. In defence of its decision not to hold any further open consultations, the Commission pointed out that the relevant technical and policy issues concerning natural gas and nuclear energy had been in the public domain throughout the course of

---

Establishing the Technical Screening Criteria for Determining the Conditions under Which an Economic Activity Qualifies as Contributing Substantially to Climate Change Mitigation or Climate Change Adaptation and for Determining Whether That Economic Activity Causes No Significant Harm to Any of the Other Environmental Objectives', C(2021) 2800/3.

47 European Commission, 'Commission Delegated Regulation (EU) 2022/1214 of 9 March 2022 amending Delegated Regulation (EU) 2021/2139 as regards economic activities in certain energy sectors and Delegated Regulation (EU) 2021/2178 as regards specific public disclosures for those economic activities', C(2022) 631.

48 EU Technical Expert Group on Sustainable Finance, 'Taxonomy: Final Report of the Technical Expert Group on Sustainable Finance' (2020), pp. 11–12, https://ec.europa.eu/info/sites/default/files/business_economy_euro/banking_and_finance/documents/200309-sustainable-finance-teg-final-report-taxonomy_en.pdf.

49 European Commission, 'Inception Impact Assessment of 20 March 2020 on Commission Delegated Regulation with Regard to the Establishment of a Framework to Facilitate Sustainable Investment', Ref. Ares(2020)1680974 (20.03.2020).

50 European Commission, 'Sustainable Finance – EU Classification System for Green Investments' (*Have your say*), https://ec.europa.eu/info/law/better-regulation/have-your-say/initiatives/12302-Sustainable-finance-EU-classification-system-for-green-investments/feedback_en?p_id=16015203.

legislative deliberations and that advanced disclosure of a draft delegated act to the public would have been likely to influence the markets. The process of getting to the Complementary Delegated Act shows the obligation of effort under the new 2021 Better Regulation Agenda to be more capable of being influenced by the Commission's discretion. It can be questioned whether, by following the Commission's reasoning, the obligation of effort to strive to promote effective public participation under the Aarhus Convention has been fulfilled.

The opportunity to given feedback on the initial draft Delegated Act was opened up to the *public at large* instead of solely to representative organisations, an option also endorsed by Article 8 Aarhus Convention. The EU's endeavours to include the public at large are especially notable given the general disinclination, pointed out by Tabb, to promote public participation in matters involving highly technical, scientific data, as concerns arise that the public may lack the necessary scientific expertise to make informed contributions.[51]

Most noteworthy in terms of the experiences with the Taxonomy Climate Delegated Act is the *amount of feedback instances* received on the draft Delegated Act. Although comparison is difficult, it can be noted that in 2020, in the same area of sustainable finance, a delegated act to introduce labels designed to help investors looking to adopt a low-carbon investment strategy received 36 feedback instances,[52] another on the obligations for investment firms to advise clients on environmental aspects of financial products received 50,[53] and another on financial benchmarks in compliance with the Paris Climate Agreement received 18.[54] With a total of 46,591 feedback instances, the Taxonomy Delegated Act stands out in terms of public involvement on the Commission's dedicated platform. Of the 46,591 feedback instances, 97.78% were given by EU citizens. However, it should be noted that

---

51 W.M. Tabb, 'Public Participation in Environmental Decision Making' in L. Paddock, R.L. Glicksman and N.S. Bryner, *Elgar Encyclopedia of Environmental Law: Volume II*, Edward Elgar, Northampton 2016, p. 314.

52 European Commission, 'Sustainable Finance – Minimum Standards for Climate Benchmarks' (*Have your say*), https://ec.europa.eu/info/law/better-regulation/have-your-say/initiatives/12020-Sustainable-finance-minimum-standards-for-climate-benchmarks_en.

53 European Commission, 'Sustainable Finance – Obligation for Investment Firms to Advise Clients on Social and Environmental Aspects of Financial Products' (*Have your say*), https://ec.europa.eu/info/law/better-regulation/have-your-say/initiatives/12068-Sustainable-finance-obligation-for-investment-firms-to-advise-clients-on-social-and-environmental-aspects-of-financial-products_en.

54 European Commission, 'Sustainable Finance – Environmental, Social and Governance Criteria (Benchmarks)' (*Have your say*), https://ec.europa.eu/info/law/better-regulation/have-your-say/initiatives/12019-Sustainable-finance-environmental-social-and-governance-criteria-benchmarks-_en.

the majority of this feedback was linked to environmental advocacy carried out by environmental NGOs, which provided a technical paper for citizens to include in their feedback.[55]

This number is perceived differently by the various actors involved. The Commission sees this high number as confirmation of the 'importance of the Taxonomy as a tool to help finance flow towards more sustainable economic activities and accelerate the transition under the Green Deal'.[56] A Member of the European Parliament noted that the draft Delegated Act's adoption had to be postponed precisely because of the many comments.[57] On the other hand, a representative of the international NGO WWF speaks of the awakening of the crowd by their enormous interest in the project, whereas an energy industrialist points out the risk of making the project extremely complex and getting lost in bureaucratic procedures due to the delays induced by, *inter alia*, the number of comments.[58] In the media, some journalists reported that the draft Delegated Act had 'failed' because of uproar during the public consultation and the threat of a veto.[59]

As learned in section 2.2, the executive is also obliged 'to take the result of the public participation into account as far as possible', with some wiggle room left for politics. Regarding the Taxonomy Delegated Act and the Complementary Delegated Act, the Commission formally explained in the memorandum attached to both acts how it took the feedback into account, in line with the Better Regulation Agenda. Apart from this general explanation, it is not easy to locate the results of public participation alongside the advice given by the Commission's different expert groups. Especially for the Complementary Delegated Act, for which no separate public consultation was held, the advice of

---

55 O. Poldori, V. Demey and G. Neveux, 'Delayed start for the European taxonomy on sustainable activities' (03.2021), p. 3, https://www.i-care-consult.com/en/wp-content/uploads/sites/2/2021/04/Expert-Opinion-10-EU-Taxonomy-I-Care-Consult.pdf. See for example the following comment: https://ec.europa.eu/info/law/better-regulation/have-your-say/initiatives/12302-Sustainable-finance-EU-classification-system-for-green-investments/F1355425_en.

56 European Commission, 'Communication from the Commission to the European Parliament, the Council, the European Economic and Social Committee and the Committee of the Regions, EU Taxonomy, Corporate Sustainability Reporting, Sustainability Preferences and Fiduciary Duties: Directing Finance towards the European Green Deal', COM(2021) 188 final (21.04.2021).

57 Quote by Sirpa Pietikainen (European People's Party), as set out in F. Simon, 'Parliament Spells out Red Lines in EU Battle over Green Finance' (09.03.2021), https://www.euractiv.com/section/energy-environment/news/parliament-spells-out-red-lines-in-eu-battle-over-green-finance/.

58 A. Hubert, 'Taxonomie de l'investissement vert: quand Bruxelles perd le contrôle', *Contexte Energie* (18.03.2021), https://www.contexte.com/article/energie/taxonomie-de-linvestissement-vert-quand-bruxelles-perd-le-controle_128912.html?.

59 F. Simon and K. Taylor, 'The Green Brief: Europe's Green Finance Taxonomy Wars, Part 3', *EurActiv* (21.04.2021), https://www.euractiv.com/section/energy-environment/news/the-green-brief-europes-green-finance-taxonomy-wars-part-3/.

the different expert groups is heavily relied upon, according to the explanatory memorandum, with the previous public consultation as part of the preparation of the Taxonomy Climate Delegated Act already being 'sufficient', at least for the technical screening criteria for natural gas.

In the end, regardless of the stance one takes on the number of feedback instances or how the feedback has been taken into account, it is undeniable that the volume of feedback increased the already lengthy timeline of getting to the (partial, with natural gas and nuclear energy sectors still missing) finished result of the first Taxonomy Delegated Act. This sheds a practical light on the theoretical dilemma of section 2, showing how time pressure conflicts with the wish and requirements to produce a sound decision with public participation. As exemplified by the request of the Member State Expert Group on Sustainable Finance to extend the deadline for public consultation,[60] which was denied by the Commission, but which itself later needed more time to get through the public feedback received, time is of the essence in the practicalities of public participation.

No time was taken for public participation in relation to the Complementary Delegated Act, an interesting fact that perhaps also shows the impact of this theoretical dilemma, regardless of the reasons formally given by the Commission for foregoing consultation on this Act.[61]

The example of the experiences under the first Taxonomy Climate Delegated Act and its Complementary Climate Delegated Act underlines the difficulty of keeping a balance between the urgency to act in complex environmental decision-making and effectively including the public throughout this process. Finding this balance becomes highly charged in the field of climate change and adaptation, the subjects of the first Delegated Act, given the strong sense of urgency stemming from the need to reach the EU's fast-approaching climate goals. Hard choices have to be made to align good governance practices for public participation with timely decision-making. In this case study, with the first Taxonomy Delegated Act having breached the legal requirement to be adopted by 31 December 2020 – instead being adopted by 4 June 2021 – and with the Complementary Delegated Act being adopted on 9 March 2022, it is evident to which side the scales were tipped.[62]

---

60 European Commission, 'Member State Expert Group on Sustainable Finance – Meetings', https://ec.europa.eu/transparency/expert-groups-register/screen/expert-groups/consult?do=groupDetail.groupDetail&groupID=3603.

61 In a questions and answers section on the EU Taxonomy Complementary Climate Delegated Act, the Commission refers to the consultation of expert groups, the fact that the relevant issues concerning natural gas and nuclear energy in relation to the Taxonomy have been in the public domain since 2020 and the 'significant' public deliberations around the Taxonomy Regulation and the finalisation of the first Climate Delegated Act. European Commission, 'Questions and Answers on the EU Taxonomy Complementary Climate Delegated Act covering certain nuclear and gas activities', https://ec.europa.eu/commission/presscorner/detail/en/qanda_22_712.

62 Articles 10(6) and 11(6) Taxonomy Regulation.

4. RE-EVALUATING PUBLIC PARTICIPATION

The case study on the first Taxonomy Delegated Act points out an important dilemma in environmental decision-making, namely the contradiction between effectively including the public on the one hand, and time constraints on the other. The EU currently handles this dilemma through capturing the Aarhus Convention requirements in a soft law approach.

From a strictly legal point of view, the flaws in the current approach are easily spotted. Participation requirements integrated into soft law leave the public with accountability issues; the case study points out the vulnerabilities of a four-week feedback period as a pre-set mould and reveals the difficulties and delays in taking this feedback into account. The case study on the Complementary Delegated Act shows the discretion the Commission retains in deciding not to let the public participate.

It can be questioned whether public participation would be better approached through hard law requirements. Opting for binding provisions could provide the public with more clarity with regard to its role in decision-making. As Armeni and Lee state, law contributes to the context, the place and the meaning of participation.[63] Moreover, public participation through hard law provisions benefits enforceability through court supervision, an issue which has remained unclear up until this point.

A switch to hard law would however be too far-reaching, as it comes with its challenges. Going past the problematic exercise of composing provisions and defining core concepts,[64] a hard law approach will be initiated by government actors retaining considerable discretion in fashioning the procedures. This leaves the question of whether the public will actually trust the process.[65] Equally important, if not more so, is the fact that a hard law approach would also leave the door open to bureaucratic 'box-checking' for public participation requirements instead of giving it meaningful potential to improve decision-making.

Furthermore, as this chapter tries to capture the spirit of the Aarhus Convention, a binding approach would go against the nature of the obligation of effort it contains, risking being replaced by a bureaucratic exercise. Indeed, as the Aarhus Convention Compliance Committee states, the Convention prescribes the modalities of public participation in a general matter but leaves the Parties

---

63 C. Armeni and M. Lee, 'Participation in a Time of Climate Crisis' (2021) 48 *Journal of Law and Society* 549, 549.

64 Tabb for example further points out the questions arising regarding the definition of the 'public' for compliance purposes: W.M. Tabb, 'Public Participation in Environmental Decision Making' in L. Paddock, R.L. Glicksman and N.S. Bryner, *Elgar Encyclopedia of Environmental Law: Volume II*, Edward Elgar, Northampton 2016, p. 314.

65 Ibid.

'with some discretion as to the specificities of how public participation should be organised'.[66]

The EU using this discretion to opt for uniformly applicable binding rules could arguably work against promoting public participation in the drafting of complex and technical delegated acts because of bureaucratic constraints and the possibility of inadequate public administration, factors possibly leading to the exclusion of the public from the process.[67]

Lastly, going further along the spectrum of bindingness and putting an explicit principle of public participation in environmental decision-making into primary law would amount to integration through law, as seen earlier, for example, in the Economic and Monetary Union area.[68] EU primary law does not provide a suitable framework to prescribe detailed public participation requirements because of their generality and difficulty providing flexibility in cases with a set timeframe.[69] Moreover, it should be questioned whether binding provisions are an adequate integration strategy for including the public in a matter as important as the environment, which inherently affects the public at large and does not leave the option to 'opt-out of participation' to a society increasingly facing the consequences of climate change.

This reasoning leads to the conclusion that the EU using a soft law approach is not necessarily a bad thing, although accountability concerns remain. Next, a few suggestions are made on how the EU, using its discretion under the second pillar of the Aarhus Convention to opt for a soft law approach, can effectively address concerns and better serve the quality of decision-making and, hence, the public interest.

Firstly, the Commission as an institution, regarding delegated acts in particular, is subject to 'horizontal accountability' enacted by the Parliament and the Council, which provided delegated power to the Commission. The loss of accountability by opting for a meaningful soft law approach could be remedied by the Commission reporting to the Parliament on how it has tried to effectively involve EU citizens in complex decision-making such as the Taxonomy delegated acts. Further decisions on effective public participation in specific cases could be made whilst providing a more democratic counterbalance to the risk of the

66 Aarhus Convention Compliance Committee, 'Compilation of Findings of the Aarhus Convention Compliance Committee Adopted 18 February to Date' (05.02.2021), p. 13.

67 A. Marzuki, 'Challenges in the Public Participation and the Decision Making Process' (2015) 53 *Sociologija i Prostor* 21, 21.

68 Example pointed out in: M. van der Sluis, 'EU Law for a New Generation?' (2016) 14 *International Journal of Constitutional Law* 480, 480.

69 B.J. Richardson and J. Razzaque, 'Public Participation in Environmental Decision-Making' in B.J. Richardson and S. Wood (eds), *Environmental Law for Sustainability*, Hart Publishing, Oxford 2005, p. 177.

Commission's opportunistic choices. As a caveat pointed out by Armeni and Lee, the relationship between participatory and representative democracy is another enormous topic, and the mere presence of Parliament does not simply resolve the dilemma of a legitimate participation procedure for citizens.[70]

Secondly, looking at complex environmental decision-making through delegated acts, it should be questioned whether it is genuinely beneficial to let the public at large give feedback, resulting in the administrative burden of a large number of feedback instances. The Commission has left the option of using representation in public participation largely unexplored,[71] despite this being endorsed by Article 8(2)(c) Aarhus Convention. (E)NGOs and business organisations representing different community sectors could channel public participation and perhaps make it more effective in influencing the decision-making process.

A third suggestion looks into citizen juries as a possibility for organising more effective public participation. A citizen jury is a group selected to represent a part of their community. They are asked to respond to a specific initiative, for which they attend a series of meetings to listen to and cross-examine expert witnesses.[72] This suggestion is not new in the realm of ensuring public participation in implementing environmental legislation, as the Commission itself also recommended this method for the implementation of the Water Framework Directive.[73] Although this does not concern delegated acts, lessons could be drawn from this experience, as citizen juries could ensure a diverse representation in public participation and a dispersion of knowledge on highly technical matters.

As a concluding note to this section, it should be remarked that the three presented suggestions do not necessitate a choice between one or the other. They are not mutually exclusive but are intended to spark a further discussion on how the EU can guarantee the effective public participation that it has vowed to ensure under the second pillar of the Aarhus Convention, even in the case of complex environmental decision-making through delegated acts.

---

70 C. Armeni and M. Lee, 'Participation in a Time of Climate Crisis' (2021) 48 *Journal of Law and Society* 549, 569.

71 B. Kohler-Koch, 'Civil Society and EU Democracy: "Astroturf" Representation?' (2010) 17 *Journal of European Public Policy* 100.

72 N. Crosby, 'Citizens Juries: One Solution for Difficult Environmental Questions' in O. Renn, T. Webler and P. Wiedemann (eds), *Fairness and Competence in Citizen Participation: Evaluating Models for Environmental Discourse*, Springer Netherlands, Dordrecht 1995, p. 158; W. Kenyon, 'A Critical Review of Citizens' Juries: How Useful Are They in Facilitating Public Participation in the EU Water Framework Directive?' (2005) 48 *Journal of Environmental Planning and Management* 431, 431.

73 European Commission and Directorate-General for the Environment, 'Public Participation in Relation to the Water Framework Directive No 8', OPOCE, 2003, p. 95.

5. CONCLUSION

The Taxonomy Regulation, adopted under the European Green Deal, has been set up to be a key instrument in mobilising funds to make the EU's green ambitions a reality. For its implementation, strict deadlines are being imposed on the Commission to devise delegated acts on technical screening criteria to determine which economic activities are considered 'sustainable'. The Taxonomy Regulation also points to a role for the public in the decision-making process. This chapter aimed to explore how the principles of the Aarhus Convention and its values, as enshrined on the European level, shape the procedure for implementing the Taxonomy Regulation.

First, an intrinsic dilemma was revealed between the strict deadlines for technical implementation and the aspiration to involve the public in decision-making. Public participation as shaped under the Aarhus Convention constitutes an obligation of effort, leaving the EU with a minimal procedural framework and discretion on how it should be organised. The stumbling block in this area is the requirement of 'sufficient timeframes', which the EU captures in a pre-set four-week consultation period, regardless of the complexity of the delegated act.

Second, a case study on the first Taxonomy Delegated Act revealed opportunities for the public at large to 'have its say' whilst also showing a large number of feedback instances becoming an administrative burden. Time proved to be a stumbling block once again, with, on the one hand, a request for more time for public participation and, on the other, the current regime already resulting in delays to the adoption of a partially unfinished delegated act. No time was taken for a separate public consultation on the Complementary Climate Delegated Act covering nuclear and gas activities, with the Commission partially relying on the results under the first Taxonomy Delegated Act for gas activities and the involvement of experts. The process of getting to the Complementary Delegated Act without a separate public consultation shows the extent of the Commission's discretion under the new 2021 Better Regulation Agenda, leaving its alignment with the obligation of effort to promote effective public participation under the Aarhus Convention doubtful.

Third, to address the procedure of public participation in itself interacting with complex environmental decision-making within a set timeframe, the EU's current soft law approach was found to be a better alternative to more binding provisions. This approach leaves room for the meaningful potential of public participation, rather than increasing the risk of it turning into a bureaucratic checklist. The accountability concerns left under this soft law approach can be addressed by, for example, the Commission reporting to the Parliament on which approach was taken in a specific case, by paying more attention to representation instead of involving the public at large and by exploring the potential of citizen juries.

To conclude, the Taxonomy Regulation delegated acts are a technical and current topic offering the opportunity to look into what public participation means in the context of complex environmental decision-making. Instead of fitting them into a pre-existing system, they give the chance to re-examine the system for European integration to fit the needs for a greener future, where it gives a voice to citizens throughout the process. In order to capture the spirit of the second pillar of the Aarhus Convention in shaping the procedure for implementing the Taxonomy Regulation, the EU is encouraged to look beyond its current focus on good governance and make meaningful use of the discretion that the Aarhus Convention has left it. Perhaps the 'spirit' of the Aarhus Convention can even be transcended to establish the new societal order the Green Deal is aiming to shape.

PROJECT REVIEW, FOSSIL INFRASTRUCTURE AND CLIMATE CHANGE

The Flemish Petrol Station Case as an Unexpected Breakthrough?

Hendrik SCHOUKENS

1. INTRODUCTION

Climate change is one of the most serious existential threats to the long-term survival of life on our planet today. The consecutive, scorching heatwaves that hit the European continent in June and July 2022, shattering temperature records in many countries, painfully illustrate that prolonged periods of persistent droughts, raging wildfires and record-breaking temperatures are becoming normal because of climate change.[1] Recent reports showcase the existence of a large emission gap, with the signatories to the Paris Agreement's current pledges only capable of reducing carbon by about 7.5% by 2030,[2] compared with previous unconditional nationally determined contributions (NDCs), whereas the Intergovernmental Panel on Climate Change (IPCC) indicated that in order to meet the internationally agreed climate targets, emissions should be reduced by 45% by 2030 compared to 2010.[3] In order to meet these objectives, however, the Parties to the Paris Agreement must double their climate efforts if they are to reach the overarching goal of limiting global temperature rise well below 2°C by the end of the century.[4]

Against this worrisome backdrop, strategic climate change lawsuits have recently emerged as a new and, in an increasing number of cases, unexpectedly successful lever to force governments to tackle climate change more decisively and systematically.[5] As of May 2022, more than 1,800 climate lawsuits have been filed in more than 40 different jurisdictions.[6] Climate litigation is usually approached as an umbrella concept covering all types of dispute that relate to climate change (touching upon both mitigation actions and adaptation measures), ranging from lawsuits focused on catalysing legal or political change at the government level to proceedings aimed at holding companies accountable for their contribution to climate change.[7] As of today, most prominent climate wins – such as *Urgenda* in the Netherlands,[8] *Neubauer* in Germany[9] and *Grande-Synthe* in France[10] – hold governments accountable for their insufficient climate policies. These proceedings definitely qualify as *strategic* climate litigation, as they aim to generate impacts that go beyond an individual case.[11] They are

1 F. Harvey et al., 'Burning planet: why are the world's heatwaves getting more intense?', *The Guardian* (18 June 2022).

2 United Nations Environment Programme, *The Heat is On. A world of climate promises not yet delivered* (Emission Gap Report, 2021).

3 IPCC, *Climate Change 2022: Mitigation of Climate Change. Working Group III Contribution to the Sixth Assessment Report of the IPCC*, 2022.

4 Ibid.

5 See for instance J. Peel and R. Markey-Towler, 'Recipe for Success? Lesson for Strategic Climate Litigation from the Sharma, Neubauer, and Shell Cases?' (2021) 22 *German Law Journal* 1194.

6 For the exact numbers, see J. Sitzer and C. Higham, *Global trends in climate change litigation: 2022 snapshot* (Policy report, June 2022).

7 See for a more in-depth analysis: United Nations Environment Programme, *Global Climate Litigation Report: 2020 Status Review* (Nairobi, 2020).

8 *Urgenda Foundation v. State of the Netherlands* (2019) ECLI:NL:GHDHA:2018:2591.

9 *Neubauer* (2021) 1 BvR 2656/18.

10 *La Commune de Grande-Synthe* (2021) ECLI:FR:CECHR:2021:427301.20210701.

11 See J. Peel and R. Markey-Towler, above n. 5, p. 1486.

increasingly based on tort law and human rights duties, which is evident given the major impact of unhalted climate change on the immediate survival chances of future generations of *humans*.[12] Only recently, the 2021 landmark decision of a Dutch District Court, in which it was ruled that the petroleum company Shell must reduce its global net carbon emissions by 45% by 2030 compared to 2019 levels, underscored the large potential for climate litigation in the realm of corporate liability and responsibility.[13]

In recent decades, however, an increasing number of climate lawsuits have been targeting legality review of specific administrative decisions, often permits or planning decisions, relating to fossil fuel production or use or other types of activities that lead to additional greenhouse gas emissions. In many instances, such cases are based on environmental impact assessment (EIA) duties or comparable planning obligations, which are used by litigants as a lever to challenge project permitting or planning decisions which have not paid sufficient attention to the climate impacts of the proposed activities. Whereas at first sight such permit-based lawsuits seem to lack the strategic potential of the *Urgenda* type of strategic climate litigation, their ground-breaking potential as landmark decisions in permitting procedures can no longer be ignored.

Arguably one of the most notable recent examples of this strand of litigation was offered by the 2019 decision in *Gloucester Resources Limited v. Minister for Planning* of the New South Wales Land and Environment Court, which revolved around the legality of a permit refusal for the construction of a new open-cut coal mine in Australia. As the mining company lodged an appeal against this decision, the latter court was asked to assess a myriad of legal arguments regarding climate change-related consideration and permit review. When appraising the legal arguments brought forward against the permit refusal, the Australian court referred, amongst other things, to the direct and indirect negative climate impacts the open-cast mine would generate. It upheld the decision, stating that it was in line with the public interest, the existing EIA rules, and, most importantly, Australia's obligations under the Paris Agreement.[14] Other similar climate-based challenges against specific projects, such as *Plan B Earth v. Secretary of State*, which focused on the climate impacts of the decision to allow an additional runway at London's Heathrow Airport, and *Greenpeace Nordic Association v. Norway Ministry of Petroleum*, where the Norwegian State's decision to grant certain offshore oil and gas development licences in the Barents Sea, produced more mixed results for climate activists. The former case initially led to a decision of the UK Court of Appeal halting the planning decision, citing its failure to

---

12 J. Peel and H.M. Oskofsky, 'A Rights Turn in Climate Change Litigation?' (2018) 7(1) *Transnational Environmental Law* 37.

13 *Vereniging Milieudefensie et al. v. Royal Dutch Shell plc* (2021) ECLI:NL:RBDHA:2021:5339.

14 *Gloucester Resources Limited v. Minister for Planning* [2019] NSWLEC 7.

take into account the UK's recent climate pledges under the Paris Agreement.[15] However, this decision was eventually overturned by the UK's Supreme Court, which held that sufficient attention had been paid to climate considerations.[16] The Norwegian climate case suffered a similar fate, with the Norwegian Supreme Court dismissing the claims and holding that future emissions from exported oil are too uncertain to bar the granting of these petroleum exploration licences.[17]

This small selection of permit-based climate litigation displays the unease of the courts when dealing with such types of lawsuits. Linking local emissions to a global phenomenon and threat, such as climate change, remains very challenging, including in legal terms. Even so, in order to not compromise the shrinking remaining carbon budgets and to keep the rising temperatures in check, national authorities will have to strictly implement their climate pledges in the permitting policies regarding potential new greenhouse gas emissions. An accumulation of many relatively 'small-scale' decisions may also lead to further unsustainable climate lock-ins, which will render the transition to carbon neutrality more difficult.

In this chapter, we use a relatively unknown decision in a Belgian planning dispute surrounding a petrol station as a lens to discuss the plethora of challenges that might arise when integrating climate considerations into specific planning and project decisions. The lawsuit at stake had to deal with the legality of an integrated environmental permit for a new petrol station in the Flemish municipality of Boechout. One of the main legal discussions concerned the question whether, and if so to what extent, climate considerations can be used as a legal benchmark to deny a planning permit for a fossil project development. In its two landmark decisions, dating back to April[18] and December[19] 2021, the Flemish Council of Permit Disputes (Raad voor Vergunningsbetwistingen) accepted the possibility of refusing a permit for fossil infrastructure with reference to climate-related considerations, even at the level of a relatively small municipality. This arguably very local-specific lawsuit is analysed against the wider backdrop of other relevant Belgian climate litigation, such as *Klimaatzaak*, in which it was claimed that a more ambitious approach to the reduction of greenhouse gases by the competent Belgian authorities was necessary to respect the human rights of the plaintiffs, among other things.[20] In section 2, the factual and legal background of the legal proceedings leading to the recent innovative jurisprudence are sketched, while the bulk of the analysis is contained in section 3. There, the legal levers that can be used to force planning authorities to carry out a project review in light of climate considerations are further outlined.

---

15 *R (Friends of the Earth Ltd and Others) v. Heathrow Airport Ltd* [2020] EWCA Civ 214.
16 *R (Friends of the Earth Ltd and Others) v. Heathrow Airport Ltd* [2020] UKSC 52.
17 *Greenpeace Nordic and Others v. Norway* (2020) HR-2020-846-J.
18 *Lauwrys et al. v. Provincie Antwerpen* (2021) nr. RvVb-S-2021-0923.
19 *Lauwrys et al. v. Provincie Antwerpen* (2021) nr. RvVb-A-2122-0276.
20 *Asbl Klimaatzaak v. Etat Belge* (2021) 2015/4585/A.

2. THE FLEMISH PETROL STATION CASE: A DETAILED ANALYSIS

2.1. THE RELEVANT REGULATORY CONTEXT AND PRECEDENTS

Flanders is situated in Belgium, a federal State, in which decision-making power is shared between a federal government, three Regions (Flanders, Wallonia and the Brussels-Capital Region) and three Communities (the Flemish, the French and the German-speaking Communities). Pursuant to Article 6 of the Special Law on Institutional Reforms of 8 August 1980 (Bijzondere wet tot hervorming der instellingen), environmental policy constitutes a regional competence. In the territory of Flanders, the Flemish Region is therefore fully competent to legislate on environmental matters, and it has done so in the past decades. However, climate change should be regarded as a cross-cutting topic and cannot be limited to the environment in the strict sense. The Belgian climate policy therefore goes beyond the regional competences linked to the environment, nature and water policy.[21]

Until recently, relatively limited attention was paid to the integration of climate considerations, as a substantive benchmark, into planning or environmental permitting procedures in Flanders. Implicitly, it was assumed that global impacts cannot serve as a concrete baseline in the context of project review, where most of the attention is directed to avoiding local nuisance. Only when a palm oil refinery facility was denied an environmental permit by the permitting authority of the Province of Antwerp (the Deputatie) in 2010, based on its global environmental impact, did the topic receive some minor attention. The provincial authority motivated that its permit was justified in light of Article 7bis of the Belgian Constitution, which stipulates that *sustainable development* is a common pursuit of all Belgian authorities, including the provincial authorities. However, after an appeal was lodged, the Flemish minister competent for the environment opted to grant the facility a permit, stating that global impacts cannot serve as a binding benchmark when evaluating an environmental permit application. Rather, the main focus is on checking whether the local impacts of the facility are in line with the applicable environmental prescriptions, set out in other tailor-made regulations. If that is the case, global impacts cannot prompt a permit refusal.[22] For a considerable time, this stance was believed to illustrate a correct understanding of the Flemish rules on environmental permitting.[23]

---

21 See more in detail M. El Berhoumi and C. Nennen, 'Le changement climatique à l'épreuve du fédéralisme' (2018) 4 *Aménagement* 61.

22 See P. De Smedt, H. Schoukens and T. Van Laer, 'Greening the constitution: the principle of sustainable development in the Belgian Constitution' (2012) *Environmental Law Network International* 74.

23 See for instance *Bvba Spielothek* (1999) 78.960.

2.2. PREVIOUS ADMINISTRATIVE PROCEDURE AND CONFLICTING VIEWPOINTS

That well-entrenched view on the substantive and material scope of the environmental permitting policy drastically changed in 2021, with the culmination of a legal dispute regarding a planning and environmental permit (*omgevingsvergunning*) for a petrol station in the Flemish municipality of Boechout. Initially, the permit application was declined by the local municipality on the basis of its climate pledges, among other things. To be more precise, the municipality of Boechout had signed the Covenant of Mayors (Burgemeesterconvenant), which included the ambition to reduce the carbon footprint of European towns and cities towards and beyond the EU climate commitments,[24] and argued that authorising a new petrol station, which moreover did not offer any options for charging electric cars, would run counter to these pledges. This decision was overturned on appeal by the provincial authority of Antwerp (Deputatie), which stated that global climate-related considerations had no role to play in assessing the compatibility of a permit application with the applicable environmental and spatial planning rules. In particular, the provincial authority held that the climate-related considerations raised by the local municipality did not qualify as environment-related considerations and could thus not be used as an argument to reject the permit application. The municipality of Boechout decided to challenge the legality of this rationale before the Council of Flemish Permit Disputes in 2020.

2.3. DECISION OF 21 APRIL 2021: CLIMATE MITIGATION AND ADAPTATION AS A DUTY OF CARE FOR LOCAL AUTHORITIES?

In a first decision of 21 April 2021, the Council sided with the municipality and suspended the permit with reference to Article 4.3.4 of the Flemish Spatial Planning Code.[25] This provision allows permitting authorities to decline permit applications which clash with the sectoral objectives and due diligence obligations that are applicable in other environmental policies. International and EU environmental or other sectoral obligations which, although they lack direct effect, force competent authorities to implement certain environmental objectives fall within the scope of the said provision. The municipality of Boechout had argued that this provision provides a legal ground for taking into account the climate pledges that were included in the Covenant of Mayors. The

24 See more on the Covenant of Mayors, below section 3.1.

25 *Lauwrys et al.*, above n. 18.

Council agreed, stating that 'care for climate' can be included in the material scope of Article 4.3.4 of the Flemish Spatial Planning Code (Vlaamse Codex Ruimtelijke Ordening). Whereas the Council acknowledged that the binding force of the climate targets embedded in the Paris Agreement remained rather ambivalent, the signing of the Covenant of Mayors reasserted a duty of care (*zorgplicht*) for climate change incumbent on the local authorities.

2.4. DECISION OF 9 DECEMBER 2021: CLIMATE CONSIDERATIONS BROUGHT UNDER THE UMBRELLA OF SUSTAINABLE SPATIAL DEVELOPMENT

In its subsequent decision of 9 December 2021, the Council reaffirmed its position by annulling the permit. However, it added two additional lines of argumentation to reiterate its earlier decision in the preliminary proceedings.[26] First, it recalled Article 1.1.4 of the Flemish Spatial Planning Code, which stipulated that the rights of future generations are to be taken into account when executing the Flemish spatial planning policy. This provision indeed puts forward the principle of sustainable spatial planning (*duurzame ruimtelijke ordening*), which ought to be at the heart of the Flemish spatial planning policy and, according to the Court, can be used as a lever to integrate climate considerations into permitting procedures. Second, the Council again repeated that the climate commitments of the municipality under the Covenant are not merely voluntary. It cannot be ruled out, the Council stated, that citizens will over time also hold local municipalities accountable for not meeting their climate targets. It is the first time that climate liability was also invoked in the context of local authorities. Third, the Council also indicated that achieving the climate pledges requires additional efforts not only on the part of the municipality, but also on the part of the inhabitants and companies present on the territory of the municipality. This was used as an additional argument for a more straightforward integration of climate considerations into the permitting procedures. At a minimum, it leaves open the possibility for municipalities to do so.

2.5. PRELIMINARY ASSESSMENT: A SOFT REVOLUTION?

Given the vigour and the conscientiousness with which the Flemish Council of Permit Disputes motivated its decision in December 2021, one can safely assume it will not be a one-trick pony. Indeed, in the preliminary legal literature on the recent shift in case law, the revolutionary nature of the decision has been

26 *Lauwrys et al.*, above n. 19.

underlined.[27] It would also be erroneous to equate the outcome of the lawsuit to a classic case of adequate motivation.[28] Henceforth, there no longer seemed to exist a principal legal argument against the integration of climate considerations into the permitting policy, even at the level of a local municipality. The novel jurisprudence underscored the fact that, while climate change definitely constitutes a global challenge, at least part of the solution is to be found at local level and equally within the concrete permitting procedures. Although the concept of 'death by a thousand cuts' was not explicitly cited as a rationale by the Council, it is hard not to link the rationale from this jurisprudence to the fact that accumulated environmental impacts can further compromise dwindling carbon budgets.[29]

Still, the recent climate-inspired decisions of the Flemish Council of Permit Disputes should be put into their proper context. To begin with, the Council did not rule that climate considerations have now become a *binding* benchmark when authorising planning permits.[30] Accordingly, the Council's rationale merely puts forward an *optional* ground for permit refusal, leaving aside the question whether and, if so, upon which substantive grounds a binding legal duty exists to take into account climate-related considerations when granting integrated permits. Furthermore, the precise factual circumstances at play should not be ignored either. It is noteworthy that the permit application concerned did not include any additional efforts in terms of renewables, such as solar panels or facilities for electric cars, which made it a rather outdated permit application. This clear lack of efforts towards further sustainability in the case file was also explicitly cited by the Council in its final decision of December 2021. The question therefore arises as to what extent a permit refusal would still have been possible in the petrol case if renewables had been included in the permit application. This question has remained unaddressed so far. Moreover, substantial doubts remain as to the material scope of this so-called 'optional' climate test.[31]

---

27 See amongst others H. Schoukens, 'Het tankstationarrest van de Raad voor Vergunningsbetwistingen als voorzichtige opstap richting een klimaattoets bij plannen en projecten: juridische analyse van een nakende paradigmashift?' (2021) *Tijdschrift voor Milieurecht* 355; L. De Brucker, 'De klimaattoets getoetst. Naar een primaat van het klimaat in het omgevingsvergunningenbeleid?' (2021) 4 *Stedenbouw Omgeving Ruimtelijke Ordening Milieu*, contribution 12.

28 See also G. Vermaercke and E. De Rammelaere, 'Mobiliteit en vergunningverlening: een symbiotische relatie' (2021) *Milieu- en Energierecht* 248.

29 H. Schoukens, 'Géén klimaatdood door duizend sneden: RvVb hint richting klimaattoets bij plannen en projecten' (2021) 2 *Stedenbouw Omgeving Ruimtelijke Ordening Milieu*, contribution 19.

30 H. Schoukens, above n. 27; L. De Brucker, above n. 27.

31 H. Schoukens, 'Voorbij de Klimaatzaak: van klimaataansprakelijkheid naar klimaattoets?' (2021) *Tijdschrift voor Ruimtelijke Ordening, Omgeving en Stedenbouw* 326, 349–50.

3. WIDER LESSONS: LEGAL GROUNDS FOR PROJECT REVIEW BASED ON CLIMATE CONSIDERATIONS

The recent jurisprudence of the Flemish Council of Permit Disputes is not only interesting from the angle of Flemish environmental law but merits a more comprehensive analysis. In the following section I sketch its potential wider relevance, focusing on the legal grounds that can be used to turn climate reduction targets into a potentially binding baseline in permit policies for projects.

3.1. THE COVENANT OF MAYORS AS AN UNEXPECTED LEVER FOR PROJECT REVIEW IN LIGHT OF CLIMATE CONSIDERATIONS?

A first bone of contention relates to the legal effects of the above-mentioned Covenant of Mayors. Many Flemish commentators were indeed baffled by the fact that the Council seemed to accord binding force to an instrument that was widely qualified as a non-binding and voluntary instrument.[32] To further assess the merits of this criticism, let us first check the roots and origins of the Covenant of Mayors, which currently unites more than 11,000 local and regional authorities across 57 countries. The Covenant was originally launched in 2008 at the initiative of the European Commission with the ambition of uniting local governments voluntarily committed to achieving and exceeding the EU's climate and energy targets. In 2014, the approach was updated in light of the Mayors Adapt initiative, which was based on a similar governance approach. On the Covenant's website, the instrument is pitched as 'a first-of-its-kind bottom-up approach to energy and climate action'.[33] It is described as 'a mainstream European movement involving local and regional authorities, voluntarily committing to increasing energy efficiency and use of renewable energy sources on their territories'.[34] As to the precise nature of the commitments, it is stipulated that 'Covenant signatories commit to adopting an integrated approach to climate change mitigation and adaptation. They are required to develop, within the first two years of adhesion, a Sustainable Energy and Climate Action Plan (SECAP) with the aims of cutting CO2 emissions by at least 40% by 2030 and increasing resilience to climate change.'[35]

---

32 See for instance L. De Brucker, above n. 27.
33 https://www.covenantofmayors.eu/en/.
34 Ibid.
35 Ibid.

Heyvaert rightly has qualified the Covenant as 'a clear example of a transnational network as it links towns and cities across Europe'.[36] In addition, she explains that the network is partly characterised by a strong involvement of the European Commission:

> [T]he participating towns and cities are partly self-regulating entities, but their organization and execution is co-governed by the European Commission, which had a decisive influence on the development of the terms of the Covenant and the institutional infrastructure, which manages negotiations and liaises between members internally and between members and external funding and technical support bodies, and supervises compliance.[37]

In light of the foregoing considerations, it is hardly surprising to note that there existed a broad consensus in the available legal literature on the *non-binding* nature of the Covenant.[38] Heyvaert, when scrutinising the regulatory nature and structure of the Covenant, cited several persuasive arguments to that effect. First, she rightly notes that the Covenant was clearly conceived to function as a facilitator for inter-municipal coordination towards a carbon-free society: it focuses on support rather than legal mandates and enforcement.[39] A similar conclusion arises when one takes a closer look at the template which the regional or local climate plans have to comply with. In this respect as well, the absence of any substantive rules indirectly underlines the non-binding nature of the Covenant.[40] To sum up, consensus in the literature was that the ambivalent, bottom-up and facilitative nature of the Covenant of Mayors does not seem to leave a single shred of doubt as to its non-binding effect.[41]

In this light, the criticism directed towards the Flemish Council of Permit Disputes when it seemed to assign legal consequences to the Covenant of Mayors in the petrol case appears justified.[42] Nowhere in the documents linked to the Covenant is it required that the signatories incorporate the international or European climate targets into their permitting policies. That said, two distinctions should be made with respect to this critical appraisal in Flemish legal literature of the Council's rationale regarding the legal consequences of the Covenant.

---

36 V. Heyvaert, 'What's in a Name? The Covenant of Mayors as Transnational Environmental Regulation' (2013) 22(1) *RECIEL* 85.

37 Ibid.

38 Ibid. See also E. Domorenok, 'Voluntary instruments for ambitious objectives? The experience of the EU Covenant of Mayors' (2019) 28(2) *Environmental Politics* 294; L. Blendin, *Orchestrating Local Climate Policy in the European Union: Inter-municipal Coordination and the Covenant of Mayors in Germany and France* (Springer, 2017), p. 241.

39 V. Heyvaert, above n. 36, p. 85.

40 Ibid.

41 L. De Brucker, above n. 27.

42 Ibid.

First, it should be reiterated that the Municipal Council of Boechout explicitly passed a (binding) decision to ratify the Covenant. The decision of the Municipal Council in itself is not without legal effects, which to some extent renders the criticism regarding the lack of binding effect of the Covenant less persuasive. Even so, critics maintain that such binding effects only arise when the Covenant is translated into a municipal climate action plan.[43] It is unclear whether in the case at hand such a plan existed, although many Flemish municipalities have adopted such plans in the wake of their accession to the Covenant.

Second, it needs to be underlined that the Flemish Council of Permit Disputes did not base its reasoning exclusively on the Covenant, but also took into account other legal norms. To be more precise, it merely stated that the signing and approval by a local municipality of the Covenant, when read in conjunction with a provision in Flemish planning law that allows for the integration of environmental objectives and due diligence commitments, granted the local municipality the discretion to integrate climate considerations into its decision-making procedures for integrated permit applications. In other words, the Council did nothing more than simply state that this commitment amounted to a duty of care (*zorgplicht*) towards the climate, which is arguably a very open legal standard. The municipality further clarified its climate-based objections to the permit application in the initial permit refusal and issued a well-reasoned advice during the appeal procedures, which the provincial authority simply rejected by stating that climate considerations have no role to play in the context of permitting policies. Whereas the rationale used by the Council still attached some degree of binding consequences to the Covenant, one might also approach the ruling from a more down-to-earth angle. In fact, the Council simply reasserted the fact that local municipalities could, through the lens of Article 4.3.4 of the Flemish Planning Code, use the Covenant as a lever to refuse potentially harmful fossil permit applications since this aligns with their due diligence obligations towards the climate.

Thus, while it might indeed be conceded that it was clearly not the intention of the European Commission to see the Covenant used as a concrete benchmark for climate review at project level, the outcome of the Flemish petrol station case only goes that far. To be clear, the Covenant can only be used as an optional lever for the integration of climate-based objections into permit decision-making procedures because Flemish planning law grants permitting authorities the possibility to do so in the first place. Most commentators assume that in the absence of such a relatively broad provision in the Flemish planning law, the outcome of the court case might have been very different.[44] That might be true. However, it remains somewhat puzzling to see the Council also refer to the international climate targets under the Paris Agreement in its first decision of April 2021. The Council seemed to

43 Ibid.

44 H. Schoukens, above n. 27.

hesitate to exclusively base its rationale on the Paris Agreement, by acknowledging that there exists a lack of consensus on the binding nature of this convention. The reluctance on the part of the Flemish court seems understandable, as the Paris Agreement in itself does not contain binding reduction targets. Even so, the Agreement is binding on its signatories, including Belgium (and, by extension, Flanders).[45] It might have been more logical for the Council to explicitly refer to the EU climate reduction targets in its decision.

In addition, it remains uncertain to what extent the recent jurisprudential move is only confined to the permit policies of municipalities that have signed the Covenant – as is the case for 90% of the municipalities in the Flemish Region[46] – or whether a similar analysis would also be replicated in those few municipalities that have not signed the Covenant. And what about the permitting authorities at the provincial and regional level, which assess the appeals lodged against planning permits issued at the municipal level?

3.2. PLANNING LAW AND CLIMATE CHANGE: AN UNEXPECTED ALLIANCE?

The Flemish petrol station case is not a stand-alone case when it comes to the potency of spatial planning law as a lever for the integration of climate change-related consideration in permitting policies. As is also the case in other permit-based climate cases, such as the aforementioned decision of the UK's Court of Appeal in *Plan B Earth v. Secretary of State* to halt the construction of a new runway at London's Heathrow Airport, national planning law sometimes contains remarkably far-reaching integration clauses which compel planning authorities to explicitly consider climate effects throughout planning decision-making procedures. For instance, section 5(7) of the UK Planning Act 2008 explicitly states that national policy frameworks, such as the Airport National Policy Statement (ANPS), must give reasons for the policy adopted. Section 5(8) stipulates that these reasons must include an explanation of how that policy takes into account existing 'governmental policy' relating to the mitigation of and adaptation to climate change. In this context, the Court of Appeal ruled that the policy framework adopted under the Planning Act 2008, which provides support in principle for the Heathrow Airport expansion, unlawfully failed to explicitly take into account the UK's recent commitments under the 2015 Paris Agreement.[47] However, in December 2020 the UK Supreme Court overturned

---

45 See on the binding effect of the Paris Agreement: D. Bodansky, 'The Legal Character of the Paris Agreement' (2016) *RECIEL* 142.

46 https://www.burgemeestersconvenant.be/.

47 *R (Friends of the Earth Ltd and Others)*, above n. 15.

the Court of Appeal's decision, ruling that the government's statement had been produced lawfully. Yet, in spite of the dismissal, the decision of the UK Supreme Court still indirectly acknowledged the importance of taking climate considerations into account when adopting policy statements. In particular, the UK Supreme Court found that the Secretary of State for Transport had adequately taken into account the Paris Agreement on climate change and had given weight to its obligations to the extent that they were covered by the existing Climate Change Act 2008. The Court gave appreciation to the fact that he had followed the advice of the independent Climate Change Committee.[48]

The relevance of regional planning law in climate-based litigation also becomes visible when comparing the preliminary decision of April 2021 of the Flemish Council of Permit Disputes with the final outcome of the case, in the annulment decision of December 2021. In an initial assessment of the decision of April 2021, I already hinted at the large potential of using the more general integration clause, enshrined in Article 1.1.4 of the Flemish Planning Code, which explicitly targets sustainable spatial development, in the context of climate change policies. To be more precise, the latter provision explicitly mandates competent planning authorities to integrate environmental considerations into spatial decisions and also pays explicit attention to intergenerational solidarity. In particular, the provision stipulated that the needs of future generations cannot be compromised by decisions regarding spatial plans and projects.[49] This stands out as an attractive lever for future climate change litigation.

Before delving into the relevance of Article 1.1.4 of the Flemish Planning Code for a more comprehensive integration of climate considerations into planning and permit decision-making procedures in Flanders, let us first recall that the application of the above-mentioned Article 4.3.4 of the Flemish Planning Code merely amounts to an optional climate integration clause. Only when the advice of a competent administration points to the incompatibility of a project with a due diligence obligation or objective from another sectoral (environmental) policy, such as climate mitigation or adaptation, can the permitting authority refuse the permit.[50] Thus, the jurisprudence of the Flemish Council of Permit Disputes does not amount to a mandatory climate integration clause; it simply states that climate considerations can be used as an argument to assess the lawfulness of a permit application.[51] As of today, the case law also fails to provide further clues on the objective criteria to be used in this regard. For instance, how should we determine the substantive and territorial scope of the climate impacts that need to be considered? Should the focus merely be on impacts related to land use changes? And should additional CO_2 emissions necessarily lead to the refusal of a permit?

48 *R (Friends of the Earth Ltd and Others)*, above n. 16.
49 L. De Brucker, above n. 27; H. Schoukens, above n. 27, pp. 355–56.
50 Ibid.
51 Ibid.

Be that as it may, it no longer appears unlikely that sooner or later a more mandatory climate test will emerge in the case law. Article 4.3.3 of the Flemish Planning Code, according to which permitting authorities are compelled to refuse a permit application that directly clashes with other directly applicable norms in other sectoral domains, is a more likely contender in this regard. However, its relevance as a lever for a strict 'climate test' (*klimaattoets*) appears limited for now. In order to qualify as a 'directly applicable sectoral norm' (*direct werkende norm*), a norm needs to be sufficiently concrete and precise. In addition, one needs to be able to establish that there is no immediate need for additional implementing measures. As of today, Article 6(3) of the EU Habitats Directive, for instance, which requires permitting authorities to refuse permit applications that might compromise the ecological integrity of so-called Natura 2000 sites, qualifies as such pursuant to the case law of the Flemish Council of Permit Disputes.[52] This means that whenever the Flemish Nature Conservation Agency is of the opinion that a project clashes with the conservation objectives of a Natura 2000 site, the competent authority must deny the permit application.[53] Would such a rationale also be applicable for climate change? The prospect might be promising for climate activists. Unlike Article 4.3.4, Article 4.3.3 of the Flemish Planning Code does not amount to merely optional integration. On the contrary, it includes a *binding* integration clause. As of today, though, it remains unlikely that the Council of Permit Disputes would state that the Covenant of Mayors amounts to a directly applicable norm any time soon. However, it cannot be completely ruled out that existing or future EU greenhouse gas reduction targets will sooner or later be qualified as such, as they are binding as Union law in themselves. As the relatively open concepts that are used in Article 6(3) of the EU Habitats Directive do not hinder the latter provisions from being tagged as 'directly applicable norms', it does not appear to be completely beyond the realms of possibility to qualify EU climate targets as such. But for now, case law has not yet reached that conclusion.

This detour brings us back to the starting point of this subsection. As mentioned above, Article 1.1.4 of the Flemish Planning Code was used by the Flemish Council of Permit Disputes as an additional backbone for the optional climate test that emerged in the decision of 9 December 2021. While this was not a remarkable move in itself, the question arises whether the reliance on this provision might also hint towards a binding climate test in a planning context in the future. As of today, the legal relevance of Article 1.1.4 of the Flemish Planning Code in permitting procedures appears relatively limited. This is not a major surprise, as the provision is premised on the concept of sustainable development, which is a notoriously broad and unclear term in itself.[54]

---

52 *nv Flanders Field Business Park* (2018) no. A/1819/0335.

53 H. Schoukens, above n. 31, p. 349.

54 J. Verschuuren, 'The Principle of Sustainable Development as a Legal Norm' in D. Fisher (ed.), *Research Handbook on Fundamental Concepts of Environmental Law* (Edward Elgar, 2016), p. 276.

We can thus posit that the protection of future generations constitutes a relatively vague norm and concept to be used as a binding benchmark for concrete project applications such as the Flemish petrol station case. The approval of one specific permit application, for instance for a petrol station, would in itself not jeopardise the rights of future generations to a healthy climate. At least, it would not always be an easy claim to substantiate. However, the accumulation of several unsustainable lock-ins might further limit the chances of a transition to a carbon-neutral society. Such a regressive permitting policy would mean that future generations would face tougher restrictions of the enjoyment of their human rights (particularly their liberties). This rationale, among others, partially prevailed in the recent decision of the German Constitutional Court in *Neubauer*, although the latter refused to accord subjective rights to future generations.[55] Since every State has a finite amount of greenhouse gas emissions that it can emit over the years – the so-called carbon budget – a refusal to block fossil-dependent projects *now* at least implies that future populations will have to meet their needs with a smaller portion of the budget. In spite of the aforementioned drawbacks, a relatively open sustainability clause in national or regional planning law might provide a useful and possibly binding benchmark in this regard at the level of the permitting procedures.

As of today, it remains uncertain whether jurisprudence in Belgium, and in particular in Flanders, will move in this arguably more intergenerational direction. Article 1.1.4 of the Flemish Planning Code, which stands out as the most interesting integration clause, has seldom been used by the administrative courts to quash planning decisions and permits, precisely because of the leeway it grants to the planning authorities.[56] Only cases where the balancing of interests has been carried out in a manifestly erroneous manner are sanctioned.[57] Recent jurisprudence still seems to opt for a more deferential approach, whereby only manifestly absurd or capricious motivations are likely to be sanctioned in a subsequent judicial review.[58] Moreover, the exact determination of a climate integration clause is likely to give rise to a plethora of questions. Should a certain threshold be applied, since in theory almost every planning decision can, at least indirectly, somehow contribute to climate change? And what about the consequences of a potential negative outcome of a climate test?

That said, Article 1.1.4 of the Flemish Planning Code might still serve as a useful lever in cases where planning decisions are taken with respect to activities which are directly or indirectly generating significant CO_2 emissions and are therefore impacting the remaining carbon budget that is available

55 *Neubauer*, above n. 9.

56 See for instance *Anné et al. v. Vlaams Gewest* (2019) no. 244.963.

57 See for instance *nv Holvoet Bouwmaterialen v. gemeente Avelgem* (2010) no. 209.558.

58 H. Schoukens, above n. 31, pp. 348–49.

for future generations. In such a context, it could be maintained that climate considerations should at least serve as an explicit consideration in a broader balancing exercise that applies when authorising such projects. Merely leaving them unaddressed or unmentioned would evidently constitute a manifest infringement on the sustainability principle enshrined in Article 1.1.4. Of course, such a jurisprudential move would not yet amount to a strict climate test, since the planning authority might still conclude that other, more pressing public interests might outweigh the climate-related impacts. Yet, in light of the ongoing case law developments in recent years, this would certainly require the competent authority to come forward with adequate motivation.[59] In this respect, the rationale present in the landmark ruling of the Land and Environment Court of New South Wales in *Gloucester Resources v. Minister for Planning* sets a new standard. As stated above, the Australian court ultimately ruled that the negative impacts of an open-cut mine project, which also included climate impacts, outweighed the economic and other public benefits of the projects.[60] However, in order to reach such an outcome before an administrative court in Belgium, more appears to be needed than a legal claim that is exclusively based on Article 1.1.4 of the Flemish Planning Code.

3.3. LINKING PROJECT REVIEW TO THE GENERAL CLIMATE LIABILITY OF AUTHORITIES?

So what other climate-related arguments are present in the recent jurisprudence in Belgium? In its annulment decision of 9 December 2021, the Flemish Council of Permit Disputes also explicitly referred to the alleged climate liability of local authorities. In this respect, it should be noted that on 17 June 2021, the Brussels Court of First Instance ruled in *Klimaatzaak* that the Belgian State and the three Belgian Regions had breached their duty of care towards the climate by failing to take necessary measures to prevent the harmful effects of climate change, but declined to set specific reduction targets on separation of powers grounds (*trias politica*). Amongst other things, the Court found the competent authorities jointly and individually in breach of their duty of care (*zorgplicht*) for failing to enact adequate climate governance. It based its decision on the civil law liability of public authorities (*overheidsaansprakelijkheid*). Furthermore, by failing to take sufficient climate action to protect the life and privacy of the plaintiffs, the defendants were also found in breach of their obligations under Articles 2 and 8 of the European Convention on Human Rights.[61] In sharp contrast with

59 L. De Brucker, above n. 27.

60 *Gloucester Resources Limited*, above n. 14.

61 *Klimaatzaak*, above n. 20.

the *Urgenda* jurisprudence,[62] however, the Belgian Court declined to issue an injunction ordering the government to set the specific emission reduction targets requested by the plaintiffs. Although the Council did not explicitly cite the ruling of the Brussels Court of First Instance in *Klimaatzaak*, the recent move indirectly aligns itself with the recent jurisprudential evolution regarding the climate liability of national and regional authorities.[63]

Obviously, a further appraisal of the legal soundness of the rather ambivalent outcome of *Klimaatzaak* falls outside the scope of this chapter. Even so, it is nevertheless relevant to highlight the fact that the acceptance in principle of the climate liability of the federal entities might also have inspired the Flemish Council of Permit Disputes in further developing its underpinning of the optional climate test in its recent decisions. As previously mentioned, the Council stated that the climate commitments of the local municipality, which were included in the Covenant of Mayors, are not merely voluntary since 'it cannot be ruled out that the municipality will be sued in court for its failure to abide by its duty of diligence towards the climate'. Even human rights duties might come into play here, as they were already used as a benchmark by the Brussels Court of First Instance in *Klimaatzaak*, albeit in the specific context of the climate liability of regional and federal entities. Whereas the ruling of the Brussels Court of First Instance did not explicitly expand the duty of care towards the climate to local municipalities – since they were not summoned in the proceedings – the Flemish Council of Permit Disputes proved to be innovative by also making a link between the general due diligence obligations of authorities towards a further integration of climate considerations at project level.

One might be inclined to state that, since local municipalities have fewer direct and comprehensive competences in the field of climate change, the rationale of recent jurisprudence on the climate liability of States, and regional authorities, is less applicable in the context of local-based climate lawsuits. Even so, replicating the *Urgenda* rationale used by the Dutch Supreme Court regarding the national responsibility of the Netherlands in the global challenge of climate change,[64] it can indeed be maintained that decisions of local municipalities also contribute to climate change and thus cannot simply turn away from climate change-related arguments in their permitting policies. For instance, land use conversion and deforestation, which both contribute to climate change, fall squarely within the competence of local municipalities in the Flemish Region. The decisions they take in this regard might affect the regional (Flemish) and Belgian carbon budget, even if the activity in itself is limited in scale.

62 *Urgenda*, above n. 8.
63 H. Schoukens, above n. 31, p. 350.
64 *Urgenda*, above n. 8.

3.4. EIA DUTIES REMAIN UNEXPLORED TERRITORY FOR CLIMATE MITIGATION AND ADAPTATION?

A topic that remained somewhat underexplored in the Flemish petrol station case is the question of the extent to which climate change-related impacts of project developments need to be taken into account in the environmental impact assessment that precedes such decision-making procedures. Since the 2014 modification[65] of the EU Environmental Impact Assessment (EIA) Directive,[66] in which it was explicitly recognised that '[c]limate change will continue to cause damage to the environment and compromise economic development', the principal discussion has now become moot. Recital 7 and Article 3 of the amended EIA Directive have clarified this. It is now clear that, prior to the granting of a planning permit, an assessment of the impact of proposed projects on the climate (for example greenhouse gas emissions) and their vulnerability to climate change should be included in the EIA.[67] Both mitigation and adaptation should be considered. Even so, relatively limited case law exists in the European Union that explicitly touches on this topic. A decision of 1 April 2021 of the Administrative Court of Marseille, in which it partially quashed Total's permit to operate a biorefinery in France and directed the company to study the climate impacts of imported palm oil, presents a notable exception. The French court ruled that the permit was based on insufficient information about climate impacts and ordered a new EIA that should address both the direct and indirect environmental effects of the biorefinery project.[68]

However, other recent cases have led to a different outcome. For instance, in the aforementioned Norwegian climate case, the Norwegian Supreme Court ultimately declined to discern a legal duty on behalf of the Norwegian government to carry out an EIA which also encompasses foreign consumption of oil.[69] In a 2022 decision of the Irish Supreme Court, a more conservative approach was also opted for. In this case, the Irish Supreme Court had to assess whether an EIA had to address the upstream consequences of the operation of a proposed cheese factory and, specifically, the milk that is necessary to supply this factory. It was argued, among other things, that the large quantities of milk that were required could only be supplied through an expansion of the national herd, which in turn would lead to additional greenhouse gas emissions. The

65 Directive 2014/52/EU of the European Parliament and of the Council of 16 April 2014 amending Directive 2011/92/EU on the assessment of the effects of certain public and private projects on the environment [2014] OJ L 124/1.

66 Directive 2011/92/EU of the European Parliament and of the Council of 13 December 2011 on the assessment of the effects of certain public and private projects on the environment [2011] OJ L 26/1.

67 Recital 13 to Directive 2014/52/EU.

68 *Association Les Amis de la Terre France* (2021) no. 180.5238.

69 *Greenpeace Nordic and Others*, above n. 17.

Irish Supreme Court accepted that the EIA Directive was designed to assist in identifying and assessing both the *direct* and *indirect* environmental effects of a specific project, including (post-2014) the climate change effects. Even so, it drew a line when stating that the 'scope of the EIA Directive should not be artificially expanded beyond this remit and, in particular, it should not, so to speak, be conscripted into the general fight against climate change by being made to do the work of other legislative measures'.[70] Ultimately, the Irish Supreme Court ruled that the indirect (upstream) environmental effects did not fall within the realm of the EIA but rather should be taken up by programmatic measures at national level.[71]

Even though EIA duties seem to present a natural lever for climate lawsuits focusing on fossil fuel projects, several caveats thus remain. Most importantly, there is the persistent confusion regarding the exact scope of the climate impacts that should be covered by an EIA. In this respect, it is essential to understand the difference between Scope 1, 2 and 3 emissions. Scope 1 emissions are direct greenhouse emissions that occur from sources that are controlled or owned by an organisation. Scope 2 emissions are indirect emissions associated with the purchase of electricity, steam, heat or cooling. Scope 3 emissions are indirect greenhouse gas emissions, both upstream and downstream, that are generated by suppliers and customers. In the absence of any ruling of the Court of Justice of the EU, it still remains uncertain whether Scope 3 emissions are also to be assessed in the context of an EIA. The limited case law at national level, briefly sketched above, seems to go in opposite directions.

In this respect, it needs to be reiterated that in non-European contexts, such as Australia and the United States, the default position appears to be that EIAs also cover downstream Scope 3 emissions. Such was the rationale used in the aforementioned 2019 decision in *Gloucester Resources v. Minister for Planning* in Australia.[72] Likewise, several courts in the United States have already ruled, in the context of fuel extraction leasing, that environmental assessments also have to address the leases' cumulative impacts, including the downstream emissions.[73]

In order to further objectivise future climate integration mandates, a further understanding of the interlinkages between EIAs and climate change remains crucial. In this regard, it is also vital to understand that an EIA in itself is but an informative, procedural tool. Even if the outcome of the EIA points to a negative impact on the climate, an authority could theoretically still decide to authorise the activity. However, recent case law developments in Belgium reveal that in order to do so, adequate motivation needs to be put in place, which somewhat

70 *An Aisce – The National Trust for Ireland v. An Bord Pleanala* [2022] IESC 8.

71 Ibid.

72 See *Gloucester Resources Limited*, above n. 14.

73 See for instance *WildEarth Guardians v. U.S. Bureau of Land Management*, 457 F. Supp. 3d 880 (2020).

limits the remaining discretion.[74] With respect to small-scale interventions, the global nature of climate change and the drop-in-the-ocean argument might often be invoked as counter-arguments. And sometimes such claims might prevail. Yet in some recent landmark rulings, such as *Urgenda*[75] and *Gloucester Resources Limited v. Minister of Planning*,[76] this line of argumentation has now been vehemently dismissed. In spite of the global nature of climate change, all greenhouse gas emissions contribute to climate change, even when they are limited in scope, some judges reason. And, most importantly, future unsustainable lock-ins might further compromise the shrinking carbon budgets of the regional or even local authorities.

4. CONCLUSION

Against the backdrop of the large gap that currently exists between the climate pledges of national and regional authorities and the actual overall reduction results, the relevance of climate litigation focusing on concrete permitting procedures will only increase. Whereas the first wave of landmark climate rulings in Europe mainly consisted of claims targeting the general failure of States to come forward with a climate mitigation framework that is in line with the recent scientific climate reports, courts are increasingly faced with challenges that focus on fossil-based projects that often give rise to unsustainable lock-ins. For a considerable amount of time, such court actions remained outside the scope of many NGOs in Europe, including in Belgium. By addressing the Flemish petrol case jurisprudence, this chapter has revealed the many challenges that arise when advocating a more binding integration of climate targets into concrete planning and permitting policies. At first sight, the outcome of the Flemish case appears to be self-evident: the decision merely reasserts the fact that climate considerations can serve as an *optional* benchmark when reviewing permit applications in the Flemish Region.

A second, more in-depth reading, however, revealed that the legal grounds used to reach such a conclusion were relatively unprecedented against the backdrop of the existing rationale in the Flemish permitting policies. No-one had expected that the non-binding Covenant of Mayors could have served as a lever for a more comprehensive integration of climate considerations into permitting procedures at the local level. Whereas the use of the Covenant as a benchmark in permitting procedures will continue to be challenged in the years to come in the Flemish Region, this chapter has equally demonstrated that a

74 H. Schoukens, above n. 39, p. 355.
75 *Urgenda*, above n. 8.
76 *Gloucester Resources Limited*, above n. 14.

combination of several legal norms, such as national planning law, EIA duties and even human rights, function as a promising legal cocktail for the advocates of a further integration of climate targets into environmental permitting and review procedures – in Flanders, Belgium and beyond. Against this backdrop, permit applications for fossil-dependent projects will probably face an uphill legal battle in Europe in the years to come. How steep the climb will be will depend on the answers to the many thorny legal questions that still have to be addressed in this context. To be continued.

COLLECTIVE REDRESS AND CLIMATE CHANGE LITIGATION IN THE EU

A Promising Future or More of the Same?

Rhonson SALIM

1. INTRODUCTION

The nature of greenhouse gas (GHG) emissions poses unique challenges for the conduct of climate change litigation. Arguably, GHG emissions result in harms affecting two types of interests. They affect the personal interests of a large number of individuals (divisible interests) as well as a collective good of a society (indivisible/diffused interest). Given these challenges, collective redress procedures[1] offer procedural flexibility to cater for the nature of the interests involved whilst promoting efficiency in climate litigation. Such procedures achieve two objectives – they facilitate access to justice for claimants who would not normally seek such justice, and they assist in the enforcement of the law in a legal system.[2]

---

1 Collective redress procedures are mechanisms which provide injunctive and/or compensatory relief for harm affecting a large group of persons.

2 A. LAYTON, 'Collective Redress: Policy Objectives and Practical Problems' in D. FAIRGRIEVE and E. LEIN, *Extraterritoriality and Collective Redress* (Oxford University Press 2012), para. 5.03.

However, the collective redress procedural landscape within the EU is not uniform across EU Member States. In particular, the architecture of collective redress procedures is diverse. Arguably, this state of procedural and conceptual fragmentation leads to uneven protection and challenges effective access to justice, particularly for GHG harms.

This chapter contends that in light of procedural reforms necessitated by Directive 2020/1828 for consumers,[3] Member States are presented with an opportunity to enact domestic procedural changes to effectively enable representative organisations[4] to better act in claims relating to climate change. The chapter argues that the Directive's approach to standing, information provision and 'redress'[5] remedies could, if transposed to the environmental sphere, enhance access to justice for climate change victims. In particular, the chapter advances an argument that effective climate change litigation for individuals can be facilitated by the empowerment of representative organisations to bring injunctive and monetary claims for the protection of divisible interests.[6] In advancing this contention, the chapter firsts sets the scene by considering the reasoning deployed, and use of the Dutch collective redress procedure, in two ground-breaking climate change cases: *Urgenda*[7] and *Milieudefensie et al.*[8] (section 2). Second, given the central importance of the concept of access to justice in the environmental sector, the chapter considers the relevance of collective redress procedures to removing or reducing some of the barriers to access to justice (section 3). Third, the chapter considers the operation of a new EU collective redress procedure in the consumer sector (section 4) and how some of the key principles of such a procedure can be usefully transposed to the environmental sector for climate change claims (section 5). Arguably, such a transposition is needed to create policy and procedural symmetry within Member States and to offer a more comprehensive response to the modern litigation and redress challenges prompted by climate change. Finally, to assist in the translation of

[3] Directive (EU) 2020/1828 of 25 November 2020 on representative actions for the protection of collective interests of consumers and repealing Directive 2009/22/EC [2020] OJ L 409/1.

[4] See section 5 below for definition of representative organisations. Representative organisations can include NGOs.

[5] Redress is defined expansively in Directive 2020/1828 and includes measures such as 'compensation, repair, replacement' (Art. 9(1). For the purposes of this chapter's discussion of climate litigation, redress is defined as referring to compensatory remedies only, e.g. damages.

[6] Where representative organisations are not currently able to bring compensatory claims for the protection of indivisible interests, this should also be revisited in light of the argument for opening up the entitlement for such organisations to act in divisible interests claims. This chapter focuses on procedural matters relating to collective redress. A discussion of substantive law (e.g. causation) is not included in the chapter's scope.

[7] ECLI:NL:HR:2019:2007.

[8] ECLI:NL:RBDHA:2021:5339.

the argument into practice, the chapter considers the main collective redress procedure in Poland[9] and suggests some procedural developments which could address some of the challenges in enabling representative organisations to bring climate change-related claims in that State (sections 6 and 7).

2. COLLECTIVE REDRESS AND CLIMATE CHANGE: THE NETHERLANDS

The *Urgenda* and *Milieudefensie et al.* cases demonstrate the benefit of using collective redress procedures as vehicles for climate change claims. In both cases, Article 3:305a (old) of the Dutch Civil Code (DCC) (collective action) was utilised. This provision is an example of a horizontal collective redress mechanism which applies across all areas of Dutch civil law and one that does not have a numerosity requirement. Of note are the procedure's rules on standing, which enable organisations with similar interests to persons to have standing to bring claims, subject to safeguards.[10] Given the procedure's horizontal scope and the liberal interpretation of its admissibility and standing requirements, it has proven procedurally flexible to enable both indivisible and divisible interest claims.[11]

Both *Urgenda* and *Milieudefensie* are examples of indivisible interest actions.[12] In *Milieudefensie*, the District Court took the view that Greenpeace NL, Fossielvrij NL, Waddenvereniging and Young Friends of the Earth NL

[9] Poland emits the fifth-largest volume of GHG gases in the EU and thus consideration of its collective redress procedures is apt due to the potential for GHG-related litigation. See https://www.europarl.europa.eu/news/en/headlines/priorities/climate-change/20180301STO98928/greenhouse-gas-emissions-by-country-and-sector-infographic.

[10] E.g. provided that the organisation advances those interests in accordance with its articles of association.

[11] Examples of divisible interest cases include financial market cases. See e.g. HR 13 October 2006, ECLI:NL:HR:2006:AW2080 (*Vie d'Or*) and HR 11 November 2009, ECLI:NL:HR:2009:BH2162 (*VEB/World Online*). The Dutch legislator envisaged this applicability of the procedure to the two different interests. 'The interests that are suitable for a grouping in a class action may be financial interests, but also more idealistic interests. A class action may protect interests that directly affect people, or that people want to advocate out of a particular conviction. In the case of idealistic interests, it is irrelevant whether each member of society attaches the same value to these interests. … It does not have to concern the interests of a clearly defined group of others. It may also concern the interests of an indeterminable, very large group of individuals' (Parliamentary Papers II, 1991/92, 22 486, no. 3, p. 22).

[12] Milieudefensie argued that Shell acted unlawfully *towards* Milieudefensie et al. (section 3 of the judgment) rather than towards the persons that Milieudefensie represented. The Court took the view that Milieudefensie's claims 'are public interest actions. Such actions seek to protect public interests, which cannot be individualized because they accrue to a much larger group of persons, which is undefined and unspecified. The common interest of preventing dangerous climate change by reducing CO2 emissions can be protected in a class action' (para. 4.2.2).

had standing because the public interest served in the claims aligned with the objectives stated in their articles of association.[13] The Court found that the interest of current and future generations of Dutch residents and of the inhabitants of the Wadden Sea area were suitable for bundling and, therefore, fulfilled the 'similar interest' requirement of Article 3:305a (old) of the DCC.[14] More importantly, the District Court denied standing to individual claimants on the basis that they lacked 'a sufficiently concrete individual interest',[15] because their interests were already 'served by the class action and they did not present independent interests'.[16] Specifically, their interest was *the same* as the common interest which the actions sought to protect.[17]

A similar reasoning was also deployed by the District Court in *Urgenda*, where the Court rejected the claim that was instituted on behalf of 886 claimants but allowed the claim brought by Urgenda on its own behalf to proceed.[18] Unfortunately, the clarity of the reasoning for standing was slightly muddied in subsequent appeals. The Supreme Court took the view that Urgenda represented the interests of the residents[19] of the Netherlands, and since these residents can rely on Articles 2 and 8 of the European Convention on Human Rights (ECHR),[20] Urgenda may also do so *on behalf of* these individuals.[21] In light of the nature of the indivisible interest that Urgenda sought to protect, specifically protection against actions that may lead to 'serious threats to ecosystems and human societies',[22] the District Court's reasoning is a more convincing explanation for Urgenda's standing. The Supreme Court's approach is more apt where divisible interests are concerned, as such interests are individualised in nature.

Nonetheless, it is noteworthy that the District Court in *Urgenda* left open the question as to whether individual residents could have standing to bring climate change-related claims. Cox argues that 'the court seems to hint that if Urgenda's own claim would not have been awarded, the individual citizens might have

13 Para. 4.2.5. The Court rejected claims by one entity, ActionAid as it did 'not promote the interests of Dutch residents sufficiently for its collective claim to be allowable'.

14 Para. 4.2.4.

15 Para. 4.2.7.

16 Ibid.

17 Ibid.

18 The Court argued: 'Even if it is assumed that the individual claimants can rely on articles 2 and 8 of the ECHR, their claims cannot lead to a decision other than the one on which Urgenda can rely for itself. In this situation, the court finds that the individual claimants do not have sufficient (own) interests besides Urgenda's interest. Partly in view of practical grounds, this has led the court to reject the claim insofar as it has been instituted on behalf of the [individual] claimants' (para. 4.109). See also para. 4.9.

19 See paras 5.9.2–5.9.3. See also para. 5.6.2.

20 The Supreme Court reaffirmed the view that the protection afforded under Arts 2 and 8 ECHR applies to both indivisible and divisible interests (para. 5.3.1).

21 The same view was taken by the Court of Appeal (para. 36).

22 Para. 4.8.

had sufficient interest and therefore standing'.[23] The recognition that individual claimants may themselves have standing leaves open the possibility that such claimants may use special purpose vehicles/non-governmental organisations to group and advance these individualised claims. That said, the District Court's approach seems to create a hierarchy of protection of interests in climate change claims in the Netherlands – claims are first to be brought to protect the indivisible interest before the courts will countenance claims for the protection of divisible interests.

Overall, the *Urgenda* and *Milieudefensie* cases demonstrate that the Dutch collective action mechanism has been at the forefront in the advancement of climate change litigation claims in the EU. However, the new version of Article 3:305a Wet afwikkeling massaschade in collectieve actie (WAMCA) applies to claims instituted after 1 January 2020,[24] and will pose a unique challenge to the commencement of future climate change claims in the Netherlands. On the one hand, it extends the remedial armoury under the collective action to allow for a claim for damages. On the other hand, it introduces stricter standing and admissibility requirements for claim organisations which may preclude further environmental (or similar types) of claims.

It is not a given that the procedural opportunities offered by Article 3:305a (old or new) can be extrapolated to all EU Member States due to the diversity of the architectures available in Member States for collective proceedings. Indeed, as the European Commission noted in its report on the implementation of its Recommendation on Collective Redress,[25] the Netherlands is one of only five Member States that adopts a horizontal framework which allows for collective compensation proceedings across all areas.[26]

---

23 R. Cox, 'A Climate Change Litigation Precedent. Urgenda Foundation v The State of the Netherlands', CIGI Papers No. 79 (2015), p. 5. Cox takes this view based on the Court's comment that 'the possibility of damages for those whose interests Urgenda represents, including current and future generations of Dutch nationals, is so great and concrete that given its duty of care, the State must make an adequate contribution' (para. 2.89).

24 WAMCA is not applicable to claims instituted after 1 January 2020 where the events giving rise to the damage concerned occurred prior to 15 November 2016.

25 See European Commission, 'Commission Recommendation of 11 June 2013 on common principles for injunctive and compensatory collective redress mechanisms in the Member States concerning violations of rights granted under Union law' [2013] OJ L 201/60. The Recommendation was accompanied by a Communication on collective redress mechanisms in Member States, which outlined the Commission's position on a range of key issues.

26 European Commission, 'Report from the Commission to the European Parliament, the Council and the European Economic and Social Committee on the implementation of the Commission Recommendation of 11 June 2013 on common principles for injunctive and compensatory collective redress mechanisms in the Member States concerning violations of rights granted under Union law (2013/396/EU)', COM(2018) 40 final. The other countries are: Bulgaria, Denmark, Lithuania and Portugal. The UK is included in this list but is no longer a Member State at the date of this publication.

3. ACCESS TO JUSTICE AND COLLECTIVE REDRESS

As indicated in the preceding section, a variety of collective redress mechanisms exists across Member States. This procedural variation means that access to a legal system differs between Member States. Thus, the question arises as to whether access to justice can be advanced by using such procedures for climate change claims. The meaning of access to justice has generated much debate,[27] with some commenting that the term suffers from 'a bad case of semantic overload'[28] in the way it is framed.

In its simplest form, access to justice can be expressed as 'the single unifying idea that, where the law in one form or another has declared rights and corresponding duties to exist, the persons to whom those rights and duties apply may expect them to be upheld and where necessary to seek their enforcement in a court'.[29] Wrbka et al. argued that access to justice is about providing persons with '*the chance* to enjoy the protection and enforcement of [their] rights by the use of law and the legal system' (emphasis added).[30] Viewed in this manner, access to justice is intrinsic to social justice,[31] and the promotion and achievement of social inclusion for individuals in the justice system.[32]

In practice, access to justice is given effect through the removal of, or provision of an ability to overcome, barriers to effective vindication of a right.[33] These barriers are of various types (e.g. legal, economic) and involve questions relating to cost of litigation, delays in dispute process and procedural complexity.[34] The need to remove barriers is also supplemented by the view that access to justice, in the environmental sector, entails an appreciation of the public interests that are involved in some types of claims.[35]

---

27 See R. Macdonald, 'Access to justice in Canada today: scope, scale and ambitions' and J. Bass, W. Bogart and F. Zemans, 'Introduction' in J. Bass, W. Bogart and F. Zemans (eds), *Access to Justice for a New Century: The Way Forward* (Law Society of Upper Canada 2005).

28 See J. Grossman and A. Sarat, 'Access to justice and the limits of law' in R. Gambatta, M. May and J. Foster (eds), *Governing Through Courts* (Sage 1981), p. 81.

29 The Rt Hon. Lord Mackay of Clashfern, 'Access to Justice', Consumers' Association Lecture, 27 July 1992, p. 22.

30 S. Wrbka et al. (eds), *Collective Actions: Enhancing Access to Justice and Reconciling Multilayer Interests* (Cambridge University Press 2012), p. 2.

31 M. Cappelletti and B. Garth, 'Access to Justice: The Newest Wave in the Worldwide Movement to Make Rights Effective' (1978) 27 *Buffalo Law Review* 181. See also J. Bass, W. Bogart and F. Zemans (eds), 'Introduction' in *Access to Justice for a New Century: The Way Forward* (Law Society of Upper Canada 2005), p. 3.

32 E. Hurter, 'Access to Justice: to dream the impossible dream?' (2011) 44(3) *The Comparative and International Law Journal of Southern Africa* 408.

33 M. Cappelletti and B. Garth (n. 31).

34 Ibid.

35 European Commission, 'Commission Notice on access to justice in environmental matters' (2017/C 275/01), para. 3.

It is here that well-designed collective redress mechanisms can mitigate or remove some of the known barriers to access to justice. These mechanisms can be designed to cater for the public interest nature of claims (e.g. through rules on standing). In divisible interests claims, the value of the interests involved may be low and this challenges the achievement of effective enforcement.[36] In this regard, collective redress mechanisms 'can level the playing field and help tackle the problems of litigation costs, under-compensation and under-regulation'.[37]

Legislative measures on access to justice in environmental matters are highly fragmented across the EU,[38] leaving the Court of Justice of the European Union (CJEU) with the burden of clarifying EU requirements on access to justice.[39] In light of CJEU case law, national courts are required to proactively interpret domestic law to give effect, in the fullest extent possible, to the objectives laid down in the Aarhus Convention.[40] Given this status quo, is there room for Member States to adopt, and adapt, collective redress architectures from other sectors so as to better enable access to justice in environmental matters, and to better enable climate change claims?

4. CHANGES TO CONSUMER COLLECTIVE REDRESS AFTER DIRECTIVE 2020/1828: REPRESENTATIVE ACTIONS, STANDING AND REMEDIES

Consumer collective redress has been a key element of EU policy for a number of years. However, the focus on consumer collective redress has increasingly come to the fore in light of mass harm incidents such as the Dieselgate scandal. With ongoing concerns regarding consumer protection, the Representative Actions Directive 2020/1828/EC (the Directive) was adopted in November 2020[41] as part of the Commission's New Deal for Consumers initiative.[42]

---

36 See C. Meller-Hannich, 'Sammelklagen, Gruppenklagen, Verbandsklagen – Bedarf es neuer Instrumente des kollektiven Rechtsschutzes im Zivilprozess?' (2018) *Ergebnisse der Legal Research Group zum 72. Deutschen Juristentag*, A3, 24, who identifies 'rational disinterest' for this occurrence.

37 R. Michaels, 'European Class Actions and Applicable Law' in A. Nuyts and N. Hatzimihail (eds), *Cross-Border Class Actions: The European Way?* (Sellier 2013), pp. 117–18.

38 http://ec.europa.eu/environment/aarhus/studies.htm; Commission Notice (n. 35), para. 7.

39 Commission Notice (n. 35), para. 7.

40 See Case C-240/09, *LZ I*, ECLI:EU:C:2011:125, para. 50.

41 The Directive is subject to a transposition delay and Member States are required to adopt and publish legislation necessary to comply with the Directive by 25 December 2022. Such legislation should apply in domestic systems from 25 June 2023 (Art. 24(1)).

42 See https://ec.europa.eu/info/law/law-topic/consumer-protection-law/review-eu-consumer-law_en.

The Directive applies to representative actions brought against a 'trader' for infringements of provisions of EU law harming 'the collective interests of consumers'.[43]

Under the Directive, a 'representative action' is defined as an action for the protection of the collective interests of consumers that is brought by a qualified entity on behalf of consumers and which seeks an injunctive or a redress remedy.[44] In such an action, the qualified entity is the claimant in the proceedings,[45] and consumers should not be able to 'interfere with the procedural decisions taken by the qualified entities, to individually request evidence within the proceedings or to individually appeal the procedural decisions of the court or administrative authority before which the representative action is brought'.[46]

The Directive defines redress measures as 'compensation, repair, replacement, price reduction, contract termination or reimbursement of the price paid'.[47] In support of the availability of redress, Member States are required to enable consumers to benefit from a redress measure in a representative action without the need to bring a separate individual action.[48]

Two forms of representative action are created under the Directive: domestic and cross-border.[49] For domestic actions, Member States retain a large degree of procedural autonomy to decide the eligibility criteria for qualified entities. However, such domestic criteria must be consistent with the objectives of the Directive.[50] For cross-border representative actions, the Directive enables mutual recognition of qualified entities and sets down criteria for standing for a foreign qualified entity to bring an action.[51] Furthermore, in line with the Directive's drive to grant procedural autonomy to Member States, States are free to choose either an opt-in or opt-out mechanism (or a combination of the two).[52] However, the Directive effectively makes the choice dependent upon whether the remedy is

43 Art. 2(1). The collective interests of consumers are defined as 'the general interest of consumers and, in particular for the purposes of redress measures, the interests of a group of consumers' (Art. 3(3)).

44 Arts 3(5) and 7(4). See also I. Tzankova, 'Collective and mass litigation in Europe: Model rules for effective dispute resolution' in A. Stadler, E. Jeuland and V. Smith (eds), *Collective and Mass Litigation in Europe* (Edward Elgar Publishing 2020) for further discussion on standing rules in collective redress.

45 Art. 7(6).

46 Recital 36.

47 Arts 3(10) and 9(1).

48 Art. 9(6).

49 A cross-border action is characterised as being one where the representative action is brought by a qualified entity in a Member State other than that in which the qualified entity is designated (see Art. 3(7)).

50 Art. 4(4).

51 Art. 6(1). Art 4(3) lists the criteria for foreign qualified entities. The criteria include requirements on conflict of interest, not-for-profit character and duration of existence.

52 Recital 43.

injunctive or redress. In injunctive cases, an opt-out approach is adopted.[53] As for redress measures, such as a claim for damages, an opt-in mechanism is required.[54]

Mindful of the vulnerability of consumers, as well as the need for consumer autonomy to be respected, the Directive imposes information provision obligations[55] on both qualified entities and traders. Consumers are to be informed about a representative action, as this is seen to be an essential element for consumers to have informed consent.[56] For ongoing claims, qualified entities bear the brunt of the burden for providing information, whilst traders are required to provide information on successful final decisions or settlements. Overall, whilst not fully revolutionary, the Directive has gone some way to removing legal and economic barriers for claimants. The following section considers the possibilities for climate change litigation should a similar model be used for climate change claims.

5. PROCEDURAL REFORMS AND POSSIBILITIES FOR CLIMATE CHANGE LITIGATION

In light of the need to introduce a Directive-compliant representative action for consumer claims, EU Member States now have an opportunity to revisit domestic policies on collective redress and to enact procedural changes to effectively enable representative organisations (e.g. not-for-profits, associations) to bring collective claims across all sectors, not only in the consumer sector. The environmental law sphere is such an area, ripe for the evolution of procedures and the transposition of a representative entitlement in the vein of the Directive.[57] Such an extension will ensure a degree of policy harmonisation between the consumer and environmental sectors in Member States. In light of the Directive, it is questionable whether an asymmetric policy approach between the consumer and environmental sectors can be sustained going forward. Some Member States have already seized the opportunity to go beyond the subject scope of the Directive to create a horizontal or generic mechanism which also grants standing to representative organisations allowing them to bring claims for injunctive and monetary relief (redress) across a variety of sectors.[58]

---

53 Art. 8(3).

54 Art. 9(2) and (3). There are concerns regarding the use of tacit consent for redress measures. See D. Fairgrieve and R. Salim, 'Collective Redress in Europe: Moving Forward or Treading Water?' (2022) 71(2) *International and Comparative Law Quarterly* 465 for further discussion.

55 See e.g. Arts 4(3), 7(2), 8(2)(b) and 13, and Recitals 58–62.

56 Recital 58.

57 Interestingly, the Directive considers the Aarhus Convention in its construction, demonstrating the influence of that Convention's obligations and entitlements (Recital 75).

58 See e.g. Italy with its class action mechanism under Law no. 31/2019. The class action model has had mixed results for environmental claims. See e.g. M. Molavi, 'Access to Justice and

5.1. EMPOWERING REPRESENTATIVE ORGANISATIONS

In indivisible interest cases, the conundrum raised by such interests is that either no one has a right to remedy the infringement of such an interest, or the relative stake of any one individual in remedying the infringement is too small to entitle them to enforce that interest.[59] As the design of Article 3:305a DCC demonstrates, the strategic framing of admissibility and standing requirements for representative entities is one way of catering for the nature of these claims.

However, this position does not mean that the violation of indivisible interests may not be the basis for pursuing redress for harms to the person (divisible interests). Arguably, there is a connection between the interests.[60] In some Member States, courts have recognised that violations of the collective good may indirectly lead to the infringement of, or threat to, divisible interests.[61] Claimants may need to translate harm to the indivisible interest into specific private individual rights – usually based in tort and/or human rights. However, the goal of the latter is to compensate an injured individual for a wrong, not to protect the environment. By framing actions on the basis of torts and human rights, the claims become an aggregation of individual rights, rather than claims based on harm to the indivisible interest (environmental right) itself. Nonetheless, it is in this individual rights space that representative organisations can play a more active, transformative role for victims of climate change.

In relation to divisible interest claims based on GHG emissions, the provision of standing to specific organisations such as not-for-profit entities or bodies of a similar character (e.g. non-governmental organisations (NGOs), environmental associations), can ensure that a public interest element is retained whilst also acting to safeguard against vexatious litigation.[62] These types of representative

---

the Limits of Environmental Class Actions in Ontario' (2020) 35(3) *Canadian Journal of Law and Society / Revue Canadienne Droit et Société* 391. Molavi argues there is limited access to justice available under environmental class actions in Ontario due to 'severe restrictions and an inhospitable legal climate' (p. 393).

59 M. Cappelletti and B. Garth (n. 31), p. 194.

60 It can be argued that an individual benefits from the protection of the general. Therefore, harm to the general interest will in some way affect the personal interest.

61 See e.g. the Polish Supreme Court decision of 28 May 2021, Case No. III CZP 27/20, where the Court found that violations of air pollution standards (though a collective good) may lead to the infringement of individual health. Some Member States have restricted the ability to bring claims for personal interests insofar as these are the same as a collective good. See *Milieudefensie*: 'the interest of the claims of individual claimants is the same as the common interest which the class actions seek to protect. Their interests are already served by the class actions and they do not have an interest in a separate claim in addition to the class actions. The claims of the individual claimants must therefore be declared not allowable' (para. 4.2.7). Interestingly, the Court took the view that the individual claimants did not have a 'concrete' interest due to the sameness between the individual interest and the public interest.

62 D. Fairgrieve and R. Salim (n. 54).

entities, therefore, can fill an important gap in the regulatory and private enforcement sphere of the legal system. Arguably, entities such as not-for-profits or NGOs fall into the conjunction point or grey space in the public–private divide, particularly if they hold charitable status. Given the nexus in the interplay between the indivisible interest and the individual divisible interest in climate change claims, it is argued that such entities are the most appropriate to have standing for climate change litigation.[63]

Granting standing to such representative entities is not alien to legal systems given current practice in the environment sphere on claims for non-monetary remedies.[64] Article 9(3) in conjunction with Article 2(5) of the Aarhus Convention guarantees interest groups access to justice in order to challenge violations of environmental law.[65] This unique position of entities has been recognised in EU law, and access to justice in environmental matters has taken the form of enabling 'individuals and their associations to exercise the rights conferred on them by EU law, and it helps ensure that the aims and obligations of EU environmental legislation are attained'.[66]

As outlined above, the Directive pushes States to go beyond the remedial limitation of injunctive relief only to enable qualified entities to initiate claims for redress for 'consumers concerned'. It is thus argued that not-for-profit representative organisations in the environmental sphere should be similarly allowed to bring collective claims for redress on behalf of individuals harmed by GHG emissions (where substantive law enables such claims). This ability can be seen as a natural extension of the existing right currently available to such organisations to bring claims for non-monetary or injunctive relief. Environmental organisations bring a wealth of technical expertise in environmental matters, and this will be of value to victims, who are likely to be unfamiliar with the intricacies of legal procedure and climate science. Coupled

---

63 It is recognised that, in line with a Member State's legal tradition, Member States may wish to leave the entitlement open to other representative associations such as shareholder associations. Such associations may wish to utilise a representative mechanism to commence litigation for redress for climate change-causing activities and/or failure to design climate change reduction policies.

64 E.g. Art. 323 Environmental Protection Act (Poland). This entitlement is longstanding in some countries, see M. Cappelletti, 'Vindicating The Public Interest Through the Courts: A Comparativist's Contribution' (1976) 25 *Buffalo Law Review* 643, 660–64. See also M. Eliantonio, 'Collective Redress in Environmental Matters in the EU: A Role Model or a Problem Child' (2014) 41 *Legal Issues of Economic Integration* 257. The French *action de groupe* is an exception which allows damages for environmental harms – see Loi n° 2016-154 de modernisation de la justice du 21ème siècle, 18 novembre 2016, and Art. L142-3-1 of the Environment Code.

65 The Aarhus Convention (Art. 9) recognises the interdependence of access to justice rights and other rights. See Case C-182/10, *Solvay and others*, ECLI:EU:C:2012:82, para. 27.

66 Case C-71/14, *East Sussex*, ECLI:EU:C:2015:656, para. 52, and Case C-72/95, *Kraaijeveld*, ECLI:EU:C:1996:404, para. 56. Commission Notice (n. 35), para. 31.

with the growing use of attribution science,[67] this new ability will enhance the enforcement armoury available to victims for GHG emissions harms. Thus, the use of a representative entity to drive divisible interest claims will bring access to justice closer to victims of climate change, enabling them to enforce their rights whilst also avoiding the risk of financial burdens (e.g. adverse costs exposure).

The ability of organisations to act on behalf of victims will help reduce the asymmetry of power inherent in claims, especially where the claims are brought against private actors such as multinational organisations, which are much more financially resourced than a member of the public. To this extent, the empowerment of environmental organisations to bring redress claims will be an invaluable procedural element should the EU Commission's Proposal for a Directive on Corporate Sustainability Due Diligence to tackle human rights and environmental impacts across global value chains take effect.[68] Under the Proposal, Member States are required to lay down rules enabling victims to bring a civil liability claim for redress before Member State courts where the harm could have been identified, and prevented or mitigated by a company, with appropriate due diligence measures.[69] The empowerment of environmental entities to bring claims on behalf of victims will support victims in capitalising upon their entitlement under a domestic civil liability regime created pursuant to this Directive. It will remove or reduce the financial and procedural burden for victims in bringing claims.

Additionally, the Directive's rule that consumers are to benefit from redress measures without the need to bring a separate action[70] can be (if transposed to climate change or environmental claims) of value to GHG victims as it removes key barriers to claimants seeking redress. The application of such a principle in climate cases will ensure that victims are not forced to re-establish liability and/or quantum in a subsequent or follow-on action for damages.[71] This reduces costs for victims and removes procedural complexity and risk in getting relief.

67 For a discussion of this, see R.F. Stuart-Smith, F.E.L. Otto, A.I. Saad et al., 'Filling the evidentiary gap in climate litigation' (2021) 11 *Nature Climate Change* 651.

68 European Commission, 'Proposal for a Directive of the European Parliament and of the Council on Corporate Sustainability Due Diligence and amending Directive (EU) 2019/1937', COM(2022) 71 final. Art. 15 of the Proposal covers climate change measures. See also Recital 60.

69 Art. 22. Art. 15 of the Proposal explicitly covers climate change and its inclusion in the plan covered by the civil liability regime under Art. 22.

70 Art. 9(6).

71 This is a concern in the consumer context. The Fitness Check Study revealed that individual consumers who brought follow-on claims for damages were still required to establish an infringement in some cases. See Commission Staff Working Document, 'Report on the Fitness Check of EU consumer and marketing law', SWD(2017) 209, 23 May 2017, carried out in the framework of the Commission's Regulatory Fitness and Performance (REFIT) programme.

Under the Directive, Member States are given discretion in the design of the procedure to be either opt-in or opt-out, although opt-in is directed when redress is sought.[72] Various approaches are taken across Member States to the question of opt-in or opt-out in procedures, although opt-in tends to be the common feature.[73] In climate change cases, given the volume of the victims and the nature and diversity of divisible interests affected, it is suggested that a degree of flexibility be maintained and a strict transposition of the Directive's direction on opt-in or opt-out should not be followed. Instead, the UK competition law approach, where both an opt-in and opt-out approach are allowed, should be adopted.[74] Under the competition law procedure, the tribunal determines whether opt-in or opt-out is followed based on the test of the 'interest of justice', in light of the specifics of the case.[75] The use of this approach in climate change claims will give courts a margin of procedural discretion and flexibility. However, it is likely that an opt-out will be the *de facto* norm as it is the most feasible option where there is a very large volume of injured parties.

With the expansion of the entitlement to bring claims on behalf of climate change victims, necessary safeguards will be required to ensure that entities maintain the appropriate balance between acting for the interests of victims and being entrepreneurial. Key safeguards will include rules on destination of funds, standing and information provision.

5.2. STANDING, DESTINATION OF FUNDS AND INFORMATION PROVISION

The existing approach for standing of representative entities under Article 9(2) and (3) of the Aarhus Convention[76] is largely mirrored in some of the minimum

---

72 See Art. 9 of the Directive. In opt-in regimes, participants have to take an active step to join proceedings and are not automatically included in the claim. In opt-out regimes, individuals falling within the parameters of the group on behalf of which the claim is brought will automatically be included, unless an expression to not be bound is made. There is debate on the merits of each option and access to justice concerns have been expressed about both: see E. Lein et al., *State of Collective Redress in the EU in the Context of the Implementation of the Commission Recommendation* (BIICL 2017).

73 See E. Lein et al. (n. 72), p. 15. Interestingly, the new Art. 3:305a (WAMCA) takes an opt-out approach as a default where domestic parties are concerned. However, it counterbalances this by requirement that a foundation must be 'sufficiently representative' when a monetary remedy is sought. This requires foundations to provide a mechanism to enable participation of persons in the decision-making process of the claim.

74 Rule 79(3) of the Competition Appeal Tribunal Rules.

75 A similar approach is taken by Belgium, although opt-in is required where physical or moral harm is alleged.

76 ClientEarth et al., *Public Toolkit on Access to Justice* (2019), pp. 4–12, http://www.justiceandenvironment.org/fileadmin/user_upload/Publications/2019/2019_Public_toolkit_on_legal_standing.pdf.

requirements in the Directive for foreign qualified entities.[77] This includes requirements that the entity's interest in the claim falls within its scope of purpose or its articles of association, its not-for-profit status[78] and/or an established history of bringing claims in a particular area.[79] These existing standing requirements could be utilised to determine a representative's standing to bring collective climate change claims for redress. However, with an expansion in the scope of operation of entities to redress, requirements on measures to avoid conflict of interest and clarity of funding arrangements will be needed to curtail ambitions of entrepreneurism by entities and to protect against the undue influence of third-party funders.[80]

With this new entitlement, and to preserve the not-for-profit element of an entity's existence, rules on the destination of any outstanding redress funds that are not recovered within established time limits[81] is advised. This will ensure that entities do not subvert the not-for-profit principle. Inspiration can be taken from the North American experience in the use of the cy-près doctrine, which allows for the distribution of unclaimed funds from compensatory claims to charitable causes. Whilst thought will need to be given to the standards for the cy-près doctrine, this option potentially opens the door to enabling Member States to direct unclaimed funds to drive public environmental initiatives.[82]

The provision of information is an important part of the personal competence of victims.[83] The provision of information enables personal recognition that a right exists. Indeed, the absence of a recognition that a right exists has been noted as a barrier that is 'especially serious for the underprivileged'.[84] As such, the transposition of the Directive's principles on information provision[85] will be important in ensuring that GHG emissions victims are afforded a degree of participation in the redress claims brought by representative organisations. This is particularly the case where opt-ins are required. It will also ensure that victims are sufficiently aware of proceedings to take adequate steps to directly benefit from a damages award after a successful claim by an entity.

---

77 See Art. 4 of the Directive.

78 See E. Lein (n. 72), where 67% of respondents confirmed that representative entities must have a non-profit-making character in their respective Member State.

79 For a survey of standing requirements for environmental entities to bring claims, see M. Eliantonio, C. Backes, C.H. van Rhee, T. Spronken and A. Berlee, *A Comparative Study on Legal Standing (Locus Standi) before the EU and Member States' Courts* (Intersentia 2012). See also ClientEarth (n. 76), p. 12.

80 See e.g. Art. 4(3)(e) of the Directive.

81 Art. 9(7) of the Directive allows Member States to establish rules for such funds.

82 This can be particularly useful for Member States with less financial resources to pursue environmental policies.

83 M. Cappelletti and B. Garth (n. 31), p. 188.

84 Ibid., p. 191.

85 Art. 13.

The section below considers how the above discussion may be translated into practice in Poland.

6. SELECTED STATE PRACTICE ON COLLECTIVE REDRESS: POLAND

Poland utilises a combination of the group action or class action model for collective redress in some sectors, with an administrative non-monetary representative action available in consumer and environmental matters. The Polish Class Actions Act[86] is available for claims relating to selected areas – consumer protection, contractual liability, product liability and tort liability[87] – providing injunctive and compensatory relief in these areas. Claims need to be homogeneous,[88] and need to be based on an identical or similar factual basis.[89] Furthermore, the procedure requires 10 or more persons to initiate a claim.[90] A commonality requirement applies in compensation claims, and class members are required to make the value of the monetary claims equal to each other.[91] The negative impact of this requirement is usually subverted by the creation of subclasses. Nonetheless, the commonality requirement has deterred the pursuit of compensatory claims and claimants often pursue a dual process of first seeking a declaratory remedy followed by bringing individual claims for compensation.[92] The procedure is an opt-in mechanism and there are stringent procedural time limits on a class member's ability to join and leave the class.[93] The Act limits the category of persons allowed to be a representative to either a member of the class or a regional consumer ombudsman.

---

86 See Act of 17 December 2009 on Pursuing Claims in Group Proceedings, Journal of Laws 2010.7.44 of 18 January 2010.

87 See also A. Trzaska, 'Poland' in C. Sanger (ed.), *The Class Actions Law Review* (3rd ed., Law Business Research Ltd 2019). Art. 1.2 Class Actions Act: claims for breaches of environmental protection law, competition law, IP law and labour law can be brought insofar as they are framed as breaches of tort.

88 See Case No. II PK 44/17, 17 April 2018, where a functional approach to the homogeneity requirement is to be taken. See also the decision of 26 April 2016 of District Court of Warsaw, Case No. XXV C 915/14, and A. Trzaska (n. 87).

89 Art. 1.1 Class Actions Act.

90 Ibid.

91 Art. 2.1 Class Actions Act. This requirement raises access to justice questions and has been critiqued by legal practitioners – see A. Kubas and R. Kos, 'Opinia w sprawie projektu ustawy o dochodzeniu roszczeń w postępowaniu grupowym', druk sejmowy no. 1829, Kraków, 20 October 2009, p. 4.

92 See M. Tulibacka, 'Poland' in E. Lein (n. 72).

93 See Art. 11.5 where class members cannot join after the expiration of the time limit for them to do so.

From an access to justice perspective, the class action procedure, in its current form, generates legal and economic barriers to justice. This is particularly demonstrated in the use of the commonality requirement and the strict time limits for opting in. However, one of the more challenging legal barriers of the procedure is the restrictive approach to claims based on harms to the personal interests of the class members.[94] With the exception of personal injury claims, class actions for the infringement of personal interests are not allowed.[95] In light of the above, it is unlikely that, in its current design, the procedure can be effectively used for divisible interest redress claims arising from GHG emissions. Indeed, Polish climate change victims have resorted to bringing individual climate change lawsuits for the breach of personal interests. In *Gorska et al.*, the claimants brought individual proceedings before different district courts, alleging that the Polish government had failed to protect them from worsening climate impacts and thereby violated a number of personal rights protected by the Polish Civil Code (life, health and property).[96]

7. POTENTIAL REFORMS IN POLAND?

The need to implement the Directive provides an opportunity for reform of the existing class action procedure, including enabling it to be used for climate change claims. The starting point would be to amend the procedure to make it Directive-compliant and adjust its scope to cater for climate-related claims. This is the most efficient solution amongst the existing procedures, as regional courts already have experience of adjudicating class action redress cases.[97] These courts have a wealth of procedural experience in the enforcement and distribution of redress remedies in mass claims and this sets them apart from the existing

94 Art. 23 of the Polish Civil Code defines the personal interests. Personal interests include health, freedom, dignity and good name, conscience, home, and creative output. See also E. Baginska and M. Tulibacka, 'Poland' in I. Boone (ed.), *International Encyclopaedia of Laws: Tort Law* (Kluwer Law International 2014), pp. 194–98 for further discussion.

95 Class action claims for personal injury are only allowed insofar as the remedy sought is a declaration of liability.

96 The claimants have additionally alleged infringements of Arts 2 and 8 ECHR as part of their claim. In these cases, an injunctive remedy is being sought. ClientEarth, a not-for-profit legal group, has been delegated by each claimant to bring the proceedings on their behalf. This delegation is based on an entitlement under Polish civil procedure for NGOs to act in cases. However, consent from each plaintiff (in writing) is required before the action is brought by the NGO.

97 This redesign of the class action mechanism is possible in light of Recital 11 of the Directive, which leaves it to the 'discretion of the Member States whether to design the procedural mechanism for representative actions … *as part of an existing* or as part of a new procedural mechanism for collective injunctive measures or redress measures'. The creation of a separate representative action is not advocated, as it will further fragment procedures in the State.

administrative procedures for environmental claims. This section identifies three key changes which will be required if reform of the class action procedure is to be pursued for climate change claims.

First, claims pursuing redress for infringement of personal interests should be allowed. Indeed, such types of interests are the most common forms of losses in tort claims in Poland.[98] As climate change claims are commonly framed on tortious grounds and/or are rights-based, harms to personal interests will likely be a main element of such claims.

Second, representative entities such as not-for-profits, including ENGOs, should be granted standing to be a class representative. This should not be a contentious revision given the existing entitlement granted to entities (including ENGOs) to bring claims on behalf of natural persons via individual mandate in civil proceedings. The granting of standing to entities to be a class representative can be perceived as 'a natural extension of these powers'.[99] It is notable that some ENGOs have been active in using the mandate facility in civil proceedings before Polish courts. As such, they would already possess capacity and expertise in acting in civil proceedings.[100] That said, the existing approach to standing requirements for ENGOs to challenge public authorities for breaches of EU environmental laws[101] leaves a degree of pessimism as to how progressive the State may be regarding the standing requirements in the class procedure.

Third, considering the importance of the Directive's information obligations for redress claims, reform of the current standard of information provision under the class action procedure will be necessary. This can benefit climate change victims, especially as the European Commission has previously lamented that 'Poland needs to make significant progress on informing the public about effective remedies for individuals and environmental associations and access to justice in environmental matters under Polish and EU law'.[102]

Nonetheless, the Directive leaves room for the Polish legislature to retain some of the existing rules of the class action procedure.[103] This is likely to include the rules on homogeneity, commonality in redress, opt-in and numerosity. Subject to the discussion above on opt-in or opt-out, the homogeneity, commonality

---

98 M. Tulibacka (n. 92), p. 15.

99 Ibid.

100 See e.g. *Gorska et al.*, *ClientEarth v. Poland (on behalf of P.N.)*, *ClientEarth v. Poland (on behalf of M.O.)*, *ClientEarth v. Poland (on behalf of P.R.)*, *ClientEarth v. Poland (on behalf of M.S.)* and *ClientEarth v. Poland (on behalf of M.G.)*. A brief outline of these cases (with links to court decisions in Polish) can be found here: https://climatecasechart.com/non-us-jurisdiction/poland/.

101 European Commission, *The Environmental Implementation Review 2019: Poland*, pp. 32–33, https://op.europa.eu/en/publication-detail/-/publication/5cf0cf1f-0ac2-11ea-8c1f-01aa75ed71a1/language-en/format-PDF/source-search.

102 Ibid., p. 32.

103 See Recital 12.

and numerosity requirements are unlikely to pose difficulties or create barriers to climate change claims given the large mass of individuals in such claims, the current approaches to damages calculation in climate change claims, and the emerging functional approach towards the procedure's requirements.[104]

8. CONCLUSION

The provision and utilisation of collective redress procedures as vehicles for climate change litigation can promote access to justice for victims of GHG emissions. In particular, effective access to justice in climate change claims can be facilitated by the empowerment of representative organisations to bring injunctive and redress claims for the protection of divisible interests of victims. This entitlement will alleviate the procedural burden on victims themselves. The need to implement a representative action that is compliant with Directive 2020/1828 affords Member States the opportunity to take stock of *all* of their existing collective redress procedures and policies, and to adjust their existing collective procedures to enable representative organisations to act better in collective claims relating to climate change. Arguably, in light of EU initiatives in the corporate sustainability, due diligence and environment spheres, such adjustments are likely to be required in the immediate future, and Member States should seize the moment.

---

[104] See A. Trzaska (n. 87), p. 162.

CLIMATE CHANGE CLASS ACTIONS IN EUROPE?

The Italian Perspective

Ander MAGLICA

1. INTRODUCTION

Climate change is undoubtedly one of the most, if not the most, pressing issues of our time, one which will fundamentally affect the future, perhaps even the survival, of humankind.[1] Since the 1992 UNFCCC Rio Convention and the subsequent Kyoto Protocol of 1997, to the Paris Agreement of 2015, up to the Glasgow Conference of the Parties (COP) of late 2021, political bodies at all levels have tried to find a way to tackle the issue through a coordinated and

---

1 See the statement of the UN Secretary General, A. GUTERRES, from August 2021 on the IPCC Working Group I Report: 'Today's IPCC Working Group 1 Report is a code red for humanity. The alarm bells are deafening, and the evidence is irrefutable: greenhouse gas emissions from fossil fuel burning and deforestation are choking our planet and putting billions of people at immediate risk. Global heating is affecting every region on Earth, with many of the changes becoming irreversible'.

efficient response. Nonetheless, the general consensus is that the measures taken so far are simply not enough.[2]

As a result, in the last few years, a growing number of climate change cases have started to emerge in different parts of the globe, in what has now consolidated itself as a worldwide movement to defend the planet's health in the judicial arena.[3] It is, after all, the judicial branch's role to intervene as a subsidiary protection mechanism once the substantive rights that have been affirmed both at statutory and constitutional level are violated.[4]

In this struggle to stop, or at least stall, climate change by means of litigation, several substantive provisions and procedural mechanisms have been employed. Among the latter, the present chapter aims to situate the debate in a richer theoretical and empirical perspective by introducing the argument that representative actions, although an imperfect mechanism, in certain circumstances may be a vital tool for social change and for the protection of fundamental rights, such as that to a safe environment.

To assess this, the chapter first investigates the social, economic and institutional barriers preventing efficient climate change litigation in Europe (section 2). It subsequently briefly presents the class action mechanism, with a specific focus on Italy, in light of the recently introduced Title VIII-*bis* from the Civil Procedural Code (section 3). Lastly, it evaluates, in a general perspective, the efficiency of class actions in overcoming the above-mentioned barriers to climate change litigation (section 4), with final proposals for social, statutory and institutional change with specific regard to the new Italian collective redress mechanisms (section 5).

2. BARRIERS TO CLIMATE CHANGE LITIGATION

As of November 2022, over 2,120 lawsuits have been brought around the world to stall climate change or receive compensation for the damage it has provoked.[5] Nonetheless, such litigation, which is still developing, has not always managed

---

2 See Working Group I contribution to the Sixth Assessment Report of the IPCC (Intergovernmental Panel on Climate Change) from 2021: https://www.ipcc.ch/report/ar6/wg1/downloads/report/IPCC_AR6_WGI_Full_Report.pdf.

3 J. Setzer and C. Highman, *Global trends in climate change litigation: 2022 snapshot*, 2022, https://www.lse.ac.uk/granthaminstitute/wp-content/uploads/2022/08/Global-trends-in-climate-change-litigation-2022-snapshot.pdf.

4 For a recent analysis on access to justice, in which the tension between courts and legislators at national and supranational level is highlighted, see B. Randazzo, 'Accesso alla giustizia e diritti fondamentali nella dimensione costituzionale nazionale e sovranazionale. Introduzione' in C. Amalfitano, L. Violini and D.U. Galetta (eds), *Law, Justice and Sustainable Development: L'Accesso alla giustizia nel quadro del SD Goal 16*, Giappichelli, Turin 2022.

5 Climate Change Laws of the World Database: https://climate-laws.org.

to achieve its final goal. This struggle can be attributed to both practical (section 2.1) and legal (section 2.2) obstacles litigants face throughout the entire judicial process: the trouble individuals or public bodies face in even accessing the courts and having their claims examined, the cumbersome and complex process of adjudication, and, even in the case of favourable decisions, the paucity of proper remedies to execute them.

2.1. SOCIO-ECONOMIC BARRIERS

As illustrated by Cappelletti,[6] law – at least from the viewpoint of the access-to-justice movement – is composed of several elements. Among them, the normative aspect certainly plays an important role, but not the primary one, which pertains to 'the people, with all their cultural, economic and psychological features'.[7] It is, in fact, essential to realise that human beings are driven by both rational and irrational incentives. Since norms are designed to regulate human behaviour, it is thus only natural to include these elements in any evaluation of legal institutions and their possible impact.

With regard to climate change, four main practical factors fundamentally discourage or limit litigation: time, information, money and organisation. These elements hinder climate change litigation conducted by both public enforcers (such as administrative agencies) and private ones (either individually or as representatives of a class).

As to the former, when the power to bring lawsuits against entities contributing to climate change (i.e. by emitting excessive quantities of greenhouse gas) is entrusted solely to public bodies, it should be considered that they may not always be up to the task. They may in principle be provided with more funding and manpower specifically recruited for climate change work, as compared to private parties, but this is not always the case. In general, it has been proven that the bureaucratic machinery over the years tends to lose motivation and become too centralised.[8] Its rigid hierarchical structure and its dependence on the legislative branch often makes it unable to adapt rapidly enough to the latest developments, to be aware of all the situations deserving of litigation, to receive direct information, or to assemble the most appropriate legal and scientific teams of experts for the specific circumstances of each case. Additionally, a dangerous tendency to fall into conflicts of interests with the possible defendants (the government itself or multinational organisations, most of the time) can be expected and, eventually, cannot be prevented either, especially if

6 M. Cappelletti, 'Alternative Dispute Resolution Processes within the Framework of the World-Wide Access-to-Justice Movement' (1993) 56 *The Modern Law Review* 282.

7 Ibid.

8 M. Cappelletti, 'Vindicating the Public Interest through the Courts: A Comparativist's Contribution' (1976) 25(3) *Buffalo Law Review* 643.

the members of such bodies are politically appointed. In particular, if the government itself is failing to comply with internationally agreed standards or violating its duty of care towards citizens, it would not be possible for an administrative body to bring a lawsuit against it.[9]

Hence, several jurisdictions correctly allow the alternative path of private enforcement. Nonetheless, this form of litigation may also have several practical (and legal, as examined in the next subsection) issues that can prevent climate change litigators accessing the judicial arena. First, litigating is expensive, in terms of attorneys' fees, court fees and scientific research, which is extensive in this kind of lawsuit. Second, litigating against States or powerful corporations (both repeat players in the litigation field that have extensive funding and lobbying networks available to them) may be very intimidating to single claimants, and such lawsuits may take an excessively long time and cost even more. There are, hence, also clear organisational obstacles. Third, information asymmetries cause most individuals to underestimate the matter and doubt their entitlement to a judicial remedy. In particular, uncertainties regarding attribution science and the proof of causation usually prevent them from seeking economic compensation for the damages triggered by climate change, even in smaller cases.[10] As a consequence, the majority of climate change cases so far have focused on the injunctive aspect and interim measures: rather than aiming at economic redress, their main goal is to prevent further future harm.

All these elements together create several significant practical disincentives for private individuals. Barring extraordinary incentives, no rational person would undertake litigation alone to save the planet,[11] but rather would expect government authorities to tackle the problem or free-ride behind the rare idealistic plaintiffs.[12]

2.2. LEGAL BARRIERS

In the event that, despite the above-mentioned hurdles, a lawsuit is filed and climate change can be discussed in a courtroom, major problems still remain.

---

9 It is the everlasting question of 'who watches the watchman?', for which the best answer is undoubtedly a larger array of options, in what has often been referred to as a 'system of checks and balances': see M. Cappelletti, 'The Mighty Problem of Judicial Review and the Contribution of Comparative Analysis' (1980) 53(2) *Southern California Law Review* 409.

10 K. Bouwer, 'The Unsexy Future of Climate Change Litigation' (2018) 30(3) *Journal of Environmental Law* 483.

11 A form of 'rational apathy': L. Vischer and M. Faure, 'A Law and Economics Perspective on the EU Directive on Representative Actions' (2021) 44 *Journal of Consumer Policy* 455.

12 L.S. Mullenix, 'Ending Class Actions as We Know Them: Rethinking the American Class Action' (2014) 64 *Emory Law Journal* 399, on the notion of idealistic plaintiffs; whereas on the free-rider problem in class actions, see L. Vischer and M. Faure, above n. 11.

Firstly, defendants could argue that climate change is a policy issue and, therefore, that it cannot be subject to the courts' scrutiny. The important theme of the separation of powers and the question of whether the judicial branch can condemn the legislative branch's decisions (or lack thereof) is relevant here. Despite the courts appearing more comfortable in still leaving a large margin of discretion to governments, several recent decisions around the globe have found the actions (or inactions) of the legislator and of the executive branch in relation to climate change to be a justiciable matter.[13]

In Italy, only one case, *Giudizio Universale*, has been filed against the State in this field. It was brought in 2021 and is still pending before the Tribunal of Rome.[14] It is worth noting, however, that both the Italian Court of Cassation and the Constitutional Court have already repeatedly stated, with regard to excessive greenhouse gas emissions by corporations, that a company's compliance with the State's provisions cannot be a relevant justification for harming fundamental rights, such as the right to health.[15] Moreover, the latter Court, in a case relating to the constitutionality of a criminal provision prohibiting assisted suicide, after suspending its decision for one year in order to give Parliament time to address the issue, finally ruled on the matter in 2019, declaring the specific provision unconstitutional and recalling that when 'confronted with a constitutional *vulnus*, which cannot be solved through interpretation – especially if it concerns fundamental rights … – the Court is in any case due to remedy it'.[16] It can thus be assumed that the same reasoning – which recalls that of other European constitutional courts, in what appears to be a growing dialogue between courts[17] – could also be applied in relation to provisions concerning climate change, should their validity be questioned before the constitutional courts.

The same goal could be reached indirectly, in a lawsuit against a corporation rather than the State itself. Such a case is also currently pending in Italy, this time before the Tribunal of Milan, and it is the *ILVA* injunctive class action,[18] filed in 2021, where the defendants – ILVA and Acciaiere d'Italia, owners of a major steel plant in Taranto – stressed their compliance with the applicable legislative and administrative provisions. The court in September 2022 rejected all the

13 J. Setzer and C. Highman, above n. 3.

14 *A Sud et al. v. Stato Italiano*, Trib. Civ. Roma, pending since 2021.

15 Ex multis, Cass. civ., S.U., n. 29298/2021; Cass. civ., S.U., n. 8092/2020; Cass. civ., S.U., n. 25578/2020; see also Corte cost., n. 35/2010, §2.3.

16 Corte cost., n. 242/2019, §4 (unofficial translation). For a more detailed examination of the decision, see B. Randazzo, above n. 4.

17 In relation to climate change, C. Voigt, 'Introduction. Climate Change as a Challenge for Global Governance, Courts and Human Rights' in W. Kah and M. Weller (eds), *Climate Change Litigation. A Handbook*, Beck/Hart/Nomos, Oxford 2021, p. 18.

18 *Zaninelli et al. v. ILVA S.p.a., Acciaierie d'Italia Holding S.p.a. e Acciaierie d'Italia S.p.a.*, Trib. Milano, Sez. spec. impresa, 10166/2021, pending, see also below n. 42.

procedural objections raised by the defendants and simultaneously suspended the decision on the merits by referring the case to the CJEU for a preliminary ruling on three questions about the interpretation of Directive 2010/75 on industrial emissions (integrated pollution prevention and control). It hence appears that first-instance judges will seek the support from the EU higher courts and rules before crossing the thin line of the separation of powers. Both cases currently pending before the courts of first instance of Rome and Milan could open the door to very interesting developments in Italian environmental and climate change litigation.

Additionally, another major hurdle for claimants, from the viewpoint of standing, is proving a sufficient connection between all the parties and the facts of the case. This concerns, on the one hand, the proof of a direct personal interest in the case, which may be complex for climate change matters, especially if the plaintiffs are filing the lawsuit as single individuals. On the other hand, the element of connection is also relevant with regard to the link between the harm provoked by climate change and the action (or inaction) of the defendant, whether a State or a private corporation. In fact, scientists concur that both the causes and the effects of climate change are global in their nature, meaning that it is extremely difficult to determine that a certain act has specifically harmed a certain individual or group of people. For instance, in its recent decision in *Smith v. Fonterra* of October 2021, the Court of Appeal of New Zealand found that 'every person in New Zealand – indeed, in the world – is (to varying degrees) both responsible for causing the relevant harm, and the victim of that harm'.[19]

The test varies in each jurisdiction. This could push both plaintiffs and defendants towards forum shopping,[20] but also indicates the key role played by scientific experts and data presented by the parties, as well as the rules on costs of the proceedings, especially during the evidentiary phase, as analysed below. Nonetheless, it is clear that a degree of flexibility and creativity is necessary from courts, which should also take into consideration the special nature of climate change litigation.[21] In particular, instead of the 'but-for' test (which requires the harmful event not to have occurred in that way without the defendant's participation), it is worth highlighting a new trend to employ attribution science studies in claims for compensation with what has been called the 'market-share liability' test.[22] A notable example of the latter test is the *Lliuya v. RWE* case in Germany, where a Peruvian farmer brought a lawsuit against RWE, the largest

---

19 *Smith v. Fonterra Co-Operative Group Limited et al.*, CA128/2020 [2021] NZCA 552 §18.

20 E.g. Shell's decision to move its headquarters from the Netherlands to the UK, coincidentally shortly after the *Milieudefensie et al. v. Royal Dutch Shell* decision from 2021 (C/09/571932, currently on appeal): https://www.ft.com/content/d932a462-2b31-479a-bd08-6e8abc02c375.

21 D.A. Kysar, 'What Climate Change Can Do About Tort Law' (2011) 41 *Environmental Law* 1.

22 C.V. Giabardo 'Climate Change Litigation and Tort Law. Regulation Through Litigations?' (2020) *Rivista Diritto e Processo* 361.

electricity producer in Germany, seeking adaptation costs of approximately €15,000.[23] That sum, which equates to 0.47% of the total costs he expects to pay for flood protection in his Peruvian hometown, was calculated based on the same percentage (0.47%) of global greenhouse gas emissions that scientific data attribute to RWE since the start of industrialisation.

Ultimately, even if the court finds the defendant responsible, it may be unable to find the appropriate form of redress. This is especially true for suits filed against States, in which courts may deem an order to draw up a stricter climate mitigation plan to be outside of their authority and against the separation of powers doctrine, as happened in the *Juliana* case in the US or in the *Klimaatzaak* case in Belgium, both from 2021.[24] A possible solution could be that adopted by the German Federal Constitutional Court in March 2021 regarding the unconstitutionality of the Federal Climate Protection Act (KSG)[25] for the insufficiency of the restrictions on emissions planned before 2030, which is also similar to the reasoning of Italian Constitutional Court in the above-mentioned 2019 case regarding assisted suicide:[26] giving Parliament, as the natural political body to do so, some time to duly implement the necessary legislation and, only as an *extrema ratio*, the court itself providing concrete regulation, should the former fail to comply with the request within the due date.

In cases against private corporations, instead, courts have been very reluctant to compensate claimants, due to the difficulty of determining the exact extent of the damages suffered, even when they have found a causative link.[27] This shows, once again, the fundamental importance of educating judges about this

---

23 *Luciano Lliuya v. RWE AG*, Essen Regional Court, 2 O 285/15 currently on appeal.

24 *Juliana v. United States* [2016] 6:15-cv-01517-TC (US District Court, Oregon) and *VZW Klimaatzaak v. Kingdom of Belgium et al.*, 2015/4585/A, currently on appeal. The former in 2020 found that '[w]e reluctantly conclude, however, that the plaintiffs' case must be made to the political branches or to the electorate at large, the latter of which can change the composition of the political branches through the ballot box. That the other branches may have abdicated their responsibility to remediate the problem does not confer on Article III courts, no matter how well-intentioned, the ability to step into their shoes' (p. 32), whereas the latter stated in its decision from 2021, '[t]hus, it is not for the judge to determine the quantified GHG emission reduction targets for all sectors that Belgium should meet in order to "do its part" in preventing dangerous global warming. In other words, while it is within the remit of the tribunal to note a failure on the part of the federal state and the three regions, this does not authorize it, by virtue of the principle of separation of powers, to itself set targets for reducing Belgium's GHG emissions' (p. 82, unofficial translation).

25 BVerfG, Order of the First Senate of 24 March 2021, 1 BvR 2656/18, http://www.bverfg.de/e/rs20210324_1bvr265618en.html. In particular, the Court deemed the KSG unconstitutional since the reductions until 2030 were too soft, consequently imposing an unbalanced burden on future generations to battle climate change and adapt to a green society, thus limiting too severely fundamental freedoms. See below nn. 60–62.

26 Corte cost., n. 242/2019, above n. 16.

27 See M. Molavi, 'Access to Justice and the Limits of Environmental Class Actions in Ontario' (2020) 35(3) *Canadian Journal of Law and Society* 391.

new field of litigation and empowering them with appropriate and sufficiently flexible procedural tools at all stages of the proceedings.[28]

3. THE CLASS ACTION MODEL

Class actions are a highly debated procedural instrument, praised by some as the 'holy grail', but condemned by others as a 'Frankenstein's monster' or a 'toxic cocktail'.[29] This chapter does not intend to unconditionally support one thesis or the other, but rather to build on them and shed light on the consideration that, in certain circumstances and with an adequate system of checks and balances against abuse, they can become an extremely valuable instrument in the fight to stop climate change. Accordingly, after a brief introduction on the legal transplant[30] of the class action model on the European continent (section 3.1), the new Italian injunctive and compensatory collective mechanisms, which entered into force in May 2021, are presented (section 3.2). Subsequently, the disadvantages and advantages of employing such class procedures to overcome the barriers to climate change litigation are considered using a comparative yardstick in relation to the other available paths (section 4).

3.1. THE EUROPEAN CONTEXT

A class action is a legal instrument typical of common law systems. It is a procedural mechanism by which an individual or an organisation acts on behalf of a group of people who have been simultaneously harmed by the same conduct of a common person.[31] Originating in the 13th century in the United Kingdom,

---

28 Economic redress is certainly not the priority in climate change litigation; however – as proven in other fields – it can have a key impact in modifying the behaviour of possible defendants. See C. Hodges, 'Evaluating Collective Redress: Models, Evidence, Outcomes and Policy' in S. Voet and A. Uzelac (eds), *Class Actions in Europe. Holy Grail or a Wrong Tail?*, Springer, Cham 2021, pp. 19–42.

29 In 2008, the Questions and Answers to the Green Paper on Consumer Collective Redress of the European Commission employed the expression 'toxic cocktail', in relation to possible abuses of the class action mechanism. See also R.B. Cappalli and C. Consolo, 'Class Actions for Continental Europe: A Preliminary Inquiry' (1992) 6 *Temple International and Comparative Law Journal* 217.

30 Expression employed by D. Hensler, 'The global landscape of collective litigation' in D. Hensler, C. Hodges and I. Tzankova, *Class Actions in Context. How Culture, Economics and Politics Shape Collective Litigation*, Edward Elgar Publishing, Cheltenham 2016, p. 3, recalling A. Watson.

31 D. Hensler, ibid. ('A representative legal procedure in which some person or organization comes forward to litigate on behalf of a group or group interest').

it only fully came to fruition in the US in 1966, with the introduction of the new Rule 23 of the Federal Rules of Civil Procedure.[32] Since then, its success in the US has been remarkable, having become established as a valuable procedural tool for the collective redress of mass damages as well as for the concrete implementation of numerous civil liberties. In today's economy and society, characterised by large-scale and standardised relationships, the class action model has thus proven to be an extremely effective means of access to justice.[33]

For several years, decades even, since its 1966 adoption, the US class action model has been a dazzling comet flying through the legal universe of substantive rights and procedural mechanisms. While in some countries traditionally close to the US culture and influence, such as Australia[34] and Canada,[35] similar models were adopted shortly after, and still seem to be thriving,[36] the European reaction was much more complex. Only recently, after decades of fiery debates and blatant scandals, does it seem like a point of convergence (although criticised by many)[37] has finally been reached in the Old Continent as well, with a gradual reversal, on the one hand, of the individual Member States, with several yet disparate and autonomous models enacted by each of them, and, on the other hand, of the EU itself. In particular, the latter, after Directive 1998/27 and Recommendation 2013/396, has recently given the green light to Directive 2020/1828 on representative actions for the protection of consumers' collective interests, aiming to set minimum standards and harmonise the playing field among the national models.

As its title indicates, however, national legislators are required to adopt class action procedures in the field of consumer law, with the consequent exclusion from their scope of application of all other rights and interests, such as the right to health or the right to live in a clean and safe environment. Unless Member States go beyond the requirements of the Directive, collective protection against

32 S.C. Yeazell, *From Medieval Group Litigation to Modern Class Action*, Yale University Press, New Haven 1987.

33 C. Piché, 'Class Actions in Quebec: Highlights of a Unique Procedure' (2021) 15 *Revista Eletrônica de Direito Procesual* 170, after a long empirical analysis in Canada, highlights three main advantages of the class action model: access to justice, judicial economy and deterrence.

34 See B. Murphy and C. Cameron, 'Access to Justice and the Evolution of Class Action Litigation in Australia' (2006) 30(2) *Melbourne University Law Review* 399.

35 For a very accurate insight on class actions and climate change in Canada, see J. Kalajdzic, 'Climate Change Class Actions in Canada' (2021) 100(2) *Supreme Court Law Review* 29.

36 S. Voet, 'Where the Wild Things Are – Reflections on the State and Future of European Collective Redress' in A.L.M. Keirse and M.B.M. Loos (eds), *Waves in Contract and Liability Law in Three Decades of Ius Commune*, Intersentia, Cambridge 2017, pp. 105–40.

37 M.J. Azar-Baud and M. Sousa Ferro, 'Directive on consumer collective representative actions: a sheep in wolf's clothing?', *EU Law Live*, Op-Ed, 2021.

climate change will therefore be difficult to achieve.[38] This circumstance may cause serious issues of inequality and even discrimination among EU citizens, as well as increasing forum shopping by both plaintiffs and defendants. Moreover, as noted by prominent authors,[39] it raises questions of constitutional legitimacy, consequently opening the door in the future to numerous complaints before national constitutional courts.

Furthermore, another legacy, in almost all the European States, of the initial diffidence towards the new collective procedural instrument is the option of relying on the so-called opt-in system, which requires explicit choice to join the class and thus to be bound to the effects of the *res judicata*.[40]

3.2. THE NEW ITALIAN MODEL

In this context, the Italian legislator – anticipating the EU's move, rather surprisingly and probably without a full awareness of its potentially disruptive impact – adopted a new class action mechanism in 2019, which entered into force on 19 May 2021. The new device – which repeals the previous one, limited to consumer law and scarcely employed – rather innovatively enhances the scope of application to all areas of law.[41]

As it only applies to facts subsequent to its entry into force, it has so far been applied in very few cases.[42] Nonetheless, several elements demand attention and make the new procedural instrument an interesting candidate not only for the protection of small-value or standardised claims related to consumer law, but also for the protection of fundamental rights and core societal interests.[43] Among the latter, the right to a clean and healthy environment certainly stands out. Thus, the next section shows how the new Italian class action can become a valuable tool for climate change litigation in the near future by overcoming most of the above-mentioned barriers (section 4).

The first necessary premise, however, is that, as its forerunner, the new collective mechanism actually consists of two instruments, an injunctive and a compensatory action. Their origins, just like their purposes, are almost opposite.

---

38 At least through representative actions.

39 S. Voet, 'Class Actions in Belgium: Evaluation and the Way Forward' in S. Voet and A. Uzelac (eds), above n. 28, pp. 131–63.

40 The alternative is the opt-out regime, which binds to the effects of the *res judicata* all the possible members of the class, unless they explicitly decide to exit it.

41 Art. 840-*bis* Italian Code of Civil Procedural Law.

42 Among them, it is worth highlighting the injunctive collective action against ILVA brought before the Tribunal of Milan in 2021, currently pending, above n. 18.

43 For a more detailed examination, see A. Maglica, and B. Randazzo, 'La *class action* all'italiana: profili costituzionali (integrati)', forthcoming.

On the one hand, the former derives from the civil law tradition and, in particular, from Ancient Rome's *actio popularis*, whereas the latter is probably the most renowned and typical procedural example from the overseas common law world. On the other hand, the former aims to stop or mitigate a certain harmful activity, while the latter's objective is an economic reparation for the harm suffered. Additionally, the recent Italian reform introduces a third crucial feature of this peculiar dichotomy: whereas the compensatory class action reflects the traditional requirements for class certification – that is, adequacy of representation, lack of conflicts of interests and, most importantly, the homogeneity of the individual rights at stake – injunctive collective relief has an even wider scope (according to some),[44] as it can be employed against any conduct, active or passive, that causes prejudice to a plurality of individuals.[45]

Thus, quite extraordinarily, the injunctive class action can be used for the protection not only of individual rights, but also of supra-individual or public interests, such as that to a clean and safe environment, which are what climate change litigation most often aims to protect. Additionally, the lack of the 'homogeneity' requirement – which already appears to be the most onerous test for achieving certification for compensatory class actions – certainly favours the admissibility of future collective injunctive lawsuits under the new regime.

Both injunctive and compensatory actions can be brought by individual members of the class or by organisations included in a specific registry established by the Ministry of Justice, which also gives them publicity and the possibility to join through a dedicated portal.[46] Injunctive claims, moreover, can be filed by 'anyone who has an interest', thus significantly enlarging the number of subjects who can commence such lawsuits.[47]

The defendants, meanwhile, can be either 'companies or institutions managing public services or services of public utility'.[48] Hence, for the moment, the possibility of bringing a class action directly against the State is disregarded. Lastly, the competent court is the section of the tribunal specialising in company matters.[49]

The most unusual features of the new procedure, which may be relevant in overcoming the above-mentioned hurdles in climate change litigation, are examined in the next section.

---

44 For further considerations, see U. Ruffolo, 'Interessi collettivi (e diffusi), azione inibitoria collettiva e "misure idonee" correttive' in U. Ruffolo (ed.), *Class action ed azione collettiva inibitoria. Commento sistematico alla legge 12 aprile 2019, n. 31*, Giuffrè, Milan 2021, p. 234.

45 Art. 840-*sexiesdecies* Italian Code of Civil Procedural Law.

46 The official platform can be accessed at https://pst.giustizia.it/PST/it/pst_2_16.wp, whereas the requirements to enter the registry were published on 12 April 2022 (G.U. n. 86, decreto del Ministro della Giustizia n. 27 del 17 febbraio 2022).

47 Art. 840-*sexiesdecies* Italian Code of Civil Procedural Law.

48 Art. 840-*bis* Italian Code of Civil Procedural Law.

49 Ibid.

4. CLASS ACTIONS AND CLIMATE CHANGE: A COMPARATIVE ASSESSMENT

The effectiveness of class actions in surmounting the barriers to effective climate change litigation should be evaluated through two lenses: on the one hand, the dichotomy between the injunctive and the compensatory remedy; and on the other hand, in relation to its three alternatives, i.e. legislative action (which is equivalent to no litigation), public enforcement and private individual litigation. Under these perspectives, the following disadvantages and advantages, of both a legal and practical nature, deserve attention.

4.1. DISADVANTAGES

The main drawbacks of class actions are the risks they entail. This procedural tool has long been criticised for its abusive use by attorneys, seeking their own pecuniary interest through settlements or large contingency fees rather than that of the class. Nonetheless, European legislators – such as the Italian one – have recently showed how this issue can be tackled through the establishment of limits or by prohibiting contingency fees,[50] as well as a mandatory approval by the court of any settlement agreement.[51]

A similar risk yet to be fully prevented is that of class actions filed by competitors who have a conflict of interest with the defendant. The recent Italian legislation provides a court review before certification,[52] but, especially in the case of third-party funding, it could prove complicated to correctly determine who is effectively financing the lawsuit.[53]

Additionally, class actions inevitably entail higher costs and, above all, still need to be fully managed by judges from the Old Continent, not yet used to their specific mechanisms nor experienced with such high-volume cases.[54] Most European countries have just recently introduced their new class action regime (and indeed had to by 25 December 2022, the deadline for implementing the new Directive) or, in certain cases, have one with a scope of application limited to consumer law.

---

50 Cass. civ., sez. II, ord. 26568/2021.

51 Arts 840-*novies* and 840-*quaterdecies* Italian Code of Civil Procedural Law.

52 Art. 840-*ter* Italian Code of Civil Procedural Law.

53 See S. Voet, 'The Crux of the Matter: Funding and Financing Collective Redress Mechanisms' in B. Hess, M. Bergström and E. Storskrubb (eds), *EU Civil Justice. Current Issues and Future Outlook*, vol. 7, Hart Publishing, Oxford 2016, pp. 201–22.

54 See A. Uzelac, 'Why No Class Actions in Europe? A View from the Side of Dysfunctional Justice Systems' in V. Harsagi and C.H. van Rhee (eds), *Multi-Party Redress Mechanisms in Europe: Squeaking Mice?*, Intersentia, Cambridge 2014.

Nevertheless, the main challenge for the new Italian regime appears to be the concept of 'homogeneity of the individual rights' at stake, a requirement for the admissibility (only) of compensatory class actions. Under the previous consumer class action, the concept of 'homogeneity' had already been at the centre of heated debates and conflicting decisions, with the last word (so far) resulting in the Court of Cassation's 2019 decision embracing a rigid interpretation that essentially equates 'homogeneous' to 'identical'.[55] This interpretation appears incorrect, since it goes beyond the wording of the norm ('homogeneous' etymologically merely means 'with the same origin'), its historical conception and, most importantly, its rationale.[56] In relation to climate change, it is thus uncertain whether the courts will deem a compensatory class action admissible, because of the 'homogeneity' requirement.

While we wait for further interpretation of this concept by the Italian higher courts, including in relation to fundamental rights, it might be advisable to limit the class, taking a lead from the recent *Milieudefensie v. Shell* case of 2021 in the Netherlands, where the District Court found that:

> the interests of current and future generations of the world's population, as served principally with the class actions, are not suitable for bundling. ... However, the interests of current and future generations of Dutch residents and ... of the inhabitants of the Wadden Sea area ... are suitable for bundling, even though in the Netherlands and in the Wadden region there are differences in time, extent and intensity to which the inhabitants will be affected by climate change caused by [carbon dioxide] emissions. However, these differences are much smaller and of a different nature than the mutual differences when it concerns the entire global population and do not stand in the way of bundling in a class action.[57]

Another problem for compensatory class actions may arise in relation to the concept of 'individual rights', since some defendants could argue that the right to a clean and healthy environment is a public and collective one.[58] However, as recalled by the German Federal Constitutional Court in a decision from March 2021 on the constitutionality of the Federal Climate Change Act, 'the mere fact that very large numbers of people are affected does not exclude

---

55 Cass. civ., sez. III civ., 14886/2019; see A. Giussani, 'Diritti omogenei e omogeneizzati nell'azione di classe' (2020) 1 *Rivista di diritto processuale* 359.

56 Ibid. In the words of Scott, 'it is a landmark in judicial sophistry to use the due process concept in the name of protecting the interests of class members, to reject the only litigation procedure capable of doing so': K.E. Scott, 'Two Models of the Civil Process' (1975) 27(3) *Stanford Law Review* 937.

57 *Milieudefensie*, above n. 20. Unofficial English translation from https://uitspraken.rechtspraak.nl/#!/details?id=ECLI:NL:RBDHA:2021:5339, particularly relevant with regard to the requirement of a 'similar interest', in the sense of Book 3, sec. 305 of the Dutch Civil Code.

58 This problem, naturally, concerns all private suits, especially individual ones.

persons from being individually affected in their own fundamental rights',[59] and 'minimum ecological standards are regarded as a precondition for a minimum standard of living'.[60] Thus, harming the environment can directly affect the rights to life and to health and other fundamental freedoms of single individuals (such as 'the possibilities for cultivating interpersonal relationships and taking part in social, cultural and political life').[61] Moreover, for smaller cases (such as the *Lliuya* case in Germany or the *ILVA* case in Italy),[62] industrial activities contributing to climate change can also directly affect the value of properties, and hence have a clear immediate economic impact on the individual members of the class.

Then again, even if the courts were to maintain a strict interpretation of the above-mentioned concepts, this issue would only concern compensatory class actions and not injunctive ones. It is also worth stressing that for the latter kind of lawsuits, tribunals can, in conjunction with the cessation order, and rather interestingly, arrange the adoption of 'appropriate measures' to eliminate or mitigate the effects of the violations.[63] With a broad interpretation, it may thus be possible to adopt economic measures, too, in injunctive actions, as the 'appropriate' way to repair damages.

4.2. ADVANTAGES

Apart from these uncertainties, which hopefully will be soon clarified by the first jurisprudence, class actions present several advantages that make them quite a valuable instrument for climate change litigation.

For instance, class actions are generally well suited to overcoming almost all social and economic obstacles.

First, the costs of litigation can be divided among all the class members: through a membership fee, for example, if the lawsuit is brought by an association, or directly through a court order for all the members who decide to opt in, like under the new Italian compensatory class action.[64] They can also be significantly decreased or not borne at all: thanks to third-party funders,[65] through the possibility of paying contingency fees to the attorneys,[66] or by means of favourable legal provisions (i.e. non-application of the 'loser pays'

---

59 BVerfG, Order of the First Senate of 24 March 2021, above n. 25, §110.
60 Ibid., §114.
61 Ibid.
62 *Lliuya*, above n. 23, and *ILVA*, above n. 18.
63 Art. 840-*sexiesdecies*, c. 7 Italian Code of Civil Procedural Law.
64 Art. 840-*sexies*, c. 1, h) Italian Code of Civil Procedural Law.
65 See S. Voet, above n. 53.
66 Although they are highly disregarded in the EU and admitted only with limitations (e.g. Art. 840-*novies* sets a maximum between 9% and 0.5%, based on the number of class members).

rule in case of loss; abolishment of court fees; charging of certain expenses related to evidence, external experts or notice exclusively to the defendant; tax exemptions).[67]

Second, better funding brings better and larger teams of legal counsel and scientific experts, as compared to other private suits. Unlike in public enforcement, the teams can be composed with more flexibility according to the specific necessities of each case and are usually more motivated, especially if they have a direct connection to it.

Third, after admissibility, settlement is made more likely by the large size of the class, with more chances to end the litigation earlier than would happen in private individual suits.[68]

Lastly, greater media coverage gives more confidence to the plaintiffs, puts the issue of climate change in the spotlight and puts more pressure on the legislative branch to address the matter. A major victory could be achieved, aside from the final outcome of the case, if new reforms were to be put in place or corporations decided to change their policies.

Moreover, representative suits have additional benefits which make adjudication and redress more likely, as can reasonably be ascertained from the recent Italian regulation.

First, in smaller cases, class actions, unlike public enforcement, have a stronger and direct connection with the specific circumstances at stake. This is initially relevant in terms of acquiring knowledge of any harmful activity, as well as subsequently producing evidence, with the involvement of the affected community. Moreover, whereas private individuals may have problems in proving they have a sufficient direct interest in the case (and hence legal standing), environmental organisations – which can be plaintiffs in a class action – are given a privileged status by the Aarhus Convention (Article 3) in seeking effective protection before a court, and can represent the whole community. The new Italian model allows organisations whose by-laws propose to protect the same rights and interests as those at stake in the specific case and which are part of a special registry held by the Ministry of Justice. The recently published requirements for joining the registry, however, require a minimum of two years to have elapsed since the establishment of the organisation.[69] This choice indeed appears to be a missed opportunity, since it does not allow for establishing – at least expeditiously – *ad hoc* associations or foundations, an option which the Dutch experience, for example, has shown to be extremely valuable.[70]

---

67 M. Cappelletti, 'Governmental and Private Advocates for the Public Interest in Civil Litigation: A Comparative Study' (1975) 73(5) *Michigan Law Review* 875.

68 See X.E. Kramer and I.N. Tzankova, 'From Injunction and Settlement to Action: Collective Redress and Funding in the Netherlands' in S. Voet and A. Uzelac (eds), above n. 28.

69 See above n. 46.

70 See X.E. Kramer and I.N. Tzankova, above n. 68, pp. 97–130.

Second, more financial resources makes it possible to call better legal and scientific experts to prove attribution, when required. According to the new Italian rules, defendants in class actions will be required to anticipate the expenses of external experts called by the court, save in exceptional and specific circumstances.[71]

Third, the new Italian class action allows the court to decide on the basis of statistical data and mere presumptions, thus making less strict the requirements for proving attribution, unlike in individual lawsuits.[72] This choice could play a crucial role.

Fourth, special rules have been introduced regarding the exhibition of documents by the defendant, in what has been described as a rather unique process 'similar to the U.S. discovery'.[73] Although not yet applied in any case, this provision could become a valuable instrument to increase social awareness of climate change. As Kysar recalls, 'tobacco defendants in the United States had faced some 300 lawsuits over a period of 40 years regarding the dangerousness of their products without losing a single case or surrendering any amount through settlement', until in 1998, in the case brought by the State of Minnesota against several tobacco companies, during discovery several documents had to be produced by the defendants. These papers later proved incredibly valuable and, once made publicly available, helped shift public perceptions of the tobacco industry into a negative light.[74]

Fifth, the last kind of barrier, the remedial one, can be overcome thanks to the class action's better flexibility in the distribution of damages. In particular, the possibility of establishing flexible forms of recovery or cy-près[75] – either through a judicial decision or a settlement plan – should be highlighted. This unusual form of recovery can be extremely valuable in cases related to climate change, in which the main goal is not economic compensation, but rather, primarily, the halting of any harmful activity (i.e. to stop or at least reduce emissions) and, subsequently, the mitigation of its effects on the planet.

Under the latter objective, the devolution of the sums recovered to an organisation (i.e. a foundation created *ad hoc* or an existing non-governmental organisation) could be better suited to tackling the disruptive effects of climate

---

71 Art. 840-*quinquies*, c. 3 Italian Code of Civil Procedural Law.

72 Ibid., c. 4.

73 Ibid., c. 5–13. In case of refusal or destruction of the documents, judges will be able apply fines and consider the facts proven.

74 D.A. Kysar, 'The Public Life of Private Law: Tort Law as a Risk Regulation Mechanism' (2018) *European Journal of Risk Regulation* 41, 55.

75 J. Kalajdzic, above n. 35, fn. 116: 'The *cy-près* doctrine in class action law permits the distribution of class members' compensation to a third party when it is impracticable to direct the payment to class members themselves. Such a distribution is to indirectly benefit the class and is thought to advance the deterrence function of class actions'.

change, both from a local and global perspective. A peculiarity of climate change is, in fact, that its effects, although certain, are yet to take concrete shape; an individual distribution of damages, however, does not allow the same flexibility in putting out wildfires which are yet to break out, creating flood barriers in zones yet to be identified or evacuating and restoring territories affected by hurricanes not yet formed.

Climate change compensation lawsuits, although still rare, are expected to rise in the coming years, and with flexible recovery mechanisms, a legal technology that has proven extremely effective in other fields,[76] it could be possible to efficiently tailor the response to the future effects of climate change, as well as to obtain their benefits (deterrence, distribution of costs and, consequently, an incentive for socio-technical advancements in industrial production).

5. FUTURE CHALLENGES IN ITALY

The recently enacted Italian class action regime certainly leaves some important questions unanswered. The most significant are those regarding the homogeneity requirement for compensatory actions, the competent court and, most importantly, the impossibility of using this procedural tool against the State itself.

As examined above, a rigid interpretation of the 'homogeneity' requirement could hinder the admissibility of most climate change compensatory class actions. Such a scenario would severely undermine the goal of the legislator when establishing this procedural mechanism: namely to facilitate effective access to justice, allowing all the individual subjective situations harmed by the same conduct to be combined into a single lawsuit, in order to restore the balance of power, which would otherwise be excessively tipped in favour of the defendant who caused the damage. The fact that the same act or conduct does not always have identical consequences is inevitable and should, rather, encourage judges to find the most appropriate solution to render the serial compensation of damages possible. There are several possible techniques, to be chosen on the basis of the specific circumstances of the case: compensation of the lowest common denominator of identicality between the positions of all the members of the class; the sum of the individual damages and the subsequent division in

---

[76] R.B. Cappalli and C. Consolo, above n. 29, mentioning *Daar v. Yellow Cab Company*, 433 P.2d 732 (Cal. 1967), regarding a taxi company in the Los Angeles area which had been adjusting its meters – and thus illegally overcharging its passengers – for four years. The court, unable to identify all the cab riders, after satisfying the proven individual damages, decided to use the unclaimed sums to subsidise the lowering of future cab rates from the defendant company.

equal parts between all the members of the class; the creation of *ad hoc* funds to cover possible future expenses; and, above all, the division into subclasses according to the injury suffered. The US experience (but not only that)[77] is full of valuable examples.

Each of these measures will necessarily involve an approximate quantification of the damage concretely suffered by each member of the class, and this is probably the reason for any reluctance to abandon the narrower interpretation of 'homogeneous individual rights'. Nonetheless, as pointed out above, the explicit choice to join the class through the opt-in mechanism already indicates an acceptance of this unusual form of lump-sum compensation and a renunciation of *ad personam* justice.

Moreover, it should be considered that the particular complexity of litigating against climate change contributions makes individual claims for compensation extremely unlikely in this field. As a consequence, the alternative to class proceedings, save for rare and irrational individual suits, will probably be the absence of climate change compensatory suits, in continuity with the barren Italian landscape for litigation in this field until now. As proven in other sectors,[78] however, the request for compensatory relief can indeed have a highly significant deterrent effect and positively modify defendants' behaviour. Hence, the outlined narrower interpretation would be highly desirable.

As to the competent judge, the Italian legislator has indicated the specialised section for company matters of the court where the defendant has a seat. This choice has raised several questions and will probably need to be amended in the future. On the one hand, in fact, it entails the risk of over-burdening the specialised section (one for every Italian region, except two in Lombardy, Sicily and Trentino Alto Adige and none in Valle d'Aosta), especially in the courts of Milan and Rome, where most of the possible defendants have their seat, as the initial case law already shows.[79] On the other hand, the choice to refer every case launched under the new class action procedure, which is characterised by a general scope of application, to a court specialising only in one kind of dispute looks like an imperfect union, to say the least: assuming judges have sufficient sensitivity to decide on matters outside the corporate realm, they will, in any case, be confronted not only with a new and complex procedure, but also with disputes which require a high level of expertise in various and very different fields to one another (among which, but not exclusively, climate change issues). It is thus doubtful that the specialised sections for company matters are the arena most suited to deciding on all class action suits.

77 See e.g. J. Kalajdzic, above n. 35, and X.E. Kramer and I.N. Tzankova, above n. 68.

78 See e.g. D.A. Kysar, above n. 74, in relation to the tobacco industry.

79 Out of the seven identified class actions started under the new regime, so far three are in Milan, two in Rome, one in Bari and one in Catania.

Lastly, it must be remarked that, at the moment, the class action instrument can only be employed in suits against private companies or entities providing public services or services of public utility. Hence, representative lawsuits against the State for its inaction in relation to climate change – like in the well-known *Urgenda* case[80] – cannot yet be brought in Italy. It might be argued that this jeopardises the right to an effective remedy and the principle of equality. Hopefully, after an initial assessment of the new procedural instrument, they will be allowed too.

6. CONCLUSION

Different weapons can be brought into the judicial arena in the fight against climate change: among them, public enforcement by administrative agencies, private individual suits, and representative, or class, actions. Arguing that only one of them should be employed in every circumstance and in every jurisdiction would simply be naïve. Rather, climate change is a crucial global matter, and, as such, it should be tackled simultaneously from different angles, ways and levels, and in different parts of the world. Consequently, the best answer is probably to have a large array of solutions and to be able to identify the advantages and disadvantages of each of them using a comparative yardstick in relation to the concrete features of each case, in what has been described, in other contexts, as an 'integrated and holistic … multilayered framework of regulation, law-making and law-application'.[81]

Among the litigious options, the contention of this chapter is that the class action model – on the rise in different European jurisdictions, although often perceived with suspicion and, so far, mostly limited to consumer protection – has the potential to overcome several obstacles which hinder effective climate change litigation and become an indispensable tool in the climate change litigator's arsenal.

The class procedure recently enacted in Italy, in particular, although still imperfect and to be tested in practice, shows potential for significant and rapid impact on the protection of the climate, especially in its injunctive form. The *ILVA* case, currently pending before the Tribunal of Milan, promises to be a first and important test to gauge the viability of the new instrument.

---

80 *Urgenda Foundation v. State of the Netherlands* [2015] HA ZA C/09/00456689.

81 S. Voet, above n. 39, p. 138; See also M. Cappelletti, *Public Interest Parties and the Active Role of the Judge in Civil Litigation*, Giuffrè, Milan 1975, p. 152: 'The answer, I believe, is that the lesson to be found is *one of pluralism*. The needs of our time are so complex and demanding that it would be foolish to rely upon any one single governmental institution to satisfy them'.

Should future case law, after the necessary corrections, support the positive analysis of the new procedural collective model, a route might be paved for legally transplanting the model into other EU national systems. In the meantime, considering the success of the *Urgenda* and *Milieudefensie* class actions in the Netherlands, several EU States when enacting the EU Directive on consumer collective redress by the deadline of 25 December 2022 may decide to expand the scope of application of their class action regime to climate change matters.

PART II

CLIMATE CHANGE LITIGATION IN EUROPE: SECTORAL PERSPECTIVES

Corporate Responsibility and Climate Change Litigation

FROM STATE TO CORPORATE LIABILITY IN CLIMATE LITIGATION

How Can *Urgenda*-Type Cases Inform the Responsibility of Private Companies to Mitigate Climate Change?

Maria Antonia TIGRE

1. INTRODUCTION

Over the past decade, climate change litigation has become a powerful tool for climate governance. In attempting to bridge the regulatory gaps in the international legal framework for climate change and the lack of ambition in international negotiations, litigation has emerged as an alternative advocacy mechanism to advance regulatory action through intentional attempts to control or influence the behaviour of governments, corporations and individuals. Cases that received a favourable outcome from courts from a plaintiff's perspective – deemed 'successful' – have pushed for more effective climate regulation or implementation of existing commitments. In its Sixth Assessment Report, the IPCC recognised, for the first time (with medium confidence), that climate litigation has influenced the outcome and ambition of climate governance.[1] The IPCC also identified climate litigation as an important avenue for actors to influence climate policy outside of the formal UNFCCC processes.[2]

Government actors are the most common defendants in climate litigation cases globally.[3] UNEP notes that paradigmatic cases filed against governments have claimed that policies or decisions are inconsistent with commitments to reduce GHG emissions.[4] These commitments can be included in constitutions, legislation or general policies. *Urgenda Foundation v. Kingdom of the Netherlands* was the first case in the world to establish a legal duty on a government to prevent dangerous climate change.[5] In *Urgenda*, the plaintiffs claimed that the Dutch national greenhouse gas (GHG) policies were insufficient to address national climate mitigation obligations. Relying on Articles 2 (right to life) and 8 (right to respect for private and family life) of the European Convention on Human Rights (ECHR) as integrated into Dutch law, the Supreme Court of the Netherlands found that the Dutch government had an enforceable obligation to protect human rights, which required the government to take steps to reduce GHG emissions consistent with limiting global warming to an average of 1.5°C.[6] The Court ruled that post-2020 the Netherlands had to reduce GHG emissions by at least 25% relative to 1990.[7]

The favourable decision in *Urgenda* was essential to recognising climate litigation as a governance strategy, filling the gaps left by regulatory failures and inaction in the Netherlands.[8] Since then, similar claims have been brought in Belgium, France, Germany, Ireland, Sweden and Switzerland. Beyond Europe,

---

1 IPCC, 'Summary for Policymakers' in *Climate Change 2022: Mitigation of Climate Change. Working Group III Contribution to the IPCC Sixth Assessment Report* (2022), p. 63, https://www.ipcc.ch/report/sixth-assessment-report-working-group-3/.

2 Ibid., p. 2230 (chapter 13–13.4.2).

3 UN Environment Programme, *Global Climate Litigation Report, 2020 Status Review* (2020), p. 13.

4 Ibid.

5 *Urgenda Foundation (on behalf of 886 individuals) v. The State of the Netherlands (Ministry of Infrastructure and the Environment)* (2015) ILDC 2456 (NL 2015) (*Urgenda* – District Court); *The State of the Netherlands (Ministry of Economic Affairs and Climate Policy) v. Urgenda Foundation* (2018) C/09/456689 / HA ZA 13-1396; *The State of the Netherlands (Ministry of Economic Affairs and Climate Policy) v. Stichting Urgenda* (2019) 19/00135.

6 *Urgenda Foundation v. The State of the Netherlands*, Supreme Court of the Netherlands, Case No. 19/00135 (20 December 2019).

7 The assessment of the 2020 emissions showed that the target was met at –25.5%. See Statistics Netherlands, *Urgenda reduction target for GHG emissions achieved in 2020* (9 February 2022), https://www.cbs.nl/en-gb/news/2022/06/urgenda-reduction-target-for-ghg-emissions-achieved-in-2020#:~:text=As%20of%202015%2C%20the%20Urgenda,with%20a%2025.5%2Dpercent%20reduction. Current targets include a reduction by 49% by 2030, compared to 1990 levels, and a 95% reduction by 2050. Government of Netherlands, *Climate Policy*, https://www.government.nl/topics/climate-change/climate-policy.

8 S. Eskander et al., *Global Lessons from Climate Change Legislation and Litigation*, 2 Environmental and Energy Policy and The Economy 44 (2021).

cases have been brought in Canada, Peru, South Korea and the United States. These claims against governments, which seek systemic changes in how governments commit to and/or comply with mitigation targets, are deemed systemic mitigation cases. In these, courts are prompted to assess whether there is a human rights obligation to urgently mitigate climate change and/or a due diligence standard for complying with human rights obligations, which can also be informed by a notion of 'fair share' or 'common but differentiated responsibilities'. Systemic mitigation cases have also relied on statutory duties or common law and tort theories. Cases have scrutinised climate commitments or targets, challenging their adequacy or effective implementation. These rulings have effects across jurisdictions and at different territorial levels of governance, articulating forms of transitional climate change regulation.[9]

As climate litigation expands, plaintiffs are increasingly targeting corporations, broadening the role of stakeholders responding to the need for a holistic and comprehensive approach to climate change. On one side, citizens, individuals and groups have a role in pursuing, enhancing and implementing climate goals. Private litigants and NGOs are bringing a growing number of cases as climate litigation becomes a tool for the engagement of civil society in climate action.[10] On the other side, corporations are becoming apparent targets, joining States as defendants as the scope of climate litigation expands.

In May 2021, the Hague District Court, the same court of first instance that rendered the ground-breaking decision in *Urgenda*, ordered Dutch-based oil and gas multinational Royal Dutch Shell (Shell) to reduce its carbon dioxide emissions by 45% from 2019 levels by 2030, as a way to limit global warming to 1.5°C.[11] Despite still being limited to a decision from a court of first instance and potentially being reversed, the judgment in *Milieudefensie et al. v. Royal Dutch Shell* (*Milieudefensie*) represented the first time a private company was ordered to comply with the Paris Agreement. The case would likely not have succeeded without the advances made by *Urgenda* years before. *Milieudefensie* contributes to a body of jurisprudence building on *Urgenda*-type cases to broaden the reach of climate litigation.

While several aspects of *Milieudefensie* are limited to the Dutch legal context, the decision has clear implications beyond the Netherlands. The decision is based on tort law (which, although constructed in the Dutch legal system, has comparable approaches worldwide), the interpretation of the standard duty of care, and international human rights and climate change law.[12] Furthermore,

---

9 J. Peel et al., *Climate Change Law in an Era of Multi-Level Governance*, 1(2) Transnational Environmental Law 245, 269 (2012).

10 Ibid.

11 District Court of The Hague, *Milieudefensie et al. v. Royal Dutch Shell plc* (26 May 2021) C/09/571932 / HA ZA 19-379, English version (*Milieudefensie v. RDS*), para. 5.3.

12 Ibid., paras 4.4.9–4.4.10.

the judgment shows how domestic litigation can contribute to 'hardening' international soft law in relation to standards of corporate conduct.[13] These aspects will be further detailed in this chapter from a comparative perspective. After the decision in *Milieudefensie*, climate litigation's future will likely include an increasing number of private climate litigation cases. Recent cases have targeted companies with high historical emissions (i.e. the Carbon Majors, which include oil and gas, coal, and cement companies) and other industries with a high carbon footprint (such as car manufacturers and livestock farming). These cases focus on the corporate responsibility to reduce emissions in the present and future and seek a court declaration that fossil fuel companies' climate change targets should be aligned with the Paris Agreement.

Against this backdrop, this chapter asks: can the emerging case law on *Urgenda*-type cases inform private climate litigation? How replicable are the strategies and arguments deployed in *Milieudefensie* to other jurisdictions? How can human rights law and international climate law be used to interpret a standard duty of care for corporations in other jurisdictions? This chapter begins by assessing the systemic mitigation 'foundation' that kickstarted the second wave of private climate litigation. Section 3 discusses private climate litigation in general before briefly analysing the decision in *Milieudefensie*. It then compares the *Shell* case with other pending cases against corporations in Europe. Section 4 discusses how private climate litigation has built on systemic mitigation cases and assesses whether similar strategies could be pursued in other jurisdictions. Finally, the chapter looks beyond the European context to debate the possibility of bringing a similar case in the Global South through an example from Brazil.

2. SYSTEMIC MITIGATION CASES

Many cases against governments fall under the 'systemic mitigation' category.[14] Systemic mitigation cases seek to compel a State or one of its organs to increase its overall mitigation efforts. These cases, which are growing in number, can significantly increase a country's mitigation ambition. Systemic mitigation cases respond to complex issues in a dynamic way. In *Urgenda*, the Hague District Court found that the Netherlands' pledge to reduce emissions was insufficient to protect the lives of Dutch citizens. There are now nearly 40 cases globally that build on the foundations laid by the decision in *Urgenda*.[15] In Europe, the total

---

13 C. Macchi and J. van Zeben, *Business and human rights implications of climate change litigation: Milieudefensie et al. v. Royal Dutch Shell*, 30(3) Review of European, Comparative & International Environmental Law 409 (2021).

14 L. Maxwell, S. Mead and D. van Berkel, *Standards for adjudicating the next generation of Urgenda-style climate cases*, 13(1) Journal of Human Rights and the Environment 35 (2022).

15 J. Setzer and C. Higham, *Global trends in climate change litigation: 2021 snapshot, Policy Report* (2021).

number as of 2021 amounts to 19.[16] Most of these are still pending, but courts in five European countries (the Netherlands, Germany, France, Ireland and Belgium) have issued judgments against their respective States (some of these are under appeal). These cases focus on either a government's level of ambition in its mitigation targets and the adequacy of the plans or its action to implement them to achieve a stated goal.

Since *Urgenda*, favourable decisions have similarly established a government's obligation to reduce emissions in other jurisdictions. For example, in *Commune de Grande-Synthe v. France*,[17] Grande-Synthe, a low-lying coastal municipality, questioned the adequacy of the French government's measures designed to meet the domestic target of achieving carbon neutrality by 2050. In 2021, the Conseil d'État found that the French government had failed to adopt the necessary legislative measures to comply with the nation's commitments of a 40% reduction in GHG emissions by 2030, compared to 1990 levels. Through an analysis of a carbon budget that provides a yearly percentage reduction of GHG emissions, the Conseil d'État found that an accelerating pathway of emission reductions would require additional measures in the short term. The refusal to take further action is incompatible with France's obligations under French and EU law. The Council ordered the government to 'take all the measures necessary' to meet its climate goals, including a 40% reduction by 2030.

In *Notre Affaire à Tous and Others v. France* ('*L'affaire du siècle*'),[18] a French court ordered the government to increase climate action to implement its international commitments. Specifically, the plaintiffs questioned the effectiveness of the government's efforts to meet climate targets. The Administrative Court of Paris ordered the government to take immediate and concrete actions to comply with its commitments to cutting carbon emissions and repairing the damages caused by its inaction (i.e. compensate for emissions over the pledges). These decisions show how courts are starting to assess States' accountability to their international commitments while also providing them with discretion to present evidence in a factual investigation and choose methods of compliance.[19]

Germany's Federal Constitutional Court presents another example of a court addressing State accountability and how international commitments are reflected in national laws. In *Neubauer et al. v. Germany*, the Court struck down

---

16 See L. Maxwell et al., above n. 14, Annex A.

17 *Commune de Grande-Synthe v. France*, https://climatecasechart.com/non-us-case/commune-de-grande-synthe-v-france/.

18 *Notre Affaire à Tous and Others v. France*, https://climatecasechart.com/non-us-case/notre-affaire-a-tous-and-others-v-france/.

19 M.A. Tigre, *A look back at significant decisions in climate litigation in 2021*, Climate Law Blog, Sabin Center for Climate Change Law (23 December 2021), http://blogs.law.columbia.edu/climatechange/2021/12/23/a-look-back-at-significant-decisions-in-climate-litigation-in-2021/.

parts of Germany's climate law as incompatible with fundamental rights for failing to set sufficient provisions for emissions cuts beyond 2030.[20] Accepting arguments that the legislature must follow a carbon budget approach to limit warming to well below 2°C, and if possible to 1.5°C, the Court found that the legislature had not proportionally distributed the budget between current and future generations. As a result, the Court ordered the legislature to set explicit provisions for reduction targets from 2031 onward by the end of 2022. The Court relied on an assessment of Germany's fair share contribution to climate mitigation in its analysis. While the German parliament quickly adopted a revised law with renewed commitments in compliance with the decision, another constitutional challenge was brought in *Steinmetz et al. v. Germany*, claiming that these commitments are still insufficient according to the most recent science.[21] This case is still pending.

Similarly, in *VZW Klimaatzaak v. Kingdom of Belgium and Others*,[22] the Brussels Court of First Instance held that the Belgian federal government, as well as the regional governments of Flanders, Wallonia and Brussels, had breached their duty of care by failing to take the necessary measures to prevent the harmful effects of climate change. In addition, the court ruled that by failing to take sufficient climate action to protect the life and privacy of the plaintiffs, the defendants were in breach of their human rights obligations. However, the court declined to set specific reduction targets on separation of powers grounds.

These favourable decisions were highly influenced by the legal arguments in *Urgenda*. However, *Urgenda* has had an impact beyond transnational climate litigation. The legal grounds have also been studied in an attempt to influence corporate behaviour and expand private climate litigation. The decision in *Milieudefensie* has proven that this strategy can be successful.

3. PRIVATE CLIMATE LITIGATION WITH THE GOAL OF REDUCING GHG EMISSIONS

The expansion of strategic climate litigation reflects the growth of cases seeking to influence corporate behaviour in relation to climate change and/or raise awareness about major emitters' responsibility. As of 11 May 2022, the Sabin

---

20 *Neubauer et al. v. Germany*, https://climatecasechart.com/non-us-case/neubauer-et-al-v-germany/.

21 *Steinmetz et al. v. Germany*, https://climatecasechart.com/non-us-case/steinmetz-et-al-v-germany/.

22 *VZW Klimaatzaak v. Kingdom of Belgium et al.*, https://climatecasechart.com/non-us-case/vzw-klimaatzaak-v-kingdom-of-belgium-et-al/. See M. Petel and A. De Spiegeleir, *Guest Commentary: Lessons from the Belgium Climate Case: the devil is in the details*, Climate Law Blog, Sabin Center for Climate Change Law (15 November 2021), http://blogs.law.columbia.edu/climatechange/2021/11/15/guest-commentary-lessons-from-the-belgium-climate-case-the-devil-is-in-the-details/.

Center for Climate Change Law's global climate litigation database includes 81 cases against corporations.[23] These are divided into four categories: (1) GHG emissions reductions (20 cases); (2) misleading advertising (9 cases); (3) environmental assessment and permitting (19 cases); and (4) disclosures (10 cases). The database also assesses cases that seek compensation for climate damages (12 cases). This chapter only analyses cases in the first category.

Of the 20 GHG emissions reduction cases identified by the Sabin Center, cases related to GHG emissions reductions with corporations as defendants have been observed in Argentina, Australia, Brazil, France, Germany, Japan, the Netherlands, New Zealand and Poland.[24] All cases are still pending. Recent cases have targeted companies with high historical emissions (i.e. the Carbon Majors,[25] which include oil and gas, coal, and cement companies) and other industries with a high carbon footprint (such as car manufacturers and livestock farming). These cases focus on the corporate responsibility to reduce emissions in the present and future and seek a court declaration that fossil fuel companies' climate change targets should be aligned with the Paris Agreement.

Of the 20 GHG emissions reductions cases identified by the Sabin Center, 12 were filed in Europe, including five in Germany (against car manufacturers and energy companies), two in France (one against a supermarket chain involved in cattle-ranching deforestation and another against an oil and gas company), two in Poland (energy companies), two in Italy (energy companies and livestock farming), and one in the Netherlands (oil and gas). Other cases are from Argentina, Australia, Brazil, Ecuador, Japan and New Zealand. These cases are forward-looking and focus on the corporate responsibility to reduce emissions in the present and future. The plaintiffs often seek a declaration from courts that fossil fuel companies' climate change targets should be aligned with the Paris Agreement.

3.1. *MILIEUDEFENSIE ET AL. v. ROYAL DUTCH SHELL*

In May 2021, the Hague District Court, a court of first instance, found a violation of human rights and a standard duty of care, leading to Shell's obligation of best efforts to reduce GHG emissions. The court ordered the Dutch-based oil and gas multinational to reduce its carbon dioxide emissions by 45% from 2019 levels by 2030, consistent with the Paris Agreement's highly ambitious goal of limiting global warming to 1.5°C. The judgment represents the first time a private company has been ordered to reduce its emissions consistent with the

23 https://climatecasechart.com/non-us-case-category/corporations/.
24 https://climatecasechart.com/non-us-case-category/ghg-emissions-reduction/.
25 *Carbon Majors*, Climate Accountability Institute, https://climateaccountability.org/carbon majors/.

Paris Agreement's goals. The court did not find that Shell's emissions were per se contrary to existing domestic regulations. However, it ruled that the company has an obligation of result and a 'significant best-efforts obligation' to reduce emissions along its entire value chain. In essence, the court extended the reasoning in *Urgenda* to private companies.

The lawsuit was brought by Friends of the Earth Netherlands (Milieudefensie) jointly with six environmental NGOs and 17,379 individuals (later dismissed by the court). The plaintiffs claimed that Shell's business operations were unlawful since its corporate policy and objectives failed to meet the due standard of care to avoid causing unjust damage to others. By not adopting more ambitious mitigation policies, Shell did not meet the standard of conduct per the goals of the Paris Agreement. This obligation arises from a violation of private law obligations by which everyone must comply with the due standard of care so as not to cause unjust harm to others (Art. 6:162, para. 2 Dutch Civil Code).

The court relied on scientific literature and climate science (i.e. IPCC reports and others), multilateral environmental agreements (i.e. Paris Agreement), reports from international organisations (i.e. UNEP, Climate Ambition Alliance, the World Energy Outlook of the International Energy Agency), the European Convention on Human Rights (ECHR) and EU targets, and other soft law instruments (i.e. the UN Guiding Principles on Business and Human Rights (UNGPs), UN Global Compact, and OECD Guidelines for Multinational Enterprises). The court found through an interpretation of the Paris Agreement's objectives and human rights that non-State actors must also 'do their part' to meet the goals of maintaining global temperature rises well below 2°C. This finding relies on the duty to cooperate, which extends to other stakeholders, as countries cannot undertake this task alone. Notwithstanding the global nature of the climate problem, the court found that Shell has an individual responsibility to reduce its emissions across the Shell group. The ruling stated that the emission reductions applied to Shell group's entire energy portfolio, including its Scope 3 emissions (i.e. indirect or downstream emissions from the organisation's production and sale of fossil fuels),[26] which account for the majority of emissions from fossil fuel companies.

Shell has since announced it will appeal the decision.[27] However, the decision is immediately enforceable and applies to Shell's entire energy portfolio.[28] The

---

26 *Corporate Value chain (Scope 3) Standard*, Greenhouse Gas Protocol, https://ghgprotocol.org/standards/scope-3-standard.

27 Shell Global, *Shell confirms decision to appeal court ruling in Netherlands climate case* (20 July 2021), https://www.shell.com/media/news-and-media-releases/2021/shell-confirms-decision-to-appeal-court-ruling-in-netherlands-climate-case.html.

28 C.V. Giabardo, *Climate Change Litigation & Corporate Responsibility. A Comment on 'Milieudefensie and Others vs. Shell'* (2021), gLAWcal, http://www.glawcal.org.uk/stories/climate-change-litigation-corporate-responsibility-a-comment-on-milieudefensie-and-others-vs-shell-2021.

company has since committed to reducing its Scope 1 and Scope 2 emissions by 50% by 2030, compared with 2016 levels, including direct emissions from owned or controlled sources and indirect emissions from the generation of purchased electricity, steam, heating and cooling.[29] These reductions do not, however, include the emissions from burning Shell's fossil fuel products, which come under Scope 3 emissions. Shell argues that these findings hold Shell accountable for a broader global issue.

3.2. PRIVATE CLIMATE LITIGATION: FRENCH CASES

In France, Notre Affaire à Tous (the same NGO that brought one of the systemic mitigation cases), along with other NGOs and a group of French local governments, has brought a lawsuit against oil and gas company Total (*Notre Affaire à Tous v. Total*).[30] The plaintiffs relied on France's corporate due diligence law (the Duty of Vigilance Act) to ask a court to order Total to recognise the risks generated by its business activities and align its conduct with the Paris Agreement's 1.5 °C target. The duty of vigilance establishes a legally binding obligation for parent companies like Total to identify, prevent, mitigate and redress human rights and environmental impacts resulting from their activities and the operations of companies under their control, subcontractors and suppliers. In addition, the law imposes the obligation to implement and publish a vigilance plan in detail or accounting for the failure to do so. The law aims to foster a broader environment in which companies have a general obligation to prevent harm caused by their supply chain. The plaintiffs allege that despite its vigilance plan, Total has not included detailed actions to curb emissions and actively cut its contribution to climate change, limiting the global average temperature rise to a maximum of 1.5°C, according to the Paris Agreement. Similar to the claims in *Milieudefensie*, the case has a preventative and forward-looking nature, intending to use the legal system as a lever to actuate a change in behaviour if Total's actions are deemed unsatisfactory. After a debate on the court's competency to decide the case, the case will next reach the merits stage.

A similar French case was brought in 2021 by an international coalition of 11 NGOs (*Envol Vert et al. v. Casino*).[31] The NGOs sued the supermarket chain Casino for its involvement in the cattle industry in Brazil and Colombia, which plaintiffs allege caused environmental and human rights harms.

---

29 Carbon Trust, *Briefing: What are Scope 3 emissions?*, https://www.carbontrust.com/resources/briefing-what-are-scope-3-emissions.

30 *Notre Affaire à Tous and Others v. Total*, https://climatecasechart.com/non-us-case/notre-affaire-a-tous-and-others-v-total/.

31 *Envol Vert et al. v. Casino*, http://climatecasechart.com/non-us-case/envol-vert-et-al-v-casino/.

The case challenges 'emissions outsourcing' by targeting entities that may have low emissions profiles in their country of incorporation but whose products cause significant pollution in other jurisdictions. The case is still in the preliminary stage. The case provides an example of supply chain litigation, which looks upstream rather than downstream, and seeks to hold companies accountable for those supply chain-related emissions.

3.3. PRIVATE CLIMATE LITIGATION: GERMAN CASES

One of the early private climate litigation cases was brought in Germany by a Peruvian farmer seeking a declaratory judgment and damages against RWE, Germany's largest electricity producer.[32] In *Luciano Lliuya v. RWE AG*, the plaintiff alleged that RWE, having knowingly contributed to climate change by emitting substantial volumes of GHGs, bore some measure of responsibility for the melting of mountain glaciers near his town of Huaraz, especially as the melting gave rise to an acute threat: Palcacocha, a glacial lake located above Huaraz, has experienced a substantial volumetric increase since 1975, dramatically accelerating from 2003 onwards. Mr Lliuya presented several legal theories in support of his claim, including one that characterised RWE's emissions as a nuisance, due to which the plaintiff had incurred compensable costs to mitigate. Acknowledging that RWE had contributed to the emissions responsible for climate change and thus for the lake's growth, Mr Lliuya asked the court to order RWE to reimburse him for a portion of the costs that he and the Huaraz authorities are expected to incur from setting up flood protections. The share calculated amounted to 0.47% of the total cost – the same percentage as RWE's estimated contribution to global industrial GHG emissions since the beginning of industrialisation (from 1751 onwards). The case has moved to the evidentiary phase, and an on-site visit was scheduled for 2022 to assess climate damages.

In 2021, the German environmental organisation Deutsche Umwelthilfe (DUH) filed two actions against the car manufacturers BMW and Mercedes-Benz for refusing to tighten their carbon emissions target and stop producing fossil fuel-emitting cars by 2030 (*DUH v. BMW* and *DUH v. Mercedes-Benz*).[33] A similar case was filed against Volkswagen.[34] The cases represent the first climate lawsuits against the car-manufacturing industry outside the

32 *Luciano Lliuya v. RWE AG*, http://climatecasechart.com/non-us-case/lliuya-v-rwe-ag/.

33 *Deutsche Umwelthilfe (DUH) v. Bayerische Motoren Werke AG (BMW)*, http://climatecasechart.com/non-us-case/deutsche-umwelthilfe-duh-v-bmw/; *Deutsche Umwelthilfe (DUH) v. Mercedes-Benz AG*, http://climatecasechart.com/non-us-case/deutsche-umwelthilfe-duh-v-mercedes-benz-ag/.

34 *Kaiser et al. v. Volkswagen AG*, http://climatecasechart.com/non-us-case/kaiser-et-al-v-volkswagen-ag/.

United States.[35] The claimants argue that by failing to clearly and irreversibly commit to phasing out the sale of passenger cars and light commercial vehicles with internal combustion engines (ICEs) by 2030, the car manufacturers are violating the fundamental right to climate protection and impinging upon the rights and freedoms of future generations, as phase-out would be necessary for the company to adhere to its allocated carbon budget. The claim is grounded in the Paris Agreement and German tort law. In addition, the claimants rely on the earlier decision in *Neubauer*, where the Court accepted that Germany has a limited total CO_2 emissions budget at its disposal.

In the cases against BMW and Mercedes-Benz, DUH asked the car manufacturers to prove carbon neutrality for Scope 3 emissions from the intended use of ICE passenger cars or refrain from placing ICE passenger cars on the market. Alternatively, DUH asked the court to order Mercedes-Benz and BMW to stop placing new ICE passenger cars on the German market after 31 October 2030 unless Mercedes-Benz can prove GHG neutrality for the intended use of said cars. The case against Mercedes was dismissed in September 2022 based on a separation of powers argument.

In the case against Volkswagen, the claimants asked the court to order the company to:

1. stop placing and to have ceased placement of new ICE passenger cars and light commercial vehicles on the market after 31 December 2029;
2. take appropriate measures to ensure that its annual aggregated CO_2 emissions (Scope 1, 2 and 3), including its subsidiaries, resulting from the development, production and distribution of passenger cars and light commercial vehicles are reduced by at least 65% by 2030 (compared to 2018 levels), and, at a minimum, to keep them below this level;
3. take appropriate measures to ensure that throughout the Volkswagen Group, i.e. across all fully consolidated subsidiaries and brands involved in the development, production and sale of passenger cars, light commercial vehicles and passenger car services, at most 25% of the total number of passenger cars and light commercial vehicles put into circulation between 2021 and the end of 2029 are ICE vehicles; and
4. ensure that the company exercises its legal and actual influence in its joint ventures (not fully consolidated shareholdings) in such a way that the goals described in (1), (2) and (3) are met.

---

35 M.A. Tigre, *The contribution of automakers to climate change: broadening the reach of private sector defendants in climate litigation*, Climate Law Blog, Sabin Center for Climate Change Law (14 October 2021), http://blogs.law.columbia.edu/climatechange/2021/10/14/the-contribution-of-automakers-to-climate-change-broadening-the-reach-of-private-sector-defendants-in-climate-litigation/.

The requested ban on the production of new ICE vehicles would take effect earlier than the 2035 effective ban proposed by the EU in July 2021. The cases are still pending.

Another lawsuit was brought against Wintershall Dea AG, an energy company, for refusing to tighten its carbon emissions target and give up the extraction of natural gas and crude oil by 2025 (*Barbara Metz et al. v. Wintershall Dea AG*).[36] The plaintiffs argued that the company was violating the fundamental right to climate protection and impinging on the plaintiffs' rights and freedoms by not adhering to a 'fair' carbon budget. Based on the company's calculated allocated carbon budget, the plaintiffs submitted that the company be asked to refrain from:

1. extracting natural gas and/or crude oil that emits more than 0.62 gigatons (Gt) CO_2 (natural gas) or more than 0.31 Gt CO_2 (crude oil) when burned (calculated as of 1 January 2021), unless the company can demonstrate GHG neutrality for the CO_2 emissions over this amount; and
2. opening new oil or gas fields, both nationally or internationally, after 31 December 2025, or (indirectly) participating in such openings through equity holdings in other companies.

3.4. ITALIAN CASES

Two cases were recently filed in Italy, further seeking broader emissions reductions. In December 2021, the NGO Rete Legalità per il Clima challenged the compatibility of the practice of intensive livestock farming with the climate emergency before the National Contact Point of the OECD (Organisation for Economic Co-operation and Development).[37] The action in *Rete Legalità per il Clima (Legality for Climate Network) v. Intense livestock farming multinational companies operating in Italy* aims to initiate a procedure before the National Contact Point directed mainly at verifying and challenging the compatibility with the climate emergency of the practice of intensive livestock farming, which generates large quantities of various GHGs, starting with methane.

---

36 *Barbara Metz et al. v. Wintershall Dea AG*, http://climatecasechart.com/non-us-case/barbara-metz-et-al-v-wintershall-dea-ag/.

37 *Rete Legalità per il Clima (Legality for Climate Network) v. Intensive livestock farming multinational companies operating in Italy*, http://climatecasechart.com/non-us-case/rete-legalita-per-il-clima-legality-for-climate-network-and-others-v-intensive-livestock-farming-multinational-companies-operating-in-italy/.

In February 2022, a group of environmental NGOs submitted another climate-related complaint to the National Contact Point of the OECD, alleging the inadequacy of the business plan pursued by the oil company ENI.[38] Specifically, the complaint in *Rete Legalità per il Clima (Legality for Climate Network) and Others v. ENI* highlights that ENI has committed to net-zero emissions by 2050, but its actions run contrary to this goal. Both cases are also in the preliminary stages. The complaint alleges that ENI has not complied with the OECD Guidelines for Multinational Enterprises due to:

1. the fact that the company's strategic plan does not foresee a sufficient cut in GHG emissions in the coming years;
2. the lack of a climate impact assessment of the company's activities;
3. the absence of transparent and adequate information; and
4. the failure to develop a plan for risk prevention and mitigation.

As the National Contact Point is a non-judicial grievance mechanism, the applicants have requested mediation with ENI.

3.5. POLISH CASE

In 2019, ClientEarth brought an action against an energy company requesting it to cease the use of lignite as a fuel for the production of energy at a power plant.[39] According to ClientEarth's petition, of the 12 units currently in operation at the Bełchatów power plant, 11 should be closed by 2030, with one to be closed no later than 2035. ClientEarth alleges that because the power plant is the single largest emitter of carbon dioxide in the European Union and has materially contributed to climate change, its alleged environmental damage action is of a scale that transcends any private interest and negatively impacts the general environment. ClientEarth also contends that this power plant has had a negative impact on other aspects of the environment, including the water and soil in the surrounding region. This environmental damage is directly linked to the use by the power station of lignite as fuel, and therefore, in order to redress the damage that has already occurred and prevent damage which will occur in the future if nothing changes, the use of lignite at this power station must cease as soon as possible. ClientEarth relies on the Polish Environmental Protection Act to substantiate its claims. The case is still pending.

---

38 *Rete Legalità per il Clima (Legality for Climate Network) et al. v. ENI*, http://climatecasechart.com/non-us-case/rete-legalita-per-il-clima-legality-for-climate-network-and-others-v-eni/.

39 *ClientEarth v. Polska Grupa Energetyczna*, http://climatecasechart.com/non-us-case/clientearth-v-polska-grupa-energetyczna/.

4. HOLDING PRIVATE COMPANIES ACCOUNTABLE FOR CLIMATE CHANGE: RELIANCE ON SYSTEMIC MITIGATION CASES AND REPLICATING *MILIEUDEFENSIE*

The systemic mitigation cases and the private climate litigation cases (when directed at reducing GHG emissions) are considered 'strategic' cases in the sense that they intend to accelerate climate action (also referred to as impact litigation).[40] Strategic climate litigation is a relatively recent phenomenon. Cases have mostly been filed since 2015, and the majority are still pending. As a result, scholarship on its effect and potential regulatory contribution, especially on whether it brings about systemic change, is still in its infancy.[41] Yet recent high-profile decisions (such as the ones mentioned here) demonstrate that these wins have an impact beyond the specific circumstances of an individual case.[42] These cases are part of a more extensive process for change, in which a case is an element of a broader strategy oriented towards attaining lasting change.[43] In particular, this chapter considers the first-instance decision in *Milieudefensie* to provide an early indication that a successful decision in systemic mitigation cases can potentially positively influence the legal arguments of GHG emissions reduction cases against private companies.

These examples follow a growing number of climate litigation cases directed at the private sector. The second wave of climate litigation focusing on holding private actors to account has emerged within a rapidly evolving scientific, discursive and constitutional context.[44] The judicial enforcement of corporate accountability for climate change, which had proven elusive in the past (see e.g. *Comer v. Murphy Oil* and *Kivalina v. ExxonMobil*),[45] is now showing more promise through recent initiatives that build on the successful decisions in systemic mitigation cases. These cases attempt to establish a form of corporate responsibility that makes corporations as subjects of international

---

40 See B. Batros and T. Khan, *Thinking Strategically About Climate Litigation*, Open Global Rights (28 June 2020), https://www.openglobalrights.org/thinking-strategically-about-climate-litigation/.

41 J. Peel and R. Markey-Towler, *Recipe for Success?: Lessons for Strategic Climate Litigation from the Sharma, Neubauer, and Shell Cases*, 22(8) German Law Journal 1484 (2021).

42 See K. Bouwer and J. Setzer, *Climate Litigation as Climate Activism: What Works?*, British Academy (2020), pp. 10–13, https://www.thebritishacademy.ac.uk/documents/2701/Climate-Litigation-as-Climate-Activism-What-Works_lnBlsWN.pdf.

43 B. Batros and T. Khan, above n. 41.

44 G. Ganguly, J. Setzer and V. Heyvaert, *If at First You Don't Succeed: Suing Corporations for Climate Change*, 38(4) Oxford Journal of Legal Studies 841 (2018).

45 *Comer v. Murphy Oil USA*, http://climatecasechart.com/case/comer-v-murphy-oil-usa-inc/; *Native Village of Kivalina v. ExxonMobil Corp.*, http://climatecasechart.com/case/native-village-of-kivalina-v-exxonmobil-corp/.

law responsible for climate change mitigation, an arena traditionally limited to States. This responsibility explicitly addresses the actions of transnational corporations, which have significant societal and environmental impacts.[46]

Milieudefensie built on the landmark decision in *Urgenda*, expanding the obligations defined to private companies for the first time.[47] *Milieudefensie* brings a new understanding of corporate responsibility relating to the risk of harm caused by companies, contribution to climate change and represents one of the first explicit judgments determining that the 1.5°C temperature limit should inform legal standards of conduct.[48] This unwritten standard of care is based on human rights and soft law instruments, such as the UNGPs. In the Dutch context, the relationship between human rights and constitutional law, the incorporation of human rights obligations into constitutional law, and the reliance on human rights standards in other cases like *Urgenda* laid the foundation for the *Milieudefensie* ruling and its application of human rights principles to the duty of care. However, that does not mean that human rights principles and international law could not be used to inform reasonableness/negligence analysis in other jurisdictions.

Milieudefensie plays a critical role in the domestic implementation and enforcement of the Paris Agreement by expanding the obligations defined to private companies. The *BMW/Mercedes/Volkswagen* cases are modelled on *Milieudefensie*, widening the scope of defendants in climate litigation to include car manufacturers in Germany. The requirement that companies have concrete and credible climate policies encompassing the net-zero goal and value chain emissions is likely to be a key element of private-sector climate litigation in the near future.[49] The plaintiffs in the car manufacturers cases argue that the latter are violating the fundamental right to climate protection and impinging on the rights and freedoms of future generations by not adhering to a 'fair' carbon budget (based on the Paris Agreement and German climate law).

The plaintiffs and petitioners in these corporate accountability cases rely on judicial decisions that affirm the national government's duty to reduce emissions. Just as *Milieudefensie* is built on *Urgenda*, *DUH* relies on *Neubauer*: the NGOs argue that the Court's finding that Germany has a limited total emissions budget creates a responsibility for companies to reduce their emissions. The plaintiffs

---

46 C. Macchi and J. van Zeben, above n. 13, p. 410.

47 T. Challe-Champiz, *Guest Commentary: An Assessment of the Hague District Court's Decision in Milieudefensie et al. v. Royal Dutch Shell plc*, Climate Law Blog, Sabin Center for Climate Change Law (28 May 2021), http://blogs.law.columbia.edu/climatechange/2021/05/28/guest-commentary-an-assessment-of-the-hague-district-courts-decision-in-milieudefensie-et-al-v-royal-dutch-shell-plc/.

48 M.A. Tigre, above n. 35.

49 J. Setzer and C. Higham, *Climate change litigation is growing and targeting companies in different sectors*, LSE Blog (4 October 2021), https://blogs.lse.ac.uk/businessreview/2021/10/04/climate-change-litigation-is-growing-and-targeting-companies-in-different-sectors/.

further argue that the duty to respect the fundamental right to climate protection established in *Neubauer* extends to corporations, given their responsibility for GHG emissions. It is arguable whether these cases could have been brought without a successful decision in a systemic mitigation case establishing an obligation from the government for emissions reductions. While the French claims were filed before the decisions in *Notre Affaire à Tous* and *Grande Synthe*, these decisions will likely strengthen the cases targeted at companies. All other cases in private climate litigation mentioned here are still pending.

Yet how replicable are the strategies and legal arguments deployed in *Milieudefensie* to other jurisdictions? Significantly, the judgment in *Milieudefensie* makes more concrete Shell's duties as regards its corporate policies on human rights and environmental due diligence and additional responsibilities set out in the UNGPs, and both are not formally legally binding.[50] This core aspect of the decision may prove essential for its replicability, as other courts may also look to these soft law international instruments to inform corporations' domestic obligations. These international standards and the common facts that comprise the basis of the case arguably make it replicable. With these emerging obligations, new claims may be brought against companies that set net-zero targets without credible short-term action.[51]

However, scholars have argued that also central to replicating *Milieudefensie* is for a jurisdiction to have a similar unwritten standard duty of care.[52] This caveat can have significant implications for the replicability of the first-instance decision in *Milieudefensie* in other jurisdictions. It can determine whether tort law is one of the key tools available for establishing climate responsibility.

For example, there is a flexible duty of care in the Brazilian context and the legal tools and doctrines necessary to replicate *Milieudefensie*. A case filed in 2020 in Brazil (*Ministério Público Federal v. de Rezende*)[53] was the first tort case filed against a private farmer regarding his responsibility for the climate damage associated with illegal deforestation (about 2,488 hectares of deforestation). Like the claims in *Milieudefensie*, the case is grounded in human rights and international climate law. The emissions from deforestation directly contribute to climate change, impacting human rights. By linking human rights violations to an unbalanced climate caused by deforestation, the petitioners argue that

---

50 C. Macchi and J. van Zeben, above n. 13, p. 410.

51 T. Khan, *Shell's historic loss in The Hague is a turning point in the fight against big oil*, The Guardian, 1 June 2021.

52 H. Van Asselt, K. Kulovesi, M. Rajavuori and A. Savaresi et al., *Shellshocked: a watershed moment for climate litigation against fossil fuel companies*, Center for Climate Change, Energy and Environmental Law (2021), https://sites.uef.fi/cceel/.

53 *Ministério Público Federal v. de Rezende*, https://climatecasechart.com/non-us-case/ministerio-publico-federal-v-de-rezende/.

each citizen, including the farmer, in this case, has a positive duty to protect the environment and is therefore responsible for the deforestation of Amazonia. The farmer has failed in his duty to collaborate on environmental protection, maintain a climate equilibrium, and not to violate the rights of traditional communities. As such, deforestation caused environmental damage and an unauthorised 1.5 million tons of GHG emissions.[54]

The case provides an interesting point of comparison to *Milieudefensie*, despite some differences in legal strategy and facts (the plaintiff is seeking compensation for climate damage and is targeting a private individual rather than a corporation), as it represents the first tort-based case in Brazil and could open the door for lawsuits against corporations in the future. A decision has not yet been issued in this case.

Lehmen has further discussed the potential for climate litigation strategies focusing on non-State actors in Brazil, given the rise in ESG (environmental, social and governance).[55] She argues that, in the wake of the increased centrality of ESG, several developments have the potential of triggering litigation, opening the door for judicial and extrajudicial cases, transnational and domestic, initiated by a myriad of stakeholders, such as shareholders, investors, NGOs, the Public Prosecution Service, the public, and, in the particular case of Brazil, other actors that have standing, such as political parties, associations and the Bar.[56]

Scholars and litigators are carefully studying the decision in *Milieudefensie* to analyse the possibilities of replicating a similar strategy in other jurisdictions and against companies in different industries. Despite jurisdictional differences, judges are increasingly paying attention to decisions worldwide. The cross-fertilisation of courts in climate litigation is gradually becoming more significant. Given the global nature of climate change, a growing feature of strategic climate cases is to include plaintiffs from beyond the particular jurisdiction where the claim is filed, including jurisdictions in the Global South that might be more vulnerable to climate impacts.[57] This is one way to expand strategic climate litigation to the Global South when a jurisdiction may not be ripe for an individual claim, similar to how the *Casino* case was framed.

54 M.A. Tigre, *Brazilian's First Tort Climate Case for Illegal Deforestation in Amazonia*, Climate Law Blog, Sabin Center for Climate Change Law (16 June 2021), http://blogs.law.columbia.edu/climatechange/2021/06/16/guest-commentary-brazilians-first-tort-climate-case-for-illegal-deforestation-in-amazonia/.

55 A. Lehmen, *Advancing Strategic Climate Litigation in Brazil*, 22(8) German Law Journal 1471 (2021).

56 Ibid.

57 J. Peel and R. Markey-Towler, above n. 42, p. 148; J. Peel and J. Lin, *Transnational Climate Litigation: The Contribution of the Global South*, 113(4) American Journal of International Law 679, 682 (2019).

5. CONCLUSION

This chapter shows how some critical judgments have a broader impact beyond the parties or that particular jurisdiction, addressing novel issues in climate governance. The cases present novel legal arguments that test the bounds of the law. Climate change policy will hardly be successful without significant private action, especially by Carbon Majors and other companies whose emissions are often more extensive than those of countries. The Paris Agreement recognised that achieving the temperature goals requires action by the private sector.[58] *Milieudefensie* significantly advanced the development of corporate responsibility in climate mitigation and companies' role in a polycentric landscape of climate change law and policy. However, further steps are required to fully engage with climate litigation's global implications, particularly regarding North–South differences.

58 UNFCCC, 'Decision 1/CP.21, Adoption of the Paris Agreement', UN Doc. CCC/CP/2015/10/Add.1 (29 January 2016), paras 117, 133 and 134.

THE LIABILITY OF FINANCIAL INSTITUTIONS FOR CLIMATE CHANGE

Legal Mechanisms and Principles for Assessing the Financial Industry's Responsibility for Global Warming

Marta ZAMORSKA

1. INTRODUCTION

In its 2022 report, the Intergovernmental Panel on Climate Change unequivocally asserts that all modelled pathways to limit global warming to 1.5°C entail a reduction of greenhouse gas emissions in all industries.[1] Scientists hold that effectively all new fossil fuel extraction projects must be halted.

The 1.5°C goal was set out in the landmark 2015 Paris Agreement, adopted by nearly 200 signatory States and thus far one of the most ambitious international binding treaties on climate change.[2] Another main objective of the Agreement, as provided in Article 2.1, is strengthening the global response to the threat of climate change by making finance flows consistent with a pathway towards low greenhouse gas emissions and climate-resilient development. The question of climate finance appears in the article establishing the temperature target. This framing attempts to underline the fact that financial flows are essential to the implementation and effectiveness of climate crisis mitigation and adaptation mechanisms. However, as the instrument is only binding for States, which often lack the funds to address the climate crisis, the participation of private financial actors is indispensable.

The financial community understands this opportunity and has begun to adopt the terms of the Paris Agreement. It is now commonplace for 'financial actors, with national and regional development banks leading the way, to talk in terms of aligning with the Paris Agreement as a necessary aspect of their business case.'[3]

Nonetheless, investments in practice still follow traditional patterns and, consequently, financial institutions continue to finance carbon-intensive

1 IPCC, 'Summary for Policymakers' in *Climate Change 2022: Mitigation of Climate Change. Contribution of Working Group III to the Sixth Assessment Report of the Intergovernmental Panel on Climate Change* (P.R. Shukla, J. Skea, R. Slade, A. Al Khourdajie, R. van Diemen, D. McCollum, M. Pathak, S. Some, P. Vyas, R. Fradera, M. Belkacemi, A. Hasija, G. Lisboa, S. Luz and J. Malley, eds), Cambridge University Press, Cambridge/New York 2022.

2 L. Reins and G. van Calster, 'Introduction – The Paris Agreement on Climate Change' in L. Reins and G. van Calster (eds), *The Paris Agreement on Climate Change. A Commentary*, Edward Elgar Publishing, Northampton 2021, p. 1.

3 N.S. Ghaleigh, 'Article 2 Aims, Objectives and Principles' in G. van Calster and L. Reins (eds), *The Paris Agreement on Climate Change. A Commentary*, Edward Elgar Publishing, Northampton 2021, p. 83.

ventures. Since 2015, large banks have invested almost US$4 trillion in coal, oil and gas companies.[4] Although financial institutions may not be direct polluters, they participate in climate change aggravation through the financing of fossil fuel extraction. It seems that if financial institutions are not made legally responsible for factually contributing to the climate crisis, their investment practices may remain inconsistent with the Paris Agreement's objectives.

This chapter considers the basis for, and the future of, the climate change liability of financial institutions and seeks to elucidate the role of various responsibility regimes that may be applicable within this context. It identifies whether, and by what means, financiers can face liability for contributing to climate change intensification based on current applicable laws and general legal and environmental principles. This analysis will consequently also reveal gaps in existing liability schemes and the chapter will canvass recommendations for policy reform and explore new directions for better tackling financial responsibility for the fuelling of carbon-intensive projects.

2. CLIMATE CHANGE OBLIGATIONS THAT ARE CURRENTLY APPLICABLE TO FINANCIAL INSTITUTIONS

The heterogeneity of financial service providers is one of the reasons why it is impossible to identify a one-size-fits-all liability regime applicable to all financial institutions that may provide financing for fossil fuel extraction.

Some financial institutions, such as banks or insurers, are already subject to stricter general regulations, and their obligations to take into account climate considerations may differ considerably. Accountability may also vary depending on whether an organisation is considered part of the public sector or a completely private institution.

Discussing all national provisions that may trigger liability for financing fossil fuel extraction falls outside the scope of this chapter. Therefore, the analysis will be limited to examples of legal obligations to account for climate considerations arising in different jurisdictions that may apply to various types of financial institutions.

---

4 Rainforest Action Network, BankTrack, Indigenous Environmental Network, Oil Change International, Reclaim Finance and the Sierra Club, *Banking on Climate Chaos. Fossil Fuel Finance Report 2021*, p. 4, https://www.bankingonclimatechaos.org/wp-content/uploads/2021/10/Banking-on-Climate-Chaos-2021.pdf.

2.1. CLIMATE-RELATED MANDATORY DISCLOSURES BY FINANCIAL INSTITUTIONS

New Zealand became the first country in the world to introduce mandatory climate-related disclosures.[5] This new legislation aims to provide consistent information on how financial organisations assess and act on risks related to climate change.[6] The New Zealand authorities determined that the regulation should apply solely to large financial institutions (around 200 entities will be affected by the new legislation) because they bear a higher level of public accountability, are already subject to the Financial Markets Authority Act 2011 and are either exposed to climate-related risks or can influence asset allocation decisions. Significantly, non-listed issuers, large greenhouse gas emitters and public entities are exempted from reporting, even though their impact on climate change-related investment is not insignificant.

The new law provides a collaboration-with-industry approach based on the comply-or-explain disclosure mechanism. Consequently, as there is no binding disclosure framework but rather a guiding code, entities may either follow the legislation or explain why they have decided to deviate from compliance. Liabilities apply only for knowingly failing to comply with the given standards. The regulation is, therefore, not looking to determine the impact businesses have on climate change and directly prevent them from making certain investments, but rather to encourage entities and investors to redirect financial flows from emissions-intensive projects to green and carbon-neutral activities.

2.2. EU ENVIRONMENTAL OBLIGATIONS APPLICABLE TO CENTRAL BANKS' ACTIVITIES

Banks are subject not only to reporting obligations but also to other regulatory requirements resulting from national and even supranational legislation. For instance, the European Central Bank, an institution with legal personality as per EU law, and national central banks of all EU Member States, altogether forming the European System of Central Banks, are legally required to support general economic policies in the EU that pursue the achievement of the EU's objectives as laid down in Article 3 of the Treaty on European Union.[7]

---

5 Reuters, 'New Zealand passes climate change disclosure laws for financial firms in world first', 21.10.2021, https://www.reuters.com/business/sustainable-business/new-zealand-passes-climate-change-disclosure-laws-financial-firms-world-first-2021-10-21/.

6 New Zealand Ministry of Business, Innovation and Employment, *Mandatory climate-related disclosures*, https://www.mbie.govt.nz/business-and-employment/business/regulating-entities/mandatory-climate-related-disclosures/.

7 Protocol (No. 4) on the Statute of the European System of Central Banks and of the European Central Bank [2016] OJ C 202/230.

In paragraph 3, that provision states that the EU shall work for the sustainable development of Europe based on a high level of protection and improvement of the quality of the environment. If read in conjunction with Article 4(2)(e) of the Treaty on European Union[8] and Article 191 of the Treaty on the Functioning of the European Union,[9] the EU policy on the environment (which includes laws designed to combat climate change) aims at a high level of protection and is based on precaution, prevention and the 'polluter pays' principle. Thus, environmental protection constitutes 'a general and overarching objective'[10] of the European Union.

The environmental protection resulting from the European Treaties serves as a horizontal policy clause (i.e. it 'must be integrated into the definition and implementation of the Union's policies and activities, in particular with a view to promoting sustainable development').[11] Although scholars generally agree that this commitment will trigger liability only in exceptional cases where environmental considerations were not taken into account,[12] one should read the Treaties' provisions in the light of the European Union's commitment to environmental protection and, specifically in the context of climate change, the EU's 2030 target to reduce net greenhouse gas emissions by at least 55% compared to 1990 levels and to achieve net-zero emissions by 2050.[13] Consequently, financial institutions subject to EU law would also be bound by the obligation to conduct a climate impact assessment before deciding on investment in corporate bonds.

This line of reasoning could have been tested before the European Court of Justice following a lawsuit filed by ClientEarth in Belgium against the Belgian National Bank over its implementation of the European Central Bank's corporate purchase programme.[14] According to several studies, the eligibility criteria on which the programme is based (namely, a market neutrality approach) involves a structural bias which resulted in over half the programme's acquired assets coming from greenhouse gas-intensive sectors.[15] ClientEarth argued that the

---

8 Consolidated Version of the Treaty on European Union [2008] OJ C 115/18.

9 Consolidated Version of the Treaty on the Functioning of the European Union [2008] OJ C 115/132.

10 M. Kotzur, 'Art. 191' in R. Geiger, D.-E. Khan and M. Kotzur (eds), *European Union Treaties. A Commentary*, Beck, Munich 2015, p. 718.

11 S. Garben, 'Article 191 TFEU' in M. Kellerbauer, M. Klamert and J. Tomkin (eds), *The EU Treaties and the Charter of Fundamental Rights: A Commentary*, Oxford University Press, Oxford 2019, p. 1517.

12 Ibid., p. 1518.

13 European Commission, *A European Green Deal*, https://ec.europa.eu/info/strategy/priorities-2019–2024/european-green-deal_en.

14 *ClientEarth v. Belgian National Bank*, Court of First Instance in Brussels, Belgium, 13.04.2021.

15 S. Battiston and I. Monasterolo, *How could the ECB's monetary policy support the sustainable finance transition?*, March 2019, https://www.finexus.uzh.ch/dam/jcr:0103ed7b-71e9-4e81-9941-ee61feefd851/ECB%20sustainable%20finance%2022%20MarchIM.pdf;

Belgian National Bank's purchases under the corporate purchase programme should be declared illegal and the bank should compensate for this illegality. In 2022, the organisation withdrew its lawsuit because the European Central Bank updated its policy on corporate bond purchases.[16]

2.3. EXAMINING CENTRAL BANKS' OBLIGATIONS AS PER NATIONAL CONSTITUTIONAL LAWS

The intertwined European legislation (along with the European Union's firm commitment toward green transition) may result in a positive legal obligation for Member State central banks to abide by the mandate of aiming at a high level of environmental protection. In a similar vein, countries and supranational organisations outside the EU also impose non-financial mandates on their central banks. However, most legislation tasks them only with supporting economic policy objectives.

According to the IMF's Central Bank Legislation Database,[17] which lists 126 institutions, as of 2022 only 14 banks, as well as one monetary union, are charged with a responsibility to explicitly promote or support sustainable economic growth or development, and

> while just 12% of the investigated central banks have explicit sustainability mandates and 54 (or 40%) are mandated to support the government's policy priorities and hence potentially sustainability, 48% of those investigated have no direct or indirect mandate demanding the central bank's engagement with climate change-related topics.[18]

Even if a mandate includes a specific duty to follow sustainable economic growth, which in turn may result in an obligation to address climate change-related concerns, the underlying policy actions might not only be politically highly sensitive and not sufficiently measurable, but they may also potentially conflict with other core objectives. In this context, the accountability mechanism with respect to a central bank's objectives cannot be particularly

---

Grantham Research Institute on Climate Change and the Environment, *The climate impact of quantitative easing*, July 2017, https://www.lse.ac.uk/granthaminstitute/wp-content/uploads/2017/05/Green-QE-policy-brief.pdf.

16 ClientEarth, *We're withdrawing our case against the Belgian National Bank*, November 2022, https://www.clientearth.org/latest/latest-updates/news/we-re-withdrawing-our-lawsuit-against-the-belgian-national-bank/.

17 S. Dikau and U. Volz, 'Central bank mandates, sustainability objectives and the promotion of green finance' (2021) 184 *Ecological Economics* 1, 9.

18 Ibid.

stringent, as it could result in decision paralysis.[19] Therefore, a bank's liability relies more on informal mechanisms than on formal *ex post* accountability regimes.[20]

2.4. CONCLUSION

Current laws, explicitly or indirectly imposing specific climate change obligations, that are applicable to financial institutions do not provide satisfactory liability mechanisms to deter further investing in greenhouse gas emissions-intensive industries. Indeed, many are too vaguely worded or rely on comply-or-explain approaches, which in turn lack sufficient clarity to institute enforcement actions. It remains to be determined if the increasing governmental commitment to climate change mitigation may trigger stricter interpretation of environmental provisions applicable particularly to central banks' activities.

3. SCRUTINY OF THE ACTIVITY OF FINANCIAL INSTITUTIONS UNDER THE 'POLLUTER PAYS' PRINCIPLE

Relatively little attention has been paid in the literature to general environmental principles that may form the basis for holding banks and other financial institutions liable for financing carbon-intensive projects.

One such principle, reflecting the concept of equity and based on corrective justice considerations, is the 'polluter pays' principle.[21] It allocates costs of pollution to a party causing or contributing to environmental hazards. Notably, the principle applies to all costs relating to pollution, which include not only those incurred in the prevention of the harm and adaptation of the environment but also compensation costs.[22] The 'polluter pays' rule became an essential frame of reference for law-makers and, consequently, depending on the jurisdiction, apart from civil liability, the polluter may face criminal charges and administrative penalties to essentially deter it from polluting activities.

---

19 Bank for International Settlements, 'Central bank governance and financial stability. A report by a Study Group', May 2011, p. 30, https://www.bis.org/publ/othp14.pdf.

20 Ibid., p. 39.

21 P. Bowman, 'On the Alleged Insufficiency of the Polluter Pays Principle', The Institute for Futures Studies, Working Paper, 2019, p. 220.

22 See e.g. Art. 8 Draft Global Pact for the Environment, preliminary draft of the group of experts, https://globalpactenvironment.org/uploads/EN.pdf.

3.1. ORIGIN AND TRADITIONAL UNDERSTANDING OF THE 'POLLUTER PAYS' PRINCIPLE

Stemming from economic studies, the 'polluter pays' principle was first referred to at the international level in 1972 in a Council Recommendation on Guiding Principles Concerning the International Economic Aspects of Environmental Policies of the Organisation for Economic Co-operation and Development, and further endorsed by the European Community in 1973. It was subsequently embedded in the 1992 Rio Declaration on Environment and Development as Principle 16, becoming since then an almost customary rule in international law,[23] underpinning national environmental policies and practice.[24] However, there is no uniform interpretation or application of the principle across jurisdictions. Specifically, no international binding definition exists regarding who a polluter is or what exactly constitutes pollution.

Under the traditional understanding, a polluter is simply the person or entity generating pollution, either as a producer or operator of a production process or as its controller.[25] In the case of climate change, a polluter would be most commonly a greenhouse gas emitter. Although the lack of definitional precision may result in legal uncertainty, it also creates a large interpretative and discretionary margin for legislators and the judiciary.

3.2. POLLUTION BY THE FINANCIAL SECTOR IN LIGHT OF A MODERN INTERPRETATION OF THE 'POLLUTER PAYS' PRINCIPLE

Amid the global financial crisis, the US House of Representatives' Financial Services Committee and Treasury Department released draft legislation providing that the costs of financial institutions' restructuring would be spread over a broad range of financial companies with assets of US$10 billion or more,

---

23 S. Kravchenko, M.R. Chowdhury and J.H. Bhuiyan, 'Principles of International Environmental Law' in E.J. Techera (ed.), *Routledge Handbook of International Environmental Law*, 1st ed., Routledge, London 2012, p. 53; contra: S. Kingston, 'The Polluter Pays Principle in EU Climate Law: an Effective Tool before the Courts?' (2020) 10 *Climate Law* 1, 2.

24 See e.g. Directive 2004/35/EC of the European Parliament and of the Council of 21 April 2004 on environmental liability with regard to the prevention and remedying of environmental damage; France, Loi constitutionnelle n° 2005-205 du 1er mars 2005 relative à la Charte de l'environnement (JORF n°0051 du 2 mars 2005), Art. 4; Clean Air Act (CAA) (42 U.S.C. 7401 et seq.); Environmental Law Centre, *The Polluter Pays Principle in Alberta Law. An Introduction & Survey*, December 2019, https://elc.ab.ca/wp-content/uploads/2019/12/The-Polluter-Pays-Principle-in-Alberta-Law-December-2019.pdf.

25 D. Heine, M.G. Faure and G. Dominioni, 'The Polluter-Pays Principle in Climate Change Law: an Economic Appraisal' (2020) 10 *Climate Law* 94, 103–04.

effectively transposing the 'polluter pays' principle into the financial sector.[26] Joseph Stiglitz, a recipient of the Nobel Memorial Prize in Economic Sciences, considers the proposition of Wall Street paying for the effects of toxic mortgages polluting the economy as a matter of equity and efficiency.[27] Indeed, economic sciences conceived the 'polluter pays' principle as a practical way of internalising negative externalities of companies instead of forcing them on society. Heine, Faure and Dominioni argue, for instance, that from an economic theory standpoint, it is possible to attribute part of the responsibility for environmental pollution to other actors, such as consumers, whose demand for products from polluting producers contributes to pollution.[28] The same 'but for' test of causation, if applicable to financial institutions, could also lead to liability attribution because, even though financial institutions do not produce, operate production sites or directly control the production processes that generate pollution, they 'provide the financial oxygen that allows the fossil fuel industry to breathe.'[29]

3.3. THE 'POLLUTER PAYS' PRINCIPLE IN CLIMATE CHANGE LITIGATION

The causal link between the damage resulting from climate change and the entities responsible for pollution constitutes one of the main challenges in establishing the liability for damages of specific corporations before the courts. It is particularly arduous to define the quantitative role of various greenhouse gases, calculate emissions from specific sources, and determine the role of gases in causing particular damage.[30] The issue has not yet been fully resolved

---

26 La Presse, 'Le principe du « pollueur-payeur » appliqué à la finance ?', 28.10.2009, https://www.lapresse.ca/affaires/economie/services-financiers/200910/28/01-915869-le-principe-du-pollueur-payeur-applique-a-la-finance.php; Reuters, 'FACTBOX: U.S. legislation on financial systemic risk', 28.10.2019, https://www.reuters.com/article/us-financial-regulation-draft-factbox-idUKTRE59Q5G320091027.

27 J. Stiglitz, 'We Aren't Done Yet: Comments on the Financial Crisis and Bailout' (2008) 5(5) *Economists' Voice*, https://doi.org/10.2202/1553-3832.1425.

28 D. Heine, M.G. Faure and G. Dominioni, above n. 25, pp. 103–04.

29 M. Campanale quoted by D. Carrington, 'Big banks' trillion-dollar finance for fossil fuels "shocking", says report', *The Guardian*, 24.03.2021, https://www.theguardian.com/environment/2021/mar/24/big-banks-trillion-dollar-finance-for-fossil-fuels-shocking-says-report accessed.

30 The case may be different with climate change mitigation lawsuits in specific tort liability cases, where causal link does not have to be established to any particular damage, see *Milieudefensie et al. v. Royal Dutch Shell plc*, District Court of the Hague, 26.05.2021, ECLI:NL:RBDHA:2021:5339.

by attribution science,[31] and a legally binding calculus has not been approved by any court[32] nor reproduced in any legislation. Therefore, even supposing that financial organisations can be considered polluters as per the economic theory approach, one may argue that it will still be unclear whether companies from the financial sector that provide funds for carbon-intensive ventures may be causally linked to the pollution.

The 'polluter pays' principle can be particularly effective in this area. First, strict liability (i.e. liability that does not require fault, either intentional or by negligence) is inherently consistent with the said principle.[33] Secondly, courts are already willing to rule that the presumption of the link of causation is sufficient to establish the liability of the polluter,[34] recognising the possibility of conveying the liability to other entities[35] or that entities may be found liable solely because they contributed to the risk of pollution.[36] The latter could be especially instrumental for establishing the liability of financial institutions for climate change, as evidently 'financial sponsorship is ... intimately part of the "cause" of corporate activities that harm the environment.'[37]

3.4. LEGAL STATUS OF THE 'POLLUTER PAYS' PRINCIPLE BEFORE THE COURTS

The question remains to what extent the 'polluter pays' principle can be directly invoked before the courts. Although considered a core precept of international environmental law, up to now the 'polluter pays' principle has been deemed insufficiently substantive to give rise to a legal obligation, violation of which would allow victims to seek a remedy.[38]

---

31 N. Durrant, 'Tortious liability for greenhouse gas emissions? Climate change, causation and public policy considerations' (2007) 7(2) *Queensland University of Technology Law and Justice Journal* 403, 403.

32 See, however, *Luciano Lliuya v. RWE AG*, Higher Regional Court of Hamm, Order on defendant's argument of 14.12.2017.

33 S.-A. Joseph, 'The Polluter Pays Principle and Land Remediation: A Comparison of The United Kingdom and Australian Approaches' (2014) 1 *Australian Journal of Environmental Law* 24, 27.

34 Case C-378/08, *Raffinerie Mediterranee (ERG) SpA and Others v. Ministero dello Sviluppo economico*, ECLI:EU:C:2010:126.

35 Case C-1/03, *Paul Van de Walle and Others v. Texaco Belgium SA*, ECLI:EU:C:2004:490.

36 Case C-188/07, *Commune de Mesquer v. Total France SA and Total International Ltd*, ECLI:EU:C:2008:359.

37 B.J. Richardson, 'Financing Environmental Change: A New Role for Canadian Environmental Law' (2003) 49 *McGill Law Journal* 146, 189–90.

38 G. Winter, 'The Legal Nature of Environmental Principles in International, EC and German Law' in R. Macrory (ed.), *Principles of European Environmental Law*, Europa Law Publishing, Groningen 2004, pp. 17–22.

In the *Beanal* case, a US district court unequivocally stated that the principle on its own lacks a universal consensus as to its binding status, especially when applied to non-State entities.[39] Thus, it seems that invoking the principle before the courts would require its direct transposition into the law or at least a legal obligation deriving from legislation that could be interpreted in the light of environmental doctrine. Nonetheless, one should not forget that the principle is already enshrined in various national or supranational rules and even enjoys constitutional status in some countries,[40] increasing its legitimacy as, at the very least, a guiding and interpretative tool for courts. For instance, in the *Urgenda* case, the Dutch Supreme Court implicitly took it into consideration in its decision, despite not referring explicitly to the 'polluter pays' regime.[41] Moreover, in the case of diffuse pollution, the principle warrants making liable the polluter that is most able to pay and not necessarily the one that directly causes the pollution.[42] This may have a deterrent effect on any new carbon-intensive project and further advance the Paris Agreement goals.

3.5. CONCLUSION

When applied to climate change, the 'polluter pays' principle faces various impediments that mostly relate to the question of who can be considered a polluter and the diffuse nature of greenhouse gas emissions. Also, at least at first sight, the principle cannot be invoked on its own.

However, courts have not shied away from expanding the notion of polluter and broadly defining the link of causation. The legal legitimacy of the principle, although resting on economic considerations, is reinforced by its presence in a growing number of international and national legal instruments. Consequently, courts refer to the principle to interpret environmental obligations that could potentially arise in submitted cases.[43]

---

39 *Beanal v. Freeport-McMoRan, Inc.*, 969 F. Supp. 362, District Court for the Eastern District of Louisiana, 10.04.1997.

40 Either explicitly, see e.g. Art. 74 of the Swiss Constitution, or by way of reference to the principle or its logic, see A. Aragão, 'Polluter-Pays Principle' in J. Cremades and C. Hermida (eds), *Encyclopaedia of Contemporary Constitutionalism*, Springer, Cham 2022, pp. 4–5.

41 S. Kingston, above n. 23, p. 26; *Urgenda Foundation v. The State of the Netherlands*, Supreme Court of the Netherlands, 20.12.2019, ECLI:NL:HR:2019:2007, paras 5.7.1–5.7.6.

42 N. de Sadeleer, 'Case C-1/03 Paul Van de Walle' (2006) 43 *Common Law Market Review* 207, 218.

43 N. de Sadeleer, *Environmental Principles: From Political Slogans to Legal Rules*, 2nd ed., Oxford University Press, Oxford 2020, p. 35.

4. PUBLIC NUISANCE LITIGATION TO REDRESS ENVIRONMENTAL CONCERNS

Originating in English common law, the other legal theory that is worth taking into consideration when assessing financial institutions' liability is the doctrine of public nuisance. Historically, the doctrine served to empower governments and courts to issue injunctions against any action that was unreasonable and could cause an injury to general welfare.[44] The US Second Restatement of Torts defines public nuisance as an unreasonable interference with a right common to the general public.[45] Consequently, the doctrine was established to allow governments to seek injunctions and abatements against a party who adopted such unreasonable conduct, while only individuals who had sustained an actual injury were allowed to claim compensatory damages.[46] Under this doctrine, private individuals are not authorised to seek abatement in lieu of the government, nor do they have standing if they did not suffer any actual harm, as the doctrine is not supposed to bring a cause of action for individuals to redress societal problems.[47] Aside from the question of standing, plaintiffs must satisfy a number of substantive requirements in order to successfully argue a claim. As a rule, a public nuisance action requires the establishment of a right common to the public, an unreasonable interference, the defendant's control over the instrumentality, and proximate causation.[48]

Gradually, the US courts expanded the notion of general welfare, and nowadays it is not disputed that environmental rights, including protection against pollution, form part of common rights.[49] Several cases have already been brought on the assumption that energy companies should be liable for greenhouse gas emissions as they amount to a public nuisance.[50] Yet, as to other elements of nuisance law, the judiciary still construes them restrictively,

---

44 *In re Debs*, 158 U.S. 564 (1895); V.E. Schwartz and P. Goldberg, 'The Law of Public Nuisance: Maintaining Rational Boundaries on a Rational Tort' (2006) 45 *Washburn Law Journal* 541, 541.

45 Restatement (Second) of Torts §821B (1979).

46 V.E. Schwartz and P. Goldberg, above n. 44, p. 542.

47 D.E. Antolini, 'Modernizing Public Nuisance: Solving the Paradox of the Special Injury Rule' (2001) 28(3) *Ecology Law Quarterly* 755, 759.

48 S. Lawson, 'The Conundrum of Climate Change Causation: Using Market Share Liability to Satisfy the Identification Requirement in Native Village of Kivalina v. Exxonmobil Co.' (2011) 22 *Fordham Environmental Law Review* 433, 439, 448.

49 R.S. Abate, 'Automobile Emissions and Climate Change Impacts: Employing Public Nuisance Doctrine as Part of a Global Warming Solution in California' (2008) 40 *Connecticut Law Review* 591, 600.

50 See e.g. *Massachusetts v. Exxon Mobil Corp.*, 462 F. Supp. 3d 31, District Court for the District of Massachusetts, 28.05.2020; *Board of County Commissioners v. Suncor Energy (U.S.) Inc.*, 405 F. Supp. 3d 947, District Court for the District of Colorado, 05.09.2019.

including when dealing with harms resulting from environmental damages.[51] Particularly in lawsuits against product manufacturers, courts have shied away from expanding the doctrine, for fear of undermining governmental powers that regulate the issue in product liability law.[52] It seems, therefore, that the (non-)applicability of the public nuisance doctrine in environmental lawsuits is more of a political question for courts than a matter of the characteristics of the doctrine itself.

As early as the 1960s, scholars were debating the flexible and broad character of the nuisance tort, which could provide a remedy for community injury.[53] In the recent string of lawsuits against Monsanto, a manufacturer of chemicals polluting the environment, US trial courts have largely rejected the company's arguments against the substance of claims brought on the basis of public nuisance tort.[54] According to Solana, who identified eight different trends in climate change litigation in relation to financial markets, public nuisance claims in tort against financiers as 'indirect polluters'[55] could be conceivable 'in the context of project finance transactions' (i.e. where funding is provided for a very specific project), simplifying the connection between the funding provider and a third-party loss suffered due to climate-related events in connection with the project.[56] Thus far, however, US judges have not had to try such a case on its merits,[57] partly because of the scale of the problem, but also due to political implications[58] in connection with the principle of separation of powers. These unduly rigid gatekeepers used by courts may further preclude climate change nuisance actions against financial institutions. Even if, in some rare cases, courts have stretched the traditional requirements of the public nuisance doctrine, notably to allow a case to proceed against a party that did not engage in the act of pollution,[59] generally they refuse to transform it into a broad and amenable cause of action.

---

51 *City of Manchester v. National Gypsum Co.*, 637 F. Supp. 646, District Court for the District of Rhode Island, 30.05.1986; *Palazzolo v. State*, No. WM 88-0297, 2005 WL 1645974, State of Rhode Island Superior Court, 05.07.2005.

52 *City of San Diego v. U.S. Gypsum Co.*, 35 Cal. Rptr. 2d, Court of Appeal of California, 29.11.1994.

53 W.L. Prosser, 'Private Action for Public Nuisance' (1966) 52 *Virginia Law Review* 997, 1005; D.E. Antolini, above n. 44, p. 779.

54 *San Diego Unified Port Dist. v. Monsanto Co.*, No. 15-cv-578-WQH-AGS, District Court for the Southern District of California, 26.03.2020.

55 J. Setzer, C. Higham, A. Jackson and J. Solana, 'Climate change litigation and central banks', ECB Legal Working Paper Series No. 21, December 2021, p. 57.

56 Ibid.

57 A.C. Lin, 'Dodging Public Nuisance' (2020) 11 *UC Irvine Law Review* 489, 506.

58 Ibid.

59 *State v. Schenectady Chems., Inc.*, 459 N.Y.S.2d 971, Rensselaer County Supreme Court, 18.02.1983.

5. FIDUCIARY DUTIES OF FINANCIAL INSTITUTIONS' DIRECTORS AND BOARDS TO CONSIDER CLIMATE CHANGE

Not only may financial institutions face liability for their actions in relation to climate change, but their directors and boards can also face lawsuits against them individually and be held responsible for failing to properly fulfil their corporate duties.

5.1. FIDUCIARY DUTIES APPLICABLE TO FINANCIAL INSTITUTIONS' DIRECTORS AND BOARDS AS PER CORPORATE LAWS

Under corporate law, obligations generally applicable to directors of firms, including those operating in the financial sector, are labelled fiduciary duties. Even though their understanding and scope vary, most notably between common law and civil law jurisdictions, the substance of these duties will generally be the same under most legal rules.[60] Thus, the governance responsibilities of corporate directors will, at the fundamental level, translate into acting in the company's best interests, which includes a standard of due care, skill and diligence that they should adopt in conducting business activities (duty of care) and an obligation not to create conflicts of interest with the firm (duty of loyalty).[61]

Fiduciary duty is an evolving concept, constantly adjusted to reflect best practices in modern business.[62] This duty is often broadly worded in legal provisions so as to not preclude its dynamic interpretation,[63] allowing courts to refer, for instance, to rules followed by a profession or in a particular sector of the economy.[64] At present, modern definitions of obligations due by directors to their companies encompass social and environmental considerations that cannot be ignored in the conduct of business.[65] Climate change is particularly relevant for these considerations.[66]

---

60 S.L. Schwarcz, A. Jones and J. Yan, 'Responsibility of Directors of Financial Institutions' in D. Busch, G. Ferrarini and G. van Solinge (eds), *Governance of Financial Institutions*, Oxford University Press, Oxford 2019, pp. 157–58.

61 Ibid.

62 L. Mehmetaj and K. Brunner, 'ESG and Fiduciary Duties of Investment Managers' (2021) 4 *GesKR* 441, 445.

63 United Nations Environment Programme Finance Initiative, *Fiduciary Duty in the 21st Century*, p. 11, https://www.unepfi.org/wordpress/wp-content/uploads/2019/10/Fiduciary-duty-21st-century-final-report.pdf.

64 Swiss Federal Supreme Court, 4A_556/2019, 29.09.2020, para. 4.3.1.

65 L. Mehmetaj and K. Brunner above n. 62, p. 445; Hansell LPP, *Putting Climate Change Risk on the Boardroom Table*, https://www.hanselladvisory.com/content/uploads/Hansell-

In the 2021 World Economic Forum's Global Risks Report, risks relating to climate change are ranked highest, estimated by both likelihood and impact.[67] Consequently, climate-related risks not only pose a material threat to companies, including financial institutions, but they also represent a direct future financial risk,[68] which is already foreseeable, making it difficult to ignore by directors on the assumption that they could not have known of the danger.[69] Corporate boards and directors are therefore considered to be under an obligation to manage and take these factors into account in their business decision-making.[70] Public authorities have already started issuing recommendations to aid the assessment of these risks. The Canadian Securities Administrators published a list of questions that boards of directors should take into account when exercising their mandate.[71] The questions help the board to collect sufficient information to appropriately oversee and consider management's assessment of climate change-related risks and to factor those risks into their investment and voting decisions. The Australian Prudential Regulation Authority warns companies that ignoring or failing to adequately assess risks arising from climate change may result in board liability.[72]

Climate-Change-Opinion.pdf; Y.H. Godiwalla, 'Corporate Social Responsibility: Theoretical Discussions' (2016) 4 *International Journal of Social Sciences Studies* 1, 5; E.M. Jamison, 'The Juxtaposition of Corporate Social Responsibility Initiatives and the Pursuit of Corporate Wealth Maximization. Note' (2011) 57 *Wayne Law Review* 1457, 1457.

66 The Hague District Court inferred corporate climate obligations from, among other factors, the UN Guiding Principles on Business and Human Rights, see District Court of The Hague, *Milieudefensie et al. v. Royal Dutch Shell plc*, 26.05.2021, ECLI:NL:RBDHA:2021:5339; in July 2022, the UN General Assembly passed a resolution recognising the right to a healthy environment as a human right calling upon States and businesses alike to enhance their efforts for a sustainable environment, see UN General Assembly, Resolution No. A/76/PV.97, 28.07.2022.

67 World Economic Forum, *The Global Risks' 16th Edition, Report 2021*, https://www3.weforum.org/docs/WEF_The_Global_Risks_Report_2021.pdf.

68 J. Setzer, C. Higham, A. Jackson and J. Solana, above n. 55, p. 21.

69 N. Hutley and S. Hartford-Davis, *Climate Change and Directors' Duties*, The Centre for Policy Development and The Future Business Council, Memorandum of Opinion, 2016, para. 14.

70 R.H. Weber and A. Hösli, 'Climate Change Liability: Comparing Risks for Directors in Jurisdictions of the Common and Civil Law' (2020) 10 *Climate Law* 152, 152.

71 Canadian Securities Administrators, *CSA Staff Notice 51-358 Reporting of Climate Change-related Risks*, 2019, https://www.osc.ca/sites/default/files/pdfs/irps/csa_20190801_51-358_reporting-of-climate-change-related-risks.pdf.

72 J. Eyers, 'APRA puts onus on directors to manage climate change risk', *Financial Review*, 26.11.2021.

5.2. SOME PARTICULARITIES OF FIDUCIARY DUTIES IN SPECIFIC FINANCIAL SECTORS AS PER FINANCIAL LAWS

Fiduciary duties of directors and boards of financial institutions will be largely the same as those stemming from general company laws or common law principles. However, they may differ in some strictly defined contexts. For example, Swiss asset managers must refrain from a range of activities explicitly enumerated by FINMA, the supervisor of the Swiss financial market.[73] Similarly, under the duty of loyalty, directors of federal savings associations must avoid specific conflicts of interest.[74]

Interestingly, one of the components of the duty of care, especially in the banking industry, is the avoidance of unsafe or unsound practices. A typical definition of the duty provides that unsafe practices encompass

> any action, or lack of action, which is contrary to generally accepted standards of prudent operation, the possible consequences of which, if continued, would be abnormal risk or loss or damage to an institution, its shareholders, or the agencies.[75]

In the aftermath of the global financial crisis, some jurisdictions decided to expand this notion to cover excessive financial risk-taking policies. It remains to be seen whether, in the future, financial institutions' investments in carbon-intensive projects in disregard of climate change risks may fall into this category, triggering lawsuits against their directors.

Financially material factors must also be considered in financial institutions' decision-making processes; thus, addressing climate change risks seems inevitable. Financial regulatory and advisory bodies have also been trying to tackle this issue. The Network of Central Banks and Supervisors for Greening the Financial System recognises climate change as a financial risk and recommends that financial institutions discuss it at board level.[76] The Bank of Canada, together with the Office of the Superintendent of Financial Institutions, conducted a project aiming to improve the assessment

---

73 FINMA, Circular 2009/1. Guidelines on asset management – Guidelines for the recognition of self-regulation in asset management as minimum standard.

74 Office of the Comptroller of the Currency, *Director's Book: Role of Directors for National Banks and Federal Savings Associations*, November 2020, p. 28, https://www.occ.gov/publications-and-resources/publications/banker-education/files/pub-directors-book.pdf.

75 United States of America Department of the Treasury Office of the Comptroller of the Currency, In the matter of Patrick Adams, Former President and Chief Executive Officer, T Bank, N.A. Dallas, Texas, Final Decision OCC AA-EC-11-50.

76 Network for Greening the Financial System, *A call for action. Climate change as a source of financial risk*, April 2019, p. 5, https://www.ngfs.net/sites/default/files/medias/documents/ngfs_first_comprehensive_report_-_17042019_0.pdf.

and disclosure of risk pertaining to climate change and evaluate financial institutions' risk management practices.[77]

For some financial organisations with a long-term horizon for their investments, climate change risks are already particularly relevant. For instance, PensionsEurope, representing 25 associations in 18 European Union Member States and four other European countries, deems climate change risk most material to the pension funds sector and supports the European Insurance and Occupational Pensions Authority bringing more focus to the incorporation of said risk by specifically addressing those issues-management policies.[78] Most significantly, retirement asset owners face growing surveillance as to their investment practices from members who do not withhold from enforcing their rights in courts. One of Australia's most significant pension funds decided to settle a case filed by a young member who claimed that the fund was putting at risk his retirement savings by not correctly assessing the financial risks of climate change.[79] The fund agreed, among other things, to align its portfolio to a net-zero goal by 2050.

5.3. LIABILITY OF BOARDS AND FINANCIAL INSTITUTIONS STEMMING FROM FIDUCIARY DUTIES

The liability regime for a breach of fiduciary obligations will significantly depend on the jurisdiction that enforces them. Generally, company law provisions will allow a firm to which a director owes duties to bring a claim. In addition, in most jurisdictions, shareholders will also benefit from the right to take legal action against directors, either through the so-called derivative action, to enforce their duties and to seek compensation for losses sustained as a result of management deficiencies, or via direct action, to redress an injury sustained personally.[80] Even more significantly, the former is brought on behalf of the firm itself, meaning that injury to the shareholders is not a prerequisite to establish standing. In March 2022, ClientEarth initiated such a derivative shareholder

---

77 Bank of Canada and Office of the Superintendent of Financial Institutions, *Using Scenario Analysis to Assess Climate Transition Risk. Final Report of the BoC-OSFI Climate Scenario Analysis Pilot*, https://www.bankofcanada.ca/wp-content/uploads/2021/11/BoC-OSFI-Using-Scenario-Analysis-to-Assess-Climate-Transition-Risk.pdf.

78 PensionsEurope and AEIP, *Comments to EIOPA's Discussion Paper on a Methodological Framework for Stress-Testing IORPs*, 21.06.2021, https://www.pensionseurope.eu/system/files/PensionsEurope%20AEIP%20input%20to%20EIOPA%20on%20methodological%20framework%20for%20stress%20testing%20IORPs%20-%20FINAL.pdf.

79 S. Pandey, 'Australian pension fund settles landmark climate lawsuit', *Reuters*, 02.11.2020, https://www.reuters.com/article/uk-australia-climatechange-pensions-laws/australian-pension-fund-settles-landmark-climate-lawsuit-idINKBN27I0DTY.

80 Editors, 'Distinguishing between Direct and Derivative Shareholder Suits' (1962) 110(8) *University of Pennsylvania Law Review* 1147, 1147.

action against Shell's board of directors, alleging it had breached its duty to promote the company's success under the 2006 UK Companies Act by failing to take the energy transition into consideration, putting the long-term success of the company at risk.[81] By the same token, in 2021, by means of the bankruptcy plan assignment, a victims' trust established to pay settlements to tens of thousands of victims of Northern California wildfires filed a suit against 22 former Pacific Gas and Electric (PG&E) directors and executives for breach of their fiduciary duties to the company and seeking liability for damages and loss of market capitalisation.[82] Directors and boards may also be legally obliged to weigh certain public interests and consider other social actors in discharging their duties, especially in countries that follow the model of stakeholder primacy.[83]

Directors and boards of corporations operating in the financial sector are additionally accountable to regulatory authorities, which may bring their own legal actions.[84] Regulators' investigative resources, combined with the deterrence and public interest objectives of their actions, mean that their suits are considered the ones most feared by the financial industry.[85] Regulatory bodies can impose substantial financial penalties on directors for breach of their regulatory obligations and may go as far as issuing a lifetime ban on assuming controlling functions in the financial services industry.[86]

The emergence of new legal concepts further raises the prospect of increased climate liability litigation against financial institutions. Banks already face lawsuits in relation to their lending practices.[87] The scope of corporate social responsibility is widening to include climate change as a material impact on a company's financial risk and return.[88] Therefore, directors' fiduciary duties and

---

81 ClientEarth, above n. 16.

82 J.D. Morris, 'Victims' fund sues 22 former PG&E officials over 2017–2018 wildfires – wants more money', *San Francisco Chronicle*, 24.02.2016, https://www.sfchronicle.com/bayarea/article/Victims-fund-sues-22-former-PG-E-officials-over-15976064.php.

83 The Dutch Corporate Governance Code, Principle 1.1; Bulgarian Code of Corporate Governance, Chapter 5; Canada Business Corporation Act, RSC 1985, c C-44, s. 122(1)(1.1); German Aktiengesetz, Art. 96.

84 I.H.-Y. Chiu, *Regulatory Duties for Directors in the Financial Services Sector and Directors' Duties in Company Law – Bifurcation and Interfaces*, https://discovery.ucl.ac.uk/id/eprint/1507830/1/Chiu_Regulatory_duties_for_directors_AAM.pdf; UK Financial Services and Markets Act 2000; Regulation (EU) No. 1093/2010 of the European Parliament and of the Council of 24 November 2010 establishing a European Supervisory Authority (European Banking Authority), amending Decision No. 716/2009/EC and repealing Commission Decision 2009/78/EC [2010] OJ L 331/12.

85 S.L. Schwarcz, A. Jones and J. Yan, above n. 60.

86 See e.g. Financial Services Authority Final Notice to Peter Cummings, 12.09.2012, para. 5.63.

87 S. Barker, J. Dellios and E. Mulholland, *Legal actions as a driver and consequence of climate-related physical risk adaptation. Liability risk and adaptation finance*, Minter Ellison and UN Environment Programme and Finance Initiative 2021, p. 44.

88 T. Clarke, 'The Widening Scope of Directors' Duties: The Increasing Impact of Corporate and Environmental Responsibility' (2016) 39 *Seattle University Law Review* 531, 541.

the debate on the future of company law are evolving around a separate corporate duty of environmental care,[89] which could correspond to the duty to avoid harm to others.[90] Against this background, banks may face particular liability risks, as their positions and roles in financial markets allow them to require in the lending process more information from a borrowing company, including environmental performance.[91] Even if a lender is protected from tort liability, it could still be held responsible for its borrowers' environmental obligations if the latter face financial difficulties. Protection of secured creditors such as banks under insolvency law does not always pre-empt other legal provisions, especially those designed to protect public health or safety from identified dangerous ventures.[92]

5.4. CONCLUSION

In a nutshell, the violation of fiduciary duties, including adequate consideration of material risks, may result in directors' or boards' liability through lawsuits brought by shareholders and sanctions from regulatory authorities.[93] Moreover, if climate-related financial risks are not correctly addressed, asset prices may be falsely evaluated,[94] ultimately becoming stranded.[95] Liability may, therefore, also arise from a violation of directors' and boards' duties to act in the company's best interests.[96]

---

89 B. Sjåfjell and B.J. Richardson, 'The Future of Company Law and Sustainability' in B. Sjåfjell and B.J. Richardson (eds), *Company Law and Sustainability: Legal Barriers and Opportunities*, Cambridge University Press, Cambridge 2015, p. 312.

90 G. Ganguly, J. Setzer and V. Heyvaert, 'If at First You Don't Succeed: Suing Corporations for Climate Change' (2018) 38(4) *Oxford Journal of Legal Studies* 841, 860.

91 B.J. Richardson, above n. 37, p. 180.

92 Ibid., p. 181; *Midlantic National Bank v. NJDEP*, 474 U.S. 494 (1986); *PanAmericana de Bienes y Servicios v. Northern Badger Oil & Gas Limited*, Alberta Court of Appeal [1991] 5 WWR 577.

93 J. Sarra and E. DeMarco, *Climate-related Legal Risks for Financial Institutions: Executive Brief*, Global Risk Institute 2021, p. 2; M. Slezak, 'Commonwealth Bank Shareholders Sue over "Inadequate" Disclosure of Climate Change Risks', *The Guardian*, 08.08.2017.

94 R.H. Weber and A. Hösli, above n. 70, p. 155; E. Campignio, P. Monnin and A. von Jagow, *Climate Risks in Financial Assets. Discussion Note 2019/2*, Council on Economic Policies 2019, pp. 23–24.

95 B. Caldecott, 'Introduction to special issue: Stranded assets and the environment' (2017) 7(1) *Journal of Sustainable Finance and Investment* 1, 2; See also the IPCC's 2022 Report, which states that coal assets are at risk of being stranded before 2030, IPCC, above n. 1, p. 37.

96 ClientEarth, *Court win in world-first climate risk case puts future of Ostrołęka C coal plant in question*, https://www.clientearth.org/latest/press-office/press/court-win-in-world-first-climate-risk-case-puts-future-of-ostroleka-c-coal-plant-in-question/; *McVeigh v. Retail Employees Superannuation Trust*, Federal Court of Australia, NSD1333/2018.

6. CONCLUSION AND OUTLOOK

One of the main legal constraints of any liability regime involving a financial institution and its role in fuelling the climate crisis is analogous to the constraint on cases involving corporate responsibility for climate change damages – namely, causation. It is already challenging to pinpoint the link between a corporation's activities that contribute to climate change and the alleged injury resulting therefrom. In the words of one district court, there is 'no realistic possibility of tracing any particular alleged effect of global warming to any particular emissions by any specific person, entity, group at any particular point in time.'[97]

Persuasively arguing the existence of causation seems, therefore, even more challenging in the case of financial institutions whose links to damage through the financing of fossil extraction projects are even more remote. The issue becomes more problematic if multiple banks or financial institutions are involved in the creation and subsequent funding of numerous carbon endeavours. Similar actions taken by various institutions render it challenging to determine which particular behaviour was the cause of the damage. Taking into consideration these difficulties, an open question is what the effect would be of preventive actions against financial institutions to mitigate, rather than compensate, climate change, based on the broad definition of the corporate duty of care.

The parallel of liability based on fault or negligence is strict liability, which can be invoked in cases of legal, albeit hazardous, activities from which the operator obtains an advantage. Loser discusses, at least from a theoretical standpoint, the idea that strict liability could be invoked in a financial crisis to render financial institutions responsible for creating certain investment products.[98] However, in the absence of specific provisions in national or international legal instruments and the impossibility of resorting to analogous application, strict liability seems, for now, unsuitable to be generally useful for all cases where financing is provided for carbon-intensive projects.

The IPCC reports already stress that 'unless there are immediate, rapid and large-scale reductions in greenhouse gas emissions, limiting warming to close to 1.5°C or even 2°C will be beyond reach'.[99] We are in exceptional circumstances, and great effort must be undertaken to reduce greenhouse gas emissions. The widely used reporting mechanism in corporate and financial laws is often based

---

97 *Native Village of Kivalina v. Exxonmobil Corporation*, United States District Court for the Northern District of California, Oakland Division, C 08-1138 SBA.

98 P. Loser, 'Financial Crisis – The Liability of Banking Institutions' (2013) 4(2) *Journal of European Tort Law* 128, 146.

99 IPCC, *Climate change widespread, rapid, and intensifying*, https://www.ipcc.ch/2021/08/09/ar6-wg1-20210809-pr/.

on the comply-or-explain principle.[100] Albeit enjoying normative force, it still allows companies to deviate from legal requirements by simply providing an explanation for their decision, effectively slowing down the process of changing corporate behaviour. In the case of financial institutions, this is not a sufficient incentive to drive reform of investing and funding praxis. Thus, the challenge for policy reform is twofold: not only to embed climate change considerations into financial markets but to effectively reform responsibility regimes to prevent finance from flowing in the direction of carbon-burning projects. Although the heterogeneity of financial service providers requires a cautious approach to a one-size-fits-all responsibility regime, some legal amendments can encompass virtually every financial institution.

Strict climate change liability for lenders funding fossil fuel extraction projects can serve as an example of a solution applicable across different forms of corporate investment. Attribution science can be used to demonstrate that damage is a result of human-induced climate change, to which emitters of greenhouse gases contributed, and to what extent this happened.[101]

To further the deterrent effect of penalties for investing in greenhouse gas emission projects, policy reforms could include a *forum necessitatis* encompassing all climate change claims, including those against financial institutions. In addition to vicarious liability, corporate law could also be amended to pre-empt the interests of stakeholders over those of shareholders, thus guiding the interpretation of director and board duties and strengthening shareholder activism. Against the current background, various impediments prevent a successful claim against financiers for contributing to climate change aggravation. Consequently, policy reforms must encompass procedural changes, as well as those relating to the merits of the financial institutions' liability regime.

100 V. Magnier, *Comparative Corporate Governance. Legal Perspectives*, Edward Elgar Publishing, Cheltenham 2017, Chapter 5, para. 5.1.3.

101 M. Burger, J. Wentz and R. Horton, 'The Law and Science of Climate Change Attribution' (2020) 45(1) *Columbia Journal of Environmental Law* 57, 147.

PART III

CLIMATE CHANGE LITIGATION IN EUROPE: THE WAY FORWARD

CONCLUSION

Climate Change Litigation in Europe – The Way Forward

Carole BILLIET, Alina HOLZHAUSEN, Matteo FERMEGLIA and Ivano ALOGNA

1. SUMMARY OF PARTS I AND II OF THIS EDITED VOLUME

Parts I and II of this edited volume provided valuable insights into climate change litigation in Europe, from not only comparative but also sectoral perspectives. Starting with Part I on 'Climate Change Litigation in Europe: Regional and Comparative Perspectives', Lavrysen and Bouquelle laid out the foundation for climate change and the courts. As became apparent throughout their chapter, climate cases will continue to be filed, especially as long as climate science confirms that States are 'not on track to deliver the Paris Agreement goals'.[1] At the same time, follow-up questions regarding the enforcement of – from the claimant's perspective successful – decisions arise. For example, Lavrysen and Bouquelle asked '[w]hat if a plan or a programme has been adopted by the government or corporation following the judgment, but is not or is insufficiently implemented?'[2] Taking the *Urgenda* case of June 2015 as an example, Lavrysen and Bouquelle pointed out that seven years after that judgment, the Dutch government has still not achieved the required greenhouse gas (GHG) emissions reduction, which makes one wonder whether this will 'give rise to follow-up cases and what types of remedies will be available'.[3]

1 Lavrysen and Bouquelle in this volume.
2 Ibid.
3 Ibid.

Next, Alogna and Billiet analysed the role of European regional courts in climate change litigation, as resulting from the expert discussion between Marc Willers KC and Judge Tim Eicke KC. Given that, as of February 2022, the European Court of Human Rights (ECtHR) has not yet issued decisions in the pending climate cases, the authors pointed out the far-reaching implications that successful ECtHR decisions might have for future European, and international, climate change litigation. Turning to the Court of Justice of the European Union (CJEU), the authors explained that whilst climate litigation cases have fallen short so far in terms of favourable adjudication, they have succeeded in catalysing public opinion and awareness around the unfolding climate crisis.[4] The experts also emphasised the remarkable differences between the CJEU and the ECtHR in terms of their objectives, powers and available remedies when dealing with climate justice claims. Ultimately, the discussion moved onto the overarching question of the role of regional courts as potential law-makers that will have to reconcile the compelling social struggle for ambitious climate action and the principles of the rule of law.[5]

Fermeglia and Alogna discussed the impact of domestic climate change cases within and outside European domestic jurisdictions on other cases based on climate change, so-called 'cross-pollination', in the chapter on the roundtable discussion 'Climate Change Litigation in Europe: Comparative Perspectives'. The authors emphasised the meaningful common legal strategies and challenges underpinning climate change litigation cases against both governments and private entities in five European civil and common law jurisdictions. Moreover, they identified and analysed emerging trends in climate change litigation both with regard to the evolving prospects of success of future strategic litigation cases and with regard to new avenues for litigation, for example on environmental permitting and to pursue corporate accountability for climate change-related action.

Continuing with Part II of this edited volume on 'Climate Change Litigation in Europe: Sectoral Perspectives', the five different sections on human rights, State responsibility, international trade and investment protection, procedural rights, and corporate responsibility covered a wide range of topics, providing a thorough overview on different trends in European climate change litigation.

In the first section on 'Human Rights and Climate Change Litigation', Lachmayer demonstrated that positive decisions of courts, such as those in the Netherlands and in Germany, illustrate the potential of a constitutional approach to climate change. At the same time, Lachmayer connected the pending cases before the ECtHR with the potential of a constitutional rights approach, arguing that these cases 'could potentially facilitate the use of Convention rights as a tool for climate change litigation before national courts'.[6]

4 Alogna and Billiet in this volume.
5 Ibid.
6 Alogna and Billiet in this volume.

Although focusing on the Norwegian case *People v. Arctic Oil* and not on a constitutional approach per se like Lachmayer, Roy and Gociu also stated that '[c]limate change jurisprudence is susceptible to transnational borrowing – it develops incrementally, and diagonally, and the decisions of lower courts, and even overturned judgments, influence court rulings in other jurisdictions'.[7]

Having shed a light on climate migration, Sprenger set out the potential for human rights law to protect climate migrants, in particular the principle of non-refoulement, including the large body of established ECtHR case law in the European context. At the same time, Sprenger recalled the need to find further solutions outside human rights law, such as a framework developed by international bodies, to offer adequate protection to climate migrants.

Rounding off the section on 'Human Rights and Climate Change Litigation', Giacomini *inter alia* pointed out that 'Indigenous rights are often overlooked in Europe'.[8] One of Giacomini's recommendations is 'a critical rethinking of the role of the European justice system … when it comes to protecting Indigenous peoples' rights, especially in the context of achieving environmental and climate justice'.[9]

In the section on 'State Responsibility and Climate Change Litigation', Garofalo set out some of the limitations of climate change litigation as a means to achieve justice in Europe, while at the same time providing 'two legal pathways that might support judges in navigating climate justice issues in mitigation cases … [i.e.] fair share calculations based on equity standards and international environmental law, and an ecological approach to the proportionality principle'.[10]

After carrying out a detailed examination of previous decisions in climate change cases, Krüßmann suggested changing the system for allocating national responsibilities for carbon emissions, as the current system focusing mostly on territorial emissions 'has proven to be unfit in recent years and in the light of an ever-worsening climate crisis'.[11] A 'carbon reduction potential', which is recommended by Krüßmann, also includes 'imported emissions'.

Van der Sluis' contribution brought together several disparate developments in constitutional law in the context of climate change litigation, proposing 'an overall perspective on the relationship between climate change and constitutionalism, in order for these debates to progress in a coherent manner'.[12]

Focusing on intergenerational justice, Handke demonstrated that 'the legal realms of national jurisprudence and international rule-making can interact fruitfully', inspiring the refinement of legal principles and the process of rule-

7 Roy and Gociu in this volume.
8 Giacomini in this volume.
9 Ibid.
10 Garofalo in this volume.
11 Krüßmann in this volume.
12 Van der Sluis in this volume.

making, for example in the context of climate neutrality and core principles of the UN climate regime.[13] According to Handke,

> balanced policies to mitigate climate change foster societal stability today and in the future. Accelerating the pace of achieving climate neutrality is the right thing to do, for both developed *and* developing countries. The protection of the freedom rights of future generations is impossible unless it is a global effort.[14]

Żukowski, who gave insights into socio-legal communication before the courts, elaborated on climate change litigation in Poland, stating that cases have not (yet) produced the successful results seen in other countries. Żukowski sets out a number of different reasons for this lack of success, before explaining how the #ClimateOurCase initiative by the ClientEarth foundation could help to 'change this state of affairs and to effect (climate rights-based) change through strategic climate litigation in Poland'.[15]

Also in this section, Thieffry shed light on procedural improvements which he considers are aimed at improving investment arbitration's greater social acceptability. An investor-State dispute settlement (ISDS) reform, which is underway on the procedural side, contains changes such 'as a code of conduct for arbitrators with an optional prohibition of "double-hatting", early dismissal of frivolous claims, security for costs, increased transparency, observation of hearings, third-party involvement through *amicus curiae* or even joinder of concerned citizens'.[16]

In the section on 'Procedural Rights and Climate Change Litigation', Schlake examined climate change litigation before the CJEU. Taking previous cases as an example, Schlake concluded that 'access to justice remains a topic that is both emotional and difficult to reconstruct'.[17] The *Plaumann* test, which was a hurdle in prior climate cases,

> has a function in the EU judicial system that goes beyond the strategic protection of acts that have been adopted through a legislative procedure. Instead, it can be seen as a structural condition for the systemic approach to judicial protection in the EU that focuses on broad access to decentralised, national courts while confining direct access to the CJEU.[18]

Thus, according to Schlake, 'in the current situation the goals of strategic climate change litigation have no prospects of being achieved through direct actions for

---

13 Handke in this volume.
14 Ibid.
15 Żukowski in this volume.
16 Thieffry in this volume.
17 Schlake in this volume.
18 Ibid.

annulment, since the concept of individual concern in line with the *Plaumann* interpretation is incompatible with a fundamental rights-based argumentation on standing'.[19]

Also focusing on the EU, Coppens analysed the EU Taxonomy Regulation and Delegated Acts against the background of public participation. According to Coppens, the 'Taxonomy Regulation delegated acts are a technical and current topic offering the opportunity to look into what public participation means in the context of complex environmental decision-making'.[20] As already mentioned in of the introduction to this edited volume, Coppens argued that the frameworks give 'the chance to re-examine the system for European integration to fit the needs for a greener future, where it gives a voice to citizens throughout the process'.[21]

Focusing on Belgium, Schoukens highlighted the increasing relevance of climate change litigation concerning concrete permitting procedures. Schoukens analysed a Belgian climate change case in which the claimants challenged the planning permission for a petrol station, in order to illustrate the challenges claimants encounter when advocating for a more binding integration of climate targets into concrete planning and permitting policies.[22]

Coming back to the EU level, Salim looked at collective redress and climate change litigation in the EU. As set out by Salim, '[t]he provision and utilisation of collective redress procedures as vehicles for climate change litigation can promote access to justice for victims of GHG emissions'.[23] In light of EU initiatives on corporate sustainability, due diligence and the environment, adjustments of existing collective procedures to enable representative organisations to better act in collective claims 'are likely to be required in the immediate future'.[24]

Lastly in the section on 'Procedural Rights and Climate Change Litigation', Maglica took an Italian perspective on climate change class actions in Europe. According to Maglica, 'the class action model … has the potential to overcome several obstacles which hinder effective climate change litigation and become an indispensable tool in the climate change litigator's arsenal'.[25] While the Italian class action procedure is 'still imperfect and [needs] to be tested in practice', it has the potential for significant and rapid impact on protecting the climate.

In the fifth and last section of Part II on 'Corporate Responsibility and Climate Change Litigation', Tigre laid out how 'some critical judgments have a broader impact beyond the parties or that particular jurisdiction, addressing novel issues in climate governance'.[26] In particular, regarding Carbon Majors

19 Ibid.
20 Coppens in this volume.
21 Ibid.; see also the introduction to this volume.
22 Schoukens in this volume.
23 Salim in this volume.
24 Ibid.
25 Maglica in this volume.
26 Tigre in this volume.

and other companies, the *Milieudefensie* case 'significantly advanced the development of corporate responsibility in climate mitigation and companies' role in a polycentric landscape of climate change law and policy'.[27]

Lastly, bringing the liability of financial institutions for climate change to the fore, Zamorska highlighted the difficulty of establishing causation using the existing liability regimes for financial institutions. At the same time, Zamorska discussed alternative ways of holding financial institutions accountable based on a broad definition of the corporate duty of care. In general, Zamorska concluded that policy reforms 'must encompass procedural changes as well as those relating to the merits of the financial institutions' liability regime'.[28]

2. FINDINGS OF THE CLOSING PANEL DISCUSSION

This section focuses on the closing panel discussion of the event at Hasselt University, during which the five workshop chairs presented key findings from the parallel sectoral sessions on climate change litigation and human rights, State responsibility, international trade and investment protection, procedural rights, and corporate responsibility.

Annalisa Savaresi (University of Eastern Finland), who chaired the workshop on 'Human Rights and Climate Change Litigation', highlighted that the session contained a 'rather diverse set of papers', which illustrated well 'the many different facets of the relationships between climate change and human rights law and the way the two intersect specifically in the context of climate litigation'.[29] According to Savaresi, as there is an ever-increasing number of rights-based climate change cases, especially in Europe, where so far most of these cases have been filed, it is necessary to 'see the big picture, and the story behind the single case'.[30] While every human rights-based climate change case has its specificities, including the different ways in which each case relies on human rights, it is also important to connect the dots between these different rights-based climate change cases.[31] The papers presented in the workshop 'are very useful to inform this future litigation and the strategies of applicants and the thinking of courts'.[32] Overall, Savaresi concluded that 'there is great potential for future human rights-based climate litigation in Europe because we have such a rich history of environmental jurisprudence before human rights bodies and courts in our continent'.[33]

27 Ibid.
28 Zamorska in this volume.
29 A recording of the closing panel is available at https://www.youtube.com/watch?v=RRNvbzPFNHM.
30 Ibid.
31 Ibid.
32 Ibid.
33 Ibid.

Sarah Mead (Urgenda Foundation) chaired the workshop on 'State Responsibility and Climate Change Litigation'. Mead identified the thread that connected the 'many different topics within that sort of broad area of State responsibility and climate change litigation' as 'the desire to explore the opportunities and the challenges associated with using climate litigation as a tool for enhancing the mitigation efforts of States'.[34] The presentations tackled important issues that arise 'in the context of actually bringing climate litigation and the kinds of difficult choices that litigants need to make when they are bringing these cases: what is really ethically fair, and what do we think that the court is actually going to be comfortable with ordering', as well as 'whether we could expect climate litigation to have an impact on the further development of the international climate change regime'.[35] According to Mead, the presentations, which form the basis of the relevant chapters in Part II of this edited volume, contained 'deep thinking on the opportunities and challenges of climate litigation against States', which is an area with a lot of scope for further research.[36] Mead concluded that:

> Europe has a particularly heavy responsibility in relation to mitigation, being a region of developed countries and also with high levels of historical responsibility. I think it makes sense for there to be a lot of scholarship and inquiring into the responsibility of European States and the possibility for climate litigation to close the accountability gap.[37]

Harro van Asselt (University of Eastern Finland), who chaired the workshop on 'International Trade and Investment Protection and Climate Change Litigation', presented some takeaways, including his own views and thoughts on the presentations. One of Van Asselt's main points was that 'the disputes and judicial proceedings in front of international economic tribunals do matter for climate change'.[38] However, these disputes and judicial proceedings matter in different ways, as there exist two different categories of cases, namely 'anti-regulatory cases' and 'assault cases'. According to Van Hasselt, with respect to the first category it can be seen that 'States are increasingly ramping up their climate policies';[39] therefore, these cases are expected to increase, especially 'when fossil fuel phase-out policies are being ramped up'.[40] In general, as set out by Van Hasselt, various sets of policies can potentially be challenged, such as policies

34 Ibid.
35 Ibid.
36 Ibid.
37 Ibid.
38 Ibid.
39 Ibid.
40 Ibid.

which protect against carbon leakage, policies which generally aim at protecting the environment or targeting the emissions embedded in products that are traded across borders, and discriminatory renewable energy support policies, which might or might not be justified by the Paris Agreement. Moreover, while, in the World Trade Organization (WTO) context, not many States have yet used the Paris Agreement or their Nationally Determined Contributions (NDCs) as a defence in litigation, 'the more cases we will get, the sooner we will actually see those defences coming up'.[41] Regarding the second category of cases, namely 'assault cases', which can be understood as cases 'where dispute settlement in international economic law could actually be used to strengthen climate action', Van Hasselt pointed out that the most well-known cases are those relating to renewable energy in investment arbitration, in which 'renewable energy producers challenge host States for reversing some of their sometimes successful renewable energy policies'.[42] Thinking beyond what has been filed in both of these case categories, Van Hasselt and the presenters at the workshop further discussed questions such as 'whether international economic dispute settlement is actually well equipped to deal with climate change cases and climate change concerns'.[43]

Marjan Peeters (Maastricht University), who chaired the workshop on 'Procedural Rights and Climate Change Litigation', highlighted the contributions' attempts to find creative ways to overcome procedural hurdles in climate change litigation, and to change procedures to achieve more efficient decision-making and more effective climate change litigation.[44] At the same time, the presentations underlined 'that substantive law is also important, of course, to be successful in procedures'.[45] Moreover, legislative developments on class actions, representative organisations, etc. show that there is 'a momentum, and there is still a lot of work to do there'.[46]

Lastly, Jaap Spier (Cambridge University and Stellenbosch University), who chaired the workshop on 'Corporate Responsibility and Climate Change Litigation', underlined that the contributions 'have in common the urgent need to explore options to overcome the deadlock in the political arena that would predominantly strike an optimistic tone, pointing to successes and hopeful developments'.[47] The presenters discussed ground-breaking cases with potentially promising avenues 'to bring States and enterprises including financial institutions to their senses', as well as the important role that the Paris

---

41 Ibid.
42 Ibid.
43 Ibid.; see also Thieffry in this volume.
44 Ibid.
45 Ibid.
46 Ibid.
47 Ibid.

Agreement can play in 'stem[ming] the tide'.[48] However, at the same time, challenges in climate change litigation were discussed throughout the workshop. Spier mentioned that '[n]ot all courts will be courageous, and causation may be a major stumbling block'.[49]

3. CONCLUDING REMARKS

Putting the above sections together, there are several emerging developments at the international, regional and domestic level in the context of climate change litigation that point to the globalisation of this phenomenon.[50] Alongside this horizontal trend of development, various sectoral, or 'vertical', strands of litigation are visible. This book, drawing on the discussions and papers presented at the Hasselt Conference, identifies some of these strands in the areas of human rights, State responsibility, international trade and investment protection, procedural rights, and corporate responsibility.

As predicted by various authors and speakers, climate change cases in these sectors and at these various levels will continue to be filed, and potentially new trends will develop. Especially in Europe, where new litigation avenues can be explored regarding, for example, Indigenous peoples' rights, and decisions are awaited from the ECtHR, climate change litigation will further develop in the near future. In fact, as mentioned throughout Parts I and II of this edited volume, the pending cases before the ECtHR, and, eventually, the decisions, could have an impact on future climate change cases not only in Europe, but also in other regions of the world because of cross-pollination of decisions.

No matter the outcome of the pending cases before the ECtHR, and future climate litigation cases in general, the route to domestic and regional courts will continue to be pursued by claimants as long as climate change continues to be a threat to the very existence of the environment and mankind. This edited volume has provided a timely discussion on notable trends in climate change litigation in Europe, thus contributing to the thriving literature on the topic, as well as to the development of legal architectures to ensure climate justice. While Europe can arguably be considered the Old Continent, it is clearly championing the collective fight against global warming by fostering novel legal concepts, strategies and, hopefully, responses to the unfolding climate crisis.

---

48 Ibid.

49 Ibid.

50 Cf. I. Alogna, C. Bakker and J.-P. Gauci (eds), *Climate Change Litigation: Global Perspectives*, Brill 2021.

INDEX

ABOUT THE EDITORS

IVANO ALOGNA is the Research Leader in Environmental and Climate Change Law at the British Institute of International and Comparative Law (BIICL) and leads BIICL's programme in this field. He is an associate member of the Sorbonne Research Institute in International and European Law (IREDIES), Sorbonne Law School. He is also a member of the World Commission on Environmental Law (WCEL) of the International Union for the Conservation of Nature (IUCN) and its Climate Change Expert Group, a member of the WCEL Taskforce on the Rights of Nature, and an expert of the 'Environmental Law and Policy' Commission, IUCN French Committee. He was the General Rapporteur of the 'Global Pact for the Environment' project (French Constitutional Council and Club des Juristes) and a member of the European Law Institute (ELI) project on 'Ecocide'. Furthermore, he is a licensed attorney-at-law at the Bar of Milan. Ivano lectures on international and comparative environmental law, climate change law and litigation, environmental liability, private law, sustainable consumer law and comparative law. He is the co-editor of the book *Climate Change Litigation: Global Perspectives* (2021, Brill). He holds a PhD in comparative and international environmental law from the Sorbonne Law School, University of Paris 1 Panthéon-Sorbonne and his PhD thesis on 'The Circulation of Legal Models in the Environmental Field: Toward a Global Environmental Law' was awarded the Special Jury Prize by the French Society of Environmental Law – SFDE.

CAROLE BILLIET is Head of the Environmental Law Unit (ELU) at Hasselt University and a member of the Hasselt University Centre for Environmental Studies (CMK), an interdisciplinary research institute. She lectures on environmental law, environmental policy, and principles of private and public law. Her main research interests include environmental enforcement law and climate change law. She is the Editor-in-Chief of the legal journal *Milieu- en Energierecht*. She combines her academic work with her position as a lawyer (Brussels Bar), where she specialises in strategic environmental litigation, including climate change litigation. She holds a PhD in legal sciences from Ghent University.

MATTEO FERMEGLIA is Assistant Professor of Climate Law and Governance at Amsterdam University, Faculty of Humanities. Previously, and throughout the development of this book, he was Assistant Professor of International and

European Environmental Law and Post-Doctoral Assistant at Hasselt University. He obtained a PhD in legal sciences at the University of Trieste and Udine in 2019. In 2017, he was a visiting scholar at Columbia Law School, where he collaborated with the Sabin Center for Climate Change Law and the Columbia Center for Sustainable Investments. In 2017, he was awarded the Raúl Estrada-Oyuela Award for Emerging Scholars in Climate Law.

ALINA HOLZHAUSEN is a Researcher in Environmental and Climate Change Law at the British Institute of International and Comparative Law (BIICL), and a PhD candidate at the University of Aberdeen. Alina graduated from the University of Bayreuth with a German diploma in law and holds a Maîtrise in international law (University of Bordeaux) and an LLM in international law and international relations (University of Aberdeen). She practised law at the German Parliament before coming to the United Kingdom in 2019. Her main research interests include human rights law, climate change law, international environmental law and public international law.

www.ingramcontent.com/pod-product-compliance
Ingram Content Group UK Ltd.
Pitfield, Milton Keynes, MK11 3LW, UK
UKHW051919100926
8556IPUK00021B/1257

9 781839 7038